A MEDITERRANEAN SOCIETY

PUBLISHED UNDER THE AUSPICES OF THE

Gustave E. von Grunebaum Center
for Near Eastern Studies
University of California,
Los Angeles

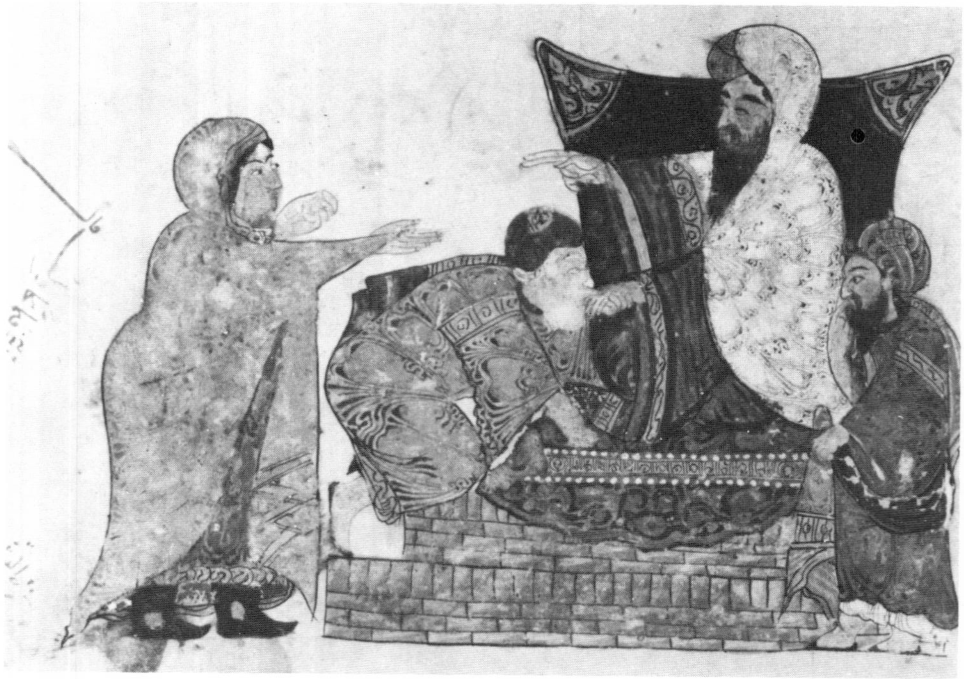

Wife pleading and husband supplicating before a judge (from the Maqāmāt of Al-Ḥarīrī manuscript arabe No. 5847, Bibliothèque Nationale, Paris).

S. D. GOITEIN

A Mediterranean Society

THE JEWISH COMMUNITIES OF THE ARAB WORLD
AS PORTRAYED IN THE DOCUMENTS OF THE CAIRO GENIZA

VOLUME III

The Family

UNIVERSITY OF CALIFORNIA PRESS
Berkeley · Los Angeles · London · 1978

UNIVERSITY OF CALIFORNIA PRESS
BERKELEY AND LOS ANGELES, CALIFORNIA

UNIVERSITY OF CALIFORNIA PRESS, LTD.
LONDON, ENGLAND

ISBN: 0-520-03265-9
LIBRARY OF CONGRESS CATALOG CARD NUMBER: 67-22430

PRINTED IN THE UNITED STATES OF AMERICA

2 3 4 5 6 7 8 9 0

In loving memory of my father

Dr. Eduard E. Goitein

(1864–1914)

"The ways of wisdom are kindness,
and all its paths are peace."

Proverbs 3:17

Preface

Writing a book on the family these days is a risk. The confusion and controversy encompassing the contemporary family, and by no means the family of the Western World alone, have left their mark on the research going on in this field. Only a misanthrope, though, would deny that we have made substantial progress in the twentieth century in the mutual understanding between the sexes and different age groups, progress manifested in social experiment, legislation, and practice. This favorable development has found expression in, and was partly put into motion by, fertile thought, often distinguished by boldness and sophistication. Anyone trying to find his place among the multitude of writers on the subject is obliged to define clearly what kind of contribution he intends to make and what results may reasonably be expected from his endeavors.

This volume undertakes to portray the Mediterranean family of the High Middle Ages (tenth through thirteenth centuries) with the aid of a great variety of letters and documents from that region and period, still largely unpublished. The authors of those writings were mostly Jews who spoke Arabic, but usually wrote that language with Hebrew characters, although for certain specific purposes Hebrew, too, was used. All the material was originally found in Fustat, or Old Cairo, the ancient Islamic capital of Egypt, but it is now dispersed in the libraries of many countries, predominantly England and the United States. The interested reader will find a full description of the Cairo Geniza, as this treasure trove of manuscripts is usually called, in the Introduction to the first volume of this publication.

The systematic historical study of the medieval family is comparatively new, even as far as Europe is concerned. For the countries of Islam it has hardly begun. The Arabic-speaking Jews, naturally, formed only a small section of the population in Islamic countries, and an even smaller one of the Mediterranean region in general. But they were old-timers, indigenous to that area, not newcomers and foreigners like the Jews in the northern parts of Europe. On the southern shores of the Mediterranean there were no geographical, occupational, or spiritual ghettos in those days. There the Jews lived, worked, and thought in daily contact with their neighbors. In medieval France, Germany, and England the Jews used Hebrew, not Latin, for written expression. In the Islamic countries of the Mediterranean even the doctors of Jewish law wrote their legal opinions and court records in Arabic, and so did the theologians, and, of course, the physicians and the students of the sciences. In short, the writers of the Geniza papers may legitimately be regarded as part and parcel of their environment, separated from it, like their Christian neighbors, by a different religious law and by a specific group ethos, which, as a social force, should be compared with modern nationalism. Thus, with the limitations just indicated, the material presented in this volume should be valued not only as a contribution to the history of the Jewish family, but also to that of the family within Mediterranean Islam at large, and, to some extent, even within the Mediterranean area in general.

The Geniza papers originated mostly in the middle and lower layers of society, which makes them particularly valuable, since we do not have much information about this, the main part of humanity, from that period. That competitive and mobile world of hardworking merchants, craftsmen, lawyers, and physicians, described in volumes I and II of this book, has much in common with our own society, and, therefore, is far less colorful and exotic than that of the feudal lords, knights, and their ladies, monks, and troubadours, who populate the medieval scene as commonly known. But precisely for this reason—that is, the ordinary character of urban Geniza society—the specific traits of its family life become an intriguing topic of inquiry: similar socioeconomic conditions do not necessarily create the same type of family.

I have characterized the work carried out in this volume as "presenting materials." I have done so because I feel that I am still occupied with spadework, with establishing the facts, as far as one can cull them out from documents often incompletely preserved and difficult to understand. The facts presented are interpreted in the way the writers themselves saw them whenever they have made this known to us. Often telling utterances are cited in full. Where the sources do not provide interpretative comments, I have tried to make sense of the facts with the aid of my general knowledge of Islam and Judaism. Sometimes matters do not fall into focus, either because our information is insufficient or, perhaps, because life itself was not in focus, was variegated and even contradictory. The society presented in the Geniza records was by no mean homogeneous. There were marked differences between the various countries and, even more so, between the different layers of the population.

Throughout the volume references to Islamic law and custom are given. Such occasional hints are made by way of illustration and should by no means be taken as attempts at systematic comparison. The time for that has not yet come since the preliminary studies for an undertaking of that kind have not yet been made. I shall be grateful to my fellow historians who explore the medieval societies on the northern shores of the Mediterranean for any comparative comments they may care to make. I crave their indulgence for the few cases in which I trespass on their precincts. This is also the place to thank David Herlihy of Harvard University for his bibliographical hints to recent research on the medieval history of the family in Western Europe, to which he himself has contributed so much.

The reader may wonder why the Jews of Yemen (now found mostly in Israel) are mentioned so often in this book. I have studied them for many years because, on the one hand, they were most intensively arabicized, and, on the other, they probably presented the traditional Jew in the purest form. Comparing and contrasting the results of my fieldwork among them with the findings of the Geniza writings was quite illuminating. The Introduction to my *Tales from the Land of Sheba* (New York: Schocken Books, 1973) gives an idea of this remarkable community.

I have tried to keep the references to Jewish law to a reasonable minimum. I did so relying on my former student Mordechai A. Friedman, now Professor of Talmud and Jewish Law at Tel-Aviv University, who has made the Geniza family, as seen in the context of the development of Jewish law and legal practice, the object of his life work. Friedman has published numerous papers on the subject, and his forthcoming book on the Geniza marriage contracts according to Palestinian custom is certain to be a major contribution. The Palestinian marriage contracts represent only a small fraction of the Geniza material relevant to family life, but Friedman's treatment is so comprehensive that it illustrates many aspects of medieval marriage (see Author's Note).

Some material bearing on family life had to be reserved for the fourth and concluding volume of this book. The trousseau lists, found in the Geniza in abundance, provide countless details about a bride's jewelry, precious utensils, clothing, bedding, hangings, copper vessels, and other household implements. This most valuable information must be studied in connection with other Geniza sources about the material civilization surrounding the medieval individual, the subject of the fourth volume of this work. Sexual mores are discussed there in the context of moral attitudes in general. The reader of the present volume should not feel cheated. Playboys, gays, and lesbians were not absent from the Geniza society, but they were not as vociferous as some of our contemporaries, wherefore I have not much to tell about them. The more intimate aspects of marital symbiosis are, of course, touched upon repeatedly in the pages that follow. Finally, legal dispositions in contemplation of death naturally deal to a large extent with spouses, children, and other relatives. But they embrace many other matters. All the multifarious details included in wills reflect a man's concern when approaching the end of his days, and consequently had to be treated as one single group.

The organization of the family had a tremendous influence on economic life. Some considerations in this respect are offered in the conclusion of B, 4 ("The Economic Foundations of Marriage"), C, 4 ("Heirs and Orphans"), and in D ("The World of Women"). Attention is also drawn to the Appendix ("The Economics of Marriage"). Beyond these, relevant material is to be found throughout this volume, which might therefore serve, to a certain extent, as a complement to volume I of this book, which is subtitled *Economic Foundations*.

A note on the purchasing power of the dinar, the gold coin mentioned on many pages, may be welcome. Because of the abysmal difference in living standards and the unstable character of our own money, a comparison with the dollar serves no purpose. A few examples of standard earnings gleaned from the Geniza might do a better service. Emoluments of 2 dinars per month for a lower community official were regarded as appropriate. A master mason could make up to 4 dinars during the same period, if he worked seven days a week. An allowance of half a dinar per month for a single person, such as a wife whose husband was abroad, was commonplace.

I feel obliged to make another technical observation. Since the various aspects of family life are closely intertwined, this volume is replete with cross references. References are made to *notes* rather than to pages, the reason being that often numerous notes occur on one page and where a mere hint to a page might entail guesswork, the note number, with the help of the running heads on both the notes and the text, will guide the reader directly to the required reference.

Leafing through this manuscript again I feel the general reader should be advised to try sections C and D first before plunging into A and B.

ACKNOWLEDGMENTS

I reiterate my thanks, expressed in the Preface to volume I, to the directors and staffs of the libraries whose manuscripts have been studied for the preparation of this volume. The photostats used were mostly acquired during the 1950s and the 1960s. New material has come to light in the Additional Series of the Taylor-Schechter Collection of the Cambridge University Library, England and the New Series of the E. N. Adler Collection of the Jewish Theological Seminary of America, New York. I wish to thank the Librarian of the Cambridge University Library, E. B. Ceadel, and also Stefan C. Reif, Director of the Taylor-Schechter Genizah Research unit, as well as Menahem Schmelzer, Librarian of the Jewish Theological Seminary, for their gracious helpfulness and the permission to use those manuscripts. I am also indebted to the Eli Michael Microfilm Center for Genizah Studies, Yeshiva University, New York, and its creator and curator, Elazar Hurvitz, especially for making disconnected and brittle pieces from the valuable collection of Westminster College, Cambridge, amenable to scholarly use.

This book was written during my stay as visitor at the Institute for Advanced Study, Princeton. It benefited much from this connection, and, in particular, from the unfailing interest and support of its former Director, Carl Kaysen and its present Director, Harry Woolf.

I am deeply indebted to Suzanne Keller, Professor of Sociology at Princeton University, for reading the manuscript of this book and enlightening me on many matters with which an Orientalist of classical training normally is not conversant. My friend, A. L. Udovitch, Chairman of the Near Eastern Department of Princeton University, took the trouble to go over the entire manuscript and suggested important corrections. Thanks are due also to Gershon Weiss, Professor of Hebrew at Temple University, Philadelphia, for his assiduous work on the restoration and copying of Geniza texts, and to my conscientious assistant Ellen J. Seidman. Part of the material used for the preparation of the Appendix was read and card-indexed by Boaz Shoshan while he was a graduate student at Princeton University. The meticulous typing of the manuscript by Sandra S. Lafferty of the Institute for Advanced Study was a great help. This volume, like its predecessors, owes its final form to the watchful eye and good taste of Teresa Joseph, editor, Gustave E. von Grunebaum Center for Near Eastern Studies, University of California, Los Angeles.

I have dedicated this volume to the loving memory of my father. What I owe him I have said in my "Life Story of a Scholar," included in *A Bibliography of the Writings of Professor Shelomo Dov Goitein* by Robert Attal (Jerusalem, 1975).

The Institute for Advanced Study
School of Historical Studies
Princeton, N.J.

S. D. Goitein

Contents of Volumes I through IV

NOTE: *A Mediterranean Society* was originally planned to comprise three volumes, volume III to contain three chapters. While working on the last volume I found it more suitable to split it in two. Volume III now consists of chapter VIII, THE FAMILY; the fourth and final volume will contain chapter IX, HOUSING, CLOTHING, FOOD, AND DAILY ROUTINE, and chapter X, THE MEDITERRANEAN MIND, as well as a glossary of foreign words, a cumulative index of Geniza texts, and a general index of the four volumes.

Contents

Author's Note

The Notes contain mostly references to the relevant manuscripts and discuss textual, linguistic, and factual problems connected with them. Occasionally notes try to anticipate questions that might arise in the mind of the attentive reader, for example, A, 1, nn. 31, 33, 35, A, 3, nn. 3–6. Hints to scientific literature other than that concerned with the sources are provided when called for by special considerations, as in A, 1, n. 93, A, 2, nn. 72, 73, C, 2, n. 1.

On how to use the Notes, the reader is referred to the Author's Note in Volume I. See also Abbreviations and Symbols in Volumes I and II for a list of the short forms used. A few additional abbreviations are listed below. A cross reference to a note often concerns also the text to which the note refers. Thus C, 3, n. 9, "see n. 7, above," refers to n. 7 in conjunction with what is said in the text.

M. A. Friedman's book on the Geniza marriage contracts according to Palestinian custom (see the Preface) consists of two parts: one deals with the subject matter in general, and the other presents the edition and translation of the texts, with commentaries. The typescript of most of the second part came into my hands only after the relevant sections of this volume had been completed; the first had not yet been seen by me at the writing of my book. The texts are referred to in my notes with the numbers given to them in Friedman's book and they bear the symbol^{+}, that is, "edited," when they appear more than once or occur in the Appendix.

Abbreviations and Symbols

The abbreviations and symbols listed in *Med. Soc.*, I, xix–xxvi, II, xv–xvi, are used in this volume.

A plus sign after the shelf mark of a Geniza manuscript means that the document has been edited and published or is included in S. D. Goitein's *India Book* or M. Michael's *Nahray* (see *Med. Soc.*, I, xxii and xxiv). Publication data on the edition or the serial number of the document in *India Book* or *Nahray* is supplied at the first appearance of the relevant shelf mark and is to be found in Shaked, *Bibliography* (see *Med. Soc.*, I, xxv [edited texts only as far as published before 1964]). An asterisk after the shelf mark of a manuscript means that the document is translated in S. D. Goitein, *Mediterranean People* (see vol. II, vii).

Additional abbreviations, not used in volumes I and II:

BT	Babylonian Talmud.
EJ	*Encyclopaedia Judaica.* Jerusalem; Macmillan Co., 1971–1972. 16 vols.
ENA NS	Elkan Nathan Adler Collection in the Library of the Jewish Theological Seminary, New York. New series.
Epstein, *Marriage Contract*	Louis M. Epstein, *The Jewish Marriage Contract: A Study in the Status of the Woman in Jewish Law.* New York, 1927.
Falk, *Jewish Matrimonial Law*	Z. W. Falk, *Jewish Matrimonial Law in the Middle Ages.* Oxford, 1966.
Friedman, *Ethics*	M. A. Friedman, "The Ethics of Medieval Jewish Marriage," *Religion in a Religious Age*, ed. S. D. Goitein. Cambridge, Mass., 1974. Pp. 83–102.

Friedman, *Marriage*	M. A. Friedman, *The Cairo Geniza Marriage Contracts According to Palestinian Custom* (tentative title), see p. ix, above.
Goitein, *Letters*	S. D. Goitein, *Letters of Medieval Jewish Traders, Translated from the Arabic*. Princeton, 1973.
Goitein, *Palestine during Its Arab and Crusader Periods* (in Heb.)	S. D. Goitein, *Ha-yishuv ba-arets ba-tequfa ha-ʿarvit we-ha-tsalbanit*. Jerusalem, 1978.
Golb, *Topography*	Norman Golb, "The Topography of the Jews of Medieval Egypt," Part II, *Journal of Near Eastern Studies*, 33 (1972), 116–149.
Gulack, *Otzar*	A. Gulack, *Otzar ha-Shetarot* (Forms of Documents) (Heb.). Jerusalem, 1978.
Ibn al-Kalbī, *Ǧamhara*	W. Caskel, *Ǧamharat an-Nasab, Das genealogische Work des Hišām ibn Muḥammad al-Kalbī*. Leiden, 1966.
Idris, "Mariage"	Hady Rogers Idris, "Le mariage en Occident musulman," *Revue de l'Occident musulman et de la Méditerranée*, 16 (1973), 45–62, 17 (1974), 71–105.
JJS	*Journal of Jewish Studies* (London).
Mann (1970)	Jacob Mann, *The Jews in Egypt and in Palestine under the Fāṭimid Caliphs*. Preface and Reader's Guide by S. D. Goitein. Reprint. New York, 1970. See *Med. Soc.*, I, xxiii.
Margalioth, *Hilkhot*	M. Margalioth, *Hilkhot Eretz-Israel min ha-Geniza* (Sources of Palestinian Law from the Geniza) (Heb.), ed. Israel Ta-Shemaʿ. Jerusalem, 1973.

Meinardus, *Christian Egypt*	Otto F. A. Meinardus, *Christian Egypt: Faith and Life.* Cairo, 1970.
PT	Palestinian Talmud.
Strauss-Ashtor, *Mamluks,* III	E. Strauss-Ashtor, *History of the Jews in Egypt and Syria under the Rule of the Mamluks,* Vol. III (Heb.). Jerusalem, 1970.
Su'ād Māhir, *'Uqūd*	Dr. Su'ād Māhir, *'Uqūd al-zawāj 'ala 'l-mansūjāt al-'athariyya* (Marriage Contracts on Ancient Textiles) (Arabic). Cairo, n.d.
TS AS	Taylor-Schechter Collection, Additional Series, University Library, Cambridge, England.
Urbach, *The Sages*	E. E. Urbach, *The Sages: Their Concepts and Beliefs* (Heb.). Jerusalem, 1969. Translated by Israel Abrahams, Jerusalem, 1975. The English version was not available at the time of the writing of this volume.
Yaron, *Gifts in Contemplation of Death*	R. Yaron, *Gifts in Contemplation of Death in Jewish and Roman Law.* Oxford, 1960.

A MEDITERRANEAN SOCIETY

CHAPTER VIII

The Family

A. "THE HOUSE OF THE FATHER": THE EXTENDED FAMILY

Introduction

The community mirrored in the documents of the Cairo Geniza was bound by a religious law developed over many generations long passed. It was surrounded and influenced by a state and a society with laws and moral notions at variance with its own. Moreover, it displayed social and geographical mobility and evinced creative flexibility in the conduct of its economic and public affairs. A community of this type cannot be expected to manifest a rigid pattern of a family system. A composite and complex situation is to be anticipated. No attempt is made here to place the family emerging from the Geniza documents within any defined sociological category.

Still, some major features are clearly discernible, shared, it seems, by other societies around the Mediterranean.

The bonds of blood were stronger than the ties of marriage. A man's family, foremost in his mind, was not the small one founded by himself but the larger one into which he was born. His family was, as is said in so many documents, "the house of his father." The term "father" included the forefathers as well as the agnates.

Law favored the paternal family. The economic security of a woman largely depended on what she had brought in from her father's (or "fathers' "[1]) house, and for her legal protection during her marriage she relied on him or on her brothers. Nor did she inherit from her husband. Although Islamic and Jewish laws differed considerably in some respects, both made special provisions for the widow, but if a man had no issue his estate "returned"—in legal parlance—to his father's house, and the wife's dowry, or, at least half of it, returned to her family when she died childless. Legal practice—although not statutory law—and commonly accepted custom made the members of the extended family responsible for one another. Finally, the widespread practice of marrying close relatives, especially first cousins, had its origin not so much in economic considerations as in the belief that such unions would provide protection for the young couple, especially the wife, and safeguards for the honor of the family.

In view of these social and psychological realities I treat the extended family first. Biologically, of course, and, therefore, so to say, logically, the nuclear, "natural," family comes first. But factually and conceptually, the latter was an outgrowth of the "father's house," it was a branch of the tree, not its root.

The Arabic of the Geniza documents has two sets of designations for the term "family," some for the extended, and others for the nuclear family.[2] Similarly, Hebrew *mishpāḥā,* "family," refers, as a rule, to the extended family, usually one with a noble pedigree, that is, one containing a number of distinguished personalities, such as high religious dignitaries, judges, scholars, government officials, physicians, great merchants, or other persons of any walk of life who had been munificent or otherwise meritorious in the service of the community. Hebrew *bayit,* "house," may designate a man's nuclear family or his wife, but the plural, in the phrase *ba'alē battim,* invariably describes the person concerned as the scion of a distinguished (extended) family.[3]

1. *Honoring Ancestors and Agnates: Memorial Services and Family-oriented Names*

In an intensely religious society man's attitude toward his family must be explored first through its place in religion. The Geniza reveals that reverence for his forefathers and for the past generations of his family was paramount and found its regular expression in the synagogue service. As a rule, prayers for a person, alive or dead, were said, not for him alone, nor for him and his immediate relatives, but first and foremost for his ascendants and noteworthy agnates, all male, to be sure, even when the person for whom the prayer was recited was a woman. We possess detailed knowledge about these procedures in the numerous "memorial lists" preserved in the Geniza.[1]

Memorial lists.—The reading of these lists must have formed an important part of the synagogue service and taken considerable time, although the complaint of a sixteenth-century newcomer to Egypt that it consumed half the service was probably exaggerated.[2] The immediate occasion for such a display was a death in the family, when, at the first attendance of public prayer by the mourners, blessings were recited for the ancestors of the deceased and for those who survived him. Here is a brief example: An "esteemed, chaste, and pious lady departed to her eternal abode with a good name and after having done good deeds" (we are not told her name); blessings were recited for her late father; an uncle, who had died young in a foreign country; a grandfather, who had been a judge; and a great-grandfather, a notable. Then "life, wellbeing, honor, and all the consolations written in the holy scriptures" were wished the mourners, namely, her husband and two sons, who were present, a third son, out of town, and to other male relatives mentioned by name. The prayer concluded with blessings for the congregation and above all for the Nagid, the head of the community.[3]

A similar service was held after the first month of mourning. A relevant document does not fail to note that two brothers of the deceased and a nephew of his had died young.[4] On the Day of Atonement, as explained in *Med. Soc.*, II, 351, when solemn prayers were recited for the caliph and for the Jewish ecumenical and local authorities, all the noble families remembered their dead. Most of the lists preserved must have been written for such an occasion since they usually contain a number of genealogies.

With few exceptions[5] these lists were hasty notes jotted down by a cantor for prompting his memory. He had recited most of the pedigrees before, as evidenced by the fact, referred to in *Med Soc.*, II, 162, that numerous copies of the pedigree of a single merchant have been preserved,[6] or that a hitherto unedited memorial list in honor of Moses Maimonides does not contain any of his titles or those of his seven ancestors; the cantor knew what he had to say, but noted only the bare names in order to make sure he had the correct sequence of generations.[7] Most of the lists are carelessly written on scrap paper, as one does for temporary use, and the four to six parallel copies of the pedigrees of prominent families which happen to be extant rarely agree with one another completely. But for our purpose this material is eloquent enough. An evaluation of its significance is included at the end of this section.

When the rationalist Moses Maimonides, in the colophons of his multivolume commentary on the Mishna, completed at the age of thirty, enumerated the seven generations of his forefathers, he did so not out of vanity, but as a tribute to the accepted notion that such an ancestorship (which included four judges) added to the religious authority of his own work. He did not repeat this in his later books.

It was taken for granted that a man tried to live up to the standards set by his ancestors. "This document must be correct, for the father of its writer was the son of the daughter of the Head of the Yeshiva." Such a statement is found in a letter exchanged between two high religious dignitaries. The principle of heredity of public office, high or low, so thoroughly familiar to the Geniza world (see *Med. Soc.*, II, 89–91, 161–162, 319), was based on the same assumption. That principle was recognized by Jewish law. The Greek inscription excavated by Raymond Weill in the vicinity of the Temple of Jerusalem, where an *archi-synagogos,* or head of the synagogue, says that his father and grandfather had occupied the same position, is an example of its ancient application.[8]

In numerous requests for help the recipient is reminded of his noble and munificent ancestors, while in letters of recommendation the person concerned is often described as of fine or illustrious stock, and one man, producing letters from Baghdad, Mosul, and Aleppo, adds: "There they know my forefathers, my house, my nobility, and all my family."[9]

A man's life was perpetuated through his sons. Sometimes all the sons of an ancestor are named in the memorial lists, not rarely as many as six sons, but more often only the direct ascendants of the person for whom the list is read are listed along with agnates who for any reason deserved mentioning. These were well-known or otherwise meritorious persons and those whose life was cut short either by an early natural death—a common occurrence—or by a disaster such as the collapse of a house, drowning, shipwreck, disappearance abroad, murder, or, especially, dying for God's sake, that is, in a religious persecution. By remembering such persons, who often had died generations ago, they were, so to say, kept alive.[10]

As a rule, a memorial list is superscribed with the name of the person or family for whom it is composed. It opens with the first ancestor who is often characterized as an important person, and is followed by his descendants for five to seven, but sometimes ten and more generations. The first ancestor in a list was not necessarily the founder of the family; different copies of the same pedigree do not always start with the same generation.[11] A simple list of ten generations is headed by a scholar and contains two names that each occur three times and two that occur twice, which manifests the cohesiveness of the family.[12]

By no means should these pedigrees be regarded as fanciful. Property deeds and other legal documents as well as books bearing notes of their proprietors were preserved in a house and helped to keep the family records straight. My own experience with emigrants from Yemen, a thoroughly traditional country, taught me that even simple people were aware of their ancestors up to five, six, and often more generations. Muslims signing Arabic papyri frequently mention not only their fathers and grandfathers but also their great-grandfathers.[13]

As mentioned, women were never listed in the genealogies. Moses Maimonides had five brothers-in-law. One of his own sisters was married to one of them. Each of the brothers-in-law is listed in the joint genealogy of the two families, with both the Hebrew and Arabic forms of their names, but nowhere do we learn the names of Moses Maimonides' wife or sister who created this union.[14] It must be noted, however, that a man's status in society depended on the family of his mother no less than on that of his father. This is expressly stated in letters and can be deduced from the memorial lists. "Ibn al-ʿAmmānī [a scion of a prominent Alexandrian family of physicians and public servants, see *Med. Soc.,* II, 245] wrote to my brother a letter full of conceit, announcing that he had married our paternal cousin—may God grant her happiness. Please tell him that she was not honored through him, but he through her, namely her pure and noble house, her ancestors from her mother's side."[15] In the genealogy of Mishael b. Isaiah, Maimonides' father-in-law, first his mother's lineage is provided through fourteen generations because her family had played an important role in Palestine, as well as in Egypt, followed later by six generations of Mishael's paternal ancestors known as scholars, physicians, and public servants.[16] In a doctor's *ʿitra,* or pedigree, the mother's lineage precedes, because it included the Nagid Samuel b. Hananya, certainly one of the most prominent figures in the history of Egyptian Jewry. The first and last name in this lineage also was Samuel. The Karaite family name "Son of the daughter of Saul" also indicates that *yikhūs,* or noble descent (Hebrew), could be transmitted through a mother. But it is always a male person to whom her reputation and that of the family accrued. The woman appears solely as a link, as daughter and mother, and is not mentioned by name. When a father of daughters is wished a son, it is said to him: "May God not wipe out the name of your fathers."[17]

The absence from the genealogies of the names of women is conspicuous because women are constantly referred to. A detailed list of Levite families, that is, families that derived their origin from the biblical tribe Levi, lists in each case whether a man's wife or mother (identified by her father's name) was from a lineage other than Levites, but nowhere is the woman referred to by her name. That omission here as everywhere is significant. A man's extended family was represented by his fathers and sons; it was a patriarchy.[18]

The naming of children.—The cohesiveness of a family and reverence for past generations were expressed by giving newborn children the names of ascendants and agnates. The Ibn Yijū family, whose most prominent member was India trader Abraham Yijū, is represented in the Geniza by letters and documents through six generations. Three biblical and two nonbiblical names recur in them as many as three and four times.[19] The sedentary Ibn Jāmiʿ family of scholars and judges in Gabes, Tunisia, is a similar case (biblical names only).[20]

Ibn Yijū and Ibn Jāmiʿ are true family names; the former was that of a Berber tribe and the latter that of a petty Arab dynasty that ruled Gabes. In both cases the Jewish family was under the protection of the ruling Muslim clan and adopted its name.[21]

The common usage was that a newborn child was named after his paternal grandfather, regardless as to whether the old man's name was already perpetuated in another branch of the family. Barhūn (I) Tāhertī of Qayrawān, a merchant, had four sons, each of whom named one of his boys Barhūn, so that four cousins with the name Barhūn (II) Tāhertī make their appearance in the Geniza.[22] Labrāṭ II b. Moses II b. Labrāt I b. Moses I was a judge in al-Mahdiyya, Tunisia (his family name, Ibn Sighmār, was again that of a Berber clan).[23] Sahlān IV b. Abraham III b. Sahlān III b. Abraham II b. Sahlān II b. Abraham I b. Solomon I (probably regarded as the Hebrew equivalent of Sahlān) was from a local Jewish family in Egypt, where the same usage prevailed, and he presided over the Iraqian Jewish community of Fustat.[24] A document such as TS 28.2, in which Solomon II b. Moses b. Solomon I declares to have no claim against Yaʿīsh II ("May he live") b. Abraham b. Yaʿīsh I (Fustat, 1018) is characteristic of this usage.

In Christian Europe it became customary among Jews to name children only after deceased relatives. Jacob Mann, who assumed that this custom already prevailed in Geniza times, ran into great difficulties.[25] The opposite is true. We find that the firstborn was named after the living grandfather in order to insure the perpetuation of his name as early as possible. In 921/2 Saadya Gaon, in a letter addressed to Sulaymān II b. ʿAlī b. Sulaymān I and his two younger brothers in Fustat, mentions that in a previous communication he had expressed to him his sympathy at the death of his grandfather.[26] The poet Judah ha-Levi writes in one of his poems: "How can Judah [the poet] forget Judah" (his grandson—from his daughter; he had no son).[27] In the examples provided above, Jacob II Ibn Jāmiʿ was the eldest, and so were Sahlān IV and Labrāṭ II, as letters and documents related to them prove. It would not be difficult to adduce other examples from the Geniza.

Naming one's firstborn son after his own father was a wonderful way to show him the filial piety that religion, Jewish, as well as Muslim, and of course Christian, imposes on us as a most holy duty. ("*You* have given life to me, *I* ensure the perpetuation of your name.") We must remember that in those days young couples often lived in the father's house, so that the old man had daily opportunity to see himself continued and, as it were, perpetuated through his namesake grandson. This idea occurred to me many years ago, when the Muslim sheikh, with whom I read Ḥadīth (Muslim oral traditions), wanted to show me his little grandson who played in the garden; he shouted: Sīdī, Sīdī ("Grandpa"); when he saw my astonishment, he explained: "I love him; so I call him as he calls me."[28]

It seems that an additional, religious, element was involved in this symbolic linking together of the generations. The Bible admonishes: "Teach your sons *and grandsons*" (Deuteronomy 4:9), and "Peace over Israel" will be when "you see sons of your sons" (Psalm 128:4). To this the Talmud adds: when religious scholarship is cultivated by father, son, and grandson, "the Torah will frequent its lodgings," that is, religiosity will stay firmly rooted in the family.[29] Hence the interest of the grandfather in the studies of his grandsons. When ʿAmīd al-Dawla ("Support of the Government"), a high official, returned from a trip, the first thing for him to do was to examine his grandson, who, to judge by the reading matter he had covered, must have been a mere child; the old man was highly pleased with the boy's attainments, at least so his teacher reported.[30]

The history of naming also seems to indicate that religion had something to do with the custom of naming a child after an ancestor or agnate. It was unknown in biblical times. Not a single king of Judah or high priest in the First Temple of Jerusalem is called by the name of an ancestor. In the genealogies of pre-Islamic and early Islamic Arab tribes and clans, which we have in the hundreds, a name is repeated in only a few exceptional cases, and then it usually has a characteristic byname to distinguish it from the first occurrence.[31]

A change came as a result of foreign influence. When the Seleucids of Syria and the Ptolemaeans of Egypt, successors of Alexander the Great, who alternately held sway over Palestine, named their sons after themselves or their fathers, and later the Roman conquerors were observed to do the same, we find that the high priests of Jerusalem, and later the Hasmonaean kings and high priests, followed suit.[32] In the pedigree of the "patriarchs" of Judea the name Gamaliel (known also from the New Testament, Acts 22:3) recurs six times, to be followed in frequency by those of Judah, Simeon,[33] and Hillel. How far the common people followed this example, we cannot say. When the custom of naming a boy after his grandfather or another ancestor or agnate became standard practice in Geniza times, in addition to strong family attachment a religious element was present: "The Torah frequents its lodgings."

In Islam something similar to what we have observed in Judaism is to be found. The endlessly repeated names from the holy history of Islam replaced the onomastic inventiveness of Arab antiquity. I do not see, however, that the Muslims had developed a system of rotating names within the family comparable with what we have in the Geniza. I scrutinized the genealogies of fifty Islamic authors from the High Middle Ages and found that only four bore the same name as their grandfathers, two, of their fathers, and two of their great-grandfathers, and these were ordinary names such as Muḥammad, Aḥmad, ʿAli, and Ḥusayn. Of fifty persons signing a document in Aswān, Egypt, in 948, and mentioning the names of their grandfathers, only nine were named after them and again with names of the character just described.[34] Thus the custom of naming a child after his grandfather seems to have been more consistent in the Jewish family than in the Muslim family of the day.[35]

Naming a son after his own father, living or dead, was not unknown in Geniza times. But it was incomparably less common than the naming after the grandfather. This difference, like the customary memorial service, seems to be an indication of a certain precedence of the extended over the nuclear family. Young parents of the 1970s, when choosing names for their newborn, usually pay no attention to either. This, too, teaches us something about the importance of onomastics for the understanding of a man's attitude toward his family.

Surnames.—Family names in the strict sense of the word were known in Talmudic times and it was assumed that they might be preserved even through ten generations. But in legal documents, in order to avoid ambiguities, not more than three generations were to be noted, for experience had shown that, as a rule, family names did not endure for long. The testimony of the Geniza seems to confirm this impression.[36]

Many types of family names appear in the Geniza, that of an ancestor's name or byname serving as such being the case most closely related to the custom, discussed above, of giving a child the name of his grandfather. A name can be identified as a real family name—and not simply as that of an ancestor—when it appears in different genealogical combinations and also is marked as such, especially by the phrase "known as," or when it is preceded by Hebrew *ben* or Arabic *ibn* and the name or names preceding it are introduced by Aramaic *bar*. The three families discussed in the following belonged to the upper middle class, the first was active in provincial towns, the two others in the capital.

"Lion" was a fairly common Jewish name (because of Genesis 49:9 "Judah is a lion's whelp"), but is found in the Geniza only in its Arabic form (Asad or Sibāʿ).[37] When the name of a person is Asad b. Manṣūr ("Victor") b. Asad, it is a regular instance of a man named after his grandfather, not a family name.[38] But in the case of "the prominent notable, "the Master of the Discerning," Abu 'l-Maʿālī Samuel *bar* Judah, *known as Ben* Asad," represented in documents dated 1133, 1149, 1150, 1151, 1153, 1164, 1165, and others,[39] Ben Asad is a true family name, for in another document the same person is called Samuel b. Judah *b. Samuel*, known as Ben Asad,[40] and in various others simply Abu 'l-Maʿālī Ben Asad.[41]

How far back does such a family name go? Not far, I suppose. The father of Samuel b. Judah b. Samuel Ben Asad most probably is identical with Judah b. Samuel b. Judah who, in 1109, wrote and signed a document, acting as notary in the community of al-Maḥalla, where we find our Samuel living later.[42] Since Hebrew "Judah" corresponds, as we have seen, to Arabic "Asad," it is likely that Judah I Asad, who in 1109 was dead, gave the family its name. There are other Ibn Asads in the Geniza, for instance, one Joseph b. Samuel Ibn Asad, but no connection can be established between them.[43]

The name of the Prophet Isaiah, absent from Talmudic onomastics, was not very common in Geniza times either, but it became the name of a great family, mostly in the abbreviated form Shaʿyā. Its members appear as great traders,[44] bankers,[45] representatives of the merchants,[46] and as government officials or agents.[47] Its last prominent sons represented in the Geniza were Abu 'l-Faḍl Sahl (Heb. Shelah) b. Yūshaʿ Ibn Shaʿyā, an influential government agent, who took care of the refugees from Jerusalem after the conquest of the city by the Crusaders in 1099[48] and Abu 'l-Munajjā, whose colorful story is told in *Med. Soc.*, II, 356.

I wonder whether this family, which might have had its origins in Syria,[49] is not alluded to in an epigram of the famous Arab poet Abu 'l-ʿAlā' al-Maʿarrī (973–1058):[50]

> If a man refrains from injuring me, then may divine bounty and mercy bless him as long as he lives.
> Let him read the Book of Moses, if he will, or let him, if he likes, conceive in his heart attachment to Shaʿyā.'[51]

I have come to this conclusion because in another epigram, which also expresses the idea that a good Christian or Jew is preferable to a bad Muslim, the Jew is alluded to by Manasse, also a personality prominent at the author's time, namely the Jewish administrator of Syria appointed by the Fatimid caliph.[52]

Whether Dāniyāl (Daniel) Ibn Shaʿyā, the author of a famous textbook on ophthalmology (recommended in a Geniza letter as worthy of being memorized) was of this family is not known to me.[53] Because of their prominence the members of this family often are referred to simply as Ben Shaʿyā, wherefore the relationships between them cannot be established. The Geniza texts referring to them all originated in the eleventh century.

How a family name derived from that of an ancestor came into being is well illustrated by "the House of Nānū." *Nānū* is a children's word like British *nanny* and served as byname of "the prominent notable, the *tājir* [or great merchant], Abu 'l-Ḥasan Adōnīm" (a rare Heb. name, meaning "Lords"). He was the son of Abraham b. Joseph; his firstborn, duly called Abraham after his grandfather, was killed, but a grandson from one of his other sons, Mufaḍḍal, was named Abu 'l-Ḥasan Adōnīm after him. The second of Adōnīm's sons, Mufaḍḍal II, had a son, Mīshā'ēl, for whom the memorial list, from which the information given above is taken, was written.[54]

Fortunately we possess documents related to Nānū-Adōnīm, dated 1156 and 1160, respectively,[55] to Mufaḍḍal I as contributor to various appeals (*Med. Soc.*, II, 481–483, App. C, secs. 30 and 31, and 508, sec. 139), to a son of the latter,[56] to Mufaḍḍal II, [57] both connected with the India trade, as well as three others, contemporaries of Mufaḍḍal II and his son. We see the family was named not after its first-known ancestor but after a prominent member who possessed an unusual byname. We are able to trace it, beginning with Nānū, through five generations, for a period of approximately one century.

In many cases it was not the name, but some special trait, physical or moral, of the person of an ancestor, which gave the family its designation. With the exception of the really "great" houses our material usually does not provide us with information about more than three or four generations of families with names such as "Blue-eyed," "Squint-eyed," "Red-haired," "With small teeth," "Long (and thin as a stick)," "Dazzler," or "Bragger."[58]

Several families "Small" were known. One, Ar. *Ṣaghīr*, was Rabbanite and prominent in the eleventh century as merchants, bankers, and philanthropists, Solomon II b. Saadya II b. Solomon I b. Saadya I Ben Ṣaghīr being the most frequently mentioned in letters.[59] His grandfather is represented in four dated documents, his father in another, and several relatives appear as contributors to public appeals.[60] Since all members of this family are called Ben Ṣaghīr, "Mr. Small," and not *al*-Ṣaghir, "Son of So-and-so, the small," the original possessor of the name must have preceded Saadya I by one or more generations. But we do not know anything about this. Nor are we entitled to assume that there was any connection between this Rabbanite family of the eleventh century and the leader of the Karaite community of Cairo with the same family name who lived two hundred or more years later.[61]

About Abu 'l-Munajjā of the Sha'yā family, mentioned p. 10, above, the Muslim antiquarian Ibn Duqmāq says this: "He was the ancestor of the Ibn Ṣaghīr family, most of whose members converted to Islam and became the physicians of the kings and sultans."[62] It is likely that the Karaite Ibn Ṣaghīrs of the Late Middle Ages were indeed of the progeny of Abu 'l-Munajjā. Many Karaites are known to us as government officials and court physicians. Thus we would have in Abu 'l-Munajjā the case of the scion of one illustrious family becoming the forebear of another.

There was another Karaite family named "Small," not in Arabic, but in Persian: Kujik (they were probably called thus because they already bore this name when they emigrated from Iran to Egypt). It already shows up in the eleventh century.[63] There was a prominent representative of the merchants in the twelfth,[64] a head of a government department,[65] and another high government official,[66] as well as an administrator of the Karaite pious foundations in the thirteenth century.[67] In the fourteenth century we hear only about converts to Islam who bore the name Ibn Kujik. One of these converts was a native of Ḥamā in Syria, but settled in Aleppo and later in Egypt; he was a great India trader and traveled five times to China, from where he returned with fabulous riches. He delighted people with the stories about his miraculous adventures and, "unlike other merchants," gave lavishly to the poor and never turned a beggar away.[68] The second prominent Ibn Kujik who renounced Judaism in this century was a physician who had become familiar with Islam because his father, also a physician, had Muslim scholars among his patients.[69] As we have seen, this is not the only Karaite family which ended in this way.

Nicknames of ancestors as surnames of their descendants.—Specific physical or moral traits of a forebear often were expressed by nicknames, which became family names, mostly under the form of "Son of a woman of this or that character," for instance, "Son of the Hot-tempered [woman];" "of Sweetmeat"; "of the Cow"; "of the Grain of Cumin."[70] These metronymics (names derived from the mother's name) should not be taken as remnants of ancient matriarchy. A nickname is a mild form of a curse or a blessing. The mother, the giver of life, has a magical impact on the destiny of her son. In a magical invocation the names of the mothers of both the supplicant and of his enemy (or his beloved, as the case may be) are mentioned (alongside with their fathers, or not).[71] When Muslims wish to anger a Jewish convert to Islam, they would say to him not "You son of a Jew" but "You son of the Jewess."[72] When a pre-Islamic, or early Islamic, warrior challenged an enemy, who had cursed his leader, he would call out to him: "I am So-and-so, son of So-and-so; the name of my mother is So-and-so; curse me and curse my mother," which meant that the fight to follow was one of life and death.[73]

Even a very personal and characteristic surname can only be taken as belonging to one family if it is confirmed by other data. A scribe calling himself Abraham II b. Isaac II b. Abraham I b. Daniel b. Isaac I (may he) r(est in) E(den), known as "The Son of the Cow," *Ibn Baqara*, or simply "The Cow," has left manuscripts now found in Oxford, Cambridge, and Budapest. He lived in Fustat in the second half of the eleventh century.[74] When a man named Isaac b. Abraham signs a document in Fustat in spring, 1034, we are not entitled to identify him as the father of the scribe, because these names were too common; but a good look at the manuscript shows that the court clerk added in Arabic characters on the margin: "The Son of the Cow."[75] When "Ibrahīm (Abraham), the Son of the Cow," is mentioned in a business letter sent from Qayrawān to Fustat during the first decade of the eleventh century, and "The Warehouse of the Son of the Cow," is mentioned in another business letter from the same place and time, we can safely assume that this was the grandfather of the scribe and a merchant living in Qayrawān.[76] He was already a member of the third generation to bear that surname. The merchants of Qayrawān were learned and some probably had (as scholars should have) a beautiful handwriting. Scribes list their ancestors in their colophons, I suppose, because they had inherited their art from them. Our analysis of the Geniza data on the Ibn Baqara family has also told us something about its history. Like many natives of Tunisia, Abraham II, or his father, left his country in the course of the eleventh century and settled in Egypt. In the sack of Qayrawān of 1057 the riches of the family had vanished, and what had been an avocation for his ancestors became a profession for the emigrant. He derived his livelihood from the copying of books, one of the worst-paid occupations in those days.

The surname Ibn Kammūna, "Son of the Grain of Cumin [fem.]," which sounds even stranger than "Son of the Cow," is quite another story. It appears first in the Geniza in the year 1121, in a report about messianic troubles in Baghdad, when an Abū Sahl Ibn Kammūna was received by the caliph and intervened with him for the Jewish community.[77] Another Ibn Kammūna, clearly a prominent personality, died in an underground prison in Wāsiṭ, Iraq, in 1204/5, reported by a Muslim historian as a noteworthy happening.[78] A third one, bearing the title "Pride of the Efficient [servants of the government]," is referred to as a benefactor in a letter by the Gaon of Baghdad, Samuel b. Eli, dated 1206.[79] All these as well as the famous oculist and philosopher 'Izz al-Dawla Ibn Kammūna, one of the most interesting authors of the Jewish Middle Ages (d. 1284), might have belonged to the same family. For all of them lived in Iraq and were connected with the government in one way or another. The philosopher's son, Najm al-Dawla ("Star of the Government"), also was in the service of the state.[80] But when in a list of indigent persons, drawn up in Fustat around 1230, an Ibn Kammūna receives two loaves of bread, he could hardly have been of that family, for he is mentioned as a native, not as a foreigner.[81] This shows that the strangeness of a name is by no means a guarantee for its uniqueness.

Family names derived from occupations or places of origin.—The observation that the rareness of a name is no proof of its uniqueness applies even more to surnames derived from occupations or places of origin. "Preparer of vinegar sauce relishes," *al-Kāmukhī*, certainly sounds odd to us, but this name was borne by at least two families, one being Kohens, that is, from the priestly clan of Aaron. The nonpriestly family of this name is represented fairly consecutively through two centuries by scholars, cantors, and others on the payrolls of the community.[82] A prospective contributor from the thirteenth century might also have belonged to this family.[83] A Kohen Ben al-Kāmukhī was on the payroll of the community in Egypt's capital around 1085; two others, father and son, one selling a book, the other, a physician making his will, appear in documents dated 1229 and 1241, respectively. Connecting links may still be found.[84]

While very specific names were borne by different families, it was equally common for ordinary names to form the distinctive marks of families represented in the Geniza throughout the centuries. For instance, Andalusī, "Native of Muslim Spain," was a frequently found surname. Still, one Andalusī family, with headquarters in Qayrawān, Tunisia, was prominent in the business correspondence throughout the eleventh century.[85] The manufacture of sugar was a favorite Jewish occupation, wherefore the name Sukkarī, "Sugarmaker," was widespread. Yet, one Sukkarī clan, active in Fustat (and working in the mint and as merchants, but not as sugarmakers), is well attested in documents and letters. The first known member, who lived in the tenth century, was known as Ben al-Sukkarī ("*Son* of the Sugarmaker").[86] In short, while doing research on the families of the Geniza, we should not disregard the surnames, but can make use of them only if their occurrence is accompanied by additional corroborating information.

The "illustrious houses."—Three types of families tended to perpetuate themselves by adhering to the same profession or by adopting one of similar status: (1) families of religious dignitaries and scholars, both high in rank, such as judges and heads of the yeshivas,[87] and lower in rank, such as cantors, scholars, and scribes;[88] (2) powerful merchant houses, such as the Tāhertīs of Qayrawān;[89] and (3) government officials and purveyors, as well as physicians, who often treated rulers and governors and thus were close to the seats of power.[90]

Naturally, the three types interchanged occupations freely. Since judges and cantors frequently engaged in commercial activities, it was no wonder that their sons might prefer business to a learned profession altogether. The prominent representative of the merchants in Fustat around 1100, Abū Ya'qūb al-Ḥakīm, "The Doctor" (in Hebrew: Yekuthiel b. Moses *hā-rōfē*), bore that surname because his father, and perhaps a more remote ancestor, was a physician. Yekuthiel's son, too, was a representative of merchants. But his grandson Yekuthiel II b. Moses II returned to his great-grandfather's profession and became a doctor.[91]

Whether the family in the poorer sections of the population was equally cohesive in adhering to the same profession or one of similar status is difficult to say at this stage of research. An analysis of the preserved communal lists has shown that, as a rule, indigent families were smaller than middle class families, the reason being that the boys had to leave the home of their parents at a very tender age in order to earn a livelihood wherever they could find it.[92] In general, the exigencies and stresses of economic life had a decisive influence on the formation and structure of families. The basic concepts about family represented one set of motivations, the economic realities quite another.

The vertical aspect of the extended family, that is, the immense significance of the patriarchs and agnates, as documented in the Geniza papers, was nothing exceptional. Ancestor worship was one of the foundations of the high civilizations of the ancient Mediterranean world, such as those of Hellas and Rome.[93] The veneration of the forefathers, entailing widespread knowledge of genealogy, was the backbone of pre-Islamic Arab tribal organization. There is also no need to point to the central position of the idea of "the merit of the fathers" in postbiblical Jewish religiosity.[94] The Geniza letters show that this notion was fully alive in the High Middle Ages, referring not only to the ancestors of the community but also to those of the person addressed, including his mother. A strong sense of the duty "to make good mention" of dead relatives, especially those whose lives were cut short, was also very much present and is to be understood within the general concepts about death, future life, and resurrection. It seems, however, that the social aspect was equally strong. "Man's success depends on his social position," as a Geniza letter has it, and this was largely predetermined by his origins, by the prominence, meritoriousness, and renown of his ancestors and agnates.[95]

2. *Horizontal Coherence: Brothers and Sisters. Endogamy*

Brothers between themselves.—"He is my brother, from father and mother, even if he breaks my bones." With these words does the brother of Daniel b. Azarya (Gaon of the yeshiva of Jerusalem and Head of the Jews in the Fatimid empire, 1051–1062) conclude his bitter criticism of the actions of his illustrious brother, actions by which he succeeded in ousting the Palestinian local leadership, with which the writer of the letter had completely identified himself.

"From the moment he arrived here, he has humiliated every colleague and every friend of mine in a manner that is well known. Yet it is my duty to be considerate toward him and to endure everything he does to me, since no one is under a greater obligation to do so than I, may God keep him, whether he does right or wrong."[1] This letter is written in Arabic, but the sentence cited at the opening of the paragraph is in Hebrew, although it is simply a common Arabic maxim.[2] By using the sacred language the writer wished to emphasize the sanctity of his fraternal duties. In the continuation of his lengthy letter he makes it perfectly clear that, whatever his brother's actions, he would never join his adversaries.

Except in letters of supplication and thanks, the Geniza people were not effusive in the expression of feelings, but kept to the facts. When it came to brotherly love, however, they occasionally turned eloquent. Here is a passage of a letter to a brother out in the Indian waters, taken there by an uncle on a business trip; the uncle fell sick and died in a foreign port; the young man took over efficiently, but, naturally, tarried overseas longer than planned.

Dear brother:

Had there been any possibility to get to you, no one else than me would come, for God is my witness, how I yearn for you. Every Sabbath and holiday, when I enter or leave the synagogue, I cry, saturated with grief, for I see all the young men getting together each with his brother, I turn left and right searching for you, but do not find you. . . . By God, my brother, most of my days pass in fasting [to fortify the efficacy of his prayers for the safety of his brother]; could I do without food, no bread would enter my mouth, but this is not possible; had I not been afraid of falling sick or making our father worry, I would have vowed not to break fast during day time, until I would see your dear face . . . and until we would be joyfully united, as we were before, when you came back from your voyage to Sicily.[3]

The writer of this letter was not a boy, but a seasoned merchant, as some strong advice that he gives his brother proves, especially one item with regard to a young son of the dead uncle, who had accompanied his father on that trip and made trouble after the latter's death. But the expressions of affection for the brother were tempered with politeness:

Kindly do not take amiss anything I wrote you in the way of advice with regard to the son of your maternal uncle, for I know that you are not neglectful in respect to him or to anything else. I permitted myself to write this because of the intimacy of our relations. Please have forebearance with my foolishness; I am writing without knowledge, for my senses have left me because of the separation from you and because of our troubles with. . . .[4]

Tender love for a younger brother, for which the story of Joseph and Benjamin in the Book of Genesis is so moving a model, is also expressed in Geniza times. The famous lines written by Moses Maimonides about his brother David eight years after he perished in the Indian Ocean have often been quoted. I have translated them in full in my *Letters of Medieval Jewish Traders* (p. 207), and the reader will find there also the beautifully informal and personal letter that David wrote to his illustrious brother from an east African port immediately before embarking on his ill-fated voyage.

Labrāṭ I b. Moses I Ibn Sighmār, judge in al-Mahdiyya, Tunisia, had a younger brother, Judah, who, like many other young men in that country, emigrated to Egypt and had some initial difficulties in adjusting himself to the new environment. The judge had given him some very outspoken instructions, both directly and through his learned friend Nahray b. Nissīm, who had emigrated to Egypt before. Here is the sequence of this correspondence. The first passage translated is from a very long letter, which opens with most joyful congratulations on the birth of Judah's first son:

You wrote, dear brother, that you were much distressed by my words of reproach. But we only criticize the ones we love, and if not you, whom is there that I should criticize? Have I not sworn to you time and again that you are not only my brother, but both my younger brother and my eldest son?[5] When will this little boy whom I made soil his feet [i.e., whom I sent on errands] and whom I punished for his misdeeds, be grown up? . . . For all the world I would not have misunderstandings come between you and me. . . . You are dearer to me than the world and all that is in it.[6]

And to the common friend sojourning in Egypt: "As to my words of excuse for my elder son and younger brother—God knows that he is dearer to me than my own soul. In fact, no blame comes to him at all. Only because of my exaggerated love for him have I used some strong words against him."[7]

About another brother, however, the judge wrote this: "In these days, because of my sins, I have become totally solitary. Our brother, may God keep him—you know the lowness of his character and nature. My attitude toward him mostly is not to have anything to do with him and to regard him as a complete stranger. These days, however, although the way caused me hardship, I went to Sūsa to attend his wedding."[8]

The last passage was translated in order to drive home the point that expressions of brotherly love were not merely traditional phrases, but reflections of strong emotions, just like the words of disapproval emanating from the same pen.

In the day-to-day correspondence between brothers, of which, naturally, we possess a great number, the writer would describe himself as "your brother, may I be your ransom," a phrase also used by parents and children with respect to one another. The idea underlying this expression is that just as close relatives must be prepared to stand up for each other in civil life, so must they be ready to bear the misfortunes that God has apportioned to their beloved—although the Psalmist (49:8) has clearly stated that God does not accept one brother as a substitute for another. This implies also that a man must be prepared to take upon himself the responsibility for his brother's misdeeds, a trait for which examples are to be found in the Geniza correspondence.[9]

Occasionally the phrase "may I be your ransom" is used in letters exchanged between persons who apparently are not relatives (although we never can be sure about this point) by which the writer wishes to emphasize that he belongs to the family of the addressee signifying that he has a claim on the other's support or protection.[10]

One kisses the hands of an elder brother.[11] If the addressee is younger, then the sons of the writer would kiss their uncle's hands and, if he was a scholarly person, even his feet, although the latter expression of reverence is not common in the classical Geniza period.[12] "My brother, master and lord," or "crown of my head" is the minimum of respect paid to a brother in a letter.[13] Longing was expressed by the usual phrases, such as "we are well and miss nothing except the look of your beloved face." Around the holidays the wording became stronger and more specific, for the holidays were the great occasions for family reunions.[14]

With the exception of these and similar phrases letters exchanged between brothers or other close relatives on business, private, or public affairs were not different from the correspondence of persons unconnected by family ties. As a rule, one wrote for a practical purpose, not for pouring out one's heart. This attitude is well expressed in the letter of a man from Alexandria thanking his two brothers in the capital for 10 dirhems they had sent to his mother and sisters living with him:

> I was told that you had complained of not having had a letter from me for a long time. But, God is my witness, I am constantly sending you letters, although there is nothing much in them except inquiring about

your well-being and your doings. I am of no use to you, for I am not in a position to give you presents, nor do I have business affairs with which to charge you. So, do not worry if my letters tarry. It is only your kindness and your love which make you worry about me. May God the exalted never deprive me of your kindness and love.

In a similar letter the writer says his relative had no reason to correspond with him because he lacked erudition (but his letter proves the contrary).[15]

The form of brotherly cooperation most in harmony with the spirit of the age was common study and worship. In *Med. Soc.*, II, 181, a colophon is translated in which a father buys a Bible codex for his still unmarried sons, "brotherly united in the striving for knowledge." A colophon in a ninth-century Bible codex states that it was copied and equipped with its scientific apparatus for two adult brothers, who, we must assume, lived together and probably had ordered the book for a family synagogue. It is noteworthy that the two copyists doing the job also were brothers.[16] Three brothers in Fustat, who had been students of Saadya Gaon (d. 942), were addressed by him as one years after he had left the country.[17] Two learned brothers in Fez, Morocco, sent their inquiries about religious law and practice to the heads of the Jewish high councils of Baghdad around the year 1000.[18] Slightly later were the learned Berechiah brothers of Qayrawān, Tunisia, in charge of the fund collections for the Jewish institutions of higher studies in Baghdad and Jerusalem.[19] They were supported in this by two of the Tāhertī brothers from the same city, one of whom was even honored with the title *ḥāvēr*, or member of the academy, conferred upon him in Jerusalem during the autumn pilgrimage.[20] Later in the century, the most illustrious example of brothers who were fellow students is provided by the Nagids or heads of Fatimid Jewry, Judah and Mevōrākh, the sons of the physician Saadya. In the same period, on a more modest plane, two brothers from Toledo, Spain, settled in Jerusalem, together with their old father, dedicating themselves to a life of devotion, the elder brother having apparently acquired the position of head of the immigrant group.[21] In the first half of the twelfth century we find the scholarly India trader Ḥalfōn b. Nethanel serving as a kind of roving ambassador for his two elder brothers, successively judges in the court of Gaon Maṣlī'aḥ, head of the Jerusalem high council, which then had its seat in Cairo.[22] A fourth brother, however, in whose hand we have at least ten letters to Ḥalfōn, was not learned, as he himself confessed. The correspondence with him reveals Ḥalfōn's assistance to him and his sons but does not contain scholarly matters. We see "the Torah is not a heirloom." Consequently, when we read in a Geniza letter to a communal leader who was not learned, but "whose house was full of wisdom because of his four sons who loved the Torah and its bearers"; or about five brothers, sons and grandsons of a *ḥavēr*, each bearing the same title, and a sixth called "friend of the yeshiva," that is, its supporter; or when poets praise three or even five learned brothers (Tunisia and Spain, respectively), we should not dismiss such statements lightly.[23] In the letters of Labrāṭ I and Moses Maimonides referred to at the beginning of this section, the intimate relationship between elder and younger brother was created not only by the former acting as fatherly guide, but also, and in particular, because he served as teacher and senior fellow student.

Brothers worshiped together and, as we have read (p. 16, above), met after the service to enjoy one another's company. A dead brother would be honored by a decorative wood panel bearing his name, placed in the synagogue, or by a Torah scroll donated to it, enshrined in a silver case, on which the donor would have engraved his own name and that of the deceased. In the cases of mourning and joy, such as wedding weeks and circumcision celebrations, services were held in family homes.[24]

The firstborn son occupied a privileged position. In the opening of letters he is often addressed together with his father, while his brothers are referred to only by number or in general.[25] Although the *kunya*, or honorific byname, had long before become stereotyped and was given even to a child at birth, it had not lost its original function of teknonymic, that is, parents calling themselves proudly father and mother of their firstborn. Thus in a letter, the firstborn Samuel "and his brother" are greeted, while the addressee's wife is referred to as "Mother of Samuel."[26] Even when the name of the firstborn was not mentioned, one would write: "Kindest regards to your boys, especially to your eldest."[27] Paying respect to primogeniture apparently was good form.

According to Jewish, but not Islamic, law, the firstborn also enjoyed economic prerogatives. This discrepancy between the two laws created delicate situations (see *Med. Soc.*, II, 389–390).

Brothers and sisters.—The relationship between brothers and sisters did not differ in many respects from those between male siblings. One exchanged the same asseverations of fraternal devotion, especially the phrase "may I be your ransom," which carried great practical implications, as will be seen presently.[28] The younger brother kissed the elder sister's hand, as he did with an elder brother; she was greeted before a younger brother, and in letters to third persons, she was referred to as "my mistress," a term similar to that used for one's mother and grandmother.[29]

In some respects, however, the brother-sister relationship was of a very particular character. Men could repudiate their wives, and often did so, but a sister was a lifelong responsibility. The noble brother was the rock on which the security of a woman rested. A Jewish woman from Yemen explained to me her situation by using these words: "A husband—I can get; children—I can bear; but a noble brother—from where shall I get him?"[30] This saying must have been widely used, for when I mentioned it in passing in a colloquium held in Salerno, Italy, in June 1973, a colleague from the Oriental Institute of Naples remarked that he had often heard it from his old mother, a native of the province of Lucania in southern Italy. The idea behind the saying has an age-old history. Herodotus tells us about a woman who, given the choice by the Persian king Darius of whose life should be spared, that of her husband, her children, or her brother, chose her brother, and for the same reason, namely, that *he* was irreplaceable.[31] In a famous passage of Sophocles' *Antigone* the heroine declares that she acted against the laws of the ruler of the city by burying her dead brother, a transgression that she would not have committed for other relatives.[32] Readers familiar with Arabic letters remember that the dirges that gained fame in pre-Islamic Arabia were those dedicated by women poets to their brothers, not to their husbands. The root of all this is that, even after marriage a woman remains, to some extent a member of her paternal family. A married woman says to her brother's wife in a north Palestinian Arab village, "You cannot prevent me from taking food from my brother's stores. It is not your money and not even his. I eat from my father's possessions."[33]

The few examples given show that the brother-sister syndrome was not confined to Egypt or to the orbit of Islamic civilization, but is a human experience well attested in the countries of the Mediterranean and the Near East. A selection from the rich material on the question preserved in the Geniza will demonstrate how it worked during the High Middle Ages.[34]

"My brother is an unsocial, bashful young man"—with these words a woman submitting a boldly worded complaint against her husband to the Nagid Samuel b. Hananya excuses herself: her natural protector was of no use.[35] The sister is the *dhimma*, or responsibility, of her brother. "You help strangers and people from outside; I, your sister, your flesh and responsibility, have more claim on your support." Thus writes a widow in Tunisia to her brother in Egypt in a time of general disaster and personal hardship.[36] In the Geniza, and also in Fatimid inscriptions, the sister is her brother's "honored dear," *karīma*, a term, which in modern Egyptian and in literary Arabic designates the daughter.[37]

Correspondence between brothers and sisters is represented in the Geniza to a far larger extent than that between husbands and wives. The oldest letter preserved, still written in Aramaic (eighth century?), is addressed by a sister to "my beloved and cherished brother, my hope and trust, my salvation from distress." When a young Tunisian, looking for work in Egypt, sends home to Qayrawān two rather detailed, but almost identical, letters, one to his parents and one to his sister, the latter can be understood only as an act of fraternal love or as compliance with etiquette.[38] A remarkable letter of condolence written by a brother to his learned sister Rayyisa on the occasion of the death of their old mother betrays a dedication which had only deepened with the years.[39] The easygoing talk of an elder sister writing to her brother in Egypt shows indeed that it was expected that a brother write to his sister in addition to his immediate family.[40] Presents should accompany the fraternal message. A long business letter sent from Tunisia to Egypt concludes thus:

> If my cousin Barhūn b. Isma'īl happens to be in town, please give him my best regards and tell him that his sister is very much yearning for him. She has not seen any letter from him since he left, nor any package; she knows about him only through the letters of others. Now, if he is on his way home, may God, the exalted, grant him a safe passage. But if he is staying on, he had better send her some cash she could use for her little ones, the girls.[41]

The married sister expected to receive cash as a present from her brother. The wife of the cantor and court clerk Ḥalfōn b. Manasse, from whom we have several letters to her brother (all written in the beautiful hand of her husband), thanks him in one of them for a gift of twelve dirhems.[42] Such presents were downright obligatory at the birth of a child when a visit from the brother was also expected. "I congratulate you on your sister having been delivered of a boy and a girl," Ḥalfōn once wrote somewhat sarcastically to his brother-in-law, "but you had better not ask me how she scolds you," evidently expressing disappointment that he had not come for the expected event or sent a present.[43] A daughter of this woman informs her uncle that she was expecting and was in her sixth month, and most urgently asks him to visit her and her old mother.[44]

The extraordinary position of the brother in past generations had its origin at least partly in the shorter life expectation in those days. The father, as we learn from many deathbed declarations providing for small children, often died young. It was the brother who accompanied his sister through life: he had to look after her in her orphaned childhood, he was bound to provide her with everything needed for her marriage, and, at old age, admitted her to his household, when, as a widow or divorcée, she had nowhere else to go. Engagement contracts and other documents show that, even in a father's lifetime, a brother often would represent his sister in the negotiations leading to the marriage. A variety of specific circumstances, such as the age or health of the father, might have been involved in each particular case. But this certainly was also a matter of decorum. Commenting on the story of Rebekah (Genesis 24:50), where her brother Laban, and not her father, confers with the messenger of her suitor, Abraham Maimonides (1186–1237) remarks: "As is well known, fathers feel embarrassed about personally dealing with the marriage of their daughters."[45]

The brother-sister relationship was by no means a one-way affair. In many cases, a married woman was economically stronger than her agnates and could serve them as a pillar of refuge. By character or other circumstances she might enjoy a position of influence within the family, and, even beyond, and thus be able to intervene in disputes between her relatives. Finally, the code of honor demanded that a person possessing authority or power should harken to the cry of help of a woman, especially a noble one, wherefore a sister was the natural intercessor for her brother.

"If I do not apply to you, to whom should I? It is up to you to spare us humiliation and to extricate us from our plight." With these words a former official of the mint in Cairo who had been reduced to abject poverty appeals to his sister.[46] The most detailed description of exceptionally cruel, prolonged, and repeated tortures found in the Geniza is addressed to a sister, with the aim, of course, to elicit her compassion and financial help.[47] That such calls for support were not in vain is proved by numerous documents, even those related to women from less well-to-do families than those addressed in the two letters just cited. In order to help her brother a woman sold her maidservant, which she was not permitted to do, since the girl was part of the dowry (and consequently her husband's responsibility); the price obtained was 10½ dinars, about half the standard price.[48] Another woman gave to her brother 3 and 10 dinars, respectively, from the purse of her husband, providing surety for these sums with her personal property.[49] When the father of a little boy was faced with the approach of sudden death, his elder daughter promised him that she would take the boy to her house, bring him up at her own expense and give him a part of the large house that she had received from her mother as a gift. The other part most probably belonged to the father and automatically went to the boy. The dying man wished that the property should be united in the hands of his son.[50]

A sister would mediate in disputes between her brothers, one instance being especially noteworthy because in this matter a man in a provincial town asks a business friend traveling to Alexandria to talk with his sister about a dispute with his brother, which he did.[51] A woman who describes herself as the daughter of the late *shaykh al-yahūd*, or head of the Jewish community in Ascalon, Palestine, asks a high dignitary in the Egyptian capital (where she sojourned), to intervene with his opposite number in the Palestinian port city in favor of her two brothers, especially one who served there as a beadle.[52] Sisters were helpful also in less urgent and sometimes even dubious situations. A married woman, together with her mother, once bought for her brother the highly estimated (and highly paid for) honor of reciting the Book of Esther during the service.[53] In two cases a sister illegally harbored a slavegirl belonging to her brother. In the first case, the master, a bachelor, had been ordered to sell her since he was not supposed to possess one in the first place. "But," the local dignitary reports, "he has not offered the slavegirl for sale, but put her with his sister and passes most of his time there."[54] In the second, the complaint of the woman with the bashful brother, she describes, among other torts done to her, how the maidservant who had been awarded to her was kept by her husband in the house of his sister. Incidents where the attachment of a man to his sisters created tension with his wife are reported in section C.[55]

The sister's son.—Affection for the sister was transferred to her son. The sister's son looms large in the private correspondence and even more so in the business correspondence of the Geniza. This phenomenon, like the brother-sister syndrome, was heavily conditioned by the medieval distribution of age so different from ours. As a rule, girls married at a tender age. By the time a woman was forty and her brother, say, thirty-five, she could easily have a son of twenty to twenty-five years, who would be able to become an associate of his uncle and some day, especially if the latter had no son, take over the business, preferably after marrying one of his uncle's daughters, if he had any.

Numerous persons (and not only Jews) are known in the Geniza simply as Mr. So-and-so's sister's son. This designation implied a claim. The nephew was to continue the uncle's work or at least his status. "Muḥsin, the representative of the merchants, son of Ḥusayn, known as Sham'ān's sister's son,"[56] most probably was called that because he had taken over his uncle's warehouse and position. For Sham'ān, too, acted as representative of the merchants in Fustat. In one document this Muḥsin is simply named Muḥsin b. Sham'ān.[57] Nathan b. Abraham, who became Āv, "Father," that is, President of the high court of the yeshiva of Jerusalem, and, for about three years (1039–1042), rival Gaon, was known as the sister's son of another Āv.[58] In the earlier history of the Jerusalem yeshiva a Gaon from a family of Kohens had himself been characterized as "R. Aaron Ben-Meir's sister's son" because the Ben-Meirs derived their lineage from the Patriarchs of Judea and through them from the House of David.[59] Moses Maimonides' son was born to him late in life, when he was forty-eight years old; therefore he took his sister's son into his house and taught him his profession, the art of healing.[60] The maker of purple cloth 'Arūs b. Joseph, a prominent figure in the Geniza world of around 1100, had no son; consequently he groomed a sister's son as his business associate. In his Arabic correspondence the young man addressed him as "my father," which was common under such circumstances, but also with the intimate Aramaic *abbā mārī* "Dad, my lord," which was exceptional. An elaborate document shows that the old man paid his sister's son's debts.[61]

According to a Talmudic saying, cited in a Geniza letter, and a popular belief, expressed in maxims found in practically all Arabic dialects, most sister's sons resemble their uncles. Should this belief have contributed to the intimacy of the relations between maternal uncles and their nephews?[62] In a warm letter addressed to a sister's son and mainly concerned with an unhappy, newly married young woman, the uncle reminds his nephew of the education given to him, the family obligations, and the love between them.[63] "Education" means the apprenticeship in business or whatever their occupation was. In a deathbed declaration a man appoints his brother-in-law as his executor, but leaves money to "his sister's son" (the son of the executor).[64] In a particularly sentimental letter, a sister's son reports to his uncle that he and his wife (the uncle's daughter) were well and healthy, but perished for longing after him and "the smell of the family." He gives indeed regards to about twenty-five persons and when acknowledging a letter of his uncle he states that its arrival was like the day he parted from him, meaning, that the letter substituted for the uncle's presence.[65]

It is remarkable that the description of a person merely as the son of the sister of so-and-so is provided even where one expects to find a fuller definition, as in a legal document, list of contributors or of passengers in a boat (three examples in one letter!), or in an important information sent from one place or one country to another. The surname was acquired even when the uncle was still alive. A Gaon of the tenth century addresses a notable in northern Iraq as "Bundār's sister's son," but, later in the letter, extends greetings to the esteemed elder Bundār, the Head of the Community, son of the late Moses.[66] In some cases we know the full name of a person referred to in a letter solely as nephew of his uncle. In others we do not. This situation seems to indicate that a sister's son often grew up in the house of his uncle who substituted for his father and whose name then served as the young man's patronymic.[67] The custom of naming a person after his maternal uncle was common in Talmudic times.

Endogamy; marriage with the niece.—In view of the extraordinary position of the sister's son in the family system of the Geniza period I expected to find frequent cases of marriages of uncles with the daughters of their sisters. This union, which was censured as incestuous by the Jewish sect of the Karaites and is prohibited by the Church and Islam, was regarded as most natural in the Talmud and is still practiced by Jews, even modern ones, both of European and Oriental extraction.[68] In the Geniza, however, I have noted only a few cases; one in Qayrawān, Tunisia, before 1055, two in the thirteenth century, one of which was about to end in divorce and the other was dissolved even before the wedding.[69] One case of a marriage with a brother's daughter, also, it seems, from the thirteenth century, appears in a letter from Damascus.[70] Thus it is likely that there was some truth in the claim of the Karaite author Sahl b. Maṣlī'aḥ (lived in Jerusalem, second half of the tenth century) that under the influence of the Karaite divines the Rabbanite Jews resolved to refrain from "the licentious union" with the sister's daughter.[71] In the eleventh and twelfth centuries "mixed" marriages between Karaites and Rabbanites were commonplace in Egypt; for this reason one probably avoided situations which would make such family connections impossible.

Marriage between first cousins.—Unlike the union between uncles and nieces, that between first cousins was extremely common in Geniza times. The marriage with the father's brother's daughter (FBD) is attested over twice as frequently as that with the mother's brother's daughter (MBD). This difference is perhaps partly to be explained by the fact that we have much patrilineal, but little matrilineal, information; the father, and occasionally also the grandfather of the bride and bridegroom are noted, but their mothers only in exceptional cases. Still the testimony of the Geniza does indeed reflect the actual situation: marriages with the FBD were common practice; *bint 'amm*, daughter of the paternal uncle, in Arabic means a wife.

Marriage with the first cousin, especially with the FBD, is a widely diffused social institution, found far beyond the confines of the Arabian world. A comprehensive discussion of this phenomenon is provided in a recent publication by Paul Bourdieu surveying the latest literature on the subject and dealing specifically with Kabyle ethnology. A critical appraisal of research in this field, written by the anthropologist Richard L. Antoun, has just appeared.[72] And a study on the subject carried out in the 1960s by Harvey Goldberg among Tripolitanian Jews is illuminating. It should also be noted that marriage between first cousins, although prohibited by most Orthodox churches, is permitted and widely practiced in the main Christian community of Egypt, the Copts. We are concerned here with the problem of why the urban society of craftsmen, merchants, and professionals speaking to us through the Geniza should adhere to this matrimonial system with the same tenacity as a tribal peasant or pastoral population.[73]

To be sure, Abraham, the father of the Jewish faith, saw to it that his son Isaac should marry a girl from his family; Rebekah, Isaac's wife, was a daughter of his first cousin; Jacob, Isaac's son, was sent by his parents to woo a cousin (Genesis 28:2). He won two, Rachel and Leah; and when Ruth was married to a man from her dead husband's kin, she was blessed with the wish that she might become like Rachel and Leah "who built the house of Israel" (Book of Ruth 4:11). This blessing, naturally, was used in Geniza letters conveying good wishes for a wedding.[74] Nowhere, however, does marriage with relatives appear as religiously motivated. Nor can the economic factors have been decisive. We do hear of properties united by marriage,[75] but any woman not related to the family would bring in houses and other valuables as dowry, receive them as gifts, or inherit them. Thus the main incentive for the proliferation of marriages with cousins and other close relatives must have been attributable to the role of the extended family and to the notion that husband and wife who belonged to the same kin would be considerate of each other and of the family at large; they would not expose their own people to shame (just as the Talmud stated with regard to the sister's daughter).[76] And since the expanded family was essentially conceived as "The House of the Father," the children and children's children of brothers were the preferred mates.

There was an additional reason for marriage with relatives, from either the father's or the mother's side: the protection of the newly wed wife, who, unless she was a widow or divorcée, normally was of very tender age. When she went into the home of people whom she knew and who had obligations toward her, she would not feel so lonely and miserable as in a house of complete strangers. It is not unrealistic to assume such considerateness for the young female on the part of the generally very egotistic males speaking to us in the Geniza. Women had a strong say in matters of marriage, and there was the duty of compassion, often invoked, especially if the bride was an orphan with not much family backing. "She has no father and brother except you," writes a relative to another relative in whose house the bride stayed, meaning that the person addressed had to replace both.[77]

In order to illustrate the times and milieus in which endogamy makes its appearance in the Geniza and how far it attained the aims assumed for it above, some relevant documents and letters are summarized here. The documents are comparatively few in number since the names of the grandfathers are rarely listed.

Marriage with the father's brother's daughter. A. Documents

1. Huge Karaite marriage contract between Solomon b. Mevassēr b. Sahl and his first cousin (expressly referred to as such) Sarah b. Israel b. Sahl, both of the well-known and rich family called al-ʿĀnī (Heb. "Poor," a name of religious significance). The matrimonial gift: 100 dinars, already paid, plus 50, delivered on the day of the wedding. Cairo 1003/4.

2. Deposition in court: a husband and his wife, who was his paternal first cousin, declare that neither any longer have a claim against a relative in an inheritance (in which both had had rights). Dec., 1026.

3. A young woman appeals to the community against her husband, a paternal first cousin, and an old man (eleventh century).

4. Official letter of the head of a local community to the authorities in the capital: The bearer of this letter wished to marry two of his motherless daughters to the sons of their paternal uncle

(i.e., his brother) and for this purpose had deposited part of their trousseaux with a married daughter of his. But the son-in-law, who had a claim against the bearer, laid his hands on the trousseaux (ca. 1130).

5. A woman, who was the paternal first cousin of her husband, complains in court that he was away without providing her with sustenance. The court awards her 1 dirhem per day, as of May 18, 1156.

6. Sitt al-Dār ("Mistress of the House"), the daughter of the India trader Abraham (Ben) Yijū, marries her paternal first cousin, seven years after her father, on his way back from India, where she was born, alerted his family that he would spare her for one of his nephews. July, 1156. See Goitein, *Letters*, pp. 201–206.

7. Engagement contract of two poor first cousins. Matrimonial gift: 5 + 10 dinars. Wedding to be held three years later. Spring, 1185.

8. The brother of a dead husband, who was the paternal first cousin of his wife, grants the childless widow (his cousin) a release from the obligation to marry him (the so-called levirate, see sec. B, 4, and C, 1, n. 223, below). 1202.

9. A *qayyim*, or administrator of a synagogue (see *Med. Soc.*, II, 77), returns to his brother's son the presents given to his daughter, after the engagement, which had lasted a long time, was finally dissolved. Nov.-Dec., 1240.

10. Marriage contract from the second half of the thirteenth century between paternal cousins of a fairly well-to-do family (name of the common—deceased—grandfather provided). Matrimonial gift: 30 + 70 = 100 dinars. Value of the trousseau: nominally 460, actually 230 dinars.

11. A case similar to no. 8.[78]

Marriage with the father's brother's daughter. B. Letters

Only at the beginning of the thirteenth century did correspondents occasionally date their letters. Therefore the chronological sequence of letters cannot be fixed with certitude, especially in the frequent cases where only one example of the handwriting of the sender is known and when no allusions to contemporary events or prominent personalities are made.

1. The head of a community in a small town of northern Syria writes to the Jewish chief judge of Aleppo, a relative of his. The writer's sister was married to her paternal cousin, a son of that couple had recently married, but experienced some difficulties with his new in-laws; the judge is requested to pay attention to this matter.

The letter is accompanied by a present of 2½ (Syrian) pounds of truffles. Early eleventh century.

2. A middle class merchant on a trip, writing to his paternal uncle, greets his wife and his mother-in-law. Late eleventh century.

3–4. A woman who was unhappily married to her first cousin asks a paternal uncle, a notable (also married to a first cousin), to let her take refuge in his home. Probably twelfth century.

5. "Your servant married the daughter of his paternal uncle." A cantor and teacher, who had been captured by the Normans (in Jerba, Tunisia, 1136) and ransomed in Egypt, writes to a benefactor.

6. A husband complains to his father about his malicious mother-in-law, the latter's brother's widow, and her daughter, his wife, who have a bad influence on his children, but against whom he is powerless.

7. A physician from Qalyūb, north of Cairo, who had opened an office in the capital, asks his *bint ʿamm*, or paternal cousin, that is, wife, to join him there. Her daughter, who also lived in the capital, was in her sixth month of pregnancy and wished her mother to assist her at the time of childbirth.

8. The judge Nathan ha-Kohen b. Solomon (see *Med. Soc.*, II, 513, sec. 17) was married to the sister of his paternal cousin Tovia b. Eli. "Your sister kisses your hand and kisses the eyes of your children." This relationship is mentioned in many letters exchanged between the two.

9. A half-brother of the judge Meir b. Hillel (1160–1171, see *Med. Soc.*, II, 421, sec. 97) married his paternal cousin.

10. A teacher and court clerk in Alexandria writes to his paternal second cousin and brother-in-law, a fledgling physician, in Cairo. Early thirteenth century.

11. The physician Abū Zikrī, son of the physician Abu 'l-Faraj, is admonished by his paternal first cousin to write to his wife (the latter's sister) and to act on her behalf.

12. The wife of the teacher and court clerk Solomon, son of the judge Elijah, was the daughter of both a paternal and a maternal uncle, that is, two brothers had married two sisters. He expresses his love for the addressee, his uncle, but complains about his unruly young wife, the latter's niece.

13. A former official in the mint of Cairo, who had been reduced to abject poverty, urgently appeals to his well-to-do-sister, who was married to a son of a paternal uncle. Oct. 21, 1219.

14. A grandson of Moses b. Joshia marries a daughter of Joseph b. Joshia. Damascus. Thirteenth century.

15. When Nahray b. Nathan, a paternal cousin of Nahray b.

Nissīm, sends him greetings from "my sister and the girls," it is evident that this was the prominent merchant banker's first wife, who had remained with her brother and children in Alexandria, while her husband, a newcomer to Egypt, was exploring his prospects for settling in Fustat. The letter contains the question whether the family should move to the recipient's place; ca. 1050.[79]

Marriage with the mother's brother's daughter

1. A cantor from Fez, Morocco, but settled in the capital of Egypt, had a maternal uncle in Damascus. Visiting there, he reports about his happy marriage with the uncle's daughter (ca. 1037).

2. A fiancé asks his maternal uncle for the postponement of the wedding with his daughter, since he had not yet accumulated the funds necessary for the occasion. Very poor people. He greets "the dowager," Heb. *ha-gevīrā*, the mother of the bride, but, of course, not the bride herself.

3. A scholar, in Fustat, whose wife was the daughter of his maternal uncle, sends books to her brothers in Tinnīs, Lower Egypt. A cheerful letter.

4. The wife of the prominent eleventh-century merchant Mūsā b. Abi 'l-Ḥayy (see *Med. Soc.*, II, 445, sec. 27, and 587, n. 20) is greeted by his brother as "the daughter of my maternal uncle."

5. On her deathbed a well-to-do young woman expresses the desire that her little boy (not yet of school age) be married to her brother's daughter. Spring, 1143.

6. Instruction to a local official that there was no legal objection to the marriage of the Kohen Elijah to the daughter of his maternal uncle. An objection had been raised in the community, but not because he was the cousin of his future wife.

7. On his deathbed a man leaves to his wife, the daughter of his maternal uncle, one-third of a house, if she does not marry again. If she does, she will receive only what was still due her from the delayed matrimonial gift. March 24, 1182.

8. For Solomon b. Elijah's wife see preceding list, no. 12.

9. A Levi marries the daughter of his maternal uncle (around 1200).

10. The son of a sister of the Gaon and nāsī Daniel b. Azarya married his daughter.

11. After the death of the India trader Abū Ya'qūb (Joseph) Lebdī, his sister's son, Abū Isḥāq Abraham b. Isaac, who had lived in his house, was betrothed to his daughter, Sitt al-Ahl ("Mistress of the Family"), with her consent, but in the absence of her brother.

When the brother, an India trader like his father, returned from his voyage, the family wished to cancel the betrothal (1118/1119).[80]

Marriages between the sons and daughters of two sisters certainly were not rare, either. But because of our lack of matrilineal information we do not read much about them. Here is an example: a father had left a maidservant to his two married daughters who lived in one house, most probably also given to them by their father. When one of the daughters died, her husband inherited one-half of the legal rights on that girl, but gave it to his son, when he married his cousin, the daughter of his father's sister-in-law. She in turn gave the other half to her daughter.[81]

Mention has been made before of two sisters married to brothers, and of a father wishing to marry his two daughters to his nephews.[82] By chance documents showing two sisters actually married to brothers have been preserved.[83] From a passage in a letter from David to Moses Maimonides I conclude that their wives were sisters.[84] Such occurrences were not more frequent than they are in our own society, and there is nothing specifically noteworthy about them.

It is well known that a sister of Maimonides was married to one of his five brothers. I looked for similar arrangements in the Geniza documents, but did not find any. No wonder. "Exchange marriages," as they are called in various Arabic vernaculars, were and are common in societies living according to Arabic tribal, not Islamic religious, law. In the former, the father gets the *mahr*, or nuptial gift, in the latter the bride does. One "exchanges" the daughters, in order to save the payment of the mahr. When the bride is the recipient, as in Islamic and Jewish laws, no such saving can be made. Maimonides' case was exceptional. Similar cases occur, albeit rarely, in our own society.

I should like to conclude this survey with two examples of endogamy preceding and following the "classical" Geniza period, but belonging to the same cultural milieu. The scene of the first is southern Italy in the later part of the ninth century. Shefaṭyā, a scholar and writer of religious poetry, also a rich and powerful man, had a beautiful and lovely daughter whom *he* wished to marry off, but his wife stalled: she would give her only to a man as learned and prosperous as her own husband. One night Shefaṭyā got up to pray and to write poetry. When Cassia, his daughter, heard this, she rushed out of her bed, brought water, and poured it over her father's hands—as was obligatory before prayer. Observing Cassia in her nightgown, her father realized that she was a ripe woman and became very angry with himself, and, of course, also with his wife that they had not yet married her off. His brother had indeed asked him to give her to his son, but her mother would have none of it. But now Shefaṭyā was resolved not to wait any longer and said so to his wife. In the morning, after the synagogue service, he told his brother, summoned the entire congregation to his house, and the betrothal was enacted. The great-great-great-grandson of Cassia, who tells us this story in his family chronicle, does not find it necessary to notify us when the young couple were informed about their fathers' decision or how they took it. He only supplies us with the title of the religious poem which her brother Amittay wrote for the occasion (we still have the poem).[85]

Our second example is less dramatic, but connected with one of the most famous personalities of the later Jewish Middle Ages, R. Isaac Luria, the great cabalist of the sixteenth century. When his father died, his mother was invited by her rich brother to stay with him in Cairo. Isaac consented to follow her because only his uncle would be able to provide him with the books needed for his studies. He was a child prodigy confounding all the wise men of Egypt with his wisdom. At the age of fifteen he was married to his uncle's daughter. This is what his biography, which, naturally, bears largely the character of a hagiography, has to tell us. But there is no reason to doubt the detail about his marriage, which is confirmed by other sources.[86]

The survey presented above seems to show that endogamy was practiced at all times and by all professional groups and sections of the population represented in the Geniza. It also reveals the fact that close relationship was no panacea for achieving happiness in marriage. We have read about engagements dissolved, hardship, and even utmost misery in marriages with a cousin, as well as about divorce. But endogamy was a fact of life, based on strong social convictions.

3. *Economic and Legal Aspects of the Extended Family*

Family attachment and claims of the individual.—In our society, the nuclear family, that is, parents with their children under legal age, form an economic commune, although husband and wife often keep separate bank accounts and other personal property rights. The situation in Geniza times was different, inasmuch as a household often comprised three generations and also included agnates and cognates. Moreover, both the government and public opinion were prone to hold a father, or brother, or an even more distant relative responsible for a man's commitments, although strict law, both Islamic and Judaic, did not recognize such a claim. This widening of the family concept was counter-balanced by the individualistic spirit of the time, the fervent insistence of nearly everyone on his full rights.

Before going into details, I should like to illustrate this situation of the Geniza family by three ordinary examples. A father writes from a Sudanese port to his son in Alexandria sending him the goods acquired there and leaving it largely to him how to deal with them. The son is admonished to take good care of his mother, his wife, and his boys, but receives only one tenth of the profit made from the goods sent, and this after some advance lump deduction for the father. Thus, the married son might live with his parents under one roof, but property is not shared in common; he is not even a partner of his father, but receives a kind of commission like an agent. The maternal uncles of the writer and their sons as well as his aunt's son greeted in the letter might have lived on other floors of the same house or close by.[1]

The troubles caused by agnates—but endured with resignation—are vividly brought home in a letter from Alexandria, addressed to the sons of a dead sister in the capital. The writer must have had a number of children, for he reports the death of the youngest, a boy, only in passing, adding drily: "May God preserve the rest." Two aged sisters lived with him, together with an orphan boy from a niece whose recent death is also reported. Another niece staying with him had a suitor whom she could not marry because she was a divorcée and had not received the legal documents needed for the new marriage. The main purpose of the letter to the nephews was to secure the missing papers (perhaps one of them had been married to the unhappy woman). As though that were not enough: two sisters of those nephews lived in a house belonging to their family in Alexandria. The house was *mayshūm*, ill-omened, probably because someone had been killed there, or had died an unnatural or premature death. No one came to visit the girls, and they lived in complete solitude, "the most miserable creatures in the entire city with no one to care for them." The writer was prepared to invite these nieces to stay with him, but their brother would not permit them to move, probably in order to have someone to look after the property. Having already been ill for five months, during which time he was able to go out to the bazaar only once, the writer had entrusted one of the sons of his dead sister with some of his business, but he had completely wrecked it. "The complaint is to God alone" (for what can one do against a close relative?). Several other relatives are mentioned in the letter in a rather sarcastic vein.[2]

The discrepancy between the belief in the legitimate claims of the extended family on a man's resources and his disgust at their conduct is even more conspicuous in this passage from the letter of a merchant who sojourned in India and for some time had been without contact with his relatives in Egypt. The recipient was the writer's cousin and brother-in-law; Mufaḍḍal, who is so prominently mentioned, was the son of another aunt of the writer.

You have given me no information about Mufaḍḍal's mother, your own mother, Umm Saʿīd [the writer's sister] . . . or anyone else. You have sent me no letter of condolence on the death of my mother,[3] nor written me who has died and who is still alive. Mufaḍḍal, yes, he has done harm to himself and harm to me, since he has lost four thousand gold pieces of mine—may God have mercy upon him.[4] But he is excused; he has become like his father; his father ruined part of my inheritance from my father, and he [Mufaḍḍal] did the same with my own property. But you have surpassed them. You have done what no Jewish man has ever done. Your story goes around here in India, let alone in Egypt. Jews arriving from Egypt, nay, even Muslims, know about your deeds.

I have sent you a kerchief and a turban with Naṣr, the Mecca pilgrim, and have approached you with regard to your middle son—the older one, he with the sound eyes.[5] Send him to me; I have a young daughter, let him come and take her and return to you. I informed you also that he could take a loan on my account and come here, where I shall pay all the expenses made by him. If your mother has died, so that you are free, take him and come yourself.[6]

This is better than that others should devour me. You have a stronger claim.[7]

I have little doubt that the writer's decision was influenced also by the consideration that his daughter could find no better mother-in-law than his own sister, back home in Egypt. But he speaks only about his fortunes, on which, he felt, his extended family had some rights.

Joint domicile.—The coherence of "the father's house" became physically visible by its members sharing living quarters or occupying adjacent or otherwise neighboring buildings.

"How good and lovely it is when brothers dwell together" (Psalm 133:1). At the time the psalmist wrote these words, they already had the nostalgic tinge of an ideal order which was no longer fully realized. Did not the Book of Genesis recount that Abraham separated from his nephew Lot (13:6), and Esau from his brother Jacob (36:7), "because the country could not support both of them dwelling together"? If those were the conditions in the pastoral and farming society of ancient Israel, what could be expected from townspeople in medieval Islam? Still the urge, and almost moral obligation, that the members of a family should live close to one another was strongly felt—as was the opposite and more modern endeavor to escape from the supervision and encroachment of relatives. Both tendencies are amply documented in the Geniza. The situation within another Jewish society inside Islamic civilization, a society of more recent date, but perhaps more pristine character, might serve as a backdrop.

In a recently published autobiography, a Yemenite octogenarian, Joseph Ḥubārāh, gives an account of the resettlement of his family, after the Jews had been pillaged and expelled from San'a, the capital of Yemen, in 1679 and temporarily banished to the unhealthy coast of the Red Sea. On the land outside the city acquired by the exiled after their return, the Ḥubārāhs, like the other families, settled together and erected in the course of time a double row of houses including a synagogue bearing their name. At the time of the exodus in 1950, nine houses, one adjoining another, were still owned by Ḥubārāhs; the others had been sold or abandoned. Thus propinquity of domicile as an expression of family coherence had endured for 270 years. It stands to reason that it had existed within the city walls of San'a for centuries before. The Ḥubārāhs were one of the minor Jewish families in the city. A look at a map of the Jewish town shows that, with a few exceptions, each of the twenty-eight or so synagogues and the surrounding streets were named after families, all well known and still extant.[8]

No such synagogues and streets are found in the Geniza documents. The twin capitals of Egypt were not the scene of mass dislocations and resettlements, as happened in San'a both before and in the wake of the temporary expulsion of the Jews from the High Yemen in 1679, which made compact clannish domiciles possible. Fustat was originally a Byzantine fortress, inhabited by Christians and Jews, and enlarged by an Arab tribal camp-city, into which ever new trickles of immigrants infiltrated. Cairo, it is true, was newly founded but, like Baghdad, was conceived from the outset as the seat of the court, the central administration, and the caliphal guards. Of the civil population only persons directly connected with the court, such as higher officials, purveyors, and court physicians, were admitted at the beginning. A document, by chance preserved outside the Geniza, tells us that the synagogue in the newly founded city was surrounded on all sides by houses belonging to one family of court physicians who had come to Egypt together with the ruling dynasty, and that the synagogue itself was under their jurisdiction. We encounter here a situation not dissimilar to that observed by us in Yemen. But this was exceptional.[9]

It stands to reason that great and rich merchant families settling in the capital of Egypt, like the three Tustarī brothers emigrating from Iran at the beginning of the eleventh century, acquired adjacent properties, although the fact that letters were addressed to all of them together should not be taken as proof of it.[10] But the ordinary immigrant did not possess the means for this manner of settlement. Migration, if it was not a flight having recourse to public charity,[11] was a protracted process. It took years for a middle class immigrant to set enough aside to acquire a domicile concomitant with his status. The son of an immigrant from Palestine became a merchant's representative; finally, on July 20, 1004, he bought one third of a house, presumably an entire story, for the then high sum of 70 dinars.[12] In 1045 the Tunisian Nahray b. Nissīm came to Egypt, and in 1066, about twenty years later, he was still living as a tenant in a mansion belonging to his two brothers-in-law. At a much later date he acquired one third of the house from one of them (the other had meanwhile died) for the considerable price of 150 dinars.[13]

If the history of Fustat-Cairo, and indeed of all the Mediterranean cities about which the Geniza informs us, was not favorable to clannish settlement, that is, to clusters of extended families, the extended family itself clearly tried hard to stay together. This is proved by the numerous documents in which neighboring houses are united in one hand or in the hands of close relatives, or where spacious houses harbored several related families. In 959, ten years before the Fatimid conquest of Egypt, a father makes a gift of two adjacent houses and two shops to his firstborn son; that property bordered on a house known to be occupied by two brothers and their families.[14] A document dated 969 shows a woman in possession of two houses located one opposite the other. In two other documents the opposite or adjacent house was described as being in a ruined state.[15] Detailed descriptions of properties consisting of three houses plus two ruins and two houses and two stables with one upper story have been preserved.[16] A house on the fashionable Nile island of Cairo, sold by a widow, bordered on one side on a property once belonging to the famous vizier Ibn Killis (see *Med. Soc.*, I, 33–34), and on the other side on that of her son.[17] A large house and an adjacent smaller one must have been a particularly popular form of family settlement. In one case we are able to trace their history through half a century; in another they form the object of a litigation between a brother and a sister.[18] In a third instance, a brother gives to a younger sister at her marriage (in 1156) one half of both a large and a small house and, later, on his deathbed, gives her the remaining halves (date not preserved). This case is particularly instructive. The houses were in the Zawīla quarter of Cairo and probably were acquired or erected by the family when they moved from the old to the new capital. They also possessed shares in a house in Fustat. Of these the dying man gave one sixth of the house to his older sister, a widow, and one twelfth to the son of a brother, both of whom certainly held other shares in the same house.[19]

In a fragmented document from Damascus, Syria, a man gives a house "on the side of my house" to a person with a different family name, presumably a son-in-law. The incompletely preserved description seems to suggest that the two houses were interconnected.[20]

Needless to say, Muslim family attachment took similar forms. When a Jew acquired from a Muslim two neighboring abandoned buildings, it seems likely that they had been occupied by various members of an extended family which had moved elsewhere. When we read, however, of the mansion of a Muslim merchant in Baghdad, destroyed by flood, which comprised thirty separate buildings as well as a garden and a bathhouse, we must remember that a large section of the Muslim population of the Iraqian capital was created by the influx of bedouins to whom a multi-domicile mansion was but an urban tent-camp of a clannish type.[21]

Useful information about the living quarters of an extended family may be derived from the lists of contributors to public appeals as analyzed in *Med. Soc.*, II, 471–509. In many cases the sponsors clearly went from house to house and from one bazaar to the next, and in their lists it is frequently evident that fathers and sons, brothers, and other relatives lived close to one another or in the same house. Number 55 on page 492 is a good example.

Since the Mediterranean house of the Geniza period, even in provincial towns, often consisted of several stories, it was the natural domicile for several branches of an extended family. Examples are provided in this book in many different contexts. The origins of joint living were of the greatest imaginable variety. A father gives an entire house to his two sons because he wishes them to stay together; the house consisted of two stories with a mezzanine in between; the gift was in two equal shares, but the document defines specifically the parts that belonged to each of the two.[22] But when we find two brothers, government officials in Damascus, living together in a mansion, we may properly assume that the property was acquired by them when they attained their high positions. They had to leave the country to escape a rapacious governor; the house became the object of a lawsuit a quarter of a century later when a son of one of them claimed his rights of inheritance.[23]

Sometimes a house was built specifically to serve more than one nuclear family. When a father gave to his daughter one half of a house newly erected by him, he clearly reserved the other half for himself or another branch of his family.[24] How the arrangement worked in practice may be seen from a detailed will written at approximately the same time: In order to attract a desirable mate for a young daughter who was widowed and had a son, her father gave her a large house (as it is called in the document); he stipulated only that he and his wife, as well as his son with his family, should have the right to occupy the uppermost story as long as they lived. The girl indeed married a great merchant choosing the ground floor for their domicile. The second floor was apparently rented out to a relative.[25]

Even very low-priced houses in a provincial town could be divided up between different members of a family. A house in Ṣahrajt, worth 10 dinars, was given by a brother to two sisters.[26] In a village a woman sells one quarter out of one third of a house owned by her to her son-in-law, who lived in the house and had already received another twelfth as the dowry of his wife. Besides the seller and the married couple, her mother and sister, and a sixth person, each owning a real, not nominal share, lived in the house.[27]

Living in the same house did not mean keeping one household, or, as our documents formulate it, "eating on one table." When a father sends his son 20 dirhems, 11 for the poll tax and 9 "for the house," and admonishes him to keep good company to his mother, wife, and brothers, it is evident that all of them ate at one table. A maternal uncle and paternal aunts and uncles greeted (in this order) might have occupied other parts of the house. When a boy writing to his father abroad sends regards from his mother, grandmother, maternal aunts, the widow of a paternal uncle, and the maidservant, and adds, "The travel of Grandpa coincided with yours so that we have become like orphans," one gets the impression that all the persons mentioned formed one household.[28] But when an elderly man with a wife and daughter stayed with his mother in order to gain the religious merit of fulfilling the fifth commandment, even though his sister (who could fully take care of her) lived in the same house and he had disputes with his sister's sons every evening, it is less clear how these people arranged their daily lives.[29] When two brothers, one married, one a bachelor, lived, worked, and "ate together at one table," it was done by formal agreement, properly stated in legal terms.[30]

The obligation to honor one's parents, that is, to stay with them and to help them, was taken very seriously by religious people. In general, letters to relatives may express the ardent wish to be united with them "in one locality *and in one house*, so that we should see one another all the time."[31] A more modern tendency which regarded separate living quarters as more conducive to good family relations is discernible in the Geniza papers. The tension between the two attitudes is evident in the conditions on domicile agreed upon between a young couple, or imposed on it, at marriage and in marital disputes on this question and the legal settlements intended to terminate them.[32]

Joint undertakings and responsibilities.—A similar contrast is to be observed in other economic and legal matters. Since a son normally followed the occupation of his father and apprenticed with him or, in his absence, with an uncle or brother, occupational cooperation between a father and his grown-up sons, between brothers, between an uncle and his nephew or nephews, or between cousins was natural, and examples for all such unions are found in the Geniza. But which legal form such cooperation assumed is rarely stated expressly. When two washers of the dead, father and son, admitted a partner to their funeral business, conceding him a quarter of the proceeds, they appear as one party to the contract, but what the arrangements were within the family we do not know.[33] When two brothers, having inherited part of a sugar factory from their father, acquired the other part from their brothers, the other heirs, and then took in two investors as partners, they formed one contracting party. There might, or might not, have existed another document showing how the brothers divided work, operating expenditure, and profits among themselves.[34] We are inclined to assume as a matter of course that they had indeed made legal arrangements to this effect. But this is by no means sure. The detailed description in *Med. Soc.*, I, 180, of a partnership between an uncle and his sister's son in the very considerable sum of 3,750 dinars (worth about half a million dollars) shows that it was conducted for years without any formal agreement, and when one was finally made, it was of extreme latitude, leaving to the partners complete freedom of action, but making them fully responsible for one another. After the printing of that volume I found a fragment of another copy of that agreement which contains the interesting stipulation that none of the partners was entitled to demand accounts from the other. Those merchants did, of course, make accounts, but insisted to be regarded as absolutely trustworthy "like two witnesses whose testimony is accepted in court" and who are not obliged to prove their depositions by accounts. Such a stipulation was of decisive importance in case one of the partners died and heirs appeared making claims.[35]

We encounter quite a different type of partnership between an uncle and his sister's son in a notary's entry where a nephew puts 26 dinars into his uncle's bank, to be used as loans against collateral. The uncle receives 13 out of 24 shares of the profit, the nephew the remaining 11 shares. Originally, profit was to be shared in equal parts. But the uncle pushed hard and the condition was changed in his favor. Losses were to be borne by both equally. These conditions were exceptionally bad for the investor and particularly revolting, because the profit was to be paid to the nephew's mother during his absence on travel, that is, to the uncle's sister. No wonder that such an agreement was registered with a notary. We see that it was not the size of the capital involved, but the character and relationship of the persons concerned which made formal and tight legal arrangements between relatives necessary.[36]

Leafing through the documents translated in my *Letters of Medieval Jewish Traders* the reader repeatedly comes across commercial cooperation, representing a firm, or a formal partnership, or informal mutual services between fathers and sons (nos. 7, 40, 57, 60, 76), brothers (1, 2, 11, 74), brothers-in-law (9, 22, 37), uncles and nephews (25, 30, 52, 64), or cousins (22, 38, 39). The material assembled there also permits us to gain an insight into how internal relationships developed. A father intent on grooming his son for independence gave him as early as possible some capital for doing business of his own, at the beginning preferably in partnership with the son of a relative or business friend overseas.[37] The general trend was toward keeping separate accounts. Between fathers and sons the separation appears to have evolved only gradually, if at all. I do not remember ever having seen in the Geniza an account made between a father and a son. The countless references to cooperation between brothers, uncles and nephews, and cousins, however, indicate that, as a rule, they took care of one another's affairs, but made exact accounts to the last penny. A case in point is the merchant of Qayrawān who, in dire circumstances, fulfills his obligations as partner toward his brother with the same rigor he observes toward his mighty partner in Egypt on whom he has to rely for his exports to that country.[38] In partnerships formed by relatives where it was stipulated that no accounting was required, as in the case of the uncle with his sister's son described above, we cannot know how the profits were shared. And in general, fine manners required that accounts should not be demanded. When three brothers and their two cousins are congratulated on their safe return from a successful business trip, a high measure of coordinated activity among them must be assumed.[39]

Having cooperated in business during a lifetime, brothers and other relatives were inclined to appoint the surviving partner trustee of their children and possessions. Numerous letters of Barhūn b. Moses Tāhertī and his brother Joseph have been preserved, as well as references to both in the letters of others, which illustrate the constant cooperation between the two. On his deathbed, Barhūn appointed Joseph as guardian of his son Moses and entrusted him with complete control over his possessions.[40] The remarkable will of a great merchant making his brother sole executor and guardian of his children is translated and discussed in *Med. Soc.*, I, 180–181. In a notary's draft a dying man asks his brother to let his daughter stay with him and to take care of her possessions.[41] How such wills were carried out is exemplified in a court record in which a merchant who was entrusted by his dead brother and former partner with his affairs and the guardianship of his four children makes this deposition: The two brothers had put a sum of 230 dinars, of which one third had belonged to him and the other two thirds to his dead brother, into a business venture with a third partner. The latter was unsuccessful and, on his deathbed, declared that he was unable to return more than 100 dinars. In view of this great loss the guardian declared that he would not take the sum due him, but share with his wards whatever would be retrieved in equal parts.[42]

Members of the extended family were entrusted with guardianships, because they had the moral obligation to assist relatives in need. The sarcastic Alexandrian, whose letter is summarized at the beginning of this subsection, harbored in his house five relatives besides his immediate family and, despite his prolonged illness, was prepared to accept two more.[43] Even a poor scholar had to maintain two sisters and a mother (a need that procured public office for him).[44] "Had it not been for the mercy of Heaven and for my brother's son Joseph, I would have been forced to take recourse to Israel [i.e., public charity]. All my days I have been a burden on him and living on his money." This deathbed declaration, discussed in *Med. Soc.*, II, 126, is paralleled by similar legal documents, stating that the benefactor had acted purely for God's sake and had not sheltered the beneficiary because he had been in any way obligated to him.[45]

The debts of a relative were an obligation that the family was expected to assume. Peraḥyā b. Joseph Yijū, himself a poor schoolmaster at that time, sends 40 dirhems to his youngest brother Samuel for the payment of his debts and for some personal expenses; in his letter to Samuel's creditor he writes: "God knows, I had to take them out of my mouth," meaning, I had to starve to be able to make this payment.[46] Abraham, the brother of the highly respected merchant Mūsā (Moses) b. Abi 'l-Ḥayy, had fled with his son from Tunisia to Egypt in the hope of opening a school there, with his son acting as the principal and himself as the assistant teacher. The son suddenly fell ill and died. The old man did not have the means for the high funeral expenses, the mourning ceremonies and other requirements. One of his brother's business friends to whom he applied for a loan refused. But another said: "Mūsā is a pious man, he is eager to acquire religious merits. This is one. I give the loan. I shall not lose my money."[47]

Brotherly affection and family honor, we see, were not always regarded as sufficient for prompting a man to act for a needy relative. Additional motives, each fitting the persons concerned, had to be adduced, the religious one, as in the case just summarized, taking pride in place. The words of the prophet Isaiah "not hiding oneself from his own flesh" was the *locus classicus* for the religious command that charity begins at home.[48] To what length one had to go in order to persuade rich relatives to do what even to us, with our less strongly developed family sense, would appear to be a most natural and elementary obligation, is evident from the passage translated below. It is taken from a letter sent by a dignitary in Jerusalem to Ephraim b. Shemarya, who led the congregation of the Jerusalemites in Fustat during most of the first half of the eleventh century.[49] A man, himself well-to-do and liberal, had lost everything in the terrible pillage by the bedouins of Ramle, Palestine, in 1025 and died, leaving three "babies," the eldest, a girl, already betrothed. When the fiancé learned about the state of the family after the death of his father-in-law, he stalled. The purpose of the letter was to secure support for the children from their relatives in Fustat, especially a dowry enabling the girl to marry. In those days a regular commercial mail service was run between the two countries.[50] A simple letter by a friend of the family to the aunt and uncle of the orphans should have been sufficient to take care of the situation. Why it was not, we can only guess. I assume the dead man had not been eager to cultivate good relations with his siblings and, in the face of this, perhaps, had left Egypt for Palestine. Thus his children had become complete strangers to the family back in Egypt. Ephraim, the recipient of our letter, was a native of Gaza, which is not far from Ramle. He might have known the father of the unhappy children before his emigration to Egypt or met him on one of his travels to the Holy Land. Here is the passage:

Since you—may God keep you—are a mine satisfying other people's needs and since you have volunteered to take upon yourself the troubles of others in matters connected with the obedience to God, may his name be praised, I saw fit to inform you about something that has just happened, with the request to deal with it so that your merits should be doubled, if God will.

Last week, a man, named Abū ʿAlī b. Azhar al-Daqqāq, died—you know him. He was a man of great liberality and praiseworthy munificence. But when the well-known happening occurred in Ramle, he became destitute until he died without an estate of any value in cash or kind. He left a baby girl and two small baby boys, who are completely lost, but I have learned that the man has a sister and a brother in Fustat, well-to-do people, of those who owe God thanks for his boon. If you, my lord, the member of the academy, may God keep you and make your honored position permanent, see fit, please approach them and explain to them the situation; perhaps the outfit for the girl might be obtained from them, so that she could be given to her husband. The son-in-law made the match on the assumption that she had an outfit. But when the true situation became known to him after the death of his father-in-law, may God have mercy upon him, he stalled from taking her. So please do in this matter what will bring you near to God, admonish the brother and the sister in the strongest terms and explain to them the rich religious merit they will acquire with this for the world to come and the gratitude they will earn here. Act in accordance with your beautiful habits and, whatever that girl will get from them, is from God and from you.[51]

Quite another motivation is invoked in a strong letter addressed by the grandfather of an orphaned girl addressed to her paternal grandfather. She was about to marry and the writer reminds his in-law that he had promised his dying son under oath 50 dinars for [each of] his children. He admonishes him to live up to the honorific titles bestowed upon him, *alqāb*, and warns him that he could not retain his honored position in society, *jāh*, nor his reputation of being one of the leading men of the community, *shuyūkh al-milla*, if his grandchildren were to marry like paupers.[52]

Whether the extended family liked it or not, the community and the government held it responsible for its members. A respectable Maghrebi, who had emigrated via Sicily to Alexandria, was operated there on his eyes, but became disabled for work. The local community supported him and his family—he had a wife and two small children—for a year and a half, but when it became known that he had relatives in the city, any further public charity was precluded and the man had to move to another town.[53] When a taxpayer absented himself or otherwise evaded his duties, the government indemnified itself through his father, brothers, or brother-in-law, as many examples recorded in *Med. Soc.*, II, 383–384, show. In the higher echelons of society a man could pay with his life for the real or alleged iniquities of a relative, as the case of Abū Naṣr Tustarī, who was executed in 1052 in the wake of the assassination of his brother Abū Sa'd, proves. A third, less-conspicuous Tustarī was spared, but financial claims against Abū Naṣr by private persons were automatically transferred to the surviving brother. For this and other examples of compulsory or voluntary family responsibility see *Med. Soc.*, I, 182–183.

Things being so, it was natural that everyone tried to protect loved ones against any possible claims that might be made against them after one's death. Hence the endless releases found in the Geniza safeguarding the rights of heirs, and, where the circumstances recommended it, also for the lifetime of a contracting party. One of the most extensive, most carefully styled, and beautifully written Hebrew documents in the Geniza is a bill of release given by Turayk ("Little Turk," a woman) to the representative of the merchants Muḥsin b. Ḥusayn, his three sons, and to his three daughters, Sarwa ("Cypress"), Fā'iza ("Favorite"), and Nabīla ("The Noble One"), and, finally, to his wife Fahda ("Cheetah"). Since Turayk had lived in Muḥsin's house for more than ten years, her heirs could argue that she might have given something to the younger or female members of the household (who meanwhile had come of age), so the release was drawn up as a precaution to forestall any claims.[54] In a complicated release given by a merchant to his partner, at the latter's request, his brother, although he had no stake in that partnership, also granted a release in general terms, testifying that the family had not retained for itself any rights except those specified in the legal instrument. The inclusion of female relatives in such documents of acquittal after the termination of a partnership, as, in one case, of the mother and married sister of one partner and the wife of the other, is particularly remarkable.[55] At the termination of his service, an employee and his master release each other from any obligation, but the employee includes in his release the sons and brothers of the employer. Nothing in the document says that the sons and the brothers were partners in the business and, hence, also employers of the former employee (in which case they, too, had to give a release).[56]

The might of the extended versus the nuclear family manifested itself in particular in the laws of inheritance. When a man died without children, a brother or any other member of "The House of the Father" being closest would take his estate, while his wife, who had served him all their joint life, had no share in it whatever.[57] A paternal cousin as exclusive heir was not exceptional.[58] "You are not your husband's heir, his daughters [who happened to be also hers] are his heirs, therefore take good care and do not give their money away to others"—in such terms a widow is warned by the elders of Damietta, when, in their presence, she gave a release to the representatives of merchants who had had dealings with her late husband.[59]

The concept underlying this legal situation is brought into relief by a remarkable disposition, made by a man either while seriously ill or before embarking on a distant and dangerous voyage. His only child, a minor daughter, was declared sole heir.[60] His wife was to be the orphan's guardian, would remain in the house as long as she lived, be maintained from the estate, and conduct its affairs without anyone entitled to interfere. This shows that the testator had full confidence in her. But if the girl died, the court would take over the property and maintain the widow out of it, or, if she preferred to marry again, pay her the delayed installment of the marital gift stipulated in her marriage contract. "The balance of the estate *returns* to my father's house." The phrase "returns" implies that a man's possessions consist in the first place in what he has inherited from his forefathers and agnates and only partly in what he has earned himself.[61]

Despite the strength of the extended family it is natural that its various members did not always live with one another in peace. Such things happened in both highly educated and low class families. Labrāṭ I, the Jewish judge of al-Mahdiyya, who has found such warm words for one of his brothers, was very critical of another.[62] In an extremely polite and well-written letter to a high personality a man repeatedly says that he could not visit him because he was afraid he would meet his brother at his house with whom he was at loggerheads, and this could become unpleasant for his host. He asks him to fix a time for his visit when he would be safely alone.[63] We read about a dirty trick played by a brother, who, abusing the common responsibility of the family, had his brother pay the poll tax for him and even about a physical attack on a brother, and this in the presence of Muslims and Christians, which was regarded as especially outrageous.[64] General complaints about being neglected by a sibling, even about "enmity", are also found.[65] There are a few insignificant instances of lawsuits between brothers, also between sisters, but they seem to be the exceptions proving the rule that the family tried to settle its affairs in private.[66] The tension created by the discrepancy between the rights of inheritance of daughters in Judaism and Islam, discussed in *Med. Soc.*, II, 399, might have given rise to many legal disputes, but here, too, the number of cases actually found is remarkably limited.[67]

I found the term "forming a brotherly relationship", *mu'ākhī*, only once, written in a letter from Jerusalem by an immigrant from Yemen. He had entered into the relationship at the recommendation of the recipient of the letter, but the adopted "brother" had died and the writer was alarmed at the possibility of the government suspecting him of concealing valuables that had belonged to the dead friend.[68] As the context shows, this brotherly relationship corresponds to the institution of the *rafīq*, or fellow traveler, described in *Med. Soc.*, I, 347–348, and thus belongs to the ambience of sojourn in foreign countries, not to that of family life. A sixteenth-century contract of friendship of two pietists who promise to be to each other like "brothers from father and mother" is essentially a religious document.[69]

I find no better quotation illustrating the attitude toward the extended family than this short sentence from a warm family and business letter sent from Alexandria to the capital: "You really are to me like my brothers or my wife"—in this order. Knowing the reluctance of those people to speak about one's wife, I was astounded to find her mentioned at all. The explanation presented itself to me a few lines later. "I felt thus toward you even before I married; how much more now, that we are relatives."[70]

B. MARRIAGE

1. *The Nature of the Marriage Bond*

The fundamentals.—A saintly Jewish woman of Baghdad, who, by her visions, was to stir up a messianic movement in that city, followed the traditions of her family in profuse fasting, prayers, and almsgiving, and refused to be married, since marriage would interfere with her rigorous religious practices. As was to be expected, the Jewish authorities did not look with favor upon her breach of social custom (not of Jewish law, for the biblical command "multiply . . . and conquer the earth" [Genesis 1:28] was regarded as obligatory only for men, not for women, "since conquest is men's, not women's business").[1] One of the highest dignitaries of the community arranged for the marriage, but, contrary to her apprehensions, the saint's marital state did not diminish her visions, which finally led to the messianic upheaval of 1120.[2]

A scholarly person, a widower, probably from Byzantium, where he had left his mother and daughter, had come to Egypt to collect a debt, but was kept there for two years. This is what he writes to a relative:

> As you know, I do not intend to remain here. But the judge Nissīm reproaches me every day, saying: "How can a person like you remain without a wife, how can you commit and bear such a sin?" [For "a man, even if he has children, is not permitted to stay without a wife, as it is written: 'It is not good that the man should be alone' " (Genesis 2:18)]. I have no answer on my tongue. If I say to him that I intend to return, he will think I am making a fool of him, since I have already been here for two years. But if I say that I do not wish to marry, I shall even more likely be a nobody in his eyes. And not only he, but all the people here say such things to me. I am afraid that out of a sense of shame I might take a wife against my will. But if I do so, what about my sin against my mother and daughter, who are waiting for me, whose eyes are on the crossroads and whose ears are open for tidings about my return? When they will hear that I have married, they will rend their garments and their eyes will shed tears. [The Egyptian wife would not be prepared to follow her husband to a foreign country, while the mother and the daughter would feel lost in an Arabic-speaking environment. Another foreigner sojourning in Egypt who yielded to the pressure of the environment and married had to divorce his local wife before returning to his home country.][3]

"May God recompense her well for her good companionship." These words conclude rather lengthy instructions from a pilgrim, on his way to Jerusalem, to his son-in-law, who lived in his house. The son-in-law is admonished to take good care of the family, and, in particular, of "the lady of the house," that is, the writer's wife, to fulfill all her wishes, and to protect her from anyone intending to do her harm. His wife, the old man emphasizes, deserves the considerate treatment since she had been such a good companion to him during the long years of a life shared in common.[4]

The elementary concept of marriage as the natural state of grown-up human beings and of the wife as being the God-given companion of her husband—laid down in the second chapter of the Book of Genesis and befitting the socioeconomic conditions of the ancient Israelite peasant—was still alive in the very different society of the Geniza world. That Jewish law made marriage obligatory—and, therefore, abstaining from it, a sin—only for men, did not change the fact that women, especially of childbearing age, were not tolerated by their environment to remain unmarried. At birth a girl was wished "to come into a blessed and auspicious house"—there was no other wish for her. An ancient stipulation of the *ketubba*, or marriage contract, is the undertaking of the husband, obligatory also for his heirs, that the daughters of his wife will live in his house, even after his death, "until they are married." No other prospect in life is foreseen for them. In practice, however, things did not always work out that way, as is shown at the end of this section.[5]

Marriage being thus taken for granted (unlike today in the United States with its fifty million singles and endless disquisitions on the subject), one would hardly expect to find in the Geniza much material about "the philosophy" of the institution. Nevertheless, the attitudes toward marriage, as well as its realities, were by no means simple. In addition to what follows immediately, some of our probings will be included in the section on the social position and spiritual world of women (D, below).

Legal documents, such as engagement agreements and marriage contracts, would hardly make good guides for us in our quest. Why certain legal forms were created, perpetuated, or allowed to fall into desuetude depended on very specific circumstances. Their existence or absence does not necessarily express the spirit of the times and the thoughts and sentiments accompanying the acts sealed by them. Yet, the legal instruments used by a society cannot be entirely disregarded.

There can be little doubt that as far as marriage between young people was concerned procreation was regarded not only as a religious duty but also as the natural thing to be expected. But only in very few marriage contracts of the Palestinian rite of the tenth and eleventh centuries is a stipulation preserved in which the wife declares her readiness "to become a mother of children," and, as of the twelfth century, this phrase seems to have disappeared altogether.[6] It was too obvious to be mentioned. Why, then, was it introduced in the first place? I assume, once it was established that the biblical injunction to multiply referred only to men, some scholars felt that the female partner was not obliged to participate in the process unless she had promised to do so in advance of her own free will. No change of attitude toward procreation, so marked in our own time, should be assumed here.

Moreover, the biblical quotation "they built and succeeded" (2 Chronicles 14:6), often formulated as "may they build and succeed," found throughout the centuries as a superscription over marriage contracts—Rabbanite and Karaite, Palestine minority and Babylonian majority rites—means nothing but "be blessed with children." For the Semitic root *bn* contains the ideas of both building and having children and is applied in this double sense in the biblical good wishes on the occasion of Ruth's marriage to Boaz.[7]

The Karaites, then a numerous and influential section of the Jewish population, were particularly explicit as to the content and scope of companionship. I translate the relevant section from a Karaite marriage contract written in Jerusalem on January 26, 1028. [but a formulary from the year 1081, and contracts issued in the capital of Egypt in 1117 and 1200, and even the text contained in the voluminous Karaite prayerbook printed in Vilno, Lithuania, 1890–1892, although differing in detail, are essentially identical with the ancient document from the Holy City.][8]

> I, Hezekiah, the bridegroom, will provide her with clothing, cover, and food, supply all her needs and wishes according to my ability and to the extent I can afford. I will conduct myself toward her with truthfulness and sincerity, with love and affection, I will not grieve nor oppress her and will let her have food, clothing and marital relations to the extent habitual among Jewish men. . . .Sarwa ["Cypress," the bride] heard the words of Hezekiah and agreed to marry him and to be his wife and companion[9] in purity, holiness, and fear of God, to listen to his words, to honor and to hold him dear, to be his helper[10] and to do in his house what a virtuous Jewish woman is expected to do, to conduct herself toward him with love and consideration, to be under his rule, and her desire will be toward him.[11]

The mutual relationship, then, contains four basic points. The husband undertakes to maintain his wife—maintenance in the widest sense of the word, while she runs the household; she is the helper; Eve was created for this purpose. Both parties promise each other sexual access to the extent accepted in their society. The different wording on the male and female sides is merely due to the Karaite predilection for expressing everything in biblical phrases. Thirdly, he vows love and affection, she—love and consideration. The verbal noun translated by me as "consideration"[12] but usually rendered with "compassion, pity," appears regularly in Karaite documents in this connection, probably meaning that the wife should have patience with her husband, even if his conduct was not quite exemplary. This brings us to the last point, namely, that the wife should listen to her husband's voice and "be under his rule" (again a biblical phrase), whereas the husband vows to make no improper use of his authority, "not to grieve[13] and not to oppress her."

In the Jerusalem contract of 1028 the groom promised (in addition to the 50 silver pieces due a virgin according to Karaite law) a marriage gift of 40 dinars, or gold pieces, of which he delivered 5 immediately, while she brought in a trousseau, described in meticulous detail and estimated as having a total value of 61-1/2 dinars. According to living standards in Jerusalem at that time the couple belonged to the lower middle class.

Comparing this with a Muslim marriage contract of the very same year, 1028, concluded in an Egyptian provincial town by a grain dealer and the virgin daughter of a miller, but listing a nuptial gift of only 1 + 1 = 2 dinars, we find companionship expressed as follows:

> "He must fear God in respect of her and render her good companionship, and, as God has ordained, do her no harm. . . ."[14] Since this contract is incomplete, I provide the continuation from a similar contract from the same environment: "He must render her good companionship and she has the same obligation toward him, but he is a rank higher."[15] The concluding phrase is taken from the Koran, 2:228, and, as the corresponding quotation from the Bible in the Karaite document, establishes the supremacy of the husband as a decree of God. The Muslim marriage contracts of the middle and higher classes (if to judge from those written in far later times and still extant, see below) probably were as verbose as those composed by Karaite clerks.[16]

The vast majority of the marriage contracts preserved in the Geniza, those written by Rabbanite notaries, are different. The usual obligations are expressed in the shortest possible way: the husband undertakes to provide his wife with food and clothing, to honor her, and to fulfill the conjugal duties, as Jewish men truthfully do, and she simply declares her willingness to become his wife. Only in a limited number of documents, mainly Palestinian and from the tenth and eleventh centuries, does the bride echo the groom by promising to serve, attend, and honor him. The word "love" is never used. Love is a gift of God, not something one can promise to do.[17]

Should we assume here a fundamental contrast between Jews and Muslims in the attitudes toward the institution of marriage? Hardly. The difference was linguistic. The Karaite *ketubba* was formulated in Hebrew, always a living medium of literary expression for matters connected with religion. The Rabbanite clerks were instructed to use Aramaic, a dead language, in documents with grave implications for family life, such as marriage contracts, bills of divorce, and deeds of manumission. This was done in order to safeguard the exact rendering of the ancient formulas established at a time when Aramaic was the language of the courts all over the ancient Near East. Thus we can only say that the Rabbanite marriage certificates do not help us much in our search for the understanding of the medieval concept of companionship in marriage. But the Karaite form—paralleled, as we assumed, by Muslim contracts emanating from corresponding social milieus—is of an importance transcending the narrow limits of a minority sect. The Karaite dispensation consolidated during the ninth century, that is, at the time of the blossoming of the new Middle Eastern bourgeoisie. The elaborate description of the marital relationship, translated above, was to the taste of a more refined and sophisticated society, and there was certainly no difference in this respect between the two branches of the Jewish community, except perhaps that the Karaites, at least those known to us from the Geniza, mostly were richer than the majority of Jews. The warm words of Saadya Gaon (d. 942) on marital love, including the sexual aspect, are indicative.[18] The insistence of the rabbinical courts on the use of fossilized formulas had its source in the apprehension that new formulations of documents on family life could lead to unforeseen complications.

The Karaite certificate from Jerusalem, 1028, is superscribed: "In the name of the living God." Similarly, Palestinian Rabbanite marriage contracts bear superscriptions such as: "In the name of our Creator," an allusion to the benediction at the wedding meal which praises God as the "Former" of Adam and Eve.[19] But the overwhelming majority of marriage contracts does not bear such a superscription nor any reference to God—so profuse in the corresponding Muslim documents. Should this indicate a secularization of the idea of the marriage bond? Not at all. The complete absence of the name of God had a specific, a technical reason. After a widow or divorcée had received all owed her, the contract was torn to pieces; in view of this the name of God was eliminated in order to avoid the possibility of its desecration by being rent. No such apprehension was in place in the Palestinian courts where the practice seems to have been to cross out the text beneath the sacred superscription after the obligations specified in the ketubba had been fulfilled.[20]

The sanctity of marriage.—Besides the fundamental purposes of providing a shelter for the wife and a help for the husband, as well as opportunity for companionship and procreation for both, medieval marriage fulfilled a number of additional functions. As our second quotation at the opening of this subsection shows, it was, above all, destined to protect man from sin, a need particularly urgent in an urban environment. "Living in Cairo without a wife is extremely difficult for blameless and chaste persons," emphasizes a Karaite husband again and again while imploring a relative to induce his wife to return to him.[21] The wife is a wall around her husband, she brings atonement for his sins and peace to his domicile—and these are only three out of twelve, mostly spiritual, goods that marriage has in store for men, as we read in a Geniza sermon.[22] The nucleus of this sermon is found in the Talmud which goes as far as to say: "When a man marries, all his sins are forgiven to him."[23] This is not a joke, for the two other changes in personal circumstances which are credited with such a consequence are the attainment of high office and conversion to the Jewish faith. This shows that marriage is conceived as entrance into a state of higher rank and greater responsibility.

The more elaborate Muslim marriage contracts emphasize the idea of the avoidance of sin in detail. Here is the introductory passage of a contract written in the Egyptian flax center al-Bahnasā in the year 1207 for a merchant who promises a nuptial gift of 35 dinars to the daughter of a clothier. Thus this Muslim marriage contract corresponds in time, locality, and social milieu to many of the relevant Geniza documents:

> Praise be to God who permitted marriage in accordance with the rules and laws of the noble religion, who helps a man favored by him to find in marriage what is permitted and to avoid what is forbidden and made it an ornament for the Muslim faith of a man.
>
> Praise be to him who made marriage a shield and safeguard against vice and prompted to it the true believers in order to keep them clean from all blemish.[24]

In another Muslim marriage contract, by which an amir marries an amira, marriage is described as instituted by God "as a protection against Satan and his host."[25]

The Geniza marriage contracts do not contain anything similar, no doubt because the same idea is expressed in the ancient benediction to be recited at betrothal and wedding. The benediction praises God for what he has permitted and prohibited in marriage and concludes: "Blessed be He who sanctifies Israel through the bridal canopy and the conclusion of marriage." Sanctifying means keeping away from sin. An ancient epithalamium from the Geniza describes this aspect of the marriage quite bluntly:

Married man, by enjoying your graceful doe,
You will stay immune from the sin of embracing a stranger.

Both the benediction and the poem are based on the Talmudic concept of the wives' role: "It is enough for us that they bring our children up and save us from sin."[26]

As stated before, procreation was a great religious duty, the first one expressly mentioned in the Bible (Genesis 1:28). Perhaps it was taken that seriously by the Jews because the very existence of the community was so often in jeopardy. But there was more to it. The aim, as is so often stated, was not merely to have children, but to be blessed with "sons studying the Torah and fulfilling its commandments;" in other words, it was not only physical, but in particular, spiritual perpetuation which was sought in the institution of marriage.[27]

Finally—from bed to board—"a man's table atones for him like the altar in the Temple,"[28] a man attains bliss in life only through his wife—as the Geniza sermon referred to above assures us. Without a proper home no Jewish religious life was feasible. The benedictions and elaborate grace accompanying the meals on working days, Saturdays, and holidays, and many other religious duties, such as hospitality and care for the wayfarer and the poor, were best fulfilled in the atmosphere provided by a household.

Yet the conclusion of a marriage was a predominantly secular affair. As explained in *Med. Soc.*, II, 163–164, the ceremony was never held in a synagogue (or a mosque, or a church) and the presence of a religious functionary was not required. The Jewish divines normally in charge represented the secular authority (see subsection B, 2, below), and the actual descriptions of marriage celebrations which we have from the Geniza period reflect their thoroughly mundane character. But the "seven benedictions" pronounced at the ceremony and repeated at the subsequent banquet, or, rather, banquets, the superscriptions over the Palestinian Rabbanite and the Karaite marriage certificates, as well as the proems to the Muslim marriage contracts translated above, prove that the religious aspect of marriage never was completely absent from the minds of the medieval people on the southern shores of the Mediterranean.[29]

It should be noted that in the Eastern churches, as well as in the Catholic church, the blessings of the Church, or even the presence of a priest, although customary, were not required for a marriage to make it legitimate, until the Council of Trent (sixteenth century) declared it to be obligatory.[30]

Choosing a mate.—I doubt whether we shall ever be able to unravel the tangled threads of family politics which were set into motion by the birth and growing up of a boy or a girl and continued to be at work until the marriage of both. The women had much say in these matters, but their voice seldom reaches us through the Geniza papers. Conscious of this deficiency, I shall now try to summarize what we are able to glean on this subject from the documents available to us.

Since endogamy, especially marriage with a cousin, was an accepted practice, the choice of a mate was largely predetermined. If a more or less suitable close relative was available and amenable, the matter was decided (see subsections A, 2, above, and B, 2, below). In any case, the relative had precedence. A postscript to a lovely family letter addressed to Qalyūb, a little town north of Cairo, contains this note: "We have saved the girl for Abu 'l-'Alā. If he is coming, have him send a message and inform us. If not, don't let him detain the girl. *And Peace.*" Then there is a second postscript: "She is not a poor girl; she is well off." The boy and girl concerned belonged, of course, to the extended family of the writer and recipient, and were not close relatives of either.[31] How deeply these sentiments about the prior rights of the cousin were rooted is illustrated by the story of the India trader Abraham Ben Yijū. As soon as he arrived in Aden back from India after many years of sojourn there he offered the hand of his only daughter (together with his riches) to any son of his brother or sister who, during his absence, had been forced to leave their native Tunisia in the wake of the Norman invasion. His moving letter is translated in my *Letters of Medieval Jewish Traders* (pp. 201–206). When no reply was received, Ben Yijū settled in Aden, promised his daughter to a boy from the first family in the town, and the girl lived in the house of her future inlaws for three years. Then word came from the family; he learned that the eldest son of a brother of his was a scholarly person. Immediately he went back on his promise to the Adenese family; but everyone understood that "the son of my brother has more rights to her than strangers." Having arrived in the capital of Egypt, communications with his family (who then lived as refugees in Sicily) again became severed, and again there were many who asked for the hand of the daughter of the India trader. But Ben Yijū remained adamant. Finally, seven years after that first offer made in the letter from Aden, the wedding between the cousins was celebrated.[32]

"Marrying out," on the other hand, was an opportunity for families to widen their connections and to enhance their strength. A son of the Persian banker Sahlawayh b. Ḥayyīm (the first name is Arabic-Persian, the second Hebrew), often mentioned in the Geniza, married Mulūk ("The Queen of the Kings"), the granddaughter of Manasse Ibn al-Qazzāz, the administrator of Syria for the Fatimid caliph al-ʿAzīz (975–996). A daughter of Sahlawayh became the wife of Ḥesed ("Grace," Heb.), better known under his Arabic name Abū Naṣr Tustarī, also of Persian-Jewish stock, the powerful brother of Abū Saʿd, the vizier of the mother of the infant caliph al-Mustanṣir (ascended the throne in 1036), and for a short period the most influential man in the empire. A granddaughter of Sahlawayh also must have married out, as proved by the very high nuptial gift assigned to her by her future husband.[33] A good example of marriage policy is offered by the scholarly and public-minded Berechiah brothers of Qayrawān (first quarter of eleventh century). They were allied by marriage both to the Tāhertīs and the Majjānīs, two strong families in that city who did not always see eye to eye, but must have found it advantageous to seek connections with the pious and highly esteemed Berechias.[34]

Marrying daughters out for the sake of creating useful family connections was particularly common in overseas relations. Mention has been made in these volumes of three enterprising young Qayrawānese emigrating to Egypt around the middle of the eleventh century, marrying there into fine old families and themselves attaining prominent positions in their new country.[35] This is what an elder brother writes from al-Mahdiyya, Tunisia, to Judah b. Moses Ibn Sighmār, when he learned about the latter's marriage in Egypt:

I took notice of the description of your blessed and auspicious wedding and understand that God has granted you to become connected with the most illustrious and finest people, those of whom one can boast in East and West. This is more precious than the earth and the fullness thereof. Thank and praise God that he has cast your lot with the grandees of Israel. You really must say: [Psalm 16:6-7] May God make . . . complete what he has given to you and make your happiness permanent, may he aid them through you and aid you through them and make you a blessing for one another. May he bless you with a male child, "may the woman who comes into your house be like Rachel and Leah, etc." [Ruth 4:11].[36]

Another letter from al-Mahdiyya, congratulating a young Tunisian marrying in Egypt, expresses the same idea: "May God strengthen you through each other; you have indeed attained a fine status."[37] Other examples of Westerners settling and marrying in countries of the East, such as Palestine and Iraq, are provided in *Med. Soc.*, I, 49.

Family politics in the selection of mates were even more pronounced in cases where girls were exported from one country to another. Tyre, Lebanon, then the busiest harbor on the Syro-Palestinian coast, was engaged in a lively exchange of goods with the capital of Egypt. No wonder, then, that business houses in the two cities were eager to strengthen their positions by establishing family relations. The Geniza has preserved a large document from the year 1051 in which a Karaite girl from Fustat became betrothed to a Rabbanite man from Qarqīsiya on the Euphrates living in Tyre, the go-between being none other than a grandson of Manasse, the administrator of Syria, mentioned above. The future husband, who promised the unusually large nuptial gift of 100 + 150 = 250 dinars, obviously was too busy to make the journey himself.[38]

The impersonality of matchmaking is particularly evident in a power of attorney written in Tyre at the beginning of the eleventh century, in which a girl—in the presence of two witnesses, of course—appoints her father as her representative to select a husband for her in the capital of Egypt. If her father was unable or unwilling to make the journey, he was entitled to appoint a substitute who had the right to appoint another substitute for himself; but the young man selected by any of the three representatives envisaged would be her legal husband. It appears, indeed, from the document that the first substitute of the father appeared before the court in Tyre, where he received the properly attestated declaration of the girl, without which, of course, he could not act in Egypt.[39]

Samuel Ibn Lukhtūsh of Spain, whose family, as indicated by its Berber name, must have been settled in the Muslim West for a considerable time, was married to a sister of Nethanel ha-Levi of Fustat, whose family produced at least two heads of the Jewish community of Egypt and at least two presidents of its high court. We know this from a letter sent by Samuel's son Joseph to Nethanel's son Ḥalfōn (Granada, 1130). There are indications that the two families in those distant countries had already been connected by an earlier link.[40]

When, by the twelfth century, Egypt had been superseded in the Mediterranean by the Italian navies, it turned eastward, to the India trade which became its most lucrative overseas undertaking. In those days we find that Maḍmūn, representative of the merchants in Aden and superintendent of its harbor, as well as head of the Jews of Yemen, was married to a sister of Abū Zikrī Judah b. Joseph ha-Kohen of Fustat, scion of a family of Palestinian Gaons and prominent India trader. Judah himself was married to a sister of Maḥrūz, a shipowner in Aden, who was in turn, it seems, closely related to Maḍmūn.[41]

Yet, such overseas connections were not always sought merely for worldly gain. By chance, a letter of congratulation on Judah ha-Kohen's wedding has been preserved. From its wording it is evident that the marriage was regarded as the joining of two scholarly families, "mixing," as the Talmudic phrase goes, "grapes of vine with grapes of vine." Maḍmūn was not only the secular, but also the spiritual head of the Yemenite Jews, and the other members of his family known to us were well read and public minded.[42]

This brings us to the genetic aspect of Geniza marriage, the endeavor to marry a girl from a scholarly family in the expectation that she would produce the desired result, "sons studying the Torah." In a long letter of congratulation on the occasion of the marriage of the son of one scholar with the daughter of another scholar, whose son also was noted for his learning, the father of the groom is first praised for "the mixing of grapes of vine with grapes of vine" (see above), secondly, he is assured that the young couple's offspring will live up to expectations, since "boys become like their mother's brother," and, thirdly, the union would be blessed because the girl was an orphan (from her mother), and marrying an orphan was an act of great religious merit.[43] In an extensive holograph to a dayyān, or judge, and his learned sons in a provincial town the Nagid Abraham Maimonides strongly recommends a young man, probably one of his former students, as a prospective son-in-law. The young man had visited the judge's place, but had received no clear answer. Yet, the Nagid emphasizes, "he still persists in his love" (of course, not to the girl, whom perhaps he had not even seen, but to the scholarly family) and was prepared, if required, to commit all his possessions for the nuptial gift—as recommended in the Talmud ("Sell all you have and marry the daughter of a scholar").[44]

Two letters of suitors to their future fathers-in-law, each remarkable for some special traits, are in the same vein. In one, a scholarly person expresses in the most glowing terms his satisfaction at becoming connected with such a personality as his "father," the recipient (whom he clearly knew only by hearsay and one visit) and ascribes his bliss to the merits of his own forefathers known to his future father-in-law. Then he emphasizes (using an inappropriate quotation) the genetic aspect of perpetuating the Torah through proper marital links. Finally he writes: "I met the cantor Ṣedāqā Ibn Nufayʿ [the matchmaker] and was informed by him about the friendly deliberations going on between you about the conclusion of the marriage. I understand that you prefer to present the younger daughter, and not the elder one, namely Sitt al-ahl ["Mistress of the Family"], may God support her. But. . . ." Here, the manuscript breaks off. One might surmise that the visitor had gotten a glimpse of the "Mistress of the Family," perhaps also talked to her and had been under the impression that she was the one destined for him and was not satisfied with the change proposed.[45]

In a society whose standard ideal was the pursuit of religious knowledge, family connection with a scholar was also sought by a person clearly lacking it. In a letter in which the sender describes himself as "the biggest man in the community"—although, remembering Proverbs 27:2, "Let another praise you, and not your own mouth," he hated to say so—he asks for the hand of the recipient's daughter, because he wished to follow the sages' advice to marry a scholar's daughter. In addition, that connection would strengthen his position. His profession obviously was not a very esteemed one, for he suggests that if his future father-in-law should wish him to do so he would open a clothing store, a clothier being the most common occupation of a respectable merchant, Muslim, Christian, or Jew. Throughout the letter the recipient was asked to treat the matter with utmost secrecy and to reply, if possible, with the dawn of next morning, for, if he was refused and this should leak out, the suitor would lose face. From other Bible quotations in the letter it is evident that the man was a widower and father of children (probably no longer living with him), a man who had gained riches and wished now to enhance his position of power by the prestige of a religious connection.[46]

In all the cases discussed thus far, choosing a mate meant deciding with which family a man wished to be connected (unless he preferred to confine his choice to his own family). It is in conformity with this situation that an elderly settler in Jerusalem, writing to his sister back in Spain about his marriage, remarks: "I am happy with those with whom I have been connected," but does not say a word about his new wife. It is not excluded, however, that the plural is used out of excessive prudery and that, in reality, the wife is meant.[47]

We would be far off the mark, though, if we assumed that the personality of the future mate did not count at all. First, one of the added benefits of the widely practiced endogamy was that cousins had plenty of opportunity to know each other before they married. This is what the schoolmaster Solomon b. Elijah writes while asking his paternal aunt for her daughter:

> If God the exalted wills, I intend to come to town to fill my eyes with the view of your auspicious countenance [that is, to see you] and to take your blessed daughter, who is so dear to me, Sitt al-Yumn ["Good Luck"], may God grant her success, as he does with those who know [him].[48] I ask you now, dear aunt, not to hold her back and not to cause any delay in her respect, for when I come to town I cannot stay more than ten days, for I have a school which brings me a good income, thank God for his bounty. So, when you make your highly appreciated arrangements, see to it that there should be no delay. For otherwise, I have to leave her and to return. Please inform me what your plans are and what you wish to have as nuptial gift, which I shall forward immediately.[49] At the receipt of these lines, send me a full statement with all your demands. I am in the best of health, thank God. *And Peace*."[50]

The writer of this letter did not get "Good Luck," who was so dear to him, and finally married another cousin.[51] From the tenor of the letter it appears that the aunt was not unaware of the feelings of her nephew and therefore could be expected to put a high price tag on her daughter, while the schoolmaster was unable or unwilling to meet her demands.

Jewish (and Christian) girls did not remain entirely invisible beyond the narrow circle of the extended family. Girls attended the synagogue service, and men talked with women afterward.[52] I do not believe that boys could speak to girls of marriageable age in the synagogue court; boys and girls would form separate groups[53] but they could get glimpses of one another. One could meet a girl in the house of relatives.[54] When an old father (without money) writes about his youngest daughter: "She is much favored [by the boys] . . . many ask for her hand, but she refuses them all," the girl cannot have been entirely secluded in her parents' house.[55] When another father suggests to his son the choice between three girls (one a divorcée), all called by name, it is evident that the young man knew them all.[56] The suitor quoted above, who inquired about the elder daughter whom he mentions by name, showed that he was not interested solely in the family connection. It is natural, though, that in a society in which it was not customary for a husband and wife to exchange written messages, such communications could not take place between unmarried men and women. Consequently, the Geniza is not able to enlighten us much about the attitudes toward the future mate and toward marriage in general, before a person took upon himself "the yoke of a household." I touch upon this question again, especially from the point of view of the bride, in subsection B, 2.[57]

Remaining unmarried.—It is occasionally stated of men that they never married. The random cases noted below occurred in different countries at different times. Three brothers, the youngest of whom was seventeen, in asking the Gaon of Jerusalem to retrieve for them a part of their father's estate, illegally held by someone else, report that they had had another brother who died without progeny, "for he never took a wife."[58] A person from Aleppo, who died in Akko, without ever having married, left two brothers in Aleppo and a nephew from a deceased third brother. The nephew appeared in the rabbinical court of Fustat in winter 1099 / 1100 to claim his share in the estate of his uncle, who was, as the document expressly states, the youngest of the four brothers.[59] A night watchman in a small town, who had never married and had no brother or other male relative, left his belongings to the daughters of his late paternal uncle. Since one of the sisters had a married daughter, the deceased must have been of a rather advanced age (Minyat Ashnā, 1150).[60] Two brothers are addressed in excellent Arabic and greatest respect by the husband of their cousin; they are praised for their munificence, but are also politely reminded that it was time for them to marry.[61] The only person of prominence who remained unwed most or all of his life was the noble and learned India trader Ḥalfōn b. Nethanel, "the center of all the leading men of his time," who visited Spain and Morocco as frequently as Aden and India, who befriended poets and scholars, and bought books wherever he could find them. Clearly, he did not need a wife and children to keep himself busy. Still, his status of an unwed person must have been a sore point, especially since two brothers were high religious dignitaries. None of his many friends and relatives whose letters to him we have—including his younger brother, whose sons already apprenticed with their uncle—dared to broach the matter to him, except a loquacious old relative who did so at a most inappropriate time: when Ḥalfōn guided the Spanish Hebrew poet Judah ha-Levi on his visit to Egypt:

> My lord—may I be made your ranson—hurry to accomplish a matter which, if its time has passed, cannot be effected any more, just as sowing, when its season has been missed, cannot be successfully done. May God watch over you—and present you with the choicest of human beings, who will resemble the lady, your mother, may God's mercy be upon her, so that the word of the scripture may be fulfilled with you, as it is written: "Isaac brought her [Rebekah] into the tent of Sarah . . . and Isaac found solace after the death of his mother" (Genesis 24:67).[62]

Although marriage was a religious duty, as we have seen throughout this subsection, a scholarly person who chose study as his love could be exempted from it. Following the Talmudic sage Ben 'Azzay, who exclaimed: "My love is Torah, let others build the world,"[63] Maimonides ruled in his Code: "A man who loves the Torah, studying it continuously all his life, and never takes a wife, does not commit a sin, provided he is not overcome by sexual desire." As so often in Maimonides' legislation, one senses a personal note. He married a woman from a very distinguished family in Egypt, where he arrived at the age of thirty, and his son and only child was born when he was forty-eight. Thus it seems that he himself tarried long before consenting to give up the life of a bachelor devoted to study. His son and successor, Abraham Maimonides, must have had a similar constitution. Abraham's son and only child was born to him when he was thirty-six, an age at which, in those days, one could easily have been a grandfather. The biblical account according to which the patriarch Isaac married at the age of forty (Genesis 25:20) was understood to mean that a man should marry only after having attained spiritual perfection, while a woman marrying for the first time at forty was believed to have no prospect for bearing a child, the essential purpose of a marriage.[64]

Girls desirous of remaining unmarried, had, I am afraid, little choice, or at least, their voice has not reached us. The saintly virgin of Baghdad who wished not to be wed in order to serve God alone, as described at the beginning of this subsection, was singularly exceptional. No other such case has come to my knowledge.[65] One must keep in mind the fact, discussed below, that about 45 percent of all the women married entered that state a second time, that is, after having been divorced or widowed. Realizing the astounding frequency of that occurrence, one wonders what percentage of divorcées and widows did *not*-marry a second time. One of my earliest and strongest impressions while doing research among Middle Eastern communities was observing how women in the prime of their lives, previously married, were leading solitary existences. Being then very young and not yet inured to the niceties of Oriental etiquette, I would ask in all innocence: "Why does a fine woman like you not marry again?" The reaction was invariably, albeit mostly in veiled form (but sometimes with a shudder): Having been disgusted by her previous experience she did not desire to try again. Should we assume the same for the Geniza period? After reading this book to its end the reader can judge for himself. Anyhow, it must be noted that both in letters and in documents, especially in the lists of beneficiaries, a great number of single women appear in the Geniza.

To illustrate the situation, I discuss here two lists of recipients of bread. Bread was distributed every Tuesday and Friday by the Jewish community of Fustat. Each time, each person received two loaves. For the clumsy word *armala*, "widow," invariably *mara*, "wife," was used, for example *marat al-shaykh al-mayyit*, "the wife of the dead elder." The first list, of which only the lower part is preserved, comprises 136 households, 48 of which were headed by women, and about 80 by men; a few cannot be identified with certainty or contain items such as "the orphans of so-and-so." By the signatures attached to it and through other indications the list can be assigned to the 1020s (see *Med. Soc.*, II, 128, 438–439, and 469). In the following I translate only the items referring to households headed by women, although single women lived also in households headed by men.

The woman from Byzantium,[66] 6 (loaves of bread). The mother-in-law of Manṣūr, 2. The sister of the wife of Sulaym, 2. The wife of Marwān, 6. The daughter of the midwife and her daughter, 3.[67] The wife of Sibāʿ and her sister, 4. Jawhara, her relative , Hiba, and Ḥasan, 8. The mother-in-law of Ṭājin, 2. The daughter of Salmūna, 2. Furayja and her daughter, 4. The woman from Alexandria and her daughter, 4. The wife of the man from Barqa, 4. Mu'nisa and her daughter, 4. The daughter of Shemaʿya, 2. The daughter of Barhūn, the Maghrebī, 4. The daughter of the man from Tiberias and her two daughters, 6. The daughter of

Manṣūr Ibn Bāna, 2. Umm Ḥalīla, 4. The [female] neighbor of Ghālib, 8. The sister of Hiba, 8. The wife of Hillel, 2. Ḥāritha, 2. Wa'd and her daughter, 4. The daughter of 'Ayyāsh, the schoolmaster, 2. The little woman doctor, 2. Umm Musharrafa and her daughter, 4. The woman from Būra and her son, 2 (!). The wife of 'Anṭūḥ, 2, his mother and his son, 3. Baqiyya, 2. The woman selling flour, 2. The wife of Jarrāḥ, 4. The woman from abroad, 2. Ṭalba, 2. The woman who behaved in an improper way,[68] 2. The two sisters, 4. The invalid and his sister, 4. The wife of the man from Ghayfa, 2. The wife of the little treasurer,[69] 4. The wife of "the little lion,"[70] 4. The daughter of Harbonah,[71] 2. The wife of Ibn Dunash,[72] 2. The daughter of the Kohen who renounced his status,[73] 2. The maternal aunt of Raḥma, 2. The daughter of Shū'ā, 2. The mother-in-law of Manṣūr, the flour merchant, 2. The daughter of the proselyte, her son, and her daughter, 6. The mother-in-law of the synagogue beadle, 4. The wife of the son of "Pain caused by medication,"[74] 2. The daughter of 'Imrān, 2.[75]

Women living alone	24
Women with a daughter	6
Women with a sister	2
Women with a son, a brother or an unidentified person	8
Women with two or more dependents	8
Total of households headed by women	48

The number of men heading a household and living alone was approximately the same (27). Compared with families headed by women, nearly twice the number of those headed by men had another person in the household, and those harboring two and more were over four times as numerous.[76] A list of a similar type written around 1100[77]—many are preserved from that period—shows this breakdown:

Women living alone	16
Women with one other person	19
Women with more than one	7
Total of women heading a household	42

The women are defined

by name, profession, or description	12
as mother or mother-in-law	16
as wife (widow)	10
as daughter	2
as divorcee	1
as spinster ("a woman who is a girl")[78]	1
	42

Some of those mentioned by name, profession, or as "wives" could also have been divorcées. But spinsters were so rare a social phenomenon that the fantastically rich Arabic language of the Geniza has no term for them. It is, however, not excluded that some of those merely called by a proper name (which is uncommon) might also have been spinsters.

Bread was distributed only to the very poor, those who were unable to do or to find work. Clothing was expensive; therefore those to whom it was distributed comprised a wider circle of needy people. A list of persons in receipt of clothing from the community of Fustat, superscribed "Leaf no. 3," and therefore representing at the most one third of the total distribution, contains the names of 81 persons, of whom 32 were women living alone. Multiplied by three, this would bring the total to about one hundred single women—a high number when we remember that only persons in need exposed themselves to the degradation of "uncovering their faces" and turning to public charity.[79]

The women of the lowest stratum of society speak to us through the lists of beneficiaries from public charity—and much can be learned from these if properly studied[80]—but the women of the middle class become known to us only through letters sent by or to them or when mentioned in letters of others. It will take a long time until this material is brought under control. My impression is that the great number of women marrying a second time after having been widowed or divorced is well exceeded by those who, after the death of the husband or after a divorce, preferred (or were forced by the circumstances of life) to remain single. This question is explored further in the subsections on remarriage and the care of fatherless children.[81]

2. *Engagement and Betrothal*

An engagement contract, preceded by a story and followed by a legal opinion.—In order to plunge the reader immediately into the social milieu in which the marriages of the Geniza period were arranged, an engagement contract is translated here in full. It was written in Alexandria, Egypt, March, 1201, and contains "the well-known" conditions under which an engagemnt was concluded in those days. The countless relevant contracts preserved from the capital of Egypt in this period are basically of the same type.

This particular document is not from the Geniza, but from the Responsa, or book of legal opinions, of Moses Maimonides. Many questions addressed to Maimonides, together with his holograph answers to them, have been preserved in the Geniza. I have chosen this document for translation because it also describes the circumstances in which the engagement did not lead to a marriage—a common occurrence—how the parties behaved in this situation, and how the law looked on the matter.

Only a few explanatory remarks are necessary for the understanding of the document. Although the names of all persons concerned are given in full, they are referred to at the beginning as "Reuben" and "Leah," which means nothing but "So-and-so"; this was customary in questions submitted to a jurisconsult; and, although the contract fixed the date of the wedding for a year after the engagement, the legal question speaks of "a fixed term" in general. "The symbolic purchase," an expression recurring in the document again and again, was an act required by Jewish law for most legal transactions. It is explained in *Med. Soc.* II, 329. "The early installment," the gift given by the husband to his wife at the wedding, is discussed subsequently.

[Question] Maimonides, *Responsa*, I, no. 88, pp. 138–144

May our master enlighten us on this question:

Reuben was engaged to Leah. A document containing the relevant stipulations was written, a term was fixed for the wedding, and a fine of 10 dinars was imposed on the side that would break the engagement.

Then Reuben traveled to Tripoli of the West [today Libya], and tidings were received that the ruler of that place pressed all the mariners of the boats into service and sent them to al-Mahdiyya on a military expedition. Reuben did not come back, and the time fixed for the wedding passed, whereupon the father of the fiancée engaged her to another man.

The father of Reuben appeared in court and sued the father of his fiancée. But the latter argued: "The time agreed upon between me and you for the date of the wedding has passed, and I cannot detain my daughter, for I am a poor man." The father of the fiancé retorted: "My son is impeded by *force majeur*: you are the side who broke the engagement, wherefore you must pay him the ten dinars agreed upon for this contingency."

Then the two parties deposited the early installment, which Reuben had paid to Leah, and the fine of 10 dinars obligatory on the side breaking the engagement, [with a third party], as well as the present which the father of the fiancé allegedly had given as a gift to the fiancée according to the local usage, namely certain victuals. All this was deposited by them until they would receive the answer of your excellency—may God give you excellence—explaining what the law prescribes.

The father of the fiancé vowed the fine of 10 dinars to be paid to the poor, binding himself to pay it from his own money and capital in case his son, after his return, did not honor his vow. Please, our lord, explain to us what is due from each party, and whether the poor have a claim on this money or not.

This is the text of the engagement contract, word for word and letter for letter:

Engagement contract. M. Japheth, the esteemed young man, son of M. Zechariah, the esteemed elder, son of M. Abraham, the honored elder, (may he) r(est in) E(den), engaged Sitt al-Turaf [Lady "cherished gifts"], the mature virgin, the daughter of M. Elazar, the esteemed elder, son of Yeshūʿā, the honored elder, (may he) r(est in) E(den). The symbolic purchase was made from Sitt al-Turaf—after true cognizance had been taken of her identity—that she had appointed the brother of her mother, M. Judah, the esteemed young man, son of David, (may he) r(est in) E(den), to negotiate all her rights and obligations resulting from this engagement.

This was agreed upon between her representative and the fiancé: "The early installment," a present to be made at the wedding, to be 40 Egyptian dinars, and the "late one" to be 100 dinars.

The wedding to be held a year after the date of this document.

The fiancé produced the 40 dinars as well as three rings, two plaited Shīrāzī rings of gold and one Shīrāzī ring of silver, delivered them to the representative, and Judah received them in our presence, we, the undersigned, as a deposit until the time of the wedding.

Then an agreement was made with the fiancé that in the marriage contract, at the time of its writing, the well-known conditions should be stipulated, namely:

that he was not permitted to take a second wife, or to acquire a maidservant his wife disliked;

that his wife was regarded as trustworthy in all matters concerning food and drink;

and that no oath, grave or light, could be imposed on her in this matter;

and that "the equal shares" be observed, meaning, God forbid, that if after entering the bridal chamber Sitt al-Turaf died without producing a living child, male or female, one half of her bridal outfit would return to her heirs from her father's house;

and that the domicile was according to her wishes; she could not be forced to live where she did not like to.

The symbolic purchase was made from the fiancé, M. Japheth, that he now give to his fiancée Sitt al-Turaf 10 dinars, out of the 40 dinars of the early installment as a gift manifested in public, which could not be annulled, to be effective if he renounced the marriage at the time and under the conditions agreed upon. [A similar undertaking was made by M. Judah for the other party and confirmed by the fiancée.]

This happened during the last ten days of the month of Adar of the year 4961 of the Creation (March, 1201) in Nō Ammōn [Alexandria] which is situated on the shores of the Great Sea.

[Three signatures, followed by the validation through the rabbinical court, also signed by three, testifying that the signatures are genuine.]

May your holy excellence instruct us what is the law in this matter and may Heaven double your reward.

Answer

According to the stipulations of this document neither the representative nor the fiancé is bound to pay any of that fine of 10 dinars, for it is not evident that the latter renounced the engagement or was impeded by *force majeur*.

Nor is the girl obliged to wait for him, but she may marry whomever she likes after the year is over. All presents given to her still extant, such as clothing, must be returned. Of victuals she has to pay two thirds of the value to the fiancé or his representative.

The father has no right to sue for the "early installment" given by his son nor to take delivery of it, except through a proper power of attorney validated in court. The poor have no claim in this matter.

Written by Moses.

This document beautifully illustrates the discrepancy between law and life. A Jewish father had the right to give his minor daughter into marriage (although such an action was disapproved by some authorities), but once she had attained sexual maturity (which was put at the age of twelve years and six months), she was a legally independent person. Therefore, Maimonides, in his answer, carefully states: "The girl may marry whomsoever she likes." But the father, in court, simply states: "I engaged her to another man," without any reference to the girl's wishes, but giving his own financial situation as the sole reason for the new engagement. (He meant to say that as "a poor man" he could not take the risk to let an opportunity for an advantageous family connection pass by. His claim of indigence must be taken with a grain of salt. As proved by other such documents, the marriage gift of 40 + 100 = 140 dinars indicates that the contracting parties definitely belonged to the middle class.)

The appointment by the girl of a representative was not mandatory. Had she been a fully grown up, formerly married woman, she could have negotiated the contract with her future husband in person. In this respect, as we shall see, Jewish law substantially differed from that of Islam. But since she certainly was a mere teenager, both decency and practical reasons made the appointment of an experienced man as mediator imperative. Unlike many other cases, where the father does the job, here a brother of the mother was chosen for it. Presumably the mother had a great say in the matter, because a substantial (or the main) part of the girl's future dowry would come from the mother's personal property or her bridal outfit. But in his appearance before court the father makes no reference to the legal representative of his daughter.

Similarly, a father, as Maimonides emphasizes in his answer, had no rights whatsoever to the property of his adult son. But as this and many other documents show, a father, a brother, or another member of the extended family would take care of the legal affairs of an absent relative, even without any formal power of attorney given to him, see section A, 3, above.

The "well-known" marriage conditions listed in the engagement contract are self-explanatory and are discussed in detail below. The last one, which seemingly gives the wife the exclusive right to choose the domicile of the couple, may puzzle the reader, and a word of explanation is offered now. Marriage was patrilocal, the wife normally moved to the house of the husband's family. When the young wife did not get along well with her mother- and sisters-in-law, the common living quarters could cause her great suffering, as is copiously illustrated in the Geniza. This clause was inserted in middle class marriage contracts to protect her.

The vow to the poor is a side issue. Since Maimonides had ruled that the girl's family did not owe a thing, the vow made under the assumption it did, had become void.

The three stages.—In principle, a marriage was achieved in three stages:

1. Engagement, a contract in which the two parties agreed in the presence of at least two witnesses on the mutual financial and other obligations and rights, fixed a date for the wedding, and stipulated fines in the event that the agreement or the date of the wedding was not honored. This was called *shiddūkhīn* (see n. 68, below) in Hebrew, and *milāk* or *imlāk* ("property conveyance") in Arabic. This legal act naturally was preceded by cautious testing of the ground, indirect and informal negotiations, and asking for the hand of the chosen mate.[1]

2. Betrothal, or legal conclusion and religious consecration of the marriage, by which the partners became husband and wife, although no intimate relations were yet permitted. This relationship could be terminated solely by an ordinary bill of divorce; "a virgin, divorced after betrothal," as a term describing the legal status of the bride, is repeatedly found in Geniza marriage contracts. Two Hebrew terms, often combined, were in use for this stage: *ērūsīn,* "betrothal," and *qiddūshīn,* "consecration." Since Muslim law does not know this stage, *milāk* or *imlāk* is used for it, too. From a case where both the betrothal and the marriage contract of a couple have been preserved it is evident that the former could be as elaborate and solemn an affair as the latter.[2]

3. Consummation by wedding, legally defined as "entering," namely, the bridal chamber, or, when said of the bride, the husband's house; or as "taking," namely, the bride as wife; or as "the procession," namely, from the house of the bride's father to that of her future husband. The Arabic and Hebrew terms for wedding celebrations designate the festivities connected with the consummation of marriage and usually do not have legal connotations.[3] On this occasion the *ketubba*, or marriage contract, was written.

In practice, stages one and two were often combined.[4] The same was done, and even more frequently, with stages two and three. The latter custom became the standard practice in the centuries after the "classical" Geniza period. Thus, as a rule, the wedding was preceded either by an engagement or a betrothal. Sometimes, though, when no contractual action had been taken before the wedding, the three elements—agreement on financial obligations and other matters, formal consecration, and leading the bride home—were merged into a single event.

Occasionally circumstances necessitated keeping the three stages separate. A document from Minyat Ghamr, a small town in Lower Egypt, beautifully written by a schoolmaster in September, 1315, tells of the virtuous woman, the pious and chaste widow Rashīda (her father was still alive), who appeared before witnesses and declared that she was prepared to marry a certain widower and to bring up his boy during the next ten years. The man had already given her 10 dinars as her first installment, promised a late one of 30, and agreed to certain other stipulations, such as the usual one of leaving her the choice of the domicile. Then the document, without noting that the widower ever appeared, states that the arrangement had become binding by the "symbolic purchase" made from both by the witnesses.

This is what happened here: Rashīda was a local woman; therefore, since everyone present knew her, she did the talking; the widower had come from outside to make the match and perhaps was not known to the witnesses. But that was not all. Both parties appointed representatives: she, her brother Rashīd (note the name!); he, a person named but not described, perhaps a brother of his late wife, who was concerned in safeguarding the rights of his young nephew. Why the representatives? Many things had still to be agreed upon: the dowry she would bring in, the cost of the wedding he would have to bear, and the betrothal gift, the *qiddūshīn,* usually consisting of a ring, or, more commonly, rings, which had to be formally delivered. Why all this was not done immediately and why the widower did not attend to these matters in person we cannot know. He probably lived in another small town, while Rashīd and the other representative had opportunity to travel to Cairo, where—we imagine—the final arrangements were agreed upon, the *qiddūshīn* were delivered, and, perhaps most important, the marriage certificate was issued by the proper authorities. On that occasion, the engagement contract from Minyat Ghamr was produced, and, having fulfilled its task, ended up in the Geniza.[5]

The legal and actual position of the bride.—Islamic and Jewish laws differed markedly on the legal and actual position of the bride. In Islam, a woman could not dispose of herself. A walī, or male guardian, had to give her away—her father, or, in his absence, the next male relative from her paternal family, or, if none was available, a man authorized by the government. Some schools go as far as to declare a marriage void if concluded without a walī. All this calls to mind the *kyrios*, or lord over the marrying woman, in ancient Athens. A Jewish girl, once she had reached puberty—which was supposed to happen at twelve years and six months[6]—was free to marry whom she wished, no tutelage and no go-between being legally required; she was "of age and under her own jurisdiction."[7] A short court record may illustrate the situation:

We, the undersigned, testify that the following happened in our presence on the tenth of Nisan, 1554, of the Era of the Documents [April 2, 1243], here in Fustat of Egypt, which is situated on the Nile River.

Mr. Joseph, the esteemed young man, may his end be blessed,[8] son of Mr. Abraham, the esteemed elder, may his end be blessed, engaged and contracted a marriage with Rebekah, the bride, the mature virgin, daughter of Abraham, the esteemed elder, the honored almoner,[9] may his end be blessed, and undertook to pay her 10 dinars as her first installment, plus the cost of the Henna,[10] the "strings,"[11] and other expenses, as is customary.

Rebekah confirmed that she had received on account 5 of the 10 dinars as a first installment. Also, that he will give a written promise to pay 50 dinars as late installment and that the wedding will take place during the month of the high holidays of the current year.[12] If he delayed the wedding, he will have to pay a fine of 5 dinars, to be waived in the case of illness. The choice of the domicile will be in her hand.

We have written down what we have witnessed, and signed and delivered the document into the hands of the aforementioned Rebekah, so that it may serve her as a proof and title of right.[13]

A few legal phrases conclude the record, which was carefully written and signed by Immanuel b. Yehiel, a prominent judge (see *Med. Soc.*, II, 515).

I translated this short record here, because it spotlights the legal situation. But it was exceptional that a virgin bride should negotiate and contract a marriage with her future husband in person. This was appropriate for an experienced woman, a widow, or a divorcée. Girls normally married at a tender age, when they knew very little about either men or money. In general, we must imagine, the choice was made by the family, the father normally having the last word, although the mother, as is natural and as we have seen,[14] was also very influential. In the absence of the father, it was usually the mother who arranged the marriage of her child.[15] When both parents were dead, an aunt or even a grandmother could act.[16] These details are important since they prove that the presence of a male person was by no means required for giving a virgin girl away.

To what extent was the girl's consent required? There is no doubt about the legal situation. A girl who had reached maturity could not be married without her consent, given before two witnesses. Most complete and better-preserved engagement and betrothal agreements and often also the marriage contracts indeed contain the statement that the bride had appointed so-and-so as her respresentative to negotiate and conclude her marriage. At that stage the choice of the mate had already been made, and the question is how far the future bride took part in his selection. Frankly, we do not know much about this point, since our sources have little opportunity to make mention of it. From the frequency of engagements broken off and betrothals dissolved one may conclude that it was not only family politics and financial considerations, but also the wishes of the young couples which influenced the final decision. Many marriage agreements say expressly "if she [not her parents or another] breaks off the engagement." No doubt much depended on the nature and strength of all the personalities concerned.

According to Qayrawānese legal practice, dislike of the groom by the bride was a sufficient reason for granting her the right to demand the dissolution of the betrothal. The Jewish courts in Egypt seem to have preferred to get a formal declaration from both bride and groom that they did not like each other. This is evident from an official letter of Elijah b. Zachariah, judge in Fustat, sent on order of the Nagid Abraham Maimonides to the Jewish judge of Bilbays in Lower Egypt. Eight months after having broken off her betrothal to a boy in Bilbays, a girl from Fustat wished to marry a young man from Cairo. Judge Elijah, before whom the case was brought, found out that the betrothal had indeed been formally dissolved, in the presence of the bride's mother, before the late judge of Bilbays, one of whose associates was his son and successor (to whom the letter is addressed). In order to be on the safe side, Elijah had the mother and the girl appear before him and had her declare that she disliked the company of her former betrothed and that she had no claims against him whatsoever. In the letter Elijah asked the judge of Bilbays to now summon the repudiated groom and have him make a similar declaration, namely, that he did not like the girl and was unable to maintain her.[17]

Some Geniza letters seem to show that the future mates were not entirely inactive with regard to the choice of their hearts. The young man from Palermo who served as the business respresentative of prominent Sicilian merchants in Egypt and married there an orphan girl serving a great family instead of one of the daughters of the house—as the letter emphasizes—probably had his reasons for preferring the orphan to riches, and perhaps it was she who had taken the first step.[18] In one of the most unrestrained letters to be found in the Geniza a father imposes on a friend to see immediately "the cursed matchmaker Mother of the Black," and to ask her to tell everyone that her story about his son was untrue; the girl had lied, and possibly "the dear lady"—her mother—had lied too; his son did not wish at all to conclude that marriage. I suspect, he wished, but the father did not find the match attractive for reasons of his own.[19]

Even where we have a detailed account of how a betrothal was initiated, we cannot be sure about the true feelings and intentions of the parties. Naturally we experience a similar uncertainty in our own society. Anyhow, what people say (or do not say) is significant for the mores of their times. The wealthy India trader Abū Ya'qūb Joseph Lebdī took his widowed sister and her son Abraham b. Isaac into his roomy house. Since the widow naturally passed most of her time in the company of the other female members of the family, Abraham, when coming to see his mother, often had opportunity to meet his cousin Sitt al-Ahl ("Mistress of the Family"). But after both his uncle and his mother had died, the situation became different. At this point our story begins. It is contained in one long document in the hand of the court clerk Ḥalfōn b. Manasse, of which, thus far, eight fragments have been identified. Abraham confided to two of his friends that he wished to remain in close contact with the family of his late uncle and asked them to help him in this matter. The two friends approached "the illustrious Rayyis Abū Sa'd," probably one of the India traders bearing that name at that time, and he was cooperative. He understood, of course, and the young man again explained that he intended to marry the girl because he wished to preserve his close contacts with his uncle's family. (To say that he liked the girl would have been improper. But did he?) The four men went to the widow's house, and the V.I.P. Abū Sa'd proposed. The widow answered that no one was dearer to her than her late husband's sister's son, but she would never marry off her daughter in the absence of her son (who was an India trader like his late father and away on a voyage). Abū Sa'd replied that after he had gone so far as to propose, he could not leave the house without having accomplished something; he suggested he would arrange the betrothal and leave the wedding until after the return of the son. At this impasse the mother intimated that Abu Sa'd and his friends should talk to the girl, which they did, emphasizing how well they knew and esteemed her. (Nothing, of course, was said about the prospective husband, or, at least there is no mention of it in the document.) Sitt al-Ahl agreed. Abraham delivered 5 dinars and two rings, one of gold and one of silver, to Abu Sa'd; the latter handed them over to the girl, who subsequently declared: I have betrothed myself to him. Here some lines are missing, but what happened is abundantly clear. When the brother returned, he disapproved of the match, or the girl, too, might have had second thoughts. The document, which has the form of a deposition in court by the two friends of the rejected suitor, ends with the declaration that Sitt al-Ahl was a legally married woman, which means, she could not get free except by a bill of repudiation, not always easy to obtain.[20]

More outspoken is the following story. A group of Karaites from Cairo had come to Jerusalem and stayed there for several months praying at the various holy sites. The group included a girl, Rebekah, and two suitors of hers, Abraham and Simon. The elders of the company decided for the former (no reasons given), but Rebekah preferred Simon. Abraham swore he would kill one of the two, if she was not given to him. The elders worried and asked the girl to stay at home or to leave the house only when accompanied by a married woman. Meanwhile they asked the father in Cairo what to do, and he replied that his daughter should be married to whom she wished. The elders tried to persuade Abraham to desist from his unreasonable demand, but he remained adamant. In this situation the elders reasonably decided that the girl should not be married in Jerusalem at all, but the entire matter should be left until the group safely returned to Cairo (which was to happen after the termination of the period of mourning over the destruction of the Temple by the "Sabbath of Consolation"—in July). At that juncture, Simon lost patience, and applied to a low official of the Rabbanite community, who, in return for a small payment, concocted a marriage contract showing Rebekah as legally betrothed to Simon and containing fake signatures of all the Karaite elders. The fraud was easily detected, and a big scandal ensued. The official lost his position and was temporarily put under ban, but Rebekah, too, became very angry and declared now she would not marry either of her two former suitors. The story is included in a letter from Jerusalem addressed to the head of the Cairene Karaite community, Aaron Ibn Saghīr.[21]

An extreme example of a girl prepared to commit actions of despair if she was married to a man whom she disliked (and was refused the one whom she preferred) is found in a letter sent from Ascalon, Palestine, to the judge Abraham, the Son of the Scholar, at the "House of Exchange" in Fustat. The letter is written in Arabic characters (probably to prevent the carrier from reading it) and the writer, Joseph b. Manasse, as the tone and contents of the letter show, must have been an intimate friend of the recipient. (He was not a relative, for he writes: "My family is your family," an expression used in urgent requests directed to a person with whom the writer is not related.)

Joseph was expected in Ascalon, but for reasons partly stated in the opening section of his letter, he was delayed. Five days before he arrived the girl whom he intended to marry (and who was known to the judge) was betrothed to another man. As we have seen before, fathers of daughters became terribly nervous when matches envisaged by them did not come through and hastened to arrange for another marriage. Joseph's arrival so soon after the betrothal had the effect of a bombshell.

When I arrived, the city stood on its head and the people did nothing but talk about me and spread the news that I would take her from them [the new groom is not mentioned, only his father, Ṣadaqa, who had managed the affair]. They were also telling all kinds of stories about her, which I refrain from repeating, whether good or bad, for I do not regard it as permissible to say anything about her. [We shall read the stories later.] Her father demanded that they should let her go, but it was Ṣadaqa who lodged a complaint against him and brought him to court, where it was decided, however, that he [the groom] should repudiate her [as is required after a betrothal]. He did not repudiate her, but lodged two new complaints, one against her father and one against me, demanding that I swear never to marry her, which I refused.

As usual in similar cases, the matter came before the Muslim authorities, who—as was also common—referred it back to the Jewish community, who finally submitted it to the Nagid (Mevōrākh b. Saadya) in the capital of Egypt. The purpose of Joseph's letter was to alert the judge to the impending arrival of the message from Ascalon and to request him to see the Nagid and to press for a decision favorable to the writer. In order to bring home the seriousness of the situation, Joseph tells now what he had heard about the girl "Nougat." [This was not the name given to her at birth, but a by-name designating her sweetness or any other trait associated with that sweetmeat.] "If he takes her on order of the authorities or otherwise by coercion, she will push her husband into a well, or take her own life."[22]

Child marriage.—A minor could not make legal actions such as concluding a marriage or appointing a representative. Consequently a father could marry off his minor daughter even without her consent since a minor could not make a legally valid declaration. In Islamic law there was no doubt about this. In Jewish law it was a moot point. In principle, the father's right was upheld, but the greatest authorities of Talmudic times stated bluntly: "A father is not permitted to contract a marriage for his minor daughter; [he must wait] until she has grown up and says, I wish to marry so-and-so."[23] The medieval Jewish doctors of law did not recognize this maxim as binding. Maimonides tuned it down thus: "Although a father is permitted to contract a marriage for his minor daughter with whomever he likes, it is improper to do so, for our sages have disapproved of this."[24]

The Geniza records reveal that child marriages, although quite exceptional, did occur. In a holograph, a religious authority rules in an answer to a query: "As to that one of whom you write that she has not yet reached maturity, but that her father wishes to contract a marriage for her, there are no legal grounds on which you may impede him; but you must endorse the marriage. There is also nothing to be afraid of in this matter [from the state authorities, since this was also Islamic law]." Clearly there was some opposition to this marriage in the community, and the local official desired to be on safe ground. An indication of a similar opposition is to be found in a declaration from the year 1049/50, in which several persons testify about the approximate age of a girl (the number of years is lost).[25]

A question submitted to Moses Maimonides tells us about a girl who was married at the age of nine and whose mother-in-law (and aunt) undertook to maintain her for ten years. Clearly, this marriage was a means for providing a home for an orphan, who also shared a property with her mother-in-law. The colorful story of this girl will occupy us later in detail.[26] Another child marriage of an orphan is reported in the letter of a *muqaddam*, or head of a local community, to his superior:

> Here is a man appealing to the community,[27] who keeps telling me that he has already been married for two years and that his wife does not permit him access. I asked her to appear in court, and she conceded that he spoke the truth, but said that she was unable to have intimate relations with a man. The girl is an orphan and approximately thirteen years old. He asks now for a divorce and she, too, wishes to be divorced, but the question to be asked from your excellency is whether he is obliged to pay her late installment or perhaps be permitted to take another wife in addition to her. Your answer is urgently requested, for this man appeals to the public day and night and incites people against me.[28]

In a third case, an orphan minor fled to her brother and her husband tried in vain to get her back. Some elders intervened, and since she was allegedly only about eleven years old, she was permitted to stay with her brother for another year. Meanwhile her dowry was deposited with the court. Two fragmentary court records from Bilbays, Lower Egypt, dated 1218 and 1221, respectively, tell about an orphan girl nine years old who was engaged on condition that the marriage take place three years later. The groom promised an immediate marriage gift of 10 dinars, and a delayed one of 60, as well as the customary contributions to the wedding expenses, such as "an entire night [of entertainment for the guests] and the saffron [for dyeing the bride's hair] and safflower [used as make-up and as an admixture to henna]." When the future husband failed to live up to his promises, the grandmother of the orphan girl refused to provide the dowry in full. Here, too, "worthy elders" arranged a compromise.[29]

Marriages of orphaned children can be understood as intended to somehow provide them with the shelter of a home, and, since marrying an orphan was regarded as an act of piety and highly meritorious, we might assume that in many cases this aim was indeed attained.[30] The examples provided subsequently show us the marriage of minors in a different light. In an engagement contract, superscribed with beautiful Bible quotations such as "I shall betroth you forever, in sincerity, truth, and loving-kindness" (Hosea 2:21) a Kohen contracts a settlement with an "esteemed, liberal, and munificent elder" "with regard to his minor daughter"—expressed in both Arabic and Hebrew and clarified by the additional note "who is, thus, under the jurisdiction of her father." The first installment of the marriage gift was 51 dinars—a strange sum—and the late one, 60 dinars (which shows these people as middle class people), while the groom would also bear the cost of the bridal ornamental costume and the henna feast.[31] The wedding was to take place *five* years after the date of the document. The defaulting party would have to pay the unusally heavy fine of 280 dirhems of *nuqra* silver, about 20 dinars. Without additional data we cannot know why the two families bound themselves for so long a period. Perhaps an aging father wished to make sure that his little daughter would marry into a good family, while the young man was sure that it would be a profitable match.[32] Similarly, when a rich, young woman, in a deathbed declaration, expressed the wish to have the daughter of her brother saved for marriage to her infant son, her will, though not legally binding, but backed by a substantial estate, certainly was heeded, as far as circumstances permitted. An interesting, but unfortunately incomplete, document foresees a waiting period of *seven* years "until she matures," but leaves it to the adolescent girl to decide whether or not to carry the match through. A brother of hers was also involved in the agreement made between the two families, but exactly how is not preserved.[33]

Sometimes the paternal authority to marry a minor daughter had bizarre or disastrous results. When a married elder sister of seven-year-old Sitt al-Dār ("The Lady of the House") died an utimely death, the child was promised to the widower. He agreed to pay 4 dinars in addition to the 16 dinars that he had already paid as nuptial gift when he married the elder sister, and to take the little girl home after three years. When he did not show up at the stipulated time, and another married sister of Sitt al-Dār died, she was to substitute for the second sister the very week she died (no doubt because the woman had left a baby who had to be attended to and, as a single girl, Sitt al-Dār could not stay with her brother-in-law). But when the community assembled for a hurried wedding ceremony, many remembered the former arrangement, and it took some time before the legal situation was clarified. On the reverse side of the document that relates this story, a beautifully written holograph by the qadi of Alexandria states that the testimony of the Jewish judge and his assistant, the cantor, had satisfied him that the matter had been properly handled.[34]

Another story of the marriage of a minor daughter by her father, told in a question addressed to Maimonides, took a more serious turn. A girl whose father was dead "engaged herself," as the text says, and a big party was given. After two months, "Simon," a relative of hers who had attended the party, appeared in court and presented a document in which the father of the girl had betrothed her to him four years before, while she was still a minor. Neither the mother of the girl nor she herself knew anything about this, and, understandably, when Simon came to ask for her hand and also sent two go-betweens to explain that, as her relative, he had more rights to her, she indignantly refused. Finally she sent her maternal uncle to him and asked him to provide her with a bill of divorce, but he would not hear of it. The court found itself in a dilemma: the document was legally valid; in addition, honoring the will of a dead person was a sacred duty. In her distress the mother applied to the qadi, who asked the Jewish judge to assemble ten of the elders of the community and thus to exercise pressure on Simon to issue the required bill of divorce. Simon gave in, but only to claim after some time that the bill was written under duress and therefore void. Maimonides, however, ruled that pressure exercised by a court was proper, while Simon's conduct constituted duress. The girl was free to marry whom she wished.[35]

This is about all I know about child-marriage in the classical Geniza period, and I do not believe that much more will be found. It was an insignificant social phenomenon, but I have treated it at some length because it is indicative of the near absolute paternal authority, which was equally operative with regard to the mature virgin who was legally independent. There must have been countless cases in which the teenage girl was shocked when her father communicated his choice to her. But I have searched the Geniza in vain for a complaint lodged by a daughter against her father with a Jewish court, a Muslim authority, or even only a relative. A father's decision was like a decree of God. It was taken for granted that God was almighty, "doing whatever he liked," but also that he was full of mercy with all his creatures; in like vein a father's authority and his love for his children were accepted as matters of course; consequently, questioning the wisdom or righteousness of his decisions, however cruel and incomprehensible they might have appeared, was impious, and, in any case, futile. *Al-'ab rabb*, "The father is the Lord [meaning, God]," says an Arab maxim.[36]

Marriage and the authorities.—According to medieval concepts matters pertaining to personal status were regulated by the law of the religious community to which a person belonged.[37] We see indeed that the great majority of engagements, betrothals, and marriage contracts preserved in the Geniza were issued by Jewish judges or clerks known to us as community officials.[38] In the limited number of cases where the writers of such documents are not known to us, we simply do not have other material from the localities or times concerned. As in most legal documents, the signatories appear as "witnesses," not in their official capacity. This absence of the indication of a communal authority was not accidental. It was not needed. According to Jewish (and Muslim) law two witnesses were sufficient for the legal contraction of a marriage. This principle was upheld even by as late an authority as Abraham Maimonides, who, in reply to a question submitted to him, ruled that a couple who in every respect behaved as non-Jews, demonstrating their apostasy by publicly desecrating the Sabbath, but who had contracted a marriage in the presence of two Jewish witnesses, were legally married.[39]

Such "freedom of contract" in family matters could have most undesirable consequences. When a girl from a provincial town, whose father was dead, wished to marry in the capital, the Nagid, or head of the Jews, who probably had been tipped off by someone, sent an inquiry to the local judge asking him to find out whether there existed any impediment to the proposed marriage. Here is the answer of the judge: "I learned that this girl was engaged several times, but it is not clear to me whether a marriage was contracted with anyone of those who proposed and became engaged to her. Her mother must be carefully examined as to what the situation was at each engagement, and if any doubts remain, further inquiries will be necessary." Had marriage registers existed in the town, or if registration of marriage had been obligatory, no such doubts would have existed.[40]

A case of two marriages contracted by one woman is explicitly referred to in an incompletely preserved court record written by the experienced clerk Ḥalfōn b. Manasse. Sitt al-Ḥusn ("Lady Beauty") concluded the contracts after the death of her first husband, but perished "in the famous murder case," together with her mother and the two men concerned. The document itself deals only with the claims of the heirs: the nephews of the mother, who asserted they were the only heirs, and others, who derived their rights from the daughter, how, is not preserved. I do not believe that "the famous murder case" was a family tragedy in the modern style. They had no revolvers in those days, and not a single case of a Jewish murderer is known to me from the Geniza. I assume the man with whom the first marriage had been contracted had been away for years, but came back by chance just when a *nahb*, outburst of pillage and murder by marauding soldiers or bandits, swept a provincial town.[41]

Under those circumstances it is natural that the authorities tried to supervise the marriages, at least of foreigners, divorcées, or in general, any couples whose personal status was not well known in the community. A Fustat court record from the year 1085 or so states that a man from Tiberias and another from al-Lādhiqiyya on the Syrian coast testified that a woman from the latter town had been divorced by her husband, who later married again and died. This testimony was required by her for her second marriage.[42] In the times of the energetic Nagid Samuel b. Hananya the procedure of marriage permits was streamlined. It consisted of three parts: (*a*) a declaration of two witnesses that there was nothing in the personal status of either the groom or the bride which might impair the validity of their marriage; (*b*) the validation of the testimony by the court; (*c*) a communication to the Nagid by the court that a fine of 10 dinars was imposed on the groom in case any impediment should become known; to this, a request to grant the permit was attached. Three such documents from the years 1153, 1159, and one whose date has not been preserved have been noted thus far from this period. All of them have as one of the two witnesses Judah, the son of Solomon the scribe. Thus it is evident that the couples were known to the communal scribe, and the testimony was a mere formality.[43]

Under Samuel b. Hananya's successors the text of the permit, or rather the testimonies leading up to it, were refined so as to specify that there existed neither a religious nor a civil impediment to the proposed marriage. One civil impediment often mentioned in the Geniza, as we shall see, was the nonfulfillment of financial obligations toward a divorcée.[44] A permit issued under the authority of the Gaon Sar Shalom (ca. 1177–1195) is noteworthy because it was given to a couple from higher Jewish society. In a letter to the same head of the Jewish community of Egypt the *muqaddam* of Qalyūb certifies that, to the best of his knowledge, there was no civil or religious impediment to the marriage of a girl called 'Amā'im, daughter of Abu 'l-Ḥasan. As the content of the letter shows, there were reasons why the Gaon ordered an inquiry. The family had moved from one place to another; the girl's sister was married to a freedman, and her brother had left Qalyūb for the Manūfiyya district, where he embraced Islam.[45]

Of particular interest is a testimony from the year 1217 preserved in two copies (one in Cambridge, England, one in New

York) about a girl who had been brought up in the house of a physician and was "not of noble descent," that is, not Jewish by birth, nor connected "with any of the families," but also not a "bastard," foundling, or "born out of wedlock."[46] What happened here is clear: the girl was originally a slave, bought by the physician as an infant, brought up in his house, and freed—a pious deed practiced also by others. He now wished to find for her a husband. Marriages with freedwomen were commonplace, but since the girl probably was an educated young woman, the physician wished to avoid the term betraying her former low social status and chose that obsolete formulation.[47]

As the document analyzed in *Med. Soc.*, II, 344 proves, the head of the Jewish community confirmed not only the marriage permits but also the special conditions attached to individual marriage contracts. But all this was of no avail as long as persons could legally conclude marriages without applying to the authorities at all. In order to preclude these anarchic procedures, especially in provincial towns and villages, anyone other than the judges appointed by the central authorities who presided over a marriage or a divorce was threatened with excommunication. Such a declaration, issued by Moses Maimonides and his court in January 1187, with regard to the judges of Damanhūr, Bilbays, and al-Maḥalla in Lower Egypt, and another one, referring to that of 1187 pronounced in Alexandria in 1235, have been preserved.[48]

The law, which regarded a marriage contracted in the presence of two lay witnesses as legal, remained in force, however, and Maimonides himself recommended its use in a situation of hardship for the parties concerned. A woman whose two husbands had died was offered a third marriage at the time of the great famine of 1201–1202. The local judge refused to marry them because of the ancient superstition that she was a "killer" and might cause the death of her third husband. Maimonides ruled: "They should contract the marriage in the presence of two witnesses, which is perfectly legal. Later the document should be issued by the court, the judge feigning ignorance of what has happened. Being strict with regard to this little offense could lead to far graver complications."[49]

By "graver complications" Maimonides meant an application to the state authorities. Such things indeed happened, and in Maimonides' own time. A Kohen, or member of the priestly family of Aaron, is not permitted to marry a divorcée. This is the law of the Torah, and nothing can be done in this matter. A Kohen in Alexandria "loved" a divorced woman and had the unheard-of audacity to "pursue his passion," and, despite all admonitions, married her before a qadi. Maimonides excommunicated him in an unusually extensive and strongly worded document. From the wording of this ban I conclude that such occurrences were exceptional, at least, in the period concerned.[50]

Basically, an application to the qadi by non-Muslims was equivalent to what we would call civil marriage. In a document issued by a Muslim court in Aswan, Egypt, in 948, a Coptic deacon married the daughter of a priest, assigning her the then high dowry of 90 dinars. Seventy-seven Muslim witnesses signed the contract; the exceptionally numerous participation in the festivity manifested the popularity enjoyed in the town by those members of the Christian clergy. Two other marriage contracts of persons with Coptic names also were issued by a Muslim authority.[51] In an interesting Muslim document from 1025 a Jewish father-in-law returns to the fiancé of his daughter the sum of 20 dinars, representing the initial installment of a nuptial gift of 70 dinars, in order to use it on a business trip; in the course of two months the prospective son-in-law has to send back 21 dinars,[52] and an additional four months of absence are granted to him. Thus the civil aspects of the marriage were arranged with the state authorities.[53] From the same period, however, a far graver case for submitting Jewish family affairs to a Muslim judge is reported. In Ṣahrajt in Lower Egypt a woman was charged with having "divorced her husband" with the help of the qadi, who also fixed an alimony for her, which the husband paid for three months. For that offense against communal discipline and religious law the woman was reprimanded and put under ban. But she went up to the capital and declared before the central court that it was her husband, not she, who had brought the matter before the qadi. Finally, it became evident that the two had agreed on this procedure by mutual consent. There is also a mutilated note saying that the man did not (or should not) have "affairs with women." Seeing that members of the Christian clergy legalized their family matters before a Muslim authority, we are not surprised to see Jews in a small town with no proper Jewish magistrates nearby doing the same.[54]

Such incidents, however, were exceptional. Family law was the domain of communal autonomy. The state authorities acted only when approached by the parties affected. The two stories told above, of marriages contracted for minors and brought before qadis, are examples.[55] Yet it is noteworthy that many marriage contracts contain the stipulation that they are binding according to

Jewish law and also to that of the state, or "the nations of the world."[56] In family matters, the communal officials represented the authority of the state.

Engagement.—The details of the engagement ceremony are best studied in a fully preserved document, such as the one by which Sitt al-Khāṣṣa ("Mistress of the Élite"), the daughter of a deceased India trader, became engaged to Ṣemaḥ ("Sprout"),[57] son of an *ʿaṭṭār*, or perfumer. It happened on Monday, that is, a day on which court meetings were regularly held, November 11th, 1146. The virgin bride was represented by her mother, but the fiancé conducted the negotiations in person, and no surety was required from his father, which means that Ṣemaḥ stood on his own feet financially.

The most urgent matter to be settled was the first installment of the marriage gift to become the bride's property on the day of the wedding. A sum of 40 dinars was deposited with a third party, also an aṭṭār, known to us from other documents. and 100 dinars were promised as the late installment. These sums, as well as the very valuable dowry and other gifts given to the future bride, show the two parties to be well-to-do.

The procedure of depositing the entire first installment with a third party was by no means common. Usually a small present, forming part of the first installment, was given to the bride's side to be retrieved in case the engagement was broken. Since this arrangement could easily lead to default by either party, it is easy to understand why people who could afford it preferred the procedure described above.

The wedding was fixed for exactly a year later. After having strained his finances to produce the first installment, the young man needed some time to earn the money needed for the wedding expenses.

As usual, the conditions imposed on the fiancé consisted of two parts, the general ones, customary in all marriage agreements made in Fustat in that century, and specific ones, imposed by Sitt al-Khāṣṣa or her mother. The future wife was to be regarded as financially reliable in all matters concerning the household, and no oath could ever be imposed on her; no second wife; no maid-servant not approved by her; in case of her death without children, one half of the dowry was to revert to her father's family. The special conditions show the strong position of the fiancée's family. Sitt al-Khāṣṣa will have the choice of domicile, both concerning the locality and the apartment to be chosen. The rents from her real estate will be her personal property and not be at the disposal of her future husband.

Finally, a fine of 20 dinars was imposed on either party in case the engagement was broken, and the "symbolic purchase," which according to Jewish law confirmed legal actions, was made by the court from both the mother and the fiancé.

But that was not all. Although a full year was still to intervene until the wedding, the fiancé took no chances. The value of each and every piece of the trousseau, about one hundred twenty-five of them, was estimated, making a total of 640 dinars, and the list was attached to the engagement document. The details about the bride's real property were listed too, although this was expressly exempted from the dowry over which the husband would have the right of disposition.

This model engagement shows us how well-to-do people arranged their affairs: they tried to avoid anything that could lead to last-hour misunderstandings between the parties; the early installment of the marriage gift was safely deposited and the dowry was estimated and approved by the fiancé and ready for delivery.[58]

Less fortunate people were not able to conclude such well-planned and tidy engagements. Most of the relevant documents reveal far less complete arrangements. In a private contract, beautifully executed by a court clerk around the year 1000, a young man makes an agreement with a father "concerning his elder daughter, call Mufaddāt." (Unlike the one we had before, this one took no chances as to which of the two daughters he wanted.)[59] The first installment was to be 25 dinars, of which 5 were a "present" to be delivered immediately, the rest to become "payable" at the time of the wedding, which was to take place in "the month of the holidays." Nothing is said about the late installment, and it seems "payable" here meant only that the part handed over at the wedding (or betrothal) was the legal means for concluding the marriage, whereas, in reality, 25 dinars was the entire sum promised by the fiancé. The father's undertaking was equally ill-defined. He promised the entire outfit, meaning clothing, of his deceased wife to his eldest daughter; the jewelry would be equally divided between his two daughters. But he promised to make an effort to add to both, and also to the bedding, which was evaluated at between 40 and 50 dinars, and the copper, which had the same value. All the objects of the dowry would be assembled in one place for the fiancé's inspection. If he was satisfied, the match would go through; otherwise, his present would be returned to him, and "no bill of divorce and no release" were necessary, that is, the agreement was not a betrothal, which needed formal dissolution.[60]

In most of the notes on engagement, however, not a word was said on the main point: the trousseau. At an engagement in August, 1132, the first installment amounting to 5 dinars out of a total marriage gift of 35 dinars was handed over, but no fine was stipulated in the event of a break. The absence of such a stipulation was unusual but is to be explained by the fact that the wedding was to be held only about two weeks later and everything—including the trousseau we might assume—was ready.[61] In another engagement, concluded at the same time before the same judge, where the wedding was fixed for six months later, a fine of 2 dinars was stipulated, the nuptial gift promised was 4 + 20 = 24 dinars, and only one silver ring was handed over to the father. Probably these were people in strained circumstances who had still to find all the means necessary for making good their promises.[62] A girl whose father and, probably, also her mother were dead (because she was represented by a paternal uncle of her mother), received two rings, one of silver and one of gold, at her engagement, and a promise of a marriage gift of 10 + 20 = 30 dinars. Thus she was not entirely destitute; nevertheless, she undertook to live with her future husband's mother and brother in one apartment, "as long as this would not constitute a nuisance to her," and nothing is said about a trousseau.[63] When another orphan girl receives at engagement her early installment to the amount of 20 dinars (12⅝ dinars in gold coins and the rest in gold and silver rings) and is promised another 50 dinars as late installment, it is evident that these were middle class people.[64]

Here, as elsewhere, the absence of any mention of a dowry must have had a technical reason. Usually, the *taqwīm,* or "evaluation," of the bride's outfit, was agreed upon in another document. Many such separate documents, characterized by their superscriptions as lists of trousseaux, have been preserved (see subsection B, 4, below). But the Geniza also contains many *taqwīms* without any superscription, which means that they had originally been attached to an engagement contract, as in the case of the daughter of the India trader discussed above. In the course of time, the two parts of the document had become separated, so that there is no way to know to whom the trousseau list refers; and an engagement or betrothal document that appears to us as strange may be explained by the supposition that another document had originally been attached to it or that it was written before or after the agreement concerned. This is especially true of engagement contracts that expressly mention the bride's outfit.[65]

In an engagement between first cousins, both mature, in which the marriage gift was as low as 5 + 15 = 20 dinars and nothing but one silver ring was given, the wedding was fixed at a date exactly three years later, and a fine of 5 dinars was imposed on the father of the boy and the mother of the girl, if either of the two fiancés wished to break the engagement or to change the conditions. From the very fact that the father, and not only the son, bore the responsibility for keeping the contract, it is evident that the latter was not yet financially independent. Agreements in which the wedding was to be held three or more years after the engagement or bethrothal, or where the father of the fiancé stood surety for his son, are not very common. Thus we may conclude that, in general, a young man was expected to marry when he was able to maintain a wife (see subsection B, 4, below). An engagement like the one just described must have been the result of special circumstances. Perhaps the father of the girl had just died, and the mother wished to arrange for the future of her child before something happened to herself.[66]

It stands to reason that an elaborate engagement agreement like that of the daughter of an India trader described above was accompanied by a festive party. But I do not remember having read anything about one in a Geniza paper. The matter was different at a betrothal. As far as the financial arrangements are concerned, a betrothal was very similar to an engagement. But by that act a woman became legally married, the betrothal benediction, discussed above, was recited, and bride and groom drank from the cup over which the blessing was said.[67] What we have are the legal documents, which betray a great variety of customs and procedures, reflecting the composite character of the community and of its legalistic heritage.

Betrothal.—An ancient example of betrothal procedures is provided by a formulary from Fustat from December 1027. Scribes created for themselves formularies by taking actual documents, omitting details not needed by them, and replacing the names by "So-and-so."

> . . . So-and-so declared before us: I wish to betroth and take as wife So-and-so, and here are the "gratifications"[68] which I shall give her. He produced three rings, one of plaited gold and two of silver. We asked him: "What is the marriage gift [meaning the one given in addition to the

formal, betrothal gift, see below]?" He replied: "Twenty good gold pieces, 10 for the early and 10 for the late installment." We asked: "Where are the first 10?" He said: "I do not have them at present. I shall give them to her, or to a representative of hers, as soon as God has them ready for me." We betook ourselves to her, and, after her identity was established by two trustworthy witnesses, she legally appointed So-and-so as her representative. Having done this, we betrothed him to her in a definite marriage bond and gave the "gratifictions" to her representative. . . .[69]

Seventeen days passed between the first and last court actions in this matter. The document shows that the bride could have acted herself. Her representative did not have to be her father nor any other relative, and situations have been found where no family relationship is evident to us. The rings may once have had a symbolic significance, but by that time their sole purpose was to gratify the bride and to serve as the formal betrothal gift obligatory at the conclusion of a marriage. Clearly this document reflects arrangements made for poor people.

An even older description of betrothal procedures, taken not from the Geniza, but from a question sent from Qayrawān to Saadya Gaon (d. 942 in Baghdad), emphasizes the role of the father. It deals with a case of which we have already had two examples, namely, that a man had more than one daughter, and there were doubts with whom the marriage was or was to be concluded.

This is our local custom with regard to marriage. If she has come of age, she empowers her father to receive her betrothal gift; if she is a minor, he does so on his own, as approved by the sages. The congregation assembles in the synagogue which the father attends and he receives there the betrothal gift for his daughter. This Reuben [meaning the father of the daughters] was a scholar and an old man, and scholars and others gathered in the house of study. [The old scholar prayed in a *beth midrāsh*, or house of study.] Simeon [the groom] stood up from his seat and gave the betrothal gift to Reuben, while the scholars from the school of the late R. Nathan were seated around. Simeon spoke up and said: "May your daughter be married to me by this ring." Those present shouted to him in Hebrew about four or five times: "Say, which: say, which," but he paid no attention to them because he was abashed, standing before the congregation and the scholars.[70]

The synagogue, it should be noted, is used here not as a place of worship but as one of public assembly and legal action. The parties concerned seemingly were low class, showing little concern about the prestige of the family and the welfare of its members.

A betrothal document written in Fustat in summer 1007 emanated from a higher level of society. Its study enables us to understand why, at certain times, it was found desirable to keep the "betrothal," that is, formal marriage, and the wedding separate. Here, again, the daughter had appointed her father as her representative. The groom (in the absence of the bride) hands over to the father 100 dinars and the rings, after the groom and the bride had agreed to the usual mutual obligations they would have to fulfill once they were united under the bridal canopy. Another 150 dinars are promised as late installment. An accompanying document no doubt contained details about the trousseau and the impending wedding.[71]

A purse of a hundred gold pieces was a very high sum of money in those days; its delivery demonstrated that the contracting parties were in earnest. We see here the raison d'être of the "betrothal": by making the marriage definite through its formal conclusion as well as its financial arrangements, it left for the wedding solely its ceremonial and social aspects: the benedictions, the other rites, and the banquets. It was a reaction against the age-old experience that "there is no ketubba that does not elicit squabbles," meaning last-minute misunderstandings about details of the dowry or the marriage gift which used to arise when the marriage was formally concluded and the contract signed at the wedding.[72]

In the preceding subsection, we saw how a well-to-do family obtained the same result by an engagement contract: the first installment of the marriage gift was presented in cash, but it was deposited with a third party, and the dowry was readied up to the last detail. For the betrothal was a grave affair; it bound groom and bride together without granting them a common life. Only a formal divorce could make them free again. This could lead to many complications, especially as the young men had to work hard in order to be able to marry and often had to travel overseas. Imagine a young man who was betrothed to a girl in a provincial town in North Africa, did business in Egypt, and decided to break off the betrothal (perhaps because he wished to marry a girl in the new country). How much could happen until he would be willing and able to have the bill of divorce issued and until it reached its destination. The Geniza tells us about such a case.[73]

Furthermore, since "betrothal" meant formal marriage, groom and bride became legally responsible for each other. When an orphan girl wished to dispose of a piece of property held in trust by the court, her action had to be confirmed by the man to whom she was betrothed (1082). In a huge document, executed in the fall of

1121, two sisters release a former partner of their late father from any claim that they or their minor sister might have had against him in respect to that partnership. The sisters' release is confirmed by their husbands, but one of these was only an *ārūs*, "betrothed," that is, had not yet led his wife home.[74]

Yet, despite these serious drawbacks, betrothals were common. Parents must have found it advantageous to bind their daughters in such a total way in order to assure for them a husband at all. There is no reason to assume that men were more in demand than women; but finding a mate befitting the social and financial circumstances of a family and its specific requirements seems not to have been an easy matter. The reader is reminded of the story opening this subsection, where a father was in a hurry to engage his daughter to another man while her fiancé tarried overseas longer than anticipated.

We have comparatively few documents from Cairo, the newly founded caliphal residence, for during the "classical" Geniza period its Jewish community was small, and the Geniza chamber was in Fustat, situated about two-and-a-half miles south of the Fatimid residence city; still, for the short span of the years 1107–1110 we have at least three betrothal contracts from Cairo. In spring 1107 a groom (whose father was dead) promised a first installment of the marriage gift worth 10 dinars, 5 of which were given to the girl at the betrothal, and a late one of 30 dinars. Thus, these were lower middle class people. No ring is mentioned; 5 dinars are, of course, an entirely sufficient betrothal gift, and their payment, as we shall see later, was regarded as a local custom. The wedding was fixed for two years later, and the young couple was to live with the girl's parents (in one *house,* not in one apartment); the parents obviously were old and had no one else to look after them besides their daughter. Moreover, the groom promised never to choose a domicile for his future wife outside Cairo. The document is in the handwriting of the eminent judge Abraham b. Nathan, *Med. Soc.,* II, 512, and signed by, among others, Abraham b. Shabbetay, another learned judge (see *ibid,* p. 47). Thus, the betrothal certainly was arranged in accordance with all requirements of the then valid law.[75]

In October 1108, another groom whose father was dead was betrothed to a girl in Cairo, this time with one ring of gold and three of silver, promising a marriage gift of 5 + 20 = 25 dinars, but retaining for himself the right to move with her elsewhere whenever he saw fit. The wedding—after a year approximately.[76]

A third groom in Cairo whose father was dead was betrothed to a girl (called Baghdad, an abbreviation of Sitt Baghdād, "The Mistress of Baghdad") in October 1110, also promising 5 + 20 = 25 as marriage gift, and, in addition, the expenses for the wedding, which was to take place seven months later. We notice that despite the great similarities, each case was different.[77]

A document from approximaely the same period (date not preserved) describes arrangements in a well-to-do family, for which we had another example in the betrothal contract of 1007, above. Here, both fathers were dead; the groom bore the honorary title "elder"; the bride, "of her free will," had appointed a brother of her mother as her representative, who received for her as "betrothal silver" 20 dinars, to be complemented, at the wedding, by 50 dinars as first installment of her marriage gift; the defective state of the manuscript leaves unclear what the second was to be, but it might have been 70 or 90 dinars or even more. In addition, she was promised a *khil'a,* or festive attire, normally consisting of a robe, a tiara, and a wimple, for the wedding. Several conditions, usually reserved for the marriage contract, are also included, such as that which makes a wife "trustworthy like two witnesses in her house and her word," meaning that no oath could be imposed on her with regard to her management of the house. On the other hand, certain parts of a compound, such as a house (or parts of it) and half a store, would be included in her dowry.[78]

I wish to conclude this survey with a few specific items. A long letter from Jerusalem, sent around 1085, contains this line: "I arranged a marriage for my younger son Abū Naṣr. It was a beautiful betrothal." The social event of the banquet seems to have been the only detail worth mentioning. From a betrothal document from December, 1093, written in Fustat by the judge Abraham, son of Isaac, the scholar (*Med. Soc.,* II, 512), we learn that a betrothal gift of 5 dinars was Egyptian local custom. This custom certainly had ancient antecedents, since the sum is referred to later in the document as "the 4 1/6 dinars." (A change must have occurred, perhaps when the money lost some of its value, and the 4 1/6 dinars were upped to 5.) In addition, the groom promised a marriage gift of 10 + 40 dinars, so that this total commitment, as the document states, was 55 dinars. In a preceding court session the bride had authorized her father to conduct the negotiations, and now the father agrees that the young couple would occupy the upper floor of a house acquired by him, as long as his daughter lived, while he and his heirs would pay the ground rent and the watchmen. (It is not stated that the father lived in that house, and the impression is that he did not.) If she preferred to live elsewhere, she would receive the rent. We see here that the choice of the domicile was the wife's prerogative, even where no difficulty with the husband's family was anticipated. A fine of 10 dinars was imposed on the party that called off the betrothal.[79]

Our second choice is a betrothal document written on a Saturday night and stipulating that the wedding was to be held prior to the forthcoming Sabbath. Again the nominal betrothal gift of 4 1/6 dinars is mentioned, but in reality 10 dinars were delivered to the father together with the betrothal ring. The remaining 10 dinars of the first installment of the marriage gift (20 + 30 = 50) were to be given to the bride in the form of two bracelets. She would follow her future husband to al-Maḥalla, the provincial town, where the wedding would be held that very week. No doubt a banquet was given also in Fustat, where the girl was betrothed. Although only a few days separated the wedding from the betrothal, a fine of 10 dinars was imposed on the side breaking the contract (Nov. 1131).[80]

The same court record notes, a few weeks later (Jan. 1132), the betrothal of a girl with the proud name Jamīʿ (an abbreviation of Sitt al-Jamīʿ, "Ruler over Everyone"), who was so poor that, at the betrothal, she, or rather her father, got nothing but a ring, and for the wedding she was promised only 1 dinar, plus 25 dirhems, the obligatory marriage gift for a virgin. But even that did not work; a postscript notes the delivery to her of the bill of repudiation (before the consummation of the wedding).[81]

A brighter outlook awaited the orphan "Beauty" (Sitt al-Ḥusn). The father of the groom undertook to maintain the couple for five years and to be responsible even for the late installment of her marriage gift (5 + 20 = 25 dinars; it might well become due after his death). No representative appeared on her side, which means that she had come of age; but, since the wedding was fixed for about two years later (betrothal: Sept. 1184; wedding: Aug./Sept. 1186), she certainly was still very young, and the two judges who signed the document watched over the financial arrangements. The young man was probably a student who prepared himself for a profession that would enable him to earn money only years later. Since the betrothal was made on the day before the Feast of Tabernacles (Sukkot), the festive meal on the evening preceding that holiday, I assume, served also as betrothal banquet (see subsection B, 3, below).[82]

When a betrothal was canceled, the parties could be in disagreement about their mutual financial obligations, as happened with the broken engagement described at the beginning of this subsection.

I summarize briefly one such occurrence reported in the Geniza because it demonstrates beautifully how much a family affair a marriage was. A man named Ṭarib ("Merry," later in the document referred to as "Abraham known as Abū Ṭarib"), represented his sister, a girl whose father was dead. When the betrothal was canceled, the groom demanded the return of 15 dinars given as the first installment of the marriage gift. A lawsuit ensued, and a board of arbitration, consisting of four prominent citizens (all known to us from other documents), decided that Ṭarib had to return 9 of the 15 dinars paid and also to renounce all claims that he, his two brothers, his mother, or his sister (in that order) might raise against the groom or against his brother (Dec. 22, 1026, which was a Jewish day of fasting, 10 Teveth). In another case a family offended by the annulment of a betrothal by the bride's side forced her new groom to give her up.[83]

All the betrothal documents considered thus far originated in Egypt, Palestine, or the Maghreb. Quite different from these and of a rather specific character are three betrothal documents written in Damascus in January and February 933 "according to the custom of the small synagogue, namely that of the Babylonians."[84] The groom's action is defined here as "he gave the ring of pledge for [*not*: to] her,"[85] and the minimum marriage gift, referred to either with the biblical phrase "*mōhār* for virgins,"[86] or simply as "in accordance with the custom of the small synagogue,"[87] was 25 gold pieces, to which the bridegroom regularly made an additional promise. This colony of merchants from Iraq who had settled in Damascus obviously wished to maintain a certain standard of living among its members, and this usage might well have been brought with them from their native country.[88] The groom in the second document, Manṣūr b. Isaac b. Sa'īd b. Phinehas (Fīnḥās), probably belonged to the famous Phinehas family of Baghdad, which seems also to be represented in Damascus by another member as party to a contract for sale of a property written by a Muslim notary around the same time (922).[89]

The details concerning the individual couples are also noteworthy. In the first contract from 933 the groom, who had promised a total marriage gift of 35 dinars, registered in the name of the bride one of four shares in a compound belonging to him, that share representing the value of the gift. Manṣūr of the Phinehas family delivered 15 dinars at the betrothal, and promised

35 for the wedding and 20 as delayed installment. The third match was concluded between an orphan and a poor man, who promised a marriage gift of 30 dinars, but was able to produce only 7 at the betrothal and 3 at the wedding; thus his delayed installment amounted to 20 dinars like that of Manṣūr. But the bride possessed an apartment consisting of several rooms, which she had inherited from her father, so the couple was at least assured of a domicile. The fathers and the guardian of the orphan promised to be fully responsible for the maintenance of the brides until their wedding. Since groom and bride had become legally married through betrothal, and since marriage made the maintenance of the wife obligatory on the husband, such promises were by no means superfluous. Yet no such stipulation is found in the many other betrothal documents studied above, although there can be no doubt that, until her marriage, the betrothed was maintained by her family. The realities of life, we see, are not always reflected in documents; in many respects, common usage was strong enough to ensure proper conduct.

These betrothal contracts from Damascus are registered, one beneath the other, on a large sheet, once forming part of a record book. Yet each is signed by a number of witnesses, the one of the groom from the Phinehas family by ten, to whom the head of the congregation added his own signature (signing last, as required by the ceremonial then in force).[90]

Similarly, on a page of a record book from the Palestinian synagogue of Fustat, dated September 7, 1043, the copy of a ketubba is signed by seven (here again, with the head of the congregation signing last).[91] This procedure, which is evident in other documents from the tenth and early eleventh centuries, emphasizes the public character of the act of concluding a marriage. Later generations obviously found it too burdensome for the witnesses to sign both the original document, handed over to the bride, or her family, and the copy preserved in the communal records. The engagement, betrothal, and marriage contracts that had been registered were then often signed either by two or more officials, or by one in addition to the clerk, whose handwriting was regarded as sufficient for making the entry a public record. No fixed system is to be observed in this matter, but it is perhaps reasonable to assume that this later practice was influenced by the Muslim example, where "trustworthy witnesses" were permanently attached to the qadi fulfilling the functions of notaries.[92]

Z. W. Falk has drawn attention to the great similarity of the betrothal procedures in the synagogue and the Eastern churches.

The Nestorians of the seventh century called the betrothal *mekhīrūthā*, "sale," "property conveyance" (from which Arabic *imlāk*, p. 69, above, might have been derived), but despite this prosaic name, it was, like the Jewish *qiddūshīn* the real consecration of the marriage bond, blessed by a priest and making the bride the groom's wife. A ring was given, a cup of wine was blessed and both groom and bride drank from the cup.[93]

Now that Jewish custom has combined betrothal and marriage, the ceremony of bride and groom drinking from the cup of blessing is performed at the wedding; but in Geniza times, when the *qiddūshīn* preceded the wedding, a blessing over the cup of wine accompanied the betrothal benediction. "The girl drank from the cup" is stated in a report on a litigation as additional proof that the betrothal was final. Normally, the documents had no reason to refer to this custom.[94]

I have preferred to illustrate the engagement and betrothal procedures largely by summarizing a number of cases. For generalizations do no good in situations that in reality are so different from one another. More examples are discussed in subsequent sections. The reader who has followed me thus far may be disappointed by the prominence of money and other materialistic matters in this story of engagement and betrothal. But these documents are not love letters; they are legal instruments by which the contracting parties try to safeguard the economic security, welfare, and peace of the young couple, as far as they are able to do so. The reader is well advised to keep this in mind now that we are about to study the main instrument for the creation of the marital junction, the marriage contract, which was written and signed at the wedding.

3. *Wedding and the Marriage Contract*

How well preserved the Geniza marriage contract is and how to study it.—Our main source for the socioeconomic conditions under which a marriage was concluded in Geniza times is the *ketubba*, or marriage contract. Many hundreds of documents of this type have been preserved, but they have in common that not two are identical; the reason: they reflect the realities of life, and life is diversified.

Unfortunately, the Geniza ketubbas share another common trait: the great majority of them have come down to us in a tantalizing state of fragmentation. Several factors contributed to this, first and foremost, of course, the general fate of decay affecting written material exposed to destruction by man and nature (see *Med. Soc.*, I, 7–9). The ketubba was especially vulnerable because it was usually longer and wider than other documents, and because its reverse side mostly remained blank, inviting paper-hungry poets and clerks to cut out a piece of the size they needed. As a matter of fact, we have to be grateful to these plunderers of the Geniza, for it frequently appears that a ketubba fragment has been saved solely because it satisfied a need for writing material. Finally and particularly, when, after the death of her husband or a divorce, a woman received all due her, the ketubba, which to all intents and purposes is a bill of debt, was torn apart and thrown into the Geniza, with only one or several fragments surviving.[1]

Since the inception of Geniza research scholars have succeeded in uniting such *disiecta membra*, whether found in various libraries, or in different collections housed in the same library. The very first item in M. A. Friedman's book on the Palestinian marriage contract consists of four different fragments of one ketubba, two found in the Bodleian Library, Oxford (previously recognized as belonging to the same document and edited by S. Assaf), and two others, one in the E. N. Adler collection, now in the library of the Jewish Theological Seminary of America, New York, and another in the Taylor-Schechter Collection of the University Library, Cambridge, England, both identified by Friedman; but all four together are still far from providing us with a complete text.

In addition to marriage contracts proper the Geniza contains *court records* drafting or reproducing such contracts or otherwise related to them, as well as *notes of judges* summarizing the main points of a ketubba in preparation for the issuance of a document. Finally, settlements arranged during marital life, or after its termination by death or repudiation, as well as dispositions in contemplation of death, often have opportunity to refer to stipulations made at the conclusion of the marriage. Occasionally such settlements are written on the reverse side of the original ketubba.

As is natural, this variegated material originated in widely different times, places, and situations. Therefore utmost circumspection is required in its study. To this *caveat* another and most pertinent consideration must be added. Both because of its legal and sentimental value the ketubba was a most valuable possession and was carefully kept by the wife or her family. When it got lost, it had to be replaced immediately.[2] How, then, did ketubbas get into the Geniza? Mostly, it stands to reason, they ended up in it when there was trouble, when the document had to be produced in court and was torn up, after the litigation had led to a settlement. And the Geniza chamber, we remember, was only a few paces away from the room where the sessions of the court of the Jerusalemite Jewish congregation of Fustat were held. Who applied to the courts? Disputes over marriage stipulations could occur anywhere. But families that were better off were able to make proper arrangements to forestall such emergencies (see B, 2, above), and preferred to settle their differences in private. It was the poor, those harrassed by dire circumstances and unable to make a good match in the first place, who were forced to have recourse to the courts. In view of this consideration, we might suspect that the general testimony of the Geniza documents on marriage is somewhat lopsided, leaning heavily toward the lower and lowest strata of society.

In order to avoid the pitfalls of both generalization and one-sidedness, we must single out specific groups of documents, each representing a reasonable measure of unity, a unity that would prevail, for instance, where documents were written by one judge or clerk, or in one single period, or originated in one type of environment, or reflected a particular situation. On the other hand, in order to form a productive object of study, the group must be fairly comprehensive and diversified. In the Appendix "The Economics of Marriage," part I, I have assembled eight groups of ketubbas and related papers which, I hope, meet those demands and thus facilitate the approach to an understanding of the realities of marriage in Geniza times.

The first group is a selection of thirty-seven documents all from Fustat and all written by the judge Mevōrākh, son of the judge Nathan b. Samuel (see *Med. Soc.*, II, 513, sec. 18, 514, sec. 22). Twenty-six are from the ten years between 1155 and 1165 (ten of them originating in the course of one summer, 1156), nine are not datable, and two are from a slightly later period but of special interest: they are acknowledgments of the receipts of trousseaux in times of unrest. They were added in order to show the situation after the pillage and burning of Fustat in 1168.

In addition to their inner coherence, Mevōrākh's documents are especially valuable inasmuch as in his court, or perhaps in his time in general, it was customary (or obligatory) to list the actual prices of the items of dowries and not sums inflated in honor of the bride or her family.

Nathan, Mevōrākh's father, wrote the more interesting and more important Geniza documents on marriage. But his total witness on the subject is not as massive and compact as that of his son. Therefore, I have preferred to select seventeen of Nathan's documents on marriage written during a period of about seven years (1140–1147) and to present them where they belong chronologically, as group 6.

Group 2 centers on court records that could be described as the marriage register of the Palestinian congregation of Fustat for the year 1186, eleven documents in all, to which are added seven from the years 1182–1185. In this group, too, the prices of the items of the dowry are realistic.

Proceeding chronologically, group 3 contains the oldest marriage contract completely preserved, issued in Damascus in 933, and eight other documents from the same city and period. In various respects this is a special group comprised of both rich and poor people.

Group 4 is widely diffused in both space and time. It comprises eight major cities: the twin cities of Cairo and Fustat; Jerusalem; Tyre, Lebanon; Aleppo, Syria; Tinnīs, one of the two eastern Mediterranean ports of Egypt;[3] Barqa, then the capital of Cyrenaica, or eastern Libya; and Qayrawān, then the capital of Tunisia. Its span of time is about eighty years (960–1039). This was a period of transition, when many of the old usages and local variations were still alive, as is illustrated by the details provided in the Appendix, group 4, and in B, 4–5, below. Provincial towns and villages are excluded. The often quoted marriage contract from the Byzantine town of Mastaura, Asia Minor, of 1022, is not listed either because its very special conditions do not lend themselves to meaningful inclusion in a schematic table.[4]

The streamlined uniformity of the twelfth century is reflected in group 5 (1105–1135). The legal framework underlying those contracts and court records is uniform; the diversified socioeconomic conditions are responsible for the variations. This was the period of the court clerk Ḥalfōn ha-Levi b. Manasse (see *Med. Soc.*, II, 231), and most of the documents listed in this section are indeed from his hand. Since the number of fragments written by Ḥalfōn and his contemporaries is endless, the group, with few exceptions, is confined to dated pieces. A glance at the sums in the list of marriage gifts and dowries shows that in this large group the number of couples belonging to the poorer strata of society was considerably higher than in groups 1, 2, 3, 4, and 6. In reality, the discrepancy was perhaps even greater, for we know both from instructions written by Ḥalfōn b. Manasse and from actual examples that in his time (or his office) it was customary to list the items of the dowry with double the actual price. This matter is discussed in B, 4, below.

Six of the documents written by Judge Nathan b. Samuel (group 6) deal with brides from well-to-do houses—a far higher percentage than that found in group 5. To this must be added that Judge Nathan, like his son Mevōrākh after him, seems to have insisted on the prices of the trousseaux being realistic.

Group 7, marriage documents from the Egyptian Rīf, clearly falls into two sections, one from larger, and another from smaller provincial towns, the latter sometimes being merely populous villages. Qalyūb, because of the nearness of the capital (see *Med. Soc.*, II, 257), is a case by itself.

Group 8, "Remarrying one's divorcée," was brought together in order to find out whether rash and ill-considered divorces were a general social evil or confined mainly to the lower social classes. The answer provided by the list is self-evident.

Part II of the Appendix summarizes the main aspects of the economics of marriage in general. About six hundred documents were examined, but since most of them are fragmentary, or do not include information pertinent to the table, the total number listed is far smaller than six hundred.

The first question to be asked in examining a marriage document relates to the personal circumstances of the young couple: was it the first or the second or still another marriage of the bride, for the socioeconomic conditions accompanying each differed considerably. It is also important to know whether or not the fathers of groom and bride were alive at the time of their wedding, for fathers tried hard to provide for the marriages of their children, both male and female, although they were not always successful.

The main topic of inquiry, naturally, is the material base of marriage: the immediate marriage gift of the husband, delivered at engagement, betrothal, or—mostly—at the wedding, the delayed one, paid at the termination of marriage, and the dowry brought in by the bride. Here, a great variety of cases, caused both by the customs and idiosyncrasies of the scribes and the fortuities of preservation, will puzzle the student of the Appendix. We are fairly well informed about the distribution of the immediate and delayed marriage gifts, although in many cases we learn only about one of them or about the total. While we have abundant details about dowries, their total values are mostly lumped with the marriage gifts; my own attempts at finding the complete value of a dowry by adding the sums attached to the individual items are often frustrated by the simple fact that not all of them are extant. A particular problem is presented by the comparative values of the marriage gift of the husband and the dowry of the parents, especially the smallness of the former and the size of the latter, so that occasionally one wonders whether the two parties have come from the same social milieu. In B, 4, below, I discuss the conclusions to be drawn from these rich, but checkered, sources of information.

What does the Geniza marriage contract tell us?—An attempt to survey systematically the contents of the Geniza ketubbas may seem futile after having said that no two are identical. It might be useful, however, to learn what kind of data we can expect to find in a ketubba, and how frequently each item occurs.

Like any other legal document, the ketubba normally opens by stating the exact time and place where it was executed. The date is given according to one or several of the various Jewish eras, in addition to those explained in *Med. Soc.*, I, 355–357, especially the era of the destruction of the Second Temple (which reminds one of the Coptic "era of the martyrs" of A.D. 284),[5] and that of the "weeks" of the Jubilee periods of fifty years (faintly resembling the Byzantine indictions).[6] The latter two are common in ketubbas according to the usage of the Land of Israel.

The locality is regularly defined geographically, such as "Fustat, Egypt, which is situated on the Nile River," but also administratively, by naming the head of the Jewish community, to whose authority the legal action incorporated in the document was subject. In Mamluk times an atrociously long list of honorific epithets was attached to the name. In the twelfth century the head of the community took pride of place in the good wishes preceding the text proper, as discussed below.

Some groups of Geniza ketubbas contain the assurances normally found in legal documents, namely, that the parties were in full command of their physical and mental faculties, that they acted out of free will, were not coerced or in error, that the document was executed in accordance with the strictest provisions of Jewish (and gentile) law, and so on; others, the majority, do not. Those matters are of interest for the history of the ketubba, but not for social history, with which we are concerned here.

The first item requiring our attention is the status of the bride. She is usually described as a virgin, which simply means that this was her first marriage.[7] They were not particular about virginity in those parts and days, or, rather, were barred by good taste from speaking about such matters. The latter conclusion seems to me more likely seeing that two modern Jewish authors from Yemen, who describe the marriage ceremonies in their native country, which stretched over several weeks, in minute detail, make no reference at all to the night of consummation or all that is connected with it.[8] In the vast mass of Geniza papers dealing with family life, M. A. Friedman and I have found only one case in which virginity formed an object of contention. The story is too funny not to be told. The husband, a Mr. Cohen—that is, of a priestly family—quarreled with his in-laws years after his wife had borne him a son. In the heat of the squabble he said: "The woman I have taken from you was not a virgin." When things calmed down, he backed down and declared that he had lied. But a new judge who arrived in the town and learned about the matter declared that Mr. Cohen's progeny was to be deprived of the priestly privileges (such as pronouncing the blessing over the congregation [Numbers 6:23–27] or leading it in the reading of the Torah). It was a gross blunder on the part of the learned judge, since only the high priest is bound to marry a virgin (Leviticus 21:13), whereas any other Kohen is only prohibited from marrying a divorcée. Finally, when the grandsons of Mr. Cohen had grown up and become respectable members of the community, a new judge appearing on the scene rectified the matter.[9]

Another case from this period, not reported in the Geniza, but known from the *Responsa* of Abraham Maimonides, was decided by the master in a way that must have deterred any groom from claiming that the bride did not have the status professed in the ketubba; not only had he no right to reclaim what he had already paid as his main marriage gift, but he was obliged to pay also what he had promised.[10] Still, it is perhaps characteristic for a rationally minded city population that the obsession with virginity, which was rampant in less-developed communities, seems to have been next to absent.

What has been just said seems to be contradicted by the Karaite ceremonial where the kerchief with the virgin blood was actually shown to witnesses and blessed. The Karaites, we remember, were the most advanced, or, at least, richest, section of the community. But here, as in many other cases, the Karaites simply took the Bible literally (Deuteronomy 22:13–21, especially verse 17), or preserved ancient custom, or were influenced by their Muslim environment, or all these three agencies acted in unison.[11]

When the bride was a divorcée or a widow, or both, or "a virgin divorced after betrothal,"[12] this was stated too, but there was no absolute consistency in this matter. Occasionally, one tried to avoid any unpleasant memories and the bride was described as "(presently) unmarried," or "the woman" (Karaites)[13] or "previously married."[14] A freedwoman, or a captive who had been ransomed also would be designated as such, and occasionally the name of a widow's former husband is mentioned.[15]

Such distinctions were necessary, because an ancient law stipulated that the minimum obligatory marriage gift to a virgin was 200 *zūz* (silver pieces) and that to any other woman, 100. In the Geniza period 200 *zūz* were regarded as worth 25 dirhems, which meant that a woman not a virgin received 12½ dirhems. Mostly it is not said expressly, or evident by the wording of the ketubba, whether these payments of the minimum obligatory nuptial gift were actually made in silver pieces or were included in the main marriage gift, which was promised and delivered invariably in gold (or its value). The Karaites made the same distinction, but fixed 50 silver pieces for a virgin and 25 for other brides. They differed from the Rabbanites in this matter not because they were richer—although that might have contributed to the distinction—but because, as always, they clung to the word of the Bible (Deuteronomy 22:29, see also 22:19).[16]

These *minutiae* of Jewish law are helpful inasmuch as they reveal to us—even where the details about the status of the bride are lost—whether a woman married for the first or a consecutive time. To my astonishment I found that about 45 percent or more of all brides of the Geniza period had stood under the wedding canopy more than once in their lives. This remarkable social phenomenon is analyzed in C, 3, and discussed in connection with the general position of women in D.

Muslim marriage contracts from this period regularly contain the remark that the bride had come of age.[17] The Karaites, whose usages were in many respects similar to those of the Muslims, do the same, and formulate this notion beautifully, "a girl able to fulfill the religious duties," for many commandments had to be observed by a married Jewish woman.[18] In most of the Geniza ketubbas, those of the Rabbanite community, this detail is provided only sporadically, although it is found throughout six centuries.[19] It was redundant because the very fact that the bride makes one or more legally valid declarations in the marriage contracts proves that she has come of age.

The personal names of groom and bride are defined by those of their fathers; their mothers are never mentioned. The reason, of course, was that the name of a man's father was his family name.

When the spouses were first cousins, their common grandfather is occasionally noted.[20] Longer pedigrees, such as those found in the marriage documents of Italian noblemen or Arab amirs, were rare exceptions.[21] In one document, the bride is characterized as *aṣīlā* (Heb.), "of noble descent."[22] Since numerous ketubbas from the best families known to us are extant in the Geniza, the absence of the reciting of genealogies at weddings (as opposed to memorial services, see A, 1, above) must have been intentional, probably in order to avoid rivalry and discord between the families newly united.[23]

The names of the fathers are usually followed by the blessings to be pronounced over a dead or a living person, whatever it happened to be. This detail is important because whether or not a person was orphaned was of considerable influence on one's socio-economic position. Here, however, we encounter the difficulty that many of our papers are drafts of notes or enclosures, such as lists of trousseaux, where the clerks did not bother to include the relevant blessings.

The occupation of the groom, or his father, is indicated, it seems, only when the occupation formed part of the name by which a person was known, such as *Bu 'l-Barakāt al-'aṭṭār* (the perfumer) or *Bu 'l-Makārim al-ṣā'igh* (the goldsmith), both followed by their full Hebrew names.[24] It is also indicated in special instances, as when a cantor marries the daughter of a beadle.[25] But even where a widow is promised that her future husband will teach her son his profession, we are not told what it is.[26]

In many marriage contracts, especially in the more ancient ones, which are executed according to the Palestinian rite, and in all the Karaite ketubbas the bride appoints a representative, and his name and those of the two persons witnessing the appointment are mentioned. The representative is called by the Greek term *epitropos* (appearing in many different forms) and, in Karaite documents, *pāqīd* (Heb.), which is the equivalent of Arabic *wakīl*, proxy, deputy, agent. In most other documents, especially those formulated according to the standard (Babylonian) custom, this detail is absent.

It cannot be sufficiently stressed that the proxy mentioned in the ketubba differs essentially from the *walī*, or guardian, of the Muslim marriage law (see B, 2, above). Epitropos was the word used throughout the Geniza period to an agent appointed by a person to serve as his or her representative. The Arabic, and later Muslim, *walī*, was the male person who had power over the female who was unable to act for herself. The witnessing by two persons of the appointment of her proxy by the bride was Jewish usage in

Palestine centuries before the advent of Islam.[27] It is possible that the Karaites adapted their legal forms to Muslim models, for this detail of having the bride represented by a pāqīd appears in their marriage contracts consistently and prominently. On the other hand, it is not excluded that they remained faithful to ancient Palestinian custom more strongly than the majority of the Jews who had adopted Babylonian usages.

Turning now to the substance of the ketubba, a note on the term itself is in place.[28] Its meaning is simply "a written statement" (on the obligations of the husband toward his spouse). Although the actual documents spell out also the duties of the future wife, mostly in general terms, the essence of the ketubba is the husband's financial responsibility, wherefore it is the wife who receives and keeps the ketubba. Some marriage contracts describe the husband's obligations regarding the delayed marriage gift to be paid at a divorce or the husband's death simply as *ḥōv* (Heb.), a debt, while a late document characterizes the dowry as a loan.[29]

Under the general meaning of obligation the term "ketubba" assumes three different meanings, two of which, strangely enough, are used side by side in the standard marriage contracts of the Geniza. First it designates the obligatory minimum gift of 25 or 12½ silver pieces, wherefore, close to the beginning of the contract this statement is found: "He added to her ketubba such-and-such a sum of gold pieces as an additional gift." Second, it comprises all the dues from the husband, including the return of the dowry, wherefore we read near the end: "Thus, the total of her ketubba, namely *mōhār* [which stands here for the minimum nuptial gift], additional gift, and dowry, amounts to such-and-such a sum."[30] Informally, in the phrase, "ketubba and dowry," the term refers to the late marriage gift that the husband owes his wife.

The stereotyped general promises made by the groom and reciprocated by the bride have been discussed.[31] It is remarkable that the full maintenance promised by the groom contains only food and clothing, but does not make mention of living quarters. The Jewish marriage contracts from San'a, the capital of Yemen, invariably included the obligation that the husband should provide a domicile for his wife inside the Jewish quarter with entrance and exits within that quarter. The absence of the stipulation in the Geniza contracts (and in most other ketubbas) had its root in the assumption that a man acquires a house, or is accommodated in his father's house, before his marriage. Maimonides' advice that a man should first have an occupation enabling him to make a living, then acquire a house, and only afterward take a wife, is based on a

Talmudic maxim reflecting Jewish life in late antiquity. By Maimonides' own time social conditions had fundamentally changed, and, as we shall presently see, the problem of living quarters looms large in the documents concerning marital relations.[32]

The groom's "additional"—in reality, main—marriage gift is broken down thus: first the total sum is given, followed by the immediate, usually smaller, installment, of which it is often stated that it had been received and acknowledged by the bride; the delayed installment, to be paid at a divorce or the death of the husband, comes at the end. Since most of the marriage contracts are fragmentary, this arrangement often helps us to reconstruct the details (see the introductory remark to the Appendix).

Subsequent to the groom's marriage gift, the bride's dowry is noted, usually detailing each item with its price, but sometimes (rarely) only providing the total value of the trousseau. The dowry is introduced by the phrase: "This is what [or simply: and] she brought in from the house of her father," the oldest and probably the most common form, occasionally replaced by "from the women's quarters."[33] That phrase is sometimes expanded to a more pious version: "This is what she brought in with her from the All-merciful and from the house of her fathers" [in the plural].[34] An ancient village ketubba simply states: "And this is what came in with her."[35] But even the very formalistic court clerk Ḥalfōn b. Manasse writes this about a virgin whose father was dead: "This is the dowry which she brought to him *from her own*." The bride concerned, ʿAmā'im, clearly was a working woman; we shall hear about her later.[36]

These economic foundations of the marriage, the husband's contributions and the wife's dowry, are studied in detail in B, 4.

The main part of the ketubba is followed by a list of stipulations, some long, some short, which fall into three categories: (1) general items, found in most documents and summarily called "the well-known conditions," or "the well-known conditions imposed by the daughters of Israel";[37] (2) fairly common items; and (3) specific items related to the special circumstances of the couple.

The first item in the first category, found in the majority of marriage contracts, is the postulate that the wife be regarded as trustworthy in the conduct of her household (and other financial matters—not included everywhere), and that no oath could be imposed on her in this matter by her husband or his heirs. This detail goes back to biblical times, when the Israelite peasant woman held the reins of the farm in her hands, while her husband went out to the fields at sunrise and did not come home until sunset (Psalms 104:22–23). The God-fearing woman of valor, so highly praised in Proverbs 31:10–31, is just a thrifty housekeeper, of whom it is said: "The heart of her husband trusts in her, and he will have no lack of gain" (*ibid.* v. 11, the first of the wife's desirable traits). The social conditions of the Geniza period, naturally, were radically different from those of ancient Israel, but the stipulation of trustworthiness still was of vital importance for marital peace and the wife's economic security.

Second and third in frequency were the husband's promises not to marry another wife and not to keep a maid disapproved by his spouse. These prohibitions, too, have a long history behind them.

Many conditions were connected with the dowry, the most common being that half of it would return to the wife's family should she die without offspring, male or female. This originally Palestinian usage became more or less generally accepted. The Karaites, interestingly, stipulated that the entire dowry of a woman dying without child should go back to her father's house; moreover, according to them, during her lifetime the husband was not permitted to take any action with the dowry without informing and consulting his wife.

Not "well-known," but still frequently found, were the stipulations in the second category dealing with such questions as the domicile of the young couple, deciding whether the husband or the wife had the prerogative of choosing it, and touching on a wide variety of other matters connected with this issue; or, whether a wife's earnings by work were her personal property, or belonged to her husband, or could be retained by her only if she provided for her clothing from her earnings; or, the condition that a husband should not travel abroad (or even outside the couple's city) without the consent of his wife and without making provision for her maintenance in his absence and in case death overcame him while away.

The third category, stipulations occasioned by special circumstances is, naturally, greatly varied: the cost of the wedding, the relationship of the spouses with members of the two families, children brought in from a previous marriage, the freedom of movement of the wife, and her treatment in general. These conditions indicate that the two contracting parties knew each other well and were taking precautions.

In addition to these three categories of stipulations, which reflect the realities of life in the Geniza period, there is a fourth which may be characterized as traditional, that is, a stipulation that was in vogue in Talmudic times and was retained solely in the ketubbas according to Palestinian (not "Babylonian," that is general Jewish) usage. Most of the laws represented by these details were still in force, but, for one reason or another, were no longer included in the common marriage contracts. One condition, for instance, provided that if a wife was taken captive (which often also meant raped), her husband was obliged to ransom her not with her dowry, but with his own money, to bring her back, and to live with her without grudge. One easily understands why such a condition, although very vital in turbulent times, was dropped from the regular ketubba.

Finally, there are stipulations concerned with religious observances, for instance, in connection with the frequent cases of mixed marriages between Karaites and Rabbanites, and, after the reforms introduced by Moses Maimonides (late twelfth century), the so-called laws of purity. They are normally spelled out at the end of the marriage contract, and the wife is warned that if she fails to observe them she will lose her marriage gift.

The social safeguards contained in the ketubba, as surveyed above, are studied in B, 5. We shall not come back to the stipulations described as traditional nor to those concerned with religious observances. The interesting divorce clause included in the ketubbas of the Land of Israel is briefly treated in C, 3.

Physical features.—In conclusion, something must be said about the physical features of the Geniza ketubba. Since it is supposed to last for a lifetime, it is written mostly on vellum, not on paper. Usually it is longer and/or wider than other documents. Although many ketubbas are poorly written, the majority display careful script and pleasant arrangement.

The signatures of two witnesses are sufficient for validating a document. But in order to honor and to please the young couple, the number of witnesses signing a marriage contract was greater and they were selected to fit the occasion. This detail is discussed below in connection with the wedding ceremonies.

A special feature is the expression of good wishes heading the ketubba, normally arranged in larger characters and often also in a different type of script (for instance, monumental and quadrangular script, with the text in cursive). The most common wish, "may they build and succeed," meaning "may they be blessed with children," has been discussed.[38] Second in frequency are the good wishes expressing the idea that marriage is a matter of luck, thus referring to the relations between husband and wife. This is formulated in many different ways: "with a good omen,"[39] "with an excellent augury,"[40] these two often combined,[41] "at a propitious hour and a lucky time,"[42] and similar phrases. The astrological background of these wishes is evident, but an additional idea is involved: if a man is successful with his marriage, he will prosper otherwise and be a blessing to his environment.[43]

This idea, that marriage is not a private affair, but concerns the community at large, is very prominent in the good wishes ornamenting the Geniza documents. The oldest ketubba fragment found thus far in the Geniza (dated 870) bears this superscription: "With a good sign for us and for all Israel, in a propitious hour here [and everywhere], with a high star for us and all Israel. . . ."[44] The most common superscriptions of the late eleventh and subsequent centuries rhyme *kallā*, bride, with *qehillā*, congregation, and, where appropriate, include the head of the community, *negīd ha-gōlā*.[45] Once the propensity for rhyming was let loose, many other good wishes having the same rhyme were added. The Karaites, always aware of the obligation to set Jerusalem above one's personal joy (Psalms 137:6), wish the young couple to be granted "to rejoice in Jerusalem's joy" and, in general, express messianic hopes in many different ways.[46] One Rabbanite ketubba (not from the Egyptian capital) is headed by a long poem—exceptional in a Rabbanite ketubba—saturated with messianic yearnings; the bridegroom was a cantor, a vocation paired with the avocation of writing poetry (see *Med. Soc.*, II, 220–221); I suspect the young man authored the poem himself and wished to immortalize it by its inclusion in his marriage contract.[47]

Another way of blessing the young couple was to adorn its marriage contract with telling verses from the Bible. To exhaust this topic would lead us deep into the intricate problem of the usage of the Bible in medieval writings. The most obvious and appropriate verse, "He who has found a wife, has found happiness and obtains favor from the Lord" (Proverbs 18:22) is next to absent because the name of God was avoided in the standard ketubba.[48] The prominent court clerk Japheth b. David used it constantly, but cut off the words "from the Lord" and wrote, instead, a rhyme "obtains favor and a propitious hour."[49] The other relevant verse from the Book of Proverbs (19:14), "House and property are inherited from the forefathers, but a capable wife is from the Lord," is rare for the same reason; as superscription, I have found it only in a sixteenth-century ketubba, far beyond the period with which we are concerned here.[50] A third verse from Proverbs (20:24) unconnected with marriage, "A man's steps are of the Lord," serves as a superscription, because it emphasizes, like the two preceding verses, that a man gets a good wife by the grace of God, not through his own merit. The reference to Elkana's love for his wife Hanna (I Samuel 1:8) is found in a poetical proem and is absolutely exceptional.[51]

Most Bible quotations selected convey the notions of joyfulness and happiness, either referring directly to weddings such as Ruth 4:11–12, and Jeremiah 33, 11,[52] or by describing the jubilant reunion of God and Israel in the simile of a matrimonial bond, as expressed in many verses in the later part of the Book of Isaiah and of several other prophets. References to the creation of Adam and Eve, such as "It is not good for man to be alone; I will make him a helper fit for him" (Genesis 2:18) are rare, and, as superscriptions, confined to Karaite ketubbas,[53] where we also find the most appropriate quotation: "I will betroth you to me forever; I will betroth you to me in truth and lawfulness, in steadfast love and compassion" (Hosea 2:19).[54]

The good wishes and Bible quotations not only expressed the notion of joyfulness, but also intended to create it by their beautiful execution. This aesthetic aspect of the ketubba needs careful consideration; it brought home the idea that the marriage contract was not merely a legal instrument conveying rights, but a bond of almost magical power keeping the newly married spouses united. We are here in a period when writing was an art exercised, as a rule, only by professional people (see *Med. Soc.*, II, 178–179, 228). Women were for the most part illiterate; men were able to read the Bible and other books written in monumental script, but the fleeting cursive used in documents and letters required unusual exertion from them, if they were capable of mastering it at all. Therefore it was (and still is) customary to read out the ketubba to the young couple (or to the bridegroom alone) at the wedding. In view of all this it was the look of the ketubba which counted. In his brilliant paper, "Arabic Epigraphy: Communication or Symbolic Affirmation," Richard Ettinghausen has shown that inscriptions on mosques and other public buildings (including the mosque of the Islamic Center in Washington, D.C.) often were executed in such a way that they could hardly be read by the uninitiated. Rather, they were destined to express the importance of the building and the greatness of God or the ruler to whom it was dedicated.[55] A similar attitude is to be assumed with regard to the ketubba: for the wife who kept it, it must have been like a charm protecting her marriage.

Take the case of the second marriage of the divorcée Turfa ("Precious Gift"), one of the poorest women mentioned in the Geniza documents. (She brought in a dowry consisting solely of clothing, estimated as being worth only 5 dinars.) But her ketubba of December 1124 is written in beautiful regular script on a large piece of vellum, 30 cm (12″) broad, and about 38 cm or more long. Wide blank spaces are left between the lines, as was customary in the Fatimid chancelleries, and the heading with the good wishes is artistically arranged: five groups of two words each, divided from one another by blank spaces of about the same size, form the first line, four, the second, and another five, the last; each of the uppermost groups is crowned by a fleur-de-lis design about twice as high as the letters. I have little doubt that the poor couple made a special financial effort for getting such a beautiful ketubba, for two contemporary ketubbas written in exactly the same arrangement for people in somewhat better circumstances are less well done.[56]

Thus far, the students of medieval ornamental art have paid little attention to the illuminations of Geniza marriage contracts. The most recent pertinent publications include reproductions of only two ketubbas from that source, and without discussing them aesthetically or historically. Because of the large size of the documents concerned and their fragmentary state any relevant publication will encounter difficulties. But I believe it is an attractive topic, as the subsequent short remarks, I hope, show.[57]

Bible manuscripts of the tenth and eleventh centuries display an attempt to enhance the beauty of the script with geometrical and floral designs, with or without colors. What we have in the Geniza ketubbas seems to be the end rather than the beginning of a tradition, or more exactly, the waning of one and the start of others. The possible connections with contemporary Coptic and Islamic art must always be kept in mind.[58]

The illuminated ketubba TS 16.73 of the year 1030/1, one of the oldest preserved, is fairly contemporary with the beautiful Bible lection discussed in *Med. Soc.*, II, 152. The script of the text is cursive, but by making the letters strictly symmetrical and vertical and by leaving four times as much space between the lines as the height of the letters, the same effect is reached as by using quadrangular letters: the text looks like a piece of textile adorned by bands. In order to avoid monotony the letter *l* is lengthened so that its long neck protrudes into the major part of the blank spaces. Those familiar with Islamic decorative writing may jump to the conclusion that this is an imitation of Arabic *l* or *al*, so often compared by poets to a slim, tall damsel. But the same aesthetic effect was already sought in the Dead Sea Scrolls, as, in the carefully written *Wars of the Sons of Light against the Sons of Darkness*.[59] It is an old scribal tradition, followed, for instance, even in the trilingual (Hebrew, Latin, Greek) tomb inscription of pre-Islamic Tortosa, Spain.[60]

The heading of TS 16.73 is in monumental script, three times as large as that of the text (1.5 cm), with the lines again separated by blank spaces about four times their own height (6.5 cm). The middle part of the second line (the first clearly visible) is decorated with a large floral medallion hovering over (originally) two horizontal *s*-shaped designs ending in arabesques. The ornamental figures and letters of this line are in gold with red contours, while the next (originally third) line is in red with black outlines. The fleur-de-lis above the middle group of good wishes (the only one visible) in line 3 has black outlines, not filled in. A line, slightly reduced in size (1 cm) and entirely in black, forms the transition between the monumental, colorful heading and the elegant, cursive text.[61]

Exactly the same tradition, slightly mixed with another, is apparent in the fragment TS 16.104, which was written under Gaon Sar Shalom (1177–1195, see *Med. Soc.*, II, 32), that is, a century and a half later. The letters are more quadrangular than in TS 16.73 and larger (2 cm, the *l*s, 5 cm), but we find the same playful mixture of gold, red, and black, alternately serving either as borders or as fillings, and the *s*-shaped arabesque designs, here encompassing one single group of blessings each in lines 1 and 3. The letters in line 7, which form the transition from the decorative heading to the text, are only 1 cm high and in red (without borders). Above and below them are lines in micrographic script, about a millimeter high, followed by another line in a similar script. This is not yet the text (which is lost), but again good wishes and Bible quotations. The use of minuscules, about which we shall hear presently, developed in Bible manuscripts, where it was necessary to differentiate between the sacred text and the learned notes destined to explain and preserve its correct reading. Soon the scribes used minute script for decorations, combining with them geometrical and floral patterns, borders, and similar designs.

A ketubba written in Aleppo, Syria, in 1107/8, that is, halfway in time between the two just discussed, differs considerably in style. The cursive of the text is ordinary with no particularly large spaces left between the lines and, consequently, with no elegant *l*'s stretching out their necks. The first three lines of the text are in large, well-done monumental script, and the superscription consists of only two lines of letters in gold with black borders, the first (originally) forming three shorter, and the second two longer groups of good wishes. Between these two lines a middle piece, forming a tablet with cable pattern, and (originally on both sides) a tablet forming a floral rinceau are posted. The one fleur-de-lis preserved is larger and executed more artistically than any one seen by me on an Egyptian ketubba.[62]

Contemporary with the Aleppo ketubba, but, naturally, standing within the Egyptian tradition, the prolific scribe Ḥalfōn b. Manasse has left numerous pieces of his ornamental workmanship. Four have been touched upon above.[63] His is also the only illuminated ketubba preserved in its entirety known to me: that of the working woman 'Amā'im.[64] It is an excellent example of what a couple in modest circumstances could expect in this matter. The good wishes are arranged in seven lines containing alternately four or three groups, each group crowned by a fleur-de-lis and divided from one another by a design of two fleurs-de-lis. Lively vowel signs soften the austerity of the perfectly drawn monumental letters. The text, written in beautiful, smallish cursive, is deftly adapted to the shape of the parchment, which narrows gradually from top to bottom. The slight curve of the right margin thus created (l. 1 of text is 24 cm, last line, l. 26, is 20 cm) is extremely graceful. This ketubba is the product of a jejune, but harmonious and self-assured, culture, and therefore, to my taste, also aesthetically more satisfactory than many of the fancy Italian, Greek, or Iranian ketubbas with their inadequate figures, garish colors, and unsatisfactory scripts. To be sure, Ḥalfōn was, in his way, a master of his art. We are entitled to judge since we have less pleasing examples from the hands of his colleagues.[65]

Besides headings, ketubbas were adorned with marginal bands bordered by lines of minute script containing Bible verses and good wishes, such as "may your heart be happy with your Creator, may the groom be happy with the bride, and she with him, and both with children, male and female, wealth and. . . ."[66] The fillings of these bands differed widely. The most common form was quadrangles or quadruple quadrangles of micrographic lines having as their centers mostly eight-petaled flowers. As already mentioned, the origin of the geometric lines in tiny script is in the tradition of Bible manuscripts, whereas the proliferation of floral designs is to be sought in the text of the headings: the basic wish, "may they build and succeed," is regularly followed by the rhyme, "and bloom and flourish."[67] Another filling consisted of Bible quotations written in huge letters contrasting with the minuscules of the borders. In one case, the band has the form of a vertical *tabula ansata* with no filling at all. In another, a Karaite ketubba, the marginal decoration consists solely of large, hollow letters.[68]

Finally, there were broad borders consisting of four or more bands, alternately filled with micrographic geometrical figures comprising floral designs and large monumental script in different colors.[69]

The most elaborately ornamented ketubba known to me from the "classical" Geniza period also signals the waning of this art: it is overdone. The border consists of six bands of different composition and colors, intersected by circles, one of which contains two stars of David (then not a specifically Jewish emblem) in different positions, and all contours realized in minute script. The sumptuous heading is equally overcrowded, with floral designs getting lost in the space, with outlined, but not filled-in, oversized vowel signs having no proper relation with the monumental letters in full colors, and a squeezed-in large medallion of three micrographic circles with a flower as center and one circle in large script as filling. When complete, the borders with the headings must have occupied more space than the text. I suspect, this baroque piece of scribal art was teamwork: the father of the bridegroom was a scholar and cantor, known to us as signatory of many documents from the years 1180 through 1191, and his colleagues might have vied in the endeavor to make the young couple happy. But the sure touch for proportion and symmetry, marking the ornamental work of the classical Geniza period, had been lost.[70]

The Geniza contains a considerable number of complete, or almost complete, illuminated marriage contracts from the Mamluk and, especially, the Ottoman periods. In these pieces the influence of the environment is clearly evident. The fragments also are worth studying.[71]

The reverse side of the ketubba was left free, but could be used for entries connected with its contents. Thus we read in a court record telling us of a married woman depositing part of her jewelry as a collateral for a debt incurred by her brother: "The court entered the deposition of these objects on the back of her ketubba."[72] An addition to the outfit of the bride, a grant to the wife of partial or complete control of her dowry, remarrying a divorcee with the same conditions as those included in the original contract, or simply a docket indicating the names of the groom and the bride are typical entries.[73]

The ketubba was given to and kept by the wife, since it spelled out the financial and other obligations of her husband toward her. For reasons of safety she would deposit it somewhere else. We hear about a woman in the little town of Malīj who entrusted her ketubba to a woman in Alexandria, but the latter proved unworthy of the confidence placed in her: she delivered the document to the husband, who made improper use of it.[74] About a Rūmi, that is, a man from Byzantium of Western Europe, married to a local wife, we read this: "Please inform my mother that the Rūmī has stolen the ketubba of my sister and not returned it. While I was about to bring him to the head of the police or the rabbinical court he absconded and disappeared."[75]

When lost, a ketubba had to be immediately replaced, and a considerable number of such second copies have been preserved.[76] Only exceptionally are the circumstances under which the loss occurred indicated, as when a well-to-do couple lost its ketubba along with other possessions during the conquest and pillage of Tripoli, Lebanon, by the Crusaders in 1109.[77] And rarely is it stated how much time had elapsed since the writing of the marriage contract; a ketubba from Baalbek, Lebanon, dated 1253, says only that it was "a long time."[78] The draft of a renewal from September 1081 notes that about five years had passed, but, there was already confusion whether the marriage gift was 5 + 15 = 20 dinars or 5 + 20 = 25 dinars. Possibly the clerk forgot to correct the draft.[79]

Wedding.—The date of the wedding was commonly fixed at the engagement or the betrothal. But requests for postponement because one of the two parties had not yet succeeded in obtaining the necessary funds were frequent.[80] In addition to fines, which were usually stipulated for a delay not agreed upon by the other party, we occasionally hear that the groom had to pay alimony to the bride for every day the wedding was postponed after the date fixed. Since the husband was obliged to maintain his wife, such an arrangement was natural. But it was exceptional; the fines normally took care of this matter.[81]

The favorite periods for weddings were the spring months March-May and early fall, September-November. A cursory survey listed fifty-five weddings for the spring, forty-three for the fall, but only twenty-five for the summer (June-August) and eighteen for the later half of December through early February. The number of weddings for the spring months would have been far higher had not Jewish custom discouraged weddings between Passover (Easter) and Pentecost (comparable to the Christian Lent). Climatic reasons aside, the summer months were avoided because several members of a family, the bridegroom included, might travel abroad on business during that period. And even in a hot country like Egypt the peak of the winter could be very uncomfortable in view of the insufficient heating facilities.[82]

Concerning the choice of the weekday one principle stands out clearly: one preferred to arrange the wedding close to the end of the week, so that there was sufficient time for the preparations and also for an additional celebration on the forthcoming Sabbath. Approximately half of all the weddings were held on Wednesday and Thursday, with Thursday taking the pride of place. Friday was not popular because the strict Sabbath rest, which began on Friday afternoon about an hour before sunset, left too little time for the proceedings. According to Islamic custom, the ceremonial procession of the bride to her husband's house and subsequent consummation took place on Thursday night, which is "the night of Friday," the holy weekday of Islam.[83]

Considerations of thrift caused people to hold their weddings immediately before holidays, especially Passover in the spring and the Feast of Tabernacle in the fall, or on Purim, which (like carnival) was a day of merriment rather than a holy day. We even read about a wedding on the eve of the New Year day, which is consecrated to prayer rather than to feasting. An examination of the cases preserved shows that they were mostly second marriages, or those of poorer couples, village people, and the like. Normally one tried "not to mix joy with joy," that is, not to hold a wedding close to the time of a holiday.[84]

It seems not to have been customary to send written invitations to a wedding, at least I have not found any. Notifications to relatives were kept short. This is what a mother writes to her son:

> I expected you and your children for the holidays, but you did not come, which disquieted me very much. Your sister misses you immensely; her eye is on the door all the time because of her yearning after you. [The sister, we remember, has special claims on her brother.] Please take notice that the little one [the sister's daughter] has been betrothed and will marry on the 25th. So make haste and come, you and your children, under all circumstances. I wish also that you ask her aunt [his sister's maternal aunt, the writer's sister] to come with you and treat her well, for she has no one in the world except God and you.

A few orders, no doubt for completing the bride's outfit, conclude the short note.[85] A letter of mixed content to a weaver and tailor has this postscript: "The little one enters her house by the end of this month. Please take notice of this."[86]

Business letters and documents occasionally mention financial arrangements necessitated by an impending wedding, but otherwise we hear astoundingly little about the preparations toward the greatest of all family events. Since the wedding was celebrated at home, one had to make room for the guests. The merchant banker Nahray b. Nissīm lived in Fustat, but also owned a house in Alexandria. When a factotum of his was about to marry, his cousin, who was in charge of that house, wrote this:

> I wish to transfer the books which you have here to the storehouse in bundles because of the forthcoming wedding, that is, Mukhtār al-Ḥalabī says he wishes to marry the daughter of the Elder Abu 'l-Ḥaqq; he already has paid him the early installment of the marriage gift and made most of the preparations. If God will, next time this will be with that one who is with you [Nahray's daughter] and at the "joy" [wedding] of Nissīm [his son], may God keep him. If you wish that I send you part of the books in a case on the Khalīj canal after the Holidays [about two weeks after the sending of the letter], please let me have your instructions.

In a letter of Solomon, the son of judge Elijah, we read that it took ten days "to bedeck the bride [the writer's daughter] with the beautifying ornaments"; I take this to be ornaments borrowed for the occasion, not the jewelry brought in by her, the acquisition of which took months and years, if not generations. For his intended own marriage Solomon had foreseen a period of not more than ten days including the betrothal.[87]

Since wedding festivities took place both before and after the bride's procession to the home of her future husband, and since the banquets for men and women were held in different rooms (or, at least, sections of a room partitioned by a curtain), both families, it seems, had to contribute to the costs, or special conditions as to who had to bear them were laid down long before the great event. In a betrothal agreement from fall 1140 a groom agrees to make all the expenditures for the wedding, "in respect of both women and men" (in that order). In a slightly earlier betrothal contract, written by Ḥalfōn b. Manasse (1100–1138), in which the groom receives one half of a property owned by the mother of the bride, but promises to buy the bride's outfit, he also stipulates that he would not provide a wedding banquet "nor any of the sumptuous luxuries of the people of Fustat." Agreements concerning the cost of the wedding are mentioned in other parts of this volume.[88]

Details of the wedding ceremonies are referred to in passing in letters and documents. We have read about the dyeing of the bride's hair with saffron and of her hands and feet with henna, her make-up, her ceremonial dress, her procession to the bridegroom's house, and the *ṣīniyya*, the tray on which money was put for the poor and for the lower communal officials during the *hanā'*, or congratulation reception.[89] One letter speaks of the custom of the congregation ceremoniously leading the groom to the synagogue on two consecutive Sabbaths (presumably one before and one after the wedding day) and "honoring" him there, that is, having him recite the most avidly sought after lections from the Bible and portions of the liturgy. On the same Sabbaths, the cantor would sing religious poems dedicated to the occasion or specially written for the bride and groom. Hundreds of such compositions have been found in the Geniza.[90]

The more ancient marriage contracts are occasionally signed by persons characterizing themselves as *shōshevīn*, "best man," of the groom, and we learn that such a relationship meant a lifelong connection involving even the best man's family.[91] Older ketubbas are signed by a large number of persons, one from Barqa, eastern Libya, dated 990, by thirty-six.[92] (This is still far less than the seventy-seven Muslims signing the marriage contract of a Coptic [Christian] deacon with the daughter of a Coptic priest in Aswan, 948).[93] The awkward signatures often found beneath the ketubbas of lower-class people prove that the friends of the young couple were honored with this function. The excellent hands that adjoined the shaky ones with equal frequency show that the presence of high-standing persons at a wedding was sought in order to enhance its glamor, as we also learn occasionally from reports about a wedding. Here is what an old aunt writes to her nephew, a physician and himself father of a marriageable girl, about the wedding of her own daughter, which the nephew was unable to attend:

> Needless to say that we cannot be really joyful when you are not present. But by the grace of the God of Israel Sitt al-Yumn ["Lady Good Luck," her daughter] had a most joyful wedding owing to the presence of our lord, the Nāsī; the betrothal ceremony was beautiful; our lord the Nāsī, our lord the judge, our lord Rabbi Samuel, and the bridegroom Hibat Allah ("God's Gift"), son of the teacher Futūḥ Ibn al-ʿAmmānī, were seated on a beautiful dais—may God grant you the same with your daughter.[94]

In general, however, reports about weddings are of utmost brevity. All a woman in Tunisia has to say about such an event to her brother on a business trip in Egypt is this: "Mawlāt ["Lady"] has married. It was a terrific wedding."[95] A man from the island of Jerba, captured by the Normans and ransomed by a notable in Egypt, writes a detailed letter to his benefactor after his return; near the end we find this note: "Your servant married the daughter of his paternal uncle on Sabbath "Comfort" [when Isaiah chap. 40, which begins with the word Comfort, is read; about a month after his return; quick work!] in the house of her father [which was uncommon; his own father had been forced to sell his house because of the bad times]."[96] Between a list of prices in Tunisia and a report about new government impositions a trader provides this information: "I asked God for guidance and married in al-Mahdiyya into a family which made high demands on me [for the marriage gift]."[97] Even more astounding is this laconic remark inserted into a lengthy report about the writer's illness: "Barhūn b. Ismaʿīl Tāhertī [a well-known member of this great Qayrawānese family] married me to the daughter of Ezra, the son of Hillel, may he rest in Eden. I ask God to make the match successful."[98]

Congratulations on weddings, too, are sometimes rather casual: "I congratulate you on the marriage of the baby [the writer's daughter], may God let you pass on to the "joy" of Abū Saʿd [his son]."[99] Depending on the circumstances, especially when the match was regarded as really good, the writers could become quite eloquent and personal.[100] Mostly, however, the good wishes were stereotype. When the communal leader Sahlān b. Abraham married in 1037, Dā'ūd (David), the brother of the (future) Gaon Daniel b. Azarya, wrote to him: "May it be a propitious sign for you, for us, and for all Israel," referring to the idea that if a man is happy in his marriage, he will be successful also in other matters and a blessing to his community.[101] We have a calligraphic letter of congratulation on a wedding by Sahlān himself; but because of its highly poetical Hebrew any attempt at a translation would fall flat; anyhow it does not contain more than the usual wishes, succinctly expressed in this letter from Jerusalem, addressed to the prominent physician and public figure Abraham b. Isaac b. Furāt, a contemporary of Sahlān. After heaping honorific epithets on the addressee in twenty-three superbly written lines, the letter concludes thus:

> I was happy to learn about the "joy" [wedding] of our elder, may God make your happiness full and complete. May the wife who comes into the house of our elder be like Rachel and Leah, who both built the house of Israel, and may God give you male children studying the Torah and fulfilling its commandments. May you see the erection of the House of God, the ingathering of the people, and the advent of the Savior.[102]

4. *The Economic Foundations of Marriage*

The obligations of the husband.—A mere glance at any marriage contract preserved in the Geniza shows that the first and foremost obligation of the husband was to provide his wife with food and clothing and to maintain her in general. Housing is not expressly mentioned as an obligation because it was taken for granted that marriage means "bringing one's wife into his own home," that is, either the house of the family of the groom's father or one owned or rented by the groom himself. "By entering my house you will become my wife," was an ancient ketubba form.[1] This assumption was so general that a Talmudic source states: "When an orphan wishes to marry, one [that is, the community] rents for him a house, provides it with bedding, and then marries him to a wife."[2] In connection with this Saul Lieberman draws attention to a lovely Jewish building inscription in Greek, which says: "May God, who has helped with building this house, help also with the marriage."[3]

The general obligation of a husband to provide for his wife finds its tangible expression at the time of the marriage, namely, in the partial delivery and partial promise of the marriage gift, usually consisting of three parts: the minimum obligatory nuptial gift, referred to either with the biblical *mōhār*, or the postbiblical *ketubba*,[4] the immediate installment of the "additional," but, in reality, main, marriage gift, of which it is often stated that the bride has already received it (as was common also in Muslim marriage contracts), and the delayed installment, to be paid by the husband in the event of a divorce or by the husband's heirs after his demise.

Naturally, the legal minimum of 25 dirhems to be given a woman at her first marriage, corresponding to 200 *zūz*, or silver pieces, in Talmudic times, cannot enlighten us on the economic efforts required from the husband. That sum was given, or at least noted, in order to fulfill a religious injunction, and, in many cases, it is not evident if this payment of silver money was actually made or was included in the main gift, which was invariably in gold.[5] Yet the legal minimum of 200 zūz conveys a message. At the time it was in force, a man whose possessions amounted to this sum had no claim on public charity.[6] In Islamic law we find a similar ceiling of 200 silver pieces for the right to receive alms; thus a common Near Eastern tradition probably existed in this matter.[7] In any case, fixing the minimum marriage gift at that sum means that at marriage a man had to prove that he was able to sustain himself.[8] To what extent this principle was adhered to in Geniza times might be learned, at least partly, from the main marriage gifts given and promised in our documents.

In *Med. Soc.*, I, 391, the question is raised why all the substantial payments connected with the marriage contract were stipulated and normally also made in gold. The obvious answer is that the relevant documents originated in Egypt, Palestine, Syria-Lebanon, Asia Minor, and western North Africa, that is, all countries that once had been provinces of the Byzantine Empire, where gold had been the standard coin; moreover, gold remained in larger supply than silver during the centuries with which we are concerned here. The Muslim marriage gifts registered in documents found in Egypt, too, are always in gold, although they often did not amount to more than 2 to 4 dinars, that is, they were given and promised by persons in very modest circumstances.[9]

Much has been written about the division of the husband's marriage gift into an immediate and late installment and the possible Islamic model for this practice. We have to discern here among the historical origins, the legal formulation, and the socioeconomic realities, as reflected in the Geniza documents. The two-stage contribution of the husband, one toward the wedding expenses and other immediate needs of the future wife and the other toward her material security after the termination of the marriage, has its roots in hoary antiquity. Talmudic law and practice laid the emphasis on the latter, on "the debt" the husband owes his wife, or, as some ancient documents have it, his "responsibility for her ketubba." The Arab-Muslim *mahr* was essentially a bride price, a payment to be made at the wedding, but one that could be deferred to one or several later installments, the dates of which, often only months or a few years, usually were fixed in the marriage contract. Thus the two institutions are instrinsically different. It seems, however that the terms "early" and "late" (installments) were adapted to Muslim usage. Likewise, the phrase found in most marriage contracts: "[he added to the obligatory nuptial gift] such-and-such a sum, of which he gave her such-and-such a sum as a gift at the time of the wedding [the receipt of which she has confirmed], while such-and-such a sum remained on his neck as a debt" is also similar in formulation to Muslim documents, although in substance it is pre-Islamic. Such an adaptation to Muslim legal parlance was necessary, for ketubbas frequently were brought before the state authorities, since in family matters the minority courts acted as representatives of the government.[10]

The overwhelming testimony of the Geniza documents proves that the minimum cash payment required from a groom at marriage was 5 dinars. We had an inkling of this above.[11] Before trying to evaluate the socioeconomic significance of this fact, the instances of immediate payments of less than 5 dinars must be briefly surveyed. These were remarriages to one's divorcée,[12] marriages to divorcées with or without child,[13] to widows with or without child,[14] in general to women marrying a second or third time,[15] orphans,[16] or women of undefined status.[17] There are a few special cases from villages and places outside Egypt[18] and others where not all the relevant data are available.[19] To these belong some carelessly written, short marriage contracts from Cairo.[20] These examples show that the customary minimum cash payment of 5 dinars was waived only under exceptional circumstances.

What does this mean? One is reminded, of course, that the standard exchange value of a dinar was 40 dirhems,[21] so that with 5 dinars we are back to the 200 silver pieces of the obligatory marriage gift of late antiquity. I doubt, however, that there was a direct historical sequence, and am rather inclined to see the connecting link in the mysterious betrothal gift mentioned in some Geniza texts of 4 1/6 dinars, which was later upped to 5 dinars.[22] This sum is clearly related to the obligatory minimum marriage gift of 8⅓ dinars (2 × 4 1/6), known from "Jerusalem" (that is, customs derived from what once was customary in Palestine), Asia Minor, and elsewhere, the equivalent of the ancient 200 zūz.[23] Such changes were brought about by monetary developments in early Islamic times and contemporary adaptation to them by Jewish law. That we shall ever be able to disentangle these complex relationships is doubtful. Here we are called upon to evaluate the fact that during most of the classical Geniza period, a minimum of 5 dinars was delivered as first installment of the marriage gift at, or before, the wedding.

In order to appreciate what this meant in practice we have to remind ourselves of the perennial scarcity of specie so often referred to in these volumes. People often experienced hardships in this matter, the wealthier because they put every available dinar to work, and the less fortunate simply because they had none. *Med. Soc.*, II, 380 ff., shows what a nightmare the yearly payment of the poll tax was for many members of the minority communities, although those in the lower groups of taxpayers had to deliver only 1 or 2 dinars. One lived on what one earned, and little was left over for extras. A gift of 5 gold pieces, on top of the expenses for housing and other matters connected with a marriage, required a serious effort on the part of a groom of the lower classes. Thus, the original purpose of the law that fixed an obligatory minimum marriage gift incumbent on the groom was taken care of by the custom evidenced by the Geniza documents: a man should not marry before he had proved that he was able to maintain a household. This is by no means a truism, since many societies are known where such an attitude toward marriage was not paramount—for one, the traditional Jewish community of Eastern Europe (from which most American Jews derive their origin), where the young couple often lived in the house of the wife's parents years before the husband became economically independent.

The customary minimum cash payment of 5 dinars by the groom becomes even more significant in view of the "delayed installment" that goes with it on the one hand, and the higher levels of cash payments on the other. A cursory perusal of the Appendix, Part II, shows that grooms paying 5 dinars as first installment usually promised late installments of 20 or 15 dinars, less often 25 or 30 dinars, and even less often, 10. Those making payments above or below these sums were exceptional. Thus the general assumption was that a man making the minimum cash payment of 5 dinars at the wedding would be able to lay aside for his wife an average of about three to five times as much during his lifetime or, rather, the duration of his marriage. The sums actually disbursed at death or divorce indicate that this assumption was not unrealistic. Naturally, we also hear of husbands who were either unable or unwilling to live up to their obligations.[24]

The picture in the next group, those making a wedding gift of 10 dinars,[25] is different. Here the average of the delayed installment amounts to less than three times the initial payment, which means that, while a special effort was made at the conclusion of the marriage contract, the economic prospects of the husband in general were not tangibly better than that of the preceding group. The two groups together represent the poor and those in modest or very modest circumstances, about one-half of the population. Beneath them were the paupers, forming about one-sixth of the total.

The next and far less numerous layer of society consisted of those who gave wedding gifts of 15 or 20 dinars to which was added a delayed installment of 40–60 dinars, the lower middle class. Persons from the upper middle class gave 30 to 50 dinars as early, and 50 to 100 dinars as late, marriage gifts. The two groups together amounted to about one-third of the whole. This distribution seems to indicate that there was a marked cleavage between the lower and upper middle classes.[26]

There was an even more pronounced gap between the well-off and the rich, those who made a cash payment of 100 dinars or more at the wedding and promised a delayed installment of about 200 dinars. With one exception, first installments of 60, 70, 80, or 90 dinars have not been noted. If you wished to show that you were really rich, you had to lay a hundred dinars on the table and come up with a total marriage gift of 300 dinars. About 5 percent of the marriage documents which contain the relevant information originated in this, the highest, echelon of society.

In the ketubba the husband mortgaged all his possessions, immovables and movables, "including the coat on his back [lit., shoulder]," as well as his estate after his death, to the debt he owed his wife. Mortgaging a specific piece of property for this purpose was uncommon. But at the sale of any immovables by the husband the wife's consent was required, a situation well reflected in the Geniza papers.[27]

Did the husband's marriage gift, as analyzed above, fulfill its economic function? Did it provide for the wife in the case of a divorce or at the husband's death? The average of 25 to 35 dinars, promised by the members of the lower classes, certainly was an awesome deterrent against divorce and thus protected the wife from rash actions of her spouse. Nor were these sums negligible as a means of sustenance. Cash was difficult to come by; therefore it was worth more than its purchasing value. A woman giving 17 and an old man providing 36 dinars bought for themselves maintenance during their remaining years.[28] Naturally, only the barest necessities were covered by such an arrangement.. Still, a young widow or divorcée with such sums in hand had reasonable prospects for a new venture in marriage, provided, of course, she possessed an outfit of her own. In general, the husband's contribution was not sufficient for guaranteeing his wife a decent living after the termination of the marriage. For this she needed the additional means provided by what she had brought with her from her father's house.

The bride's dowry.—"Give your daughters to husbands," says the Prophet Jeremiah, 29:6. "Is the daughter in her father's hands [so that he can 'give her away']?" asks the Talmud (with reference to the accepted opinion that a father should not marry off his daughter as a minor, but should wait until she grows up and makes her own choice).[29] Answer: "Have him give her something and provide her with clothing and cover so that the young men will jump [be eager] to marry her."[30]

This little disquisition illustrates the legal situation: the ketubba, the husband's obligation, was religious law; the *nedunyā*, an ancient Near Eastern term for the dowry, was a matter of practical wisdom and local custom. Consequently, while the tractate on the ketubba is one of the more extensive parts of the Talmud, there is no section in that vast body of legislation dedicated to the nedunyā, and very little is said about it in general. This means that the material about the dowry found in the Geniza documents is hardly influenced by ancient law, but reflects actual situations varying according to place, time, and individual case.

The variety of circumstances is mirrored in the multiplicity of terms. Besides the Hebrew-Aramaic nedunyā ("that which is given"), which appears in marriage contracts and other legal documents throughout, and another Aramaic term,[31] mostly Arabic words are used. *Jahāz* or *jihāz*, "outfit," used also for equipping an army, fitting out a ship, or supplying a traveler with provisions, is the term commonly found.[32] The word *raḥl*, literally "luggage," can designate the dowry in general, or the clothing and bedding, as opposed to the jewelry.[33] Equally frequent is *shuwār* (or *shiwār*), also originally denoting travel equipment, but assuming perhaps the specific meaning of trousseau because it was confused with an almost identical word meaning beautiful clothing.[34] A fourth Arabic term is of North African vintage, not surprising in view of the constant influx of Tunisian and Moroccan Jews into Egypt.[35]

Lists of trousseaux not included in marriage contracts are mostly headed by the word *taqwīm*, "estimate," or "estimation," already met with above in connection with the engagement agreements.[36] The procedure followed at the taqwīm is evident from numerous documents. The bridal outfit was assembled in one room, knowledgeable men (thoroughly briefed, no doubt, by even more knowledgeable women) made the assessment of the monetary value of each item in the presence of the groom, who then had to express his consent with the evaluation, for it was he who was responsible for the preservation of the precious objects received. The reverse side of one such list, which enumerated twelve items of gold and silver jewelry, thirty-four of clothing, four of bedding, and thirteen of copper and other household goods, representing a total value of 145 dinars, contains two statements: one of the father of the bride (named Sitt al-Suʿadā, "Mistress over the Happy Ones") stating that all "gold, silver, copper, clothing, silk, and other valuables listed overleaf" had been given by him to his daughter as an irrevocable gift and were now her exclusive property, and one by the groom, that he was obliged to keep all this as "iron sheep," meaning something to be returned in full, for which he bore responsibility. According to the law there was no need for such declarations, for what they said was partly implied and partly expressed in the marriage contract. But this particular "estimation" was made in a small provincial town, where the local judge, who wrote the document, preferred to have these matters clarified in straight, simple Arabic, since the Rabbanite marriage contract was formulated in Aramaic, the ancient language of the courts.[37] A similarly styled document of assessment, written, it seems, by a son and assistant of that judge, states that the groom was satisfied with the evaluation made. This declaration, too, was redundant and is, therefore, absent from practically all similar lists, but, like the father's additions to the estimation, illustrates the actual procedures.[38]

When did the taqwīm, the assessment of the trousseau, take place? In the case of a well-to-do couple we have found that it had already been done at the engagement, a full year before the wedding.[39] When a taqwīm document lists the early, but not the late, marriage gift of the husband, it stands to reason that it too was written some time before the final preparations for the marriage.[40] From the wording of most relevant documents, however, the assessment of the trousseau seems to have taken place in connection with the wedding, or, at least, the betrothal. One court record expressly sets the date for the assessment two days before the "consecration," which denotes either the "betrothal" or, rather, the betrothal combined with the wedding.[41] When the evaluation of a dowry was made on the evening of Sunday, September 2, 1244, two days before the Day of Atonement, there can be little doubt that the strange date was chosen because the wedding was scheduled for the first possible day after that day of fasting, namely, the subsequent Sunday, which preceded the Feast of Tabernacles by one day. We remember that the eve of a holiday, and even more a day before that, were favorite dates for weddings of couples in modest circumstances. This surmise is confirmed by the fact that the next entry in that court record, written overleaf, was a wedding held on the next Monday, the eve of the Feast of Tabernacles.[42]

A properly executed and well-preserved appraisal of a dowry is apt to provide us with a complete picture of the economic circumstances of a marriage. It lists the price of each item and, where needed, describes it by provenance, material, color, and size. The totals of the main groups, such as gold and silver jewelry, clothing, bedding (including hangings and carpets), copper, and other household goods, are often noted. The total of the entire outfit is followed by other possessions of the bride, such as houses, or, usually, parts of houses, one or more maidservants, and, occasionally, books. Finally, the document notes the contributions of the groom and concludes with the grand total, that is, all that will be due from him or his heirs at the termination of the marriage.[43]

The assessment lists were drafts to be entered into the final marriage contracts and to be preserved in the record books or archives of the communities. In both cases there was no reason to tear them up, as had to be done with the ketubba after it had served its purpose as proof for the obligations of the husband. Moreover, unlike the ketubba, a taqwīm was usually written on both sides of a leaf. Thus, there was no inducement for people looking for paper to cut it according to their own needs. These technical circumstances explain why the taqwīm lists, second in number but not in importance, to the marriage contracts themselves, represent a most valuable source for our knowledge of the brides' trousseaux.

Of similar character and value, but limited in number, is another type of document, named "dowry receipt." In times of insecurity, or for other reasons, people occasionally found it advantageous not to include the specifications of the dowry in the marriage contract, a document read out in public at the wedding. Instead, the groom acknowledged receipt of the dowry and of his obligation to pay the delayed marriage gift in a separate document, explaining his doing so by his "apprehension of the vicissitudes of the time." Such receipts were written, for instance, in the years of the administration of "the Monk," the Fatimid finance director notorious for his rapacity (see *Med. Soc.*, II, 281, 348), during the transition from Fatimid to Ayyubid rule, and in the middle of the thirteenth century, again a time of upheaval.[44]

The main repository of information on the bride's dowry is, of course, the marriage contract, the ketubba. To make up for its generally poor state of preservation we are rewarded by the mass of detail it yields. The picture of the material civilization emerging from the Geniza is derived largely from ketubbas and cognate documents that describe the possessions of women, the furnishings of houses, and the implements of the kitchen, each with its price. Here, however, we encounter a serious difficulty. In many parts of the Islamic world, including the countries in which the Geniza papers originated, it was customary to assign fictitious, highly inflated values to the outfit of the bride and to its individual items to enhance the prestige of the families concerned. Descriptions left us by medieval Arabic historians speaking of donkeys carrying empty boxes in the festive procession of the bride to her future husband's house, are tangible illustrations of this custom.[45] Nor was this an innovation of Islam. The Talmud leaves it to the discretion of the parties involved whether to list in the ketubba the real values or to double the prices; and Saadya Gaon (d. 942), in his book of legal forms, partly preserved in the Geniza, reports that in some places the former practice prevailed and in others, the latter.[46]

The picture emanating from the Geniza is even more complicated. In a formulary written by the clerk Ḥalfōn b. Manasse around 1130 it is expressly stated: "We evaluated each item doubling its price ["2 dinars being 1 dinar"], as is customary in our place." Consequently, when slightly later, in 1145, a widow reclaimed her dowry and late marriage gift totaling 552 dinars, the court remarked: "This means that what is really due her amounts to something above 250 dinars." A ketubba written at Saladin's time (ca. 1190) contains this note: "The outfit can be reclaimed only at half the evaluation listed."[47] These documents were issued in Fustat. But outside the capital other customs were attested to. In a court record written on August 10, 1204, from Bilbays in the eastern part of the Nile Delta, it is stated that the wardrobe of the bride was appraised there as being worth four times its real value and her gold, silver, and copper two times as much. In the same period, in Alexandria, the entire outfit was priced at four times its worth. In the district capital al-Maḥalla the situation was even worse: the prices were wildly exaggerated, but there was no fixed custom in this matter.[48]

Fortunately, in most cases we are able to get at the real prices. The vast majority of marriage documents originated in the Egyptian capital, and there we find that when the prices were doubled, a Hebrew phrase "2 dinars are worth 1" was added to the trousseau list. Such an addition is presupposed in the formulary of Ḥalfōn b. Manasse referred to in the preceding paragraph. In some cases it is stated explicitly that the husband's responsibility is to be understood in this sense.[49] Conversely, numerous marriage documents, including many of the most detailed and valuable ones, say expressly: "1 dinar is worth 1 dinar, real price, no duplication." One list, after providing the real values of the entire trousseau, adds: "The parties asked the sums to be doubled; consequently, the total will be such-and such."[50] Moreover, where documents sum up the liabilities of the husband—marriage gift and dowry—in dinars "of full weight and worth, approved by an assayer," it stands to reason that the real worth is intended. Wherever doubt remains, we are able to check the items against those listed in documents explicitly fixing the prices realistically, as well as by circumstantial evidence: the size and appearance of the document concerned, the number and type of the items listed, additional gifts of houses or their absence, conditions imposed on husband and wife, and so forth. But even lists suspect of blowing up their prices are not without value. First, it is interesting to know which objects they name and describe; second, the relative values of the various items are instructive.

Besides appraisals of dowries, receipts for them by the groom, and marriage contracts, there were sundry other types of documents describing the outfit of a bride: agreements made when a husband granted his wife exclusive disposition of her possessions;[51] claims for an outfit or parts of it deposited with a third party;[52] receipts for an outfit after the termination of a marriage, or in the case of an inheritance;[53] and special cases, partly those whose circumstances could not be determined with certainty.[54]

The traditional sequence of the main sections of the bridal outfit—jewelry, clothing, bedding, and copper—is maintained in most marriage documents, but there are, of course, exceptions.[55] In numerous lists the sections are headed or summarized separately, or both, but even very long taqwīms dispose of this convenience.[56] The lists regularly conclude with a chest or trunk "and its contents," meaning, the bride's lingerie, varying in value between 1 and 50, and, in one case, even 80 dinars.[57]

An examination of the comparative value of these sections reveals a number of socioeconomic facts. Clothing was expensive and was the husband's main responsibility besides food. It was the wife's chief prerequisite and pride; occupation with her wardrobe was her favorite pastime. Consequently, clothing was by far the largest item in the bride's outfit, a rule confirmed by only few exceptions.[58] The second largest group, also manufactured mainly from textiles, was formed by the furnishings, all those sofas and lounges with their cushions and reclining pillows, the mattresses with their blankets and covers, curtains and other hangings, rugs, and carpets. One did not sit on a chair and at a table, we remember, but on a sofa along the walls or simply on the floor. A house did not have many rooms; curtains provided privacy; wall pictures, so common in Hellenistic and Roman civilizations, were next to absent; beautiful hangings made the house friendly. In this bedding group the discrepancies among social classes and among individual cases were even more blatant than in clothing. It could occur that a rich bride brought in bedding valued over twice as much as her clothing or more than her clothing and jewelry taken together.[59] More uniformity is to be observed in the last group, copper utensils and other household goods, of which even otherwise rich outfits are often conspicuously poor. About twenty-five objects appear regularly on the lists, but a single trousseau practically never comprises them all, while about another twenty-five occur only sporadically. Costly pottery serving as tableware could not be included in the dowry (which represented a lifelong obligation on the husband), because of its perishable character, while inexpensive crockery was not brought in by the bride for obvious reasons.

The widest divergency prevailed in the first group: jewelry and silverware. More than a few brides possessed no ornaments at all.[60] Objects made of precious metals, as a rule, represented only about one tenth or less of the total value of trousseaux estimated as being worth between 60 and 120 dinars.[61] But in the taqwīms of rich girls jewelry is regularly second in vaue only to clothing, and, in that of a very rich girl, it comes first: worth 471 dinars, "real worth, no duplication," as against 373 dinars for clothing.[62] Although even within the opulent class the differences are great, they are still more marked in the ketubbas of the lower middle class, where we find jewelry worth 9 dinars in a total outfit of 203 dinars, as against one of 53 dinars in one of 160 dinars, the latter being a ratio more commonly found with well-to-do girls.[63]

The perplexing story of the Geniza trousseau becomes meaningful when we consider how it was brought together and how it compares with the marriage gift of the husband. A look at the Appendix reveals that there was a tendency to fix a round sum as the total value of the dowry. This shows that, as a rule, the bride's dowry was not simply what she possessed but what had been agreed upon, probably after long pourparlers. In many cases, the individual sections, too, totaled round sums, which points in the same direction. A distinct class stratification is evident in these totals, ranging from the destitute who had no dowry at all,[64] to the rich with 500 dinars and more, and the very rich who brought in 1,500 dinars, plus maidservants and parts of houses.

Occasionally we learn that a certain total was "local custom." Particularly instructive is the following case. In a Hebrew document written in Fustat on June 23, 982, the son-in-law agrees to state in the marriage contract that he has received objects in gold, clothing, and furnishings worth 150 dinars, "as is customary in the ketubbas of this city," although what actually was brought in amounted to only 50 dinars. Correspondingly, the father-in-law gave him 20 dinars in cash and a promissory note of 80 dinars, which had precedence over all his other obligations. This local custom could not affect everyone, of course, since more than half the brides of Fustat represented in the Geniza brought in 100 dinars or less. Thus, a parent who belonged to a certain class had to send off his daughter with an outfit worth not less than 150 dinars. It is characteristic of the socioeconomic unity of the southern shores of the Mediterranean that in the same century a marriage gift of 150 dinars was customary among the Muslims of Qayrawān and could be claimed in court.[65]

Cash never formed part of a dowry during the classical Geniza period, and evidence of the practice did not begin to show up until the fifteenth century, probably under the influence of immigrants from Spain and other Christian countries.[66] In the June, 982, document just discussed, money only substituted for the girl's outfit, which the father had been unable to acquire before her marriage. This restriction of the dowry to personal belongings of the bride was of vital social importance, as the next subsection shows.

An example illustrating how an outfit was acquired reveals characteristic aspects of that fateful step, no doubt one of the more decisive factors in the economic life of Mediterranean society. Early in June, 1156, the grandmother and guardian of an orphan girl received from the merchant with whom the court had deposited the orphan's inheritance the considerable sum of 238 dinars in order to buy her the marriage outfit. In mid-August of the same year she married with a dowry amounting, according to the almost complete list, to 723 dinars. The total was probably 750 dinars. Thus the major part of the dowry must have come to her from her mother or even her grandmother, and this situation, as is presently explained, probably was the rule rather than the exception. On the other hand, an agreement on the size of the dowry must have been made in advance so that it was necessary to supplement it with the inheritance. Finally, a period of two months seems to be somewhat short for the purchase of jewelry, clothing, and household goods amounting to 238 dinars, considering that even in the trousseaux of wealthier brides items valued at 2 dinars or less were by no means rare. Thus the marriage booms of spring and autumn must have created quite a stir in the bazaars.[67]

The analysis of the husband's marriage gift has revealed a high degree of uniformity within each social class and also a fair measure of regularity in the relationship between the first installment presented to the bride at the beginning of the marriage and the delayed portion to be delivered when it was over. The case is different with the relationship of both to the dowry.[68]

With few exceptions, the bride's dowry amounted to five, ten, twenty, thirty, and more times as much as the groom's early installment, ten times as much, approximately, being the most common relationship. This seems natural, since the groom presumably was at the early stages of his economic independence, whereas the father of the bride was at the height of his earning capacity and her mother would either part with some of her own dowry, or pass on to her daughter movables or immovables inherited or received as gift. But the matter is more complicated. Two important aspects of the Geniza marriage emerge. The first is demographic. The groom, as a rule, must have been considerably older than the bride, for even the modest cash gift expected from him at the wedding, together with the other expenses connected with the marriage, required an effort of several years of work. But the situation was entirely different from that of fourteenth-century Italy, made familiar to the student of medieval marriage by David Herlihy's writings, where the demands on the bridegroom were incomparably higher. This resulted in a far wider disparity in the ages of the spouses with all the grave demographic, moral, and cultural consequences entailed. In the Geniza world, the lion's share in the initial economic makeup of a marriage was contributed by the bride's family; consequently, the groom was not forced to spend too many years preparing his share.[69]

Second, the wide differences in the relation between cash wedding gift and dowry found within the same stratum of economic capacity proves that money was not the sole, and in many cases not even the main, consideraton in the negotiation of a marriage. It is even more conspicuous when the relationship between the delayed installment and the dowry is examined. When a widow or divorcée, possessing an outfit of 795 dinars—a sum large enough to maintain a family for thirty years—marries a man who gives her 5 at the wedding and promises 10 dinars at the termination of the marriage, she must have had a special reason for accepting those terms. Her precise motivation, I leave to the imagination of the reader. But she certainly did not marry for money.[70] When a mother, assisted by her brother, gives her orphan daughter, a virgin, to a husband presenting jewelry worth 10 dinars at the wedding and promising a total marriage gift of not more than 20, when the dowry is worth 774 dinars, very particular circumstances must have influenced their choice.[71] Since such disparities are by no means uncommon, we must conclude that "imponderables" played a very great role in the arrangement of marriages. In order to get an inkling of the motives that might have been behind such decisions, I examine some of the family papers of persons known from the Geniza in other contexts. This will give us the social backgrounds of the economic facts emerging from the ketubbas, lists of trousseaux, and cognate legal documents studied thus far. But before doing so, a topic usually forgotten, must be briefly considered: the economic role of the wife.

The economic role of the wife.—Seemingly, the wife is a recipient, not a provider, of economic benefits: her husband makes her a gift at the beginning of the marriage and owes her a payment at its termination, her family fits her out, and, in addition, she might receive an inheritance, or a gift, or both, during her marriage.

In reality, the situation was different. In her marriage contract the bride promised, among other things, to serve her husband. For this service she was compensated by both her maintenance by the husband and his obligatory gifts. Consequently, a wife was bound to work, "even if she had a hundred maidservants," and the Jewish doctors of law, who always tried to capture the realities of life in neat legal paragraphs, defined exactly which chores she was obliged to perform. The doctors were, however, reasonable enough to distinguish between work to be done by poorer women, such as grinding wheat, and those better-off, who sent their grain to the miller or simply bought flour. Naturally, the economic value of the wife's work for her husband differed widely, ranging from doing or supervising the household chores to substituting for him in his business affairs when he was ill, or teaching children when he needed help.[72] According to age-old custom and statutory law spinning was one of the duties of a wife; it was still mentioned as such in a marriage document from the Fayyūm, Egypt.[73]

Besides "serving" her husband, the wife could earn by work done (at home or outside the house) for other people. The remarkable amount and sophistication of Talmudic discussion devoted to the problems of the wife's earnings demonstrate the economic importance which this source of family income had assumed in the impoverished society of late antiquity.[74] The very saying "he who expects to maintain himself by the earnings (lit., wages) of his wife, will never see blessing in his life," betrays the extent of this phenomenon.[75] A wife's earnings belonged to her husband in compensation for the support provided by him, or, as the ancient formula has it, "her food against the work of her hands."[76]

As far as the Geniza period is concerned, it seems that the instances of working women were very rare during the tenth and eleventh centuries. They became more common during the twelfth, and are encountered with great frequency from the thirteenth onward. The first instance noted by me is a request submitted in Aramaic to the Nagid Mevōrākh b. Saadya around 1100 asking him to approve certain conditions to be included in a marriage contract, the most conspicuous of them being "that he should under no circumstances demand from his spouse her earnings, and, if she worked, they belonged to her" (see *Med. Soc.*,

II, 344). About thirty years later, but on the same sheet, such a request, reiterated in Arabic, and addressed to the Gaon Maṣlīah, was written by the court clerk, Ḥalfōn b. Manasse.[77] In a marriage contract (in Aramaic, of course) by Ḥalfōn it is indeed stated that the husband had no rights to his wife's earnings—a divorcée—but that she had to furnish her clothing with her work.[78] Even more significant are court proceedings recorded by Ḥalfōn, from which we learn that a betrothal had broken down because of this question of the future wife's work. The groom was dismayed that the place of her work was far away from his own living quarters; by the time of the agreement, however, he agreed, under oath, never to interfere with her work or to take her earnings. Nothing is said about clothing.[79] A few years later a document written by the judge Nathan b. Samuel tells about a divorce caused by a dispute about the wife's work and a remarriage on condition that she provide her clothing with her earnings; the husband would be free from this obligation "whether she was employed or not."[80] In 1157 Nathan's son Mevōrākh wrote a betrothal agreement, in which the bride, who was the daughter of a cantor, received the right to keep her earnings, while nothing was stipulated about clothing, which could only mean that it had to be provided by the husband.[81] Finally, in a petition from Cairo to the Gaon Sar Shalom (ca. 1177–1195), the wife of Abu 'l-Ḥasan, the miller, known as "Son of the Spindle Maker," also the daughter of a cantor, requests that he should not have the right to tell her, "go and do embroidery in the houses of other people and bring me your earnings," and if she worked, she should be permitted to retain her wages.[82]

This short survey has shown that the question of the wife's rights on her earnings occupied the Jewish courts throughout the twelfth century. When we consider, however, the mass of marriage documents extant from that century, we receive the impression that this aspect of the wife's position was not yet a major issue. By the middle of the thirteenth century, however, working women must have become so common that a statement on the wife's earnings appears as a constant item in the marriage contracts. A ketubba written in 1260 by Judge Immanuel b. Yehiel contains the fixed formula "the work of her hands against her clothing" (it was the second marriage for both spouses and the bride undertook to educate her stepdaughters).[83] How far things had gone may be gauged from this statement in a ketubba written on September 11, 1296 (Tishri 13): "She has taken upon herself that her earnings should belong to her husband." This was the law; there was no need for such a declaration; but the opposite, namely that the wife should go to work and use her wages as she saw fit, or as was agreed upon in her ketubba, was so accepted at that time that acting according to the law had to be expressly stipulated.[84] Equally frequent were statements saying that the groom had renounced his rights to the bride's earnings, or, as was commonly formulated: "Her earnings belong to her and he is held to clothe her."[85]

Most marriage documents from the Mamluk period (1250–1517) contain a reference to the wife's work.[86] Not only widows and divorcées, or poor women, but also brides with a large trousseau would stipulate the retention of their earnings and free their spouses from the obligation of providing them with clothing.[87] Richer brides, though, more commonly received this privilege without renouncing their right to clothing. At the end of this period, and probably under the influence of immigrants to Egypt, it became customary to insert into the marriage contracts the stipulation: "Her earnings belong to the groom, and he is obliged to clothe her." This return to statutary law was explicitly noted in contrast with the practice prevailing in the country before.[88]

Notice that the standing formula in Talmudic times was "her *food* against the work of her hands," whereas throughout the Geniza documents it is the *clothing* that was to be provided by the wife if she wished to retain her earnings. This change may have been brought about by the different socioeconomic ambiance. In Islamic times the Jewish woman was more confined to her home, where she occupied herself with needlework and dyeing textiles, as well as with exchanging items of her outfit for other materials needed for her wardrobe. Providing clothing for herself, both by home production and exchange, was therefore in comparatively easy reach. The Jewish woman of Late Antiquity was able to sustain herself and provide her own nourishment since she had wider options for making a livelihood. I have not found, however, a corresponding stipulation in Islamic marriage documents, while one Geniza document makes the earning woman responsible not only for her clothing, but also for the rent of the premises and the supply of drinking water.[89]

I am still hesitant to draw final conclusions from the changes in the attitude toward working wives apparent in the Geniza documents from the tenth through the sixteenth centuries. Work entailed the wife's contact with other people, undignified exposure, and this is what was frowned upon by the Jewish husband, as we know him from the Talmud, a tendency probably intensified by the Muslim environment. He was prepared to let his wife die of hunger rather than to permit her to work.[90] Thus it is reasonable to assume that only dire necessity compelled husbands of the lower classes to grant such permission or even to demand from their wives to work outside the house, as is revealed by the Geniza documents of the twelfth century. When this tendency becomes widespread from the middle of the thirteenth century on, one seems to be justified in assuming that this change reflects the increasing impoverishment and misery of the population in general and of a minority group in particular. To be sure, one must also take into consideration that once a formula has crept into legal documents, it has a tendency to perpetuate itself. On the other hand, the permit granted to brides with large trousseaux to keep their earnings is not as preposterous as it appears at first sight. Such excellent nineteenth-century observers as E.W. Lane and Freiherr von Maltzan report from Cairo and Jedda (the seaport of Mecca), respectively, that even the richest Muslim women did not refrain from selling the products of their artistic needlework and even received orders.[91]

One matter, though, appears, to be self-evident: a wife's earnings by work could have been of substantial, even vital, value only in families with small income, for a woman's wages were minimal; in the higher classes the wife's economic power stemmed from her property. A wife's possessions consisted of her dowry, or, rather, all that she brought into marriage, her husband's wedding gift, which became her personal property, and gifts and inheritances that she received during her married life. The legal rights on each of these items are defined by law and are partly stated in the documents written at an engagement, betrothal, or wedding. But the very much variegated realities connected with them are more clearly apparent in court proceedings recorded when the wife's possessions became the object of litigation. I prefer, therefore, to relegate this topic to the subsection "Husband and Wife" (C, 1, below).

From the family papers of persons known otherwise.—The economic foundations of marriage and their social implications have been studied thus far in a general way. In the following, some individual cases of persons indentifiable from sources other than their family papers are considered.

Naturally, we know most about personalities from the higher echelons of the society. The Karaite Japheth b. Abraham b. Sahl, who married around 1030 the daughter of a *Nāsī*, a member of the Jewish nobility which traced its origin back to King David, is none other than Ḥasan, the son of Abū Sa'd al-Tustarī. After the assassination of his powerful father in November 1047, Japheth-Ḥasan embraced Islam and became a vizier of the Fatimid empire.

The Geniza document reports that Japheth honored his bride with a wedding gift of 100 dinars and promised a deferred installment of 200, making a total of 300 dinars. In the highly poetical introduction to the betrothal document (in Hebrew, of course, since the parties were Karaites) not only the father, but also the two uncles of the groom (known from other Geniza documents) are highly eulogized, which implied that the two families united by the new bond were of equal status. The grandfather of Japheth-Ḥasan, Sahl b. Israel b. Jacob, had emigrated—also accompanied by two brothers—from southern Iran to Egypt. The proem of our document alludes to this origin, and has God say to the emigrant: "Do not be afraid of going down to Egypt, for there I shall make you a great people" (Genesis 46:3, said to the Patriarch Jacob). The bride bore the name of Amat al-ʿAzīz, "Maidservant of the Almighty," not found elsewhere in the Geniza. An aristocratic girl had to be different.[92]

At approximately the same time, Ḥusn ("Beauty," a common name) b. Ḥayyīm II, the granddaughter of another Karaite of Persian origin, the often mentioned and highly esteemed banker Sahlawayh b. Ḥayyīm I, received a marriage gift of 100 + 200 = 300 dinars. The documents referring to the matches of the son and the daughter of Sahlawayh do not contain the relevant details.[93]

In 1080 the daughter of a government "treasurer" (*gizbār* in Heb., *jahbadh* in Ar., both derived from the Persian) was married, probably in Tyre, to a man from Damascus with exactly the same marriage gift.[94] These sums appear a fourth time two years later in the ketubba of the nāsī and temporary head of the Egyptian Jews, David b. Daniel b. Azarya, when he married a Karaite girl Geveret ʿAlāmōt ("Queen of the Girls," a Heb. rendering of Ar. *Sitt al-Banāt*) who brought in a dowry of almost 900 dinars. Knowing the straitened circumstances in which the far more prominent father of David had often found himself, I suspect that the marriage gift was actually provided by the Karaite father-in-law, to enable the groom to keep up appearances and to present the 300 dinars expected from a member of his class.[95]

When, in 1033, Dā'ūd b. Abu 'l-Faraj ʿImrān b. Levi ha-Kohen, who is none other than the Karaite notable David b. Amram, married Naẓar ("Control, Competence"), the daughter of another Karaite, he gave 200 dinars as wedding gift and promised 300 as the late installment. The social position of this David b. Amram may be gauged from a Hebrew letter addressed to him, where the writer (well known from other epistles of his) says he had come to Egypt to seek help from Ḥesed, that is, Abū Naṣr Tustarī, who was murdered shortly after the assassination of his illustrious brother Abū Sa'd (see above), and that after those catastrophes only David and his brother Mevōrākh remained in a position to render assistance to the writer. A letter from Ramle, Palestine, written by the brother of the Gaon Daniel b. Azarya, shows that David played an influential role in the communal rivalries that led to Daniel's election.[96]

A total marriage gift of 500 dinars crops up again about a hundred and twenty years later in a taqwīm describing the richest trousseau found thus far in the Geniza. The bride could have been the daughter, or daughter-in-law, of the Nagid Samuel b. Hananya, since the writer of the document was the judge Nathan b. Samuel, the Nagid's confidant. The same sum was offered at approximately the same time, by Khalaf b. Bundār, an Adenese merchant and notable, who wished to have the only daughter of the Maghrebi India trader Abraham b. Yijū for his son.[97] The amount is found a fourth time, this time in a Muslim document in 1334, when a noble amir, enumerating his ancestors up to the mythical progenitor of the Arab race, married an amira in Aswan, Egypt, and presented her with 100 dinars at the wedding, agreeing to pay her another 400 dinars in ten yearly installments.[98]

A similar correspondence between the amounts of Muslim and Jewish marriage gifts is to be observed with regard to the middle class, of which we know mostly the scholars who served as communal leaders or merchants who left much of their correspondence in the Geniza. Scholars in comfortable circumstances were those who also were active in business or banking. We have the ketubba from January 1050 of Abraham, the son of Isaac, the scholar, so often mentioned in this book. The marriage gift amounted to 80 dinars, of which he presented 30 at the wedding. The value of the dowry was approximately 640 dinars—which would seem to be out of proportion to the marriage gift. But his father-in-law was not mistaken in his choice. Abraham became overseer of the "House of Exchange" and judge of the community, and we still find him in this double capacity in the fifth decade of his married life.[99]

A few years earlier, in September 1037, Sahlān b. Abraham, a very prominent communal leader, head of the Babylonian congregation of Fustat, a scholar and liturgical poet, married the granddaughter of the Jewish judge of Sijilmāsa, Morocco. Her father obviously had emigrated to Fustat and acquired there, perhaps through marriage, an old house (or one-half of it) about which a document dated 959 exists. The girl received an outfit worth 240 dinars and one-half of that old house, which was included in the dowry. Sahlān presented 25 dinars as wedding gift and something between 40 and 50 as delayed installment.[100] Similar marriage gifts (20 + 50 = 70 dinars) were received by the elder daughter of the judge Ephraim b. Meshullam (*Med. Soc.*, II, 513, sec. 20), and given by the scholarly nephew (who later became a judge) of the India trader Abraham Yijū, when he married the latter's daughter.[101] All this tallies with statements in a book of Muslim legal opinions from Qayrawān to the effect that the marriage gift of well-to-do *'ulamā'* (Muslim religious scholars) oscillated between 50, 100, and 120 dinars.[102]

Merchants whose lucrative activities were not impeded by scholarship or exertion for the common weal did better. An *'aṭṭar*, or "perfumer," marrying an orphan girl from an old family of India traders produced 40 + 100 = 140 dinars as marriage gift and received 640 as dowry (November 1146). Shortly afterward, two other men undistinguished by public office or learning offered 50 + 100 = 150 dinars and obtained even higher dowries. When the prominent representative of the merchants in Fustat, Jekuthiel b. Moses, settled, after protracted litigation, with his divorcée for 75 dinars we can be sure that the deferred marriage gift promised by him had been at least 100 dinars, if not much more.[103]

The marked differences found between groups within the upper and middle classes and illustrated by individual cases are also to be found in the lower strata of the society. In *Med. Soc.*, II, 219–224, it has been pointed out that the cantors (comparable with the Christian lower clergy, or the Islamic *imāms*, or leaders of the congregation in prayer) formed a large and heterogeneous group of religious and communal officials. This is evident also in the family papers of persons of this profession. David b. Shekhanya (the father of Japheth, one of the most prolific scribes known from the Geniza) notes, in 1013 in a renewal of his lost marriage contract, a gift of 15 + 20 = 35 dinars and a dowry of over 100. But in addition to being a cantor, he served as court clerk and supervisor of two slaughterhouses, that is, he had a steady and assured income. We have the ketubba of the second marriage of a cantor in similar circumstances (in addition to his main job he served as clerk and a kind of treasurer to the community). In it he provided only the minimum wedding gift of 5 dinars, added 25 as late installment, and had to content himself with a dowry worth 55 dinars; but the bride Khibā', "Hidden Treasure," a virgin, promised to bring up the widower's daughter. Khibā's father was a beadle known from many Geniza documents and head of a large family.

The two cantors whose daughters were expected to contribute to the family income with their earnings, as described above, probably were poor members of this profession.[104]

Some general conclusions.—The foundation of a nuclear family had formidable economic implications not common in our society. The husband's responsibilities and how he was able to meet them have been discussed above. A word must be added here on the wife's dowry. A cursory reading of the Appendix brings home the fact that in many cases the amounts represented by the bride's outfit could not have been raised by the efforts of the father alone. The husband's contributions and undertakings show what a man was able to save by his work. But the dowry was usually many times a multiple of the husband's wedding present and often also of his total marriage gift. This was possible because the jewelry, clothing, bedding, and copper brought in by the bride were largely heirlooms passed down through generations. For this reason, many trousseau lists contain specific items characterized as "new"; the majority obviously were not.[105] Most of the ketubbas in which the item is extant stipulate that one-half of the outfit reverts to the wife's family if she dies without offspring. Originally, being "the custom of the sons of the Land of Israel" (see *Med. Soc.*, II, 6), this stipulation was accepted everywhere, although the law that ultimately prevailed in all Jewish communities was Babylonian-Iraqian, not Palestinian. The Karaites went a step further and ruled that the entire outfit of the wife returns to her family if she died childless. A stipulation to this effect is to be found in all relevant Karaite documents from the Geniza seen by me. All this taken together and combined with the material presented in this subsection and the reports about the actual returning of dowries to widows and divorcées (see C, 3, below), leads to a number of conclusions:

1. The contribution of the extended family: Looking with reverence upon the preceding generations was not merely an act of piety; it had practical implications. The dead took care of the living. A similar observation was evoked by the role of the pious foundations providing the community with means for charity (see *Med. Soc.*, II, 121–122). The impact of past generations on the material well being of their own posterity was even greater.

2. The parents' burden: Yet the demands on the fathers of daughters were very heavy, especially if more than one had to be

provided for—a circumstance for which the Geniza contains numerous examples. The birth of several daughters was an economic disaster, which explains why their arrival often was greeted with mixed feelings. More about this in C, 2, and D, below.

3. Stability of prices and durability of materials: It is astounding that the bridegroom could take upon himself responsibility for returning the full value of the dowry after the termination of the marriage, which normally would occur decades later. In the few passages of the Talmud dealing with the *nedunyā* it is assumed that the prices of the individual items could change during the short period between the engagement and their actual purchase.[106] The monetary chaos of late antiquity is not unknown. By contrast, prices in the Geniza period tended to be remarkably stable. Although settlements leading to a reduction of the husband's obligations are fairly common, the courts acted on the supposition that he was obliged to pay the sums stated in the marriage contract.[107] Reductions were granted for a variety of reasons, but never, as far as I can see, because of a change in the value of the currency.

The fact that demands were made for restitution of the outfit in kind, including items not only of gold or silver, but of copper and textiles as well, and the common occurrence that mothers left such items to their daughters point to the durability of the materials concerned.[108]

4. Hoarding precious metals and textiles: Large quantities of precious metals were thus taken out of circulation and hoarded in the form of jewelry representing savings made for the protection of the so-called weaker sex. Since textiles served widely as types of payment, this consideration to a certain degree also applied to them.

In addition, items of the outfit often served as collateral for debts incurred by the husband, or were used by him for commercial undertakings, and as such contributed to "the movement of the markets." As far as the testimony of the Geniza goes, this occurred mostly in low-income families.[109]

5. The bridal outfit a stimulus to arts and techniques: It has been emphasized above that during the classical Geniza period (tenth through thirteenth centuries) the dowry was always delivered in kind, never in cash. I have no reason to assume that the Muslim and Christian compatriots and contemporaries of the Geniza people acted differently, although I am not yet in a position to

prove this, since their marriage contracts refer to the husband's obligations, not to the contributions of the bride's parents. This social habit must have had a tremendous influence on the development of gold-silver-and coppersmithing, as well as on the textile industry in all its aspects, including dyeing (the production of durable colors requiring much technical skill). Attractive and durable goods had to be produced in large quantities. No wonder that Islamic civilization excelled in the small arts, and that many Jewish craftsmen worked in those industries.

6. The wife's possessions and her work, indicators of socio-economic conditions and changes: The relative values of the different sections and even items of the trousseaux varied widely according to the social class to which a couple belonged. A study of these differences is apt to reveal much about the daily life of the various classes of the population.

The fact that the economic importance of a wife's earnings increased steadily from the twelfth century on seems to point to the mounting impoverishment of the Jewish community or the population in general, perhaps also to a slight change in the attitude toward women.

7. No excessive disparity in age between husband and wife: The groom, as a rule, must have been somewhat older than the bride since he was expected to earn the wherewithal for the wedding present. Since this gift was comparatively modest, the age gap normally could hardly have been very great.

8. Money not the sole, or even main, consideration for making a match: A study of the economic foundations of marriage is of necessity concerned with its material aspects. But the very testimony of these aspects—in particular, the often observed disparity between the low value of a marriage gift and the high value of the corresponding dowry and the comparatively limited contribution of the husband in general—seems to prove that considerations other than money must often have been operative, and even decisive, in bringing about a marriage. Were eligible husbands in short supply? Were widows and divorcées, even with money, not desirable? These and similar questions occupy us in the subsequent sections.

9. The economics of marriage reveal a rather rigid stratification of society: The clerks and elders who assisted at fixing the amounts to be contributed by the groom and by the bride's family must have

possessed well-established yardsticks with which to measure the economic capacities of both, for we find a good deal of conformity within each social group. The round sums set for the marriage gift in most cases, and for the dowry in many, point in that direction. Seven steps on the economic ladder stand out: the entirely destitute, and two groups each within the lower, middle, and upper classes. The imponderables referred to in the preceding paragraph softened the boundaries between the categories.

10. Muslim and Christian parallels: Islamic and Judaic marriage laws and legal forms differed considerably. The Jewish representative delegated by the bride to receive the minimal obligatory marriage gift, whose appointment is not mandatory, is essentially different from the Muslim male guardian of the female, without whom no marriage can be contracted. Also, the "debt," or ketubba, payable by a Jewish husband at the termination of the marriage should not be equated with the Muslim deferred *mahr*, payable at a stipulated time after the wedding according to evidence in Muslim marriage contracts contemporary with the Geniza documents. Finally, it is highly significant that a trousseau list or its total value (sometimes also subtotals of its sections) is included in the Jewish but not in the Muslim marriage contracts. This inclusion emphasizes the property rights of the wife to whom the dowry reverts at the termination of the marriage.

A minority speaking the language of the surrounding majority is naturally likely to adapt its legal nomenclature and procedures to theirs, as has been observed. There remains the question of how accurately the Geniza material is able to illustrate social conditions prevailing in the population at large. Instructive parallels have been noted: a customary local dowry valued at 150 dinars, the maximum amount of 500 dinars for both Jewish and Muslim dowries found thus far, and the similarity in the amounts of the marriage gifts presented by the divines of both religions. To them should be added the marriage gift of a Coptic deacon to the daughter of a Coptic priest in Aswan amounting to 15 + 75 = 90 dinars. These parallels are noted here simply as prelude. More such comparative material is presented in the examination of the social aspects of married life.[110]

5. *Social Safeguards*

Two examples of "conditions".—The social safeguards, like the details about marriage gift and dowry, were usually included in the ketubba. Separate agreements exist on the "conditions" under which a match was arranged: documents written at an engagement or a betrothal and sometimes even earlier. Before going into detail, two examples of the "conditions" are rendered here.

A calligraphic draft with additions in another script

In [Your] na[me], oh All-mer[ciful]. These conditions were agreed between us, namely:

Immediate marriage gift: 40 dinars, to be a gift [i.e., the wife's personal property] as from the wedding; the delayed gift: 60 dinars.

Complete and absolute trustworthiness [of the wife].

No other wife; no concubine; no slave girl may be purchased except if she chooses so.

If she dislikes living with his father and mother, he has the decision about the domicile in a place which she will select.

We [the bride's side] do not impose other conditons on them [the groom's party].

Marriage on Purim, if God wills.[1]

These are all the conditions which will be entered into the marriage contract. Any new conditions are invalid, and we have no right to make them [additions in another script made by another scribe:] nor may they impose any other condition on us. As to the outfit: if there will be no child and, God beware, death occurs, *one half of the dowry* will go *to the house of her brother* [or: father, corrected: *mother*, with an unfinished reference to the mother, written between the lines].

His father stands security for him. *And Peace.*

If she dislikes living with his mother, the decision is in his hands.[2]

The absence of date and names and the presence of the words "And Peace" close to the end prove that, despite the meticulous script, this is not a formal document, but a draft, or, rather an instruction, given to a clerk by the judge, or other official, who presided over the proceedings, leaving it to him to write out the final agreement. The seemingly repetitious addition at the end concerning the domicile was necessary in order to make it clear that the husband had the last word in this matter. That here only the mother-in-law is mentioned as the one with whom the young wife might wish to part company should not be understood as a correction to what had been said previously; normally her main contacts were with her mother-in-law. The usual condition that one half of the dowry returns to the father's house in case the wife dies childless is expressed with a Hebrew phrase, which was, however, changed in a rather garbled way. The double reference to the bride's mother suggests that the father was dead, that the mother had provided the outfit, at least in part, and probably retained certain rights on it. The incomplete state of the passage gives the impression that further clarifications were expected on this point. The additional stipulation that the father of the groom takes upon himself the responsibility for his son's future actions is by no means commonplace. One sees that "the well known conditions" found in most contemporary marriage agreements were complemented by special stipulations according to the circumstances and wishes of the contracting parties. Such a particular situation is even more apparent in the following example, which, because of its repetitious wording and fragmentary state is presented in summary.

A betrothal agreement

1. Should separation occur, the document freeing Sitt al-Dalāl ("Lady Bold") will be produced by her husband without delay.[3]

2. She is trustworthy in her statements concerning everything and no oath of any kind may be imposed on her.

3. He will not marry another wife [nor keep a slave girl disliked by her].[4]

4. He will not beat her.

5. He will not leave Fustat and travel anywhere [except with her consent].[5]

6. Before setting out on a journey he will write her a conditional bill of divorce,[6] and deposit the delayed installment of her marriage gift as well as the sums needed for her maintenance during his absence.

7. The young couple will live in her parents' house. The husband owes a yearly rent of 6 dinars and will never be late in paying it.

8. He will not separate her from her parents, as long as the latter are alive and cannot force her to live anywhere else.

9. A fine of 50 dinars is imposed on him in case he fails to fulfill any(?) of the preceding conditions.[7]

The wife's trustworthiness.—In the two agreements translated, and in countless other marriage contracts, the foremost condition imposed on the husband was to trust his wife, in legal terms: her word was "like that of two witnesses," that is, it was final, it required neither a proof, nor an oath. In our analysis of the ketubba (subsection B, 3, above) we traced this stipulation back to remote antiquity, when the peasant was out in his fields all day long while his wife supervised the management of the farm. By Geniza times, the wife was involved but little in her husband's craft or business, but there were other weighty considerations that made this condition of trustworthiness essential. Because of the strong attachment of the wife to her paternal family she could be suspect of pilfering from her husband's house for the benefit of her own kin. In Muslim folktales from Yemen noted by me this appeared to be a constant cause of marital discord, and examples from the Geniza are not lacking.[8] Second, the husband was responsible for his wife's outfit. But since this consisted mostly in jewelry, female clothing, and kitchenware, it was she who had constant control of these valuables: items could easily disappear through sale or otherwise, while the husband stood security for the dowry's full worth. Third, if not otherwise stipulated, the wife's earnings by work went into the common pool, which meant, for all practical purposes, that they belonged to her husband. Since these earnings were mostly derived from needlework, spinning, or weaving, or from serving as a sales woman to other women, it was difficult for her husband to know her actual takes, and suspicion might raise its ugly head. Finally, at the termination of the marriage, when considerable payments were due the wife, counterclaims, such as that she had received loans, partial payments of the late marriage gift, or partial or full disposition of her dowry, could be made. The stipulation, summarized under the Hebrew term "trustworthiness," aimed at the protection of the married woman from such and similar allegations and, thus, at the preservation of marital peace.

This stipulation was formulated in different ways, and, consequently, had different scopes: "She is trustworthy in her statements, in the management of the house, with regard to her outfit and all other implements used by her in every respect and against any claimant, [in particular] her husband and all his heirs after his death; she has the status of two trustworthy witnesses whose testimony is accepted in court; no oath may be imposed on her under any circumstances, not even a ban in general terms." Although the document from which this passage is taken was merely a betrothal agreement, the stipulation was provided in full, because the bride was a girl from Fustat married to a husband in a provincial town and, consequently, in particular need of protection.[9] The same full text of the stipulation was provided by the same clerk, Ḥalfōn b. Manasse, in the case of a poor orphan girl.[10] That this stipulation was not a mere technicality, thoughtlessly copied from a formulary, may be gauged from a third betrothal agreement written by Ḥalfōn, worded exactly in the same way, with the exception that it says: "[Trustworthy etc.], but *not* with regard to her outfit." Unfortunately, only the end of this Geniza fragment is preserved so that we do not know the circumstances explaining the exception made.[11]

The many instances in which the item "trustworthiness" does not appear in a marriage agreement should not be regarded as careless omissions. When a mother of children sends a letter in Arabic characters (the scribe was a man) with an addition in Hebrew letters: "I am trustworthy in this matter, having the status of two witnesses whose testimony is admitted in court," it is evident that that status was by no means taken for granted.[12] Similarly, when a woman, after marital strife, asks in a petition to the head of the Jewish community that, as first point in the forthcoming settlement, "trustworthiness" should be conceded to her, clearly her ketubba had not contained that privilege. By chance, the communal record of her marriage has been preserved; it details her marriage gift and dowry, but says nothing about trustworthiness.[13] Finally, the many deathbed declarations in which a husband grants, or reconfirms, the status of incontestable trustworthiness to his wife prove how precarious this privilege was.[14]

A short comment is required concerning another formulation of the item "trustworthiness" found in a number of marriage agreements. It runs like this: "She is to be held trustworthy by her husband during his lifetime and his heirs after his death with regard to all food and drink prepared in the house and any claim founded on surmise [and not on proof]. No oath might be imposed on her etc." When I read this first in the engagement contract of the daughter of a well-to-do India trader, which granted her special privileges, among them exclusive rights to the immobile property she owned, I surmised that the formulation was intended to further strengthen her position. In reality this different version is a matter of legal definition based on the socioeconomic realities of late antiquity. The item "claim founded on surmise [and not on proof]", Heb. *ṭaʿanat shemmā*, is based on Mishna Ketubbot 9:4: "He who has his wife keep a store or appoints her as manager of his affairs may impose on her an oath at any time [even without having a proof against her]," and Shevuʿot 7:8: "These must give an oath, although no claim based on a proof is made against them: partners, sharecroppers, managers, and wives doing business for their husbands." The wife as shopkeeper is a figure familiar from the East European Jewish *shtetl*, as it was in Talmudic times, but does not fit into the Islamic society of the Geniza period. Since this right of the husband was enshrined in the law books, however, some judges regarded it as necessary to protect the wife against it.[15]

The condition of the wife's trustworthiness, so prominent in the Geniza marriage agreements, is not paralleled in the relevant documents of the Islamic environment. A stipulation that a wife is to be believed when she claims that her husband has maltreated her is found in Cordova, Spain, around 900.[16] Islamic custom could dispense with the general clause of trustworthiness because the

Muslim husband did not carry that heavy load of responsibility for the repayment of the wife's dowry as his Jewish counterpart and, in general, because the division between the properties of the spouses was more pronounced in Islam than in Jewish law. The situation was different with regard to the next common stipulation in the Geniza marriage agreements—that referring to the wife's possible rivals.

No second wife, no maidservant without the wife's approval, no concubine.—Ancient Jewish, like Islamic, law permitted polygyny. Unlike Islam, Judaism, as practiced in the Geniza period, strictly prohibited sexual relations between a master and a slave girl owned by him, which, of course, was also the law of the Church. Since the social customs of a surrounding majority are apt to be accepted by a minority, the prohibition of marrying another wife, included in a Geniza marriage contract, was regularly accompanied by the provision that the husband should not keep a maidservant disliked by his wife or should not acquire any without her approval. There even exist marriage agreements that contain the clause concerning the slave girl but not that against polygyny, which seems to demonstrate that the latter was less a threat to a wife than the former.[17]

An examination of the oldest testimony for the polygyny–slave girl clause known thus far confirms this impression. After four specific conditions, including one that I have not yet found elsewhere ("If she makes something, it belongs to her"), the text continues: "[He undertakes] not to buy any maidservant except with his wife's consent, and whenever she will demand to have her removed from the house [i.e., to sell her], he will do so; also, not to take another wife, and if he does, he will pay her the delayed installment [of the marriage gift] in its totality and write her a document that will set her free from him, although she [and not he] demands the separation." No wonder that the clause regarding the slave girl came first. She was an investment, the wife is a liability. A slave, if displeasing to her master, could be sold and yield money; a divorce entailed great financial obligations. Therefore, matrimonial peace had to be protected against concubinage with slaves not less, and perhaps even more, than against polygyny.[18]

M. A. Friedman, who has contributed a number of papers to the problems of polygyny and the slave girl syndrome in the Geniza, makes the important observation that the clause referring to both does not make its appearance until the beginning of the twelfth century.[19] This observation is not undermined by his later discovery of a case in which a man from Ramle, Palestine, promises in the year 1078/9, under penalty of a fine "to the poor," not to take a second wife.[20] For there is a great difference between such a stray item and a fixed legal form appearing in numerous documents and referred to as "the well-known conditions." Friedman also draws attention to the story of the Sicilian Jew who was married in Damascus but was obliged to have a wife in the Egyptian capital if he wished to enter government service (as related in *Med. Soc.*, I, 68). The rabbinical court of Fustat informed the applicant that, *according to local custom*, he could not take a second wife without the consent of the first or his repudiation of her.[21] The early existence of this custom is attested by another document written during the years 989–1089.[22] Complaints or reports about polygyny are almost completely absent from the documents of the Geniza of the eleventh century, although the majority of the material, at least the letters, originated at that time. A petition by a woman whose husband had taken a second wife, "whose tears never dried," and who asked for "a strong document" safeguarding her rights, was written early in the twelfth century.[23] Thus that local custom probably had been in force for many years. Special circumstances must have caused its formulation into a stereotyped condition to be inserted in a marriage agreement.

I assume that the change came about at the time and probably on the initiative of the Nagid Mevōrākh b. Saadya (ca. 1095–1112), whose vigorous communal and religious leadership replaced that of the Jerusalem yeshiva (see *Med. Soc.*, II, 30). The oldest formulation of the slave girl–polygyny clause translated above was written when he was in office. It was executed calligraphically and on a separate sheet, no doubt in order to be submitted to the Nagid for approval.[24] Its insertion into a marriage agreement could be only a recommendation, not legally binding, and it is characteristic of the history of legal usage that the final, or, at least, the most common form of the clause—with polygyny mentioned first—appears only under the authority of Mevōrākh's son, the Nagid Moses.[25]

What did the monogyny clause give to the wife? First, the husband had to pay her (or to deposit in court) her delayed marriage gift. This was, of course, a most effective deterrent, inasmuch as the sum stipulated could be saved by most husbands only in the course of many years. Second, the wife had the right to compel her husband to grant her repudiation, although he did not wish to do so. Third, fines usually in amounts out of the reach of most husbands were stipulated. It seems, however, that this applied only in the case of mixed marriages between Rabbanites and Karaites.[26] As Friedman has rightly emphasized, the acceptance of the late marriage gift by the wife did not necessarily imply that she demanded a divorce. The choice was hers. This is the plain meaning of the regular monogyny clause, and some documents say explicitly: "He will pay her the delayed marriage gift in full. If she willingly consents to remain married to him together with that other wife, she may do so. If not, he is obligated to write for her the bill of release by which she will be set free."[27] But would any wife agree, out of her free will, to share her husband with another woman? To the many observations made with regard to this aspect of polygyny I should like to add one of my own. While studying the society of a Yemenite weavers' village, which, in 1950, was transferred almost intact from Yemen to the hills of Judea, I was astounded to find two women, widows of one man, living together for no other reason than that they were good friends. The first wife had been barren, the second was the mother of several children. The latter described their married life to me thus: "We two women were like two doves. The man was one week with her and the next with me. I did embroidery, and she the household work. I produced the children, and she reared them." When the woman felt that I may have misunderstood or misheard her, she added: "Very simple, she loves children and I love to do needlework."[28]

In general, however, the right of the husband to take additional wives was a curse, and it is therefore no surprise that even in the ancient Near East fathers made provisions protecting their daughters from this calamity (Genesis 31:50).[29] Islamic law and custom found various ways to empower the first wife to rule over the second or to obtain a divorce either for the second wife or for herself (the husband transferring his right of repudiation to his first wife).[30] A few actual marriage contracts from the ninth century bearing these conditions have been preserved on Egyptian papyri, while collections of responsa by Muslim jurisconsults in Cordova, Spain, refer to that clause at approximately the same time.[31] It stands to reason that the countries between Spain and Egypt followed a similar course; the clause in question is indeed known as the Qayrawānese condition (named so after Qayrawān, then the capital of the country known today as Tunisia). It must be conceded, however, that none of the published Egyptian marriage contracts contemporary with the Geniza documents bearing the polygyny–slave girl clause contains a similar stipulation. The very fact that this clause was called "the well-known conditions of the daughters of Israel" and the existence of a local statute prohibiting anyone from taking a second wife without the consent of the first seem to indicate that polygyny was more generally condemned in the Jewish community than in its environment. Our report on marital life in the light of the Geniza documents (C, 1, below) shows that it was a minor social evil. Conditions in marriage contracts concerning life with two wives are also described there.

The spouses' residence and relations with their mutual families.—Where a married couple lived, and with whom, are aspects of married life that loom large both in the documents made out before or at the marriage and in the reports about what was happening later. The socioeconomic realities and the provisions made by contracts or the courts as reflected in the Geniza papers bear much similarity to those known from Islamic sources.

Normally the bride "goes out [of her father's house] to [that of] her husband."[32] A bridegroom in Tripoli, Libya, whose father had been forced to sell his house in a time of famine, writes mournfully to a benefactor in Fustat: "Your servant married the daughter of his paternal uncle in the house of *her* father."[33] Since this was the accepted practice, there was no need to stipulate explicitly that the bride moves to the house of the husband's family. Where we do find such conditions, the reference is to joint living quarters "in the company of" one or two of the husband's parents or other relatives. The wife's agreement could be made unconditionally, or she would even expressly promise never to demand separation from the husband's parents. That situation is foreseen when a groom imposes on his bride "never to separate him from his mother."[34] More common was a rider to the contrary, namely, that the arrangement was valid only so long as it was not harmful to the young wife, or, more precisely defined: the husband had to move out of his parents' house if she wished so, or to divorce her if he refused her demand.[35]

The situation with regard to domiciles provided by the wife's parents was more complicated. In many instances the wife brought in one or several houses (more frequently: shares in houses) either as part of her outfit or as her personal property, the income from which was hers to the exclusion of her husband. In the numerous relevant documents it is usually not stated whether the newly married couple chose to live in those places or not. Sometimes it is stated that they occupied a floor other than that inhabited by the wife's parents.[36] Staying in her father's house for a year or two after the wedding was stipulated when the bride and her husband planned to move to another city or, perhaps, when she was young and needed time to overcome the trauma of getting married. In one such marriage contract, written in Tyre, Lebanon, the father had given his daughter a house in Acre, to be occupied by the young couple. But the father retained the right to live in that house, too, temporarily or permanently, either alone, or with his wife and children, if he happened to return to Acre, where he had been domiciled before.[37] Similarly, in a Muslim marriage agreement the father stipulated that the couple stay in his house until his daughter got accustomed to her husband.[38]

Mostly, however, one has the impression that the condition obligating the newly married couple to live with the wife's parents was made for the benefit of the parents, probably because they had no one else to look after them. This is never said so expressly. The documents simply say: "Living quarters with her parents."[39] But when we read as the very first condition in a rather detailed marriage agreement, "she will never cease to live with her mother and never part from her; even if the girl, God forbid, should desire this, she will not be supported in this demand," it is obvious in whose favor this stipulation was made.[40] Also, when a girl brings into the marriage half a house on condition that her mother lives with her, we may assume that the widow had no other accommodation.[41] In many cases, however, the young couple stayed in the house of the wife's parents simply because the husband, as the bridegroom in Tripoli quoted above, had no house of his own.[42] Then the question arose whether he had to pay rent, as he would have done if he had lived elsewhere. It must have been a widely accepted Muslim custom that a son-in-law living with the parents of his wife did not pay rent.[43] This explains why the second example of a social-conditions agreement summarized above emphasized so strongly that the husband who had to pay his in-laws a rent of 6 dinars a year, that is, half a dinar per month, was expected to pay punctually, without any delay or argument.[44] Two marriage documents, one Karaite and one Rabbanite, two centuries apart, contain the stipulation that the husband living in a house belonging to his wife was not bound to pay her rent. The second document adds, however, that if the husband preferred to live elsewhere, he had no rights whatsoever on the house and the wife might make use of the rent as she saw fit.[45]

The condition most frequently imposed on a husband concerning his residence was the prohibition to settle with his wife anywhere except in the town agreed upon. Her family desired to be near the couple in order to be able to watch over its doings and, if necessary, to interfere. "She will live in Miṣr [Fustat] to the exclusion of Cairo"—thus we read in the engagement contract of a well-to-do bride. Only two and a half miles or less separated the twin cities, but they were so different in character that they could be regarded as remote despite the geographical proximity.[46] Other documents prohibit (or give the right) to move *from* Cairo.[47] When a bride followed her husband to a provincial town, or vice versa, her or his obligation to do so had to be stated explicitly in the engagement or betrothal document.[48]

Since the choice of the domicile was one of the main causes of marital friction, it became customary from the end of the twelfth century onward to insert a clause in the marriage document stating whether he or she had the right to choose. This stipulation was formulated in different ways. "He will settle her in a place which she will select" seems to mean that the wife selects the apartment, but he has the final word.[49] Such wording obfuscated the matter, as is proved by our first example of social-safeguards documents, where the future husband's prerogative had to be reiterated at the end.[50] The opposite formulation, where the wife's consent is required, also lacks precision.[51] Finally, a common form of this clause became the blunt statement: "The choice of the domicile is in the hand of the groom" (or "the bride"), sometimes fortified by the addition "wherever he likes." Even when the bride follows the groom to his hometown, she might be given the prerogative of the choice of the domicile.[52] Muslim marriage customs also foresaw stipulations granting or denying the husband the right to move to another city, or authorizing the wife to demand that she should not share living quarters with her husband's parents.[53]

The question of the couple's residence was largely one of the relationship between the two families to which each partner belonged. Mostly, tensions and discord between the families became apparent only during married life and, therefore, were rarely referred to in the marriage agreements. A Muslim marriage contract from the year 878 stipulates "he will not prevent her from visiting her family, nor her family from visiting her"—obviously a stereotyped clause, only exceptionally echoed in Geniza marriage documents. A native of Alexandria, who followed his wife to the capital, got her consent to visit his family in the Mediterranean port together with him once a year. Both parties were divorcées. The agreement was necessary. Clearly such agreements were occasioned by special circumstances since we find others where the wife was exempted from the obligation to visit the husband's family.

Understandings reached after marital strife tell more about these matters.[54]

Restriction of the freedom of movement of wife and husband.—The right of the wife to see her relatives was part of a larger complex: the question of how far she was free to leave the house and to go wherever she liked. M. A. Friedman has made a comprehensive study of this aspect of married life in Geniza times.[55] After carefully examining the situation in pre-Islamic times, he arrives at the conclusion that both in practice and in theory, the Jewish family had to adapt itself—to be sure, only to a certain degree—to the stern rules of seclusion prevailing in the Muslim environment. Maimonides in his Code, first states, in accordance with Jewish law, that the wife has the right to leave the house and go to her father's residence, to gatherings of mourning or festivities, to be attentive to her female friends and relatives, so that they may also come and visit her; for, Maimonides adds, she is not a prisoner to be prevented from going and coming. The latter remark seems to be an allusion to a passage in Muhammad's famous "sermon of farewell," pronounced at his last pilgrimage to Mecca, where, in introducing his reforms in favor of women, he said: "Your wives are like prisoners of war; they have no free disposition over themselves."[56] The same allusion is found in a circular of Maimonides' contemporary and adversary, the Gaon Samuel b. Eli of Baghdad.[57] But after having stated the wife's rights, Maimonides adds—apparently without being authorized to do so by a Talmudic precedent—that the husband may not permit his wife to leave the house more than once or twice during a month, "for there is nothing more beautiful for a wife than sitting in the corner of her house, as it is written (Psalm 45:14): 'The most honored place for a princess is inside.' "[58]

Al-Ghazālī, the great teacher of Islamic ethics, deals with this topic repeatedly, and, specifically in his chapter on jealousy, which, according to him, is both a vice and a virtue. A wife may leave the house with permission of her husband, but staying (he says: sitting) at home "is safer." "For leaving the house merely for sightseeing and other unimportant matters is detrimental to [the husband's] *muruwwa*, 'manliness,' and may lead to immorality [on her side]."[59] Screening one's wife from the outside world was a matter of pride for her husband. Such an attitude was present in Greece and in the Jewish society known from Talmudic literature. Probably under Iranian influence it became far more pronounced in the Islamic world. When a debtor, who could not let himself be seen, writes in a Geniza letter, "I am hiding in my house like women," he refers to a commonly accepted attitude. But whether this remark reflects the actual situation in the Jewish (and Muslim!) society of the Egyptian capital during the High Middle Ages, or is merely a proverbial expression, needs further investigation.[60]

Stipulations in marriage agreements restricting the wife's freedom of movement are rare, and are to be understood as owing to special circumstances. In order to bring this point home, I translate one such engagement agreement in full:

With good luck and success!

This was agreed upon between R. Ephraim, the scholar, son of (his) h(onor), g(reatness), and h(oliness), our master and teacher Meshullam, the wise and the prudent, (of) b(lessed) m(emory), and R. Yeshūʿā ha-Levi, son of R. Ṣedāqā, al-Ramlī, with regard to his elder daughter Sitt al-Fakhr ["Glory"]: Early installment—15 dinars, being a *gift* [her personal property], plus a present worth 5 dinars, consisting in rings. No conditions to be imposed on him except her trustworthiness regarding food and drink. The late installment 50 [corrected above the line:] 60 dinars in accordance with local custom.[61] They will live with her parents, as long as he chooses so. If he moves out, he has to bear the cost of the living quarters, nothing else. He undertook to observe 'the ritual bath.' She will leave the house only with his permission."[62]

The agreement is written in the unmistakable hand of the judge Nathan ha-Kohen b. Solomon, and the groom was to become the prominent judge Ephraim b. Meshullam (see *Med. Soc.*, II, 513, secs. 17 and 20). Since the grandfather of the bride was dead in 1134, but is not referred to as such in this document, it was probably drawn up some time before that date. The father of the bride was a highly respected member of the community, renowned for his piety, learning, reliability, and expert knowledge of building operations, wherefore he was entrusted with the supervision of repairs carried out in a building belonging to a charitable foundation.[63] His byname indicates that he was a native of Palestine.[64] It explains the extremely strange fact that the observation of the laws of purity (the monthly ritual bath of the wife taken after a prolonged period of continence) was imposed on *him*, a scholar; for the Egyptian Jews were notoriously lax in these matters before Maimonides' reforms, carried out approximately half a century after the writing of our document. Ephraim took up residence in the house of his father-in-law in Fustat, perhaps because the Meshullam family house was in Cairo, where his brother, and later his nephew and grandnephew served as judges, or simply because his paternal home was already filled with other young couples. The unusual stipulation that "Glory" may not leave the house except with her husband's permission, probably was occasioned by Ephraim's desire to prove that, although he was now domiciled in the house of her family, it was now he, and not her papa, who was the boss.[65]

Unfortunately another marriage document in which the bride agrees, out of her free will and choice, to leave the house solely with her future husband's permission and approval, and even concedes him the right to lock her in whenever he wished, is so fragmentary that no guess is possible as to the circumstances that led to so extraordinary a measure. The delayed marriage gift was 20 dinars, which means that the couple belonged to the lowest stratum of the society. The document seems to state also that the wife must accompany her husband on his travels whenever he asked her to do so. Thus, anticipated frequent absences might have nourished exaggerated apprehensions with regard to the wife's faithfulness.[66]

Conditions restricting a wife's freedom, or restoring it to her after attempts of her husband to deny it, mostly make their appearance after marital squabbles or a hasty repudiation. The matter is taken up again in C, 1.

More surprising is the comparative rarity of stipulations in marriage contracts regulating the husband's travels away from his wife. For absenteeism of the husband was the most widespread cancer of marital life as known to us from the Geniza. The precautions taken in the second example of social-safeguards conditions translated above, are rarely found elsewhere and for a variety of reasons, principally perhaps because law and custom had foreseen such exigencies. A conditional divorce, setting the wife free, if the husband did not return at a fixed time, was common practice among Muslims and Jews.[67] In connection with this, in the agreement just referred to, another obligation was imposed on the husband: to deposit the late marriage gift. This, too, was exceptional, both as a condition and a praxis: the young husband normally did not possess that much money. The third condition: leaving to the wife all she needed during her husband's absence, before his departure, is also rarely found in marriage contracts; again, because of the lack of cash, other arrangements were preferred.[68] Only occasionally a condition such as "he will not travel away from her abroad except with her consent" is inserted into an engagement contract, and that without fixing a penalty in case the promise is broken.[69] References to these conditions are found in letters and court records. "My wife does not permit me to travel [from Alexandria to Cairo] except when accompanied by her and the children," writes a man to a sister.[70] Or, a woman named Khulla, "Friendship," appears in court conceding her husband the right to travel for about a month after he had presented her with three quarters of a dinar for her expenses during his absence. Her marriage contract probably had provided that he needed her officially certified agreement before setting out on a journey.[71]

Conduct of the spouses.—This topic, too, appears in marriage contracts only under very specific circumstances. When "Sitt al-Ahl ["Mistress of the Family"], the virgin bride, promises to behave with deference toward her father-in-law Samuel, the father of the groom, never to treat him with disrespect, to listen to his commands, and to accept his moral guidance," we must have a closer look at her ketubba in order to find out what might have necessitated the clause. Her own father was dead, thus she was probably accustomed to a higher degree of independence than other girls. Old Samuel was a synagogue singer, perhaps a comical figure, not averse to the bottle, as was not unusual among the members of that vocation or avocation (see *Med. Soc.*, II, 223–224). Thus, a stipulation on deference to him was not out of place. On the reverse side of her ketubba we read that, seven years after the wedding, the husband had hastily pronounced an oath to repudiate her but regretted it immediately; since oaths had to be honored, a writ of divorce was written, delivered to her, and immediately torn up, whereupon a new marriage ceremony with all its accouterments was held. All this shows that the persons with whom "Mistress of the Family" became connected were of a somewhat peculiar character.[72]

A clause not to utter a hasty oath harmful to one's wife is indeed included in a marriage contract. Other instances where thoughtless swearing led to compulsory repudiation are reported in the Geniza. I see here the influence of the Muslim environment where swearing to divorce one's wife was a common form of confirming any assertion and where even such an oath pronounced in drunkenness made repudiation obligatory.[73]

Two marriage documents, almost a century apart, one in eloquent Hebrew, the other in plain Arabic, presented here in abbreviated translations, seem to indicate that members of the jeunesse dorée of the Egyptian capital sometimes needed a warning that entrance into the marital state demanded a change in their style of life. My feeling is even that the wordy Hebrew version is nothing but a variation of an Arabic formula probably found also in Muslim and Christian contracts. In the first document the groom's family name was *(Ibn) Zaffān*, dancer, jester, buffoon. But no relationship should be sought between this name and the conditions spelled out in the groom's agreement, for the Zaffāns were a respected family of merchants and physicians, known from numerous Geniza papers of the tenth and eleventh centuries and referred to also in a Muslim source.[74]

The first document, written on November 22, 1047, runs approximately thus: "When Fā'iza ("Favorite"), my betrothed, enters my house, I shall behave myself toward her as virtuous Jewish men behave toward their virtuous wives. I shall walk the straight path and avoid everything crooked and wicked. I shall seek the company of decent people and avoid those of rotten ones, I shall not enter the houses of frivolous and licentious persons, nor of one known for ugly deeds and licentiousness, nor shall I share with them food or drink, or anything else." In case of violation of this agreement the court is empowered to punish him "with Heaven's [God's] judgment," that is, any action recommended by the circumstances, although not enacted by law.[75]

Our second choice is a full-fledged engagement contract, containing the usual stipulations concerning trustworthiness of the wife, slave girls, and polygyny, and fixing the marriage gift at 20 + 40 = 60 dinars, which puts the contracting partners into the upper lower middle class. The wedding was deferred for two full years. The first special clause states that the groom cannot make any condition or demand with regard to the outfit to be provided by the bride's father. Then the text goes on: "He also took upon himself to walk in praiseworthy ways and not to make friends with people whose company is obnoxious. Whenever any revolting behavior on his side is established, he must deliver 10 dinars to the girl [his future wife] as a personal gift." Finally, her father had the right to break off the engagement whenever he deemed fit. One wonders why the father agreed to the match at all, when he had such strong doubts about the character of his future son-in-law. The young man was perhaps a close relative and, therefore, the customary first choice.[76]

Exceptionally, a very specific provision of conduct is inserted into a marriage agreement, such as one on wife beating, or another one freeing a wife from sharing her husband's bed at a time when he breaks his promise not to take another wife or concubine (meaning, until the matter is settled in court). Normally such matters come before the courts (and to our knowledge) when they pop up in the course of married life and are, therefore, treated in subsection C, 1.[77]

Mixed marriages.—Intermarriage between Muslims, Christians, and Jews normally took place only when one of the two partners, or both, converted.[78] But the three communities contained different sects, churches, and schismatic bodies, and here mixed marriages were common and needed regulation by statute, contract, or judicial decision. During most of the classical Geniza period Egypt was ruled by a Shiʿite caliph while the majority of the population remained Sunni Muslim, and in North Africa the Shiʿites became, in the course of the eleventh century, a cruelly persecuted minority. There was another Muslim sect in North Africa at that time, the Ibāḍī branch of the Khārijites, which was small, but vigorous, and has remained so until the present day. And there were other splinter groups. Mixed marriages between orthodox Muslims and others, regarded as schismatic, occupied the divines frequently, and their rulings varied from toleration or recommendation of conversion to outright prohibition.[79] The Coptic Church demands from members of other Eastern churches, or Latin Catholics, the acceptance of the Coptic faith at marriage (and, in our days, from Protestants, even renewed baptism).[80]

In view of this situation the rich Geniza material on Rabbanite-Karaite mixed marriages gains significance. It ranges from marriage agreements devoted almost entirely to the religious observances of the two contracting partners to others where no mention is made of religion at all and where the fact of intermarriage is recognizable only by the distribution of a stipulated fine between the poor of the Karaites and Rabbanites. This topic is treated in volume IV, chapter X. No case of intermarriage with a Samaritan is known to me from the Geniza, although, in Mamluk times, the head of the Jewish community had jurisdiction also over that small schismatic group.[81]

Squabbles over marriage agreements.—Considering the many economic and social safeguards that had to be taken into consideration at the conclusion of a marriage we are not surprised that the Talmudic saying "no ketubba without squabbles" finds its confirmation in the state of numerous Geniza documents. When we find a beautifully written ketubba with the sum of the delayed marriage gift entered in another, irregular and ugly script, it is evident that the item concerned was an object of contention until the very last moment.[82] In another ketubba that entry is left blank altogether.[83] Again in others the original sum is replaced by another one written above it, sometimes without the former being crossed out.[84] Occasionally the numbers are written in such confusion that the reader is unable to decide what was finally intended.[85] Stipulations are added in another script after a previous statement that no further conditions would be imposed on either side.[86] Even to a judge's note a new item is added in a different hand.[87] A rider is put on a ketubba on the very day of its writing, or a second version is found on the same sheet.[88] When a complete ketubba bears no signature at all, and another, only one, there must have been a hitch in the procedures, for even a copy had to list the names of at least two witnesses.[89] Invited to the wedding of a relative in another town, a man replies that his wife was expecting and he himself was extremely occupied, but he would still undertake the journey if he could be sure that the bride's outfit was completely ready.[90] Occurrences where it was not ready on time are reported in our documents.[91]

Thus, occasions where the jubilance of the wedding day was dimmed or spoiled by undignified haggling over the marriage stipulations must not have been uncommon. But this did not diminish its significance. The wedding was "The day of joy" (Song of Songs 3:11), the one great day in a man's life. Whenever unmarried sons are mentioned in a Geniza letter the writer adds the wish that God may keep them alive and let their father see *afrāḥhum*, "their joy." If my memory does not fail me, I have never seen that wish with regard to a girl. There the wish was that she should "enter her house," or "come into a blessed and auspicious home."[92] "Making the bride happy" was of course a religious obligation no less than that statutory requirement with regard to the groom. The good wishes and quotations written at the head and in the margins of the marriage contracts state this emphatically. The Talmud tells quite astonishing stories about how great divines tried to fulfill this commandment, one even taking the bride on his shoulders and dancing with her.[93] In the Islamic ambiance female merrymakers had to do the job. But the difference in the good wishes for boys and girls reflects a reality. Marriage for the husband was a change: together with the acquisition of a source of possible happiness, he took upon himself "a yoke," but essentially he remained within the same male society to which he had belonged before. For the wife it was a shock; she became uprooted and was thrown into a strange environment with entirely new functions, physical and otherwise. We must keep this difference in mind while turning now to the study of married life as revealed in the Geniza records.

C. "THE HOUSE," OR NUCLEAR FAMILY

1. *Husband and Wife*

"Baby" and "Mistress of the house."—Can we ever hope to penetrate the arcanum of married life in an age and region so removed from us as the High Middle Ages in Egypt and other countries of the Mediterranean area? The Cairo Geniza, the tool of enquiry used in this book, provides us with letters and documents. Documents such as contracts, declarations, pleas, and court records reveal to us the realities of life and are invaluable. But normally one goes to court or makes out a written settlement only when mutual trust has become weakened or when things have gotten out of hand altogether. Consequently, the testimony of documents is slanted; it is unable to tell us the whole story.

We are even worse off with letters. The postulates of propriety, as understood in those parts and days, put stringent limitations on the freedom of expression of letter writers. A man was at liberty to address his mother or sister as he liked, but not his wife. We possess only a few examples of personal letters sent by a husband to his wife, meant for her eyes (and not to be read out to her by a man). Three such letters are translated in full at the end of this subsection to enable the reader to listen to a medieval couple exchanging their thoughts and feelings when they were, so to say, unobserved. An allusion to intimate relations has been found by me only once, in a letter which is remarkable also for several other reasons, but which was never sent off. While reading it through again, the writer must have decided that it was not dignified to commit such matters to paper. [1]

As a rule, when a man was away from home, he wrote not to his wife but to his mother or a male relative, referring to his wife most sparingly, if at all—for instance, inquiring after her health, making arrangements for her maintenance, or simply sending her regards. Under no circumstances would he call her "my wife"; that expression would carry too improper a sexual connotation. He would send greetings to his children "and their mother," or would refer to her as "the house," "the residence," "the inhabitants of the house," or use other awkward expressions. In Hebrew, where the word "inhabitants" is rendered not by a singular collective term, as in Arabic *ahl,* but by a plural, *baʿalē ha-bayit,* "masters of the house," the prudish circumlocution sounds particularly strange to us. [2]

During most of the "classical" Geniza period, when writing to a relative, even to a son or a brother, one would not refer to the recipient's wife with this term, but would allude to her with the phrase "the one who is with you"—the usual term—or other indirect expressions. Even a husband writing home could say "greet my uncle [meaning his father-in-law] and the one who is with me," meaning his wife; she was then actually far away from him.[3] The name of a man's wife was never mentioned. Strict Jewish etiquette prohibited sending greetings to any woman, and, as can be seen from the correspondence of scholarly merchants of the eleventh century, this taboo was then taken very seriously. Thus it happened that we have over two hundred and fifty letters addressed to, or written by, Nahray b. Nissīm, many from close relatives and intimate friends, yet we never learn the name of his wife—and he had three, two whom he mourned, and one who survived him.[4] In the warm, personal letter of the judge Labrāṭ I b. Moses I of al-Mahdiyya, to his younger brother, of which a passage is translated above, he expresses regret that he has never met his brother's "house," who had just borne him a boy. But he sends regards to his brother's father- and brothers-in-law, and even to the newborn, but not to his brother's wife. Only "the girl," meaning the judge's wife, sends greetings to her brother- and sister-in-law.[5]

Happily we are able to observe in the Geniza a gradual erosion of this rigid taboo. In many letters we do find regards to the recipient's "house," or to "the one who is with him," or to the mother of his children. In this respect the concluding passage of Moses Maimonides' long letter to his beloved disciple Joseph b. Judah is particularly noteworthy. After having stated that even the maidservants in the house pray for him and wish to see him back, Maimonides adds: "Although the religious law forbids to send greetings to a woman, it does not forbid to pray for her, therefore 'Peace upon you and peace upon your house' (I Samuel 25:6)," meaning the disciple's wife.[6] Exactly the same words are found at the end of a Geniza letter, addressed to a judge, and the quotation from I Samuel often stands for regards destined for a woman.[7]

But there is more to it. Beginning with the later half of the twelfth and especially in the thirteenth and later centuries women are freely mentioned by name and greeted, and not rarely the names of a whole bevy of women appear in one letter. One no longer needed to beat about the bush, but could speak freely about "your wife" and "my wife,"[8] and messages by and to women become frequent. This change cannot be attributed to the weakening of religious discipline, for the Late Middle Ages were characterized by strictness and bigotry rather than by laxity. Nor can it be explained by the immigration of French Jews to Egypt and Palestine (beginning around 1200), for it was too tiny a trickle to exercise such an impact.[9] Nor do I believe that this change was confined to the Jewish community. I am rather inclined to see in it one of many expressions of a social transformation caused by generally worsening economic conditions and the subsequent weakening of the bourgeoisie, which had endeavored to keep up standards of dignified behavior inherited from the ruling class and the courts. In subsection B, 4, above, another indication of this change connected with the one studied here, namely the increasing importance of the wife's earnings, is tentatively explained in the same way. The straightforward talk of lower classes now creeps into the correspondence of scholars. This development is completed in some of the later sections of the *Arabian Nights,* also written in Egypt, whose sordid vulgarity is surpassed only by certain American best sellers of the 1960s.

The Geniza as a source for the customs of married life fails us entirely when we search for letters written by women. The question of female literacy is discussed in section D, below. Here suffice it to say that while we have few personal letters addressed by husbands to wives, we have none in the opposite direction. The letters wives sent to their husbands are dictated and factual. The most a woman would dare to say in such circumstances was a phrase like "It is strange to me that you should be in one town and I in another."[10] We have reason to assume that women who were able to write did write personal, and perhaps even intimate, letters to their husbands. But it is easy to understand why such letters have not been deposited in the Geniza.

Adverted to the limitations imposed on us by the nature of our sources the reader will be indulgent with the insufficiency of the forthcoming remarks.

"The baby is well, and so are the babies," we read in a cheerful report from Jerusalem sent to a husband abroad.[11] An extensive business letter by a learned merchant describing his frightful experiences at sea ("the water stood in the boat to the height of two men") and expressing his yearnings after his babies, concludes with the urgent request from his business partner to buy a pair of beautiful earrings of the Isfahān type for "the baby," his wife.[12] Even after having borne several children the young wife is still referred to as "baby," *ṭifla,* "girl," *ṣabiyya,*[13] "the little one," *ṣaghīra* (as opposed to *kabīra,* "the great," or "old one," namely, the mother-in-law, as long as the latter is in command of the house)[14] and even *al-ṣughayyira,* "the little, little one."[15]

Such expressions of endearment are of course familiar from common American speech, where ladies in their seventies are still referred to as "the girls," but these terms carried an additional connotation in the Geniza period: the wife was treated as a child, to be educated, guided, and dominated by her husband and his family: mother-, father-, and sisters-in-law. When the father of a newlywed girl writes to his son-in-law, "I have only one request, be considerate with your maidservant [meaning, the writer's daughter], for, you know, she has no one in the world except you [being a stranger in your town]," he emphasizes the wife's subservient role: *jāriya,* "maidservant," was then the term commonly in use for "slave girl."[16]

This attitude toward the young wife had its root and justification in plain facts: normally she was a teenager with no experience in life. Even after a wife had borne three living children, her husband, on his deathbed, appointed not her, but her mother (his mother-in-law), as sole guardian of her children and executrix of his will; as the document explicitly says, the dying man relied on the old woman's efficiency (besides her piety and her love for her grandchildren); clearly, he could not expect such knowledge of the world from his wife, who perhaps had not yet reached the age of twenty at that time. Additional examples of such situations could easily be adduced.[17]

On the Sabbath of the wedding week the groom was honored in the synagogue with the recitation of the beautiful story of Rebekah (the future wife of the Patriarch Isaac), who, when asked by a traveler to let him have a little sip of water from her jug, not only let him have his fill, but ran back and forth to the well, until she had drawn water for all the ten camels forming the traveler's caravan. Poems in honor of the groom referring to this custom have been preserved in the Geniza.[18] The ideal young wife was the one who did her chores with enthusiasm merely because of her good character (and probably also her good education), and we have no reason to doubt that there were many like Rebekah, "found perfect in the house of her father-in-law and running home all the time, reporting her success to the house of her father."[19] Yet the "baby"-complex has its pitfalls. A teenager certainly needs guidance; but adolescence is also the age when the young woman feels herself becoming ever stronger, physically and mentally, and, consequently, less and less inclined to bow to the authority of her husband or his family. Marital strife setting in soon after marriage, as described so often in this chapter, must be understood against this background.

Another term for "wife," occurring at least as often as those characterizing her as a child or a girl, reveals quite a different aspect of married life. I am referring to "house," repeatedly mentioned above.[20] "I entered my house" means "I married."[21] However prolonged a husband's absence from his home might have been—and sometimes he absented himself for years—his "house" was the place where his wife resided. This was the attitude of the government, the Jewish authorities, and the population at large.[22] In the life of many couples the Hebrew maxim " 'his house' means his wife" took on quite a literal connotation, namely, that the newlyweds moved away from the groom's family into separate living quarters. This important aspect of married life is discussed below.[23]

A third group of terms describes the wife as "the mistress of the house," and this is to be taken literally. When the young wife moved into the house of her parents-in-law, or even when she remained in her own father's house, she became a subordinate rather than a mistress: "You have made her a servant", writes an uncle, who was dissatisfied with the treatment of his niece by her husband's mother, who put her to work despite the young woman's connections to her aunt by various other family ties.[24] A father writing to his son-in-law (who shared living quarters with him) would call his own wife "lady of the house," but his daughter "the one who is with you," and a father addressing his married children would express himself similarly.[25] This was natural, since a mother was addressed and referred to as "my mistress." When, however, the years went by, and, especially after the death of the husband's father, the mother-in-law herself would refer to the wife as the mistress of the house, and a son writing to his mother would send regards to his wife using the same epithet.[26] Naturally, everything depended on the circumstances and the personalities involved. From "baby" to "mistress of the house" was a long way, and it was an uphill struggle. Some never made it. In not a few Geniza papers women of old age appear as oppressed and miserable as they probably had been in their youth. Others, especially those domiciled away from their families and having a husband living up to the promises made by him in his marriage contract, fared better. The Geniza people were very much aware of the fact that marriages were arranged by God, or, as they emphasized even more frequently, were a matter of luck.[27] King Solomon in his wisdom has said: "He who has *found* a wife, has found happiness" (Proverbs 18:22). But when he was in another mood, he wrote: "I *find* the woman more bitter than death" (Ecclesiastes 7:26). "*Found* or *find*"?—this was the question the young husband was asked by his friends some time after his wedding, meaning, is the new life joyful for you or full of bitterness.[28] In the following subsection I investigate what might have induced husbands and wives to answer this and similar questions in one way or another.

Affection and conjugal relations.—I do not attempt to prove the obvious, namely, that love was present in the Geniza world just as in our own. But it is perhaps worthwhile to inquire how these matters were felt and expressed in a society so different from ours.

There is no need to emphasize that the nature of love prevailing in those days and its rhythm of growth were diametrically opposed to those we consider ideal. For us love is a bond between equals, not much different in essence from true friendship between persons of the same sex; subsequent intimate relations may enhance or diminish feelings previously entertained. Couples in Geniza times had little, if any, opportunity for premarital friendship, although seclusion, as shown above, was by no means complete.[29] As a rule, marriage was the beginning, not the crowning, of an alliance. And it was an alliance definitely not between equals, but between a master and one commended to his care. When mutual satisfaction prevailed and, in the struggle of life, the wife became more and more her husband's support, marriage grew into companionship, into a bond between equals, or, rather, nearly equals. When Geniza husbands speak of love, we should take them seriously. They were not people from another planet.

Once again taking our clue from the Rebekah story, recited on the wedding Sabbath, we read in Genesis 24:67: "He [Isaac] took Rebekah as his wife. And Isaac loved her and thus found solace after his mother's death." The verse indicates more than a sequence, namely that love comes with marriage and does not precede it: replacing the mother, the wife becomes the mature companion of her husband. A wish to this effect expressed in a Geniza letter is cited above.[30] When a schoolmaster living far away from home apprises his old mother of his marriage and writes that he was absolutely happy and that his young wife, besides being beautiful, had all the good and noble character traits of his mother, we feel that his innermost desires had been satisfied, and also that "love at first sight" was not entirely out of reach of medieval people.[31] Normally, the relationship as expected at the beginning of a marriage was as expressed in this plea of a father-in-law: "I need not commend to you the one who is with you; treat her, as I know you will, with kindness, tenderness, and consideration."[32] But in the first of the letters translated at the end of this subsection, a scholar, apparently married for a short time, writes home freely "a wife who knows that her husband loves her," and "I have no one who loves me except you." In a fervent incantation a husband asks the three Angels of Love to see to it that his wife preserves her love for him.[33] And the two other letters translated there, one by a young husband, and another by an old one, when speaking of love, reveal an almost natural sense of equality.

Even a purely legal document, a question submitted to Moses Maimonides, states: "She did not cease loving her husband until his death." The letter requesting the early issue of a death certificate wished to make it clear that the woman concerned desired to marry soon, not because she had cast her eye on another man, but because she had no means of subsistence.[34] The marital relationship is strikingly described in this good wish inserted in a business letter addressed to Nahray b. Nissīm: "May God make her an individual blessing, *khāṣṣiyya mubāraka,* for you and give you success with each other." The term *khāṣṣiyya* designates something possessing a specific nature or having been specifically prepared. They understood, as we do, that happiness in marriage depended on the concord of the personalities of husband and wife.[35]

What did a Geniza man seek in his wife? The usual Hebrew laudatory epithets—woman of valor, pious, virtuous, and chaste, as they were understood in those days—are apt to convey a fairly correct idea. First, a young wife should be a Rebekah, doing willingly and effectively the work expected from her, or, as we read in one letter: "I was happy to learn that your wife is efficient, clean, solid, and doing her chores well."[36] The term "pious," *ṣaddeqet,* comprised the additional nuances of charitable, lenient, considerate (with everyone, especially, of course, her husband, something similar to the considerateness stipulated in the Karaite ketubba).[37] "Virtuous," *keshērā,* referred to sex and religious observances in general. "Chaste," *ṣenū'ā,* should perhaps be best translated as "unassuming," "knowing her place," also "one who knows to keep a secret." The beauty of a wife could be mentioned solely in a personal letter addressed by a son to his mother, and even that was exceptional.[38] Flattery of the bride's beauty in wedding songs consisted of stereotyped phrases and was meaningless. The most specific reference to a married woman's looks a poet could permit himself is one found in an encomium for the head of a yeshiva. After having borne him three sons and two daughters (all already married at the time), the poet says, she still was joyful and blooming, neither withering, nor shriveling.[39] A wife was expected to make herself attractive to her husband by keeping her hair well combed, applying kohl to her eyes, and perfuming her body.[40] The costly lingerie of fine Egyptian linen, "betraying the breasts beneath them," which well-to-do brides brought with them into marriage, probably served the same purpose.[41] A wife became most lovable to her husband when she gave him many healthy sons (if he could afford to have them).[42]

A wife expected her husband to be tender, kind, and considerate, to show her "love, approval, and a generous mind."[43] "Treat her well, and she will be attracted to you." The husband should be a gentleman, should have *muruwwa*, "manliness," meaning the character of a man who, because he knows he has power, does not use it against someone weaker.[44] This attitude should be expressed in presents, small and large, routine and special. Since the husband did not give his wife household money, but did the shopping himself, the Geniza women were not in the fortunate position of our grandmothers who deftly saved here and there from their weekly allocations and then surprised everyone in the house with the wonderful things they bought with them. Instead, a husband, when drawing up his shopping list for the weekend, would add to it the item *salwā lil-mar'a,* "cheering money for the wife."[45] Another husband notes in his accounts of monthly household expenditure a regular item "for the wife."[46]

The most common opportunity for a gift to the spouse was the return from a journey, and the Geniza people, we remember, were great travelers. Naturally, we hear about such presents only when the traveler makes a last minute order or is reminded of his duty. We had such a case above. Similarly a sister in Qayrawān, Tunisia, admonishes her extremely busy brother sojourning in Egypt not to forget to buy presents for his two daughters and "their mother," adding politely that the reminder was redundant.[47] A traveler from Qayrawān, arriving in Alexandria, was shocked when he noticed, still on board, that he had not brought with him what his wife had desired to have: a Qayrawānese robe, cap, veil, and mantle, that is, a complete attire, and he now asks the addressees to send the items with the very first caravan setting out, adding: "This is my most urgent request." The wife's wish had not been made to him directly in a letter, but was conveyed to him by a brother of the addressees, who had traveled from Egypt to Tunisia.[48] There were other occasions for gifts. When a husband tried to induce his wife to follow him from the city to a provincial town, he writes to her: "Sell the wine and buy a silver bracelet for its price and put the bracelet on your wrist." The selling and buying was to be done by a male relative.[49] In view of all this we understand why a husband on his deathbed found it necessary to declare that all clothing and other presents given by him to his wife during their married life were her personal property.[50]

Conjugal relations were regulated by custom that had the force of law. Since they were stipulated as a duty in the marriage contract, the frequency of marital relations that could be regarded as a sufficient fulfillment of that obligation was discussed by the sages of the Talmud. They were reasonable enough to posit a wide range of alternatives according to the occupations of the husbands and similar circumstances. They agreed, however, that for scholars once a week was enough and that the proper time for the fulfillment of this duty was the night belonging to, that is, preceding, the weekly day of rest. Since everyone regarded himself as a student of the holy law, this measure became standard. An India trader, away from home for years, writes to his impatient wife: "I do not believe that the heart of anyone traveling away from his wife has remained like mine, all the time and all the years—from the moment of our separation to the very hour of writing this letter—so constantly thinking of you and yearning after you and regretting to be unable to provide you with what I so much desire: your legal rights on every Sabbath and holiday. . . ."[51] The lonely husband whose letter is translated at the end of this subsection felt particularly miserable on Friday nights. A young and scholarly husband who became very angry when he discovered that he had to pay rent to his father-in-law with whom he stayed, used to absent himself during the week, but for the Friday-night dinner he had to come home. Of a woman temporarily separated from her husband it was said: "She has no holiday and no Sabbath."[52]

Similar customs prevailed in Islam and Christendom. Thursday night, which precedes the Islamic weekly holiday, was set aside for conjugal enjoyment, to be followed by a bath and perfuming on Friday morning—before the solemn noon prayer which was to be attended by all males. In Christian Europe, in social classes adhering to traditional ways, Saturday night had a similar role. The statutory three monthly visits to their wives incumbent on Athenian husbands in classical times imply a similar frequency of connubial relations. These customs, spread over such wide areas of time and space may at the outset have had their origins in hygienic assumptions, which later, in monotheistic societies, were surrounded with a religious halo.[53]

The Karaites regarded sexual activity on the Sabbath as a grave desecration of the holiness of the day. Therefore, in the many documents on mixed marriages found in the Geniza the Rabbanite partner undertakes to honor this religious susceptibility of his or her spouse. The socioeconomic inducements for mixed marriages had to be pretty strong to overcome age-old social habits in so vital a matter.

The Karaite stance had ancient antecedents in the pre-Christian Book of Jubilees, which has certain affinities with the Dead Sea Scrolls. The Book of Jubilees was translated into Ethiopic and exercised some influence on the tenets and practice of the church of that country. As a curiosity I may mention that in *The Book of Light*, ascribed to Zar'a Ya'eqob (Jacob), emperor of Ethiopia (1434–1468), the injunction of sexual abstinence binding for Saturday was extended to Sunday, the Christian Day of the Lord.[54]

Inability of a husband to perform his matrimonial duties is attested in various Geniza documents. Two examples are given. The first is a legal question, submitted by an official in a small town or village to his superior.

> Whenever she is alone with him [i.e., whenever he tries to approach her], he falls down and shakes convulsively and remains in this state until the fit is over. The girl is constantly in great distress because of intense fear. Since this state of the husband persisted, she was unable to remain with him any longer. She appeared before the court and released him from the payment of the late marriage portion which he owes her according to her marriage contract. She requested him to set her free by writing her a bill of repudiation as required by the law of *Moses, son of Amram, may he rest in peace*. The girl declared also that this husband of hers to whom she was married did not have sexual intercourse with her and that she still was *a virgin and no man had known her*.
>
> Please provide us with your legal opinion whether her divorce in the described manner is obligatory or not, Also, whether the gift of the early marriage portion made to the girl is void and returns to the husband after he incurred debts for the girl on her wedding expenses and on what she needed for marriage, whereupon she found him to be in such a state that it was impossible to remain with him. This illness is chronic since he was taken by it, but she had neither observed nor known of it before. Please provide us with your legal opinion.[55]

The second item is a scrap of paper in the handwriting of the judge Nathan b. Samuel on which he jotted down the very words used by the complaining female, Milāḥ, "Queen of the Beauties": " 'I am thirsty, no one gives me to to drink'—This happened about two months ago. 'I am a thirsty woman, the man is useless; let him separate, let's annul.' She has been thirsty for nine months." Such vulgar language could not be used, of course, in the illustrious presence of the judge; it was conveyed to him by two witnesses from Cairo, where the woman lived and where her declaration had been taken down about two months earlier. The judge noted that other witnesses about the case were available.[56] The list of the poor, analyzed in *Med. Soc.*, II, 448, sec. 33, makes mention of a girl called "Daughter of the Thirsty Woman," meaning, daughter of an impotent father, one of those ridiculous nicknames, being a conjunction of contradictory terms, of which the mockery-loving Egyptians were so fond. It corresponds exactly to "Son of the Mule," another such byname found in the Geniza.[57]

Prescriptions for satisfactory intercourse and amulets against witchcraft or the evil eye impeding it are not absent from the Geniza. How serious magical interfering with sexual performance was taken is evident from an official petition by the teacher and court clerk Solomon b. Elijah summarized below.[58] A case of female incompetence because of young age has been cited above.[59] I may have overlooked a stray reference to interrupted intercourse and abortion, but those matters apparently occupied the Jewish courts of the Geniza period less than they did their Muslim counterparts.[60] The escapades of husbands with slave girls, prostitutes, and pleasure boys, as well as the question of female faithfulness are discussed in Vol. IV, chap. x see the Preface, p. x, above.

One consideration, however, is not out of place. Because of the religious, moral, and social convictions held in the world described here, the married wife's role as provider of sexual satisfaction was far more pronounced than it is in our modern, semipromiscuous society. This applied in particular to Christians and Jews, who did not have the legal outlet of concubinage with slave girls as did their Muslim contemporaries. To be sure, the vast majority of the Muslims was in the same situation: the purchase of a desirable concubine was beyond the means of the common man. Naturally, this role of the wife greatly enhanced her position and influence. ("The companion of the night is stronger than the counselor of daytime," says an Arabic proverb. More picturesque versions were also in vogue.) When she failed in this respect, her misery could be extreme. Many of the petty discords reported in the subsequent pages might have had their real root in reasons quite different from the issues overtly contended.

There was one biblical book whose story was well known to the women of the Geniza period and whose moral, I presume, was well heeded by them: the Book of Esther. Three women, each sharply contrasting with the other, are the main actors. The proud queen Vashti, who brazenly disobeys her foolish drunkard of a husband, is dethroned and repudiated at the advice of all the counselors of the King; if Vashti had her way, the women of the Empire would rise up against their husbands in an all-comprising rebellion. Zeresh (in the Geniza a byword for a wicked woman), the wife of Haman who is the villian in the story, misguides her husband by sinister advice, and, indirectly, causes his downfall. Esther always seems to do what she is told to do; she is obedient to her uncle, to the eunuch in charge of the harem, and, of course, to her husband, the King; but she is successful in everything: the refugee Jewish girl becomes a possible choice for the throne of Persia; the King prefers her to all other girls; and she engineers the destruction of the archenemy Haman. Esther knows how to behave, but she is not a timid woman. When necessary, she dares to defy the rules of the court and is prepared to suffer death.

This type of a woman, who is outwardly pliable and accommodating, but strong and resolute in mind, is the one who has prospects for success in a patriarchal society, where men believe that it is up to them to rule the house ("like a king," as Maimonides writes in his Code). At marriage the husband remains in the safe haven of the family of his father. It is the teenage wife who has to brave a new and often unfriendly environment and to accommodate herself to it—a tough task, as the next subsection shows. A woman must be an Esther if she wants to survive.

Problems with the couple's relatives and residence.—The new family into which a young husband entered was destined to become for him an additional source of strength and support. Quotations to this effect are provided in section B, 1, above. This was not merely a matter of social status and economic opportunities, but of the emotional aspect of family life as well. The same seasoned merchant from Tunisia, who was so glowingly congratulated by his elder brother back home on the advantages gained by his new connections, is addressed by him in another letter thus: "My boy, understand your new situation. Replace me with your father-in-law and accept him as a substitute for your own father, may he rest in Eden, and for myself, and accept your mother-in-law as a substitute for your mother, may God have mercy upon her."[61]

The situation of the young wife was somewhat different. In the poetic dreams of the biblical Song of Songs 3:4, 8:2, the female singer who composed the songs of that book fancies bringing her beloved into the familiar and protective ambiance of her "mother's dwellings." The Geniza documents reveal a reality that often was the opposite. The young wife became a "lonely stranger," yearning after her distant mother. As Sophocles has a woman say in his (mostly lost) tragedy *Theseus:* "As soon as we reach our youth and our mind begins to awake, we are sent away from home . . . far from the gods of our fathers, far from those who brought us into the world, to live among strangers." Similarly the Geniza: "Dear sister, arouse longing for me in the heart of my mother; since you have left me, I have become a lonely stranger; there is no one who talks to me; death is better than this"—thus a newlywed ends her message, dictated, of course, to a male member of the household she had joined not long before.[62] Even after a young woman had borne a child who had died (after having been able to walk) and after a visit of her mother, her husband writes this to his mother-in-law: "I need not commend to you your daughter. You know how it was when you left her, while her heart was bound to yours, and how she suffered because of the little one. Due to your absence she has neither night or day. Separation and loneliness have closed her off from the world. No one comes to see her. You remember, had it not been for your presence, she would have had no one to keep her company. So, by the obligation God has imposed on you, do not treat us any longer as strangers, but come without delay."[63] A young wife whose father-in-law was also her uncle and who had a brother who lived in the same town (and, it seems, house) asks her mother in the most urgent terms to visit her, concluding: "If she does not come, neither God nor men will approve it."[64]

In general, of course, it was expected that the female members of the new household would recreate the homely atmosphere of "the mother's dwellings" for the young wife. She was "the trust" given to her mother-in-law to be kept as her most precious possession.[65] A young husband expected a relative (the exact relationship is not evident from the letter) to bestow upon himself the "fragrance" of his mother and to become for his wife "a mother and sister." Similarly, a woman marrying a widower promises to become like a sister to the future wife of a stepson.[66] The model relationship between mother- and daughter-in-law was that made eternal in the biblical book of Ruth. How considerate they were to each other! Throughout the book they constantly bore in mind the well being of the in-law. When, on a little strip of paper found in the Geniza an old judge asks a younger colleague to write for him a funeral oration for a lady which he had to deliver the next morning, he assigns to him as topic "Naomi (and Ruth)." The old woman certainly was renowned in the community for the kindness shown to a daughter-in-law who had come from another town.[67] Remarks that "the little one is in a thousand states of happiness" are not rare in letters, but that does not say much. Detailed reports are usually available only when something went wrong.

The Geniza husband, as we have seen, expected his wife to live up to the image he had of his own mother. But the newcomer to the house might have received quite a different impression of the old woman and might have hated the comparison, whether meant as praise or blame. That a wife should be like a man's mother is, of course, a human propensity also found elsewhere.

> I want a girl just like the girl
> That married dear old dad,

says an old American song. But in the generation-bound Geniza society this attitude was particularly strong.[68] The most common actual complaints of a wife were that the mother-in-law was not considerate, did not honor her, imposed on her too much work, and suspiciously supervised her comings and goings. Astoundingly for us, but in complete conformity with the notions of the Geniza world, the relationship with the sister-in-law was even more complicated. The special attachment of brothers to sisters is discussed in detail in subsection A, 2, above. To this we must add that the only females of approximately the same age with whom a young bachelor could talk intimately were his sisters; no wonder, then, that, after marriage, he still would find their company more congenial than that of his new wife, especially when the sisters were older and more mature, as appears to have happened in the light of various reports. It seems, too, that the newlywed had not rarely to live under one roof with spinsters, an additional aggravating circumstance. All this explains the young wife's sufferings and her endeavor to move away from her husband's family.

Such situations were foreseen in many engagement, betrothal, and marriage contracts.[69] Even more do we hear about them in complaints and settlements made in the course of married life. An example from a well-to-do and educated family may open our survey. The young husband is described as a scholar. On the wife's side an uncle conducted the pourparlers, even though her father was still alive, perhaps because it was regarded as more dignified. At the marriage of Sitt al-Nasab ("Lady of Noble Birth") it was stipulated that she had the right to coerce her husband to move with her to another place, if she did not get along well with his sisters (and his mother; in one phrase the mother is mentioned in the second place, and in another she is omitted, suggesting that the difficulties were with the sisters). The change indeed occurred a few months after the wedding and the husband moved out of the family house and rented another apartment for his wife and himself.

As the document states, however, "his heart remained divided," namely, between his sisters and his wife. In addition, the extra rent was a burden. Therefore, at the intervention of Sitt al-Nasab's uncle, a new agreement was reached, which is characteristic in various respects: Sitt al-Nasab returned on condition, *(a)* that she would live in a separate apartment, which was on a different floor and looking out on the inner court, while the family of her husband would occupy the part of the house facing the street; (*b*) that none of his sisters should enter her place, not even to ask for a match;[70] (*c*) that the preparation of food and all other household activities should be separate; (*d*) that her husband's living quarters should be separate from those of his sisters; (*e*) that in case of new trouble the husband had to move out with his wife to another house; (*f*) that in case of nonfulfillment of any of these conditions her husband would pay without any delay a fine of 50 dinars—an enormous sum—to be distributed to the poor of Fustat.[71]

A quite different atmosphere prevails in another settlement written by the same scribe, the frequently mentioned Ḥalfōn b. Manasse. Here the husband undertakes to prevent his mother, sister, or any other relatives of his from entering his wife's premises, or from harassing or harming her. He on his side will not "stretch out his hand against her," nor run away, nor hide himself as if he was a runaway. She on her side will not leave the house except with his permission, and, in general, the spouses will behave properly toward each other; otherwise, the court will intervene. Here the harassing of the wife by the female members of the husband's had almost led to the breakup of his marriage.[72]

A third marriage settlement written by Ḥalfōn b. Manasse, unfortunately preserved only in part, reveals a new aspect of family relations. Again the sisters of the husband are denied access to the wife's living quarters except with her permission, and he himself is warned never to curse or to beat her. Here, however, the wife's mother had intervened, had given part of a house to the young couple on condition that her daughter should share the apartment with her, should be free to leave the house whenever she liked, and should have exclusive rights to her earnings. The old woman also stipulated a number of items for her own benefit.[73]

A fourth, and even more fragmentary, agreement made out by Ḥalfōn b. Manasse must be considered here in view of its specific implications. The court accepted the demands of the girl's father that she must be moved away from the living quarters of the husband's mother "to the new house" (to whom it belonged, is not said). But the husband insisted that his own furniture should not be moved "to the new house"; only his wife's outfit should go with her on condition that he was no longer responsible for it. As in our first example, it was regarded as entirely feasible for the husband to remain in the house or apartment of his own family, while his wife occupied a place by herself. I assume "the new house" adjoined one of the existing houses of one of the two families.[74]

A frightening picture of the suffering of a young wife is revealed in this complaint to a judge: the husband (known as a pauper from a communal list) maltreats and curses "the little one." Things had reached these extremes: his sister hits her with her shoe (or is it her foot?), his father calls her names, whenever he sees her, and, in general, "she has no esteem or home with them." In order to torment her, the husband threatens to marry another wife, and "every day he drives her out of the house." On top of all this, he spreads rumors about her and gives her a bad name. They even brought the midwife to examine her, but, "thank God," she found her to be pure.[75]

This epitome of marital strife, caused or aggravated by the interference of the husband's family, is fittingly concluded by a cry for help uttered by the luckless woman. It is the story of a family interconnected by two, and very probably, three marriages with paternal first cousins. The writer's mother-in-law was a sister of the addressee and was married to her cousin. The writer's mother had a bad reputation, which she had probably acquired after the death of her husband, a brother of the young woman's father-in-law. I have little doubt that this mother of hers was another sister of the uncle; for otherwise one can hardly understand why she expected to find in him support against closer relatives. From the tone of her letter and its repeated statement "I still have a claim on you," I conclude that her uncle had taken her into his house and brought her up after the adventures of his sister, her mother. We can even go a step further and imagine that the dashing widow was more successful as a woman, than her sister, the unhappy girl's aunt and mother-in-law. This would go a long way to explain that "interminable enmity" of which the letter speaks. The writer calls herself Umm Sitt al-Nās, "Mother of 'the Mistress of Mankind' "; she might once have had a little girl by that name. Here is the letter:

My lord [her uncle], I am unable to describe to you how miserable I am. Even if I had been the daughter of a slave girl,[76] you would have protected me, in particular, for my mother's [uncle's sister] sake.[77] That enmity should have come to an end long ago. I have not left Dammūh[78] of my own free will. This was the beautiful choice of your sister [her mother-in-law, who is her own mother's and uncle's sister]. I had nothing to do with this. . . . Do not ask me how he [her husband] treats me; I pray to God that he reward him for this. First, we all moved into one house. Soon my mother-in-law[79] began to work against me, isolating me from everyone and putting enmity against me into the heart of her son. The least she did was that she said to me: "Go away and become like your notorious mother." You know the noble character of your cousin [also her father-in-law]. He [the father-in-law] suspected me with my elder cousin! You remember well how everyone reacted to your sister Baqā ("Long life").[80] In short, I cannot describe to you my state until God brings us together and I shall tell you what your sister has done to me this year, she and her son.

You [plural] know that I have no one in the world except God and you. Do not neglect me, for I still have a claim on you. I left the house, not having on me even a cap, and I am staying now with a widow. I am afraid I am getting a grave palsy on my hands.[81] So, absolve yourselves of the religious duty of almsgiving by collecting for me a woman's cap, a mantle, and 20 dirhems to enable me to travel to you. Do not let me down [singular], for I am still commended to your care, having no one else to whom I can come, no other uncle on father's or mother's side. Answer this letter soon. You are charitable to strangers, how far more to me, your child.[82]

The recipient of this letter, Abu 'l-Faḍl (Mevōrākh b. Abraham) Ibn Sabra signed documents in Zawīlat al-Mahdiyya (a suburb of that Mediterranean port) in the years 1049, 1063, 1074, and later appears in many letters and documents as resident of the Egyptian capital down to 1090. He was a parnās, or honorary welfare official, in his Tunisian hometown, and "head of the parnāsīm" in Fustat (see *Med. Soc.*, II, 80, top, and *ibid.*, p. 455, sec. 60). His business correspondence betrays him as being fairly well-off. Incidentally, he, too, had trouble with his marriage. While in Egypt, probably during a longer sojourn there on one of his many business trips, he divorced his Tunisian wife by proxy. I assume she was not prepared to follow him to a strange environment. But, as his representative writes from al-Mahdiyya, her family was not angry with him, and his new marriage in Egypt was a success. Another Ibn Sabra emigrating from the Muslim West to Fustat repudiated his Tunisian 'wife' (from betrothal only) in 1034. All in all we see that the family tragedy described in the letter translated above was a middle class affair.[83]

The reader who has attentively followed the story of Ibn Sabra's niece, as told above, may wonder why two of his sisters had followed him from Tunisia to Egypt when his wife had remained in her native city. It was not exceptional. Moses Maimonides, when leaving Morocco or Spain for the East, was accompanied by at least two sisters, and another prominent Westerner going East, Nahray b. Nissīm, traveled with his sister. Brothers were trusted more than husbands.[84]

Examples of wives refusing to follow their husbands to a foreign country are numerous, a few already having been mentioned. Arye b. Judah, probably a European Jew, as his name indicates, had married a woman in Cairo and wished to take her with him to Palermo, Sicily, which, at that time (January 1095) was under Norman domination. The young couple had visited there, but, once back in Cairo the young wife took refuge in her father's house and refused to return. Arye swore that he could not live in Cairo and finally arranged with her father to repudiate her. He returned her outfit, and she restored the early installment of the marriage gift, as was the duty of a wife who declined to follow her husband "to his house," as the document states.[85] A Tunisian who had married a woman in Constantinople, but was imprisoned there and suffered other hardships, "which two camel loads of paper would be unable to describe," had to divorce her before leaving the country, although she had borne him a boy, who had died, and a girl, who was still small. The reason: he intended to leave Byzantium for good. "May God never let me see the Land of the Rūm again," he writes from Jerusalem.[86] A girl from 'Ibillīn, a village in western Galilee (still in existence), who was married in al-Maḥalla, Egypt, to a man from Aleppo, Syria, wrote an urgent message to her mother in the capital, asking her to come quickly or to dispatch a proxy: her husband wished to take her to his native city, which she was by no means prepared to do.[87]

Following a husband to another place in the same country was no less shunned, and for a variety of reasons. We already know that stipulations regulating this aspect of marriage were often included in engagement contracts and ketubbas. Here some cases that popped up during married life are considered. It was not always the pressure of the wife's family which counted. There was the young wife who was an inveterate city dweller and was not prepared to move with her husband to a small place out in the provinces, or could not endure remaining there. In one such instance her uncle, who had arranged the marriage because he was both a relative and friend of her husband, threatens her with the usual nightmares: her spouse would either marry another wife or leave the country altogether.[88] Another letter tells about a wife who ran away from al-Maḥalla, a district capital, and returned to Fustat because she could not stand the Rīf, the province. Her husband retorted that Fustat was too expensive; the most he could cope with was Damietta, the Mediterranean port.[89]

Then there were also women who were reluctant to go from country to city. In the first of the three letters translated at the end of this subsection, the wife, a daughter of the *dayyān,* or Jewish judge, of al-Maḥalla, refuses to follow her husband to the capital. At home she was a queen; in Fustat, a girl from the countryside. In a similar situation a woman from the Rīf writes to her husband, who had tarried in the capital too long (and had not written her): "You fancy that I will come to Miṣr. I shall never go up there. For if I do so, we shall not live in peace with each other—may God never plant discord between us."[90] But even inducing a wife to follow her husband from one provincial town to another required action by the authorities.[91] A summons to a woman asks her to appear in court and to explain why she refused to accompany her husband (where to is not stated). As we have seen, it was her duty to do so if provisions to the contrary had not been made in her marriage contract.[92]

The Geniza material presented thus far shows the wife relying on her family for protection against her husband. Naturally, the battle lines were not always drawn up that way. Often the wife had reason to complain about her own kin, especially when they were tardy in making good the promises made in the marriage agreements. A lovely little letter from the countryside complains about the people back home who had not yet delivered "the textiles and the copper" listed in the ketubba, so that the newlywed girl had to serve the meals to her husband in earthenware, which caused her no end of embarrassment.[93] A more serious situation is revealed in an ancient court record where the wife declares that her father had appropriated her outfit, for which reason she frees her husband from any responsibility for it.[94] In a magnificently written Hebrew fragment a woman called Esther (probably a foreigner, since Egyptian Jewesses did not bear biblical names) appoints her husband as her proxy for suing her brother who had not delivered what he had promised in her betrothal contract.[95] Other cases about nonfulfillment of economic stipulations in favor of the bride are extant and some of them are described below. One brother even laid claim on part of a house sold by his mother to his married sister, certainly because he did not acknowledge the property rights of his mother and did not care to make trouble for both.[96] When an uncle, warning his niece that she could not reckon on any support from her family, writes to her, "A wife has no one in the world except her husband," he certainly described a situation that was not exceptional. The Yemenite women say: "Hell with my husband is better than Paradise with my family."[97]

Another quite natural, situation where the women in a household felt drawn to one another and formed a common front against the menfolk is discussed in section D.

Possessions and pecuniary obligations of husband and wife.—The economic aspects of married life were another factor that made either for cooperation and happiness or for discord and misery. We learn about these matters mostly when marital strife led to litigation, or otherwise when action in court had to be taken. Arrangements made shortly before or after the demise of the husband or at a divorce must also be considered (see C, 3, below).

The discussion of the economic aspects of marriage, as revealed in engagement, betrothal, and marriage contracts (B, 2–4, above), has shown complicated legal arrangements and multifarious stipulations intended to cope with them. Actual life revealed a similar picture. I feel that many actual or alleged encroachments on the rights of the other spouse had their roots not only in outright greed or dire circumstances, but also in misunderstanding of the legal situation. A full elaboration of this point is, however, beyond the scope of this book.

In the Rabbanite marriage contracts the husband mortgages all his possessions, present and future, immovable and mobile, to the payment of his marriage gift and the restitution of the wife's outfit. The Karaites went a step further and stipulated that no use of the outfit could be made except with the wife's knowledge and consent. In reality, it appears, the husband's obligations and responsibility created a similar situation within the main section of the Jewish community. Moreover, a wife had possessions not included in the common pool, such as the first installment of the marriage gift, given to her by the bridegroom at the wedding or before, gifts from her family explicitly excluded from her husband's jurisdiction, or pieces of inheritance or gifts coming to her during married life under the same circumstances. How did all this work?

It worked well, as long as mutal trust and affection prevailed between the spouses and as long as their material circumstances were not too strained. True, the strings of the purse and of the sacks of wheat were in the hands of the husbands, and, as we learn from the letters of husbands away on travel and from many court records, they were tightly held. Male relatives or friends substituted for the master of the house in his absence; the monthly allocations of money and wheat were standardized, and usually modest.[98] Current expenses such as purchases and payments for repairs, were usually made or supervised by him or by his male representatives. This created a high degree of dependence of the wife, but was not necessarily always regarded as such: the husband was the errand boy of the wife. In a public appeal to the community a woman's first complaint was that her old husband vexed her by sending her out of the house to do for him this or that.[99] Assurances of a husband that he will be "the obedient slave" in the house and she "the mistress and queen" are not absent from Geniza letters.[100] Does not a widely diffused Arabic proverb advise the newlywed: "Be a slave to your husband for a week, and he will be your slave all his life"? Yet, the husband was the breadwinner and supporter. This was his duty, but also the source of his power. It was the general order of things and, therefore, probably was felt as less oppressive than it is to us.

The economic power of the husband also encompassed the wife's dowry, since he had the right of usufruct (using the income from the wife's property). But this power was limited by the obligation—extended to his heirs—to restore every dinar of it in case of a divorce or his death. In fact, the dowry represented a strong bond between the spouses and gave them a constant opportunity for cooperation. The bride's extensive wardrobe, bedding, furnishings, and kitchenware spared the young couple from incurring large expenses at the start of their married life. Part of the jewelry, usually comprising a number, and often a considerable number, of ornaments of the same type, could be, and was, used as collateral for her husband's mercantile undertakings. And her houses, or shares in houses, when included in the dowry, brought rent, supplementing the family budget. Any use of the wife's jewelry required her cooperation. It cannot be stressed enough that during the classical Geniza period the dowry did not consist of cash given to the husband, but of the wife's objects, thus emphasizing that it was her property, not his. Add to this the fact that the dowry was usually a multiple of the marriage gift—immediate and delayed—provided by the husband, and it becomes evident, that the middle-class dowry and other possessions of the wife made her position quite comfortable.[101]

A wife's transactions, such as the purchase or sale of a house, had to be confirmed by her husband, but the opposite was also the case, since his property was mortgaged to her. Many documents illustrating this situation have been preserved.[102] He was not even permitted to remove from the couple's domicile the furnishings belonging to him, since it could represent an attempt to evade his obligations. Explicit statements to this effect are extant.[103] Throughout the centuries we read about a wife granting a loan or a gift to her husband, selling to or buying from him, standing security for him, or vice versa, or engaged in other transactions—all situations showing her as disposing of a purse of her own. A few examples on loans illustrate. The first example does not credit much the male partner. Sitt al-Dār ("Lady of the House") had given a loan of 10 dinars (in the presence of two witnesses, of course) to her husband, whose family name was "Son of the Trustworthy," al-ʿAdl. After an initial denial he admitted that the sum had been given to him—10 gold pieces in number, 9 in weight—but only in order to enable him to pay her the delayed marriage gift in case she requested him to repudiate her. The end of this unpleasant story is lost.[104] In a huge calligraphic document, mostly consisting of legal verbiage, Nājiya ("The Saved One"), called Sitt Ḥidhq ("Lady Efficiency") releases her husband from all obligations resulting from her marriage contract, and releases both him and his son from the repayment of loans given to them—in return for what, is not said. Most probably it was a house. Women were fond of houses which provided them with a lifelong domicile and income.[105] A man remarrying his divorcée gives her a loan of 5 dinars, against a collateral consisting of a gold bracelet, to be paid back in installments of half a dinar per month. No doubt, she was a working woman.[106] On his deathbed a silk-weaver releases his wife from a debt to him of 3 dinars and gives her 15 dinars as a last installment of his marriage gift.[107] To conclude with an example from Mamluk times: a wife grants a loan of 40 "Florentine gold ducats" to her husband to be paid back within a few months.[108]

A common cause of marital dispute was the husband's control of the dowry. The conflict would be settled, not always permanently, by the husband relinquishing this right, partly or totally, and the wife releasing him from any responsibility for her possessions. Such situations would arise when the wife was no longer an inexperienced girl, but was eager to take her affairs into her own hands, when the husband went abroad for an extended period, or when the wife's family was not satisfied with his management or simply did not trust him. Then "the iron sheep," as the outfit entrusted to the husband was described, had to be converted into *melūg*, the wife's personal possessions, an Akkadian term that had a history of at least three thousand years before it appeared in the Geniza papers.[109] These terms are used in the draft of a document in which Ḥusn, "Beauty," releases her husband from all responsibility for her outfit, specifying items running up to about 540 dinars. The dowry also included a house. The marriage had been concluded in the year 1030 / 31.[110] "In the presence of her entire family and with their consent," a woman receives from her husband control of her dowry, she may sell it and buy whatever she likes "[a house], a room, a place"; he would make no claim on any proceeds accruing to her (1109–1118, the last digit is not preserved.)[111] The story of a woman who came to blows with her husband over this question and obtained control of her possessions four and a half years after her wedding is told below.[112] Her contemporary, *Sitt al-Kull*, "Ruler over All," daughter of Mr. "Blessings," got all her jewelry, furnishings, and other outfit back and the right to sell them and buy whatever she chose, but her husband, a synagogue singer, also received the ominous warning from the court that if he tried to take another wife, he had to pay her the late installment of the marriage gift, that is, to repudiate her. The settlement did not work: she was divorced two years later.[113]

Sometimes, it was not family strife or other personal considerations that induced a husband to divest himself of his responsibility for his wife's possessions. In the insecure times of the late 1120s a woman was granted the right to dispose of any part of her dowry she saw fit and to buy immovables for it. Silverware and jewelry were excluded from this agreement, probably because they could be entrusted to the good earth or to another safe hiding place. The wife was declared as "trustworthy," that is, no claim could be made against her with regard to her actions, while the other obligations of the husband, which were fixed in the marriage contract, remained in force. A relative of that husband was renowned for saving communal property from the hands of "the Monk," a rapacious finance director, the cause of "those insecure circumstances."[114] The opposite reaction appears to us more natural, namely, that in precarious "changing times," such as summer 1175, the beginning of the Ayyubid rule of Egypt, a wife should entrust her husband with money belonging to her as her personal property.[115]

When love waned, cooperation would turn into conspiracy, each side trying to grab as much as possible. The more vulnerable partner, the wife, was specifically under suspicion of such desperate steps, for which reason, as we have seen, she was explicitly protected in her marriage contract against suspicion and mistrust.[116] But husbands were no less prone to protect, or enrich, themselves through encroachment on their wives' property or rights. As is only human, the misbehavior often was mutual; and there even existed a term to describe it, *mughābara fi 'l-raḥl,* "trying to outdo one another in grabbing the other's possessions." A document using this term describes a typical solution for such marital strife: (*a*) the husband promises to return all the belongings that he had removed from the house;[117] (*b*) all the furnishings, carpets, jewelry, and copper that the wife had deposited with her mother or with any other members of her family will be taken off the list of her possessions for which the husband was responsible; (*c*) in the future she will dispose of such items only with his consent and in the presence of two witnesses; (*d*) he will dispose of her things or his own belongings only with her consent and in the presence of two witnesses. The wife was present and confirmed the agreement in person, but was represented by a Tunisian. The two signatories were Eli b. Amram, the head of the Jerusalemite congregation of Fustat, and Abraham b. David b. Sighmār, a relative of Labrāṭ I, the Jewish judge of al-Mahdiyya, Tunisia, repeatedly mentioned in this book. Perhaps the two families originated from two different countries.[118]

A similar situation may have prevailed in the following case. Mubāraka ("The Blessed One") b. Samuel of Gabes, Tunisia, had sold her maidservant for 20½ dinars and given the money to her brother, who embarked on a business trip to the West. This was done with the husband's consent, but apparently with some misunderstanding on his side. The husband brought her to court in Fustat, "and asked her many questions." It then appeared that only 10 of the 20½ dinars were mortgaged to her ketubba, whereupon she empowered her husband to sue her brother for the remaining 10½ dinars and for the profit made with that sum.[119]

The sad story of a physician, told in a long letter of his to an old uncle, concludes this chapter of marital distress. His beloved wife, "dear to the family and the town," had died, leaving him with a little boy of three. He settled in al-Maḥalla in order to study there with Ibn Sabra, a famous physician, and also to cure himself of an illness that had plagued him for years. For various reasons, in particular to provide a mother to his orphaned child, he married a woman from Ibn Sabra's family, but the marriage was not a success. The wife soon discovered that her husband was not as rich as she had imagined and began to remove his belongings to the house of her own family. She "ate up" all he had brought with him, to the amount of 150 dinars. He asked for a divorce, of course, without paying her dues, and received a legal opinion confirming his rights from no less an authority than Moses Maimonides. But it is a long way from a legal opinion to its implementation by a court. Our physician left the place and for two years tried to establish himself in another town. Meanwhile the wife had borne and weaned a girl, and the family induced him to join her again. On court order all his belongings were returned and his little boy, who had been sent to his dead mother's family, was brought back. Soon, however, the old story began again. Finally, the writer of the letter despaired and, like so many other husbands, disappeared and went underground. All he asked his paternal uncle—and he had done the same with the family of his former wife—was to keep his whereabouts secret. There was a small, or not so small, other request: the boy, who meanwhile had become seven, was now going to school; the uncle is asked to present the fledgling scholar with the family Bible.[120]

Wife-beating.—In the preceding sections reference has been made repeatedly to husbands beating and cursing their wives. This serious aspect of marital life requires more than passing attention. One must be aware, of course, of the legal implications of such references found in engagement contracts and in settlements after marital strife. They served as a warning to the husband that he could be forced by court action to divorce his wife (and to pay her the late installment of the marriage gift) if a suit of this nature was brought against him. Thus the frequency of such references in legal documents does not necessarily reflect a similar frequency of occurrences in life. Wife-beating is very rarely mentioned in letters.[121] Yet, the testimony of the documents cannot be easily dismissed.

Rabbis writing in medieval France and Germany were very outspoken on wife-beating, branding it an un-Jewish practice. The famous Rabbi Meir of Rothenburg, Germany, went as far as to recommend cutting off the hand of a husband who habitually committed this crime, since hitting a woman was a graver sin than injuring a man. Still, the evil was not unknown in the Jewish communities of Europe, since a considerable number of jurisconsults dealt with it in their legal opinions. It even led to the creation of a statute that proposed forcing the culprit to separate from his wife and to support her until he reformed.[122]

Under Islam, the situation was apparently different. The Koran (5:33) permits, or perhaps recommends, beating the wife if she is inaccessible to milder forms of correction. It must be noted, however, that the Muslim courts protected her against an excessively cruel husband. Readers of *The Arabian Nights* may remember the beautiful story of the good-natured cobbler Maʿrūf, whose shrew of a wife is forever running to the qadi, falsely accusing Maʿrūf of beating her, whereas, in reality, he was the meekest and gentlest of husbands. And Ibn Baṭṭūṭa the great traveler, himself repeatedly holding the office of a judge, describes how a colleague protected a woman with a similar complaint.

Since the holy book of the ruling faith had acquiesced to wife-beating, however, an atmosphere was created, which may have induced some Jewish authorities in Islamic lands to take a similar view. Yehuday Gaon, the first reputed author of a post-Talmudic code of law (eighth century), writes: "A wife should never raise her voice against her husband, but should remain silent even if he beats her—as chaste women do." Even Maimonides wrote in his Code: "A woman who refuses to do the work to which she is obliged may be forced to do so, even with the stick." To this his Provençal critic, R. Abraham b. David, remarks: "I have never heard that it is permitted to correct women with a stick." "I have never heard" means: there is no legal support in the sources for Maimonides' ruling. The Talmud, indeed, says nothing of the kind, and in the numerous Geniza records, in which women bring complaints before the courts in this matter, the latter invariably reprimand the husbands, occasionally imposing fines on those who relapsed.[123]

Surveying the Muslim, Christian, and Jewish literary sources known to me I am not convinced that wife-beating was more rampant in Mediterranean Islamic countries than in medieval Western Europe, nor that the legal situation was much different. If the Geniza material produced below gives a different impression, it should be noted that it mostly concerns couples from the lower and lowest strata of society. Poverty breeds discord, easily erupting into violence. Maimonides is a special case: coming from the Muslim West with its stern mores, he was dismayed by the easygoing manners of Fatimid Egypt, and since "idleness leads to lewdness" (repeatedly quoted by him), he took a particularly hard stance—unwarranted by the law—with regard to a woman who refuses to do her household chores (which were mandatory).

In order to understand the situation we must keep in mind that the newlywed wife was usually a mere teenager, who by nature was disposed to be stubborn and even "impudent" (as one letter has it). The husband, to the contrary, who had to work a considerable time to make a livelihood and to earn all or part of the marriage gift, was already hardened by life. Since the stick was a legitimate instrument of education, a husband was easily disposed to use it for the correction of a spouse who, to him, was still just a child. Even a man like the court clerk, cantor, and teacher Solomon, son of the judge, Elijah, scores of whose records are preserved in the Geniza, is scolded by a relative for having behaved in this way against his teen-age wife.[124]

Usually, complaints about wife-beating were made, when there was deep discord between the spouses, mostly about their common or respective possessions, but also about other matters. The wretched woman whose petition to Maṣlīaḥ, the Head of the Jewish community in Egypt (1127–1138) is translated below, is a case in point. The note is beautifully written, probably by a schoolboy, just as she dictated it to him in straightforward Arabic vernacular, similar to that spoken today.

In the n(ame of the) All (merciful)

May God grant peace to our master and teacher Maṣlīaḥ ha-Kohen, the Head of the yeshiva "the Pride of Jacob,"[125] *may his rule endure forever.*

Your maidservant has been married to this one for fifteen[126] years, and has never received from him a thing, not even a piece of silver for going to the bathhouse; he bought me no clothing, not even a cap, and I complain about vexations and beating. He keeps saying to me: "Buy your freedom [by renouncing the marriage gift]"—may God punish him for what he is doing[127] to me. He must pay me my marriage gift; fifteen years I have been suffering by his bad character and his vexations. Now I throw myself upon God and upon you. I am a captive. Free me.[128]

The Gaon, like many a caliph and sultan, held a public audience; the woman would appear in person, hand over the note to an attendant, whereupon the Gaon would send a cantor or another lower religious dignitary to the house to examine the matter and, if necessary, order a court action. Clearly the complaint about beating was secondary to the woman's general unhappiness with a husband unwilling or unable to provide for her properly.

By chance, four other such complaints have been preserved from the same period. Two deal with financial matters. A woman, also belonging to the poorest section of the community, had inherited something from her father; according to Jewish law, the estate becomes the personal property of the wife and is not to be included in the dowry brought in at the marriage; the husband obviously thought otherwise, and the couple quarreled; the court formally enjoined him not to beat or to curse his wife, but to honor her and to provide her with everything she could rightfully claim; whether or not a fine was imposed on him for relapse is not evident because the document is fragmentary.[129]

A similar case in which misunderstandings about the nature of the wife's personal property led to strife, wife-beating, and court action, is described below.[130]

A complete story of domestic trouble is recorded on the reverse side of a beautifully written and completely preserved ketubba, now in the Bodleian Library, Oxford. The virgin 'Amā'im ("Turbans," meaning "Ruler over the turbans," that is, over the menfolk) married in May 1128, and received as immediate marriage gift 5 gold pieces, while the late installment was fixed at 25 dinars. She brought in a dowry worth 46 dinars; thus these were lower middle class people, but by no means destitute. Being an orphan and probably also a working woman, she was dismayed when she discovered that, as a married woman, she no longer had a free hand over her own belongings. A fight erupted and after four and a half years, in January 1133, as reported in the court record occupying the entire reverse side of her marriage contract, her husband returned the dowry to her (with the exception of a few household items, such as a lamp and a bucket), granting her complete disposition to do with them as she liked. She, on her side, exempted him from any further responsibility for these valuables, while he promised to keep good companionship with her, not to beat her, and, of course, to pay the late installment of the marriage gift in full.[131]

Two other relevant court records, presided over by the same judge and written by the same clerk as the one just discussed, have been summarized on previous occasions, and other documents referring to wife-beating are known.[132]

Women from strong families did not acquiesce in the brutish behavior of their husbands; they simply ran away. Then it was up to the husband to show contrition and humbly to try to get her back. Three such cases, each from a different century and situation, conclude this unsavory topic.

In the first a cantor and Kohen confesses to have beaten and cursed his wife and to have falsely accused her of filching money and utensils from his house. He recanted completely, promised to mend his ways, and formally undertook to pay her the late installment in full and to set her free in case he relapsed.[133]

A similar agreement was made under very special circumstances about a century later, in September 1252. The husband, a man from Damascus living in the capital of Egypt, had been guilty of insulting, cursing, and beating his wife and was forced to divorce her. The first six lines of the bill of repudiation had already been written. Then well-meaning elders intervened, the husband promised to reform, and in case he relapsed, the witness of one man, an almoner and public figure known from other documents, would be sufficient to prove him guilty. The total of the wife's late installment and dowry amounted to 70 dinars. The court record dating the story is written on the reverse side of the bill of repudiation.[134]

The only example of wife-beating known to me as occurring in a better middle class family is recorded, as in our first example, in the form of a strongly worded declaration of repentance by the husband. The left half of the document, and with it the date, are lost, but the handwriting of the clerk known from several dated documents puts it around 1100. Here is an abridged translation, shortening in particular the legal verbiage:

> Write down what I tell you, sign the document, and give it to my wife Sitt al-Dār ["Lady of the House"], daughter of Solomon: I declare herewith before you, out of my free will, etc., that should I ever travel away from my wife without her consent, or [marry] another [wife] as long as she is with me, or beat her, or harm her otherwise, I have to pay 40 dinars as a vow and donation to the two synagogues in Fustat in equal shares, I, Abraham b. Hananel.
>
> We wrote it down, signed, and gave the document to Sitt al-Dār b. Solomon.
>
> When no one is between them, [the proof of innocence] is on him. Confirmed.

It is easy to reconstruct what happened here. The husband wished to go abroad (or, at least, to Alexandria, for instance) and to take his wife with him. As usual, she did not agree to leave the capital, where most probably her family lived. Then he threatened to marry another woman in the new place, a hollow threat, since the Jewish authorities would not have permitted him to do so. Finally, the altercation got out of hand.[135] The man, from the important al-Amshāṭī ("Maker of Combs") family, is known from a contemporary document and may well have been a brother of Joshua b.

Hananel b. Abraham al-Amshāṭī who donated the beautiful woodwork in the Geniza synagogue which is still extant.[136]

The accusation of wife-beating is usually paired with that of cursing her and calling her names. Verbal insult was viewed as damaging and degrading as physical attack. Several Arabic words were used for this misdeed; I have never found a Hebrew term for it in the Geniza. Beating and cursing wives must have been a lesser social evil in late antiquity than it was in the Middle Ages.[137]

The absent husband.—Absence from the house of one of the two spouses, mostly, of course, of the husband, was the family problem represented in the Geniza documents more than any other. The material on this topic is vast, sufficient to fill a volume. Engagement and marriage contracts, though, make less mention of it than one would expect.[138] For practical reasons I am treating the subject under two headings, being aware that the dividing lines cannot always be drawn with precision: first, absence occasioned by economic necessity or troubles, or by other reasons not directly connected with the mutual relationship of the spouses; second, absences related to marital strife, neglect, and desertion.

Traders, big and small, were forced by the very nature of their occupation to travel frequently and often for prolonged periods, and even craftsmen, as well as professionals, such as physicians, scholars, teachers, and cantors, often had to seek their livelihoods outside their hometowns. To the material on this aspect of Mediterranean society, assembled in *Med. Soc.*, I, 47–59, numerous other pages of this book provide illustrations, and additional information is contained in the texts subsequently discussed. Agreements made before the undertaking of a voyage stated the frequency and duration of the periods of absence and foresaw arrangements for the maintenance and other expenses of the family back home. In the case of extended travel, especially overseas, a conditional bill of divorce set the wife free if her husband failed to return at the date agreed upon. Some other stipulations, in particular safeguards for the security of the dowry and other obligations toward the wife, were included in such settlements, which, it seems, were made in court (and, thus, come to our knowledge) mostly when previous experience with the husband was not propitious.[139] Letters, legal opinions, and court records tell us how such arrangements and agreements worked.

Commercial travel to the Rīf, the Egyptian countryside, or, rather, to provincial towns, was one of the common occupations of the lower sectors of the capital's population. This court record shows how it looked from the wife's point of view. The husband had to stay at home two weeks, the period left free by the Jewish laws of purity for intimate relations during a month. He was not permitted to absent himself for more than a month, during which he had to pay his wife her expenses every week. Failing to do so, he had to deliver to her the final marriage gift immediately and in full. She promised "to attend to her house and her work and not to go out." In case of contravention she faced divorce.[140]

When the husband traveled overseas it was also customary to set a limit to the time he could absent himself. In July (Tammūz) 1045 a native of Barqa (Benghazi, Libya) appeared with his wife before a notary in Fustat and received permission from her to be away until the forthcoming Passover (April). Moreover, he empowered the notary to write a bill of divorce and to deliver it to her in case he did not return in time.[141] This instrument of precaution, used by both Muslim and Jewish courts, has already been referred to more than once.[142] It seems that even at the beginning of the twelfth century, a statute was in force in the Jewish community of Fustat which made such an arrangement obligatory.[143] How it worked, may be learned from this passage in the letter of a trader who had suffered shipwreck, got stuck in Sicily, and was prevented from returning to Egypt by a state of war in the Mediterranean:

> If she accepts the divorce, I shall send every year the alimony for the boy. But if she prefers not to accept it, deal with this matter discreetly in a way deserving my thanks: ask her whether she is prepared to settle with me in Sicily. [In case she does], let her confirm this by oath and inform me accordingly. I shall then sell my place and bring her here together with my boy. By God, I did not write her the bill of divorce because I hated her, but because I was afraid of the punishment of the Creator [that is, a violent death].[144]

In many instances it was not practicable to fix a term for the husband's absence, particularly when the husband moved to another place to try to establish himself there and left his wife and children back in the family home until he was sure of the success of his new venture. That must have happened frequently, for we often find situations where a husband lives in one town and his family in another, to be visited by him from time to time. Here is an agreement made in Tyre, Lebanon, in the fall of 1102. Jerusalem had been conquered by the Crusaders in July 1099. Tyre, then the greatest port city on the Lebanese coast, was to be their next target, although it was not until 1124 that it finally surrendered. Under those circumstances it is easy to understand why a merchant who could afford it tried to move to the capital of Egypt.

These were the conditions imposed on our husband who wanted to go from Tyre to Fustat: Every month the wife received three waybas [about twelve gallons] of wheat, together with the cost of its grinding; a Shāmī [Syro-Palestinian] pound of oil [for food and lighting; this pound weighed about six times as much as the Egyptian or present-day American pound]; also wood for fuel, and, per week, 20 dirhems (of local issue), worth one-sixth of a dinar, plus one-half of a qīrāṭ (see below). To these economic stipulations were added social safeguards. The wife was given exclusive use of the upper floor of the house, which she had occupied with her husband and his parents, and "her father-in-law and his wife" had to move downstairs to the middle story and were not to intrude on her. She would get someone to stay with her and to serve her. The husband's parents were not to interfere with visitors calling on her and, when speaking of her parents, were always to mention them with the blessing due the dead [such as "may he rest in Eden"]. This agreement was to be in force "even for a hundred years" until the husband asked her in writing to join him in his new domicile or came in person to fetch her. Since a fragment of the marriage contract of that woman has been found in the Geniza, it is likely that her husband fulfilled his promise and brought her, indeed, to Egypt.[145]

The exchange rate of local issues was extremely unstable and its equivalent therefore had to be fixed in gold. The strange sum of one-sixth of a dinar plus one-half of a qīrāṭ as payment for one week, if multiplied by four, results in three quarters of a dinar, a monthly alimony found elsewhere in settlements made with absentee husbands, in one case, together with 3 waybas of wheat.[146]

In the agreements made between lower class spouses, the wife's earnings were an important factor. I translate a short court record from September 1133, regarding a native of Caesarea, Palestine, probably a craftsman:

Abu 'l-Faraj b. Ghazāl al-Qaysarānī appeared in court and pledged—of his own free will, without any coercion—to pay to his wife, Mawadda ("Love"), the mother of his children, 20 dirhems a month, in installments of 5 dirhems per week, together with 2 waybas of good wheat and the cost of grinding it. For her part, she pledged to pay, out of these 20 dirhems, his poll tax, the rent for their apartment, and her household expenses. She would not claim anything from him in addition to this, after he had paid her that sum through the court; nor would he lay any claim to her earnings from work or spinning, not even as much as a penny. The two were in full agreement about this, and the symbolic purchase [sealing any legal action] was made in the established way.[147]

A question addressed to Moses Maimonides (late twelfth century) tells of a husband who went away without assigning anything to his wife and mother of his children except her own earnings and the rent of a house forming a part of her dowry, both legal sources of income for the husband. The wife found she could not manage and incurred a debt, and, in addition, claimed that the rent was hers.[148]

To avoid ambiguities, an India trader setting out for Yemen states explicitly that the income derived by his wife from a house was hers, since he had sold it to her. The agreement shows how well-to-do people arranged their affairs. The wife received for herself, her two daughters (still small children), and a maidservant 25 dinars per year plus 5 irdabbs of wheat (equivalent of 30 waybas, or about 120 gallons). This tallies with the 30 dinars per year and 12 irdabbs of wheat assigned to another woman (with a small boy) of the same class.[149] In addition, however, the wife of the India trader received her late marriage gift, which amounted to 60 dinars (actually she got only 55 with 5 remaining as a debt against the husband), and her dowry, which was evaluated at 400 dinars or more (the tens and single digits are lost). Naturally, a new marriage contract had to be drawn up. The only date on the incompletely preserved document is that of the original ketubba, summer 1157, but another document, a conditional bill of repudiation, given by the same husband to the same wife before setting out on a journey in summer 1169 (and written by the same scribe), probably coincided in time with the financial arrangements just discussed. The bill of repudiation included a clause for the girls: the father's obligations were binding also in regard to any of them.[150]

When a year had passed after an absence agreement had been drawn up, the wife had to confirm before witnesses that she had received all due her. This was done both for the protection of the husband and of the relative or business friend who had made the actual payments. In one document the wife declares that she received from her husband all the food, clothing, [drinking] water, oil, and rent he owed her and her children for twelve months.[151] When no formal settlement had been arranged before the husband's departure or when he absented himself longer than provided for, the courts intervened, although reluctantly, and assigned alimony to the wife according to her social status. In summer 1126 a wife with a daughter received 20 dirhems per month (no wheat or other matters mentioned), "the absolute minimum," as the document states.[152] In a case from approximately the same period, where the husband stayed away longer than expected, the wife received payment for service, "since she was of fine people, who stay at home."[153]

Merchants, professionals, and craftsmen of the middle and lower classes, while setting out on a journey, hoped to be able to sustain their families at home from the profits made while abroad. How this was realized is illustrated in my *Letters of Medieval Jewish Traders*, pp. 249–251, and in messages of travelers specifying the items sent and how to use them.[154] Many times, however, their hopes were not realized. The letters in which husbands excuse themselves for tarrying longer than planned, or for sending only part of the allocations promised, or nothing at all, are legion. Unemployment, mishaps, danger on the roads, or failure of the friends back home to live up to their promises were the usual reasons given. "I have not left a thing for the children," observes a merchant abroad ruefully, asking a business friend to look after his family.[155] When Mevōrākh b. Nathan, the scribe so often mentioned in this book, came home from a journey, he found the house stripped of everything, "not even a mouse could find something to eat," because the friend who had undertaken to provide the family with wheat had himself gone on travel and forgotten to pass on his task to someone else.[156] A husband away in North Africa assures his wife that he has not forgotten her and vows not to wash his clothes, to cut his hair, to drink wine, or to enter a bathhouse before seeing her.[157] Another traveler tarrying away from home pledges to fast during daytime until he gets back.[158] Such vows, I am afraid, did not fill empty stomachs.

How the family at home managed is well illustrated in the letter translated below, written by a boy, proficient in Hebrew and Arabic scripts (sons of merchants were taught both), as dictated to him, no doubt, by his mother. The recipient, ʿAllān b. Ḥassūn, an India trader known from other Geniza records, had traveled to North Africa and had sent money home, but, for reasons not specified, it was not delivered to the family. The situation was aggravated by the absence of the only other adult male member of the household and by the costly and dangerous process of weaning an infant. Under the circumstances, the wife sold implements and furnishings and leased the upper floor of the house, which was occupied, when the menfolk were in.

In Your Name, oh All Merciful!

The letters of the Presence of my illustrious lord, my father, have arrived—may God make me his ransom from all evil and give him success and unite me with him in His kindness and mercy, if God will.

As to what you wish to know my lord: We [meaning, "I, your wife," plural of modesty, still used in Arabic speech] are in great distress, owing to bad health and loneliness. We have weaned the baby—do not ask me what we suffer from him: trouble, crying, sleepless nights, so much so that the neighbors—God is my witness—are complaining. We incur great expenses for him: the doctor, medicaments, and two chickens every day. We have sold the levers [see the note], the "swords,"[159] and the cupboard, and have let the upper floor; the proceeds, however, are really not sufficient for the baby's expenses and for what we also need. After all this, I hope [here the wife becomes informal], he will remain alive—God is my witness, you would be happy to look at him.[160] By God, do not tarry any longer. My eyes are lifted upon God, the exalted, and upon your return.

The dinars, sent by you from the West, have arrived, but nothing was given to us. Do not forget the beads for Zayn al-Dār ["The Ornament of the House"],[161] do not forget the maidservant. I [the boy speaks], kiss your hands, and so does my mother, my grandmother, my maternal aunts, the wife of my paternal uncle, and everyone in the house. It happened that both you and 'the elder'[162] departed simultaneously, so that we remained like orphans without a man."

Here the boy had come to the bottom of the page and could have continued overleaf, as was customary. Obviously, his mother asked him at this juncture to read out to her what he had written and, finding the letter unsatisfctory, dictated a new one. Thus, this sheet, instead of going to North Africa, remained in the house and, finally, landed in the Geniza. Before taking down the dictation, the boy had written: "To the Presence of my lord, the elder Abu 'l-Ḥasan 'Allān b. Ḥassūn—His son Zayn al-Dār, may he be his ransom!"[163]

Naturally, the opposite situation where the absent husband claims to have provided all the family needs and asserts that complaints to the contrary were mere calumny, is also encountered. In an eloquent letter a traveler details all he had sent: 6 irdabbs of wheat (making 36 waybas per year, or 3 per month, as so often reported up to now), 4 "gold dinars," and several smaller remittances in silver, totaling 51 dirhems; here one or two lines are lost, no doubt containing the remaining 30 or so dirhems which could make a grand total of 6 dinars, again half a dinar per month. The writer gets very excited. "I should neglect my wife?!" he exclaims, adding: "Has not God said [Proverbs 11:17]: 'He who wrongs his flesh [meaning: wife, Genesis 2:23] is a cruel one?!" and, quoting Proverbs 22:23, he invokes God to punish those who give him a bad reputation.[164] One traveler even asserted that his wife had been given too much and told the addressee, a close relative, that he would sue him for the balance.[165]

The runaway husband.—An orderly absence, carefully prepared by notarial agreements written before departure and made bearable by correspondence while away on travel, differed substantially from those innumerable instances where the husband vanished, leaving the family without sufficient support, or no support at all, and without knowledge of his whereabouts and doings. Such disappearances occurred when the husband was unable or unwilling to maintain his family, or defaulted in paying his debts to private creditors or the tax collector, or both, or fled for personal reasons, such as a danger forcing him to go underground, conflicts with his wife, or, simply, "because he found someone"—usually a slave girl—"more beautiful than her."

"Your brother quarrels with his wife. He went on a journey, and no one knows whereto he traveled." The casual way in which this tragedy is reported (in a letter sent, in Sept. 1212, by a learned cantor in Alexandria to an even more eminent colleague in Fustat) shows how common such occurrences must have been. When such situations arose, the authorities intervened, trying to find the fugitive, bring him to court, induce him to return to his family, or, at least, to send those at home what was due them. Failing all this, a court would force him, by threat of excommunication, to write his wife a bill of repudiation, thus redeeming her from an intolerable bond. But usually this was a very protracted affair: until the wife and her family made up their minds to publicize their troubles by suing the culprit; until the authorities acted; until trustworthy and concerned travelers were found, who were prepared to carry the messages to the relevant localities; until the courts approached took action; and finally, until the husband put into effect what he had been induced or forced to do. Even then it could happen that a court record or a bill of divorce, or another vital document, or a consignment of money, got lost or otherwise did not reach its destination.[166]

Many examples are represented in the Geniza. This social evil was rampant in the lower and lowest ranks of society, but not entirely absent from the higher echelons.

Absenteeism of the husband could occur even when he was still in town. I have read about one, who, after physically mistreating his wife, promised, among other things, "not to hide as if he were a runaway,"[167] In an appeal to the community, translated below, a woman asserts that her husband never stays overnight at home.[168] These were people from the slums. But we also have an extraordinary letter of a wife to her husband whom she described as "a man of perfect character and high social rank"; a letter written in excellent script and style, possibly by herself, but reflecting a situation not dissimilar to the one just mentioned. The young husband was angry that he had to live in her family's house and also had to pay rent. Probably the engagement contract had not stated that detail with sufficient clarity. In order to force the issue, he stayed away, coming home only for the Sabbath—when his absence could have led to a lawsuit, since love on the Sabbath night was the wife's legal right. She writes that the rent could be returned and that she was prepared to move with him to another place, for she had learned from the warning example of her sisters (who obviously had had trouble with their husbands for similar reasons). But, she added, she went on a hunger strike (more exactly: she would not eat during daytime), until the matter was settled. She wrote the letter after the wayward husband had once absented himself even on the Sabbath. On the reverse side a hasty answer is written: "If you do not break your fast, I shall come neither on the Sabbath nor on any other day."[169]

A father who was aware of the tension between his daughter and her husband sensed that he was intent on desertion and posted a guard at the gate of the city. The fugitive was captured and brought to court together with his belongings which he had tried to take away with him.[170]

The young man to whom the following missive, a mixture of an official summons to court and a fatherly admonition, is addressed, probably did not get very far either:

> My boy, Bu 'l-Makārim ("Man of Noble Deeds"), Moses b. Ezekiel, (may) G(od) k(eep you). The very moment you read these lines come to court and do not tarry even for a single hour. If you will be late in returning to town, you will get a heavy fine from our lord [the Head of the community], for you left before we [the court] settled your wife's claim that you have taken away her silver. Also, you still owe her 13 dirhems from the alimony stipulated, as well as the total alimony of your daughter, from the day you left to this very day. You cannot eat and drink while those committed to your care go hungry. Where are you and where is God?!
>
> Nathan ha-Kohen b. Salomon, (may he) r(est in) Eden.[171]

The full misery of a woman tormented by repeated desertions of her husband is revealed in this story of Hayfā' ("Slender Wisp"), daughter of Sulaymān Ibn al-'Arīq ("Man with Deep Roots," of noble descent), native of Acre (Akko) in the Holy Land. After she had been forsaken by everyone, her husband and her own family, she begged her way to the Egyptian capital, where she hoped to receive material as well as legal support. She gives the impression of a fighter rather than of a woman in despair. This is a slightly abbreviated version of her complaint, addressed to the head of the Jerusalemite congreation in Fustat:

> I am a poor foreigner reporting what I had to endure from my husband, Sa'īd b. Mu'ammar ("Lucky, son of Long-lived"), the silk weaver. He left me pregnant and traveled away. [No mention of a birth is made here.] Then he came back and stayed a while until I was with child. He left me again, I delivered a boy and took care of him until he was a year old, whereupon Sa'īd came back. Then there was that incident with Ibn al-Zuqilliya,[172] who drove us out of our place. We arrived in Jaffa, where Sa'īd abandoned me, leaving me alone in a town where I was a stranger. Thus I was forced to get back to my family. From them, however, I suffered their hard words which only God knows. I decided to leave and, uncovering my face [that is, living on public charity], I finally arrived here, where I learned that Sa'īd had come to Malīj, where a brother of his lives. I went there, but was told that he had returned to Shām [the Holy Land]. I ask you now to write to someone there who would induce him to have compassion on me and my child; for the boy is now like an orphan; anyone looking at him has compassion with him and blames his father. If he responds, fine; otherwise, have him set me free. I do not blame him. I call upon God as judge, day and night. I am now looking forward to the action to be taken by you and ask God to accept my prayers for you in his mercy.[173]

A sequel to this complaint seems to be preserved in a letter sent from Malīj to the successor of the judge whom "Slender Wisp" had addressed. The letter is hopelessly mutilated, but enough is evident from it to indicate that the husband was expected to be in Acre (Akko) or Tyre, that a bill of divorce had been lost, court records could not be found, and that the issue at stake was a boy, three and a half years old, for whom the father should either send support or arrange to be taken under his care. The question of children from broken marriages is treated in C, 3 and 4.[174]

We are in a better position with regard to two other documents related to our topic and showing people commuting between Egypt and the Holy Land. They concern a man called Hiba ("Gift," Heb. Nathan) of Fustat, son of Israel the Lame, who lived in Ramle, Palestine, and was separated from his wife, who had remained in Egypt. On Sunday, August 7, 1065, he appeared before an assembly of twelve notables in Ramle (all signing the document concerned) and declared that he was well aware that they disapproved of his staying without his wife. In view of this he appointed a representative traveling to Egypt who was supposed to induce his wife to join him and to accompany her on her expected trip to the Holy Land.[175] What actually happened is evident from a letter from Ramle, written several years later by Eli I ha-Kohen b. Ezekiel I, a scholar from whose hand many papers are extant.[176] The Egyptian wife, as usual, refused to leave the country; Hiba was forced to divorce her, took as wife a daughter of Eli I, and had two or more children with her. But the times were catastrophic. Palestine was overrun by Seljuks and Turkomans. Tyre was surrounded, and no one could travel even from Jerusalem to Ramle. This was no time for a merchant to stay in the country. Hiba returned to Egypt, leaving his wife and children with his father-in-law, but without providing for them. Two years had passed without his having sent even 1 dirhem, when, as Eli mournfully remarks, it would have been his duty to support them (as hungry residents of the Holy Land), even if they were not his children. Nor was Ramle cut off from Egypt. In the same letter Eli conveys to his son-in-law the advice (to be transmitted to him by the recipient of the letter) to send his flax not via Jaffa where it would be seized by the commander of the Fatimid army, but through Ascalon. Thus it was not lack of communications which prevented Hiba from providing for his family; it was neglect.[177]

In the preceding, the term "Holy Land" was used repeatedly because the wish to settle there on account of its holiness was often a cause of separation—or served as an excuse for those who wished to get rid of their families. Because of the constant anarchy life in the country was almost unbearable. In one of his most beautifully styled letters the Gaon Solomon b. Judah, writing from Jerusalem, tells about a scholar of a noble family who had settled in the Holy City, and had left his wife in Egypt because he wanted to make sure first that he could establish himself there with the means at his disposal. After this was assured, he had sent for his wife, but was not successful. Now the Gaon appeals to a confidant to approach the woman, who was of a fine family, beloved by her husband and loving him. "She should not say 'how can I leave my native country and the house of my father and travel to a place where I do not know what will happen to me,' but should rely on God and come."[178] In a letter written in June 1016, long before he became Gaon, Solomon had to report about another settler in Jerusalem whose Egyptian wife was not prepared to follow him, but did not accept his conditions for a divorce.[179]

No wonder that such a situation served as a pretext for desertion. The cases described above are complemented here by a few telling examples. In spring 1015 a woman in Ramle appoints a representative to sue her Damascene husband who had disappeared two years before without leaving her anything; she was prepared to renew their common life, or else demanded a divorce, with all the payments involved, including the cost of maintenance for two years.[180] Another Damascene husband, who had settled in the Holy Land (as the text says) and went bankrupt in Ramle, was sued by his Egyptian wife, whose attorney, appointed in Fustat, was to extract alimony from him for the year of desertion, 20 dinars as delayed marriage gift, and a bill of divorce (summer 1024).[181] More tragic was this story told in an almost poetic letter of a Gaon, perhaps also Solomon b. Judah. A woman deserted by her husband for many years had brought up an only son and when he was old enough had sent him out to find his father. But the boy perished on his way. Along with attempts at consolation the Gaon refers to a debt of 300 dinars and losses incurred by the recipient of his letter (whose name is not preserved.) These details, together with the style of the letter, which required a thorough knowledge of Hebrew language and literature, proves that they were upper middle class people.[182]

Solomon b. Judah's own family was not spared its share of misery. One of his daughters was married in Jerusalem to a man of a fine Egyptian family, who was far more advanced in age than she. The man left her and the country. In the beginning he contributed to her maintenance. But at the time the Gaon writes again about this, three years had already passed without any communication from the husband. The Gaon's son, sent after him to Egypt and addressing him and his brother, "the notable," was not successful in persuading him to return to his wife. The Gaon, being the highest juridical authority, found himself in an embrassing position. "They say to me 'you take care of everyone's suits, why do you not take up the case of your daughter?' " Nor was he more successful with another son-in-law: after having spent his wife's dowry (how is not said), he died leaving her with two daughters and a boy. Thus the aged Gaon, as he writes, had "five women in the house," and this in years of famine and constant warfare.[183] The question of how strictly a wife was obliged to follow her husband to the Holy Land, and vice versa, is discussed in detail in the Talmud and reflected in Geniza documents.

Several cases presented above are marked by the length of time husbands were away from home without contacting their families. Many more such instances are reported, and some deserve mention because of special circumstances involved. A woman in Damascus, a mother of four, had been deserted for three years by her husband, a Karaite turned Rabbanite, who was believed to be living in the capital of Egypt.[184] A communal official is reprimanded by a religious leader because his sister's son had forsaken his wife for seven years; it was the official's responsibility to have that matter set right; otherwise he could hardly serve as a model for the community. We remember the special relationship between a man and his sister's son.[185] When a man died in India after a sojourn there of nine years, he left a wife and a girl of eleven, which means that his wife must have been comparatively young during that long period of absence.[186] Another India traveler did not write home for ten years, and the question was asked whether his wife was permitted ("since the times were so bad") to marry another man. The husband had become a Muslim and before setting out for India, his wife had demanded a divorce, but he refused, arguing that he would come back soon. The Muslim judge to whom this question was addressed apparently referred it back to a Jewish court, for a Jewish wife whose husband embraced another religion cannot marry without having received a bill of divorce from him drawn up according to Jewish law.[187] I have already remarked in *Med. Soc.*, I, 58, that a father-in-law addresses a deserter absent for twenty-three years as though he had been away for only twenty-three weeks.

Even more remarkable is this story of reconcilation. A man had stayed away from his wife for eighteen years "like a runaway," that is, he did not let her know about his whereabouts and never sent her a thing. During the entire period she maintained herself by her own efforts. When he finally came back, "worthy elders" made peace between them and they decided to be together "as before." The only thing the husband had to do was to write her a bill of debt that he owed her 100 dinars, which comes to about 6 dinars per year or half a dinar per month, the usual alimony for a wife among people with modest means. This is simple arithmetic. But one wonders how the wife had passed eighteen years during the prime of her life as "a widow while her husband was alive and not permitted to marry another man."[188]

Thus far, our attention has been centered on the deserted wife. What about the neglected children? There was little opportunity to mention girls since their education was entrusted to their mothers. But this silence should not be taken as an absence of fatherly feelings. We have read above the mournful words of a scholar from Byzantium separated from his wife and daughter by adverse circumstances.[189] Another man from that country stranded in Egypt writes that his thoughts were given to his only daughter day and night, while a Tunisian who was forced to repudiate his wife in Constantinople because he had left that city for good remarks somewhat casually: "Only an infant girl of mine has remained there."[190]

The situation was different with boys. The obligation to teach one's son was taken very seriously and looms large in the correspondence of absent fathers.[191] When tension prevailed between the traveler and his wife at home, he was particularly concerned about his son's education.[192]

An extraordinary example of this relationship is provided by a calligraphic letter from Damascus, presently preserved in the University Museum, Philadelphia. The time was the first quarter of the twelfth century, when the country was in complete turmoil because of the Seljuk devastations and the subsequent invasion by the Crusaders; prices were exorbitant. A scholarly scribe in Tyre, Lebanon, father of five, was one of the victims of the hard times. In order to feed his family he sold his wife's jewelry, his own better clothing and furnishings, his books and Bible codices, pawned other codices in order to borrow money, and took out other loans not covered by collateral. When everything was exhausted, he traveled to Damascus, where his scribal art had better prospects for success. This worked for some time, and he sent home whatever he could "for the kids." But the Damascus community was plagued by the ransom of captives, the most costly charity (see *Med. Soc.*, II, 137), and by inner dissension, indirectly caused by the constant state of war. Orders for the copying of books ceased, and other sources of income (such as doles to wandering scholars) were discontinued. Thirteen months had passed without our scribe having been able to send home any substantial contributions. In the face of such calamity he resolved to try his luck in the capital of Egypt, a city renowned for its opulence and charity. But now that he was intent on traveling to a remote country he wished to have his eldest son with him. The boy, no doubt in connivance with his father, escaped from the house of the grandfather, where the family lived, and had already reached Saida, Lebanon (about twenty miles north of Tyre), on his way to Damascus, when his mother sent after him and had him brought back. In the letter, which the scribe wrote to his father-in-law, he implies that the boy's mother was prepared to desecrate the Sabbath in order to prevent the boy from joining him because the day he was brought back was a rainy Friday in winter, close upon the beginning of the Sabbath. The mother understood, of course, that once the boy was with her husband, he would not be so eager to come home. In his ire, our scribe had vowed that unless the boy was sent to him he would never return to Tyre and would even repudiate his wife. In his meek and respectful letter to his father-in-law he regrets having made such a foolish vow, but brazenly demands the boy to be sent to him, for vows cannot be gainsaid. The reverse side of the letter is blank; it bears no address; it was never sent off. Its deposition in the Cairo Geniza shows that its writer made good his threat to emigrate to Egypt. Whether he was followed there by his boy or by his entire family, or by no one, we may perhaps learn some day. A calligraphic court record written by him in Tyre in fall 1102 has been discussed above.[193]

Except in the higher echelons of the Geniza society, where overseas marriages formed part of international mercantile policies, women, as a rule, were not prepared to follow their husbands to a foreign country, as we have come to learn earlier in this chapter. It is astounding, though, that the dangers of travel are almost never invoked as an excuse. This passage from an unfortunately very much damaged letter sent from Tunisia to Egypt is an exception confirming the rule: "Your wife came to me to consult me whether she should travel to your place. She is undecided, since her brothers disapprove of her leaving. Then your letter to the elder Abu 'l-Faḍl arrived, in which you express apprehension that the sea voyage might be dangerous for them [Abu 'l-Faḍl and his company], knowing their state. If *you* are afraid, what do you expect from women? I made this suggestion to her: I shall send. . . ." Here the manuscript has a hole. At the end of the letter, as usual, the writer recapitulates: "If it is right with you that she comes, she will come. It depends entirely on your decision. Do not rely on my advice. Of course, the choice is in the hand of God [meaning, that men's decisions are reached by God's decree]." Clearly, some extraordinary circumstances made a sea voyage at that time inexpedient. The Geniza women were as assiduous travelers as their menfolk. It was not the dangers to be incurred on a journey which made wives reluctant to join their distant husbands.[194]

What could happen to a wife moving with her husband to a foreign country is well illustrated in three lengthy documents, all referring to a woman of true valor, a mother of three, who had emigrated from Qayrawān, Tunisia, to Egypt. She was the daughter of a physician and he a scion of a prominent family of merchants and scholars, originating from Msila (today in Algeria), called al-Jāsūs ("The Spy"). Both husband and wife bore the name "Happy" (he, Surūr, she, Surūra), but their marriage, at least after their arrival in Egypt, did not bear out such auspicious nomenclature. Surūr separated from his family; but before he was able to leave Egypt, he was brought to court by Surūra, in Fustat on Sunday, February 10, 1040. Three questions had to be settled: her delayed marriage gift, a balance from her dowry (the lion's share had already been salvaged by her), and maintenance for the time the family had been deserted. Her delayed marriage gift was exceptionally high: 200 dinars; the balance of the dowry amounted to 100 dinars. The husband was unable to produce such sums, and instead, sold her the upper story of a mansion in Qayrawān, which he had inherited from his father, worth 295 dinars, leaving him with a debt to her of only 5 dinars.[195] In another document, also made out in Fustat, Surūra sold that apartment to a man from Gabes, Tunisia.[196] For the maintenance expenses Surūra was ceded one half of a bill of debt given in Qayrawān to her husband's father by a merchant from Alexandria in summer 1029, clearly a bad debt. She presented that bill to the court in Fustat with the request to have it collected in Alexandria. Surūra's trouble with her insolvent husband recalls the Arab maxim "when a Jew goes bankrupt, he searches the old account books of his father." Anyhow, they show the risks incurred by a wife leaving her native city for a foreign country.[197]

Actions in court, then as today, were excruciating, and especially with regard to runaway husbands. A woman in Alexandria who had been deserted by her husband appointed her brother as her attorney. Accompanied by the two witnesses to this arrangement the brother traveled to Fustat where he appointed a cantor and clerk of the court as his sister's permanent representative. The sequence of this case, which started in the fall of 1039, is not yet known.[198] Similar appointments of attorneys going from Alexandria to Fustat, and even from Fustat to Cairo, are known.[199] Three documents illustrate the tribulations of the Tunisian Sittūna ("Little Lady") b. Ḥayyīm al-Raḥbī, who had been left as a grass widow in Egypt for years. Her husband, known from a sizable business transaction carried out between Fustat and Qayrawān, had partly sold and partly pawned her jewelry so that she was in dire distress. Finally he turned up in Spain, where a Fustat welfare official, who happened to travel to that country, was to take up her cause. "Little Lady" had become so poor at that time that the clerk who made out the power of attorney given by her to the traveler noted that he took no fee for the service.[200]

How frustrating the search for a runaway could be even within a country is brought home by the correspondence between authorities on one case. A woman in Alexandria, whose husband had fled his creditor and gone to the capital, complained that she had been deserted for a long time, that she had to maintain herself and a little girl (with special needs, it seems), to pay rent, and on top of this, was sued in court by the creditor of her husband. The

Alexandrian authorities, in the most polite terms, address their masters, the judges in Fustat, to do a pious deed by approaching the chief judge for action in this matter. On the reverse side of the document and referring to it, the judge Samuel notifies the Nagid, or head of the Jewish community, that he had sent several summons to the man, but since both the High Holidays (approx. September) and Hanukka (approx. December) had passed without response from him, sterner measures were now required, and, to the judge's dismay, the Nagid had to be troubled. The matter was of utmost seriousness since the Alexandrian wife asserted that her husband had married another woman and was living with her in Cairo. Clearly, the police now had to be instructed to bring the man to court by force. But only the Nagid, as official representative of the state, was authorized to give that order.[201]

The most frightful aspect of this dark side of family life in Geniza times was the constant menace of the vanishing husband, leaving his wife a grass widow, socially and psychologically, a cripple. Even a scholar and succesful lecturer, the writer of the first of the three letters translated at the end of this subsection, is not ashamed to conclude his assertions of love and yearnings with the threat to abscond to a foreign country. Still more astounding is the fact that persons addressing the highest authorities have the cheek to speak openly of their intentions. In a letter to a Nagid written in Arabic characters the writer describes himself as indebted and unable to support his family of six "in these bad times"; "the knife has reached the bone," and if the Nagid does not help, he will flee and travel away, "and the little ones will die of hunger."[202]

If we can empathize with that cry for help, we are revolted by this letter of a Karaite scholar to "King Ḥisday," the head of his community. It is in the form of a request for a legal opinion, but in substance is a demand to be granted a divorce with payment of the marriage gift in installments (which, in fact, meant never completely). Reasons given: in the first place, he had been forced to marry his wife and had done so under duress. Moreover, he had suffered from her bad character and mean deeds for three years, which were to him like twenty, and he hated her. All this was topped by the arrival in Alexandria, where the couple lived, of his mother-in-law. If his demand was not granted, he would travel to a faraway country, never to see his wife again, and she would remain deserted for all her life. The Arabic letter concludes with a Hebrew quotation: "I have demolished my house, its stones and beams, and gone to foreign parts, never to return."[203]

I crave the indulgence of the reader for having tormented him with so many pictures of human misery. But I feel that only actual situations, each different from the other, are able to convey a full idea of the devastation caused by the phenomenon of the runaway husband. Clearly the society was incapable of dealing effectively with this problem, because it was bound by an ancient law, which appeared to be the more God-given since it was in conformity with the social notions held by everyone in the wider environment.

Polygyny, levirate, and sororate.—Unlike absenteeism, polygyny or its threat was not a major trouble for wives. By custom, albeit not by law, the Geniza society was essentially monogamous. Our discussion of the relevant stipulations in the marriage contracts has resulted in this observation.[204] Threats to the effect that a husband might take another wife were not entirely absent, but they were rare, and, one has the impression, not taken too seriously.[205] Since polygyny was legal, though, it could create situations not very dissimilar to "triangles" commonplace in modern society, which is so different in law and outlook from that of Geniza times.

In December 1089 a man appeared in court in Fustat and told this story. He had quarreled with his wife, and the matter had ended in divorce, inclusive of the settlement of the financial matters involved. But he still had tender feelings for her and wished to keep her as a wife. Wishing to mollify her and also on behalf of their son, he assigned her monthly payments in cash and yearly deliveries of wheat for four years. The payments and deliveries were to be made through their son or in any other way she preferred. If, however, God ordained that she should agree to return to him, which he desired, the stipulation was void, since, as a husband, he was in any case obliged to maintain her. That December day of 1089 had a special signifiance for him; on that very day he married another wife.[206]

This document reveals the benefits of polygyny. We cannot know, of course, why the man chose to marry another woman. According to the notions of the society to which he belonged the most likely reason was that he wished to have more than one son, a desire that his aging wife was unable to fulfill. On the other hand, he hated to be separated from his lifelong companion, while she, understandably, was outraged by his decision. She too, he felt, would one day prefer sharing life with him in company of another woman rather than missing it altogether, also out of consideration for her son, who was apparently dedicated to father and mother alike. Although regarded as undesirable, under certain circumstances polygyny provided the frame for the regulation, however imperfect, of natural human relationships.

Some actual cases of bigamy are reported or referred to in legal documents as well as in letters found in the Geniza. The reasons given or implied were the wife's barrenness, proved after ten years of marriage, her being unfit for cohabitation, or inability to take care of her children because of insanity or other impediments, in which case the second wife undertook to look after them. There were also special circumstances lying outside the husband's power of decision: we have read about a government official who was obliged to have a family in Fustat, while his wife lived in Damascus, and there was, for Jews, the sacred obligation of the levirate, marriage to the widow of a brother who had died childless, see below. Very rarely does one read about a husband running away with another woman and marrying her against the orders of the authorities.[207]

The conditions under which a wife would agree to her husband's marriage to another woman were approximatly these: first, a separate, fully furnished, domicile from which nothing could be removed without her authorization; second, safeguards for all the rights stipulated in the marriage contract; there was even a case where the first wife was paid her delayed marriage gift with the condition to repay it if the second marriage was terminated; third, equal rights with regard to clothing, especially on weekends and holidays, and conjugal relations; finally the right to receive a divorce if she wished so.

A list of Levis, that is, persons regarded as belonging to the biblical tribe of Levi, contains this item: "Khalaf, the chicken dealer, has three sons: Ma'ānī etc.; their mother, "the daughter of the woman with the makeup," is Israelite (not a Levi). Ma'ānī has two wives; one is a freedwoman, from whom he has a daughter and a son; the second is the daughter of his maternal uncle, a son of the woman with the makeup. Ma'ānī has from her a son called Sa'īd." For reasons we cannot know, perhaps because she was still too young, Ma'ānī was unable to marry his cousin, as was customary. Meanwhile he took a freedwoman and had two children with her. But only his son from his own kin is called by name. The other obviously was not regarded as a Levi.[208]

These people might have belonged to a lower stratum of the society. But the family name Dajājī, chicken-dealer or -farmer, became common from the thirteenth century onward, and India traders bearing the name are known. One, Ma'ānī al-Dajājī, may even be identical with our bigamist, and another, Abū Sa'īd Levi b. Abu 'l-Ma'ānī al-Dajājī, might have been his son from his cousin, mentioned above, for in that late century they used Sa'īd and Abū Sa'īd indiscriminately.[209] If these identifications are correct, and there is little to be argued against them, the story of the bigamy is simple. Ma'ānī went off to India as a young man, and there bought, manumitted, and married a local girl. Years later, when he came home with his wife and children, he wished to have a son of his own. The daughter of his maternal uncle might even have waited for him. Sa'īd, the son from this second marriage, became an India trader like his father and reached the Coromandel coast of southeastern India.[210]

Be that as it may, our second story of bigamy certainly refers to a leading Jewish family in the Mediterranean area. The man, Mūsā (Moses) b. Jekuthiel the Andalusian, was most probably the son of the Spanish Maecenas of Hebrew letters, immortalized by the poems of (Solomon Ibn) Gabirol, for the name Jekuthiel is not found elsewhere in Geniza documents except as perpetuated by Mūsā's son and great-grandson. Mūsā was the father of Jekuthiel, better known as Abū Ya'qub al-Ḥakīm (the doctor), representative of the merchants in the Egyptian capital and one of its most prominent V.I.P.s during the last quarter of the eleventh century. The first Jekuthiel was executed in Spain in 1039, an end common to rich and influential people in those days and parts, and his son Mūsā left his native country and moved eastward, also usual in such cases. There, in Fustat, we find him signing a court record and being referred to in others in 1041 and 1043. In a letter from Jerusalem to his colleagues on the bench in the Egyptian capital, he writes about public and private affairs, about his meetings with the head of other members of the yeshiva, the central Jewish council, and about his intention to proceed to Tyre, Lebanon. In documents related to his son Mūsā is referred to as a physician (always in Hebrew, meant as an honorific title) but, like other physicians, he was involved in business, and might even have become conspicuous in that field like his renowned contemporary Abū Zikrī al-Ṭabīb ("the physician").[211]

We learn about Mūsā b. Jekuthiel's family on the occasion of his death, which was almost as violent as that of his father. A report about this event is included in a letter from the tiny Jewish community of the village, *ḍay'a*, of Qalhā, or Qalahā, situated on the canal connecting the fertile region of al-Fayyūm with the Nile (still existent).[212] The letter is addressed to "the" parnās, or social welfare officer, in Fustāt, no doubt Eli ha-Kohen b. Yaḥyā, with whose father Mūsā was closely connected.[213] During the pillage of Fayyūm, *nahb al-Fayyūm,* referred to in the letter as an event known to everyone, Mūsā had lost most of his belongings and had tried to escape with his family from the district. But on their way they were assaulted by bandits, stripped of their clothing and everything else, and badly manhandled. The dying Mūsā was visited in Qalhā by his son Abū Ya'qūb, the representative of the merchants, who, on his trip (whether from or back to the capital is not stated) also suffered indescribable hardships. After a month in the village, Mūsā died penniless. He had been accompanied by two wives, one from a noble Karaite family, by whom he had a daughter, and another, by whom he had a girl and a boy. A sister of the second wife had also traveled with them. Like their father the two girls died in the village, probably as a result of physical maltreatment. The noble woman, the letter goes on, could not be left in a place like Qalhā. Therefore the villagers had hired one of them to accompany her to Cairo where a paternal cousin of hers was a *kātib*, a government official, or to any other larger Jewish community. The boy, however, could not be sent (with his mother and aunt), since, as the letter states, he was in danger of sexual abuse from the Negro bands on the rampage in the country.[214]

We are here in the terrible time of famine and civil war, 1069–1072, when the rioting Sudani regiments had overrun most of upper Egypt, systematically destroying the country. It explains why Mūsā b. Jekuthiel lived with his family in the Fayyūm. The great famine, which started in 1065, hit the capital in particular, because it found itself mostly in a stage of siege owing to the clash of the various military factions; therefore people tried to find relief elsewhere, especially in a place like the fertile Fayyūm. I refrain from offering an explanation for Mūsā's bigamy because I have the feeling that further Geniza research will provide us with additional information about this important family. So much is evident from the letter summarized above that Mūsā's son Abū Ya'qūb Jekuthiel, the representative of the merchants, was not the son of any of Mūsā's two wives caught in Qalhā. Jekuthiel probably was born in Spain, and like many another man in his position, used the relations of his father with his native country to first represent the merchants from there until he became recognized as a leader by the community of merchants in general. What happened to his own mother we may learn some day.[215]

Getting permission to marry a second wife was a very complicated matter, as we learn from a letter written in Minyat Ghamr, a town in the Nile Delta. An unhappy husband pours out his heart.

His wife was ill; for twenty years he had suffered, and the major part of his life had already passed. Arriving from Jerusalem in Minyat Ghamr (which probably was his native town), he had found a suitable match for a second marriage. The local judge, who knew his story, had compassion for him, but did not dare to act in such a delicate matter. Our man went down to Alexandria to submit his case to the next higher legal authority, but Anatoli, the French rabbi who was in charge there, stalled. "You know his character and his 'dryness,' " the unhappy man writes. Meanwhile he had already contacted the highest authority, the chief judge Menaḥēm in Cairo, but was told he had to come up in person. He could not do so because he could not leave his newly opened store for the time required for such an undertaking. Therefore he asked the recipient, the future judge Elijah, to draw up a petition to the chief judge, which Elijah was able to do since he was familiar with the nature of the illness of the writer's wife and the hardships endured by her husband. Elijah, like the writer, had lived in Jerusalem. The illness probably was mental; it was next to impossible to repudiate an insane wife, since the repudiation had to be accepted by her. The writer understood that he would have to come up to Cairo for the wedding (which involved the drawing up of various legal documents in such a case); this shows that he was hopeful for the success of his plea. On the other hand, he asked Elijah to keep the matter secret, which seems to indicate that some hurdles were still ahead.[216]

When a man married a second wife without permission of the first and the approval of the authorities, he was liable to excommunication. How unpleasant an experience it could be might be learned from the story of an excommunicated husband who fled to Qūṣ in Upper Egypt, arriving there . . . with his original wife, as told in *Med. Soc.*, II, 333. Still, there must have been husbands hoping to escape the watchful eye of the authorities even while hiding with a second wife in the very capital of the country.[217]

Since polygyny is an ancient Middle East institution, both Arabic and Hebrew have a term for the rival wife, *ḍarra* (Heb. *ṣārā*), "trouble," "enemy." I searched the family papers of the Geniza for this word, but, thus far, have not been very successful. A mother who had accompanied her young daughter from the capital where she lived, to a provincial town, the daughter's domicile, informs her son in Fustat that his "little sister" was with child. In view of this, her son-in-law (she writes, of course, always, in accordance with the fine manners of the time, "your brother-in-law") did not keep his promise to bring the mother back to Fustat. When we arrive at the end of the letter, we understand the husband's reason. There she repeats: "Your sister is pregnant," and adds, "I cannot stand her being oppressed by the rival wife." The old story of Sarah and Hagar (Genesis 21:9–12): the oppression of the pregnant second spouse by the barren first. A woman from Byzantium, forsaken by her husband who was about to marry a local woman, writes: "Who is this woman that is prepared to enter a household with a rival wife and two daughters?"[218]

An important cause of bigamy in Geniza times was the levirate, the marriage of the brother-in-law to the wife of a brother who had died childless. In Islamic society, levirate was a custom, but only in Judaism, in that time and region, was it a law.[219] The surviving brother was free to refuse the marriage to his sister-in-law by undergoing the ceremony described in Deuteronomy 25:7–9. But first, the brother had to be found, and, second he had to be prepared to free the unhappy widow. Since many economic arrangements were connected with this: the widow's rights derived from her marriage contract, and the brother's prerogatives as the heir, endless chicanery and trouble could be endured by the widow before she was set free. Moreover, the surviving brother could be a child, a minor unable to perform a legal act; in this case the widow was forced to wait for years until anything could be done on her behalf. The Geniza contains considerable material about these matters.

The student of Islam is reminded of the koranic law prescribing that a husband cannot retake his wife after he had repudiated her unless she has concluded and consummated a marriage with another man. The law intended to protect the wife against a hasty repudiation, made in an hour of quarrel and anger. The intention was good, but the legal instrument created for its implementation was a disaster, a constant irritation and ailment of Islamic society. Similarly, the levirate marriage was well suited to the peasants' world of ancient Israel with brothers sitting together on a piece of land (Deuteronomy 25:5), where a widow had nowhere to go after the death of her husband. It became a monstrosity in the urban society of Geniza times. The Karaites were reasonable enough to outlaw the levirate altogether by applying to the relevant Bible passage the intricate methods of Islamic (Muʿtazilite) Koran interpretation.[220] The Rabbanite divines of Egypt ruled that the levirate did not override their antibigamy statute. In others words, if a man wished to marry the widow of his brother, he had first to divorce his wife and to pay all her dues; this attitude made levirate marriage destitute in practice. Moses Maimonides, however, decided that the levirate was a religious duty and, as such, takes precedence over all other considerations. Because of the great authority of the Master this decision prevailed, at least among Oriental Jews.[221]

In the early 1930s, when it was still possible, I made a painstaking case study of the levirate, then fully alive among the Jews of Yemen, great admirers and followers of Maimonides. I was astounded to learn to what length both partners to the levirate, the brother and the widow, went in order to fulfill a heavenly commandment, which seemed the more sacrosanct and meritorious the more senseless and harmful it was in practice.[222] Remembering that experience of mine I fancy that at least some of the persons about whose sufferings by an outdated law we read in the Geniza might have been indemnified and fortified by a similar religious posture. A number of cases of levirate marriage are described in the note.[223]

How the levirate entailed bigamy is impressively illustrated in a marriage agreement made between a Nagid, or head of the Jewish community of Egypt, and the widow of his brother, the Nagid who preceded him. This happened on June 5, 1482, near the end of the Mamluk period of Egyptian history, with which the office of the Nagid also came to an end. In accordance with Maimonides' ruling, Faraj ("Relief"), the widow of Yeshūʿā ("Salvation"), son of Joseph (who, too, had been a Nagid) married her brother-in-law Solomon under the usual conditions of equality between the two wives ("one night with this, one night with that") and the continuation of the prerogatives resulting from her former marriage contract. There was, however, an additional stipulation, necessitated by the office of the Nagid. At the yearly pilgrimage to the holy shrine of Dammūh the Nagid was, of course, accompanied by his wife. It was one of the rare occasions of her public appearance. Who of the two should be the companion? Here the wife of the former Nagid received some preference: not more than two days of the festive week was the new holder of that office to stay with his first spouse.[224]

The levirate—a man replacing his brother—was matched by the sororate, its female pendant. That a sister should take a dead wife's place was neither law nor custom. But the actual occurrence of those unions must have been frequent, if we are to judge from the casual way in which relevant actions are reported. Apparently it was regarded as natural for a father to give a daughter to a bereaved son-in-law, even when she had already been promised, engaged, or betrothed to another man. We have already read the bizarre story of the minor girl who was supposed to substitute for one elder sister who had died, and then for another.[225] Even more revealing is this report about prolonged litigations involving the Muslim authorities in Qayrawān, Tunisia. A girl had been betrothed to a youth still under his father's control (but not a minor), when her father learned that his future in-laws had suffered great losses in dealings with Rūm, probably Italians. In order to dissolve the connection, the father argued that his daughter did not like her future spouse, which, according to Qayrawānese Jewish (probably also Muslim) custom, was sufficient reason for demanding a divorce (as needed after a betrothal). The Jewish judge to whom the case was submitted did not regard the girl's pretended dislike for the betrothed as sufficient reason for a divorce. In this impasse, the father came up with another idea which appeared to be more acceptable: the girl had to substitute for her sister who had died a few months earlier, leaving babies who had to be taken care of. The Muslim authorities to whom the case was submitted, as usual, sent it back to a Jewish jurisconsult of high rank, who was more inclined to accept the first argument: the Qayrawānese custom. Old women were sent to the girl, and when they found out that she was adamant in her refusal to marry the youth to whom her father had betrothed her, the jurisconsult ruled that he was obliged to set her free, and the bill of divorce was written.[226]

How a marriage with a wife substituting for her dead sister worked can be learned from the documents about the woman from Ṣahrajt which are discussed above in connection with the supervision of family life by the authorities. Both her sister and the latter's child had died; thus we see, it was not only caring for babies which made for the "female levirate." A house belonging to the dead sister and her daughter had been inherited by the widower, as was the law. But the newlywed resented being a stranger in a house that had been the property of her own family, and took possession of the deeds. This was not the only source of friction, and a divorce settlement was arranged before a Muslim judge in that little town. The case came before the rabbinical court in Fustat which ordered further inquiries, the results of which have not yet turned up. One has the impression that the woman agreed to marry her brother-in-law in order to regain the family house. Sororate was so common in Islam that Arabic has a special term for it: "He replaced her with her sister."[227]

Settlements and appeals.—When husband and wife did not get along well together and things were approaching the breaking point, both sides were prodded by the counsel, warnings, and outright threats of relatives and friends to make peace with one another.[228] The result was called Peace with a capital P, I mean, the Hebrew word *shālōm* appearing in an Arabic text. Naturally, the credit for having achieved it is given to God. "We were happy to learn that you and your wife intend to visit us so that we all shall be united in one place, and, in particular, that God has put Peace between you and her. May it never cease to persist" (from a letter to a relative).[229] A father in the Egyptian capital whose daughter was married in Alexandria receives this report from a friend: "For some time now misunderstandings have occurred between Shabbat ("Sabbath," the recipient's son-in-law) and the girl, and a divorce was impending. I approached him and his brothers, may God keep them, and talked with them amiably again and again, and they, the brothers, were not remiss in their duty. You, may God guard you, must now write to them and thank them for what they have done. I have settled the matter in a way you would have liked. They are now completely happy, be assured in this respect. I am here more than as a brother or friend, for I am indebted to you, as is everyone who visits Miṣr [the capital], may God make you always like this."[230]

Since disputes about the material possessions and claims of the two parties were one of the most common causes of marital conflicts, these could be easily resolved by submitting the case to a legal authority. As we have seen above, this could be done anonymously, without specifying the names of the persons concerned. How this worked is beautifully illustrated by a letter of thanks sent from the little Delta town of Malīj to a parnās, or welfare official, in Fustat. The mother of a newly married girl who was having difficulties with her husband had traveled to Fustat and consulted the official, who subsequently obtained a legal opinion from an acknowledged authority. She brought home with her a letter containing that opinion, which then was read out in the synagogue in the presence of the local judge, the cantors, some notables, and anyone else who cared to attend. The details of the dispute are not stated; it only said that if the husband wished a divorce the legal authority obliged him to pay the delayed marriage gift in full. This was enough to induce him to give in. "The boy cooled off [literally, broke down, Ar. *inkasar*] and kissed my head and the head of her mother [the writer's wife, who had traveled to Fustat]; those present brought about an agreement between us, and we all cooled off."[231]

When a court was approached, the judge sent a lower official to the house first in an attempt to restore peace. Here is such an instruction by a judge: "So-and-so appeared before us suing his wife. Please send for her immediately and look into the matter. If the complaint of the husband is justified, rebuke her and bring about a settlement restoring Peace. And tell her what she has to expect if, after the date of the settlement, she in any way relapses. If no agreement is reached, have her come to court accompanied by her husband."[232] When we find on top communal accounts in the hand of a cantor the laconic remark "the Baghdādī has made peace with his wife" (an Arabic expression is used), we may assume that the official concerned succeeded, or believed he had succeeded, in his errand.[233]

Often, or, probably, mostly, a wife was spared the unpleasantness of appearing in court together with her husband. As is proved by numerous examples, she would appoint a brother or, in his absence, someone else to represent her. When we find that the husband, too, is represented by another person, special circumstances must have been involved. In a carefully executed court record dated August 5, 1028, both wife and husband appoint their fathers as their attorneys; moreover, the fathers are made responsible for any financial obligations falling on their children; finally, if one of the parties stalled in absolving himself of these obligations, "the court and the community," twice emphasized, will permit the other side to approach the state authorities. Clearly, high sums were involved, too much to be handled by the young husband in person. By chance, a list of the wife's trousseau, signed by her father (extremely unusual), has been found. It must certainly have been an enclosure to the dossier to which the court record just described belonged. The marriage gift was 20 + 30 dinars, and the outfit was valued at 676 gold pieces, a high sum indeed.[234]

The preceding subsections contain many examples of marital conflicts brought before the courts and of the actions taken by them. During the procedures the dowry sometimes had to be deposited with the court.[235] Two settlements are described here in full, one from the countryside, concerned mainly with the social aspects of marriage, and another from Fustat, settling financial matters, but touching also on the personal relations of the spouses.

The first document is from the Fayyūm, from the end of the tenth, or, perhaps, the very first years of the eleventh century, and still written in Hebrew (in a quite lively style), probably because the local scribe had not yet mastered Arabic legal parlance. It is a real story from the countryside, one of a haughty girl from the capital who treated her rustic in-laws with condescension, or outright contempt, and could not submit to the deferential manner in which a wife in the Fayyūm was supposed to serve her husband. In a fit of indignation she had torn up her marriage contract, which was of course a very foolish thing to do. Now, it was up to her to retract and to mend her ways.

She came before us and said: 'I have sinned, make peace between us.' She wept, she and her son, in the presence of the community. Everyone prodded her husband Abraham, saying: 'Why do you not take her back?' Said he: 'She treats me with contempt, me and my family, my brother, my sister, and their sons, and all my relatives.' We investigated this statement and found that it was true. Consequently, we had her make the symbolic purchase [required for making a commitment binding], by which Salma, the daughter of Nathan, took upon herself the following obligations toward her husband, Ibrahīm b. Salām: She will stand up in his presence whenever he enters or leaves a room. She will serve and treat him with respect, be neat, and not refuse to do any work usually done in a house. When she sees him sorrowful, she will not argue with him, nor will she ask him to buy her expensive clothing, which he is not able to provide. She will not scorn him with contemptuous and derisive words, but be submissive toward him and his relatives. When mentioning his name or that of his relatives, she will add the honorific epithets due them [such as 'may God enhance his honored position']. She will not improperly disobey him, in word or deed, and leave the house only with his permission. She will not demand that they move to the capital or any other place, unless he himself wishes to do so. [This was probably promised when they married]. In general, she should honor and serve him with respect, and never sit idle in the house, but either occupy herself with work on flax and wool, or the household, such as baking and cooking. Salma, the daughter of Nathan, undertook all these obligations unconditionally. Whenever she fails in any one of these, her husband is free to divorce her with no court refusing him the permission to do so. Abraham b. Salām, on his side, promised to be with her with all his heart, with undivided attention, and, like virtuous Jewish men, to honor her and treat her with respect, also, to buy her clothing, as far as his means permit.

This tenth-century document from the Egyptian countryside shows how a weak male tries to insure his superiority over a strong female.[236]

Quite a different world confronts us in a settlement made in Fustat about a century and a half later, in summer 1142. Its outcome is included in a terse note in the hand of the judge Nathan b. Samuel, whose scrapbook, now dispersed all over the Geniza, is a most precious source for social and legal history. This was an agreement arranged between poor people, a father, his daughter, and her husband, after misunderstandings about the financial arrangements made at the marriage had led to serious trouble. The father, unable to provide his daughter with a proper outfit, had given her a house instead, and sold those items of the dowry which his daughter disliked. Three questions had to be settled. The father had yet to register the house with the state authorities in the name of his daughter; who would pay for the fees and taxes at that transaction? The house needed repairs; who would have a say in the way these repairs would be carried out and who would pay for them? Finally and most important: the husband had to understand, once for all, that he would have no right of usufruct of the house, but that the income from it would be used for his wife's clothing.

The agreement reached was as follows: The father had to register the house in the name of his daughter within three months; the taxes and fees, amounting to 12 gold pieces, a very considerable sum for poor people, had to be borne by the couple (customarily the buyer paid the transfer costs); of these, the husband paid 3 and the wife 9 dinars, reason not stated; although she was entitled to keep the rent for herself, he would inherit the house, or one half of it, in case she died before him childless. He renounced his right of usufruct, and if he so much as mentioned such a demand, he would pay "to the poor" a fine of 3 dinars. The son-in-law had no claims as to how the repairs should be carried out; on the other hand the father-in-law was not entitled to ask him or his daughter to share in the expenses for them. Finally, the father had to hand over to his daughter the sums received from the sale of objects from her outfit. In case the father failed to meet these obligations the marriage was terminated and the husband's delayed gift forfeited. The warning to the husband not to beat or curse his wife meant that the court would force him to repudiate her if any such complaints against him were to be established. We see that agreements, even between common people, show a high degree of "freedom of contract" not envisaged by the law.[237]

Naturally, settlements, even if arranged by the most competent judge, did not always endure. We had such cases before. One, which particularly impressed me, serves to conclude this topic. It concerned the moot question of the wife's freedom of movement: the woman bore the proud and utterly exceptional name Ẓāfira, "Victorious," or Victoria. The document lacks beginning and end, but is written in the late style of Ḥalfon b. Manasse, around 1135, or perhaps even later. This is what remains:

Between Ẓāfira, daughter of the honored elder Japheth, the cantor, and her husband things had happened which almost led to a divorce, until finally *peace* was restored between them. They made peace, after he had bound himself never to mention any obligation to stay at home and not to prohibit her from going to any place which a respectable Jewish woman could visit, such as a synagogue, public baths, gatherings of congratulation or condolence, or going out to buy or sell flax. Nor would he forbid her to go to the house of her sister to see how she was and to pay her a visit, whenever she liked, nor would he forbid her sister to come to his house. . . .

Thus I was sure that Victoria had remained victorious. But when I visited the Institute of the Peoples of Asia in Leningrad, 1965, I found her bill of repudiation, written on January 26, 1145. I assume her sister, who loomed so prominently in the fragment translated above, was the real winner in the struggle.[238]

Since the courts were kept busy with the complaints of married women, we understand that they sometimes failed to take action in the case of real grievances. When a woman, especially one of the lower sectors of the population, one who had no family backing her, despaired of obtaining her legal rights in court, she adopted the extreme measure open to anyone wronged or otherwise suffering: she appealed to the community. We have already encountered appeals by an orphan and her minor sister, both driven from their house by their own family, and by a captive just ransomed, in need of the most essential necessities of life. Here is one by a woman totally neglected by her husband:

In Your name, oh All Merciful.

Oh Community of Israel, I appeal to God and to you.

I am a young woman, whom God the exalted—whose judgments we accept—has made miserable by marrying a man known as Joseph b. Kulayb [or: Caleb], the brother-in-law of Ibn Ṭarsūn, the cantor. He is my paternal cousin, an old and senile man, who vexes me with errands outside the house, small and large.

You know what the Scripture says: [a man must provide his wife with] food, clothing, and conjugal relations [Exodus 21:10]. Not only does he not provide any of these, but he never stays at home at night.

An orphan girl lives with me and keeps me company.[239] Two years ago he promised me to pay me half a dirhem per day; but he keeps saying: wait a month or two until God will help and I shall be able to pay you. But the two months have become two years. Therefore I am asking now the "Head of the Assembly"[240]—may God make his honored position permanent—and the community—may God keep them—to secure me my rights; otherwise, I shall have to go to a gentile court and secure my rights there.

During ten years he has given me no clothing except one wimple. My mother took care of me during this long period. He relied upon her and acquired a good reputation [as one who maintains his wife].[241] Then, three years ago, my mother died. I sold all my dowry and maintained myself by this, but now nothing has remained with me except turning to God and to you, oh Israel.

Had I said less in this matter, it would have been sufficient.

Peace be upon you. "May God increase your number a thousandfold and bless you as he has promised you" [Deuteronomy 1:11]. Amen. Selah.

There are other such complaints, preserved in the Geniza.[242]

Marital strife was not the only cause of friction that occasioned settlements in court. There were many varied reasons why couples found it advisable to have their mutual agreements legalized by a notary or a judge, for instance, to forestall claims by or against heirs, to protect property in time of general insecurity, or, simply, to safeguard rights that, for any reason, needed clarification. Settlements normally required several actions, as when a spouse made a gift of a house to the other spouse which needed registration before both a Muslim and a Jewish authority, or when a husband ceded to his wife full disposition over her dowry, or released her from a debt she owed him. The nature of the Geniza, which, remember, is not an orderly archive but its opposite, means that we usually have only one document of two or more referring to a settlement. For example, in June 1244, Labwa b. Abū Ghālib ("Lioness, daughter of Subduer") renounced to her husband all he owed her from her marriage gift, dowry, and other obligations, such as a debt to her, and, on top of this, undertook to maintain their younger son for ten years and their elder son for two years, including the payment of the latter's poll tax and expenses for his apprenticeship in the art of silversmithing. Their father had only to provide the boys with clothing. Against all this, the only thing he did in this settlement was to release Labwa from all claims he might have had against her—before men or before God. The claims had been spelled out, of course, in another document. They are referred to here in a general way to explain the extraordinary sacrifices made by the wife.[243]

Such partial testimonies to settlements made out of marital cooperation are included in many Geniza papers. Wills and deathbed declarations were other legal ways for expressing such relationships, see subsections C, 3 and 4, below.

Three letters.—As promised earlier, three letters of husbands to their wives are given here in translation. The first concerns a young couple, he a scholar, she the daughter of a judge. The second was written by a man of somewhat lower rank, a cheerful cantor and father of a boy, writing to the daughter of another cantor. The third letter was exchanged between mature spouses, married a second time. She had grown-up sons from a previous marriage, and he was a religious and learned merchant, a man of that group which formed the backbone of the society described in this book.

"Praise," the daughter of the Jewish judge of al-Maḥalla, certainly knew how to read, for, if the letter had to be read out to her, its writer could never have permitted himself the outspoken expressions of love which we read in his letter. The young scholar most probably was chosen by his father-in-law to succeed him as judge in the provincial town. But he had higher aspirations; he was after an appointment in the capital, where his wife was not prepared to follow him. This is the background of our letter. The ugly threat at its end is jarring. But it reveals the reality of life as it was lived in those days.

I am writing to you, my lady, my dear, crown of my head and my pride—may I never be deprived of you, for you cannot imagine how I yearn for you. May the Creator, the exalted, make easy what is difficult and bring near what is far away, for he knows what is in my heart.

Of late, my yearning has become so strong that I am not able to bear it any more. I want you to know this. Therefore, put your trust in God and come to me, solely because you rely on him and for no other reason. For I am confident that God, the exalted, will not forsake me, even when I am alone, far less when I shall be accompanied by *a pious and valorous woman* such as you. Therefore, do not tarry, but come. A woman, who has a husband whom she knows is religious and God-fearing and loves her, is expected to assist him. I spare you by saying no more in this matter.

. . . R(abbi) Aaron has arrived. The books are with . . .

(Lower part of page torn away)
(Written on margin and top)

Please do not neglect me, but reply to everything I wrote and do not make me unhappy. As to the ḥanbal carpet, you can buy it after your arrival here, according to your own taste.

(Verso)

The members of the two synagogues came to listen to my *lecture,* through which I acquired *a good reputation.* I was only sad that you were not present. The brother of *the divine* did not come and paid no attention, and whenever people ask me about him, I am in a most disagreeable position; he breaks my heart and does me harm also in other ways.

In short, there remains no one who loves me, oh Umm Thanā

("Praise"), except you. Therefore, come; otherwise I shall leave this country and disappear. *And Peace!*

(Address, written upside down, first line in Hebrew, the second in Arabic letters)

To al-Maḥalla, to the house of the *Judge*
To al-Maḥalla, to the bazaar of the perfumers.[244]

The letter of the cheerful cantor is in Hebrew. The cantors were the Hebraists of the day, for they had to produce liturgical poetry, which, of course, had to be in the holy language. It may be, too, that he was a native of Europe and not yet fluent in written Arabic expression. The unusual form of address on his letter seems indeed to betray him as a foreigner. Like other cantors, he traveled to the small towns of the Egyptian countryside in order to make some money by singing at weddings and Sabbath services. His epistle has a definitely humorous flair, achieved by twisting familiar biblical and postbiblical quotations. His dedication to his wife, clearly a literate woman, is evident. But when he remembers his little boy, his pen glows.

Abundant greetings and wishes for speedy salvation come from East and West to my pure and chaste wife. Now I know how good your doings are, although I have no mouth to express this in words. I am sure you are well, but my well-being is bitter,[245] because of my separation from you and from the eyes[246] of the boy, my dear, beloved, and most cherished son. I weep and groan and cry, day and night, and lift my eyes unto the four quarters of the world, but there is no one who has mercy upon me, except the Holy one—blessed be he. Although you need no admonition from me, please lift your eyes to Heaven and act for the sake of your soul by taking utmost care of our cherished and dear boy, and do not neglect him. This will be the best proof of your love.

Please, do not worry about me at all. For if I could, I would ride upon a swift cloud and come.[247] But if the Lord ordains it, I shall complete my work soon and come back quickly, with Heaven's aid, without a full purse, but with a happy heart.[248] I trust on Him that said: "Let there be the world," and there was the world, and when all gates are closed, the gates of tears are never shut.[249]

Please talk amicably to Mrs. Umm Thanā ("Praise")[250] and advise her that as soon as I shall return, I shall finish [copying] her Pentateuch.[251]

Greet everyone who inquires about me, in particular my lord, our h(onored), g(reat and) h(oly) Master and Teacher Abu 'l-Bayān, the cantor, the wise and prudent—(may his) R(ock) k(eep him).[252] And upon you let there be the lot of the righteous, and peace.

Written in Sammanūd on the New Moon day of Kislev (November-December), may it be a good sign for us and for all Israel.[253]

I passed Saturday in Benhā.[254] No food entered my mouth from the time of my departure on Thursday until the Sabbath night [i.e., Friday evening].

(Verso)

Isaac b. Baruch (may his) R(ock) k(eep him) wrote this. He is sad.

This letter should be brought to Etan ha-Ezraḥ[i] [name of a Temple singer, Psalm 89:1; here an honorific title for the cantor] to . . . Abu 'l-Bayān the cantor in Miṣr [Fustat].[255]

The woman to whom our third letter was addressed did not write her letters to her husband herself, but dictated them. This does not at all mean that she was illiterate. Even merchants whose handwriting we know dictated their letters, or wrote drafts, which friends with a better hand copied. There can be no doubt that this letter, like the preceding ones, was destined for the recipient's eyes. The man who took her first letter down was none but "The Diadem," the judge Nathan b. Samuel (*Med. Soc.*, II, 513, sec. 18), whose wife was the maternal aunt of the writer of the letter translated here. The perfect calligraphic script betrays a man who was accustomed not only to write business letters, but was proficient in drawing up documents of legal and communal character. The extensive references to liturgical poetry show that he was also accustomed to lead congregations in prayer. All this was to be expected from a merchant belonging to the elite.

As to our study of married life, this document of a second marriage seems to reveal a stronger and more personal relationship than anything read before. To us this appears to be quite natural; for a medieval society such a situation is noteworthy.

I[n Your name].

[May God avert from you all evil for the sake of his] glorious and awe-inspiring [name].[256]

This is to inform you that I am now well and in good health, after having suffered various illnesses and serious ailments. There is no point in describing them at present. I shall write about them in another letter. For I would not like to disquiet you and increase your apprehensions, considering your frailty and incapacity to bear what has been imposed upon you. I mentioned that illness only so that my letter should be a substitute for my presence and because God, the exalted, has already relieved me of it.

Your dear letters have arrived, after I had been without letters for a long time—which caused me anguish [lit., tore my heart], one in the handwriting of my lord *The Diadem, may he be remembered [by God] with blessings*, and another written by the elder Abū Manṣūr, *may his Rock preserve him*. They were brought to me by a muleteer, whom I paid for his services.[257] I was extremely glad and happy with them even before opening them. Then my mind became troubled, before I read them, for fear of disquieting news—*God forbid*! I read them and thanked God for your well-being and good health, although I had doubts, knowing you, whether you would hide things concerning yourself, in order not to worry me.

There were, however, in your letter, some expressions that hurt me, namely, where you speak about your yearning, solitude, and separation, and the sickness of the heart which brings about the sickness of the body. By God, there was no need to say these things. For, God knows, I am not one who has to be aroused to compassion and tenderness, as I possess of these more than I am able to describe. Moreover, I am in a state the like of which I never suffered since I was born and had dealings with people, caused both[258] by a deep depression, never experienced before, and by solitude and loneliness. Everything I undertake becomes entangled. Thus, when I sell something, I do not attain relief, for I buy in its place other merchandise, which I cannot sell in our town without loss. Relief comes only when I get a merchandise with which one can travel and sell in any place. All this I do in order to speed up my return, and because I have compassion with your state of mind, and out of fear that one of us may be overtaken by death, while the other is away.

I have also troubles with my meals. When I prepare something and put it on the fire, it does not turn out well, because of my fatigue, preoccupations, and worries. Then, when I stretch out my hand to take something, I think about you and your sufferings and your loneliness and the loneliness of each of us. God knows, how I eat and drink and sleep. Most of the night I do not sleep. When I sleep a little, I wake up and remain awake alone, although the night is still long; then I recite a *litany*,[259] *a hymn, a religious poem*,[260] a prayer, or a *dirge*,[261] or whatever comes to my mind, wishing for the morning to come, but the night is long. Sometimes I am too weak to recite, then I remain silent and think, until God bestows upon me the morning, or I slumber again for a short while. There are also times when my mind is too disturbed by loneliness; then I go, once a week, and stay overnight with your boy Abū (Is)ḥāq in the dyeing workshop, finding some diversion for a moment, God knows.

However, the hardest thing I experience is every Friday night. When I light the candle and put upon the table whatever God bestows, and think about you, then only God knows what happens to me.[262]

I know I have talked too long about things for which shortness would be more fitting, but I speak to you about myself, as if you were present, for consolation and as if I were with you and talking with you—may God bring this near! And I also let you know my situation that you should not think—as you have said [in your letters]—that I lead here a good life, selling and buying, and not worrying about you. No, even if this had been the case, I could not forget you a minute; nor could my mind be quiet while being separated from you, and I would have been impatient without you; how much more now that I am in an opposite state.

Another matter. A *Muslim* known to me, called Abū ʿAlī, arrived here and told me that you came to his store in the company of Abu 'l- . . . and wept. This was hard for me and caused me anguish, very, very much. I ask you by God—although I do not want to entreat you under oath—have patience and be not unduly worried about me. Pray to the Creator—may he be exalted—to facilitate my affairs and to unite us soon. Maybe, when I come home, you will regret and repent and say: "I wished I had let him stay longer!" Moreover, the Creator already has facilitated many of my affairs and I am now on the point to be relieved soon, if God will. I am not able to fix the time for you, but *his salvation—may his name be praised—comes quick like the twinkling of an eye*.[263] Had I finished today, I would not wish to stay on for one day more. Maybe I can leave here something in bond or take it with me.

I should not be blamed for anything said here, for I write every letter with the messenger standing over me. In addition, I am worried for reasons of which I have mentioned some and of which there is no point to write more. [The last line of the second page is torn away. As usual, the letter is continued on the margin. The last words of the lost line no doubt were: greetings to you and] to everyone under your care. Convey my greetings to all our friends, to the *judge* and to the sister of my mother,[264] to *Maʿānī* with all his troubles, to Abū ʿAlī, the son of the sister of my mother, to the elder Abū Manṣūr[265] [seven others mentioned, among them two women and another son of his wife] and others, for whom to mention no space is left.[266] *And Peace*!

When I read this letter, after having completed it, God alone knows what I feel.[267]

2. *Parents and Children*

The value of children to parents.—A recent study on the value of children to parents by Lois Wladis Hoffman of the University of Michigan produced some enlightening insights, which might serve as a backdrop to the testimony of the Cairo Geniza. Open questions such as "What would you say are some of the advantages or good things about having children, compared with not having children at all?" were put to 1,571 American women under forty with at least one child and to 461 of their husbands. The answers were sorted into nine groups, four of which stand out either by frequency or rarity. Besides the natural aspect of affection, giving and receiving love (rating: 66 percent, women; 60 percent, men), one group of responses by far outstripped the others: "Children are fun," they provide their parents with stimulation and joy (60 percent, women; 55 percent, men). Utility, economic and otherwise, got a poor average of 9 percent of the respondents, and moral and religious incentives a negligible 6.6 percent.[1]

For the Geniza, naturally, I am unable to provide statistics. A further disadvantage of the subsequent inquiry is the discouraging fact that my "respondents" are almost exclusively male, a disadvantage somewhat lessened by the observation that in the Hoffman national survey the answers of men and women differed only slightly, which might indicate that given the same cultural ambiance the opinions of spouses about the advantages of having children are pretty much the same. Our lack of statistics is compensated for by the clarity and emphasis with which the basic values emerge from our documents.

The massive evidence of the Geniza proves that children, that is, sons, formed a prominent, central, and, so to say, public component in a man's life to a far higher degree than is customary in our own society. When you write a business letter to a person who has no sons, you pray that God may give him "male children studying the Torah and fulfilling its commandments." When he has sons, you wish him that God may keep them, or you may add that the father should "see their Torah," that is, success in study, "their good works, and their 'joy,' " that is, wedding. If they are grown up, greetings must be extended to them, each in accordance with the circumstances. Even a complete stranger, writing a begging letter—and many have found their way into the Geniza—first carefully inquires about the family of the addressee in order to insert the proper wishes for his progeny.[2]

The religious merit of having children is discussed above.[3] Procreation is an explicit commandment of the Bible, and God's law can be preserved only if it is studied and kept, now and forever. Hence the great emphasis not only on children but also on grandsons and great-grandsons. It seems strange to us that in letters in which fathers are wished to witness their son's study and marriage they are wished also to see the same from grandsons and great-grandsons, as happened to Joseph (Genesis 50:23) or Job (42:16).[4] Those wishes sound especially odd in a letter of congratulation on the circumcision of a boy eight days old.[5] Underlying all this is the Talmudic idea that "he who hears a lection from the mouth of his grandson is like the one who has heard it [from God] on Mount Sinai."[6]

The precedence of "study" over "good deeds" in the wishes for success with children should not be taken too literally. It is the ancient Socratic idea that one has to know what is good in order to be able to act in accordance with it. Simple wishes that the addressee's children grow up as righteous and honest men are not lacking either.[7]

Alongside religious and moral motives, the utilitarian and egotistic incentive that a son become a support and source of strength for his father appears frequently in letters. This wish is regularly expressed with the phrase "may God strengthen your (upper) arm through him," written in Arabic or Hebrew, and found throughout the centuries.[8] The phrase originated in ancient times, when, during tribal warfare, a multitude of sons was the safest protection for an aging father, but it also had its legitimate place in the urban society of the Geniza period: family partnerships, presided over by fathers, were the strongest business firms, craftsmen worked together with their sons, and professionals and dignitaries enhanced their prestige and influence when they had sons ready to take over their positions, which they themselves often had inherited from their fathers.[9] The Bible verse most frequently quoted in the Geniza is Psalms 45:16: "Instead of your fathers shall be your sons [you will make them princes all over the country]." This is said not only in letters to high dignitaries, such as a Nagid, a judge, or a great scholar, like Maimonides, where it is common, but also in simple family letters.[10] Another biblical phrase, "may he [the son] sit on your [the father's] chair" (I Kings 3:6 and elsewhere) is also used in this connection, even in addressing a low community official, such as a cantor, who is wished this with regard to his two sons and his future grandsons and great-grandsons.[11]

In the Hoffman survey this "expansion of the self" is rated 35 percent, the third strongest incentive for the desire to have children. In the Geniza period, taken together with the utilitarian-egotistic motivation of which it forms a part, it should be regarded as powerful as the religious and moral considerations—if not more so.

Paternal affection is expressed in terms of endearment by which a man would refer to his son, or which would be used by others addressing the father. "My son, the joy of my eye" (which is idiomatic Arabic, and not a translation of the corresponding biblical phrase, Ezekiel 24:25, Lamentations 4:2) and "the dearest to me of all mankind" are the most commonly used expressions.[12] "The lovely flower," "the blossoming rose," originally perhaps said of children, can refer also to grown-up sons; *muhja,* "lifeblood," is another strong term.[13] The most common word of endearment for son is *ḥamūd,* "delight," so common that the Hebrew letter *ḥ* stands in memorial and other lists simply for "son of."[14]

Here is the opening of a letter of congratulation on the birth of a son. Labrāṭ I b. Moses I in Tunisia, whom we have already met repeatedly,[15] writes to his brother Judah in Egypt:

> Your letter containing the great news and joyful tidings about the blessed, blissful, and auspicious newborn has arrived. We had here much joy, music, and congratulation gatherings because of this. . . . Yes, my brother, you are to be congratulated, and very much so. May God bestow on me that both you and he will live and may God make him a brother of "seven and even eight."[16] May God strengthen your arm through him and established by him your honored position and fulfill in your case: "Instead of your fathers there shall be your sons, you will make them princes all over the country." May God avert from you and from him the effects of the evil eye and may he never let me hear anything undesirable about the two of you all my life.[17]

Later in the letter we read about the spiritual side of the festive occasion. A family Bible, lost in the pillage of Qayrawān (1057), had been "ransomed" from the marauders, the missing folios replaced, and the costly manuscript sent to Egypt as a gift to the baby son.

A letter of congratulation on the birth of a son, written in perfect script and language and entirely dedicated to the subject, is even more exuberant. Opening with Psalms 127:3–5, ("like arrows in the hand of a warrior are the sons of one's youth . . ."), verses that extol the role of sons as defenders and supporters of their fathers, it enumerates all the secular motivations for having sons in highly stylized rhymed Arabic prose. It concludes with the wish that through the boy the happy father may have a numerous family. The writer, no doubt a professional scribe, adds that he has written a charm, *ḥirz,* "a protection, but the Protector is God," for the safety of the boy and his mother and also sent a *mezuzah* (the biblical verses Deuteronomy 6:4–9, and 11:13–21, put into a container and affixed to the frame of a door), certainly destined for the room of the baby and his mother. A newly born was particularly exposed to the evil eye.[18]

But what about girls? It is not easy to answer this question. I have not found a letter in which a father is congratulated on the birth of a girl, or where he is wished that God may keep a daughter of his. At the birth of a girl the father, or the family, is congratulated on the mother's *khalāṣ,* deliverance (not: delivery), meaning that she did not die nor was she harmed, in childbirth. Only once, in a letter of a sister writing to her brother overseas, are good wishes expressed for a newly born niece, and lovely things are said about the addressee's daughters. But even in that feminine missive the recipient is wished that God may give him something "to lift up his heart, namely a manchild" (lit., "a male son," see Jeremiah 20:15).[19]

The reasons for this discrimination are obvious. In the house of worship Jewish girls, like their Christian compatriots, were confined to the women's gallery. They did not actively participate in the services; they could profit individually from what they were able to perceive, but they did not "study." "The men to learn, the women to listen."[20] Thus the religious motive of spiritual perpetuation did not apply to girls. From the utilitarian-egotistic point of view they were a net loss: a father had to work all his life for readying appropriate outfits for them. In a deathbed declaration a man assigns 100 dinars to each of his three minor daughters for their future outfits, leaving the rest of his property to his two sons; but how hard had a man to work in those days for earning even a quarter-dinar![21]

Finally, as to the motivation of physical continuation, an ancient maxim, both Jewish and Arab, says: "The sons of sons are like sons, the sons of daughters are not."[22] How deep-seated such notions were even among mothers was brought home to me when I read this passage in the letter of a noble old woman, writing from Raqqa on the Euphrates to one of her sons in Egypt: "You [plural] have left me with your sister and this you yourself have wished, but how long can a person live in other peoples' houses?!"[23]

Compare this with what the same woman writes in order to express her yearnings after her son, who had failed to communicate with her during the entire summer (when letters were carried by travelers): "Send me your worn shirts and with their dirt, so that I may revive my spirit with them," that is, by looking at them and inhaling their smell, a reminiscence of the Islamic (not: biblical) Joseph story, where Jacob is revived and his blindness is healed when Joseph's shirt, sent to him from Egypt, is cast over his face.[24]

No wonder, then, that a report about the death of a girl is regularly followed by the wish that she may be replaced by a boy, sometimes accompanied by the consolation that God might accept the child's death as an atonement for the father's sins. (It was believed that babies die for their fathers' sins, since they could not have committed a sin themselves.) "The family is fine and in good shape after the disaster that occurred with the little girl. They are composed. May God in his beneficent ways give them male children instead."[25] "I was informed about the deliverance of Abū Saʿīd's wife, praise be to God for this. As to the girl's death, nothing can be done about it. May God soon give them a male child instead. Congratulate them all on her deliverance."[26] Even more telling are these two terse lines squeezed into a business letter, which is addressed to a relative: "The little one [the writer's wife] is fine, God has given a boy as a replacement."[27]

Naturally, that is not the whole story. If affection, giving and receiving love, has been found to be the strongest motivation for the desire of having children in contemporary U.S.A., how much more must that have been so in a time and place where the elementary human urges were far more pronounced. Girls, especially when they are small, often are more lovable than boys. "I prefer girls," said Rav Ḥisdā, a prominent Talmudic sage. His medieval commentators, perplexed by so preposterous a dictum, explained that Ḥisdā's sons-in-law were greater scholars than his sons. But, the context suggests, that the sage preferred girls for their own sake, and similar opinions are recorded in the name of Muslim authorities.[28]

The relationships between parents and daughters, as emerging from the Geniza, are discussed below. Here it should be noted that even among common people blaming a wife for producing a girl must have been regarded as improper. A very simple man, who quarreled with his wife because her father had not made the payments promised to the young couple, absented himself and refused to return until the payments were made. A lawsuit was pending at the Nagid's court. During his absence a girl was born: This is his reaction in a letter to his wife:

> "Oh Sitt al-Faḍl ("Noble Woman"), give up your bad feelings and seek *reconciliation.* I am happy with my child.[29] What?! Because the first one is a girl I should hate her? God forbid! What I say is this: God has made my lot pleasant. It is an auspicious *sign* for me and for you. . . . But even if it had been a boy and he would have been described as exceedingly beautiful, I would not come home and would not look at him, as long as you dislike me. I ask God, the exalted, to take away that bad feeling between us and make us good to each other.

Despite this attempt at reconciliation the letter ends with the assurance that the writer would not come unless there was money enough for both to have a good life.[30]

A girl as the firstborn is auspicious (our writer quotes here the Talmud, or, rather, a familiar Talmudic phrase), because she averts the evil eye from the family, so much feared at the birth of a boy.[31] Moreover, she is a little mother for the sons expected to follow.[32]

Genuine love for a daughter is expressed in the calligraphic letter of a young cantor who was away from home, successfully seeking an appointment in another town. Sitt al-Bayt ("The Lady of the House") was a naughty little girl, and the members of the household in which she lived with her mother (the letter is addressed to a young brother) sometimes said nasty things to her. But "curses," even when not meant seriously, might have detrimental affects, and our writer was worried. This is what he writes after having described his successes in the town visited:

> Thank God, I am perfectly well, but yearn after my family [wife] and child[33]. . . . The people here are happy with me, but my mind is troubled. I wished I could fly to you, tell me, what I can do. Please write me how you are, especially my daughter and her mother, for, when I am alone, I cry all the time because of my separation from them. . . . Do not neglect Sitt al-Bayt and do not curse her; I am very much troubled because of her, and while I am writing this, my tears are running down.[34]

The feelings of this young cantor for his little daughter match those of his colleague for his son in the letter translated at the end of the preceding section.[35] We have read above about a scholar who refused to marry out of consideration for his mother and daughter.[36] And an ascetic from Byzantium, who lived in Jerusalem as a "mourner of Zion." writes that he must return to his country to look after his only daughter.[37]

In greetings and good wishes extended to a man, or in reports about the family, the children usually precede the wife. In some cases the wife is referred to as the children's mother; in most others she is mentioned in this connection as "the one who is with you" or with other circumlocutions.[38] Shall we conclude from this scribal custom that children somehow were regarded as "closer relatives" than wives? A comprehensive study of the numerous references of this type would be desirable in order to appraise these emotional evaluations.[39] I should like, however, to draw attention to a remark in the commentary of the Nagid Abraham, the son of Moses Maimonides on Genesis 31:17: "Jacob mentions children prior to wives, for children are the purpose of being with women, although in reality they come later, while Esau mentions the women first, because his thoughts are given to them." It is the patriarch Jacob who, of course, does the right thing. Thus, the pious Nagid Abraham seems to have regarded the custom of mentioning children prior to wives as religiously commendable.[40]

Bearing and rearing.—Attempts at family planning were not unknown in the Geniza society (as probably in any cultivated ambiance). An Islamic textbook on commerce, quoting a saying ascribed to the prophet Muhammad, lauds the convenience of a small family, an attitude probably not unknown among the Mediterranean bourgeoisie of the High Middle Ages. When a very young husband, who already had a daughter, is warned not to be too eager in siring children, lest his quest for a boy might result in producing a girl every year, clearly ways and means were applied to forestall such occurrences.[41] That such practices were not very reliable may be learned from the demand of a woman with many children who left her husband the choice between complete continence or divorce.[42]

Examples of records on conception, birth, and weaning are occasionally found in the Geniza. Here is one:

> The blessed appearance [of pregnancy][43] took place on the 6th of Shawwāl 484 [Muslim year] corresponding to [the Hebrew month] Kislev. . . . Nov. 21, 1091; the blessed birth—Tuesday, 12th Rajab 485, corresponding to Elul, Aug. 18, 1092; the blessed weaning—Thursday, 16th Rabīʿ al-awwal, corresponding to Nisan[44], April 5, 1094; the blessed miscarriage—Thursday, 20th Rabīʿ al-akhīr, corresponding to Iyyar, May 9, 1094.

A miscarriage may be blessed either because anything decreed by God is blessed or because of the well-known maxim of Arabian folk medicine that a miscarrying woman is quick in conceiving again, or for both reasons.[45] The note is in the unmistakable, unreadable hand of ʿArūs b. Joseph, a merchant repeatedly mentioned in these volumes, and is written beneath accounts on the lower end of a double page of his account book. On the top of the reverse side is another note about the beginning of a pregnancy and a birth, continued immediately by accounts. No names of the new arrivals are given. Girls were probably born; in various letters ʿArūs is wished a "male child."[46]

The following notes are of a different type. They are written in calligraphic script on a special piece of paper. A space of about eight lines is left blank between them.

> A male child was born to the elder Abū ʿAlī Ibn al-Dimyāṭī [native of Damietta] and was named Abu 'l-Fakhr, Thursday morning, the fifth hour of the day, the 25th Marheshvan, called by the Muslims Dhu 'l-Qaʿda.

The appearance of [the pregnancy of] Sitt Ghalb ("Lady Overcoming," Abū ʿAlī's wife) was perceived in the middle of Shawwāl, known as [the Jewish] month of Teveth. Then it was established for Marheshvan [two months earlier]. I vowed that if it were a boy, I would give as alms at his circumcision a hundred pounds of bread and a lamb, and I would call him Abū Saʿd after my brother, may God have mercy upon him."[47]

The happy father was none other than Abū ʿAlī Ezekiel b. Nethanel Ibn al-Dimyāṭī, the brother of the scholarly India trader Ḥalfōn b. Nethanel. Ḥalfōn was a bachelor and took his nephew Abu 'l-Fakhr, the boy listed above, into his business. Since that happened in the 1140s, the date of the first note written above must have been 1129 or 1130, for only in those two years did the Muslim and Jewish months mentioned coincide. Abu 'l-Fakhr probably was named after his maternal grandfather; it is very likely that "Lady Overcoming" had stipulated this at her marriage.

The erratic way in which these notes were written explains perhaps why so few of them have survived.

Women wrote freely about their pregnancies and so did their husbands, and good wishes were extended to them. "I am in my sixth month," writes a woman (who had a married daughter) to her maternal uncle, asking him urgently to visit her, "for death and life are in the hand of God."[48] Another woman with child asks her sister and mother to take more interest in her because of her condition. In the two letters in which she makes this request she also speaks about her children, a girl and a boy.[49] "Your daughter is well and in her fourth month" writes a son-in-law from Alexandria to his uncle and father-in-law in Fustat and immediately adds: "We are upset because of the plague in Fustat, about which we have heard here."[50] Labrāt I b. Moses I, in the letter quoted earlier in this section makes this short remark: "The girl who is with me [his wife] is busy [pregnant]. I wish her safety."[51]

It is natural in an extended family for the woman of the house and her daughter-in-law to be expecting at the same time. With Isaiah 66:7 they are wished to give birth to a male child before being in labor. The well-wisher, a relative of the dowager, asks "for her month"; if he can manage, he will try to visit at the time of the birth. Such remarks are frequent.[52]

The women of the Geniza period seem to have inherited something of the robustness of their ancestors prior to the Exodus from Egypt, of whom it was reported: "They are vigorous and give birth before the midwife comes to them" (Exodus 1:19). Considering that the entire Geniza correspondence is pervaded by reports about bad health and illness, I have always wondered why we hear so little about the inconveniences of pregnancy and death in childbed. It cannot be a taboo concerning things female, since illnesses of women are reported as much as those of men. There are a few references to the deaths of mothers at delivery, or shortly after, but far fewer than one would expect.[53] Yet the risk of childbirth was great. We have wills of pregnant women (one declaring that she was entering her ninth month) made in anticipation of the possibility. Two wills provide for the child, "male or female," who would survive the mother, one also giving generously to charities and relatives, and one turning over the testator's assets to her mother on condition she brings up the newborn, while the husband will be free of any obligation. The idea behind this will was, of course, that the husband would soon marry again and that a grandmother would be a better substitute for a mother than a stepmother.[54]

The subject of birth appears in the Geniza mainly as a social event. We hear little about the physical or medical aspect. "Son of the Midwife," "Son of the Little [female] Doctor" are family names, but we do not learn anything of importance about the activities of these professionals attending a woman at childbirth.[55] The main concern of the family was to receive properly the many women who came to see the young mother.[56] In the case of the birth of a boy, the circumcision ceremony, following eight days later, was a great affair, second in commotion only to a wedding. Solemn and protracted additional prayers were recited both on the Sabbath preceding the circumcision and during the ceremony itself; we have reports about what liturgies were read at such "a tremendous assembly."[57] The privilege of leading the circumcision ceremonies (and receiving the honorarium going with them), mentioned in *Med. Soc.*, II, 86, seems to refer to the recitation of prayers rather than to the actual operation. Attendance at the ceremony was a very sensitive matter of prestige for high and low; hence the letters of inquiry and apology sent on such an occasion.[58] Poems with good wishes were read out, of course, in anticipation of a reward. A circumcision ceremony was also a good occasion for sending in a begging letter, and we have already read about an expecting father vowing a festive meal for the poor.[59]

As an aside I should like to mention that a Jewish judge in Alexandria (who was also a physician) was accused by an adversary of wasting his time circumcising Christian, that is, Coptic, boys, instead of a attending to his duties at the Jewish court of the city.

Coptic circumcision has its roots in antiquity. Female circumcision, practiced among Copts, is unknown in Judaism.[60]

Birth registers do not seem to have been kept by the religious communities, let alone by the government. The government became interested in its non-Muslim male subjects when they were old enough to be charged with the payment of the poll tax. But the proud father would list somewhere the exact date, preferably according to the various eras of his own and other communities known to him. Thus one birth is listed according to the Coptic, the Muslim, and two Jewish calendars, another according to four Jewish eras (Creation, Era of the Documents, Destruction of the Second Temple, and Jubilee Years) and Muslim chronology, and is, in addition, accompanied by a horoscope.[61] A carefully executed horoscope, written by the learned cantor and clerk Hillel b. Eli, certainly was ordered from a professional astrologer of the scientific type.[62]

The names given to children are discussed in various parts of this book.[63] It is noteworthy, however, that the newborn is referred to neither with his Arabic nor his Hebrew proper name, but with his honorific byname, such as Abu 'l-Barakāt, "Blessed," or Abu 'l-Fakhr, "Glory."[64]

Nursing, as far as the Geniza has opportunity to refer to it, is invariably done by the mother. Both Jewish and Islamic law foresee two years as the period normally needed for this phase of the child's upbringing, and this is confirmed by the Geniza documents. The widow "Beauty" appears in court in summer 1120 and declares that her little daughter "Glory," about a year and a half old, still needed nursing; taking care of the baby and nursing her consumed all of the mother's time and she was therefore unable to earn her livelihood.[65] In the note of the well-to-do purple maker 'Arūs b. Joseph nineteen and a half months had passed between birth and weaning.[66] When in a letter to her husband abroad a mother writes, "We are in great distress, owing to poor health and loneliness, we have weaned the boy," she uses "the plural of modesty"; it was she who had nursed the baby. Weaning was a dangerous stage in the child's life (we should recall that the patriarch Abraham gave the big party at the weaning, not at the circumcision of his son Isaac [Genesis 21:8]; the doctor, as she writes, had to be constantly consulted, and a soup, cooked from two chickens, served as a daily replacement of the mother's milk.[67] During nursing a woman was not supposed to do heavy work. But a husband who had given his divorcée alimony of 15 dirhems and 3 waybas (about 12 gallons) of wheat per month, as long as she nursed his baby, demanded to be freed of providing the wheat after the weaning.[68]

Occasional notices about the upbringing of children are dispersed throughout the Geniza and it would be worthwhile to collect them.[69] A considerable number were brought together in my *Jewish Education in Muslim Countries* (Heb.), but more can be found and have been found since the publication of that book.[70] One paid attention to the feelings of a child. When a distinguished woman in Jerusalem died, leaving a boy of two and a half years, he was claimed by his paternal aunt, who was none other than the wife of the Gaon Elijah b. Solomon. But the Gaon himself ruled that the boy should stay where he was because he would feel better in his accustomed environment. No doubt, female members in the widower's household had looked after him during his mother's last illness, and in the same letter we read that her sister was already on her way from Egypt to Jerusalem, probably to fill the dead woman's place.[71] A widow with a little boy in Minyat Ziftā, a town in the Egyptian Delta, receives from her future husband this contractually confirmed promise: "He will feed and clothe this orphan and teach him a craft. He will be to him like the children borne to him by the bride, he will not turn him out, or beat, or humiliate him with words."[72] And how lovely is this report from Damascus about a boy who was left by his father with relatives when he traveled to Egypt: "He is happy and gay in the company of our children. He goes to school with them, dresses like them,[73] and plays with them. He is not a stranger. Everyone loves him. They all sleep on one mattress. She [the writer's wife] shows him love more than she does to her own children."[74]

Usually the fathers away from home insist that their young sons at home should not play or be on the street "with the boys," but should be in school all day long. To the examples provided in *Med. Soc.*, II, 174, others could be added, for example, one, in which the mother is admonished also to watch that the little one, who still needed assistance in washing his hands, should say the proper benedictions over bread, wine, and water.[75] A father mourning his son, who died at the age of six, eulogizes him for never playing in the street or at home, for running to the gate of the house to welcome the needy and share his food with him, "whether he had plenty or little," and for delighting his father with intelligent questions. The father was a member of the yeshiva; higher learning, we remember, consisted in asking questions about a text studied.[76] A father in a dirge on his daughter remembers the days when he taught her the Bible: "When I remember the quickness of your mind, your knowledge of the Torah, your deeds of charity, and the gracefulness of your diction, I say: 'Would that I could listen to you again as at the time I taught you the Torah and questioned you on its knowledge by heart' and cry out 'Let me see your countenance, let me hear your voice' (Song of Songs 2:14)."[77]

When we see here fathers eulogizing not only the intelligence, eagerness to learn, and actual knowledge of their children, but also their love for charity, we must assume that the parents used practical methods to implant this love in the hearts of their children. The one just quoted, namely, that a small boy willingly shared his food with a beggar standing at the door of the house, is a good example. When a father in al-Mahdiyya, Tunisia, on the eve of the New Year sends his daughter's old clothes to Fustat, Egypt, where they were to be sold and the proceeds sent to Jerusalem for the maintenance of orphans, we can hardly fail to see in this an educational intention. At the beginning of the new year, a girl received one or several new dresses. Her old dresses were hers; she could sell them and buy herself something she liked; but she was taught better: she should think about girls who had no father to buy them a new dress, about girls far away. Was this not a very practical way to teach children both altruism and love for the Holy City?[78]

The alertness of a child, in particular his attentiveness to members of the extended family, is a topic occasionally touched upon in letters. A man in Alexandria writes to his brother in Fustat, after another brother had died, about his own boy Mūsā (Moses), who bore the same name as his dead uncle: "The little one begins to speak clearly, and this is what he says all the time: 'My uncle, my uncle Mūsā.' May God have mercy upon Mūsā [the dead uncle], and give life to Mūsā [the child]."[79] In two other letters from Alexandria, sent by Nathan b. Nahray to his illustrious second cousin Nahray b. Nissīm, Nathan describes how his little son, also called Nahray, always inquires about *rabbēnū* "our master" (as the visitor was addressed in the house after the latter had departed). "My boy Nahray is angry with us and is always saying, 'When do *rabbēnū* and Abū Sa'd [the latter's boy] come?' And he says, 'Bring me to him.' We say to him all the time, 'They are in the synagogue; presently they will come.' " Little Nahray cannot have been more than three or four years old, for at that age he would have accompanied his father to the house of worship. This short passage also shows that then, as always, one told little lies to children.[80]

A most important aspect of the upbringing of children was their constant participation in the life of the adults. During the week the boys were in school, where also the prayers were said. But on Sabbaths and holidays the boys were taken by their fathers to synagogue and attended service there even when the father was abroad.[81] Girls frequented the women's gallery with their mothers.[82] Invitations to weekends, holidays, and family events invariably included "the little ones."[83] And the very early participation of teenagers in economic life brought them into constant contact with the world of the adults.

It is difficult to provide exact data in this matter since our sources speak about the adolescent mostly in general terms and do not indicate his years. It was taken for granted that a girl of ten and her elder sister, who already had attained puberty, would work (in embroidery, in the case concerned).[84] When, in a legal opinion, it is said of a girl of nine years, "She spins with them every day and earns with this her livelihood *and more*," one has the impression that this was regarded as exceptional.[85] A Karaite court decision from the year 1004 has this to say about a boy of fifteen: "Although this master Aaron is only fifteen years old, he is possessed of common sense, shrewdness, understanding, and prudence, and knows how to handle commercial transactions. Still it is the general opinion [of the experienced merchants assembled to opine about the case] not to leave his part in the inheritance in his hands."[86]

Strict law was different. This is a question submitted to Maimonides, about two hundred years after the case just mentioned: "A boy of fifteen came to the synagogue [where the court was held]. A man produced a document issued a year before showing that the boy owed him money. . . . Some said that he was a minor and his transactions were not valid. Then it was established by witness that he was fifteen. Some opined that he [i.e., his capacity to act legally] should be examined. . . . The matter remained undecided until we receive your instructions. . . ." Answer: "He is to be regarded as one who has come of age since this has been established by witness. His mental capacity need not be examined."[87]

Maimonides decided here in accordance with the law that identified puberty (assumed to be reached by boys at thirteen) with legally coming of age. Only certain transactions with immovables were excluded from the adolescent's free disposition until he reached the age of twenty.[88] In a court record from Bilbays, Lower Egypt, from spring 1217, an elder brother receives the administration of a minor sibling's share in their father's inheritance and takes it upon himself to maintain him "until he reached maturity at thirteen." It should be noted that Maimonides, in a postscript to his voluminous commentary on the Mishna, reports that he was thirty at the time of its completion, but began to write it at the age of thirteen.[89]

In a highly interesting contract of apprenticeship from spring 1027 a father in Fustat hires out his son to a weaver for four months, in return for a monthly payment of 15 dirhems to be changed to the regular wages of a workman afterward, and both father and son make legally binding stipulations (which proves that the latter was more than thirteen years old).[90] According to the law a father has no jurisdiction over his mature son. But here, as in the case of the Karaite court ruling of 1004, quoted above, and in countless other cases,[91] matters were decided according to practical considerations. When, in summer 1232, witnesses testify that an adolescent was "mature and displaying eagerness and endeavor to earn his own livelihood," they clearly referred not only to his physical maturity but also to his mental capacity. After having been in business for sixty years a man boasts that as a boy whose beard had not yet become apparent he was already renowned for his probity. All in all, it becomes apparent that both girls and boys entered economic life at a very early stage. Childhood came to an end soon, or, rather, it was an imperfect stage in a man's lifespan. The sooner it was terminated, the better. But the education of adolescents was no less a concern than that of children.[92]

The size of the nuclear family.—What was the average number of children in a nuclear household? By that we do not mean the number of children born. We cannot know this, for children stillborn or dying early normally do not appear in our documents.[93] Moreover, we must remember that daughters were never mentioned in memorial lists and rarely greeted in letters. Often we learn about them only circumstantially. Thus we might conclude that Moses Maimonides had only one brother and one sister, but a Geniza letter to him by his hitherto unknown sister Miriam in which she greets his sisters shows that he had at least three sisters.[94] Finally, most of our information comes from normal, fairly well-off families. We learn about poor people when a man complains about his big household, which he is unable to support, or from lists of paupers, where only a few members live at home, in many cases certainly because the boys had to leave their parents at a very tender age to seek a livelihood.[95]

The Geniza is rich in information about the size of the nuclear family, and over the years I have collected much material about this question. But the more I gather, the more I am convinced that only full and systematic research can do justice to the topic. Here I must confine myself to a few general remarks, illustrated by characteristic examples.

We are best off with legal documents in which there is reason to be specific with data about children, documents such as releases, wills, settlements of inheritance claims, or inquiries addressed to authorities about them. The release from any claim, given by a woman called Turayk, or Little Turk, to a representative of merchants, specifying the names of his three sons and three daughters, is discussed above.[96] An India trader, before setting out on his voyage (on which he was murdered), makes detailed provisions for his three sons and three daughters.[97] A will makes the dying man's wife guardian with far reaching rights over his three minor daughters and two sons.[98] Two married daughters and three adult sons were the heirs of a man from Qayrawān in 1034; one married daughter and four sons appear in an inquiry about the estate of their father; another four sons and a girl are mentioned in a question about the inheritance of a poor parnās; and at least five brothers shared the inheritance of a house in 1238.[99] We have wills for a single child, one for a son, another for a daughter, and one for a single daughter inheriting the entire estate of her father.[100] Between the extremes of families with five or six children and others with only one there are, of course, many intermediate examples in legal documents.

Instances of seven children mentioned in connection with cases of inheritance are rare. A man from Alexandria, whose brother had died on board ship en route to Yemen claims a share in the estate, emphasizing that his household consisted of nine souls, which probably means that he had seven children. A question submitted to Maimonides speaks of five sons, two of whom had come of age, two daughters, and a widow left behind by a man who had appointed two executors of his will.[101] I have not noted a will, or a similar document, made for eight children as heirs.

Appeals to authorities, or to the community at large, in which the supplicant mentions the number of his or her children as a reason for the request, have a semi-official character and should also be regarded as fairly reliable. A community official in Acre (Acco) who had five daughters, but no son, complains that he had lost much of his income since the Crusaders (who had conquered the city in 1104, not long before the letter was written) did not permit the ritual killing of animals, from which he derived a considerable part of his income.[102] A widow who had lost four grown-up sons applies to the community after her fifth and only remaining son had been killed by the Ghuzz, or Seljuks.[103] A man apparently from Europe had left six hungry children, four daughters and two sons, in Alexandria, being forced to flee from there because of debts and the pursuit by the collector of the poll tax.[104] These are the highest numbers of children found in requests by needy people.

Family correspondence is another source when it is extensive and had reason to mention the entire nuclear family, as when a man writes from abroad to a brother and sends regards to the other siblings. Abraham Yijū, the noted India trader, had two brothers and two married sisters. Ḥalfōn b. Nethanel Ibn al-Dimyāṭī, another great India trader, had three brothers but no sister.[105] His namesake Ḥalfōn b. Manasse, the court clerk and cantor, had two brothers and, at least, two unmarried sisters.[106] Labrāṭ I b. Moses I, judge in al-Mahdiyya, Tunisia, was one of three brothers and they had one married sister.[107] Of the two men mentioned in these volumes more often than any others, Moses Maimonides had one son and Nahray b. Nissīm, one son and several daughters, of whom only one grew up to be married. In the cases in which a man wished that God preserve "his only delight [son]," we cannot know whether daughters, too, were in the house.[108]

A single family letter going overseas after the sender and recipient had been separated for a prolonged period can also be useful because the parties give each other exhaustive reports about their families. Since it was customary to recapitulate at the beginning of a letter messages previously received, we usually hear about both sides. Thus, from a letter sent from Jerusalem to Toledo, Spain, in 1053, we learn that the writer had a brother in the Holy City, and another brother and two married sisters in Spain.[109] A letter received in Alexandria from North Africa 1089 shows that the sender had two married daughters from his first marriage and two teenage sons and a married daughter from his second wife, whereas the recipient had two sons and two married daughters.[110] A man from Tlemcen, Algeria, who had not heard from his brother in Egypt "for years," reports, around 1050, that both the country and the family were flourishing, that he had two sons, and his deceased sister two sons and a grown-up daughter.[111] In none of those letters have I read about more than five children in a nuclear household.[112]

Greetings in business and private letters, praises in poems, and data in genealogical lists—our most abundant sources—are of limited value, since only sons are mentioned as a rule. Genealogical lists have the additional disadvantages that they are usually hastily executed and exhibit no system according to which agnates are mentioned or omitted. Consequently, memorial lists can be used only for what they say, not for what they omit. Yet, a trained demographer might extract useful information from these unrewarding materials.

Four, five, or six sons were not uncommon in families of government servants, judges, physicians, or merchants bearing such titles as 'Delight of the Yeshiva," or "Pride of the Community," that is, who were well to do enough to be munificent.[113] In the same circles families with two sons or one were even more frequent.[114]

All in all there seems to have been nothing extraordinary in the size of the Geniza family. It was quite similar to that accepted in the Western world about two generations ago. It could not compare with the abundant fertility of the monogamous family of the nineteenth-century bourgeosie in Western Europe and, of course, not with that of the Muslim ruling class of the Middle Ages with its widely practiced polygyny and concubinage, made possible by power and riches. The Geniza people, high and low, tried hard to have as many sons as possible, but the grim realities of economy and hygiene put strict limitations on their hopes. I have not yet encountered in a Geniza letter the fulfillment of the wish to a newborn child that he may become "a brother of seven or even eight" [brothers].[115]

Relationships between grown-up children and their parents.—Adult children showed their reverence toward their parents by kissing their hands, or hands and feet—at least in letters.[116] Mutual affection was expressed by kissing the eyes.[117] Children were expected "to serve" their parents, that is, to stay with them and to extend to them any help they needed, as it is written, "like a father who loves his son, who serves him" (Malachi 3:17). Consequently, father and mother were addressed or referred to as "my lord" or "my lady," whatever the language used—and not only in letters. A weaver writing to his wife, quotes his son: "My boy Manṣūr came to me and said: 'My lord. . . .' "[118]

As might be expected, we hear about filial obligation mostly when the writer was unable or unwilling to fulfill it. In a lovely letter from Tyre, Lebanon, a young cantor who had found a job in a small Lebanese town writes to his parents in Alexandria, excusing himself over and over for being separated from them. It was not his wish, God had decreed it, for he could not find work in his native city and hated to stay idle. Finally, he goes as far as to say that he was marrying a poor orphan girl for the only reason that his future wife should not come from a family that would impede his returning as a dutiful son to his parents.[119] Of particular interest is the letter of a humble schoolmaster apprising his mother of his marriage.[120] He apologizes for being unable to come and to serve his mother, prohibitive cost and other reasons being the causes. The mother lived with two of the writer's brothers, so it was not her need but his failure to live up to his sacred duty which prompted his excuses. Failure to travel to one's mother for a holiday needed a special apology. To their son's assurances of attachment parents would reply: "You never cease to love us, whether far away or staying with us."[121]

How a son, himself elderly, attended to his father may be learned from this passage of a letter he sent from Jerusalem to a sister in Toledo, Spain: "Our father is in a state that one would wish only for one's enemies. He has become paralyzed, blind, and feeble-minded, and suffers much. The bearers of this letter will tell you about him and about my care for him. He does not lack a thing, for he is well served and cared for. I do not rely on anyone else to concern themselves with him. My bed adjoins his; I get up several times every night to cover him and to turn him, since he is not able to do any of these things alone. May God, the exalted, reward him for his sufferings."[122]

Straightforward statements to the effect that a man is unable to travel because he cannot leave his parents occur occasionally.[123] Caring for one's parents could be a heavy burden, but "God visits him that he loves" (Proverbs 3:12), and "honoring parents," that is, providing for them, was not only a religious commandment but also an element in a man's *muruwwa*, or gentlemanlike behavior.[124]

A profuse expression of filial dedication is found in this letter sent from Egypt to Aden; to a father who, on his way home to Egypt from India had stopped in the south Arabian port: "Please, with the help of the Almightly, may the reply to this my letter be—the sight of you, if God wills. Be not enticed by business so that you forget us. For—by my faith in Heaven—every day more of your absence takes a year from our lives. Consider, the life of the son of man is nothing but light. You are our light. If you are not with us, how can we live?"[125] Another son writes this to his father, who had journeyed from Egypt to Palermo, Sicily, where he had a nephew: "Had we known how much we would be afflicted by the separation from you, we would not have let you travel in the first place."[126] Even more characteristic perhaps is this passage from a letter of a communal official to the Nagid Mevōrākh: "Your servant passed these days in utmost distress because of your being away from your noble hometown and from the company of the Rayyis Abu 'l-Bayān [Moses, the Nagid's son], may the Keeper of the souls of the righteous preserve him."[127] A son should be constantly in attendance. Ideally, father and son should never separate.

The mother's claim to her children's attention seems to have been regarded as even stronger than that of the father's. "I intended to stand before my mother [i.e., to serve her] and to acquire through her religious merit," writes an old man, himself a father.[128] The mother's honored position should by no means depend on her state of being the woman of the house. A son, sending an urgent invitation to his widowed mother, leaving her an almost unlimited number of alternatives for carrying out the visit, writes this: "You know, and everyone knows, the high regard in which you are held. Now you are even greater than when you were the woman of the house; there is no one who does a thing except on your command." The woman's young grandson, who yearns for his grandmother, is the only attraction the writer dares to offer.[129] When a boy from Alexandria runs away "to the army," his father in urging him to come home reminds him three times of his obligations toward his mother.[130]

In this respect, no difference between sons and daughters can be detected. The very specific and strong attachment of the learned woman Rayyisa to her mother is evident from the letter of consolation addressed to her by her brother on the occasion of their mother's death.[131] A woman disconsolate over the death of her husband is assured by her brother of relief from God "because of her kind ways with her mother and everyone."[132] The lack of consideration by daughters toward their mothers was particularly resented, as will presently be seen.

In addition to its religious value, which put reverence toward parents on the same plane as service of God, or rated it even higher,[133] there were socioeconomic circumstances that strengthened the bonds between parents and children. In their youth and early adult life children were dependent on their parents more than is commonly true in our own society, and in old age the parents (especially the mother) often had to rely on their children, as much as they strove not to.

Girls could not expect to make a reasonable match or be secure in marriage, widowhood, or as a divorcée without strong financial and moral support from their parents. The very health of a woman frequently depended on the willingness of a father or mother to make a significant contribution to her treatment.[134]

But a son, too, looked forward to paternal assistance. The law obliged the father to arrange his son's marriage.[135] This meant, in the first place, that the father ceded to him a part of his house, or made him a gift of a separate home, where he would live with his new wife, as many Geniza documents illustrate. A physician gives his son a house, newly erected by him in the Street of the Chain in the Mamṣūṣa quarter of Fustat (both frequently mentioned in documents), as a *ṣadaqa,* or religiously meritorious gift.[136] An "entire house," situated on "the blessed *khalīj* (canal)" of Fustat, was given to a son, but was partly under reconstruction.[137] An old house bordering on the properties of two Muslims and one Christian in the "Fortress of the Rūm," is given by a father to a son, a physician; another son had no share in the house, for he rents from his brother a closet for 12 dirhems per month, a considerable sum.[138] In a magnificent, but unfortunately fragmentary, document, a father gives a property (apparently consisting of a big and a small house) to two sons, partly as common property and partly assigned to either of them.[139] A similar donation to two brothers is attested in a document from Tyre.[140] When a woman, with the consent of her husband, gives a small house plus an open space (used for dyeing, bleaching, tanning, and similar operations) to her younger son, we can safely assume that she had earlier given another property, probably the adjacent larger house, to an elder son.[141]

It should not be forgotten that a father's gift was automatically an act of generosity on the part of the mother since a married man's property was mortgaged to his wife's ketubba and any disposition of it required the wife's consent.[142] A concise but complete document, signed and written by the experienced court clerk Mevōrākh b. Nathan, illustrates this relationship. First, the wife gives her husband complete freedom of disposition over one half of a house belonging to him, which was also serving as their domicile. Second, the father gives this half to a son. Third, the son is not permitted to sell or give away that half during his father's lifetime. This left the son the option of leasing it in the event he wished to separate from the family and derive income from the rent.[143] In a beautiful fragment from Alexandria, a father gives an entire house to his son Jacob "borne to him from his wife Rafī'a ("Sublime");" no doubt the lost part of the document contained a declaration by Rafī'a granting her husband free disposition over the property.[144]

A married woman could only make a gift of property not forming part of her dowry. Thus the "Mistress of Iraq," whose exaggerated concern for funeral arrangements shows that she expected to depart this world soon,[145] gave one quarter of a house to a son, another quarter to a daughter, and stipulated that her husband had the right to live in those parts (on condition he keep them in repair), but emphasized that he otherwise had no right to them whatsoever.[146] Stipulations that the parents had the right to live in premises given to a child are also found elsewhere.[147]

A typical example of how parents with moderate means tried to provide shelter for their children is contained in this question addressed to a jurisconsult: "A man possessed a house with three apartments, south, east, and west. He gave the southern one to his daughter as part of her dowry, the western one to his firstborn son. He remained in the apartment to the east. He had three other boys. When he died, his sons became his heirs." The rest of this question is only partly visible. But cases like this, where a father died after having fulfilled his paternal obligations toward a daughter (who normally married at a tender age) and toward a firstborn son, but before he was able to provide similarly for his younger children, must have been frequent. See subsection C, 4, below.[148]

Besides the moral and material support received from parents there was another benefit derived from them which a medieval man must have prized most highly: their blessings, or, rather, their prayers. Of a man who succeeded in life the Yemenites say: "His mother has prayed for him."[149] Compare this with a short note from the Geniza sent from the Egyptian capital to a brother living in the countryside: "This is to inform you that the Lady [meaning: their mother] is fine. . . . Your mother prays for you; may God accept her sincere prayers on your behalf." This reference to the intercessional prayer of the mother implied also that the old woman was pleased that her faraway son had remembered her and inquired after her health.[150] In the conclusion of a long business letter a father writes to his son: "May God let me always have good news from you and grant you safety. May he accept my sincere prayers on your behalf, give me what I ask for you, and ordain you *a long life* [as promised in the fifth commandment, Exodus 20:12]." The tone of the letter shows that, despite some fatherly advice, the writer was perfectly content with his son's performance.[151] A particularly warm family letter to a son overseas ends thus: "By these lines, I do not deprive you of intensive prayers, you, your brother and your children, Peace upon you, and God's mercy and his blessings." Only God can grant blessings. But the parents are the natural pleaders for their children.[152]

The biblical stories of the blessings of the Patriarchs (Genesis 27:26–29, 48:15–20; 49:1–28)—familiar even to the present-day generation through the paintings of Rembrandt and other great masters—reminded everyone of the power of paternal intercession. But children are not regarded worthy to pray for their parents; they have not yet accumulated enough merits to be worthy pleaders. Although children in the Geniza ask their parents to pray for them, or are assured by them that they do, I do not remember having read of the reverse.[153] Children might offer themselves as ransom for their parents' sins. An ancient Palestinian prayer book, found in the Geniza, instructs children to include their parents in their private supplications for forgiveness. But the official prayer for the dead, the Kaddish, now so prominent a part in the synagogue service, especially in the United States, and made widely known through the musical creations of Maurice Ravel and Leonard Bernstein, acquired that function in late medieval Christian Europe. In Geniza times the Kaddish was a solemn doxology, including a prayer for the *living*, and, in particular, the spiritual leaders of the community.[154]

The wishes that children should be like their parents and, even better, more successful, or of greater renown, expressed in letters to both parents and the children themselves, are mundane rather than religious. This is evident from the wording of the wish and also the biblical reference to it, the words spoken to the dying King David: "May God make Solomon's name more famous than yours and make his throne greater than your throne" (1 Kings 1:47).[155]

"When your son is grown up, let him be your brother"—this beautiful Arabic maxim, which has Hebrew and ancient Near Eastern antecedents, is reflected in the Geniza correspondence exchanged between parents and children.[156] No wonder. Since the sons entered economic life early, they soon became the helpers, collaborators, or partners of their father, or took over altogether. Our letters reflect the stage reached by the son and, of course, also the characters and situations of the persons involved.[157]

Naturally, fathers often had reason (or believed they had reason) to be dissatisfied with their sons. "Stop occupying yourself with marriage plans and such idle things," writes a father, reminding his son, a fledgling physician, that he had not yet made enough money for such ventures.[158] The judge Elijah b. Zachariah, after admonishing his sons to stop quarreling with one another and bringing disgrace to the family, ends by saying: "I am sick and tired of preaching to you" (and they, perhaps, were too).[159] The old Gaon Solomon b. Judah writes to his son Abraham, who served as his official emissary: "Keep to yourself what has happened between me and you." But when the Gaon worked for a peaceful settlement with the Karaites, and the younger leaders advocated tough measures, Abraham publicly sided with the latter.[160]

Mothers, too, could be critical of their sons. A woman in Alexandria, after sending to her son in Fustat a long list of errands to be done for herself and other members of the family, warns him not to anger his younger brother and to be patient with him.[161] Another, writing from Palermo, Sicily, to Barqa, Libya, reminds her son that he was now in his father's place, and, therefore, had to be considerate both toward his younger brother and herself, and to honor those who did her a favor; he should also show gratitude to those who helped him and take heed of his enemies; in general, she assures him, she was satisfied with him.[162] An old woman in Fustat adjures her son in the countryside "by the milk with which I have nursed you, do not neglect your boy" (who was probably studying in the capital and staying with his grandmother).[163] Of particular freshness is a letter from Aden, southern Yemen, in which a mother scolds her son in Fustat for going abroad—something done only by fools—and especially for sending her a worthless dress, which made her the laughingstock of the town. She repays him with a lot of gossip and some useful instructions.[164]

Occasionally, friction between children and parents came into the open. "I was sad when I learned that you quarreled with your father—but he is your father!"—we read in a personal letter to a man who is otherwise praised for his actions described as noble and in accordance with the traditions of his family.[165] A rather impersonal business letter concludes with this remark: "Best regards to Abū Kathīr Ephraim; tell him that his wife and son are well, may God punish the man who put enmity between him and his son."[166] An extraordinary document of estrangement between father and son is contained in a long letter of an overseer of the Sultan's ships describing his manifold calamities. The son loved music, Italian wine, and bad company, and, of course, was always in debt; all attempts of the father to correct him: presenting him to the qadi of Alexandria, taking him on a trip to Tunisia, sending him to the countryside on administrative work, suggesting to him travels to Yemen and to Syria—were of no avail. The young man of twenty-two was not a mere good-for-nothing. He was allergic to his father. "As long as you are alive, I have bad luck. As soon as you are dead, I shall be successful." Nowhere else in the Geniza have I read such terrible words addressed by a son to his father. But the father, too, secretly hoped that the wastrel would perish on one of his travels.[167]

In general, however, the families tried to hush up conflicts. Lawsuits between parents and children are rare and were clearly regarded as outrageous. In a court record of December 31, 1100, a son agrees to renounce all claims to an inheritance from his mother, grandmother, or great-grandmother in a Muslim court to which he had brought his litigation, and the father is to deposit one half of all his possessions, movables and immovables, with the Jewish court. After the settlement in the Muslim court the objects of litigation are to be divided in equal shares. Fines were imposed for failure to carry out these stipulations.[168] In a fragmentary record from summer 1045 another lawsuit over an inheritance is settled. The father agrees to have his son live in his house for three years, but without providing him with food; should the father sue the son again, he will have to pay a fine of 15 dinars to the alms fund of the congregation. The circumstances under which a father was compelled by a court decision to pay his daughter 1 dinar per month for her baby boy during eighteen months are not clear (summer 1065).[169] A long letter from Qayrawān reports on an argument between a Muslim shipowner and his son over a bale that disappeared from the customs house of the port of al-Mahdiyya. The father brought the son before a merchant court of elders, who rebuked the young man and scolded him for acting ignominiously toward his father, but the son remained adamant. Finally the bale was found.[170]

A son who sued his mother in court was a monstrosity. A judge in Alexandria informs an assistant of the Nagid Mevōrākh of such a case, in order to ask the Nagid's intervention. A man from Barqa, Libya ("the Wild West"), had induced a young compatriot to sue his mother for the father's estate. The mother had brought up the children by her own work and had them study the Torah on her account (as the judge emphasizes twice). First, the boy took from his mother a Bible codex (a precious object in those days), which, however, he was forced to deposit with the court. Publicly reprimanded, the evil man from Barqa then brought the boy's case before the qadi, who, as usual, sent it back to the rabbinical court. Reprimanded a second time, the Barqī threatened to approach "the Sultan," that is, the administrative court of the governor, but the boy, along with a brother and another relative, disappeared from the city. At this dangerous turn of events (the boy might sue his mother in the capital), the Nagid was alerted. Since Alexandria was plagued by the rivalries within the various Mediterranean communities meeting there, the judge notes that the Barqīs keep aloof from their mischievous compatriot.[171]

An opposite case, namely, that of a widow instituting a long litigation against her three sons until she got from them what was due her—her late husband's marriage gift and her own dowry, "consisting of jewelry, clothing, merchandise, and other goods"—is reported in a Hebrew document from the late tenth or early eleventh century. The woman's name was Khazariyya, which did not mean that she was a Khazar but that her mother thought that she was, or should become, as beautiful as a Khazar (Turkish) girl. Her late husband, however, was Ṭāzān the butcher, a very outlandish name indeed. Lawsuits between children and parents seem to have been essentially foreign to the civilized Geniza society.[172]

With stepsons the matter was different. They could easily have been older than the young widow of their father and could have had good reason for distrust. Lawsuits of this type occurred in families of repute. The position of stepchildren in general is discussed in C, 3, below.[173]

Foster children.—Adoption in the strict sense is unknown to both Islamic and Jewish laws. But persons called foster child, *rabīb,* of a man or a woman, are mentioned in the Geniza frequently. Often we are able to ascertain that they were stepchildren, sometimes we cannot. We have, however, clear examples where persons reared children with whom they had no family connection whatever. In time of great calamity, probably at the beginning of the Crusaders period, when many female prisoners had to be ransomed and cared for, a woman, herself a mother of three girls and two boys, took a little girl into her house and brought her up "in order to acquire a religious merit." Unfortunately, the story did not end as beautifully as it began. After four or five years, when the girl matured, one of the two boys asked her to marry him. But the marriage lasted only a few weeks. She refused to return to her husband, exclaiming, "even if he pours gold pieces upon my head." The pressures exercised by the family and the authorities were of no avail. Finally, she was driven out of the house by her foster siblings.[174]

A record of an actual adoption proves that the Jewish courts had considerable experience in these matters. The wife of a stranger died sixteen days after she had given birth to a girl for whom the bereft father was unable to provide. He "sold" her for 5 dinars to a prominent lady, who agreed to bring her up. The father promised to allow the foster mother complete freedom in the education of the girl, he would never demand the return of the girl, nor even come near the place where she lived. He would have no claim on any gains made by the girl or on any other income accruing to her from the house of her benefactors, from a marriage gift, or from compensation given to her for a disgrace or an injury inflicted upon her. If the girl died, no claim of negligence could be made against the woman. An incomplete last sentence seems to say that the father would return all her expenses to the foster mother if the girl, when grown up, wished to return to her father's family.[175]

According to both Jewish and Islamic laws no free person, whether one day old or grown up, could be sold. The word was used in order not to put the unhappy stranger to shame: he made a deal, he was not a receiver of charity. But he certainly could make good use of the money. As to the motives of the lady, I do not believe that she was barren; if she were she would have adopted a son. Raising an orphan girl in one's house and marrying her was a tremendous religious merit, for it fulfilled the biblical ideal of one "who does a good work every minute" (Psalms 106:3).[176] In addition, I assume the lady's children were already married and she felt herself young enough to have a child around the house, who would then be a companion to her in her later days. There is nothing special in all this. What attracts our attention is the elaborate legal formulation with which the document (an incompletely preserved draft) is drawn up and the many circumstances considered in it. Only a good amount of court experience with such cases could have produced this document.

When the foster sons of the "illustrious lord al-Afḍal" ("The Noble") receive charities from the community, it is safe to assume that they were not close relatives of his. From the relevant document it is evident that the payments were regular. The bringing up, and later manumission of slavegirls has been described before as a form of adoption.[177]

It is appropriate to speak about "the informal adoption of parents" as a constant feature of the Geniza correspondence. Just as a man would address a friend to whom he was not related as "my brother from both father and mother," so would he call an older person on whose guidance, advice, or support he counted "my father," *wālidī,* literally, "my progenitor," and himself "your son," using even the term of endearment *ḥamūdō* (Heb.), "your delight." This usage strikes me as particularly strange when in the same letter the writer makes mention of his real father or when he refers to himself as "your son, brother and friend."[178] This form of address, familiar from the Bible (2 Kings 2:12, 5:13, 6:21, and elsewhere) and the ancient Near East, and lingering in present-day Arabic speech, should not be overrated; it occurs in the Geniza in profusion. Yet this extension of family terms to human relationships in general (to which also the term *'amm,* paternal uncle, belongs) is an indication of the intensity of feelings for the family itself.

3. Widowhood, Divorce, and Remarriage

Widowhood.—We read much about widows in the Geniza, but little about widowers. The reason for the difference should not be sought in a higher rate of male mortality.[1] It was caused by the entirely different situations in which husbands and wives found themselves after the demise of their spouses. A husband's social and economic status was affected hardly at all by the death of his wife. If not otherwise stipulated, he was heir to her dowry and other possessions, and was freed from the obligation of paying the delayed marriage gift, a heavy financial liability. As to the domestic chores, a household was comprised mostly of female relatives besides the wife: a mother, a sister, a grandmother, an aunt; in their absence a maidservant or an elderly hired free woman did the work;[2] or the husband would take a second wife soon after the first had died, especially if he had children.

For the wife the death of her husband was a disaster. She lost her support and even her domicile and could rely only on the remnants of her dowry, her other possessions, and the promised late marriage gift, all of which were often uncertain and insufficient assets. Indigent widowhood was a calamity for the woman concerned and an imposition on the community. It is for this reason that so many Geniza papers contain complaints of widows or describe actions to improve their lot.

On the other hand, widowhood or divorce freed a woman from the yoke of marriage. She was now free to act on her own in financial as well as other matters; for instance, she could marry whom she liked and on conditions she imposed, or could even have an affair. But freedom was sweet only if fortified by adequate means. The well-to-do widow or divorcée was another social figure prominent in the Geniza records.

At marriage a husband mortgaged all his possessions, "even the coat on his shoulders," and, after his death, his estate, to the "debts" he owed his wife: her delayed marriage gift and her dowry, the income of which he had been entitled to use for the duration of the marriage. In reality, this agreement frequently proved to be unenforceable simply because the husband was unable to acquire the means for the payments guaranteed. Consequently, when the end of life approached, we find settlements made in which the amount of the late marriage gift to be paid was reduced, sometimes to half the original amount or even less. The reductions involved concessions on the husband's side, usually the granting to the wife of the status of "trustworthiness," which protected her from being troubled by heirs and courts with demands to render account of any property of her husband held by her.[3]

The frequency of such occurrences must have induced husbands to reiterate on the deathbed what sums they still owed their wives from their marriage contracts, a very common practice.[4] Moreover, a gift to the wife in addition to the payments due her was customary. This was often done on condition that she remain unmarried, at least as long as the children were young and had not themselves married. People from all layers of the society adhered to this expression of love and appreciation. An extreme case is that of a rich man giving his second wife and the mother of three of his children (he had a son from a first wife) 200 dinars if she did not marry again, but only 50 dinars (her delayed marriage gift, the obligatory payment) if she did.[5] The poorest of the poor would provide a gift of 1 dinar, or a sack of wheat; a testator with limited means would release his wife from a modest debt she owed him.[6] In the middle class gifts of 10 dinars seem to have been considered as a decent sum, whether the debt owed was 30, 50, or 60 dinars.[7] But "the illustrious doctor, the well-known physician Abu 'l-Maḥāsin Segan ha-Kohanim ["the leader of the Kohens"] b. Abu 'l-Faḍā'il al-Kāmukhī," makes a gift of only 5 dinars in addition to the debt of 5 dinars "written in her ketubba"—not all the practitioners of the medical profession got rich. The great emphasis with which, in the document concerned, the dying doctor protected the widow from any claims on the part of her own sons shows that even that modest gift must have appeared to the latter as exaggerated in view of the dire circumstances of the family.[8]

In wills to a second wife we find legacies made to a child from a previous marriage, as when the stepson of a merchant receives 30 dinars.[9] Gifts made to the wife in kind, in addition to the payments due her, were also usual. A wealthy man gives to his wife the wardrobes in the house, a maid, and a male servant, the latter being a very exceptional occurrence. The slave was probably the merchant's agent, who looked after the master's business during his illness.[10]

The terms "I give," "I will," were used in deathbed and similar declarations in an entirely different situation, namely, when the husband left all his possessions to his wife because their total value hardly covered what he owed her. A perfumer in Fustat gave his wife full disposition over his house and all that it contained (the latter having no value, according to him), thereby paying all that was due her from her marriage contract; neither heirs nor courts could interfere, "even if it was found that nothing was left for the orphans."[11] A goldsmith in the same town left everything he possessed to his wife "as payment toward what was due her from her ketubba," and freed her from all oaths (a widow was obliged to swear that she had not received such payments before or that she had not appropriated some of her husband's belongings).[12] In a court session before Sar Shalom ha-Levi, then the head of the Egyptian Jews, witnesses testified that, on his deathbed, a man in Alexandria had made a gift to his wife of all his landed property in that city because he did not possess anything else.[13] Even a proprietor of houses of considerable value could die without leaving his wife a thing; in such a case the court would empower her to indemnify herself with those properties (if she could, since they would usually be mortgaged).[14]

Other than in grim circumstances like these we rarely read that a husband makes his wife his sole heir. When ʿArūs b. Joseph, a prominent public figure, did so before setting out on a business trip to the Muslim West, he had a special reason.[15] In the same document he empowered her to bring up his children (he had only daughters) and to provide them with dowries as she saw fit, as well as to marry them off to whom she preferred.[16] He certainly must have had full confidence in her character and financial acumen. Her father, Abraham Ibn Ṭībān, and brothers were respectable members of the community, frequently appearing in Geniza papers as contributors to public appeals (often together with ʿArūs himself).[17] Unlike other fathers, ʿArūs did not assign fixed sums for the outfits of his daughters in his will, because he had reason to assume that his wife would be in a better position to judge what would be necessary or appropriate in each case, when their time for marrying arrived.

We are able to reconstruct ʿArūs's reasoning because we have his dispositions on this matter as specified above, in addition to many letters and documents from and about him. It is likely that other men of his class held similar views. We do not know. In the fragment of a remarkable letter a judge reports that a merchant who had died in a foreign country had left all his belongings to his wife. In a previous letter written by the judge the widow had empowered the recipient, a man who had taken care of the merchant's affairs during his last illness and after his demise, to collect all his assets and to have his body carried to Jerusalem at a cost of up to 17 dinars. Apparently no action had been taken in this matter, whereupon the widow appointed her maternal uncle as her representative to exhume her husband's "bones" and to transport them to the Holy City for interment. We do not learn anything about the husband's motives. But we see the widow acting as an heir with full powers.[18]

Normally a husband would not appoint his wife as heir, for if she remarried and died, the estate would go to another man.[19] There was, however, another way by which the wife's abilities and the husband's trust would give her full disposition of his possessions after his death: her role as executor and guardian, sometimes preceded by that as caretaker during his last illness. A notable leaves to each of his three minor daughters 100 dinars for their bridal outfit, his two sons to be the heirs of the balance of his property, and his wife, whose father was still alive, to function as executor for all his children, "to bring them up and to look after their affairs." She was to be "administrator and executrix for all his possessions;" no court would have a right to supervise or to restrict her actions, nor could a court, or her children upon coming of age, impose an oath on her, that is, sue her to give an account of her actions.[20]

In another disposition in contemplation of death a man appoints his wife as executor (and guardian of an only daughter) giving this reason for such confidence: "She understands the child's circumstances better than others, she is more experienced in her affairs, and has more compassion for her."[21] We see such an executor in action in a large contract between the aforementioned ʿArūs b. Joseph[22] and a noble woman called Amat al-Qādir ("Maidservant of the Almighty") and her stepson Japheth (who at that time, it seems, was old enough to understand business, but had not yet fully come of age for acting independently). In the document Amat al-Qādir explains that her late husband had entrusted her with the management of the affairs of his son and also bequeathed to her one third of his possessions.[23] She and Japheth first released ʿArūs from all obligations resulting from his previous transactions with her late husband and then handed over to him 300 dinars as their share in a *commenda* partnership for a business venture in Yemen, where ʿArūs then proceeded.[24]

It is natural that on the other end of the social ladder, with people of modest circumstances, the wife took care of her husband's affairs during his illness and after his death, until the courts, the statutory guardians of orphans, came in and clarified the legal position. The workshop of a silk-weaver described in *Med. Soc.*, I, 86, was "in the hands" of his wife until she was requested by the authorities to make an inventory of what belonged to her boy, the heir.[25] A *ḥazzān*, or cantor, who served as a kind of funeral director, wished to have confirmed by witnesses that a dying man had earmarked 10 dinars for his burial. The money itself was "with his wife."[26] Thus, it is no wonder that in a court record a woman who "had been entrusted by her husband with all his affairs" had to confirm that she would carry out his dispositions in case he died.[27]

When a widow was not granted the status of executor or other special privileges by her husband, she was likely to get into trouble. As soon as her husband closed his eyes, she ceased to be the lady of the house. Everything in the house now passed into the possession of the legal heir, whether it was a son, a daughter, a brother, a paternal cousin of her late husband, or someone else. Her claims were debts against the estate of the deceased, but people often were tardy in living up to their commitments, especially toward a creditor in a weak position, like a widow. This attitude toward a widow's claims is already expressed in an ancient law of the Israelite peasants: "Payments for torts are made with the best field, for debts with that of middle quality, and for the wife's ketubba, with the worst."[28] To counteract the law, the marriage contracts preserved in the Geniza normally contain the stipulation that after the termination of the marriage the wife has to be indemnified with "good gold dinars of full weight," that is, with the choicest of her former husband's possessions. Thus far, I have found only two documents in which the groom agrees to pay his late marriage gift in dinars "of the worst sort", using the legal term occurring in the ancient law cited.[29] But the attitude persisted, and is even expressed in wills, where the husband assigns to his wife the price of objects difficult to sell or of limited value, such as household goods or books, while objects of more value were available for other purposes.[30]

Before a widow could get out anything from the heirs she had to show which of her late husband's possessions were "under her hand," so that these assets could be offset against the heirs' obligations. If not otherwise stipulated or agreed upon, she had to confirm this by taking an oath that she was hiding nothing, "the oath of the widow" so common in the Geniza documents and a most hated affair. The courts went to great lengths in this respect, locking away everything in the house and inquiring not only about small pieces of furniture or kitchenware, but even about the wife's earnings from work during her husband's life, which were legally his.[31]

One widow even learned that she could not be indemnified for nursing her child (which made it impossible for her to earn by working), for this was a service she owed her husband, besides, "the heirs have precedence [over the widow]," and "law knows no mercy."[32] This attitude of the courts was dictated by the meticulous care they exerted for the protection of the rights of the orphans, but it could be hard on their mother. In a picturesque, but incompletely preserved, query addressed to a legal authority this story is told: a widow holding a statement making her trustworthy in every respect was advised to lock the gate of the house to the judge and the elders coming to make an inventory. She refused to let them in, but witnessing her grief the visitors asked her not to make any changes and said that they would return later. She then declared that she held nothing of her husband's possessions. The seemingly superfluous question, whether she owed "anything," meaning had she taken the widow's oath, probably was occasioned by an incomplete or unclear formulation of the "document of trustworthiness." We have another question about such a document, which seems to show that uncertainties in these matters were not uncommon.[33]

Uncertainty or outright ignorance of the law could have disastrous consequences. A woman had permitted her husband to give as collateral for a debt a house belonging to her personally (not being a part of her dowry). She had acceded in order "to do him a favor" and "to have a quiet life with him," after he had coaxed and pressed her to accept what appeared to be a temporary measure. But when the husband died without having paid the debt, even the great judge Menaḥēm b. Isaac b. Sāsōn, in a responsum written in his hand, could not but decide that her property was forfeited.[34]

To protect a woman from ambiguities, we find husbands and heirs making legally ratified clarifications. "The half a house in which I live is written in my wife's ketubba; it is hers. The jewelry given by me as a collateral is hers; it must be ransomed with the money of the orphans."[35] Abu 'l-Ḥajjāj Joseph, son of the late "Great Master," the "Head of the Masters," Elazar, confirms that his mother had given to a brother a three-year-old maid born in her house and brought up by her, and that neither he nor any of the other heirs had any claim to the girl. Similar documents confirming a widow's property rights are extant.[36]

Clarifications were the more needed as husbands often left their wives in unfavorable or in ambiguous legal conditions. In a detailed deathbed declaration a government supplier makes his second wife trustworthy retroactive to the time of their marriage (a stipulation very much needed, see below), as well as for the future, with the exception of the "principals." When asked of what the principals consisted, he explained: "Immovables and merchandise, namely, pepper, lead, collaterals given to me, and jewelry of silver and pearls [a list of which had been deposited]." Concerning these, her own children (who were also his) could, when grown up, demand an account from her, but not his other children. If needed for the household, or "cases of illness, school fees, clothing, or unforeseen expenses," she could sell some of those principals, but only under the supervision of a relative named, or two witnesses appointed by the court. How to spend the money thus received was her business and no one had the right to tell her what to do. She was a woman of circumspection and mercy.[37]

While these arrangements of an experienced merchant sound fairly reasonable, although they were perhaps not fully satisfactory for the widow, we are shocked when a man wills that his business partner should lock up everything in the house, sell it, and from the price obtained give his wife what he had assigned her.[38] Very special circumstances must have caused a wife, introduced by her brother to the three witnesses present, to agree to the reduction of her delayed marriage gift from 70 to 20 dinars, and, on top of that, to renounce the title of trustworthiness granted her in the marriage contract. Apparently, she had plundered her husband's house during his lifetime. Similar accusations, including one against the mother-in-law living in the house, are extant, but this woman was the daughter of the prominent notable Abraham b. Nathan the Seventh, "Favorite of the Yeshiva" and "Favorite of the Congregations," and one wonders what relations existed between her and her husband.[39]

Sons from a previous marriage were inclined to be suspicious of their stepmother. In a document written in Fustat in March 1034 an heir, brother of two married sisters and two brothers, claimed that the widow of his father in Qayrawān had manipulated and laid hands on his estate; he therefore sent a representative to "the community" in that city to sue her.[40] When, in 1132, a widow produced in court a list of her claims (including a gift to her on deathbed of 5 dinars)[41] and one showing what she held of her late husband's belongings, the stepsons retorted by asserting that she had cheated her husband in the conduct of the household. An oath that she was not guilty of this offense was imposed on her, but the end of the story most probably was that she renounced some of her demands and the sons freed her from the oath.[42] We have other such settlements between heirs and a widow. In one particularly complicated and intriguing case, a son frees his mother from her widow's oath; she was content to receive her delayed marriage gift of 30 dinars, while she renounced what was still left of her dowry and other dues to the amount of 20 dinars. To a minor son was left the choice of demanding of his mother the widow's oath upon his coming of age, in which case he would have to pay her one-half of the dowry she had renounced. All seemed settled when rumors reached the court that the deceased had left gold unaccounted for. To underline the serious nature of the proceedings the holy Torah scroll was taken out of the ark in the presence of the widow and "a ban in general terms" was pronounced against anyone who might have laid hands on the belongings of the dead man. But the widow did not budge.[43]

Complaints about heirs who did not pay a widow her dues or did not otherwise come to terms with her are, of course, found in the Geniza, but fewer than one would expect.[44] More common are releases in which the heirs declare that they have no further claims against the widow and the latter declares that she has received all owed her. Many such documents have been preserved. Expressly or by implication the releases show that they had been preceded by lawsuits, sometimes of long duration.[45] A trousseau list, written with a thick pen and greyish ink, in which each somewhat faded item is gone over with a fine pen and black ink, looks as if it had accompanied such a release, whether for a widow or a divorcée we cannot know.[46]

After having been cleared by the heirs and the courts, the widow had to overcome another hurdle: collecting the sums assigned to her. Except for the rich a man's assets consisted mostly of partnerships, other forms of investment in business ventures, promissory notes, and the like; and, of course, there were often counterclaims. Of the numerous relevant documents, a few characteristic of the period are briefly described. In a tenth-century letter, probably from Damascus, fifteen elders admonish a community in another country to bring to court a merchant against whom a widow held no fewer than twenty documents of indebtedness. His claims against the orphans, offset by counterclaims, had to be dealt with separately.[47] In a letter in Arabic characters connected with this case, the orphans (but in reality the widow speaks) ask a *ḥāvēr* to pronounce a "ban in general terms" against anyone submitting falsified documents to a Muslim judge.[48] A similar complaint, that the partners of her late husband had bribed Muslim authorities and divided almost the entire estate between themselves, leaving next to nothing to her for her three daughters and minor son, is made in a letter from Alexandria to the Nagid Mevōrākh. She seemed more critical of the Jewish judge of Alexandria "and his son," repeatedly referred to with his father,[49] than of the qadi, whom she had approached in person at a certain stage of the litigation, and who, according to her, declared that the orphans enjoyed precedence.[50] This letter is perhaps the most detailed account found in the Geniza of the struggle of a widow with the former partners of her late husband.[51]

How protracted such litigation could be is evident from an instruction by the Nagid Abraham Maimonides to a provincial judge. In a previous note the Nagid had advised him to settle the accounts with the debtor and to submit them for examination. After approval and an order to arrange the payments, still nothing happened, and the widow, the mother of a child, was again forced to travel to the capital. This time she carried home with her a strongly worded letter by the Nagid, addressed to both the judge and "the holy congregation," containing quotations like "do not wrong any widow or orphan" (Exodus 22:21), or "for their redeemer is strong, He will plead their cause against you" (Proverbs 23:11). Judging from another piece of correspondence of the Nagid Abraham Maimonides with a local authority one doubts whether even this letter had the desired result.[52] To conclude this sad topic on a happier note: we have a document in which a widow appoints an agent to claim merchandise left by her late husband with several merchants who were sojourning "in Yemen."[53] And we also have a bill of release in which a widow confirms having received all the goods carried for her from that distant country.[54]

After the fight for their basic rights was terminated, a new and protracted struggle began for many, if not most, widows. The majority of widows about whom we read in the legal documents of the Geniza were mothers of minor children. The courts, in their endeavor to preserve the property of the orphans, entrusted it to executors or administrators, if it had not been done by their father, and assigned to the household of the widow alimony of mere subsistence level. But even these scarce means of livelihood were often not delivered on time, or in full, or they proved to be totally insufficient. Subsection C,4, below, describes some of those hardships.

A widow with adult sons usually lived in the house of one of them. Numerous family letters and legal documents reflect such a situation. Staying with a married daughter was less frequent, but not as rare as one would be inclined to assume in view of the popular prejudice against such an arrangement.[55]

For widows from a second marriage—an extremely frequent occurrence, as will be seen presently—special arrangements had to be made to provide them with a domicile. For well-to-do people this presented no difficulty, since they normally possessed several houses or parts of them. "I also will that my wife should stay in the house in which I am at present, in one of the apartments which my brother will choose for her, if she wants to live there; but if she prefers another place in our compound, my brother will put her into lodgings agreed upon by her and him; and there she will take with her all I willed to her and her son." This we read in a comprehensive deathbed declaration of a wealthy man with minor sons from a first marriage.[56] Another notable gives to his wife a small house (overlooking the *Khalīj*, or canal, of Fustat), which was adjacent to his own, large one.[57] When a man who possessed five eighths of a house gave one eighth to his wife and her son as lodgings, "belonging to them forever," the intention probably was to make a gift to the stepson rather than to the wife, for she was also the mother of the donator's children. For reasons unknown to us she might, of course, have preferred to live as widow with her son from a first marriage.[58]

Poorer people had no such choices. A widower who was about to marry but who had a grown-up son stipulated that his new wife could stay in his house after his death, but that he would not be able to provide her with separate "widow's lodgings," a privilege normally expected to be granted under such circumstances.[59] Grave conflicts could ensue when the legal situation was not as clearly stated as in that document. In a mournful but strong letter to a Nagid the widow of a cantor asserts that besides suffering because of insufficient food and clothing, she and her boy had been without a permanent domicile for three months, because a son of her late husband attacked her physically, and in a dangerous way, whenever she tried to enter the house to which she had a claim. She was writing now because when she cried for help the last time, only a Turk passing by saved her from her stepson, who would otherwise have killed her. We have, of course, no way of checking these assertions. That they could have been made at all is testimony enough to the plight of widows, and so is the conclusion of the letter: "If you help me, so good; if not, I trust in God, the exalted, and go my way."[60]

Most of the women who were forced to have recourse to public welfare were widows. For the term "wife of" in the lists of receivers of bread, wheat, clothing, and handouts of money and other benefits described in *Med. Soc.*, II, 438–469, means "widow of," and most of the single women with children registered in those lists must have belonged to this category.[61] A benefit granted to them was the right to live in a house belonging to the community (for which, however, a rent had to be paid), and, in one document we even read about a house occupied, with one exception, solely by women, comparable with the Muslim houses of widows known from later times.[62] One wonders why so many more single women than men were "exposed" to public welfare. The problem is touched upon in section D, below, where the position of women in general is discussed. There we consider also the opposite social phenomenon, the independent woman with means, widowed or divorced.

Divorce.—"God hates divorce," says the Bible (Malachi 2:16), and one is not surprised to find the Geniza courts trying hard to settle matters between husband and wife before granting them a divorce. "Take with you some of the elders, go to her, talk to her heart [an untranslatable biblical phrase], and reason with her, hopefully they will make peace with each other." Such attempts are found during all the phases of the juridical process leading to divorce.[63] But the very extensive space occupied by these matters in the Geniza documents proves that divorce was much more common in those times and places than in the Jewish families of Europe and America until the last generation. E. J. Worman, the Curator in Oriental Literature at the University Library Cambridge was so impressed by this fact that at the beginning of this century he assembled into one collection from the Geniza forty bills of repudiation, ranging in time from 1024 through 1279.[64] But such bills and related material are dispersed in great numbers all over the Geniza. As a matter of fact, the oldest document found thus far is a note of repudiation, given in Jerusalem in the year 872/3 by a man from Baghdad to his wife, a native of Nesībīn (modern Nisib) in northern Mesopotamia.[65]

The wish to separate when a common life becomes unbearable is a natural human urge. In a society that prohibits or ostracizes divorce, people restrain themselves (or find other solutions). In the Geniza world divorce was disapproved, but abundantly practiced. Several reasons seem to account for it. The example of the surrounding Muslim environment no doubt was a strong factor. The Copts, an ancient and enduring Christian community, practice divorce, even though it is banned by the Church. Egypt, their country, had become thoroughly Muslim, and the mores of a majority exercise an overwhelming influence.[66]

First marriages we remember, were normally arranged by the parents or other relatives to form an additional link in the connections existing between the two parties through family or occupational ties. But what happened to the wife when those ties themselves became strained or severed altogether? In a long letter from Jerusalem, containing much news, we read this: "The member of the High Court, R. Ḥayyīm, behaved in an ugly way toward his brother-in-law. The matter ended up in separation [from his wife], but God provided the girl with a replacement better in every respect: religiosity, means, and scholarship; these days she is entering her new house."[67] A note to a judge, signed *yeshū'ā,* "salvation," the motto of the Gaon and nāsī Daniel b. Azarya, strikes a similar note: "Mufrij b. Sulaymān appeared before me and complained that a brother-in-law of his treated him with contempt. The wife also does not like the husband [This, it seems, was a matter of secondary consideration]. They [brother and sister] have decided to separate from him. You, our master—may God strengthen your honored position—are best fit to summon the parties and to settle the matter in a way conducive to the welfare of all concerned."[68] In an unusual letter to her husband away on travel a wife expresses her yearnings for him and wishes to be united with him in health and happiness, but reveals to him that his parents and his brother urge her "to release" him. The manuscript breaks off with the words: "Now, if I divorce you. . . ."[69]

In view of such occurrences one wonders what happened to those "diplomatic" marriages arranged by eminent professionals and business people.[70] To restore peace between the two yeshivas of Baghdad, Hay Gaon, the leading figure in the Jewish ecumene during the first third of the eleventh century, married the daughter of Samuel b. Hofni, head of the other yeshiva. But after the latter's demise, relations between Hay and his brother-in-law became extremely strained, a situation that caused bewilderment even in faraway Qayrawān, Tunisia. How the woman placed between these two men faired is not reported.[71] David b. Daniel b. Azarya, for some time head of the Jews in the Fatimid empire, repudiated the girl betrothed to him, although it was his father-in-law who had procured for him, a stranger in Egypt, the means needed for his success. Our source, which was hostile to David, cites this as another proof of his vile character, especially since the girl's mother was dead and she had been betrothed to him for two years.[72] David's contemporary, Jekuthiel b. Moses, better known as Abū Ya'qūb al-Ḥakīm, "the Doctor," the leading Jewish merchant in the Egyptian capital, repudiated his wife Munā, daughter of Samuel b. Nahum, probably of the Nahums, one of the most influential Jewish families of Alexandria at that time.[73] Another prominent contemporary of David b. Daniel, Japheth b. Abraham, "the Pride of the Community," a banker who served as administrator of the caliphal mint, saw his daughter Sitt al-Fakhr ("Lady Glory") divorced, under which circumstances we do not know; for the time being we have only her bill of repudiation.[74] Anyhow, we see that the matchmaking of the great families was not always a success.

The extreme, physical mobility of the Geniza society was another factor undermining its family life. Young men of all walks of life often had to leave their wives for months and years, and wives usually were not prepared to follow them to foreign ports. The subject is extensively treated in the subsections on the absent and runaway husband, above.[75] Here, a few examples of bills of repudiation sent from one country or locality to another underline the fact that separation caused by travel was apt to lead to divorce. In a lengthy letter, mostly in rhymed prose, Joseph ha-Kohen b. Solomon Gaon, writing from Jerusalem or Ramle, informs the Jewish chief justice of Aleppo that it had taken seven months to find the husband whose wife in the Syrian city had demanded a divorce; the bill had now been made out and entrusted to a man who would deliver it to the woman.[76] A husband from Fustat, while in Aleppo, divorced his wife, who had remained in the Egyptian capital; we have both the court record dealing with the case and the actual bill of repudiation.[77] When the freedwoman Dhahab ("Gold") received the bill of repudiation sent to Fustat from a provincial town, the official dealing with the matter found it necessary to ask the Nagid for further instructions.[78]

Mobility had another negative effect: it resulted in marriages, probably often hastily concluded, between persons from different places who were not compatible.[79] The 872/3 bill of repudiation from Jerusalem already mentioned, the most ancient one found thus far, reflects such a situation. In a bill from Fustat a woman is repudiated by her Alexandrian husband in the small town of Ṭatay, renowned as a holy shrine (Feb. 1052).[80] An immigrant from Yemen, who had married a woman in Bilbays, Lower Egypt, divorced her in Jerusalem, "after much suffering and paying her more than was due her" (ca. 1214).[81] A man from Jabal Nafūsa, a mountainous district southwest of Tripoli, Libya, repudiated a "Maghrebi" woman, probably from Tunisia, in Fustat (Dec. 1214).[82] A marriage between a husband from Ascalon, Palestine, and a woman from Alexandria, Egypt, was terminated in Fustat in 1223/4.[83] A woman from the Egyptian capital, married to a native of Qūṣ in Upper Egypt, who had settled with him in Bilbays, was repudiated by him in that little town (Feb. 1279). She married another man, was again divorced, but remarried the divorcé; the ceremony was held in the house of the Nagid, who probably had taken a personal interest in the case (Feb. 1290).[84] Some of the Geniza court clerks mentioned the places from which the parties hailed, the majority did not. Had all clerks adhered to the custom of noting the parties' countries of origin, the dangerous effects of mobility on marital life would have become even more patent in the relevant documents.

Finally, a contributing factor to the frequency of divorces in the Geniza period might have been the greater attentiveness to a wife's sufferings, to be expected in a cosmopolitan bourgeois society, coupled with the notorious Mediterranean sensitivity to "what people say." A bad marriage was a disgrace, because such matters never remained a secret for long. Its termination was preferable to the shame it brought to the families concerned and, in particular, to the husband.

"Separation should be agreed upon by the two of you. . . . Living together without mutual consent is like prostitution.[85] You behave as if you are doing us a favor, and as if we have got you and yours into a quagmire. In reality, we shall feel as if released from the stocks, for this is heartbreak and hell. Our lives and yours are in your hands. Put an end to it, and relieve the people of gossiping about you."[86] Thus writes a man who had married his orphan niece to a very intimate friend and relation of his after the marriage had gone awry and become public gossip. We have a plethora of correspondence about this couple, the husband being none other than Solomon, the son of judge Elijah, he complaining about the bad, incorrigible character of his wife, and his friend coaxing or censuring him and instructing or scolding the spouse.[87] Solomon's brother, the physician Abū Zikrī, was an equally difficult husband. When he absented himself for an unseemly long period, his brother-in-law wrote him this:

> I sent you several letters about your wife and received no answer. Every letter was written with blood running from the eyes. She throws her yearnings on me and seeks my companionship.[88] But how can I help her? What can I do? Every letter she sends you only increases her misery. Do not ask how she passed the holidays, holidays without you! . . . This is what she says to you: I ask you by God, my cousin, do not stay away any longer. Do not visit upon me the iniquities of others. [he had probably quarreled with his in-laws]. You know well that I have no control over this.

When God brings you back safely and you come home, Doctor, I shall not tell anything to anyone about you. [A veiled threat: otherwise your marriage will become town talk like that of your brother].[89]

The dominant position of the husband was sealed in Islamic and Jewish law by his right of unilateral repudiation. Ancient Near Eastern (and Jewish) law knew more humane forms of separation. The Aramaic marriage contracts of the Jewish community of Elephantine, southern Egypt, written in the fifth century *B.C.*, provide the wife with power to initiate divorce proceedings similar to that of the husband. Traces of such legislation are found in the Talmud, and M. A. Friedman's painstaking study of the marriage contracts according to Palestinian custom found in the Geniza has shown that its last vestiges were still alive well into the eleventh century.[90] Whether caused by the impact of the environment (Iranian or Muslim), or by a too literal and generalizing understanding of a passage in the Bible ("when . . . he writes her a bill of divorce . . . and sends her out of his house" [Deuteronomy 24:1]), the overwhelming testimony of the Geniza proves that only an action on the part of the husband could terminate a marriage. The courts could coerce him, but if he remained obstinate, or could not be found, the wife was condemned to the life of "a widow whose husband was alive," which was worse than that of a widow, for she could never marry again. Islamic law foresees separation ordered by the courts under certain circumstances without the cooperation of the husband.[91] Obviously with this in mind a man of little learning writing Hebrew asks whether a woman, who was deserted by her husband with whom she had lived for ten years, but from whom she had not received a bill of repudiation, or otherwise been separated, may marry another man.[92] I wonder whether this confused question is not connected with the one mentioned above and written, of course, in Arabic language and characters, in which a Muslim jurisconsult is asked whether a Jewish woman whose husband had converted to Islam and disappeared in India for ten years, may not marry again, seeing that she had no other way of maintaining herself.[93] Another Jewish India trader converted to Islam after his marital strife had reached the Sultan's court in Aden, South Arabia. But Khalaf b. Maḍmūn, the Jewish representative of the merchants in that port city, intervened, the husband issued the desired bill of repudiation, and Khalaf took the girl into his house awaiting her father's arrival.[94]

The term "unilateral repudiation" needs qualification. In order for it to become effective, the bill of divorce must have been received by the wife. Many such documents preserved in the Geniza confirm, on the reverse side, that "it has got into her hand."[95] How fastidious the authorities were in this respect may be concluded from two reports about the delivery of the bill, one an official document and another a letter reminding the addressee of how it was performed. At least three men acted, two serving as witnesses and one as the actual deliverer. The official document describes the three as entering the hall of the house of the woman concerned, while she was sitting in an adjacent cabinet;[96] the proxy of the husband entered the room and put the bill into her hand while the two others looked on.[97] The letter describes four persons, including a ḥāvēr, or divine, waiting on the landing of a staircase behind a door; the wife opened the door, and the writer put the bill into her hand, but took it back in order to keep it in a safe place.[98] The same meticulous attention to detail was observed when the husband was present at the delivery.[99]

The acceptance of the bill of repudiation by the wife was seemingly a mere formality. What else could she do, since her dowry and her delayed, that is, main, marriage gift were in the hands of the husband? Similarly, if a woman writes, as we have read above, "if I divorce you," or the same expression is used in documents referring to what a woman says, the meaning can only be that she agrees to accept the repudiation.[100] Does not the Mishna rule: "A wife is divorced irrespective of her will, but the husband divorces only willingly?"[101] An accusation directed against a woman in a small town who had divorced her husband before a Muslim judge "according to her own wish and against his will" underlines this attitude.[102]

In reality, the acceptance of the bill of repudiation by the wife, required by the law, was more than symbolic. In many, if not most cases about which we have more detailed information, one gets the impression that the female partner was the initiator of the divorce proceedings, mostly, to be sure, by renouncing what was due her. In each of the three instances mentioned in which the courts tried to make peace, it was the wife who had to be talked into it.[103] Before ordering the writing of a bill of repudiation a man gave his wife "three fifths of a mill which he possessed and all furniture, clothing, Bible codices, and other books found in the house, and everything belonging to him under the sky" as compensation for all that was due her and, in addition, declared that he had no claims against her in any respect.[104] This and similar statements do not sound like unilateral repudiations. Of course, she might have made life so miserable for him that he preferred to divest himself of all his possessions rather than keep her—advice given in the Talmud to wives wishing to get rid of their husbands.[105] A silk weaver in Alexandria had to declare himself bankrupt before being permitted to repudiate his wife. These were the conditions agreed to by him: after taking an oath of bankruptcy he would pay his future divorcée 15 dirhems of good silver every month (approximately 1 dinar; her late marriage gift amounted to 30 dinars). If unable to do so, he would give her half his daily earnings. He was not permitted to leave Alexandria for four years. For the rest of his life he could not retake his first wife, who lived somewhere out in the country. His clothes were sold, and their price, 137 dirhems, given to the wife. If he failed to keep any of these stipulations, he would be excommunicated. The court record states expressly that this was a settlement "agreed upon by the two after long discussions and disputes," not a court decision imposed on the parties. One can hardly fail to see here a strong woman in action (her name was Sitt al-Kull, "Mistress over All"); after living with her, the husband felt that his first divorcée had not been so bad a wife after all, and, therefore, was forced to vow not to marry her again.[106]

Jekuthiel b. Moses, the representative of merchants usually referred to as "the Doctor," was a hard bargainer, as we know from numerous documents, but he found his match in his tough-minded wife Munā. Court sessions preceding the divorce had been unable to settle the matter. She claimed that he still owed her money due from her marriage contract as well as some silver jewelry, and he asserted that she kept some of his belongings. Munā produced some clothing and household goods in court and declared that that was all she had. "The Doctor," not satisfied, demanded that she swear the obligatory oath of the divorcée. The judge warned and intimidated her, as was usual in such cases; the bier and the trumpets (actually: ram horns) were brought in to remind her of death and the Last Judgment, but Munā remained adamant: "I swear." Finally, worthy elders intervened, to avert the ominous event of a false oath. "The Doctor" agreed to pay 75 dinars and both parties renounced their claims. The repudiation procedures followed immediately. Jekuthiel asked the judge (none other than Abraham b. Isaac the Scholar, see *Med. Soc.* II, 512, sec. 10) to write the bill—a short piece of about thirteen lines or less—and Eli b. Yaḥyā, the parnās, or welfare official, to serve, together with someone else, as witnesses for its delivery. All acceded to these requests. Munā received the bill from Eli's hands and produced her marriage contract. During all these procedures, Jekuthiel was sitting in the courtroom. At the end, he received the marriage contract and tore it to pieces.[107]

One gets the impression that even the divorce settlements in which a wife makes great concessions, such as waiving the cash payments due her from her marriage contract, were initiated by the female partner. The Geniza texts and contemporary sources use an Islamic legal term for this procedure: *iftidā'*, "ransoming herself," getting herself free by monetary sacrifices (Koran, 2:229). In my review of the edition of Maimonides' *Responsa* I warned that the use of Arabic terms does not prove the borrowing of Muslim institutions. For what could non-Muslims writing Arabic do but use Arabic terms?[108] The entire question has now been taken up by M. A. Friedman in a solid study, which shows that, according to established Jewish statute, a wife, as *mōredet*, "revolting" against her husband's rule, could initiate a divorce by renouncing her delayed marriage gift, whereupon the husband would be forced by the courts to accede to repudiation. Most likely, both the Arabic and Jewish practices are compromises between an ancient Near Eastern tradition which gave the wife the right to separation on the one hand and the principle of unilateral repudiation by the husband on the other.[109]

The financial arrangements at a divorce were of the widest possible variety, and many documents describing them have been preserved. A wife initiating the divorce would usually not forego all her rights, but only some of them, or would permit payment in installments (sometimes insured by guarantors).[110] This permission was not easily approved by the authorities, for experience had taught them that a man in that situation and eager to marry another wife was often not punctual in fulfilling his obligations toward the first. This evil, too, is illustrated by numerous documents. Two examples: A detailed list of receipts shows that in the course of two years and five months a divorcée had received 3 1/2 instead of 10 dinars. In another fragmentary court record, the wife is promised 3 dinars per month, but the reverse side shows only one payment of half a dinar.[111] When a husband claimed that his wife, a former widow, had infected him with her illness about which he had not known before the marriage, and that, in view of his state of health and poverty, he asked either to be freed of the payment of the late marriage gift altogether, or to be permitted to do it in installments, one suspects that there was no great difference between the two alternatives. The same is true in the case of a man who applies for this permission because of the alleged bad character and atrocious behavior of his wife.[112]

Two basic documents were needed to make a divorce legal, or rather, to enable the partners to remarry: a declaration from the wife that she had received all due her from her marriage contract or other financial dealings with her husband (including alimony in case she was pregnant or had children from him), and the formal bill of divorce given by the husband, a brief, standard document, called *geṭ* (Heb., pronounced similar to English *get*). The wife's declaration is usually referred to by the Arabic term *barā('a)*, "release," which, in informal speech occasionally seems also to designate the *geṭ*.[113] When the husband had counterclaims, as so often happened, he had to acquit his wife. A mutual release seems to have been the standard procedure.[114]

The bill of divorce was of tremendous religious significance: for a married woman to be with another man was a deadly sin; that piece of paper made it permissible for her to belong to someone else. And it was even commendable that a divorcée should marry again.

Besides these two types of documents which represented the termination of divorce procedures were others that show them to us in progress, mostly because one party was unable or unwilling to meet the demands of the other. I do not see that they contribute much to the understanding of divorce in Geniza times, but still would like to provide some examples.

Fā'iza ("Favorite"), the daughter of the banker Solomon, son of Nathanel (called in Arabic: Kathīr), was about to be divorced by Barhūn b. Sahlān, another banker.[115] Part of her dowry, especially utensils of silver and copper, as well as some textiles, had been given by her husband as collateral and had to be redeemed. Other items formed the object of a lawsuit. The first document, undated, deals with these matters. After they had been settled and Barhūn delivered the other objects still kept by him, he would receive the desired release.[116] On January 23, 1028, Barhūn declared he had received a release but could produce it only in the next session of the court.[117] Three months later, however, on March 28, Fā'iza declared that she was prepared to accept the divorce only if and when her husband delivered the sums and objects still owed by him.[118]

A more cooperative spirit is apparent in a court record describing a settlement between poorer people, the astrologer Ṭāhōr b. Nāmēr (Heb., "Pure, son of Leopard") and his wife. She releases him from all claims, except 3 dinars still owed to her out of her total delayed marriage gift of 15 dinars, while he promises not to woo another woman before having paid her that sum and delivered the bill of repudiation to her.[119]

Three letters, one addressed to the Nagid Abraham Maimonides and two emanating from his office, deal with a man taking a second wife before paying the delayed marriage gift to the first. He is described as "the tax farmer of Sanhūr" (an inland town near Alexandria), but we find him both in Alexandria and in the provincial capital al-Maḥalla. His wife, the daughter of another tax farmer, must have been married for a long time, for she had a grown-up son, and had come to the capital with a boy of seven in order to give him a good education. In her petition to the Nagid she expresses the apprehension that her husband would take the boy away from her and marry another wife without paying her her dues. She later came to see the Nagid in person and produced a court record showing that her late marriage gift had not yet been paid. The Nagid acted, sending warnings that no local official should marry that man before he had absolved himself of his obligations toward his first wife. He also wrote one or several personal letters to the Jewish judge of al-Maḥalla where the tax farmer was supposed to marry, and summoned the culprit to the Nagid's court to determine if he would deny the charges of his wife. But that judge, as we learn from the third letter in this matter, had not reacted to the several reminders, and we are left in the dark as to how the affair ended.[120]

These examples show that then, as now, divorce actions were protracted affairs. In this connection attention must be drawn to those strange instances of finding two identical bills of divorce for the same couple, separated in time from each other by a day, a month, or two, three, or even nine months. Together with these must be considered other bills that lack the signatures of witnesses or where the signatures are cut away.[121] There was a legal situation that required the writing of a second bill of repudiation. According to the law intimacy between a man and his divorcée invalidated the divorce, and a new bill had to be written. We have a detailed report about such a case, when a Kohen was suspected to have met with his divorcée, "the daughter of the hunchback woman," a woman about whom we shall hear presently. He denied the charge by an oath, but the authorities, to be on the safe side, arranged for a second divorce.[122]

But the cases detailed in note 121 were different. The fact that the second bills were written exactly one, two, or three months after the first means that even after the writing of the bill of divorce, and in some cases even after its signing, either both parties, or one of them, had second thoughts. Then the judge told them: "Come back after a month, two months," or whatever he deemed fit under the circumstances. We see that at the second trial it could happen again that someone got cold feet. Therefore we understand why a question addressed to Hay Gaon emphasizes that in order to be valid a husband must order both the writing and the delivery of the *geṭ*. A mere request to write the bill might be only a stratagem on his part to frighten his wife and extract concessions from her.[123]

Divorce was indeed used as a means for exercising pressure, as we learned from the story of the girl from Fustat married to a man in the Fayyūm.[124] Equally instructive is a letter of a foolish woman asking a learned relative to arrange for a renewal of her marriage (which had been dissolved by the good services of the same scholar). She would put into the new contract: "Whenever he speaks to me about divorce, he must pay me a fine of 50 dinars [a sum this woman certainly had never held in her hands], whereas I shall never impede him from marrying again, and if I do so, my late marriage gift will be reduced from 20 to 5 dinars." One sees how the two spouses intimidated each other before the abortive divorce.[125]

One would like to know something about the duration of a marriage ending in divorce. Naturally, there were traumatic experiences, causing a girl to run away a month or so after the wedding and adamantly refusing to return to her husband.[126] Something of this sort might have happened when a man traveling from Alexandria to Cairo and south writes home: "I received a letter from which I learn that Hārūn (Aaron) has divorced Yumn ("Good Luck"). Praise be to God, you [plural, meaning, the family] marry off and divorce while I am away on one single trip."[127] When father or mother appear in court together with the future divorcée and do the talking for her, or when the father even provides guarantees for the case that his daughter, after becoming more independent, would sue her former husband, it is apparent that she was still very young and had been married for only a short time.[128] But such situations were not very frequent. At a divorce the wife normally acted on her own. As customary as it was that the betrothal be enacted in the absence of the bride, the divorce, by contrast, required her presence. Once, when a mother at a divorce action pretended that her daughter was ill, the court sent a messenger to her house telling her that she was liable to lose her rights if she did not appear in person.[129]

Divorce did not sever the relations between the two spouses completely. Payments to the divorcée in installments have been discussed above, and the remittance of child support looms large in the Geniza. The divorcée was regarded as dangerous. A Kohen, in a letter to the Nagid Abraham, expresses the apprehension that his divorcée, who visited in his neighborhood frequently, might harm him through witchcraft, and requests that she be prohibited from visiting there; he fears too that he could hardly avoid meeting her, which was forbidden by law.[130] A son writing to his father (who had married again) regrets that the old man had so much trouble with his divorcée ("had I been there I would have given her hell").[131] A social welfare official charged with the delivery of alimony to a divorcée, was instructed to tell her that 30 dirhems per month for a baby was more than that adjudicated by the court, and to warn her, and her family, not to give her former husband a bad name. (Was not one of the purposes of separation to reestablish a man's standing in society?)[132] Finally, reconciliation after a hasty divorce required much coming and going between the two parties before it could be effected.

Remarrying one's divorcée was widely practiced, but only in the lower strata of the society, as a glance at Table 8 of the Appendix, part I, suggests. In order to see this phenomenon in the proper perspective, one must know that, according to Jewish law, a husband is not permitted to retake his wife after she has been married to another man. Therefore, couples considering remarriage had to make haste. In a case where we have both the bill of repudiation and the new marriage contract, nine months had elapsed between the two.[133] "Cancellation of the divorce" rather than "remarriage" would be the proper description of this action. In Muslim society it was so common that it was designated by a special term. Whereas the marriage gift at the "retaking" in Muslim North Africa was normally smaller than at the original marriage, we find in the Geniza the opposite situation. In most cases, it seems, the husband had to make an effort to get his divorcée back.[134]

I have come across a condition imposed on a bridegroom never to repudiate his future wife only once: when an old woman manumitted and married off her slave girl. This stipulation was well meant, but foolish: since the husband's formal repudiation was required for any separation, the wife, too, was bound forever. But similar provisions are found in ancient Near Eastern law.[135]

In conclusion, the reader is reminded that the tribulations leading up to a divorce—the disappointments, miseries, complaints, and abortive reconciliations responsible for the breakdown of a marriage—are treated in the subsection "Husband and Wife" (C, 1, above). Here, some causes for the frequency of divorces in Geniza times have been discussed, and the divorce procedures themselves have been subjected to a critical examination. All in all, the resulting picture is dark. The authorities certainly tried to protect the wife from the consequences of a law that gave the husband the unilateral right of repudiation. But the authorities were not well organized and did not have much power. The dire reality is touchingly compressed in one phrase of a letter by a particularly unhappy woman: her husband had placed her, together with a girl of eight, in a Muslim environment, had forsaken but not divorced her, had taken away her son, who died while with his father. Moreover, she was ill. This is the advice which was given to her: "Cut your hair and buy yourself free." When a woman cuts her hair and sends it to a man in power, he must act. For this was "the strongest possible form of entreaty," since the hair of a married woman should not be exposed to the eyes of a stranger, let alone to his hands. The women in the caliphal palace did so when the Fatimid empire was threatened by complete anarchy and dissolution. Here that wretched woman is advised to do the same: her preparedness to waive her rights was not enough; she had to move the authorities to act on her behalf by humiliating herself.[136]

Strong women—strong in character and strong through their family connections and possessions—no doubt often had the upper hand in their quest for divorce, and some of them have been presented in this subsection. It was, however, the helpless and poor women who mostly left us records of their fate, naturally, and that possibly is why divorce in Geniza times seems so dark, darker than it actually was.

Remarriage.—Death terminated the marriages of the Geniza period earlier in life and divorce more frequently than was common in Western Europe and America a generation ago. For these reasons the problem of a second or third marriage arose for many, especially since religion and society generally were not in favor of the unmarried state for able-bodied persons.[137]

Research on this matter must remain woefully lopsided and incomplete. We have many details about the second marriages[138] of women, for a marriage contract normally indicates whether the bride had been previously married, and, in many cases, whether she was widowed or divorced, or both.[139] Nothing comparable exists on the male side. A previous marriage of a husband is implicit in a marriage contract only when children from that union are mentioned. Otherwise, references in deathbed declarations, in letters, or in combinations of data form our sources. We have a letter of condolence on the death of his wife addressed to the merchant banker and scholar Nahray b. Nissīm when he was an elderly man, but also a legal document, written about ten years after his death, in which his widow buys a maidservant. This proves that he was married at least twice. A newly discovered letter shows that in his youth, Nahray was married to his cousin, a girl from Tunisia; it was his Egyptian wife, who was mourned in that letter.[140] The Nagid Mevōrākh b. Saadya was a younger stepbrother of the Nagid Judah b. Saʿadya. Thus Mevōrākh's mother, a remarkable woman, was Saadya's second wife.[141] When a son, who himself had a married son, expresses regret that his father had troubles with his divorcée and advises him to move with his present wife to a stepbrother of his, it is evident that the old man had married three or, probably, four times.[142]

The most urgent reason for a single person with children to marry again was the need to give to the orphans a mother or a father. Contracts where the bride agrees to bring up the groom's children or vice versa, or where both parties provide for their offspring from a previous marriage, are frequently found in the Geniza. They are discussed in the subsection on the lot of orphans (C, 4, below).

The number of widowed or divorced fathers marrying a second time must have been infinitely larger than that of mothers. This seems to be proved by the fact that we have next to no references to fathers making, or trying to make, arrangements for their orphans (except remarriage, as just noted), while the Geniza is replete with reports about unmarried widows or divorcées having children. This contrast is understandable since a busy man normally is not free to deal with small children; a single woman forms a household, a single man does not; the "house-husband" had not yet been invented. True, on travel, the merchants had to look after themselves and do the cooking. But at home, when no wife, or daughter, or another female was around, one complained: "I have no one to hand me a cup of water."[143]

Being married was the normal state of an adult. Marrying again after a previous marriage had been terminated was therefore the natural thing to do. Single fathers with children, we have asserted, were far less numerous than single mothers. But we have no demographic data for gauging what percentage of the male population entered matrimony more than once in life. For women, as alluded to above, we have at least the semblance of some statistics. Scanning my card index for first and second marriages, I find these results:

First marriage ("the virgin bride")	103
Second marriage	
Not known whether widow or divorcée	63
Widow	32
Divorcée	23
Divorcée marrying former husband	22
Total	140

About six hundred documents were examined, but only 243 contained the information sought.[144] In order to be truly representative, references to marriages in letters, such as congratulations or reports on weddings, should be added to first marriages, when the circumstances allow us to assume that the bride had not been married before. For second marriages, too, are known to us not only through the fragments of ketubbas, but also by indirect evidence, such as information on inheritance. I estimate that the 103 figure for first marriages should be augmented by a half to 155, while that for second marriages (excluding return to first husband) amounts to 118, about 45 percent of the total (of 155 + 118 = 273). Further Geniza research will augment these figures, but I feel that the percentage reflects the realities of married life in Geniza times.

No direct statements displaying social prejudices against second marriages, especially against a woman formerly married, have been found by me in the Geniza. To the contrary, a father suggesting to his son a choice among three girls, mentions "the divorcée of so-and-so," and a woman in Jerusalem who remarried soon after her divorce is hailed as having made a good swap.[145]

The judge Nathan b. Samuel he-ḥāvēr, one of the most prominent members of the community in his time, was married to a wealthy divorcée. Three documents concerning this woman prove that at least twelve years had passed between her divorce and her marriage to Nathan.[146] The tables in the Appendix show that marriages with widows, and specifically divorcées, were far more common among the poor than among the better off, and that remarriages of one's own divorcée were almost entirely confined to the lower classes. Well-to-do widows marrying again appear in the Geniza more frequently, but the rich divorcée al-Wuḥsha, represented by several documents, never married again, perhaps because of her dubious reputation.[147] Occasionally widows say that they do not wish to marry again, but are forced to do so by their dire economic situation.[148] In a somewhat enigmatic letter the widow of a physician, a distant relative of the Nagid Samuel b. Hanaya, implies that she will be compelled to marry against her will (apparently to a man beneath her station), unless the Nagid assists her in redeeming half of her house, which had been mortgaged against a debt.[149]

The strangest motive inhibiting a divorcée from marrying again I found in a letter from North Africa about the plight of a middle-aged woman who could not overcome her intense resentment against her former husband, who seems also to have been a relative. She stayed in bed for three months, did not go to any wedding or other party, visited the bathhouse only once a month (instead of every week), and when her father suggested she marry another man, she refused, "so that *he* will be punished for my sins in the world to come." (A husband was responsible for his wife's conduct toward God; he was, for instance, entitled and, under circumstances, even urged, to annul her vows.) This looks like a medieval form of expression toward a relationship not unknown to contemporary divorcées.[150]

Regard for the children's welfare has been noted as a main reason for a second marriage. The same consideration could have the opposite effect, namely, that a mother alone preferred not to remarry in order to dedicate herself exclusively to the upbringing of her little ones. I vividly remember a young widow of perfect beauty from a Yemenite weavers' village, a real flower of the fields, who declined all suggestions for a second marriage because of her children. When I visited the village twenty years later, she was still single; the baby in the house was a grandchild. That similar attitudes prevailed in Geniza times is proved by the great number of single women with children mentioned in the documents. While many of these women simply might not have found a husband willing to take care of another man's offspring, others might have been motivated by regard for their children. The opposite, marrying without sufficient safeguard for the children, was disapproved. Two letters, emanating from the same pen, tell about a widow with children intending to marry a person who obviously had not too good a reputation. The judge warned her: "You will be his slave." She replied: "I wish to be his slave." The writer reporting this summarizes thus: "She has set her mind on marrying and has forsaken her children."[151]

The legal impediment to remarriage, that no one could enter a new union before being cleared by a release from the previous spouse, has been detailed above. Similar precautions were made for children. When a widow wished to marry, her son had to free her from the widow's oath, if that had not been done before.[152]

Jewish (and Eastern Christian) law prohibited a woman who had illicit relations with another man from marrying him (or to remain with her husband). We hear very little about such matters in the Geniza.[153] Illicit relations of a man with a maidservant and the subsequent problem of marrying her were more common.[154]

The popular belief that a woman widowed twice was "a killer" and should therefore not be permitted to marry a third time is mentioned in the Talmud and was adhered to by some judges in the Geniza period, much to the objection of Maimonides, especially with respect to a younger woman, even if she was widowed more than twice. To soothe the scruples of those who were apprehensive of contravening the authority of the Talmud, Maimonides recommended the practice commonly accepted in Spain, following the Jewish authorities there: the couple should marry outside the court in the presence of only two witnesses, and then report to a judge, who would legalize the union post factum and arrange for the religious ceremony.[155]

A considerable number of second marriages listed in the Geniza documents seem to be contracts between two aged persons who decided to form a common household. She brings in little and he gives and promises even less. These were probably people doing some work, as much as they could find and were able to do, or lived on public charity, or both. But this interpretation, like the question of poverty in the Geniza in general, needs further study.

No difference in the professed main aim of marriage, the procreation of offspring, is discernible between first and second marriages. The Geniza tells us about husbands who sired more children in their second than in their first marriage, and vice versa. It all depended, of course, on the circumstances, such as the age of the spouses and the respective duration of the two unions.[156]

The same is to be said about compatibility. I have told the story of the unhappy physician who longingly remembers the wife of his youth when his second marriage turns out to be an unmitigated disaster. On the other hand, the most personal letter of a husband to a wife seen by me thus far in the Geniza was written to a woman who had two sons from a previous marriage.[157] At a second marriage the prospective spouses certainly had had more opportunity to know each other than at a first, although for a union of that type, too, matches were made between persons in different places who probably had never met. Thus a physician in a small provincial town empowers the judge Elijah in Fustat to betroth for him a widow from Marrakesh, Morocco, who lived in the capital. Competition among physicians was sharp, and we learn elsewhere that they did not dare to leave their clientele even for a short time.[158] When a brother arranges a marriage for his half-sister in another town under very trying conditions, the future husband certainly had not seen her, since a special penalty was stipulated should he refuse to marry her after she traveled to his place.[159] In general, however, the detailed arrangements made, especially by spouses with children, give the impression that the persons concerned knew what they were doing when they entered a second marriage. The relevant agreements are discussed in the next subsection.

4. *Heirs and Orphans*

The process of succession.—Our studies of the disposition of property made in the face of widowhood and divorce have shown how the Geniza people tried to adapt existing legislation (Jewish and Muslim) to their own social notions or personal wishes.[1] In this subsection, which is mainly concerned with the lot of orphans, first the actual course of the transfer of property from the dead to the living is scrutinized. I purposely use this general phrase because it is not always evident whether a claim was based on a law of inheritance or on a will.

Orphans, of course, were not the only successors to a property left. First, the Muslim state had to be reckoned with. Immediately after the death of a non-Muslim, the Office of the Poll Tax and Estates had to be informed. Actual death announcements found in the Geniza are from the second half of the thirteenth century.[2] It is doubtful whether so rigorous a procedure was followed in Fatimid times. Then not only did a greater leniency toward minority groups prevail, but the general policy (or lack of policy) of the government was one of reluctance to interfere in the affairs of its subjects, and that left the legal handling of estates to the religious authorities of the non-Muslim communities. The interference of the government was feared at all times, and bans were pronounced against persons applying to it in a case of inheritance, or fines were imposed on them. Not until the thirteenth century did the Muslim authorities take the matter into their own hands, thus assuring for themselves whatever portion of an estate they could lay their hands on. Not only was it a question of an inheritance tax, but also the share claimed by the government, especially from female heirs, or heirs who allegedly could not be found, or persons leaving their possessions for charitable purposes indicating that they had no legal heirs.[3]

A Muslim source reports that Saladin (1171–1193), who put an end to Fatimid rule, was approached by the Jewish authorities with the request that their long-standing right to deal with the estates of their coreligionists, especially those whose heirs were absent, not be taken from them. This indeed shows that an attempt in this direction was made by the new ruler, who needed funds for his incessant wars. A Geniza fragment from this time describing an attempt to retrieve the estate of the orphans of a *kātib*, or government official, from *al-dīwān al-ṣāliḥī* (Saladin's administration) seems to refer to such a situation.[4] Saladin consulted the doctors of Muslim law, who confirmed that the demand of their Jewish counterparts was justified. Whatever Saladin ruled in that matter, the examples reported in *Med. Soc.*, II, 396, prove that shortly after his death the Muslim authorities acted in a rather high-handed manner with regard to Jewish estates. From that time on, as is well known from literary sources, in this, as in other respects, the situation of the minority groups deteriorated steadily.[5]

Before trying to show how the authorities speaking to us through the Geniza documents handled the claims of heirs, some special cases of inheritance must be considered. According to Jewish law a husband inherited from his wife, but not vice versa.[6] We hear surprisingly little about this. Probably, agreements made at the wedding, or later in life, took care of the wife's succession.[7] The natural thing for a husband to do was to turn over his wife's estate to their common children. Elazar b. Elazar of Damascus gave clothing, bedding, and copper, as well as a maidservant, inherited from his wife Fakhr ("Glory"), the daughter of a cook, to his two daughters Ḥasab ("Distinction") and Kifā' ("Reward") in equal shares. The division of the items was made by lot, handled by a servant of the court, under the supervision of two judges (Fustat, 1182). A share (besides the maid) amounted to only 11 1/8 dinars. Thus, these were poor people; the late Fakhr possessed no jewelry; we should not suspect Elazar of keeping the gold and silver for himself.[8]

For a similar case (even in the names), but on a higher social level, we turn to a document written in Qūṣ, Upper Egypt, in 1216. The physician Abū Manṣūr Elazar b. Yeshuʿā ha-Levi gives to his two infant daughters Nasab ("Nobility") and Kufū (voweled thus) the entire trousseau of his wife left to him, worth 200 dinars, and consisting of "clothing, gold, silver, copper, and other things . . . as noted in her marriage contract." The declaration was made "in the house of Abū Sa'd Saadya, in the presence of the latter's son Abu 'l-Mufaḍḍal the Scholar," I assume, the physician's in-laws. The widower probably intended to marry again and wished to safeguard the outfit of his late wife, who had died in her youth, for her young daughters.[9]

When a man sues his mother-in-law for the estate of his wife, allegedly held by her, the document emphasizes three times that the dead woman was "the mother of his children." It was in their name that the demand was made.[10] Even more far-reaching was the case of Manṣūr b. Mukhtār ("Victor" son of "The Chosen"), who appeared in court in January 1046 with his boy and made him a gift of the entire estate of his wife Dhukur ("Treasure"). Having done so, he claimed from his brother-in-law, a banker, all she had left with him, particularly 100 dinars that she had allegedly given him for repair of the family mansion. If retrieved, these sums would be administered by the court as the guardian of minor orphans. Incidentally, these two examples show again that a wife was supposed to keep possessions over which she had the right of disposition with members of her own family.[11]

It is characteristic of a period of transition, like that of the Geniza, that ancient laws and notions continue to exercise their force as new ideas come to the fore. We have repeatedly had opportunity to discuss the legal and social position of the firstborn son, to whom Jewish law gave a double share and who was treated by the family and outsiders with special respect.[12] Here must be added some data related to the process of inheritance. In a fragment written by Ḥalfōn b. Manasse at his best, a father testifies that he had never married anyone before the mother of his firstborn, nor had he sired any child before him. My assumption is that the document had been requested by this man's divorcée who wished to protect the prerogatives of her son. In any case, we see that the rights of the firstborn were upheld, at least in principle. The same is evident from a large fragment of a responsum in which an elder brother is described as "simple, not a firstborn" (that is, preceded by an elder sister), and therefore not entitled to the special privilege he apparently claimed. To be sure, a father was entitled to distribute his possessions in equal shares to his children (in Judaism, not in Islam), a privilege often taken advantage of in Geniza times.[13]

A mutual release contracted among a firstborn, his younger brother, a stepbrother, and a stepmother stresses three times the privilege of primogeniture. The parties declared that it was a free agreement, not one imposed by a court, and also had it confirmed by a Muslim notary. But all the young man—son of a butcher—got was 11 dinars; one sees the notion of primogeniture was deep-rooted, though rarely applied.[14]

A similar ambivalence prevailed with regard to the inheritance of daughters. The legal aspects of the matter have been discussed.[15] Here, it must be noted that daughters as sole heiresses or receiving equal shares with sons appear in numerous documents. From the tenth through the beginning of the thirteenth century these matters are handled as though no outside interference was anticipated. Where it was, an interested party applied, or was expected to apply, to a Muslim court. The heiress of Barqa (990) and the daughter of an India trader (ca. 1100), among others, have been mentioned above.[16] In 1028, a woman in Fustat is declared the sole heir of her father who had died in Acre (Akko), Palestine; in 1031, a woman in Damascus acknowledges receipt of her father's estate; in 1050 another one receives all the rights to the estate of a relative in Aleppo, Syria, a maternal cousin of her father, since her father was the sole heir of that cousin and she, of her father.[17] At approximately the same time Qurra ("Delight of the Eyes") b. Solomon, as sole heiress of her father, asks to be assigned 20 dinars out of the 35 deposited by him with a representative of the merchants in Ramle, Palestine. Her stepmother would receive 15 dinars due her from her marriage contract. From another, perhaps previous, document in the same affair it appears that Qurra had a minor sister.[18] Banāt, daughter of Japheth Abu 'l-Riḍā, a man who went down in a shipwreck on his way back from Spain to al-Mahdiyya, Tunisia, taking with him 300 dinars out of a partnership of 1,000 dinars, sued Musāfir b. Samuel, the partner, for 350 dinars still owed to her father. The relevant document was sent from Tunisia to Tyre, Lebanon, where the Gaon Elijah had validated it shortly before his death (1083). But the matter came before the rival court of the nāsī David b. Daniel in the capital of Egypt, where Musāfir happened to be staying, and the case was presented quite differently from the way Banāt's representative (her husband) had done.[19] In the same court the attorney of Thāmira ("Fertile," a rare name) of Alexandria sued a debtor of her late father, since she and her (minor) sister were the only legal heirs (spring 1088).[20] Finally, in November 1217, Sitt al-Thanā' ("Lady Praise"), a virgin come of age, confirms in court that she had received from the executor all her father had left while she was an infant, including the rents collected from the property during her infancy.[21]

None of these comprehensive documents alludes to the fact that the daughters' claims were not in conformity with the law of the majority population. The additional observation that the absence or presence of relatives eligible as claimants in such cases according to Muslim, but not Jewish law, is not referred to in these papers suggests the assumption that, in the period concerned, daughters as sole children were regarded as having the same rights to their fathers' estates as sons.

The egalitarian spirit is reflected in the numerous cases where males and females receive equal shares in wills, or other forms of gifts, from relatives, near or distant. A father wills 74 dinars, as well as jewelry, clothing (male and female), bedding, and copper in equal parts to a boy and a girl from a second marriage.[22] Again, a father leaves one quarter of a house to an infant daughter, and a similar share to a son, and another does so with regard to a sixth of a house.[23] A mother makes gifts of two quarters of a house, one to a son, another to a daughter, and a grandmother in the little town of Malīj does the same. A mother in Qayrawān, Tunisia, divides a valuable upper story in the same way.[24] An uncle gives his possessions in equal shares to the sons and daughters of his dead brother and appoints their mother as his executor.[25] Another uncle divides a sum received from a partner of his late brother in equal shares among three brothers and one daughter.[26] A schoolmaster assigned equal sums to the four children of a son and to the two of a daughter.[27]

In the thirteenth century, when the government began to meddle more and more in the estates of the minorities, a father, in his will, might assign one third to a daughter and two thirds to a son, both minor, in order to forestall lawsuits before the qadi when they came of age. In Islamic law, we remember, a female inherited one half of a male's share. It is doubtful, however, whether this sporadic measure of precaution indicates a change of attitude. We find such discriminatory treatment occasionally far earlier, as when a father gives one half of his estate to his daughter and the other half to his own brother, again, because in Islamic law a daughter can never inherit more than one half of her father's estate. These provisions are contained in a will referred to in an abortive settlement dating from April 1103.[28]

When a father had sons and daughters, how he distributed his property among them depended on the circumstances. When the daughters were married, it was assumed that their dowries and other gifts (such as a house or a part of it) received at the wedding represented their share in their father's possessions. They did not inherit; at most, they received a small legacy as a token of love. If they were unmarried or minor, the father earmarked fixed sums for their outfits, or left the action to his wife, or a son. The heir was obliged to see to it that the orphaned girls were married in accordance with their station. The courts, the guardians of the orphans, watched over the fulfillment of this obligation.

No fewer than four court records, all written in the course of six weeks in the spring of 1156, deal with a single case of orphan girls. Abū Zikrī Judah Kohen, the noted India trader and representative of merchants in the Egyptian capital, left a son, Sulayman, from an earlier marriage, and two minor daughters from his second wife, the daughter of a *kātib,* or government official. He assigned to each of the girls 200 dinars as their dowry and 50 dinars, with which a share in a house should be acquired. Until their marriage, the two together were to receive a monthly allowance of 2 dinars.

The court acted immediately. As long as the immovables were not acquired, Sulayman volunteered to add another half dinar to the monthly allowances (which shows, by the way, that an investment of 100 dinars in a house was assumed to bring 6 dinars as yearly rent). He undertook to give the girls their dowries not "at marriage" (as the will obviously had stated), but as soon as they came of age "according to Muslim law, so that they were able to release him in a legally valid fashion." If, however, the mother applied to a Muslim court, or to another government authority, or used her influence with persons in power to exercise pressure on him, the gift would be void. As collateral, Sulayman had to deposit with the court the deeds of his house, as well as those for a quarter of another house he possessed. Shortly thereafter the mother acknowledges the receipt of the allowances. Finally, about six weeks after the first action recorded, the purchase of a property for one of the girls, one eighth of a house worth 50 dinars "on the little Market of the Vizier in the Street of the Wine Sellers," was completed to the satisfaction of the court. Despite the great care for the girls, a patriarchal social system, conveying the father's absolute hold on the family purse to the son, is manifest.[29]

In the case just discussed the father had ordered that immovables be acquired for his daughters. In a similar situation, a brother in the small town of Ṣahrajt declares in court that although the ancient law required that "a daughter maintained by her brothers receive one tenth of the family immovables . . . in our time" she may be indemnified with money. He, however, would give his two sisters a house. Incidentally, one sees again that landed property was regarded as indispensable for the economic security of a woman.[30]

When a father did not fix the amounts of the dowries of his daughters, but gave their elder brother general instructions, leaving it to him to make the final decisions, he must have regarded his son as being of the same discernment and love for his siblings as he himself. In one magnificent Hebrew document written in October 1006, the father also empowers the elder son to give his younger brother his share in the estate only when he, the executor—not the courts—was satisfied that the boy was ready for the responsibility.[31]

The discriminatory treatment of daughters in matters of inheritance was imposed by an ancient law and seems to have been at variance with the egalitarian trends of the Geniza period. Yet that preferential attitude toward males had its place in that society, inasmuch as the majority of females were either minors and teenagers, who were in need of a guardian, or married women, who again had a special status, having received their fair share, and often more than that, in what their fathers were able to provide. In any case, inheritance was a strong factor, negative and positive, in defining the place of women in Geniza society.

The actions of the courts and other agencies with regard to the administration of estates and their proper distribution were largely conditioned by the very nature of things, and, consequently, in many respects, probably were not essentially different from what happens in other societies that have a mercantile economy and possess a fairly well-organized juridical system. Since the supervision of succession was one of the main concerns of the Jewish courts, the Geniza material about this topic is extensive. I have tried to confine myself to matters that have a bearing on the specific conditions, attitudes, and techniques of the age.

Immediately after the death of a person an inventory of his possessions was drafted and the court's seal was put on them. The Geniza reports a case where this was done even before the burial, another, where the seal was put on the multifarious belongings of a rich goldsmith on the day of his demise, and a third, where Moses Maimonides had ordered registered all that was found in the house of a dead physician during a holiday week, when normally no legal documents were written.[32]

It is evident that other inventories were made close to the death of their proprietor. "This is what we found in the house of R. Joseph after his sudden death," says a list of assorted clothes and household and grocery goods, concluding with the remark that certain pieces of clothing were "taken out," obviously for the needs of the family.[33] When Isaac b. Moses, judge in the town of Sunbāṭ, who derived most of his livelihood from his drugstore, died in October 1150, two inventories were made, one of his very extensive library and another of his not so richly studded storeroom.[34] There is the letter of an heir addressed to the dayyān Ḥiyyā (b. Isaac) informing him that "because of the rumors" (presumably, that he intended to get the better of other heirs) the writer locked his place, awaiting the judge's instructions.[35]

The widow's mandatory declaration, or oath, that she did not hold any of the belongings of her husband, was another measure of precaution. It was matched by the confirmation of the heirs which released her from all claims in this respect.[36]

These measures were only the first step in the endeavors of the authorities to preserve an estate for its legal heirs and legatees. Usually, not all of a man's possessions were kept in his house, and, often, they were not fully or properly listed. Attention has been drawn before to the aversion of Mediterranean people to count exactly what they have.[37]

A common device of the courts was the promulgation of "a ban in general terms" against anyone who held possessions of a deceased person without returning them, or who failed to report any knowledge of them. A letter from Alexandria, written around 1080, says that every Monday and Thursday following the death of a person the local Jewish judge pronounced a ban against anyone who knew of a document or an account book noting the assets of the deceased, or of things he had deposited with anyone. It was to no avail, and neither was a similar "warning" issued by a judge of al-Maḥalla to return books (it seems of a bookseller) for the benefit of orphans.[38]

Since business was international, a ban was not confined to one place or country. A ban on behalf of a merchant who had died in Egypt was proclaimed in all provincial towns of Palestine, and in Jerusalem on the peak day of the pilgrimage to the Holy City, when the highest degree of publicity was available (ca. 1060).[39] While in these and other instances from the eleventh and twelfth centuries this expedient of the ban was applied only when warranted by the circumstances, by the thirteenth century it had become almost mandatory. When, in December 1258, an official was sent by the Nagid David b. Abraham Maimonides to Damīra, a town in Lower Egypt, to settle a matter of inheritance, he first assembled ten persons "at least" in the house of a local notable, a government official, and pronounced a ban against "any Jewish person, male or female, who held a deposit, silver, gold, a business connection, movables, or real estate, or anything else of value belonging to the deceased without confessing it," whereupon all those present said "Amen." What the letter really shows is that the value of the estate, in cash and kind, had been established before. The business at hand was its distribution. One of the three sons of the dead man was a minor. The boys already of age could have freed their mother, or, rather, stepmother, from the oath of the widow, so that she could receive what was due her from her marriage contract; a minor could not. But before imposing that loathsome oath, the official preferred to consult the Nagid.[40]

Estates, like marriage gifts and dowries, prices of houses, and often even amounts of loans, were estimated in gold, the specie of constant value.[41] The Damīra inheritance, just discussed, consisted of 1,500 dirhems, partly pure silver, *nuqra*, partly alloyed silver, *waraq*, wares, implements, and household goods. It was estimated as being worth a total of 94 dinars at the exchange rate of 1:40 (dinar: waraq).[42] One hundred and fifty years earlier, in July 1108, the small and modest family of a seller of potions valued the inventory of his store, along with 169 dirhems in cash found there, at 11 1/2 dinars; this estimate was necessary, for half that sum was due a minor brother; years would pass before he came of age; by then the price of the silver specie might have undergone a marked change.[43] Again, about a hundred years earlier, in summer 1007, a sum of 164 dinars and 10 qīrāṭs, representing the value of the estate left by the scholar Jacob Rōsh Kallā b. Joseph b. Isaiah,[44] was sent from Damascus to Fustat and delivered to his son Joseph who had come of age and lived in the Egyptian capital. The document states that the father had left things with several persons and emphasizes twice that the sum had been brought together, obviously by the executor Moses b. Shahryār, "from various sources," or "under different titles." Similar cases, where estates were valued in gold coins, or actually converted into that specie, are found throughout the centuries. In one case this was done even with regard to a new house, left by an aunt to two nephews, one of whom was a minor. I understand this custom prevailed in England well into the nineteenth century. When James Smithson, the father of the Smithsonian Institution in Washington, D.C., died (1829), his estate reached this country in the form of 105 bags each containing 1,000 gold sovereigns.[45]

Today, accession to one's inheritance is a wearisome legal process. In Geniza times, the matter seems to have been different. When an inheritance was not contested, or otherwise problematic, when the collection of the assets caused no difficulties, and when no minors were involved, the courts stayed out. At least, I have not read anything to the contrary—not even about an inheritance tax.[46] One should not argue that our documents had no reason to make mention of them because these taxes were collected by the Muslim government. The poll tax, too, was levied by government agencies, yet the Geniza is replete with information about it. The intervention of the qadi was dreaded so much because once he had laid his hands on an estate, it was difficult to get it away from him. He would take from the substance of the estate under whatever legal pretext he could find, and there were, of course, the various tips and bribes routinely expected. Even with regard to the highly respected Alexandrian qadi al-Makīn (Makīn al-Dawla, died 1134 after a prolonged incumbency) the intervention of the Nagid Mevōrākh b. Saadya was repeatedly sought to retrieve estates held by him.[47] But we do not read about inheritance taxes on non-Muslims, which certainly would have been accompanied by additional extortions had they existed in the period considered. In any case, the Jewish authorities certainly had no right to impose an inheritance tax, and thus had no reason to interfere in the process of succession, unless it was made necessary by specific circumstances.

When an inheritance was contested, the courts had first to find out who the legal heirs were. Since such cases usually were complicated, and, we have only one, mostly incomplete, document about each action, not much can be learned. In one fragment, a man who died a martyr's death during the Crusaders' siege of Acre (Akko, 1104) had one heir who had drowned in the Indian Ocean, and a sister who was, or had been, married to the claimant who appeared in court. Declarations about sole heirs are common.[48] Four generations of males and females related by ramified family connections appear in one document and five in another.[49] In a record concerning two sisters and two brothers one sister was married to the paternal uncle of a claimant. After she and her husband had died, each of their two daughters retained 1,000 dinars from the estate of their parents, giving the rest to their maternal aunt. With this, the latter married a man who had sons from a previous marriage, to whom he allegedly owed money. He stipulated that they should get what he received from that aunt at their marriage. But he died first, and she gave her belongings to one of her two brothers. This one had no children, but wished to leave his possessions to the sons of his dead brother. This is only the beginning of the story that came before the court. It was perhaps worth recording, because it again shows that the bonds of blood were stronger than the ties of marriage.[50]

Sometimes, the instructions given by the testator were ambiguous. If so, the decision was left to the legitimate heir. Thus Japheth b. Meshullam Ibn Ḥirbish ("Rattlesnake") of Damascus had invested 350 dinars in a business venture of Musāfir b. Samuel, the trader mentioned before, advising him that in case he died, one third should be given to his son, another to his brother's children, and a third (lost). The note produced in court had neither the form of a legal gift, nor that of a will, wherefore the sum was awarded to Japheth's son Nethanel, the legitimate heir.[51]

When the various claims were established, either by mutual consent, or after litigations, often before both Muslim and Jewish authorities, the heirs appeared again in court and released each other from any future obligations. Numerous such items have been preserved. In December 1026, husband and wife, who were cousins, acquit a relative in connection with an inheritance.[52] In March 1049, a man releases two paternal uncles and their mother.[53] A maternal aunt is freed by her nephew from any claim on the estate of her father, real estate and movables.[54] Even in the case of poor people, such as that of the firstborn of a butcher, described above, a concurrent document was made out before a Muslim authority.[55]

Acquittals are of limited value for our understanding of the process of accession, since they represent only its final stage. We are in a better position where we have more than one document about a case. A man died, leaving no children, but two sisters, a mother, a maternal aunt, the latter's children, and several more distant relatives. The estate was divided into three equal shares among the two sisters and the mother. According to Jewish law, in the absence of direct male heirs, women got the entire estate. The details of the distribution among the three must have caused difficulties. In one document, written on Monday morning, July 5, 1227, the son of one of the sisters stood security for his mother, to wit, that, having received her share, she would not make any additional claim against any relative, either in a Muslim or a Jewish court. If she did, all losses caused to the other parties would be borne by him. On the following Thursday evening the three women appeared before the judge and his associates and released one another from any possible claims.[56]

The courts were kept busy by heirs appointing attorneys to handle inheritance releases after they had received their shares from the carriers or keepers. These procedures were not essentially different from the claiming of regular debts or deposits and the acknowledging of their payment or receipt. A few examples illustrate some common types of documents.[57]

The prominent merchant Manasse b. David of Qayrawān owed Judah b. Joseph Janūnī (Guenoun) 1,400 dirhems. Both died, and Judah's brother and heir Israel sent a power of attorney to Nahray b. Nissīm in Fustat, Egypt, to sue Manasse's son, Abū Zikrī Judah, who lived there, for this sum. The Qayrawānese document, one of the finest in the Geniza, recounts in detail how the debt originated, before which authority in Qayrawān the inheritance was confirmed, and what the exact prerogatives of the attorney were (1054/5).[58] Before Nahray could act, Israel, too, died, whereupon his two sons sent a new power of attorney to Egypt, referring, of course, to the one issued by their father.[59]

A model of a power of attorney in matters of succession is the one given by an Ibn al-Maqdisī ("Son of a Native of Jerusalem") in Fustat to a man who was to claim for him the estate of a daughter of a paternal cousin who had died in Alexandria. Ibn al-Maqdisī gave his attorney as a symbolic gift "the threshold of his house in the Tujīb quarter of Fustat, known as the domicile of his father" and "together with it" conveyed to him a long list of rights to act as his substitute, including the one to sell on the spot everything he retrieved, movables and real estate (April 1215).[60]

In a court record written about a century earlier (spring 1116) we see how the authorities acted after receipt of a power of attorney. Two brothers in Aleppo, Syria, claimed the share in a partnership of their late brother from his two partners, one a prominent merchant of Fustat, Yaḥyā ha-Kohen b. Samuel al-Baghdādī, and the other a banker, Abu 'l-Ḥusayn al-Ḥalabī ("of Aleppo"), also repeatedly mentioned. Since the Aleppo document was in the hand of its chief Jewish judge, Baruch b. Isaac, "the Great Rav," and validated by him and his associates, the Fustat authorities could act without making further inquiries. According to the products noted (yellow myrobalan and galbanum), the business venture concerned was made on the trade route to India, on which the brother whose estate was claimed had probably perished. As was common in such cases, the matter was complicated. The entire partnership had been taken over by another well-known India trader, also a Ḥalabī, on his way to the East, and the main part of the court record preserved deals with the settlement between him and Yaḥyā. The record is truncated and its continuation is missing.[61] Incidentally, the Geniza contains a complete record on an exactly opposite case, namely, the action of a court in Fustat preparing a claim to an estate in Aleppo, to be made by a man residing in the Egyptian capital.[62]

Here are a few telling examples of the many releases to keepers or carriers of shares in an inheritance. Two brothers having come of age confirm that they had received from "Sahl, Joseph, and Saadya, sons of Israel b. Jacob, renowned as the Tustarīs," all the property from the estate of their late father deposited with them by an elder brother, who had meanwhile died. The Tustarī brothers, one of whom, Sahl, we remember, was the father of the vizier Abū Sa'd, crop up in other documents as keepers of the estates of orphans (early eleventh century).[63] In January 1037, Isaac b. David, of the great Ibn Sighmār family of al-Mahdiyya, Tunisia, confirms in Fustat having received for Banīna, sister of a Maghrebi merchant who had died in Tyre, Lebanon, and whose executor he was, two remittances sent by Ibn Abī Qīda, representative of the merchants in that Lebanese city. He had already confirmed the first, the price of the personal belongings of the dead man, 4 dinars, 2 qīrāṭs, less 1 ḥabba (1/74th of a dinar), but the relevant document had been lost. The second sum, 6 1/2 dinars and 1 qīrāṭ, was the price of dried spikenard. Now, receipt for the two remittances was made out, and, accordingly, the carrier of both, a Mr. Small (of the noted Ben Ṣaghīr family), was released from any responsibility for the sums carried.[64] In a Cairene court under the authority of Samuel ha-Nagid (1140–1159) two brothers confirm having received from a maternal uncle, the physician Elazar ha-Levi, 12 1/2 dinars, representing the price of a maidservant left to them by another maternal uncle.[65]

A document illustrating a single phase in an inheritance lawsuit may prove revealing. In a Judaeo-Persian court record from July 951 (the oldest clearly dated document known so far in that language) one Samuel sued his two brothers for a share in their uncle's estate. The brothers retorted that Samuel owed the uncle money. Before dealing with the matter, the Karaite court ordered the two parties to take an oath that they would not apply to any other authority (which probably meant not only the qadi but also the rabbinical court). That being done, an account book of the dead uncle was produced, but it failed to supply clear evidence. Finally, Samuel agreed to grant his brothers three months to study all the account books of their uncle to prove their case. The record probably was written in Ahwāz in southern Iran and came into the Geniza when one of the persons concerned, like so many other Persian Jews, emigrated to the West, specifically to Egypt.[66]

A similar interim settlement, and again mostly among Persian

Jews, but this time in Fustat, and about a hundred years later, was made before "the Great Rav" Judah b. Joseph ha-Kohen in April 1057. A man of the Ibn Ezra family had died, leaving assets with two brothers of Ḥayyīm II b. Sahlawayh II b. Ḥayyīm, whose ramified family connections have been described above. The two brothers, too, had died, probably simultaneously, perhaps on a sea voyage, and without having left children, for Ḥayyīm II was their heir. Ḥayyīm II appointed then the banker Ibn Sha'yā, also a Persian, for he was known as Ibn al-Tawwazī (native of a town in Iran) as auditor with the instruction to examine the account books of the three dead persons and to pay to Ibn Ezra's heirs whatever was due them. The accounting was to be made under the supervision of another banker, the great Abū Naṣr Ibn Ṣaghīr ("Mr. Small"). We see in these examples the businesslike way in which experienced merchants went about matters of inheritance.[67]

Conversion to Islam was not widespread during the classical Geniza period.[68] Therefore we hear very little about the succession to an inheritance by Jews who had embraced Islam. According to a well-known principle of Islamic law, "the adherents of different religions do not inherit from one another," but the Fatimids were Shi'ites who gave neo-Muslims special rights to the estates of their non-Muslim relatives. They ruled: A Muslim inherits from an "infidel," but an infidel cannot inherit from a "believer." This legal situation might be reflected in two Geniza records, both from the middle of the twelfth century. When 'Ammār b. Makhlūf of Damietta, the Mediterranean seaport, was sued by a neo-Muslim relative in a matter of inheritance, he promised to pay him 20 dinars, if he forced another relative, Abu 'l-Mufaḍḍal, son of the ḥāvēr Peraḥya, and himself styled "Delight of the Yeshiva, Head of the Munificent," to give an oath concerning the same sum. Abu 'l-Mufaḍḍal swore, but 'Ammār was imprisoned for some time in connection with this affair. The record concerned deals with a side issue. 'Ammār in public withdrew his accusation that it was Abu 'l-Mufaḍḍal who had caused his imprisonment and otherwise harmed him.[69]

Our second document is an account by a trustee of the court, and we must try to reconstruct the story behind it from the data provided. A poor widow had died, leaving her sister 164 dirhems with the provision to pay the expenses for her burial from this sum and to take the rest for herself. No doubt, her personal belongings were also bequeathed to the sister. But hardly had that old woman closed her eyes, when her "renegade" sons laid claim to her inheritance. First, an agreement had to be made with them on how much should be spent on the burial.[70] Every detail had to be argued with them, including 1 3/4 dirhems for the tailor who sewed the shrouds. Finally, a total of 104 dirhems was agreed upon for the burial. Then the text continues: "For the bribe for the qadi—10 dirhems; consideration for Abū Muhammad (the qadi's servant)—1 1/2 dirhems." These sums were delivered to the servant in the presence of three persons listed by name. Subsequently, and again in the presence of three witnesses, 40 dirhems were given to the "renegades" in the way of an agreement, 6 to the (Muslim) attorney, 2 to the official messenger of the qadi, and 5 to another qadi who drew up the relevant document. This left an overdraft of 4 1/2 dirhems, which the trustee paid out of his own pocket. I assumed that personal belongings, too, had been bequeathed because if the "renegades" took everything left after the various Muslim officials were compensated, there was no point in speaking about an agreement.[71]

A peaceful settlement, *ṣulḥa*, reached after long negotiations, concludes this subsection on inheritance. The central figure in this lawsuit was a grandmother, called Sitt al-Kuttāb, "The Queen of the Scribes," who had, besides an adult grandson from a married daughter, minor grandchildren from two sons who were under the tutelage of three guardians, after their fathers had died. Sitt al-Kuttāb's husband had died some time before, bequeathing a house plus 100 dinars to his daughter. He owed his wife 100 dinars from her marriage contract and, in his last will, had presented her with two clasps with pearls. At his death the guardians of the children of her sons laid their hands on all he left. Her daughter appointed her son (not her husband, probably from a second marriage) as her attorney, but seemingly without much success. Then, as the record states, "The widow Sitt al-Kuttāb arranged this peace after she said to us [the court] many times: You cannot get a settlement from me unless you first settle with my daughter." On one day the daughter received the deed of the house while the guardians agreed to register it as her property with both Jewish and Muslim authorities; on the next day the gold was brought in, whereupon the daughter released the guardians from any further obligation. Finally, Sitt al-Kuttāb received her clasps and 60 dinars, the remaining 40 to be paid later; her marriage contract was torn up as a token that everything was settled. She was solemnly released from the oath of the widow and all other obligations toward the heirs. A concluding formality was the agreement of the guardians to stand security against any claims of the orphans on the day they came of age and a declaration of the daughter's husband that he confirmed all the actions of his wife. This happened in Alexandria, Egypt, in the month of May 1207. As the honorific name of the grandmother indicates, she probably came from a family of government officials.[72]

In many, if not most, of the cases of succession described in the preceding pages, orphaned minor heirs were involved. In the following, we learn about the specific conditions affecting the lives of orphans.

The administration of the possessions of orphans.—"The judge is the father of the orphans."[74] This Talmudic maxim,[75] cited in our documents in various forms, explains why the Geniza is replete with material about fatherless children.[76] How far this role of the courts was effective and beneficial might be gleaned from the forthcoming examples selected for illustration.

In addition to the actions taken for the protection of any heir (see the preceding subsection) the first duty of the judge was the appointment of an executor or executors for the minors, unless it had already been done by their fathers. A classic case is represented in a detailed and complete Hebrew court record from spring 1026, fortunately complemented by a document in Arabic, written thirteen months later. The Hebrew record concerns a minor, four years old, the Arabic document his elder siblings who had come of age but were not yet able to take care of their financial affairs. The court did not act of its own initiative. Yeshūʿā b. Sedāqā (possibly the orphans' maternal grandfather, see below) "and others" remonstrated against the inactivity of the authorities and demanded the appointment of a guardian, since the orphans' father had died intestate. In the Arabic document the minor's siblings appoint their maternal uncle Joseph b. Yeshūʿā (see above) as their representative (July 1027). But with regard to the minor "the judge and the elders" acted differently. They appointed Eli b. Japheth, "known as Bar ʿAdī," but not otherwise described, as guardian, with the banker Solomon b. Saadya Ibn Saghīr ("Mr. Small") as his supervisor. The assets collected were to be deposited with the latter and he and the judge had to approve any payments to be made from the orphan's estate.[77]

A similar procedure, namely, the appointment of a supervisor (also a member of the Ibn Ṣaghīr family) over a representative in matters of succession, has been noted in a document written thirty-one years later, in 1057.[78] A responsum by the nāsī Daniel b. Azarya (Gaon 1051–1063) makes mention of a judge who had appointed two guardians to be directed by two supervisors with whom the sums collected were ordered to be deposited. One supervisor gave the other the sums with which he had been entrusted, but, when the latter's house was looted (the Arabic term used indicates that this happened in a time of civil disorder), the orphan's money, along with some belongings of the supervisor, was lost. Daniel states, first, that no judge can devolve his own responsibility of supervision on anyone else and, second, that he was not satisfied that the supervisor had displayed the measure of precaution to be expected from a man in his position of trust. As the question addressed to the Gaon shows, the man had not hidden the gold beneath the floor, in a wall, above the ceiling, or in any other safe place, but had kept it in the house, because he had just received it and wished to check the amount.[79]

In a cause celèbre, represented in the Geniza by at least six documents, a dying merchant appoints two guardians and one supervisor for his only son. In their early actions, when approaching debtors of the dead man, the guardians cooperate with their supervisor. In the later records the supervisor is not mentioned. I wonder where the office of supervisor of guardians originated. Since the Hebrew document of the year 1026 referred to above uses an Aramaic term for it, I assume that this was a pre-Islamic, ancient Near Eastern institution.[80]

I have termed it a cause celèbre, because persons from different countries, religions, and professions were involved, several Jewish and Muslim authorities were approached, public appeals were made, and the affair dragged on for a number of years. An Andalusian merchant, Samuel, in Arabic Isma'īl, ha-Levi b. Abraham, when in Fustat, felt his end approaching and assembled "a big crowd" of Karaite and Rabbanite Jews, as well as of Muslims qualified to testify before a qadi. In their presence, he appointed a Baghdadi with the family name Nīlī (dealer in indigo) and a banker as guardians of his only son Abraham. A man whose grandfather was called Yazdād ("God-given," Persian), that is, from a family native in Iran, was chosen by him as their supervisor. A Rabbanite judge was also present. The guardians were Rabbanites, the supervisor probably a Karaite. They were given complete freedom of action, were not obliged to make accounts, nor could any oath be imposed on them. Two fragments of the official document serving as the legal instrument for these appointments are extant. They are entirely in Aramaic, which also seems to indicate that the office of a supervisor of guardians was pre-Islamic.[81]

Three documents show how the guardians fulfilled their task. The first two are letters to former partners of the deceased. The writers emphasize that they had taken upon themselves the hard task solely out of compassion and affection for the orphan (that is, not for any compensation) and expected a similar attitude from the recipients, whose piety and probity had been lauded by the dead merchant. Following a court order they should transport the merchandise held by them for the partnership to the writer's place or, if that was too difficult, to bring its price in cash. One letter concludes with the admonition: "Live up to your reputation." The names of the partners addressed have not been preserved.[82]

The third document, a huge Hebrew court record, shows the effect of the guardian's action. A merchant known otherwise as commuting between Tunisia and Egypt, had had a partnership with the deceased Andalusian worth 1,043 dinars, part of which had reverted to him during his lifetime. A careful examination of the relevant papers and account books showed that a sum of 136 1/2 dinars was still owed. The amount was delivered to the guardians, and the partner was released from the oath due to the orphan with regard to any amount owed to his father on condition that he be prepared to take it, if requested to do so by the latter, when he came of age.[83]

The affair did not end as harmoniously as it started. The orphan Abraham b. Samuel al-Andalusī was declared of age in January 1026 when still a teenager and began to make trouble. At his instigation, the guardians were forced by the government to produce their accounts and were threatened with flogging, or were actually flogged, by a Jewish court. On December, 1027, Abraham again brought them before a court and demanded that a balance still due be delivered. They refused unless a proper release be given to them before a Jewish judge and a qadi. They were not prepared to produce additional accounts, since they had been expressly exempted from this duty by the orphan's father. A committee of three, headed by Samuel ha-Kohen b. Ṭalyūn (Avṭalyōn), head of the Iraqian congregation of Fustat, was to look into the matter, but nothing came of it.[84]

The next document is dated Monday, December 18, 1027, but in between something else had happened. A proper court, composed of the heads of the two congregations and a third person, called Samuel, The Delight of the Yeshiva, probably identical with the eminent merchant-scholar Samuel (Isma'īl) b. Barhūn Tahertī of Qayrawān, was to end the affair either by mutual agreement or by a decision imposed on the parties. Many outsiders came, complaining about the nuisance caused by the young man with his public appeals in the synagogues and elsewhere, but The Delight excused himself as being busy "and other reasons." The session was adjourned for two weeks at most, and the guardians were warned not to bring Abraham before a Muslim court. When one of them remarked that it was Abraham who had approached the governor, *al-qā'id,* with the request "to assemble the Jews" to consider his cause, he retorted that he had done so because he wished to have a decision according to Jewish law.[85]

Unlike the case just described most of the others are represented by just one document. But taken all together a fairly consistent practice of the courts regarding the care of orphans emerges. The judge retained constant supervision, although this duty was not always exercised in an efficient manner. The attorney who was to retrieve the estate, the guardian with whom the child was put, and the keepers who held the orphan's assets would be replaced by others if the judge saw fit, or, rather, if he was approached by a complainant with the request to do so. Preserving the capital left seems to have been the foremost concern of the authorities. If feasible, it was put into the hands of more than one person; the keepers had to provide collateral, usually real estate, sometimes also guarantors. No remuneration was expected for this service. Alimony was in accordance with the amount of the estate, but always modest. When the support of the orphan had to come out of his capital, each payment had to be approved by the judge or his representative. The red tape often caused great hardship, since the authorities did not always act promptly when the widow or guardian approached them with the request to release the amounts approved. At maturity (boys at thirteen, girls at twelve and six months) the orphan was given legal possession of the estate, but the court "and the elders" retained actual supervision until they were satisfied that he or she was able to make use of it responsibly.

A lengthy draft describing the appointment of the Trustee of the Court 'Ullā b. Joseph as *wakīl,* or representative, of an infant in Damietta, whose father had died in Fustat, shows the procedure in detail. First, the choice of 'Ullā is elaborately justified. 'Ullā was pious, reliable, eager to do good works and to exert himself for others, and also to gain merit before God; he was knowledgeable in the ways of business and cooperative with others, experienced in dealing with tough customers in and out of court, and trained in the pursuance of lawsuits. 'Ullā was reminded that his task would be merely a deed of charity, whereupon he could not but accept it. (One should never *ask* for such an appointment.) Then all the legal powers and obligations of the executor were specified and accepted by him, especially his duty to constantly make accounts with the judge on all that was accruing to the orphan and expended on his maintenance, and to put the sums received at the disposal of the court. His office would come to an end at the orphan's maturity.[86]

A widow, contemporaneous with ʿUllā, complained to the Nagid Mevōrākh that her brother-in-law, who had been appointed by her late husband as executor for her children, was too weak to deal with a hard bargainer like "The Doctor" (the representative of the merchants Abū Yaʿqūb al-Ḥakīm), a business partner of the deceased. For the sake of God, the Nagid should spend an hour of his precious time in dealing with this matter, for "he had the wisdom of an angel of God" (II Samuel 14:20). The personal intervention of the Nagid was needed, for the law made it obligatory to carry out the will of a dying man, wherefore the judges had been reluctant to take the office of the executor from the uncle of the orphans and to entrust someone else with it.[87]

The transfer of orphans' capital from one trustee to another was an easier matter. Samuel, "The Master of the Discerning," who is none other than the often mentioned Ben Asad,[88] served as "guarantor" for a banker in al-Maḥalla in whose keeping orphans' money had been deposited. Under circumstances not specified Samuel handed over the amount to another trustee, who was advised not to make any payments from it except upon a written order from the court.[89]

The role of guarantor is also present in a venture on behalf of an orphan, undertaken by Samuel Ben Asad together with his son Eli, probably with the intention to groom him in deeds of charity, which might also prove to be a bit profitable. The orphan had reached maturity, but was not yet regarded by the court as able to manage the estate. An amount of 56 1/2 dinars, perhaps only a fraction of the whole, was entrusted to father and son, who stood security with their own possessions, real estate and movables, and one for the other, "the living for the dead, the present for the absent, and the well-to-do for the indigent." The document states that the orphan was present in court during the procedures.[90]

Entrusting the property of orphans to two persons, each responsible separately for the total amount, seems to have been a common practice of the courts in those days, for we find Samuel Ben Asad a third time in such a role. Again a widow applied directly to the Nagid, this time Samuel b. Hananya, because it was a case in which the will of a dying man had to be changed. The father of the orphans had left them, among other items, shops in the town of Malīj, from whose rent they should be supported. The minimum required for their support was 1 dinar per month (the number of orphans is not stated), but the rent brought less. Under these circumstances the two Jewish chief judges of Fustat, on order of the Nagid, advised Samuel Ben Asad and his fellow trustee to deliver ten pounds of silk worth 20 dinars from the orphans' estate to their paternal uncle. The latter would trade with this merchandise, add the profit to the income from the shops, and provide 1 dinar per month for his nephews. The instructions of the chief judges were carried out before a proper court of three in the town of Minyat Ashnā, where, I assume, the family concerned lived (Jan. 1151).[91]

In the document just discussed it is assumed that one who held money belonging to orphans would make some profit with it, part of which would be used for their maintenance. The undertaking of the holder to return the amount in full implies that the orphans participated in the profits, not in the losses. That was the law.[92] The degree of security demanded from a man entrusted with an orphan's property depended, of course, on his financial circumstances and on his standing in the society. For a man like Samuel Ben Asad a declaration that he was accountable with all his possessions found in a certain locality was sufficient.[93] Less wealthy and less trusted people had to provide more substantial security. In a detailed note in the hand of the judge Nathan b. Samuel a certain Zikrī b. Ḥalfōn (not known to me otherwise) receives 50 dinars from funds belonging to two orphan girls to be kept by him until they were ready to be betrothed. He promises to provide for their maintenance an amount to be fixed by their guardian. As collateral for this loan, Zikrī had to mortgage the apartment where he lived, namely, quarter of a house belonging to him, and his share in another house, one eighth of it, before both a Muslim and Jewish court. The deeds were delivered to the guardian, who would hand them over to the judge in case of default. The latter, in consultation with three elders (required to sign the relevant document), would sell as much as needed for the compensation of the orphans.[94]

Such measures of precaution were taken even when close relatives were placed in charge of the estate of fatherless minors. An old woman appointed by the court as guardian of her grandchildren received cash and utensils left by her son and, as collateral, mortgaged her home. Not enough with this, another son of hers agreed to be her guarantor. The role of women as guardians and executors in general is discussed in D, below.[95]

The matter was different when a person was appointed as executor and guardian by the testator. In such a case, much depended on the strength and authority enjoyed by the local judge. When a man died in Bilbays, Lower Egypt, in spring 1217, leaving a wife, a grown-up son, and a minor boy, the house was properly sealed. But when the judge wished to proclaim the customary "ban in general terms" (see *Med. Soc.*, II, 340–341), the elder son, a well-off merchant, protested: "God has not put me in a position where I need to take anything from the share in the estate of his father from the orphan, my minor brother." The share of the orphan, according to him, was 80 dinars, which was to be kept by him until the boy came of age. Moreover, as an act of charity, for which he hoped to be rewarded by God in this world and in the world to come, he would provide his brother with food, clothing, and anything else needed to the amount of a minimum of 15 dirhems per month. This would mean about 4 to 4 1/2 dinars over a year against possible profits to be made from the 80 dinars. Since no security was given for the principal, this was obviously an undertaking of no great religious merit.[96]

We have read about cases where a dying man appoints a wife, a son, or a brother as plenipotentiary executors, explicitly or implicitly freeing them from the supervision of the courts.[97] We have also seen that despite such provisions courts did intervene.[98] The general procedure seems to have been that immediately after a death the customary precautions for safeguarding the rights of heirs, and in particular orphans, were taken, but as soon as the legal position was cleared, much depended on the circumstances, including the power yielded by the authorities dealing with the case.

When orphans possessed real estate, the courts, according to the circumstances, either converted it into gold, or tried to preserve it, even if keeping it in repair required spending most of the gold left to them. The most eminent experts on housing would be consulted and their advice followed, whereupon the trustee would be advised to release the amount agreed upon. We read once about an expenditure of 50 out of 74 dinars possessed by two orphans needed for the repair of a house belonging to them. In the letter requesting the intervention of the Nagid Mevōrākh in an inheritance case in Alexandria, discussed above, the purchase of "a little caravanserai" and the half of another one, which would bring a monthly revenue of 3 dinars is suggested for the orphans. The port city Alexandria, which was also a terminal for the North African caravan route, was supposed to provide regular income from the traders using those facilities. But when we read so often in letters from that city that no ships had arrived and all business was at a standstill, one doubts whether real estate was such a safe investment after all. As we have read, the rent of shops in

Malīj, which a father thought was sufficient to take care of the maintenance of his children, had to be supplemented by another source of income. Finally, if the property was conspicuous, or belonged to a person connected with the government, it was always in danger of attracting the attention of rapacious officials, with the usual catastrophic consequences. In one such case, the executor, again Abu 'l-Ma'ālī (Samuel Ben Asad), had to spend 220 dinars in order "to get back" the property, which he then sold for 300 dinars. The uncle of the orphans bore the title Raḍiyy al-Dawla ("Pleasing the Government"), and the father of their guardian was a *kātib*, or government official. Probably the orphans' father had been in a similar situation, which explains the fate of his real estate.[99]

Often the cost of supporting an orphan was to come out of the capital deposited for him with a guardian or a trustee. In such a case court supervision was particularly rigorous. The cost had to be kept as low as possible, and each withdrawal from the principal had to be approved. An uncle who held the estate of his late brother, and whose orphaned nephew lived in his house, was permitted to take from it only 20 dirhems per month for food and general living costs, while clothing had to be approved separately. A list of the withdrawals was to be submitted to the court.[100] When the money was held by a trustee, he received from time to time an order to pay the alimony approved to the guardian, in one case 3 dinars for a period of four months, which would result in about 30 dirhems per month, or 1 per day (in reality, often somewhat less). The boy concerned was the son of a goldsmith.[101]

When the orphan came of age, the trustee was ordered to deliver to him the balance of the estate. This balance was substantiated by the acknowledgment of the receipt of the money deposited with the judge as well as by the *riqā'* (Ar.) *bēth dīn* (Heb.), the orders of payment, issued by the court for the cost of the orphan's food and clothing.[102] Declarations by orphans reaching maturity, male and female, that they had properly received all due them from an inheritance, have been discussed above in various contexts.[103]

The material presented thus far shows how the administration of estates by courts affected the lives of minor heirs. There is more to come on this subject in the subsequent pages. But before considering the lot of orphans specifically, it is perhaps proper to ask how the handling of cases of inheritance by the courts influenced the economy of the Geniza society in general.

The system of the administration of law in those parts and times, which did not know the institution of an attorney general and all that goes with it, was susceptible to procrastination. As a rule, the courts acted when they were approached. True, the sealing of the property of a deceased was customarily done immediately after his death and at the initiative of the authorities. Presumably it was effected in connection with the burial, in which a divine, or his representatives, participated.[104] But once that was done, it was up to interested persons or public minded notables to elicit further action. When an orphan stayed with a mother, a grandmother, an uncle, or a grandfather, who had not been appointed as executors, the property could not be touched until someone was selected for that office by a court. We have read how a court was urged to do so.[105] When the executors and their supervisors or guarantors had been selected, the most difficult part of their job was to assemble the minor heir's estate, a process often woeful not only to him but also to anyone who had had dealings with the deceased. Since a minor could not act legally, his executors had to guarantee that they would be liable if the dead man's debtors or partners were sued by the orphans come of age. Often a contested property had to be left untouched until a settlement or decision had been reached, or even until the minor was able to act.

A case like that, where a merchant in Egypt, who had become involved with an orphan in Sicily, had to apply to the Jewish authorities in his own country, in Tripoli, Libya, and in Jerusalem, is described in *Med. Soc.,* II, 395–396. Another one encompassing different countries must have dragged on for years. A noted writer of liturgical poetry, Nahum b. Joseph Baradānī, was elected head cantor of the great synagogue in Baghdad at a time when he happened to be in Qayrawān, Tunisia, probably as an emissary of the Iraqian yeshivas, but certainly also earning money for himself by singing. He must then have been an old man, for Hay Gaon, in a letter written in 1006, mentions him as his schoolmate, with whom he grew up in friendship, and Hay was at that time in his late sixties.[106] Nahum sent merchandise and Hebrew books (the latter a great article of export from Qayrawān) to Egypt and subsequently appointed an agent to sell them in Palestine. The agent sold the merchandise, but kept its price for himself, claiming that the dead cantor owed him more than the books had brought. Then he took the books to Jerusalem (where they would be sold to pilgrims from all over the world), but still did not settle the matter. Meanwhile, the old cantor, his son, daughter-in-law, and granddaughters had died. When the grandsons, Joseph and Nahum Jr., came of age, they empowered the Jewish judge of Palermo, Sicily, who happened to visit Hay Gaon in Baghdad, to sue, on his way back home, their grandfather's agent at the high court of the Palestinian yeshiva in Ramle, Palestine. This he did, and it was agreed that the agent should receive—what, is not preserved, but most probably part of the books. Much time elapsed before Joseph and Nahum Jr. again appeared in court in this matter, but what happened then is lost. By the 1060s the Baradānī brothers, like so many other Iraqians, had moved westward; we find them in Tyre, Lebanon, Jerusalem, and Egypt. Whether the rest of the books belonging to them had been sold, returned to them, or spoiled by rainwater (as happened occasionally in Jerusalem), we may learn some day.[107]

Goods in which orphans had a share remained sequestered until released by the courts. This endangered their very preservation, physically and otherwise. A document recording a settlement specifically refers to such risks. A trader had brought merchandise from Tripoli, Lebanon, to Fustat and deposited them in various warehouses. A short time after his return he died, leaving a teenage son, who had been declared capable of dealing with movables (but not yet real estate) and another son who was a minor. The teenager received his share in a settlement with a representative of the investor. The rest of the goods remained sequestered until the investor arrived in town. He suggested a generous division between himself and the minor, taking what was due him and releasing the minor from all future responsibility, "for if the goods remained in the warehouses until the little one comes of age, anything could happen to them" (July 1094).[108]

An especially serious cause of delay in the freeing of an estate was the frequent disagreement between judges or jurisconsults about the rights of the parties concerned.[109] An extraordinarily strong letter written by the Jewish judge of Gaza, Palestine, and signed by him and fourteen (twice seven[110]) associates, to Ephraim b. Shemarya, head of the Palestinian congregation of Fustat, illustrates. A man in the Egyptian Fayyūm died childless, survived by a brother in Gaza, three nephews from a sister, and a niece and grandniece from a stepsister. As the letter emphasizes, the two sisters had been outfitted and married by their father. According to Jewish law, the legal situation was therefore beyond doubt: the surviving brother was the sole heir. But Ephraim refused to release the estate, and our letter was destined to accompany the man of Gaza, who traveled to Egypt in order to transport the bones of his brother for burial in Jerusalem. Ephraim's reasoning is not provided. According to Muslim law, we remember, the sisters' progeny had a claim on the inheritance. Two of the nephews seem to have been minors, possibly also the grandniece. It could be argued that the minors, when coming of age, could get a favorable settlement by threatening to apply to a Muslim court. Anyhow the estate must have lain fallow for a long time.[111]

The widow complaining to the Nagid Mevōrākh about her inefficient brother-in-law who was unable to secure her children's estate from his partner, expresses the apprehension that the latter, too, might die, and getting something out of orphans for other orphans was next to impossible.[112] In a strongly worded directive the Cairene judge Abraham b. Nathan warns a local judge not to wrong the partner of a deceased merchant who had left minor children "even to the amount of a penny," for the sages had said: "Orphans who eat what is not theirs should go after those who left them." Another Geniza letter emphasizes that awarding to orphans what they are not entitled to was as great a sin as depriving them of their rights.[113]

We in our own times are only too familiar with the troubles to be incurred in the settlement of an inheritance. The difference is that the economy in those days was so much weaker. In order to prosper, the little that people possessed had to work all the time. Its prolonged sequestration in favor of minor heirs was a disaster.[114]

The lot of orphans.—Because husbands ran away so often, for many children orphanhood began when their fathers were still alive. It was so common that the Arabic language coined a special term for it: *aytām al-aḥyā*, "orphans whose parents are still alive." In a list of beneficiaries at a communal distribution of wheat "an orphan whose parents are alive" appears as a legal term, meaning that the minor was eligible for public charity just like a regular orphan.[115] A letter written by the teacher and court clerk Judah al-ʿAmmānī in February 1228 conveys to the judge Elijah b. Zechariah and the Nagid Abraham Maimonides the complaint of a woman from Byzantium who was deserted by her husband in Alexandria, after he had sired her two daughters. He had not left her a penny, in a city where she was a complete stranger, and she had to take recourse to communal welfare; she had not heard from her husband for five months, "but how long can one live on public charity?" Twice in the letter the girls are described as orphans, once with the term mentioned above, and once with an even stronger expression: "His daughters, who are a piece of flesh cut off from the body, orphaned." One is reminded of the biblical "one flesh," meaning one family (Genesis, 2:24). How the authorities acted in these matters is described above.[116]

In most Geniza texts mentioning fatherless children they appear as living with their mothers. The boys would pass their days in the

Bible school. If the family was indigent, the fees were paid by the community to individual teachers, or there were special classes for orphans, where admission was free.[117] An orphan started to work early. A court record signed by the judge Yehiel b. Eliakim (1213–1233) speaks of an orphan to be examined "by the masters of the craft," it seems, because two orphans were involved, and a choice had to be made between the two.[118] The girls kept their mothers company, learning or perfecting themselves in the techniques of spinning, weaving, and especially embroidery, while a teacher—paid by the community if necessary—came to the house to provide a minimum of religious education.[119] Girls, too, started to earn money early. When a judge in Malīj, Lower Egypt, reports to his superior in Fustat that "the little orphan girl does embroidery every day," he meant that she worked in other people's houses.[120]

When a widow died, her children normally found shelter in the house of a relative, the father's brother being the "natural" choice.[121] In this matter, too, the courts acted as the orphans' guardians. We find one put in the house of a person not characterized as a relative even though a paternal uncle was extant; or, when a widow in a small place died, leaving a girl of three (together with a small house), the judge in the capital, among other questions, asked for a report on who took the orphan into his house and cared for her.[122] We have read about a decision made by a high authority refusing to give a small boy to a woman who claimed to be his next of kin, but ordering him to stay in the house where he lived before his mother's death.[123]

When the family was not able or willing to provide a home, or when no appropriate relatives were available, the orphans were put with a trusted family, preferably that of a teacher or cantor, or the widow of one. Even the judge Elijah b. Zechariah kept an orphan in his house, to be sure, a relative, the son of a physician in Bilbays, who went to school in the capital.[124] Lists of indigents in receipt of handouts from the community contain such items as "the orphans in the house of the cantor," "the teacher and the orphan girl who is with her," or "the orphans with the sister of Abu 'l-Faraj, the son of the astrologer," probably the sister and assistant of a schoolmaster.[125]

This little notice from the chancellery of the Nagid Joshua Maimonides (1310–1355) conveys a Dickensian atmosphere. The "elder" Isaac obviously was a close relative of the orphan Mūsā (Moses), but not eager to keep him. Probably the boy had already once run away from his house. "To the cantor Faraj Allah ["God has saved"], may God keep him. Please take notice that the bearer of this is the orphan boy Mūsā. Ask the elder Isaac about him. If they [sic!] refuse to give him shelter, please send a messenger immediately and let me know, so that I can proceed against them in accordance with the law. Beware of being remiss in this matter. And may God, the exalted, help you." Strict law did not require relatives to give shelter to an orphan, but the acknowledged moral code of behavior had almost the force of law.[126]

There is no mention of an orphanage in the Geniza. The number of orphans remaining after the relatives had done their duty was small and did not call for the creation of one. Moreover, the notion that children belonged in a house with a family, even if it was only an adopted one, was too strong to permit placing orphans in a barracks-like place. The so-called orphanages erected by Muslim rulers in a later period were often nothing but training schools for future soldiers.

Numerous Geniza letters are cries for help of orphans and their mothers, lacking food and clothing, and sometimes even a proper place to live. The father had died without leaving a thing, the rations fixed by communal charity were insufficient, and, not uncommon, the payments due from estates under the administration of the courts had not been made in time or in the required amounts. Such pictures of misery are often topped by the woeful excuse that the mother was unable to work because of illness ("your maidservant's eyes are sore and have been bandaged for the last forty days") or general incapacity.[127]

The judges, it seems, released money for the orphans only when approached. A concise, but instructive letter of recommendation by a local official states that the bearer, Sālim b. Hārūn,[128] had admitted the three orphans of his late brother to his house, but for some time nothing had been paid out of the estate, because he, Sālim, was away in Gaza, Palestine, on a business trip. Meanwhile, the children had lived at his and his mother's expense. But now wheat and clothing had to be bought for them. Sālim applied for the release not of the money held by the judge but for that entrusted to a local man called "the Son of the Pious."[129] With that amount he would again travel to Gaza, and from the profit made buy what was necessary for the orphans. Sālim, the official assures the judge, was a reliable man, "punctual in fulfilling his obligations."[130] Proper bills of debt would be made out before Muslim and Jewish notaries.[131]

Twice in this letter it is emphasized that the clothes to be bought for the orphans would be of cotton. The textiles usually worn in Geniza times were linen, wool, and silk. Cotton, although imported to Egypt in those days, was the clothing of the indigent. In another letter of a local official a widow wishes to have a cotton dress for her little daughter.[132] An orphan girl whose father had remarried was so destitute that her bridegroom, himself an orphan, had "to pull out" one of his own robes and clothe her with it.[133] When a Nagid is asked to authorize a collection on behalf of an orphan girl about to marry, and for whom only a "polo tunic" and a *malḥafa* (which served both as mantle and blanket) was needed, one wonders what she wore at the time of the request.[134]

To be needy and miserable seems to have been regarded as the predestined lot of orphans and their mothers—and not only those from poor families. In the model of an appeal to the community an unnamed[135] widow and mother of four, who had taken loans she was unable to pay, asserts that she and her children had never before "uncovered their faces" by asking either private persons or the public for support. After all that has been reported above it is not difficult to imagine what had happened here. Real estate belonging to the family had dwindled in the process of succession, and its remnants were ruined by lack of repair. The cash left to them had been eaten up, if not lost, by the negligence or dishonesty of the administrators. Since the widow had seen better days, credit had been extended to her—until it became evident that she was a hopeless case.[136] We read, indeed, about a widow and mother of orphans who was imprisoned, no doubt for debts she was unable to pay (a Muslim judge was involved).[137]

When I studied Yemenite communities in the early 1930s I was astounded to hear orphans described as wild, dangerous, and even cruel.[138] I then was reminded of the bands of orphan boys who made Eastern Europe unsafe after World War I, and whose rehabilitation was promoted and studied in the writings of the saintly Polish-Jewish physician and educator, Janusz Korczak.[139] Nothing like it is to be observed in the Geniza world. An orphan boy who wished to eat had to be registered for the two weekly distributions of bread and other handouts. Our analysis of these registrations has shown that the authorities were very strict in these matters.[140] The great care of the community for the schooling of orphans certainly had its origin also in the desire to keep them off the streets and away from mischief. Payment for professional training was perhaps confined to the sons of deceased community officials.[141] Since facilities for organized charity were not easily available in provincial towns, indigent widows with small children frequently moved to the capital, as is amply proved by the detailed lists of beneficiaries of the communal chest. This explains perhaps why we find a collection for the orphans in the capital made in a place of the Egyptian countryside. The heavily burdened community of Fustat was forced to devolve some of its load on the congregations of the Rīf.[142]

The orphan girl was the poorest of the poor. Since the position of a wife depended largely on the strength of her family and the means she brought into the marriage, the female orphan's prospects in life were dark. Her natural refuge was a position as a domestic in a friendly household. But people seem not to have been eager to employ orphans, and we read little about it in the Geniza. For understandable reasons the community insisted that orphan girls be married as soon as possible. (Nowhere have I read about an orphan girl becoming a prostitute.) Things being so, it was not practicable to a household to employ a domestic who would leave precisely when she would become fully capable of doing the chores. One preferred slave girls. In this light must one understand an emphatic passage in Maimonides' Code of Law, where he declares that the keeping of slaves means sin and iniquity, day in, day out, while employing orphans and the poor turns every hour into a good and meritorious deed.[143]

Naturally, sometimes an orphan serving in a household would attract the attention of a visitor, especially if he was a stranger on travel, whose family was far away and could not guard him against so foolhardy a step as marrying a penniless orphan.[144] When anything of that kind occurred, people could become quite apologetic: "Your son has done nothing wrong. He was ill, suffering pain, and had no one to look after him. Therefore he decided to hire an orphan girl who would take care of him. Later he married her on condition that, when he preferred to return to his country, he would divorce her." The girl gave birth to a boy who died. A female relative who reports this to the family back home adds: "It was all his doing. You accuse me in vain. Have I married him to my own daughter?"[145]

The eagerness of the community to get rid of unmarried orphan girls could have disastrous results, especially in small towns where the surveillance of the courts was loose. Sometimes the teenager was married before she was prepared, physically or mentally, or both, to perform what was expected of her.[146] Or she was given to an unworthy stranger, as, for example, when an orphan and her child were deserted by a husband from the Egyptian capital, who disappeared together with the little money she had saved.[147] A man from Aleppo was betrothed to an orphan in Cairo, promising to marry her after a month. The month became three, and then six, and, at the end, the girl had to be content with 5½ instead of 10 dinars, imposed by the court as the fine for nonfulfillment; otherwise the man would not have given her the bill of repudiation required after a broken betrothal.[148] A lonely orphan who had been married ("they have married me . . .") to an unworthy man for ten years, describes her plight to a Nagid in an eloquent letter, possibly written in her own hand. The man lived on what she earned, and when she refused to go on with this any longer, he gave her a bad name. She was prepared to buy herself free by renouncing her late marriage gift, on condition "a ban in general terms" was pronounced against anyone impugning her honor, but this request was turned down by the judges. She now approached the Nagid in person, asking him to free her "from a hell which only God knows."[149]

Yet, marrying an orphan was regarded as a deed of great religious merit. Of the pietist disciple of Abraham Maimonides this is reported as done solely for God's sake.[150] A traveling cantor asserts that he married an orphan so that he would not have in-laws to impede him from returning to his parents and serving them.[151] In a letter to a notable a man is commended as worthy of support because he was going to marry a lonely orphan.[152] In all these cases, I am afraid, a cynic would assume that piety was propped up by poverty.

In families with means and prestige an orphan could not always be sure that her relatives would exert themselves for her.[153] But we also find substantial gifts to an orphan with a view to enable her to marry, and when the women of the community brought together the outfit of a poor orphan bride, they made an effort that she have on her wedding something to make her happy.[154] The conditions under which the orphan "Beauty" was married promised a modest measure of well-being in life.[155]

Motherless orphans rarely are the subjects of Geniza documents. Female relatives in the house, occasionally also domestics, would carry on where the deceased had left off, until the father, by remarriage, gave his children a new mother.[156] But established practices must have existed for the care of motherless children whose fathers possessed no facilities for their upbringing. In two documents found thus far, orphans are entrusted to two women living together who do the upbringing (not the supporting, of course) as a deed of charity. The children, especially the girls, probably were regarded also as being or as capable of becoming of help to their elderly foster mothers, or, as in one case, the children were accompanied by a maid. The first document contains no financial arrangements. In that one, two women, seemingly not related to each other or to the widower, agree to join in bringing up his daughters "in friendly companionship"—a phrase used in marriage contracts and elsewhere for the relation between husband and wife. If one of them broke that agreement, she would be committing a sin before God: The record was read out to them and they confirmed it by the usual "symbolic purchase." On the reverse side payments for the children's support are entered: five payments during one week amounting to 7½ dirhems, making a monthly total of 30 dirhems, a normal allowance for two orphans. In addition, however, on Friday chickens for 3½ dirhems and olive oil for 1⅛ dirhems were bought. So these people were not entirely destitute. This unassuming pact between a father of orphans, two elderly women, and God as guarantor, is one of the heartwarming papers of the Geniza (February 1043).[157]

The second document is more businesslike. Two sisters, widows, one with a grown-up son, and another (the elder one) with an infant, admitted to their house two boys and a girl of a widower together with the slave girl "Kinky," who would "serve" the orphans. The record is a release in which the sisters confirm having received from the widower all due them for food and drink, clothing, rent, school fees, and all other things needed by male and female children until the end of the month of Tishri 1356 (Sept. 25, 1044). The mother of the infant boy also confirms having received the rent for that period for one half of a house she owned in which the widower lived. Moreover, it is stated emphatically that "Kinky" was the exclusive property of the widower. Nothing is said about any remuneration for the sisters, which means that their services were given gratuitously. Finally, the grown-up son of the other sister stands security for all the consequences emanating from this record. I assume the widower had remarried, either in that very month of Tishri, the month of the High Holidays, when many weddings were held, or, more probably, some time before, and that his new wife had been given a period of respite to enjoy married life before taking upon herself the additional task of playing mother to three minors. Our document marks the end of the orphans' stay with the two widows and probably the beginning of life with a stepmother.[158]

Marriages of fathers or mothers of orphans were not always concluded for the benefit of their offspring. We have read of persons bereaved of their spouses who entered new unions which were regarded as detrimental to their minor children or which created problems for the grown up ones.[159]

Contracts deal mostly with financial matters. Consequently, the majority of ketubbas terminated by stipulations on orphans brought into a marriage concern the children of the bride, since, as a rule, they had to be maintained by their future stepfather. Even a rich Karaite widow with a dowry of 719 dinars stipulates that "her daughter will live with her in her living quarters until she marries, and she will be provided by him [the groom] with food and clothing."[160] Another ketubba, of which only the end is preserved, states that the groom will support the bride's two daughters until their marriage.[161] Orphans of whom it was stipulated that "they will eat with him on one table" were brought in by a bride whose assets (dowry and marriage gift) amounted to 118 dinars.[162]

Promises for the good treatment of the stepchildren are mostly found in the ketubbas of poor couples. "The groom agrees to bring up the son of his spouse [a divorcée] in his house, he will provide this orphan[163] with food and clothing and teach him a craft. The boy will be to him like the children whom he will have with his bride, he will not drive him out of his house, nor beat, nor humiliate him." This we read in a marriage contract from the provincial town of Minyat Ziftā, written in summer 1110. The divorcée received 1 dinar as immediate, and 5 dinars as delayed marriage gift, that is, practically nothing. She renounced all her dues in favor of her boy.[164] In a postscript to a ketubba with seven signatures in which the bride received only 1 dinar as marriage gift, the groom takes the boy "under his wing" and promises to treat him as his own child (1053/4).[165] Similarly, in a contract in which a groom agrees to maintain the daughter of his bride for ten years, and her son for five, she receives only 2 dinars. That document also contains the curious stipulation that she was not permitted to leave Fustat. Was this a measure of precaution against the eventuality that she would run away leaving him with another man's children (1244)?[166]

Agreements like these were not always included in marriage contracts because they were clearly taken for granted. When a man was reminded on the day of his wedding that his future stepson, when grown up, might wish to sue his mother for the inheritance of his natural father, he drew up a document in which he declared: "I have brought this orphan up, he is my relative from father's and mother's side [one of the boy's parents was a relative of that man's father and the other a relative of his mother], and I love him more than anyone else. All you [the court] ask me to do for him [meaning, permitting him to sue his mother], I will do." Moreover, he agrees to provide the boy with food and clothing as long as the bride remains his wife (Nov. 1089). This additional document proves that the groom had found it unnecessary to include his obligation to support the boy in the marriage contract.[167]

Frequently a young orphan possessed an estate inherited from his father when his mother entered a new union, and that had to be regulated. A Karaite ketubba contains the laconic statement that the groom would take care of his stepson's capital, amounting to 463 dinars, as if it were his own.[168] These matters were normally regulated by separate agreements. In one document the widow Sitt Al-Ḥusn ("Beauty"), upon marrying a notable, styled "Pride of the Congregation, son of Head of the Congregation," stipulates that as long as she lived all income from business conducted in a store adjacent to the gate of her house was hers, and that her minor son would have no share in it. Moreover, the rent from the store would accrue to him only after maturity. This Beauty must have been an energetic woman, for, in a document written when her former husband was still alive, she received from him the permission, "in view of the insecure times," to sell as much as she deemed fit of her dowry and to buy real estate with the money.[169] When a woman who had brought a boy and a girl into a second marriage died, her father was apprehensive lest her husband lay his hands on the movable and immovable possessions of her orphans and tried to prevent such a calamity.[170] A widow with three grown-up sons, who married a person whose father had borne the rare honorific title "Elder of the Congregation," made sure that no false claims were made on any side. She declared that her husband owed her nothing except the usual obligations undertaken in a marriage contract plus his promise to let her live in his house for five years after his death. Her sons would have no claims whatsoever (on that house), while her husband had no right to sue her sons (for what would be bequeathed to them by her).[171]

Fathers with orphaned children would remarry with the intention of providing them with motherly care.[172] But express stipulations to that effect are rarely included in marriage contracts and then, again, only in those of people with limited means. A bride in Minyat Ghamr, Lower Egypt, agrees to bring up her future husband's son for ten years "and to do for him all he needs" (Sept. 1315).[173] A fragmentary ketubba ends with the addition that the bride "will bring up the groom's children until. . . ." Her dowry, as far as preserved, shows that she came from a family of modest circumstances.[174] Since the term "bringing up" is ambiguous and may imply support, the bride's obligation is repeatedly formulated thus: "She will live with his daughter (or: daughters) in one domicile and eat with her (or: them) on one table." One betrothal contract stipulates that the wife would lose her delayed marriage gift if she decided not to live any longer with the husband's daughter in one place. It may be that in these cases the children had already reached maturity.[175]

Instances where both spouses had children from a previous marriage also must have been frequent. In the case of a well-to-do merchant, the sons of the two spouses from former unions were well provided for.[176] In noting the details concerning a couple about to marry, a judge lists casually, "His children are with her, and her boy is with him until he marries."[177] In a late engagement contract a future stepfather will supply his bride's girls with food for five years (unless they married before), but not with clothing, while the bride would look after his boys, one an adolescent, and another five years old. The bride possessed a house in which the couple was expected to live.[178]

A man's son or daughter from his wife's prior husband would be called "the son [or: daughter] of the wife," and this designation could become a personal or family name. For instance, *Bishr ibn marat al-ālātī*, "B., the stepson of the musician" (in a list of beneficiaries), and, as a name, *Abu 'l-Faraj Ibn al-mara*, "A.-F. Stepson" (in a list of contributors), *Bint al-mara zawjat 'Ammār*, "Stepdaughter, wife of A." (in a letter).[179]

A common designation for a stepchild from either father or mother was *rabīb(a)*, "foster child," for instance, *ibn imra'at al-Wāṣiṭī rabībuh*, "the son of al-Waṣiṭī's wife, his foster son." The same word is used of a woman's stepson in a letter to Maimonides.[180] And again, as a family name, *Abu 'l-Fadl Ibn al-rabīb*, "A.-F. Fosterson" (in a list of names, written on the reverse side of a letter in Arabic characters to the Gaon Nathan b. Abraham).[181]

One wonders whether the term was not also used of a person brought up in a house without being the stepchild of one of the spouses. Orphans from a foreign country admitted to a family as an act of charity have been mentioned before.[182] One is reminded also of Moses Maimonides' sister's son, who was brought up by his illustrious uncle, instructed by him in the medical arts, and treated by him like a son.[183] And of an orphan from the countryside who stayed with his relative, the judge Elijah, for his education.[184] In view of those examples, "Hilāl, 'Newmoon,' the foster son of the Rāv" (in a census for the poll tax), or "Surūr, 'Happiness', the foster son of the judge" (in a letter from Alexandria), were probably relatives of those divines, but not necessarily their stepsons.[185]

Looking back over the data presented in this subsection (which may be complemented by the detailed description of communal social services in *Med. Soc.*, II, 91–143), we ask ourselves how in fact the Geniza society did provide for its orphans. The answer must be, first, that their care was certainly regarded as a religious commandment of the very first order, and both the community and individuals were eager to earn "merits" by this deed of charity. But even conceding that our information is one-sided, because misery is clamorous whereas well-being is reticent, our general verdict must be negative. We read too much about the sufferings of the orphans and their widowed mothers. The reason for this was partly factual: the weakness of the economy and the looseness of the juridical and communal organizations. In addition, however, conceptual shortcomings, religious and social, must share responsibility for that unsatisfactory state of affairs. God has decreed death for the father, the maintainer of the family; we human beings may try to alleviate the consequences of God's decree; we are not supposed to change it. The individual's strength was derived from his family: when the family was impaired by the death of the father, the survivors became weakened, if not destroyed. Furthermore, society was competitive and self-reliant; everyone had to look after himself. If the orphan wished to survive, he had to fight. In this book have been cited quite a number of articulate orphan girls who brought their claims before the highest authorities or even to the community at large. Finally, this was a male-oriented society; when the father died, his dependents became, as it were, outsiders; they had no rights, only a claim to charity. But human charity, as a prayer has it, "is scarce in providing, but plentiful in causing shame."

D. THE WORLD OF WOMEN

Outside men's purview.—The men who left us their writings in the Geniza believed that "the princess' place is in the innermost corner of the house," that women should be confined to the narrow circle of the family. Whether and how far the actual experience of these very men tallied with their ideas about the women's role in society is the topic of the study undertaken in this section.

Recorded history seems to suggest that human males have a tendency to form more or less compact groups, from which the individual derives a position of strength. Such strength is needed and used in manifold ways, among them to help the male overcome the female. Whether this drive to form groups is inherent in the very nature of the male, as opposed to the female—perhaps even in his biological makeup, as has been asserted—or is activated in each society by specific socioeconomic conditions, cannot be discussed here.[1] The medieval civilization reflected in this book certainly was one characterized by its strong and compact groups of males. Warriors, courtiers, men of religion, scholars, physicians, merchants, and craftsmen were brothers to one another, and, like brothers, often fought among themselves. The women were attached to the groups of their fathers and husbands, but they did not belong. A man's company consisted of men—or, at least, so it seemed.

I wish to illustrate this world of males by two tidbits from Arabic literature, one from the first century of medieval Islam, and one from the last. The newlywed wife of a caliphal crown prince (who had, of course, other wives and concubines) perceived that her husband was a great lover of wine. She procured the best wine to be had and prepared for him a dinner of fish with a salty sauce. The prince was delighted with the food, but remarked that the fish wished to swim. She brought out the wine and the prince was delighted. "But there is still something missing." "What is it?" "Someone to talk to." She brought in her two brothers. The prince liked them, they became his boon companions, and she his favorite wife.[2]

The male's incapacity of "talking" to a woman is depicted again—centuries later—in a different setting. A volume, *Women's Liberation,* published in Cairo, 1899—one of the most moving Arabic books I have read—describes and deeply deplores the plight of the husband who was unable to communicate with his wife because she lacked even the barest contact with his social and spiritual ambiance.[3]

The existence of male groups does not preclude the formation of female groups within or alongside the world of men. It is precisely this question which must ultimately occupy us in studying the women of the Geniza society. How deeply were they integrated in the male ambiance around them, how much did they identify themselves with it or live lives apart—all this should become clarified with the aid of the additional Geniza sources presented in this section, taken together with the materials studied on the preceding pages.

Men were supposed to know only the women of their own household or extended family. Consequently, a woman appearing in court or before a notary was introduced, in principle, by the phrase "after we have taken [proper] cognizance of her," a phrase never mentioned in connection with men. It was taken for granted that the men knew one another. Since this phrase is rendered not only in Arabic and Hebrew, but also in Aramaic, the language spoken in Southwest Asia before the advent of Islam, it is reasonable to assume that the practice was pre-Islamic. One suspects, however, that the phrase is often added only out of reverence for traditional attitudes and not because the judge or his associates actually did not know the woman before them. This assumption becomes reality when we find the phrase repeated on the second day of a lawsuit after a woman had already testified in the presence of the same court the day before, or when three gentlemen first talk a girl into a marriage, assuring her that they knew her well, and when she agreed, and the formal betrothal was concluded, the clerk again notes "after having made proper cognizance of her."[4] In numerous court records referring to women this clause is missing altogether.[5] All in all it seems that the judicial practice based on the notion that women were known only to their own menfolk did not quite correspond to reality. This is not surprising, since women, rich and poor, single and married, were involved in economic activities, which required their presence in the offices of notaries and in courts. These were places frequented by many men, since legal actions required publicity (and aroused curiosity).

Before exploring the common meeting grounds of men and women, we should like to hear the voices of the women themselves. But how to do this, seeing that, as a rule, men wrote the Geniza papers that have come down to us? We have one direct access to the world of women: the names they chose for their daughters. For names then, and in particular those of women, were not what they are today: they were keys to the innermost thoughts of those who gave them.

The message of women's names.—Today we choose a name because we imagine it sounds attractive, or because it is traditional in the family, or has some other connotation for us, but, as a rule, we pay no attention to its meaning, which, in most cases, is unknown to us. In the Geniza, to the contrary, female names were living words, each with a distinctive connotation, of which those who gave them were well aware. The meaning of a name and the frequency of its occurrence are therefore true indicators of what a woman wished for her daughter and, by implication, for herself.

The large number and wide variety of female names given at birth immediately attract attention. Thus far I have noted no names that appear as often as twenty times and only eight that occur ten times and more. The average seems to be a recurrence of two to five times, with many found only once. Add to these the many telling nicknames given to women during their lifetimes which then stay with their descendants as family names, and we gain the impression that these medieval women, far from being colorless, had much character and individuality.

In another context I have drawn attention to the rich onomasticon of ancient Israel and pre-Islamic Arabia, both well known to us. The equally abundant treasure of female names in the Geniza period is derived from neither. It is entirely different from both. It originated independently owing to the specific situations, the stirrings and aspirations of the women within the new civilization which matured in the Near Eastern and Mediterranean Islamic cities during the High Middle Ages.[6]

A second trait that catches the eye is the complete absence of biblical and other Hebrew names among the Jewish women of Egypt. In the rare times when they are found it can be shown that the family originated in Palestine, Tunisia or other North African country, Spain, Byzantium, or Western Europe, where biblical names were occasionally given to females. This startling deficiency would seem to demonstrate a chasm between the popular local subculture of the women and the worldwide Hebrew book culture of the men. The dichotomy is even more emphasized by the purely secular character of the female names, which, with very few exceptions, confined to upper class, mostly Karaite, families, do not contain any reference to God or other religious concepts.[7]

I must add that I have made the same observation with regard to the Jewish women of Yemen, among whose husbands religious learning was more diffused than had been so with the Jews of Egypt in the Geniza period.[8] One must therefore reckon with the possibility that the absence of biblical and theophoric names among women was originally not a matter of free choice but was a taboo imposed by males, and became an accepted custom only in the course of time. But that is mere surmise.

Names from Arabic classical or popular narratives also are seldom found. There is Laylā, the heroine of the stories of the love-mad poet Majnūn, ʿAblā, the beloved of the great warrior ʿAntara, ʿĀtika, the favorite wife of the caliph ʿAbd al-Malik, and Bānūqa, the boy-like daughter of the caliph Ma'mūn.[9] The very rare occurrence of those names induces doubt that they were taken directly from the narratives concerned; the names were probably chosen because they were in general use, just as today a mother will call her daughter Angelica without having the faintest idea that she is the heroine of Ariosto's *Orlando Furioso.* With this I do not wish to imply that Jewish women did not listen to Arabic folktales.[10]

The third, and most surprising aspect of the female Geniza nomenclature is the prevalence in it of the ideas of ruling, overcoming, and victory. Most of these names are composed with the word *sitt,* "mistress," "female ruler," originally an honorary title added to a name, which became the personal name of a girl given to her at birth.[11] The word Sitt was often omitted, so that strange forms of female names result. Above, we had *'Amā'im,* "Turbans," abbreviated from *Sitt al-'Amā'im,* "She who Rules over the Turbans," namely, the men.[12] A girl belonging to the class of government officials was called *Sitt al-Kuttāb,* "Mistress of the Clerks," in short, *Kuttāb,* "Clerks," the daughter of a big merchant, *Sitt al-Tujjār,* or *Tujjār,* "Merchants,"[13] one of the higher class in general, "Lords" (*Sādah*), or "Upper Class" (*Khāṣṣah*). Hence the strange names born by girls: such as *Mulūk,* "Kings" (frequent), or those of countries, cities, or peoples. We have several times *Sitt Baghdād,* "The Mistress over Baghdad," and simply *Baghdād,* or *Ramle,* the same for Iraq (*'Irāq*), the Muslim West (*Gharb*), Byzantium (*Rūm*), and the Persians (*Furs*).

Names describing their bearers as ruling the house (*Dār*), the household (*Bayt*), the family (*Ahl*), the clan (*'Ashīr*), brother or sisters, or boys or girls in general, are natural, and therefore frequent. A most common female name in the Geniza is *Sitt al-Kull,* "She who Rules over Everyone," paralleled by *Sitt al-Jamī',* which means the same, *Sitt al-Nās,* "Mistress over Mankind," *Sitt al-Zamān,* "Mistress of her Time," and *Sitt al-Aqrān,* "Ruling over her Peers." The names *Sitt A'dāhā,* "Mistress of her Enemies," and *Sitthum,* "Their Mistress," are particularly noteworthy.[14]

The group of names describing a woman as ruling over certain types of people or all of them is matched by another composed of Sitt with an abstract noun. Here again the idea of eminence is found throughout. The most common names of this type were *Fakhr,* "Glory," *Thanā',* "Praise," *'Izz,* "Fame," followed by similar notions, such as *Ri'āsa,* "Leadership," *Naṣr,* "Victory," *Naẓar, "Control, Supervision,"* *Ma'ālī,* "Excellence," *Ghalb,* "Overcoming," and so forth. Telling names in this context are *Qā'ida,* "[female] General," *Wazīra,* "Vizier," and *'Alam,* "Flag" (at the head of an advancing troop, common). *Labwa,* "Lioness," not found in pre-Islamic Arabia, probably also belongs to this category.[15]

How shall we explain the female names, considered thus far, which come to almost 70 percent of the material? Do they represent a cry of protest against the oppression to which the women might have been exposed, or are they an admonition to fight for dominance in the household and for leadership in general? A favorite topic of old Oriental wisdom and rhetoric was the observation that woman is not frailty, but the most powerful force on earth, stronger than riches, wine, wisdom, and kings.[16] Like the biblical Queen Esther, however, she must show her strength in ways different from those fitting her male partner (see pp. 292–293, above). It should be noted that the proud names presented above were not particular to Jewish women.[17]

Some names display opposing and unexpected traits. "Bashfulness," the allegedly intrinsic characteristic of women,[18] is represented by the names *Ḥayā'* and *Khafar,* which are less common than one would expect. Twice as often as both together we find the opposite: *Dalāl,* "Coquetry, taking liberty with someone, boldness," or *Fā'iza,* "Successful [with men]," *Khulla,* "Lover," *Haẓiyya,* "Favorite," *Mawadda,* "Love." The names *Mūnisa,* and, even more remarkable, in the masculine form, *Muwānis,* "Good Company," "Intimate Friend," probably also contain a wish for success in marriage. As an Arabic (and Judeo-Arabic) saying has it: "Enchanted by his beloved [wife], a man neglects his [male] companions."[19]

Chastity and Fertility, regarded by men as the most praiseworthy attributes of a women, are all but absent from the female onomasticon of the Geniza. Many men are called "Pure," *Ṭāhir* (Ar.) or *Ṭāhōr* (Heb.), or "Chaste," *'Afīf,* but I have not yet come upon a Ṭāhira or 'Afīfa.[20] *Thāmira,* "Fertile," has been met with only once.[21] These things were taken for granted by women. It was their lot, imposed on them by God, to be faithful to their husbands and to bear them children. There was no point in expressing it as a special wish embodied in a name. But that their menfolk should remain pure and chaste was indeed a deep concern for mothers, since concubinage with slave girls was the most dreaded source of marital conflict.

Names designating noble lineage, such as *Nasab, Nisāba,* and *Ḥasab,* were common. Especially in families that had seen better days the emphasis was not redundant. *Karīma,* "noble, distinguished," had in the Geniza period the additional meaning of "sister" (unlike modern Arabic, where it means "daughter") and is found as a female name also in a Muslim marriage contract of 1028.[22]

There is no need to survey here names with general connotations which are found all over the world. We all greet the newborn as dear and beloved. Hence the name *'Azīza,* "Dear," and many other derivatives from the same or similar roots. "Pearl" and its synonyms were as common then as they are today.[23] But when we find occurring in the Geniza most frequently the girls' names *Turfa,* "Cherished Gift" (also in the plural *Turaf*), *Ghāliya,* "Precious," *Munā,* "Wishes Fulfilled," *Mu'ammala,* "The one hoped for," *Ghunya,* "Gain," *Yumn,* "Good Luck," I suspect here a female protest against the male prejudice that only boys should be born, and that girls represented unfulfilled wishes, dashed hopes, and financial loss. Many names express the wish for a long life, the most impressive of which is the very common *Nājiya,* "Saved," indicating the dangerous times through which the Geniza people often had to live.[24] Others carry a wish for happiness, joy, and contentment.

Girls should be beautiful. And since *nomen est omen,* since names have magical power, numerous names describe the newborn as a paragon of beauty, especially the extremely common *Sitt al-Milāḥ,* "The fairest of the fair," often abbreviated as *Milāḥ.* Beauty is expressed in many ways: simply and directly, such as *Jamīla,* "Beautiful," by numerous variants of the notion of light,[25] also "Moon," in early, and "Sun" in later Geniza times, or by the names of graceful animals, in particular "Gazelle," or trees, especially "Cypress." Since Turkish slave girls were renowned for their beauty (only the prettiest were imported, of course), Jewish mothers called their daughters *Turkiyya* or, as a sign of particular affection, *Turayk,* "Little Turk" (in the masculine), or *Khuzayr,* "Little Khazar" (a Turkish people partly converted to Judaism).[26]

Many names were common to males and females. These names mostly express general notions and wishes, such as "Blessings," *Baraka,* "Good Tidings," *Bushr,* "Gift," *Hiba,* "Well being," *Salāma,* "Happiness," *Sa'āda,* "Long Life," *Baqā,* "Substitute" (for a child that had died), *Khalīfa,* "Beauty," *Zayn.* Several names expressing the idea of eminence, mentioned above, such as "Glory," "Praise," "Victory," appear also as male names, but then mostly preceded by *Abū,* "Possessor of." These identical names of males and females also probably demonstrate the proud mother's contention that she did not care whether she had given birth to a boy or a girl. The same applies to feminine forms of male names, such as *Maymūna,* "God Auspice," paralleling *Maymūn,* made famous through Maimonides.

Genealogies, we remember, were confined to males. A woman was identified by the name of her father, not of her mother. We are therefore not in a position to know whether female names were transmitted in a family in the same way as the male ones. A woman from Qayrawān writes to her brother on travel abroad that a girl was born to one of their brothers "and I called her by the name of my mother *Surūra* ("Happy")"[27] Thus, this girl was named after her *paternal* grandmother. We find the same in a contemporary family chronicle from southern Italy (where the names, of course, were not Arabic, but Latin or Hebrew) in which a girl is called Cassia like the mother of her *father*.[28] We should not generalize. It stands to reason, however, that the custom—unknown in biblical times—of strengthening the family attachment of a newborn by giving him the name of an ancestor or other relative was observed in the Geniza period also with regard to girls.[29]

Changing fashions in the preferences for certain names or groups of names for girls can be observed throughout the "classical" Geniza period. On the other hand, the longevity of some names, even rare ones, is remarkable. *Umm al-Khayr,* "Possessor [literally, "Mother"] of Goodness," found thus far only once in a Jewish document, dated 1029, appears again as the name of a Muslim noble woman, married in Aswan three hundred years later, in 1334.[30] And some female names from the Geniza, especially those composed with Sitt, have lived on well into the second half of the twentieth century, at least in the Karaite community of Cairo (whose weekly with its family news I had opportunity to read in the 1950s).

The messages contained in the female names of the Geniza period must be heeded by anyone trying to penetrate into the secluded world of its women.

Historical antecedents.—In order to put the women's world of the Geniza period in its proper historical context some of its antecedents must be considered, if only in the barest outlines.

The women of ancient Israel, as they appear to us in the Hebrew Bible, were disadvantaged by polygyny and all that went with it, but they played a far more vital role than their female progeny in postbiblical times.

In that pristine peasant society the wife was "man's helper, his counterpart." (This is the proper rendering of Genesis 2:18.) He produced the food, she made the clothing. He was afield, either tilling the soil, from daybreak to sunset, or deliberating with the elders "at the gate," sometimes also participating in a war; she ran the house, planning, storing, buying and selling, spinning and weaving, and dispensing help to the needy and advice to whomever sought it. A look at the praise of the woman of valor in Proverbs 31:10–31 brings that situation home.

Second, there was no education gap between men and women. The wisdom of both was practical. "Heed, my son, the admonition of your father and do not forsake the teaching (in Hebrew: Torah) of your mother" (Proverbs 1:8).

Third, love was robust and outspoken. Joseph was the manifest favorite of his father Jacob because he was the son of his beloved Rachel. "Am I not better to you than ten sons," the barren, but preferred Hannah is consoled by her husband (I Samuel 1:8). The wife was her husband's "companion" (Malachi 2:14). Hence the many and unforgettable portraits of women presented by the Hebrew Bible. Those men paid attention to their women. They knew them.

Finally, marriage in biblical times, unlike that of the Geniza period, possessed the halo of permanence. "Your clan will be mine; your deity will be worshipped by me. Where you die, I will die, and there I will be buried; even death will not separate me from you." This is the vow of the bride (Ruth 1:16–17, where the attachment to the dead husband is extended to his bereaved mother). The wife leaves the house of her father and clan and becomes a member of the husband's family. This severance was so strict that a woman of the progeny of Aaron, when married out of the priestly clan, was no longer permitted to partake of the sacrificial meal restricted to Kohens, and her parents and siblings were not allowed to "defile themselves" by following her bier. She on her side agreed to be buried in the common tomb of her new family. The husband's vow equally stressed permanence. "I betroth you to me for eternity, I betroth you to me in equity and justice [you will get all due to you] in love and mercy [and more than that], and I betroth you to me in steadfastness [a reiteration of the everlasting character of the marital bond]" (Hosea 3:19–20; here said by God to Israel).

Israel's *religion,* however, was not favorable to the fair sex. A woman could enter the temple and pray, as Hannah did, but the immediate service of God was reserved for male priests. Women could be possessed by God's spirit; they could become prophets, like Miriam, Deborah, and Hulda (2 Kings 22:13–20). The very last prophet mentioned in the Bible by name, No'adya ("Meeting with God"), was a woman (Nehemiah 6:14). But they were exceptions. In the sanctuary men alone were permitted to officiate. The reason for this, I believe, was the obsession with ritual purity (endangered by the women's monthly menstrual cycle), an obsession shared by other ancient peoples. The oracle of Delphi, Greece, was pronounced by a woman prophet, but the priests were men. The women of ancient Israel reacted against the antifeminism of the national religion by turning to foreign gods. They baked cakes and offered libations and incense to the sweet "Queen of Heaven" (Jeremiah 7:18, 44:15–19), and mourned Tammūz-Adonis, planted gardens in his honor, and rejoiced in his rebirth (Ezekiel 8:14, Isaiah 17:10).

The missionary spirit accompanying the religious revival preceding and following the Babylonian exile affected the women as well as the men. In all the teaching and other public assemblies women were expressly mentioned among those present, even prominently (Ezra 10:1, Nehemiah 5:1, 8:23, 12:43) as was foreseen in the book that contains the program for that revival (Deuteronomy, 29:10, 31:12).[31] Women now become the protagonists for the salvation of their people, like Esther in the Bible and Judith in the apocryphal book named after its heroine, and in the Synagogue and the Church the mother of the seven Maccabean martyr brothers, who died after encouraging her sons not to yield to idolatry (Second and Fourth Books of the Maccabees), is the prefiguration of the woman-saint dying for her faith.[32]

Unfortunately, however, the trend unfavorable to the participation of women in the community's religious life became strengthened by a mighty new influence: Hellas. High cultures, characterized by rational reasoning, are prone to abase their women. For as soon as the men begin to ponder the low state of their women, a state partly inherited from an earlier stage of civilization, they feel the urge to explain and to justify the situation, and by this to exonerate themselves of this imbalance. Thus, they add theoretical demeaning to actual oppression. The Greeks, who thought deeper and more systematically than preceding cultures, came up with manifold theories. Aristophanes and Plato, each in his own way, even visualized the possibility of almost complete equality. There seems to exist also, with regard to women, a strange contrast between Greek art and poetry, which magnified and idealized women, and life and scientific theory, which reduced them to a lower rank. Be that as it may, the conviction that woman is inferior, biologically and mentally, became the dominant trend, with the practical consequence of excluding her from participation in the pursuits of men.[33] With the Hellenization of the Mediterranean world this conviction resulted in the deprivation of women of their right to a proper education. The Jews were one of the peoples affected by this influence.

Studying and expounding the Scriptures became the very core of rabbinical Judaism, as it developed in the centuries before and after the destruction of the Second Commonwealth (A.D. 70). The discussion whether "a man has the duty to teach his daughter Torah" or "the woman's wisdom is for the distaff, not more" and "better burn the words of the Torah than give them to women" went on for some time but, in practice, was decided in favor of the second alternative.[34] The propitious beginnings of female participation in the religous revival at the beginning of the Second Commonwealth were stifled by a new spiritual situation, when popularized Greek scientific theory combined with ancient Near Eastern prejudices to push the women into a dark corner. Something similar happened in Islam. Muhammad, in his missionary zeal, addressed women frequently and strove to enlist their participation. He also bettered their lot by legislation. But when the Arabs moved out into the sedentary countries of the Near East, which were infected by an antifeminine bias, the reformatory spirit of Islam became blunted, and the excessive concubinage indulged in by the conquerors degraded womanhood irreparably. In Judaism, the exlusion of women from the study of the Scriptures, which was the main expression of piety, inevitably had a degrading effect.

Yet the ways of the spirit are inscrutable. The reader who has followed me till here is reminded of Paul's First Letter to the Corinthians: "Women should keep silence in the churches. They are not permitted to speak, but should be subordinate, as the Law says. If there is anything they desire to know, let them ask their husbands at home" (14:34–35). Yes, women should not open their mouths in the church, but the letter implies that they were present there. And very much so, as we know from their tangible role in the diffusion of Christianity. The same happened in the Synagogue. The mosaic inscriptions in the synagogues of late antiquity show women as frequent donors, and the zeal of women in helping their husbands and sons to acquire religious learning is highly praised in the Talmud. Rabbi Aqiba, the most popular of the Talmudic sages, is reported to have said to his disciples pointing to his wife: "Mine and yours is hers." A subordinate role, if acquiesced in and successfully performed, can be very satisfactory.[35]

The socioeconomic character of the Jewish community, and, with it, the position of its women, also changed markedly in postbiblical antiquity. Farming still was prominent, both in Babylonia-Iraq and in Palestine, as was recently brought home again by the astonishing find of an unusually large agricultural inscription near Beth-Shean, Palestine, believed by the editor to have been executed in the seventh century (probably, however, somewhat before).[36] But the process that converted the Jews into an almost exclusively urban population was already in full swing. It was completed in early Islamic times, during the eventful, but obscure, seventh through ninth centuries, when much destruction and some rehabilitation were under way, the results of which are revealed to us in the Geniza papers.

The women of the Geniza world cannot be regarded as a unified group, either geographically or in rank. Iraq and Iran, with their Persian traditions, insisted on strict seclusion and subordination of women. On the other hand, it was the opulent Karaites and other rich and influential Jews who emigrated from those parts to Syria-Palestine, Egypt, Tunisia, and farther afield, and, as is natural in well-to-do families, their daughters gained from this affluence and became more independent than many women from the local populations. There was a similar migration movement to the Mediterranean countries among the Muslims of the East.[37]

Visitors to Egypt from the religiously strict and zealous Muslim West, Morocco and its dependencies, were shocked by the easygoing ways of the Egyptian capital, where wine was publicly sold and women enjoyed much freedom. To explain the latter phenomenon a somewhat malicious legend was invented. When, by God's decree, Pharaoh and his hosts were drowned in the Red Sea, the slaves of the dead Egyptians approached the widows proposing marriage. The widows agreed but on one condition: that the Egyptian husbands always be slaves of their wives. The account concludes: "Have you ever made a deal with a Copt? When you are sure that the matter is settled, he says to you: Wait, first I must go home and consult my wife." Copts are brought in here not as Christians, but as the indigenous Egyptians. The Muslim women of Fustat were notorious for their license. "Every wife has two husbands," exclaims Muqaddasī, the great Muslim traveler from Jerusalem, the holy city, whose people, again according to him, were "the most virtuous of all mankind."[38]

It was unfortunate for Jewish women that rabbinical Judaism took shape mainly in Iraq (Babylonian Talmud, the Gaons), and was codified by Moses Maimonides, who came to Egypt from the Muslim West. On the other hand, the Babylonian scholars, living within a highly developed economy, had a practical and mundane mind, which beneficially influenced legislation in family matters. By his deep erudition and keen understanding, Maimonides was able to mitigate his rigorous codification through humane guidance and gentle admonition. The decisions of the judges preserved in the Geniza generally appear to us as practical and humane, too, but they could not prevail against a Godgiven law and widespread social notions which the Geniza world had inherited from late antiquity and early Islam.

This book has shown how women fared within the family. Before trying to draw some general conclusions, the common meeting grounds of men and women and female activities not directly connected with family life must be briefly examined.

Women in economic life.—In discussing the economic role of the wife[39] we came to the conclusion that, as far as the Geniza documents go, the problem of the working woman was virtually absent during the tenth and eleventh centuries, became acute during the twelfth, and paramount from the thirteenth on. This was partly explained by the progressive impoverishment of the minority groups, or perhaps of the population at large, and partly also by the loosening of standards of propriety, as men grew less reluctant to expose their wives to the outside world.[40]

The professions open or specific to women, as surveyed in *Med. Soc.*, I, chap. ii, sec. 6, were limited and brought only small income. Women's possessions were mainly acquired through gift, dowry, or inheritance, and for many also through communal charity. But it was precisely this derivative character of their participation in economic life which constantly brought women in contact with the world of men.

The number of widowed, divorced, or deserted women who had lost their struggle for a decent livelihood, or had never possessed one, was very considerable.[41] They could not sit at home, awaiting help. They had "to uncover their faces," as the phrase went, to show up in public, in order to secure their rights, or to obtain a minimum of sustenance. Our analysis of the functioning of the communal social services has shown that in order to be eligible for public welfare a person had to be registered; these registrations were frequently checked and changed. The semiweekly distributions of bread and the occasional handouts of wheat, clothing, and cash were not delivered to the homes, but had to be picked up at the synagogue compound. All this required much moving around and unavoidable contacts with the men in charge of supervision, registration, and distribution.[42]

A concise note, two inches high, written and signed by the judge Samuel b. Saadya, illustrates: "The administrators of the Compound of the Jerusalemites are advised to pay to 'the Mother of Abraham,' better known under the name 'the Mother of the Little Calf,' 9½ dirhems, her share in the revenue from the Compound of the Jerusalemites for the year 1477 [of the Seleucid era, A.D.

1165/6]. And Peace."[43] Sixty-six years had passed since the Crusaders had taken Jerusalem. Normally, no Jews lived there. But the community of Fustat possessed a compound (sometimes referred to as a row) of houses whose rents served as alms for the Jewish poor of the Holy City. I have not yet found a direct statement as to who the poor of Jerusalem were after the city was taken by the Crusaders. But we have two other notes written by that judge in the same year and awarding the same sum from the same source to two male persons, one of whom had the family name al-Dimashqī (from Damascus).[44] So we may perhaps be justified in assuming that foreigners, especially of Syro-Palestinian descent, were regarded as eligible for these benefits.

In order to substantiate her claims, 'the Mother of the Little Calf' (her son was probably a big fat man,) had to find witnesses who were able and prepared to testify about her status (descent, poverty, no family in a position to support her, unable to work) and to present them to the court. An application by a woman to a judge for her share in the revenue from that compound was written approximately at the same time.[45] With the note of the judge the woman had to find one of the administrators who had cash ready to pay her—or, who would give her a promissory note to a tenant or a grocer. All this for a sum sufficient for two or three weeks, at most.

The men in charge of social welfare were only a small section of the male world with whom single poor women had contact. It was their fellow poor whom they constantly met while making use of the communal services. When I started to study the organization of public charity in the Geniza documents, I expected to find separate lists for men and women and separate days designated for the collection of food, clothing, and cash by the members of each sex. Nothing of the kind was found. All the lists show that women and men mixed freely while receiving their welfare benefits. This seems to strengthen the earlier surmise that numerous marriage contracts may have been contracts of convenience between indigent old men and women to form a common household. As we have seen, they had much opportunity to meet one another.[46]

Private charity was different. The Geniza contains countless begging letters written or dictated by men, none by women. Women appealed to the heads of the community, to judges, or welfare officials, and, naturally, also to members of their own family, but not to strange individuals. Considerations of decency closed this avenue of economic support to women. Private charity was extended to women, sometimes in grand style, but it could not be solicited in the impersonal way permitted men.[47]

Women of all classes appear in the Geniza documents as being in possession of immovables. They receive as a gift or donate, inherit or bequeath, buy or sell, rent or lease houses (more often parts of houses), stores, workshops, flour mills, and other types of urban real estate, and also take care of their maintenance. This most prominent aspect of the female role in the economy of Geniza times deserves closer study.

When it is said of a girl that she "enters her house," the reference is not to a house belonging to her but to the domicile of her husband, which generally was on the premises of his family home or otherwise provided by him. Yet, to some extent, the husband's house was hers, morally, because she was to become "the mistress of the house" and to take charge of its management, and legally, since the house, like all other possessions of the husband, was, as stated in the marriage contract, mortgaged to his obligations toward her. In early deeds of sale the wife is mentioned first as the seller, even when the property at issue was not brought into the marriage by her. In one document it is expressly stated that the house concerned was inherited by the husband from his father.[48] By mentioning the wife first it was indicated that she had lifted her mortgage from the real estate sold and would lay no claim on it after her husband's death or a divorce. The wife's mortgage rights could become grim reality when the husband had no other means of absolving himself of his obligations toward her. Relevant examples have been adduced above.[49]

In some instances, an apartment brought in by the bride, either as part of her dowry or as her personal property, served as the residence of the young couple.[50] But this was the exception rather than the rule, since, ideally and normally, the husband provided the family's domicile.[51] The primary purpose of providing a woman with real estate was the creation for her of enduring economic security, which would make her financially independent. This is self-evident in the numerous cases in which a woman possessed more than one piece of property. For example, when a widow (or, less likely, divorcée) brings into the marriage, besides a valuable bridal outfit, "an entire large house in the Fortress of the Candles" (the Byzantine nucleus of the city of Fustat), another "large house in the Grand Bazaar opposite the Funduq" (merchant's hostel), and a quarter of a house somewhere else (where, not preserved);[52] or when the daughter of the India trader Abu 'l-Barakāt Lebdī, at her engagement, is given five out of twenty-four shares in a mansion that once had belonged to her grandfather, plus one half of the house of her late father, on condition that the rent of both will be hers to the exclusion of her future husband (Nov., 1146);[53] or when Abū Ya'qūb al-Ḥakīm, the often mentioned "Doctor" and representative of the merchants in Fustat, on his deathbed bequeaths two houses to an adult virgin daughter of his (ca. 1100).[54] There are other examples, like a woman donating a house for religious and charitable purposes while she stayed in an apartment she had acquired, or three Christian women selling the remaining share in a house belonging to them to a Jew who previously had acquired the other shares; the women lived elsewhere.[55]

Real estate as investment must be assumed, of course, with properties not normally serving as living quarters. A noble young woman sojourning in Jerusalem possessed several stores there; she died in days of disturbances when it was dangerous to carry her body to the cemetery, and it was suggested that she be buried in one of those places (ca. 1065).[56] At approximately the same time a woman in Fustat (seemingly unmarried, no husband mentioned) sold one quarter of two stores belonging to her to Abraham, son of the President of the High Court and some time Gaon, Nathan b. Abraham, for 35 dinars. Many notables signed the document (1066).[57] The widow of the India trader Abu 'l-Barakāt Lebdī, mentioned above, acquired one sixth of two stores (one of which served as the office of a physician) for 53¾ dinars in 1143.[58] A father buys a quarter of a flour mill for his unmarried daughter (thirteenth century).[59] A Muslim woman receives a monthly rent of 28 dirhems for a drugstore from a Jewish pharmacist (Oct., 1334).[60] In an Arabic document from March 1519, Samrā ("the Dark Brown," a mark of beauty,) sells a workshop for dyeing clothes in the village of Baḥṭīṭ to a Jewish dyer, as well as one (nominal) half of each of two houses belonging to her in the nearby town of Bilbays, Lower Egypt.[61] The same system, we see, was adhered to throughout the centuries, with no difference to be observed among the various religious communities.

Even in documents dealing with only one house, it is often evident that it was acquired for the revenue it was expected to bring rather than for living quarters. To adduce again an example from the story of the Lebdī family, Joseph, Abu 'l-Barakāt's father, first rented (and sublet to several tenants) and then bought a house worth 500 dinars from Nājiya, the wife of an important personage (spring 1102). This house was clearly an object of investment for both the seller and the buyer (Joseph Lebdī bought a quarter, worth 300 dinars, of another house in the same year).[62] Naturally the same is true with engagement or marriage contracts in which it is stipulated that the revenue accruing from a property brought in by the bride is hers. When "the Daughter of the [male] Cheetah" sells to "Lady Gazelle" one (real) half of her house with the concurrence of both husbands, we cannot know whether the property sold had been a source of income (which is more likely) or formed part of the residence of the seller. The price was 117 dinars, paid in cash, with the exception of 9½ dinars still due, and the expenses to be borne by the seller (Hanukka, Nov. 1132).[63] But in a similar case, when a woman sold to another woman a nominal quarter of a house which her father had given her as part of her dowry and of which she had previously sold one half to the same buyer, or when a woman buys, "with the permission and in the presence of her husband," a nominal quarter of a house for 1,000 dirhems, it is likely that the properties conveyed were objects of investment.[64]

In numerous documents women are depicted as vigorously taking charge of their properties. Sitt Naba', "Lady Excellence"[65] of the renowned Amshāṭī ("Comb Maker") family, leased two of her properties, one an orchard with a modest building, and another, a *qā'a,* or one-story house, overlooking the Nile, for a period of seven years against a rent of 52½ dinars, that is, 7½ dinars per year. The tenant was not to pay rent but to put the two properties into good repair. By the time of the document, spring 1231, three and a half years had passed; the repairs had been successfully completed, an upper story had been added to the modest building in the orchard "with her permission and consent," and the townhouse had been renovated. Sitt Naba' now declares in court that the tenant may keep the properties for another four years, may gather the fruits of the orchard for himself and sow there what he liked, and if she were to sell one of the properties, or both, she would restore to him the balance remaining from the rent already paid by the tenant plus his expenses. Throughout the document Sitt Naba' speaks. At the end, her husband confirms her actions.[66]

Concern for keeping her property in good repair also prompted the action of Sitt al-Milāḥ, "the Fairest of the Fair," daughter of a man named Ephraim ha-Levi with the honorary epithet "Head of the congregation."[67] She sold many objects of gold, copper, and clothing from her bridal outfit, no doubt with the consent of her husband (although it is not directly stated) and used most of the proceeds for repairs of a house in the Khandaq (Trench, Ditch) quarter in the residential city of Cairo. For 5 dinars she also bought bees, probably to replenish depleted swarms she kept in an orchard she owned near the city (Sept. 1110).[68]

Of particular interest is a story contained in two documents written by Ḥalfōn b. Manasse (1100–1138), both unfinished, certainly because of the delicacy of the subject matter. A common trick of Islamic legal practice for circumventing the prohibition of taking interest was this: A sold his house to B with the right of buying it back after a fixed period. Meanwhile A remained in the house and paid B rent at an exorbitant price; in reality, that was the interest. The same practice was adhered to, though to a limited extent, by Jews, mainly from the twelfth century on. Jayyida ("First Rate") possessed a house—or rather two thirds of it, for the other third belonged to a Jewish pious foundation, as we know from a slightly later Arabic document.[69] Jayyida needed 50 dinars (for what purpose, is not stated), got them from David, the dyer, and sold him her house for two years with the promise to pay him a total "rent" of 16 dinars, 8 per year, in other words a usurious yearly interest of 16 percent. When Jayyida arrived in court, she did not beat about the bush, but stated bluntly: "I took a loan etc." This was bad form, and after a few lines the court clerk broke off.[70]

The second testimony conformed even less with the ideas of propriety held by the courts. Two or more witnesses tell about their visit to Jayyida's place:

> We responded to her request and went. She locked us all in, brought the above-mentioned Mr. David and seated him and herself close to the door behind which we were, so that we should hear word for word what each of them said. She said to him: "Da'ūd [Arabic form of the name David], listen, no one is between us. Return to God [i.e., behave as a man should], and do not claim something on which you have no right. I owe you only 50 dinars. How come you sue me for 66? Have we [meaning, I, pl. of modesty] received from you anything above 50 dinars as price of the house? So why have you made out a writ of debt in my name to the amount of 66 dinars?"

Jayyida had the witnesses listen in order to accuse David of taking fixed interest, a flagrant breach of the law of the Torah. But the clerk discontinued writing in the middle of the line, because the circumvention of the law habitual in the Islamic environment had also been accepted in Jewish courts and could not be treated as a crime. I wonder what Jayyida's husband, who was a scholarly person, thought about this initiative of his enterprising wife.[71]

Real estate could be turned into cash and then be invested in commercial undertakings. We do not know (yet) how Nājiya used the 500 dinars she obtained from the sale of a house to Joseph

Lebdī.[72] Her contemporary Amat al-Qādir invested 300 dinars belonging partly to herself and partly to a teenage stepson in a business venture of a merchant traveling to Yemen.[73] Most of the money of the *dallāla,* or business agent, Wuḥsha was invested in loans for which she had received a large number of precious collateral.[74] Women as providers or receivers of loans are frequently encountered in the Geniza. The first case of a loan given on fixed interest and noted in a record book of the rabbinical court of Fustat (May 1156) is that of a woman lending 27 dinars to another woman and her son for the duration of six years, to be paid back in monthly installments of ½ dinar. This makes a total of 36 dinars, including fixed interest of 9 dinars, which corresponds to about 11 percent per year.[75] A wandering preacher fulminated against the women of a town he visited as being usurers who lent money on fixed interest.[76] An opposite case, a woman (and her husband) arranging for a fictive sale of a house in order to secure a loan of 50 dinars against interest has just been cited.[77]

Such operations could end in a disaster. A case, interesting in more than one respect, may be summarized here. Bahiyya ("Radiant"), the daughter of Ya'īsh ha-Kohen, probably a relative of Eli b. Ya'īsh ha-Kohen, the social welfare official so often mentioned in this book, had taken, in partnership with a Muslim, a loan of 42 dinars from a Jew before a Muslim court. When the business venture in which the money was invested failed, long law suits before the rabbinical court ensued, since the issues were ambiguous. In order to save Bahiyya from being dragged through Muslim courts, a compromise was reached: the creditor would demand from Bahiyya only 30 dinars and get the remaining 12 from the Muslim. Since Bahiyya did not have the cash, the sum was to be paid in equal shares by her husband and her brother Jacob.[78] But her husband stalled. Finally, he agreed to pay 11 dinars, while the brother bore the lion's share of the burden of family responsibility (summer, 1057).[79] A brother sometimes felt this duty more strongly than a husband. The reader is reminded of sisters providing financial support for their brothers.[80]

Women regularly appear in the Geniza documents as buyers or sellers of servants, but those transactions should not be regarded as commercial activities. To be sure, slaves, like houses, represented a financial investment, but they were acquired for domestic services, wherefore it is natural that women dealt with such matters, whereas male servants acted as business agents and aides to traveling merchants. For the problem of slavery in Geniza times and the share of women in it *Med. Soc.*, I, chap. ii, sec. 7, should be consulted. Often the slave girls changing hands were minors, destined to be brought up and groomed for service in the house of the purchaser—almost like a child. Thus a widow, who obviously did not foresee that she would need her help, sold a minor girl for the considerable sum of 18¾ dinars, whereas a wife acquired from her husband a slave child, probably born in the house during the husband's previous marriage.[81] When a mother sells to her son a mamlūk, a male slave of European extraction, no doubt the reason was that the slave, having been the business agent of her father or husband, had come into her possession by way of inheritance or as part of her delayed marriage gift. She had no use for him, since it was not customary in Jewish houses to keep male domestics.[82]

Since women often possessed commercial experience, it is natural that we frequently find them appointed as guardians of their children and executors of estates. We have found not only wives in these capacities, but also a mother-in-law, a grandmother, and a sister-in-law.[83] When a widow who happened to be the daughter of a scribe and the wife of another, acted as guardian for her two daughters, as well as an executor, the estate she had to manage was probably very limited in size. In the document concerned she received books and Torah scrolls, probably copied by her late husbnd, which had been deposited with a physician. In a postscript in Nagid Abraham Maimonides' own hand she is warned that the items were the property of her daughters, the heirs, not of hers.[84] But when a communal official in Malīj informs his superior in Fustat that "last week" a man had died after appointing his wife as guardian of his minor son and executor of his possessions, and that he had had deposits with the banker Ibn Sha'yā and goods with the Tustaris—two of the most prominent names in the commercial world of Egypt during the first third of the eleventh century—it is likely that the management of this estate required some experience in business matters.[85] Sometimes a wife took care of her husband's affairs during his last illness. Hence the deathbed declarations that no claims could be made by the heirs of the husband, in particular with regard to actions taken by her during his illness. Exceptionally, his wife managed whatever business or workshop he had. When a man appears in court and declares that he had no claims against his wife "with regard to any dispositions she made in my house and all she managed for me," that situation probably formed the background.[86]

All in all though, the woman's share in economic life was restricted. The derivative, indirect, and often insignificant means by which her possessions were acquired also characterized their use. A woman invested mainly in real estate, she lent money, concluded partnerships, also sold and bought textiles, jewelry, and other items included in a bridal outfit, but she was not in the mainstream of the economy—the large-scale production and exchange of goods. Moreover, a married woman, so far as she did not possess means outside the common pool of the nuclear family, depended entirely on her husband, and, in his absence, on his male relatives, even her own sons, or his business partners or friends. This dependence was both humiliating and occasionally even precarious. Yet many women, married and unmarried, had means of their own and made varied use of them, which made contacts with men outside their own family unavoidable.

Women in court.—The question whether, as a matter of regular practice, women were free to fight for their rights in person or had to rely on others, that is, whether they were represented in the courts by men, or acted on their own, deserves closer examination. "I went to the qadi," writes a widow from Alexandria quite casually, and this in a letter destined for the attention of the Nagid Mevōrākh. Other Jewish women applying to Muslim courts have been mentioned throughout this book.[87] Muslim women are regularly portrayed in Arabic literature as appearing in courts. How much more must this have been the case in the Jewish community which was a closely knit society of limited size, where everyone knew everyone, where women regularly attended the house of worship and were not required to veil their faces. Muslim and Jewish court records differed characteristically in the practice of giving a description of the physical identity of the parties. This procedure is never found in Jewish Geniza records but the Muslim courts followed a tradition represented in the Greek papyri. They also had need for it in view of the larger public they served. No attempt is made in the following to compare Jewish with Muslim practice concerning the appearance of women in court. I have drawn attention to it only to emphasize that what follows here should not be regarded as exceptional, although it might have been, to a certain extent, specific.[88]

When two women come to the rabbinical court of Fustat in December, 1132, to settle the sale of a property, they are accompanied by their husbands. But the men play a secondary role; the women act, the husbands only confirm the transaction after its conclusion.[89] The energetic woman Jayyida, whose story has been told above, might have acted without the consent, or even knowledge, of her scholarly spouse.[90] About a hundred years after these two cases, we see again one woman selling a piece of property to another, but they do not appear in court. Both are represented by their husbands.[91] Should we assume here a change of the times? Not at all. The same clerk described Sitt Naba' as acting entirely on her own,[92] and records portray women, even unaccompanied virgins, speaking and acting in court.[93] The husbands were present because transfer of real estate required the consent of the spouse, husband or wife.

Two conflicting notions governed the attendance of women in court sessions: One was the holy principle that no party should be listened to by the judge without the other one hearing every word said. The other was the wish to protect the woman, either because she was noble, or aged, and for these reasons not in the habit of mixing with people, or because she was in grief over a loss endured (in either of which case two witnesses would come to her house and take down her declaration); or because she was young and inexperienced, or otherwise incapable of action, wherefore a representative, mostly a relative, would take up her cause. Much depended on the circumstances, more specifically on the legal character of the litigation. In general, however, the demands of justice and proper procedure triumphed over consideration, or, rather, there was no need to be considerate, for the women were neither weak, nor inexperienced, nor overly shy or snobbish.

Where the interests of another party were directly involved, as in the numerous instances of releases and their like, the presence of the woman must have been regarded as specifically desirable. Many documents of this type have been preserved. A father bequeathed a house to his married daughter. At his death three deeds, written, of course, in Arabic, were deposited with a man called Ibn al-Muhandiz, son of the surveyor, who probably followed the profession of his father.[94] This might have been done by the dying man himself, or, rather, by a court, because the legacy was contested. Releases mostly marked the end of a lawsuit. Now the daughter appears in court, receives the deeds, and releases their keeper from all future responsibility. She was accompanied by her husband, a government official, and her brother.[95] This should by no means be understood to signify that women, like minors, had to be represented in court by a guardian. The husband had to share his wife's responsibility, while the brother, by his presence, acknowledged that the house was a deathbed gift, not an item inherited (in which case he, and not his sister, would have had a claim).

Moreover, it was characteristic for the extended family of those days that releases were often given to and by relatives not directly involved.[96]

When a widow and mother of three released her second husband from all claims that her sons might raise against him on her behalf, and he acted similarly for the benefit of her progeny, she spoke and acted first, taking up nineteen broad lines of the document, whereas he got only two. This shows why her presence was required: the main purpose of the action was to protect the husband.[97] From the same couple, however, another document has survived, which calls for comment. Concerning a house belonging to them in equal (nominal) shares it is stated that each of the two spouses has complete proprietary rights to his or her share and may sell or donate it, as either chooses. Here the wife's attendance was imperative, since the declaration implied that both sides renounced their rights of preemption.[98]

Women giving security or safeguards to and for others were normally expected to do so in person, and many such actions are recorded in the Geniza. A case where a release for a partner is combined with a guaranty that a minor sister, when reaching maturity could not sue him is reported above. The two sisters giving the guaranty make the declarations in the presence of the partner of their late father; their husbands only confirm.[99] When a widow brought one (nominal) sixth of a house into the new marriage, her husband was afraid that the widow's sons and a Muslim who held the other shares in the house might some day claim that he, the husband, occupied more than one (real) sixth and ask him to pay them rent. His wife, he announced in court, was prepared to indemnify him in such an emergency. She was present and made the appropriate declaration. The record is in the handwriting of judge Nathan b. Samuel, who, as often, did not sign the document itself, but its validation.[100] When two unmarried sisters made a settlement with their brother over the estate of their father, they were introduced to the court by their mother ("and also by someone else on whom we rely"). The mother stood security for her younger daughter, who had reached maturity, and was therefore able to make a legally valid declaration, but was not yet old enough to be fully responsible for her actions.[101]

Undertakings accompanied by the threat of severe punishment in case of nonfulfillment made an appearance in court unavoidable. A grain dealer comes before the court together with his divorcée, promises to pay 4 dirhems every week for his five-year-old boy, who was staying with his mother, but stipulates that the boy visit him on a Sabbath ("weekend," mentioned first) or a weekday, when he, the father, wished. Against this, the divorcée acknowledges having received from him all due her and agrees not to give him a bad name, nor to sue him before a Muslim court or a state authority. In case of default she would be banned and excommunicated.[102]

In numerous cases women did not sue in person, but appointed a representative, mostly a relative or a communal official.[103] There is nothing specific about this: men did the same. A great variety of reasons compelled a person to make use of a proxy. The party sued was out of town or had to be found. Real estate or other matters that required action in a Muslim court formed the objects of contention. Or the matter concerned was too complicated for action by an ordinary person. In all such instances no difference is to be noted in the Geniza documents between men and women, and the number of men appointing a proxy is larger than that of women—for the simple reason that we have more lawsuits in which men only were involved. A special reason for a woman to employ the services of a representative was the necessity to sue a close relative such as a brother or a husband.

A woman appointing a proxy could do so in court, as when Ḥasnā ("the Belle") b. Ezekiel b. Masʿūd al-ʿAqrabānī (from ʿAqraba, Palestine) appointed a cantor, who probably served also as court clerk, to sue "the daughters of Isaac ha-Kohen, the butcher," for having taken possession of a house left to her by her father. This happened in 1024/5. Whether this was the same house of which Ezekiel had acquired one third twenty years earlier, in 1004, or how those women could lay their hands on another person's property, we do not know.[104] The document states only that Ḥasnā appeared "before the judge and the elders" and, at the end, that her action was confirmed by her husband, as required in all matters affecting real estate.[105]

Teenage girls, who were supposed to be, and certainly often were, bashful, were saved the annoyance of making declarations in public. A beautiful example of this is the appointment of a maternal uncle as proxy by two siblings who had come of age, but were still too young to take care of the estate of their father. The boy made the appointment in court, after the judge explained to him what the action involved. For the girl several persons, certainly acquaintances of the family, two of whom are mentioned by name, were sent to the house, and then, in court, put her declaration on record.[106] The appointment of proxies conducting the financial arrangements for the conclusion of a marriage usually took place in the house of the bride, as when a girl appoints her brother to receive from the groom her immediate marriage gift and to negotiate with him the late one.[107] That a virgin, that is, a girl not previously married, should deal with her future husband directly was exceptional.[108]

Occasionally, married women or widows would arrange the appointment of proxies at home. "We betook ourselves to the house of So-and-so, where his wife transferred all her rights on a house inherited from her mother to her husband so that he could extricate them from the present holder"—this is a legally valid statement, although it is signed by only one person (Mishael b. Uzziel, who happened to be the son of Maimonides' sister), for the handwriting of the notary proved that he was the second witness present at the declaration.[109] When a widow wished that her maternal uncle, who was going to the country where her husband had died, should take care of his estate and carry his remains to Jerusalem for burial, "she asked us to come to her house," as the judge writes, where the formalities took place.[110] The situation was somewhat different in a document written on vellum with utmost care, in which a widow released a debtor of her late husband, after having received from him 31 gold pieces. The declaration was made in her place, and the writer, a prominent judge, states that he knew the widow. Releases were highly sensitive matters, and were therefore normally enacted in open court. Here, I assume, the woman was still in mourning, wherefore the judge, taking two or more witnesses with him, arranged the transaction in her house.[111]

Our survey has shown that, with the exception of teenage girls, those "pearls still hidden in their shells," women were as active in court as men. Sometimes one gets the impression they were even a bit overzealous in keeping the courts occupied. In an angry letter the Gaon Sār Shālōm ha-Levi rebukes the *muqaddam*, or head of the Jewish community of al-Maḥalla, for neglecting essentials in favor of trifles, and cites as examples two women, one sending a proxy to the Gaon's court over a matter of 1 11/24 dinars, and another vexing her son-in-law by intrusion into his house, unfounded accusations, and suits before Muslim courts.[112]

Women on travel.—A good many men were engaged in commercial activities requiring travel, within a country and, to a large extent, beyond its borders. Moreover, as explained in *Med. Soc.*, I, 42–59, the Geniza society was characterized by its mobility. Consequently, travel and seafaring occupy a prominent place in the papers of the Cairo Geniza (see *Med. Soc.*, I, chap iv). While women, unless they chose to separate, accompanied their husbands when moving to another town or country, their day-to-day occupations did not require travel, and, in general, they preferred to stay in their hometowns, where they felt protected by their families. Thus, with regard to travel, there was a marked difference between the two sexes, incomparably greater than that still existing in our society today, and this difference between husband and wife had a profound impact on family life.

Yet, the Geniza shows that women did travel for a variety of reasons and to a larger extent than we would expect. If married, they were not always accompanied by their husbands. Owing to the population's mobility, the extended family became dispersed, a situation that provided many opportunities or pretexts for travel. What a woman in Fustat, married to a man from Alexandria, could face in this respect is reported above: she was obliged to be ready to visit her in-laws in the Mediterranean seaport for one month (but not more) during the course of a year. Thus the couple would pass the month of the High Holidays, which comprised seven days of complete work stoppage and five half-holidays, with the husband's extended family.[113] These family visits requiring travel, for holidays and even weekends, formed a conspicuous aspect of social life in Geniza times.[114] Women had to travel unaccompanied by their husbands, and often for prolonged periods, in order to visit a married female relative in another town who was either expecting a baby, recuperating after delivery, ill, or suffering by being in an unaccustomed or unfriendly environment.[115]

Another common occasion for female travel was a visit to a holy shrine, or even to the city of Jerusalem. A detailed statute about the festive days at Dammūh, a Jewish sacred place south of Cairo, rules that no woman unaccompanied by a husband, brother, or grown-up son was to visit there unless she was "very old." A statute would not have been needed, had not the women visited there all too frequently.[116] When a woman is called "the Pilgrim," I assume it was because she had made the journey to Jerusalem alone, as a widow or otherwise unaccompanied by a husband. For, unlike Islam, in Judaism this honorific epithet was not normally applied to a person who had made the pilgrimage.[117]

In addition to these commonplace occasions for female travel we find others whose reasons can only be guessed, or about whose circumstances we know nothing except that the husband felt helpless without her (as we would today in like circumstances). "You mentioned that 'the family' has gone on a journey. I regretted to learn that you have been left alone by 'them.' " writes one great merchant to another.[118] In two cases we see that the absent housewife was replaced by a male relative visiting the house. A husband in a small town sends this cry for help to his wife staying with her son in the capital: the wall of a neighboring house had fallen down and damaged the environment; the family home was in a desolate state; her brother, who had been staying with the writer, had left; the tenants had traveled to Minyat Ziftā; "and I am alone in the house;" and, above all, the business season was in full swing. A more cogent combination of reasons for hurrying home could hardly be invented.[119] When a wife is visiting the writer's "paternal uncle" (i.e., father-in-law) and several other persons are greeted, but not the wife's mother, we may assume that she was dead, and that the daughter was keeping her father company while her husband, as he writes, enjoyed the visit of another paternal uncle over the weekend.[120] The strange condition imposed in the marriage contract of a widow with two small children, that she was not permitted to leave Fustat, seems to show that a young mother traveling away from home was not extraordinary.[131]

The *kabīra*, the old lady, or "dowager," was the female traveler par excellence. She kept the extended family together and could get away more easily than the younger women in the house. A warm letter of a man in Fustat to his brother in the countryside opens: "The *kabīra* has safely arrived and told me what has happened to you. Don't worry." One gets the feeling that the old woman was the bearer of a message best not confided to paper.[122] Receiving a visit from mama seems to have been a point of honor for a young couple. An extensive and profuse letter by a cantor in a provincial town to his widowed mother in Cairo is entirely devoted to this topic. Here are a few excerpts.

I have no tongue—my witness is God—to describe how much we are longing and yearning after you, Mother. I adjure you by God: do not tarry any longer, for our eyes are lifted only to God and to your coming. . . . We wish to move to our new place; but we said: "Let's wait until she comes" . . . Had it not been for my duties, I would have come in person instead of sending this letter. Please, do not disappoint us. Take a Nile boat down to Jawjar, this is convenient and comfortable . . . or, I am in Malīj for Pentecost [the Shavuot holiday, at which the cantor would officiate in that town] and shall remain there for a week. If this is agreeable to you, come to Malīj, and we shall travel home together, or I shall get up to your place—whatever you command me to do. Or I shall send a Jewish muleteer, paying him the fare, he will bring you to Malīj, where I shall await you. Whatever you command me to do, send me a note before

Pentecost. . . . The little one and his mother [the reference to the writer's wife had been forgotten and is written above the line] kiss your hands and eyes and send you most special regards.[123]

Once having arrived at her destination, a kabīra would not be in a hurry to return, a situation seemingly reflected in a letter where a mother staying with her son is requested in the most urgent terms to hurry back to her husband, who was seriously ill and could die at any moment. A postscript adds: "Otherwise you will feel regrets, when regrets will be of no avail." Clearly other letters asking her to return had preceded.[124]

Women living outside the capital had another reason for travel: the need to appeal to the authority whose decision was final. The divorcée from Ṣahrajt, who had been banned because she had allegedly "divorced her husband" before a Muslim judge, or the mother of a newly married girl in Malīj who brought home from the capital a legal opinion which restored peace in the family are such cases.[125] A Muslim book of responsa tells about a woman who tried to flee from her village to Qayrawān, Tunisia, seeking justice in a dispute with her husband.[126] Some Geniza records showing women designated as provincials appearing before a court in Fustat might concern persons not resident in the capital who had come there in order to argue their case in person.

Exposing women to the dangers of sea travel was always a matter of concern.[127] When Belisar, the great general of Emperor Justinian I, set sail for conquering North Africa (533), he took his wife on board with him in order to manifest that his undertaking was safe and promising success (it was).[128] Muʿāwiya, the future caliph, did the same and for the same reason, when the Muslims tried for the first time to cross the sea for a naval attack (and he, too, was right).[129] By Geniza times, sea travel for women had become common. Mostly, of course, they were wives accompanying their husbands or traveling to join them in a foreign country. About a merchant who was found at another time in the Sudanese part of ʿAydhāb we read this in a letter sent to the India trader Ḥalfōn b. Nethanel: "Your nephew Abu 'l-Faḍl b. Abu 'l-Faraj is sailing from Tyre [then occupied by the Crusaders] to Alexandria. His wife is with him." I understand the concluding remark as meaning that Abu 'l-Faḍl had wound up his business in the Lebanese seaport and was returning to Egypt for good.[130] The case of a merchant who was expected to bring his wife from Tyre to Egypt or have her follow him there is explained above in detail.[131] When Ḥayyīm b. ʿAmmār, representative of merchants in Palermo, Sicily, traveling with his wife from

Egypt to that island, was overtaken by pirates, he returned home "naked," that is, stripped of his goods, money, and good clothing, but nothing is said of his wife. Ḥayyīm b. 'Ammār appears in numerous Geniza papers as commuting between Sicily and Egypt. Whether his wife accompanied him because she was a native of that country (which is likely), or for another reason, we do not know.[132]

Single women traveling overseas, even those who had not yet been married, are mentioned in the Geniza as a matter of common occurrence. When Christian ships were taken by Muslim freebooters, there were among the Jewish captives brought to Alexandria the wife of a physician, accompanied by her husband, another married woman, and a girl.[133] No wonder. Unmarried girls had the opportunity to brave the dangers of sea travel because overseas marriages were a deliberate policy of the mercantile class. Naturally, the girls did not travel alone. But men, too, on sea and on land, normally traveled in the company of friends. Overseas marriages were arranged by the fathers. But the contracting parties were interested in the success of the match, and not every father is a bad judge of the character of his daughter. Who knows, some girls may have liked the idea of being married overseas. The spirit of adventure inspiring the teenage sons of the Geniza traders to some extent perhaps infected their daughters.[134]

A Muslim handbook of market supervision orders captains carrying women in their ships to set up a partition between them and the men.[135] A Greek savant humorously describes how a very religious Jewish skipper from Alexandria actually put up a dividing screen on his boat—to the chagrin of the male travelers, for the girls were comely. The year was A.D. 404.[136] I have not yet read about such arrangements in a Geniza text. Female passengers had to carry their marriage certificates (or similar identity papers) with them when they traveled in the company of their husbands. Otherwise, the couple could incur unpleasant experiences.[137] When a report of a shipwreck tells that twenty persons, women and men, perished, it puts women first, obviously because not every ship carried female passengers.[138]

The bravest of all female travelers were those needy women who did not accept their dire lot, but set out to try their fortunes elsewhere. A widow with two children from Damascus traveled via Ascalon, Palestine, and Bilbays, Lower Egypt, to Cairo, receiving letters of recommendation wherever she went.[139] The story of a deserted woman from Acre (Akko), Palestine, who came, via Jaffa and other places, to Fustat together with her boy, then was off to

Malīj trying to find her husband there, and finally returned to the capital fighting for her rights—has been told above.[140] The moving appeal of a captive mother with a boy from Palestine is translated in *Med. Soc.,* II, 169–170. The lists of beneficiaries of public welfare analyzed in *Med. Soc.,* II, Appendix B, contain many female foreigners, and one wonders how they all found their way to Fustat. The cost of their donkey rides or passages by sea (for many came from Europe) probably was borne by the Jewish communities through which they passed.[141] But how did they otherwise fare on their woeful journeys? Anyhow, whether girls proceeded to their new homes overseas, or old women alone were on their way to visit their progeny, whether wives accompanied their husbands, or went up to the capital to sue them, whether a devotee (or seeker of adventure) was on a pilgrimage, or a wretched, but determined pauper on the outlook for relief—the landscape in Geniza times was never completely devoid of women on travel.

At home.—The household chores of the Geniza women were apparently not excessively heavy, and left them considerable time for other activities. Grain was stored in the house, but the handmill, that eternal symbol of female servitude, not long ago so woefully prominent in the life, song, and folklore of the women of Yemen, is practically absent from the Geniza inventories of household implements. One brought one's grain to one of the mills found everywhere in the city. Bread, the main fare, could be bought in the market. If prepared at home, its baking was done in a bakery nearby. In general, food was simple, and since fuel, because of the scarcity of wood, was expensive, one preferred, for weekday consumption, to bring home a warm dish from the bazaar.[142] Washing and cleaning, too, cannot have been too burdensome; the fuller, *qaṣṣār*, using fuller's earth, *ṭufāl*, took care of the heavier textiles.[143] Spinning and weaving, the labors theoretically incumbent on all women, are hardly ever mentioned, except with regard to individuals who were professional weavers.

The rearing of children, too, was perhaps less exacting than one might imagine. Women were praised for their eagerness to give their boys a good education, or scolded for neglecting them, but complaints about "the pains of raising children," to use a Talmudic phrase, are practically absent from the Geniza. The troublesome boys were packed off to school, even in poor houses (since the community took care of the fees), whereas girls were expected to play nurses to their younger siblings, or to be otherwise useful. Boys went early to work and girls usually married in their teens. Most households comprised more than one female adult, and any regular middle class family possessed a maidservant.

The occupation most frequently referred to in connection with women was embroidery, and here we should remember that, even at the time of our own grandmothers, there was not a single piece of household linen or lingerie which was not embroidered or otherwise embellished. This preoccupation with decorative work must have had a healthy impact on the inner life of women: it made for continuous search for new models, hence, inventiveness, for comparison with the work of others, which entailed sociability, and for pride in one's own creations, hence, a feeling of success. And there was the soothing effect of steady and quiet work. Embroidery was a luxury, produced by one's own efforts; it formed the female counterpart to the modest amount of leisure obtained by the bourgeois male and used by him for his spiritual and other pursuits.

The trousseau lists describe comparatively few items of bedding and clothing as embroidered, whereas many hundreds of others are noted without this detail. This could mean that the pieces of a bride's outfit bought in the bazaar usually were plain. It was left to the future housewife to adorn her pillows, linen, and personal wardrobe in the way she chose. Male clothes, too, could be richly embroidered. But the texts seem to indicate that this was done by professional embroiderers, not by housewives.[144]

As the trousseau lists show, even a middle class bride often brought into the marriage numerous pieces of clothing of the same type; richer girls—quite bewildering quantities. What did they do with them? In those days clothes were not put on hangers; they were kept in beautifully decorated trunks or chests. For the very preservation of those pieces it was necessary to take them out from time to time and to expose them to fresh air. On such an occasion, could a woman resist the temptation to try them on one after another, preening before her jeweled mirror (also forming part of her bridal outfit), and posing before the other female members of the household or visitors invited for the occasion? I do not mean by this to taunt female vanity. As their letters prove, even scholars of the Geniza times could be transported by the beauty of the colorful men's clothing, often manufactured from precious materials.[145] I wish only to emphasize that preoccupation with her extensive bridal outfit must have consumed a considerable part of a housewife's time.

This activity was not confined to the home. Although the total cost of the trousseau was noted in the marriage contract as a liability of the husband, its individual items could be and were often exchanged, of course, with his consent, for more desirable items. For this purpose the services of agents and brokers could be used, but the Geniza women insisted on their right to do so in person if they wished. While the daily household errands were done by a servant or by the husband, who regularly went to the bazaar, the selling and buying of textiles was a pleasurable pastime for the woman of the house, just as shopping is cherished by many of the women of our own time.

There were many other occasions for leaving the house, as is evident from the documents dealing with the struggle of the wife for her freedom of movement. The first place mentioned as suitable for being frequented by a respectable woman was the synagogue.[146] On Sabbath all work, whether household chores or embroidery, was forbidden. What better way to kill time than by attending service? There, a woman could hear her father, brother, husband, or son recite a lection from the Bible or sing a portion of the liturgy—she might even have bought such an honor for him;[147] she could watch the proceedings, especially the opening of the holy ark, when the Torah scrolls were taken out and God was near, so that the most secret wishes of the heart could be conveyed to him, so to speak, in person;[148] or she could listen to discussions about communal affairs, which took place during the service; then, coming down from the women's gallery through the "secret door," she might enter the synagogue courtyard for a chat with members and friends of the family.[149]

Visits to the public bathhouse were of similar frequency (normally once a week) and of even wider social significance.[150] Less regular, but probably more time consuming, was attendance at wedding celebrations and visits at childbirth and mourning, also expressly included in the lists of proper occasions for a woman to leave the house. Finally, and perhaps most frequently, women went out in order to see their families and female friends, and in return expected to be visited by them.

"Tell me what you do, and I will tell you who you are." We would like to know what the women did when they got together. Besides tentative inferences such as the one made above with regard to needlework and to the Geniza women's rich trousseaux we are left in the dark. I cannot use my experience with the village women from Yemen, whose human ambiance was far more variegated and colorful, and whose daily chores brought them into constant contact with nature. The pastime of the Geniza women, I assume, was to gossip rather than tell beautiful tales—although they might have done that, too, occasionally—and to talk about their purchases and sales rather than sing poetry. Some might also have played chess, as was enjoyed by that beautiful and wicked Jewish woman in *The Arabian Nights* who constantly defeated her Christian paramour, until she had taken from him all his possessions (they played chess for money in those days). One thing is sure. With few exceptions, the women known to us from the Geniza papers did not come together to study the Bible.[151]

The independent woman.—The enticing chess player just mentioned is representative of the independent woman who plays the heroine in certain types of longer stories found in *The Arabian Nights*. She became independent either because her husband absented himself frequently and for prolonged periods, or because she was a divorcée or widow who had inherited riches from her father or other relative. As the Geniza documents and contemporary sources prove, these women could be found in all layers of the society. Usually we know them only from the transactions they made or the cases they litigated, many of which have been studied in this volume. Here I present two intimate portraits, one woman from the poor section of society and one well-to-do, one married, the other divorced. A letter by a woman from a pietist family reveals the spiritual aspects of female independence.

My first example is derived from two legal inquiries submitted to Moses Maimonides, which are particularly revealing inasmuch as one presents the case from the point of view of the wife, and the other from that of the husband. As was common, no names are provided. In his book of *Responsa*, the two inquiries are separated from each other by ten other items.[152]

It was a fantastic story, in many respects characteristic of prevalent social conditions and notions. It begins with a child marriage, arranged in order to keep a property together, but certainly also with a view to provide a home for an orphan.[153] A woman arranged the marriage of an orphaned relative, nine years old, who had a share in the house in which she and her sons lived, to one of her sons, promising to maintain the young couple for ten years. After seven years she declared that she was no longer able to keep up her obligations. At about that time, the girl gave birth to a son. When the child was about nine months old, the husband vanished, traveling to Palestine, Damascus, and other places. He absented himself for three years without leaving his wife money "sufficient for one supper." When he came back, he did not earn a penny, but sired another son. He was so poor that sometimes his brother and sometimes his young wife or his mother had to pay the poll tax for him—otherwise he would have been thrown into prison. As another indication of his utter penuriousness the letter indicates that he never lighted a lamp for his wife ("not even with linseed, let alone with olive oil"). If she wished to see light, she had to visit the apartments of her mother, or brother-in-law, who, we remember, lived in the same house. A year and a half after the birth of his second son the man disappeared again and roamed around the world for another three years.

Meanwhile, the young wife had reached the age of twenty-five years. In one respect she had made good use of her loafer of a husband: she had learned from him how to read the Bible, and perfected her knowledge during his absence. Her brother, a schoolteacher, accepted her as partner, and this arrangement lasted six years. Then her brother left town, and she ran the school alone for four years, employing her elder boy, who by then was seventeen, as her associate. This she did, as the letter is careful to stress, "so that he could talk to the fathers of the schoolchildren, while she would take care of the mothers."[154]

During the years she taught school her husband stayed with his mother. When he happened to have some money, he would spend it on himself and his mother, but never on her and the children. He never provided them with clothing ("not even shoes"), bedding, school fees, or the poll tax. All he bought for the household during twenty-five years of marriage was—a mat. She stayed with her boys on the school premises, which she rented for 14 dirhems (per month).

The lawsuit reflected in the two letters to Maimonides started at that juncture and probably went on for some time. The good-for-nothing complained, (*a*) that it injured his dignity for his wife to be a school mistress, and (*b*) that he had no one to serve him. She should give up her teaching and stay with him; otherwise, he should be permitted to take an additional wife. To this she retorted that she could not leave the school to her son "even for one day," for the parents sent their boys to her school because of her, not because of him. If her husband agreed with this, she was prepared to live with him, either in her own apartment in the family house or on the school premises, and if the latter she would permit him to take for himself the rent of the apartment belonging to her. She was also ready to accept a divorce. The idea of a second wife was preposterous.

From the letter in favor of the husband it becomes evident why he preferred a second wife to a divorce. Naturally, nothing is said of his inability or unwillingness to maintain his family. We read only that during his repeated travels (on business, of course) his wife became a school mistress, with the result that she had constantly to meet with the fathers of her pupils, which he abhorred, "both in his own interest and in hers." He further complains that she failed to provide him with the services expected from a wife (including the conjugal duties) and that she neglected her children. He was unable to divorce her because of her share in the family home; she would "take it with her" and marry another man, whereupon his sons might lose their inheritance.

To this Maimonides replies that the husband was not permitted to marry someone else without the consent of his wife. But the school mistress should be instructed by the local judge in the strongest possible terms that the demand of her husband that she desist from teaching was endorsed by the law and therefore could never be a claim for a divorce.[155]

The answer to the letter in favor of the wife was different in tone and emphasis, but essentially the same in substance. If a husband did not support his wife, he would be forced to set her free and to pay her the delayed marriage gift. On the other hand, he had the right to forbid her to teach, whether a craft or "reading." The way for her to get free was a declaration that she could not live with him, in which case she would lose her marriage gift (which she had little prospect of receiving anyway). As a divorcée, Maimonides concludes, "she would have disposition over herself, she could teach what she liked and do what she liked." This sounds as if it was not so much the concern for the teacher's chastity as the regard for her husband's social susceptibilities which inspired the decision. One must keep in mind, however, that sexual intercourse of an unmarried woman, although improper, was not a sin.

The story of the poor schoolmistress shows how a woman of resolution could preserve her independence and provide for herself and her children under the most trying circumstances: indigence and marriage to an unworthy husband.

A quite different story is that of Karīma ("The Dear One"), daughter of ʿAmmār ("Longlived"), known by the name of al-Wuḥsha ("Object of Yearning," Désirée) the Broker. Five full-fledged documents deal with her affairs, while numerous others either refer to her in passing, or are fragments of papers devoted to her in their entirety. No other woman gets so much space in the Geniza as she does.[156]

Al-Wuḥsha's father, known in Hebrew as "Amram, the banker, son of Ezra, Head of the Congregation, the Alexandrian,"[157] signed a document in Fustat involving a man from Alexandria, in July 1093, and is referred to as dead in June 1104.[158] He had at least three daughters and two sons, which might explain why our first document concerning al-Wuhsḥa, the list of her trousseau, is not very impressive, although it contains some rarely mentioned and particularly precious pieces of jewelry. The total dowry is noted as being worth 316 dinars, but an examination of the individual items seems to reveal that, at least in part, the estimate is exaggerated. The real value probably was half of the sum listed, about 150 dinars, which would be proper for a family in easy but by no means rich circumstances, which had to provide for three daughters.[159]

The groom, Arye b. Judah, and his marriage gift were even less impressive. He was a stranger in Fustat like al-Wuḥsha herself; the gift presented at the wedding consisted of only 10 dinars, and that promised as delayed installment was not more than 15 dinars, which shows him to be a man without means.[160] Why the match was made, we cannot know. It must have been occasioned by very special circumstances, for instance, that al-Wuḥsha had already been known as inclined, perhaps, to being too independent.[161]

The marriage cannot have lasted long. In a fragment showing a transaction between a Mr. Goldsmith from Alexandria and "Karīma, named al-Wuḥsha the Broker," she is designated as the divorcée of Arye b. Judah.[162] Arye tried his luck with another woman in Fustat, but again was not successful, as described above.[163] That divorce action took place in January 1095, just about when al-Wuḥsha had given birth to a son from an irregular liaison. From this, as far as we know, her only marriage, al-Wuḥsha had a daughter named Sitt Ghazāl ("Lady Gazelle"). We know that, because at the head of a document from December 1132, in which Sitt Ghazāl buys half a house, the judge, in order to identify her with the name under which she was commonly known, wrote in bold letters "Bint (daughter of) al-Wuḥsha."[164]

Not enough with this, al-Wuḥsha's fame lived on in her granddaughter. In a document from July 1150, a woman described as the daughter of the daughter of al-Wuḥsha, makes arrangements for repairs in a house of hers in the Zuwayla quarter of Cairo.[165]

We do strike a snag, though. In al-Wuḥsha's very detailed and completely preserved will, discussed below, in which several relatives and other beneficiaries are named, no mention is made of a daughter. It can mean only that mother and daughter had become completely estranged, whereupon Lady Gazelle was disinherited. Such things happened.[166] Even if Lady Gazelle had been married with a rich dowry (which, I assume, she was, since she had money to buy half a house), her mother would not have failed to make her an additional gift on her deathbed. The two certainly became alienated only after the daughter's marriage, perhaps because Lady Gazelle may have made nasty remarks about her mother's conduct.

The cause of al-Wuḥsha's notoriety is self-evident. As her constant nickname "The Broker" indicates, she was a business woman, moving around in the company of men. Poor female agents and brokers were common. Well-to-do ones were exceptional. A court record from April 1098 describes how on a Wednesday (when normally no session of the court was held) al-Wuḥsha went into the synagogue compound, where she met three men: a beadle, a Bible schoolteacher, and the son of a judge. She told them angrily that she had received a summons to the court, because ʿUlla b. Joseph, the well-known trustee, sued her for a trifling sum. The men, who knew her, understood that a person like al-Wuḥsha did not wish to be bothered with such small matters. The court record was made because al-Wuḥsha did not honor the summons.[167]

Another court record, dated June 30, 1104, reveals her involvement in a large business venture. One of her brothers had concluded a *commenda* partnership for 800 dinars with the India trader Joseph Lebdī[168] and a third person. The brother died on the voyage undertaken for that business venture. At the time of the lawsuit goods worth 300 dinars had already been sold, and al-Wuḥsha claimed her "share" in them. To understand this claim, one must know that it was customary for partners in a commenda to let other investors participate with smaller amounts in the larger share for which the partners were responsible. The court record makes mention of another venture in which al-Wuḥsha participated, and from which twenty-two camel loads (11,000 pounds) had already arrived. In this lawsuit al-Wuḥsha was represented by an agent, not because she was a woman, but because the checking of the arrival and sale of large quantities of wares required handling by an expert.[169]

The most informative document about al-Wuḥsha is her last will, written by the cantor and court clerk Hillel b. Eli.[170] It shows her as a well-to-do woman, possessing 700 dinars at least, of which 300 pieces were "in gold" and kept by her at home (certainly buried in a safe place). Sixty-seven gold pieces were deposited with another woman, while the rest consisted of loans for which collateral had been given and was held by her.

These were her last dispositions: her brother received 100 dinars; a sister, 50; the daughter of a paternal uncle, 5; another sister (in this order, probably a stepsister[171]), 10 dinars. With the exception of the last, the relatives also received personal gifts, such as rings (exactly described) and pieces of clothing (including a mourning dress for the sister); the cousin gets, among other things, "the bed on which I lie, but not the carpets." The sisters receive less than the brother, because al-Wuḥsha certainly had contributed lavishly to their bridal outfits, but other considerations might also have prevailed.

Communal, religious, and charitable institutions are properly provided for, the cemetery[172] getting 25 dinars, four synagogues the same ("for oil so that people may study at night"), and "the poor of Fustat," 20 dinars. In the way of private charity "Joseph's[173] wife and her two brothers" receive 5 dinars each, and a distant relative, an orphan in Cairo, 2 dinars. The total of 87 dinars for charities represented about one tenth of al-Wuḥsha's estate. A religious person should tithe his property for charitable or otherwise meritorious purposes. Al-Wuḥsha wished to live up to accepted standards.

The main part of the estate, namely the collateral holdings, the gold, and all the rest, "including the rugs and carpets," belonged to al-Wuḥsha's boy, Abū Sa'd. Should he die as a minor, the estate was to be divided in two equal shares between the family on the one hand and the synagogues and the poor on the other. To Abū Sa'd's natural father Ḥassūn of Ascalon (Palestine), "not one penny should be given," but two promissory notes on debts amounting to the very considerable sum of 80 dinars should be returned to him, in addition to a gift of 10 dinars.

A large section deals with the funeral, for which the exorbitant sum of 50 dinars is designated. Every piece of the burial attire should be new, and is exactly defined and its prospective price fixed. Then there were the expenses for the coffin, the pallbearers (the way to the cemetery was long), and, especially, the cantors, "walking behind me" (and chanting), "each in accordance with his station and excellence."

Al-Wuḥsha's last thought, as befitting a mother, was given to the religious education of her boy. But she was a practical woman. Abū Sa'd should know the Bible and the prayer book "as was appropriate for him"—but not more, he need not become a scholar. A Bible schoolteacher, an old acquaintance mentioned by name,[174] should live with the boy in the house, for which service he would get a sleeping carpet, a blanket, and 5 dirhems a week—the utmost minimum of a living at subsistence level (as was proper for a person engaged in such an unprofitable occupation). But she was reasonable enough to leave this detail to the discretion of "the [orphans'] judge and the elders."

The lengthy will concludes with the declaration that three Arabic documents detailing al-Wuḥsha's assets and liabilities, as well as the actions to be taken with respect to each, had been dictated and authorized by her. The notable who took the dictation is otherwise known.[175]

Al-Wuḥsha dealt with other women, and by no means only in small matters. Part of her gold, as stated in her will, was deposited with "Lady Choice," under what circumstances is not said.[176] In an enormous document, of which, unfortunately, mostly the legal verbiage is preserved, al-Wuḥsha releases a "Lady Beauty" from all obligations she might have incurred while making transactions on her behalf. A gift was also involved, probably of real estate, for al-Wuḥsha, her son Abū Sa'd and her other heirs are obliged to defend Lady Beauty's rights, if any claim is made against her.[177]

The story of al-Wuḥsha's love affair came before a court—and thus to our knowledge—after she had closed her eyes. The matter in hand was to prove that Abū Sa'd, her son, was the issue of a relationship that was irregular, but not incestuous, or otherwise of a nature to disqualify him from marrying a Jewish girl. Only one page of the relevant court record is preserved. Its end and, with it, the date are lost. The document deserves translation in full. The cantor with the title "The Diadem," who plays such a decisive role in the story, is none other than Hillel b. Eli, al-Wuḥsha's confidant, who wrote her marriage contract and other documents related to her, and also her last will. He accompanied her throughout her adult life.

The elder Abū 'Alā Japheth, the . . . , the son of the elder Maṣlī'aḥ—may he rest in Eden—appeared before us and made the following deposition, while we were constituted as a court of three. He said: "I was with the cantor, 'The Diadem'—may God accept him with favor[178]—when al-Wuḥsha, the broker, came in and said: 'Do you not have any advice for me? I had an affair[179] with Hassūn and conceived from him. We contracted a marriage before a Muslim notary,[180] but I am afraid that he may deny being the father of my child.' She then lived in the house of Ibn al-Sukkarī[181] on the uppermost floor. He [the cantor] said: 'Go and gather some people, and let them surprise you with him so that your assertion might be confirmed.' She did so, gathering two who surprised her with him, and confirmed her assertion. She was then pregnant with this Abū

Sa'd, her son, whom she had conceived in her illicit relation with Ḥassūn. I know also that on the Fast of Atonement she went to the synagogue of the Iraqians, but when the Nāsī[182] of blessed memory noticed her, he expelled her from the synagogue. I know all this for sure, and deposit herewith my testimony to this effect."

There appeared also in court the ritual slaughterer Abū Sa'īd Ḥalfōn ha-Kohen, son of Joseph ha-Kohen—may he rest in Eden—and deposited the following testimony in our presence: "I was living in the house of Hibat Allah[183] Ibn al-Sukkarī—may God accept him with favor—on the ground floor for many years, while al-Wuḥsha, the broker, had her domicile in the uppermost part of the house. In those days, she came down once to one of the tenants, namely Abū Naṣr, the Kohen, the cantor Ibn al-Kāmukhī,[184] and to Abraham the Jerusalemite, known as the son of the Murahhiṭ,[185] and said to them: 'Please, come up with me to my place for something.' The two went up with her and found Ḥassūn sitting in her apartment and . . . wine and perfumes. . . ."[186]

Here the manuscript breaks off. The reader of these two complementary depositions wonders why al-Wuḥsha found it necessary to legalize her liaison before a Muslim notary and did not simply marry her paramour Ḥassūn, since she was a close acquaintance of the scholarly and highly honored Jewish divine Hillel b. Eli. Ḥassūn no doubt had a wife in his hometown Ascalon, and the Jewish court in Fustat did not permit him to take a second wife without the permission of the first, and she certainly refused, if Ḥassūn cared to ask her at all. I suspect, however, that al-Wuḥsha told a lie, in order to make her alliance a bit more respectable. For had she contracted a marriage, Ḥassūn would have taken a big chunk of her estate, and, according to Islamic law, a legal heir cannot be disinherited. Be that as it may, the most important interest of this record is its social setting. The five men present at al-Wuḥsha's appearance and straightforward declaration: the cantor, the two witnesses, and two reporters, do not get excited about what they hear (which, of course, they had known before), do not feel induced to ostracize her, and those asked to go up to her room are not hesitant to do so. The expulsion of al-Wuḥsha from the synagogue on the Fast of Atonement seemingly was against the law, since even excommunicated persons are permitted to join the community on that day of forgiveness. But the Nāsī did the right thing: he wished to demonstrate that even a rich woman may not permit herself to violate accepted rules of behavior. Al-Wuḥsha seems to have understood this. In her last will, the synagogue from which she was expelled, that of the Iraqians, receives the same donation as the main synagogue, that of the Palestinians.

Since al-Wuḥsha's daughter and granddaughter were named after her, we are not surprised to find, in a legal document, Abū Sa'd referred to simply as "al-Wuḥsha's son."[187] More remarkable are two complete court records from the years 1133 and 1148, that is, many years after her demise, in which one of the two parties, a respectable banker, is described as al-Wuḥsha's sister's son or as her relative.[188]

Al-Wuḥsha certainly made an impression on her contemporaries because, on the one hand, she was an exceptionally successful businesswoman, her estate being about five times as large as her marital outfit, and, on the other hand, remained unmarried most of her life; on top of it, she had a love affair which produced for her an heir. She, her husband, and her lover all were strangers in Fustat. She was unique also in that she appears as a contributor to a public appeal—the only woman in over a hundred such lists. (As is to be expected from her, her contribution was of medium size, neither stingy, nor particularly generous.)[189] Yet we should not regard al-Wuḥsha's case as totally exceptional. She happened to live at a time from which more and better executed documents have survived than from any other period of the "classical Geniza." Our survey of women in economic life has shown that other women might have been as successful and independent as she. We must concede that the nature of our sources woefully restricts the range of our knowledge.

The limits set by the nature of our sources are even more painfully felt when we wish to examine another type of female independence: that reached by participation in the spiritual pursuits of the male ambiance. Most of the documentary Geniza consists of legal papers, business correspondence, or family letters of a practical nature. One wrote for a purpose, not for the expression of thoughts or feelings. For spiritual matters we must consult the vast literary treasures preserved in the Geniza which are probably more than ten times as comprehensive as the documentary ones. But, as far as I know them, they are mostly traditional, and, as a rule, impersonal.

Women in Geniza times could become visionaries rousing a popular movement, but they were even rarer phenomena than the women prophets of ancient Israel.[190] Throughout the centuries we find a woman occasionally described as a Nazirite, a person who vows to abstain from wine and other intoxicating beverages, which in those days must have been a rather trying vow, since bread and wine formed the staple food. I surmise that the vow, like that taken by Karaites living in Jerusalem, also included abstinence from meat, the idea being that as long as the Temple was in ruins, and God was not honored with the obligatory libations of wine and sacrifices of meat, his servants, too, should not enjoy such luxuries. But all we know about the Nazirite women is their designation; one woman described as a Nazirite made private donations for orphans and the communal chest; another gave a house to the community for charitable purposes; the son of still another is found in an ancient list of receivers of handouts of bread. We do not learn what induced them to make the vow nor what it meant to them. There were also male Nazirites.[191]

Individual women are described in letters, and especially in dirges, as pious, devout, or saintly. They certainly were, but nowhere do we read in which specific ways these qualities were expressed. When a man is called "the son of the devout woman," or when a mother is described as "the pietist," we can be sure that these women were as conspicuous in their religious comportment as al-Wuḥsha was in her commercial undertakings. But we do not know their stories.[192]

To give the reader a feeling of the spiritual makeup of a pietist woman of that period I translate a letter written by the daughter of one when she felt her own end approaching. Piety in Judaism (and originally also in Islam) was paired with knowledge, namely of the holy scriptures and the "oral" teachings derived from them. "An ignoramus cannot be pious."[193] This may sound strange to people with some popular concepts of Hasidism and Sufism, but any serious book on these topics will teach them better. The writer of our letter wants her baby daughter to receive *ta'līm*, formal instruction, so that she might be able to emulate her pious grandmother. Since she believes that her days are numbered, she asks her sister to take care of it. But the sister clearly was of the common set and inspired the writer with little confidence.

This is to inform you, my lady, dear sister—may God accept me as a ransom for you—that I have become seriously ill with little hope for recovery, and I have dreams indicating that my end is near.

My lady, my most urgent request of you, if God, the exalted, indeed decrees my death, is that you take care of my little daughter and make efforts to give her an education, although I know well that I am asking you for something unreasonable, as there is not enough money—by my father[194]—for support, let alone for formal instruction.[195] However, she has a model in our saintly mother.[196] Do not let her appear in public, and do not neglect her Sudanese nurse, Sa'āda, and her son, and do not separate them from her, for she is fond of her and I have willed the Sudanese nurse to her.

However, the younger slave girl, ʿAfāf, shall be given to Sitt al-Sirr—but nothing else—and this only after our debts to Abū Saʿd and others have been paid. Cursed be he who acts against my dying wish.

[I say this], for I have noticed more than once that you like the elder one more than the younger one; however, you know well that I took an oath more than once—and the last one in her presence—that I shall not will anything to Sitt al-Sirr, for reasons that I cannot mention, but which you know.

My lady, let Abu ʾl-Barakāt[197]—may I be his ransom—come and treat me, for I am in a very serious condition.

Please do [pl.] not act against anything I have mentioned to you [pl.]. Cursed be he who separates the old servant from my younger daughter, by selling her or otherwise.

My lady, only God knows how I wrote these lines!

It is highly probable that the ill woman had written this letter with her own hand. Her mother had been a pious woman—*ʿābida* in Arabic—and it is therefore not surprising that she had given her daughter a religious education, which included reading and some writing. The writer's elder daughter, Sitt al-Sirr, had obviously gone astray, and the mother had, therefore, disinherited her. Thus, she was all the more eager that her younger daughter get an education, which would lead her on the right path, and that she not appear in public—which the elder daughter apparently was doing much too often.

It seems that the writer's sister was more akin to the type represented by Sitt al-Sirr than to the pietists in the family. Therefore, the writer uses the strongest form of entreaty, *curse*, should the request be refused.

Another interesting feature is the writer's order that the younger girl not be separated from her old Sudanese nurse and her son, because the little one was fond of her. Obviously, she had more confidence in the educational capabilities of the old slave than in those of her sister.

Education cost money; teachers of the elementary stage of Bible study and of calligraphy, letter-writing, and arithmetic were paid. The higher stages of education were normally free.

As the letter does not contain any concluding formula, not even the word *shālōm*, "peace," it was probably not dispatched. Possibly the writer, in reading through what she had written, backed off when she realized that she had twice pronounced a curse.[198]

A world within a world.—"Women are a nation by themselves." This piece of Near Eastern popular wisdom, quoted in the Talmud, expresses man's inability or unwillingness to understand his womenfolk or to let them participate in his own pursuits. (The female counterpart, "Men are locked chests," is more optimistic: if you find the key, the chest can be opened.)[199] The question whether this attitude or reality was present in the society known to us through the writings of the Cairo Geniza must be answered to a large extent in the affirmative. Man's first and foremost duty, his raison d'être and pride, was the study of God's teachings, leading to the fulfillment of his commandments. Women, allegedly because of their unremitting chores, had fewer obligations, and were therefore exempted from study.[200] To use a Greek notion (which, historically, was largely responsible for that attitude), the woman was the *banausos*, the drudge, who, by definition, did not enjoy the privilege of liberty and leisure required for learning. As a rule, the women were uneducated. Of the letters found in the Geniza, a few dozens at most were sent by women; of only a few of them is it likely, and of none absolutely certain, that they were personally written by a woman.

The exceptions cited confirm the rule.[201] "Does your mother pray?"—I once asked a Yemenite girl. "Yes." the girl replied, "but she says to God what *she* wants," meaning not what is written in the prayerbook. In Geniza times, it seems, women of all classes knew the basic Hebrew prayers. But it did not amount to much. Upper class girls, circumstances permitting, certainly received some formal instruction. The twelfth-century author Samuel al-Maghrebi recounts that his mother and her two sisters knew how to read and write Hebrew and Arabic. Samuel emphasizes writing because even among men the art of writing was acquired only by certain classes of people. (Of 'Ā'isha, the favorite wife of the Prophet of Islam, and of another of his wives, it is reported that they knew how to read but not how to write.)[202] The girl with the richest trousseau found thus far in the Geniza brought into her marriage a pen box made in China with all its accessories, probably to be used by her.[203] The letter of a mother concerned for the education of her daughter has just been discussed.

In the poorer sections of the population there was the *mu'allima*, the female Bible teacher, usually a relative of the teacher who owned the school. She fulfilled the double task of assistant, probably taking care of the smaller boys, and manager negotiating with the mothers bringing their children to school. A family letter in the Geniza is addressed to *kanīsat al-mu'allima*, literally, "the synagogue of the woman teacher" (since school often was held in the synagogue compound, the school itself came to be called synagogue) "to the elder Abu 'l-Manṣūr ("Victor"), known as Son of the Schoolmistress." This is a case similar to the one told before, where a woman became an independent owner of a school after her brother, who had accepted her as his associate, left the city, whereupon she brought up her son as a schoolteacher.

That same Abu l'-Manṣūr Ibn al-Mu'allima was entrusted with a historic mission. When Jerusalem was conquered by the Crusaders on July 15, 1099, not all the Muslims and Jews were slaughtered, as one reads in the textbooks; the prisoners who were taken and the books that had been looted had to be ransomed. Ascalon, the south Palestinian port, which had remained in Fatimid hands, was where the transactions were made. The Nagid Mevōrākh, upon receiving the terrifying news, tore his clothes and sat on the floor, as was proper to do at the receipt of such tidings; then he asked his visitors to collect the money needed for the ransom payments in Ascalon. A first installment was immediately brought together. The question was how to send the money to Ascalon. The communications by land and by sea were in utmost jeopardy, not only because of the Franks, but in view of the general anarchy in the Fatimid empire caused by the defeat and, in particular, by the devastating epidemics that had plagued the country for four years. The schoolmaster known as "the Son of the Schoolmistress" undertook the perilous mission. As the letter addressed to him shows, he was not entirely penniless, for a relative asks him for assistance "to get over this hard year." But we might be right in assuming that Abu 'l-Manṣūr volunteered not solely for idealistic reasons. The scribe left the space for the name of Abu 'l-Manṣūr's father blank. He knew the man solely as "the Son of the Schoolmistress."[204]

The very testimony of Maimonides that the teaching of women was not worth much points to its presence. The story related above exemplifies, however, that teaching by women must have been a desperate attempt to gain a livelihood rather than an expression of yearning for a higher form of existence.

The educational gap between male and female was the ultimate source and manifestation of the repression of womanhood in civilized societies. Only the Western world has overcome this obstacle in the advancement of human destinies. Starting in the Late Middle Ages and the Renaissance, making slow, and then mighty progress in the eighteenth and nineteenth centuries, and consummated in our own times, full access to the treasures of the spirit has been gained by the women of Western Europe and the United States, a process now emulated all over the globe. The Geniza society was not essentially different from other literate societies contemporary with it, perhaps if we disregard faraway Christian Europe with its nunneries and their princely abbesses, institutions foreshadowing in some ways female independence.[205] More detailed comparisons with societies closer to the Geniza world are difficult, because too little research has been done on the women of medieval Islam or those of the Oriental Christian communities. What we know concerns mostly the women of the ruling classes. The few women saints and visionaries mentioned in the Geniza have many counterparts in Islam.[206]

The prominence of women in the affairs of Fatimid Egypt and Zirid Tunisia is remarkable. ʿAzīz, the first Fatimid caliph to reside in Egypt during his entire reign (975–996), was married to (among others) a Christian woman who was so influential that she obtained the appointment of her two brothers, one after the other, as patriarchs of the Melchite Church. Her son, the maniac al-Ḥākim, became his father's successor (996–1021). Al-Ḥākim's sister, Sayyidat al-Mulk ("The Mistress over the Kingdom"), was suspected of having engineered his murder and she ruled the country after his death for four years. The Sudanese mother of the caliph al-Mustanṣir (1036–1094), who originally had been a slave girl in the possession of the Jew Abū Saʿd al-Tustari (who later became her "vizier"), held power while her son was a minor.[207] Al-Mustanṣir himself, on his deathbed, put the Imamate, the religious and temporal leadership of the empire, into the hands of his sister, who then swore allegiance to al-Mustaʿlī, the youngest and therefore, most amenable, of the seven sons of her dead brother.[208] Al-Muʿizz, the most splendorous ruler of Zirid Tunisia (1016–1062), was brought up by his aunt Mallāl, also known in the Geniza papers as al-Sayyida, "The Mistress," or "The Ruler," who acted as regent until her death in October 1023, and there were other prominent women of the Zirid court.[209] The role of women at the courts of eleventh-century Egypt and Tunisia was so conspicuous that Ibn ʿIdhārī, the noted historian of the Muslim West, dedicates a special chapter to the topic.[210]

Women in public affairs could not escape the attention of the subject population, in particular the circles of the higher government officials, physicians in attendance, court purveyors, and others who had direct access to the men in power. These contacts were extended to their womenfolk. When the mother of the Nagid and court physician Mevōrākh is praised in a dirge for having placated the ire of the King, this influence probably was exercised through the women of the court.[211] In a legal settlement the daughter of a late government official is warned not to use her relations with either the government or persons connected with it for impairing the rights of her stepson.[212] In a letter from the Ayyubid period some women are requested to be helpful through their good relations with the wives of some close servants of the Sultan.[213] When the welfare official Eli ha-Kohen (*Med., Soc.,* II, 78) was in doubt whether he could arrange the marriage of a proselyte freed woman with a Jewish man, he was given a guarantee by the mother of Sa'd al-Mulk ("The Good Star of the Kingdom") that she would take up the matter for him should any difficulty arise. Needless to say, the two prominent judges who validated her declaration did so in her home.[214]

The influential position of women of the higher class seems not to have been matched by spiritual attainments. Neither the literary nor the documentary Geniza seems to contain a single piece of writing, religious or other, attributable with certainty to a woman. Tens of thousands of pieces of liturgical poetry have been preserved in the Geniza, but we never hear of a female poet. (A Jewish woman writing Arabic poetry in Spain is known through a Muslim source.)[215] When an encomium says of the wife of a Gaon, a mother of six, that "God is pleased with the offering of her songs," psalms from the Bible or other prayers are intended, not songs composed by her.[216] One may argue that a woman's voice was not to be heard in the synagogue. Thus, there was no "seat in life," no incentive for the creation of a religious poem by a woman. It is also true that the more important families tried to live in Cairo, the residential city, far away from the Geniza chamber. Still, the complete absence from the Geniza of any spiritual matter created by, or even for, women cannot be taken lightly. The Arabic and Hebrew folktales found in the Geniza (some of them interesting) are pastimes and mostly belong to the international stock of entertainment literature. Anyhow, most of these tales, as their contents show, cannot be classified as women's lore.[217]

Thus, the inner worlds of men and women certainly were separated from each other. But the gap was not as deep as the preceding considerations might induce us to imagine. The spiritual concerns of the men of the Geniza period are studied in *Med. Soc.,* IV. There were certainly learned merchants, highly cultured physicians, and government officials of refined secular erudition. But the rank and file of men and women alike were consumed by the pursuit of material gains—tempered by the service of God; common interests created many occasions for the meeting of members of the opposite sexes and perforce made for similar mentalities. To some extent, women lived in seclusion. But men, too, were secluded.

A respectable merchant sat in his house or his office in the bazaar, while brokers and agents did the auctioning and haggling. The nobler a woman, the more she had claim to being served by persons doing her errands. But there was no strict segregation. The Jewish houses in Fustat described in the Geniza documents, with few exceptions, had no women's quarters. There was privacy, but no purdah.

Beyond the economic meeting ground there was religion which bound men and women together. The first prerequisite of a town suitable for a wife to live in was the synagogue. Female attendance was regular. Women donated Torah scrolls for the service, oil and books for study, and houses for the upkeep of synagogues.[218] All this is indicative. There was no God to turn to other than the God of men. The husband was the priest in the house. His officiating at the benedictions before and after a meal and at other ceremonies was essential for the spiritual comfort of the female members of the household. Milton's "He for God only, she for God in him" is valid also for the Geniza society.[219]

This should not be understood to mean that the woman's contact with the world was made only through her husband (as assumed for the Athenian wives in the time of Pericles in a recent treatment of the subject).[220] Within the world dominated by men there was another one created by the women for themselves. The Geniza women were of a very sociable nature. They constantly flocked together, whether in the women's gallery in the house of worship, the bathhouse, the bazaar, the gatherings on happy or mournful occasions, or through the visits of friends and relatives. No wonder that a women, even a young one, could become "dear to the family and the town."[221] The Geniza woman was not the slave of her household. She had a life beyond her family.

The forthcoming fourth and concluding volume of this book forms the direct continuation of this one, it complements it, so to say, both from the outside and the inside. Volume IV describes the towns and houses, the clothing and food, and the daily routine of the Geniza people in times normal and abnormal. It also explores their inner life, their motivations, attitudes, and behavior, as well as their higher aspirations, as far as they are recognizable in the letters and documents that form the source material of this book. After the family of the Geniza period has been studied in this volume, and its economy and communal life in volumes I and II, the concluding part is devoted to the individual, his physical environment and spiritual world.

Appendix

THE ECONOMICS OF MARRIAGE

Appendix

Part I. Eight Groups of Documents on Marriage

See pp. 97–100 above.

If not otherwise indicated, the documents analyzed were written in Fustat (Old Cairo).

Sums are in dinars (d). (For its purchasing power see Preface.) The immediate and delayed installments of the marriage gift of the husband (designated A and B) and their total are indicated thus: 50 + 100 = 150. Sums in parentheses are arrived at by calculation. Thus, 50 (+ 100) = 150 means that in the document analyzed only the numbers 50 and 150 are visible. Where only one of the two installments or only the total is preserved, the fact is indicated thus: A:50. B:100. Total:150.

"Incomplete" means that one or several leaves of a record book are missing; "frag." signifies that the paper or vellum on which the document is written is only partly preserved; "not completed" means that the writer of the MS did not finish.

M.c., marriage contract (*ketubba*); m., marriage; GT, grand total.

GROUP 1.

THIRTY-SEVEN DOCUMENTS AND NOTES ON MARRIAGE IN THE HAND OF JUDGE MEVŌRĀKH B. NATHAN (1155–1165, 1169, 1171, AND UNDATABLE)

Dated Documents

	Ms mark and description	Date	Marriage gift	Dowry and other details
1.	TS 20.8 – 12.552 M.c., frag.	Oct. 10, 1155	A:15	360, including m. gift, plus 1/4 house donated by brother.
2	Firkovitch II, 1700, ff. 3*a*, 5*a*	Summer, 1156	—	Brother promises to provide each of his two half-sisters with 200 in addition to immovables willed to them by their late father.
3.	*Ibid.*, ff. 18*a*, 28*a*	Summer, 1156	—	He buys for one sister property worth 50 and undertakes to do so for the other.
4.	*Ibid.*, f. 10*a* Engagement	Summer, 1156	2 + 15 = 17	No dowry indicated. The bride an orphan from father and mother.
5.	*Ibid.*, f. 13*b* Incomplete	Summer, 1156	20 + 40 (= 60)	Of the trousseau list, only the jewelry (50) and beginning of clothing entries preserved.
6.	*Ibid.*, f. 14*b* Settlement	Summer, 1156	—	Wife acknowledges to have received from husband part of her dowry worth 30.
7.	*Ibid.*, f. 16*a*	Summer, 1156	3 + 5 (= 8)	No details; even the girl's father is not mentioned.

8.	*Ibid.*, ff. 24*a*-25*b*	Summer, 1156	50 + 100 = 150	Jewelry	124
				Clothing	196
				Bedding	96
				Copper and furniture	84
				Total dowry	500
				Maidservant	20
				GT (with m. gift)	670
				Plus two halves of two houses in Cairo, given to her by her brother.	
9.	*Ibid.*, f. 15*a*	Summer, 1156	—	The bride was an orphan. About two months before her marriage her grandmother and brother received 238 from the orphans' court to buy her outfit.	
10.	*Ibid.*, ff. 25*b*-26*b*	Summer, 1156	50 + 100 (= 150)	The dowry of this orphan: 209 + 262 + 234 + 18 incomplete. Total dowry, as far as preserved: 723	
11.	*Ibid.*, ff. 27*a-b*	Summer, 1156	20 + 50 (= 70)	Jewelry 150; only the beginning of the section on clothing is extant. The daughter of an India trader is married to her cousin, who was a scholar and refugee.	

GROUP 1. *(Continued)*

	Ms mark and description	Date	Marriage Gift	Dowry and other details
12.	BM Or 5536 II Betrothal	April 9, 1157	10 + 30 = 40	The future wife (daughter of a cantor) will retain her earnings. A fine of 10 on the party not ready for wedding, twelve months later. Although father is alive, the mother alone is present and undertakes to pay the fine.
13.	TS 8 J 5, f.18*d* Incomplete copy of M.c.	Aug. 27, 1157	10 + 40 = 50	Only first seven items of dowry preserved. Valuable.
14.	TS 12.457 M.c., frag.	March 6, 1158	5 + 20 (= 25)	Dowry not preserved.
15.	TS 13 J 3, f. 10, item III Incomplete trousseau list	Spring, 1159	30 + 80 (= 110)	Jewelry 155. Forty items of clothing, valued ca. 100, preserved.
16.	*Ibid.*, item IV Settlement between husband and wife	Spring, 1159	5 + 17 (= 22)	Dowry 20 (22 items, some valued only 1/2 dinar).
17.	*Ibid.*, item V Settlement	May 5, 1159	B:30	A widow receives her late installment in the form of household goods left by her husband and brings these in as dowry into a new marriage.

18.	TS 8 J 9, f. 17*a* Settlement	1160	5 + 20 (= 25)	Dowry 25, many details. Grand total 50.
19.	*Ibid.*, f. 17*c*, item II* and *d*, item I Settlement	1160	B:10	Dowry 73 (originally 75). Prices, it seems, overvalued (2 = 1)
20.	TS 8 J 5, f. 22* Engagement	Nov. 29, 1161	10 + 20 (= 30)	Dowry not indicated. A ring of silver and one of gold given "as a deposit."
20*a*.	Bodl. d 66 (2878), f. 77	Ca. 1161	—	Dowry 30 (itemized).
21.	TS 12.443 End of m.c., frag.	—	10 + 20 = 30	Only a few items of the dowry preserved.
22.	Merx, *Paléographie hébraique*, pp. 39-43 Renewal of m.c.	Feb. 18, 1164	B:10	Dowry 13 1/2. Blind husband destroyed ketubba. The new ketubba lists the value of the dowry as still extant.
23.	BM Or 5561 B, f. 2 Incomplete m.c.	June 9, 1164	10 (+ 30) = 40	Dowry not preserved.
24.	*Ibid.*, f. 3 Incomplete m.c.	(1164)	5 + 10 = 15	Many items of dowry with realistic values.
25.	Bodl. f56 (2821), 14*v*, 18*v* Central piece of m.c.	1164/5	Total 40	Many items of dowry with realistic values.
	Renewed acknowledgments of the receipt of the trousseaux given to wives after the burning and pillage of Fustat in 1168			
26.	PER H 20	Oct. 18, 1171	—	Dowry of 56, most detailed.
27.	ULC Or 1080, Box 5, f. 15 See B, 4, n. 44	—	B:50	530 (total debt of husband: 580). Many details.

GROUP 1. *(Continued)*

Ms mark and description	Date	Marriage gift	Dowry and other details	
Documents in which the date of marriage is not indicated or not preserved				
28. TS Box K 15, f. 65, pp. 1-2 Trousseau list	—	5 + 20 (= 25)	Jewelry	6
			Clothing	25½
			Bedding	13
			Copper	10
			Perfuming vessels	5½
			Total	60
			Freedman marries freedwoman, see Goitein, *Letters*, p. 336 n. 1.	
29. TS Box K 15, f. 65, pp.3-4 Trousseau list	—	10 + 30 (= 40)	Jewelry	10
			Clothing	40
			Bedding	18
			Copper	19
			Perfuming vessels	10½
			Total	100 (actually 97½)
			Grand total	140

30.	TS 12.526 M.c., frag.	—	10 + 20 = 30	Dowry, incomplete.
31.	TS 16.86 M.c., frag.	. . .] 6/7	—	Dowry divided into sections marked off by signs.
32.	ENA 1822 A, f. 10 M.c., second leaf	—	—	GT 95. Seven items of bedding visible, worth 19 and all copper worth 11 1/2
33.	ENA 3626, f. 6 Trousseau list	—	10 + 30 = 40	210 (GT 250). Dowry divided into sections.
34.	ENA NS 3 vellum, f. 5 M.c., frag.	—	—	GT 140. Part of outfit preserved.
35.	TS 12.585 Settlement at departure: arrangements for conditional or final divorce	1169 (marriage probably 1157)	B:60	Dowry 400+. See C, 1, n. 150
36.	TS 13 J 3, f. 14 Divorce settlement, Cairo	March 1170	B:10	See C, 1, n. 110.

In all cases in which the relevant statement is preserved (nos. 1, 8, 16, 18, 19, 21, 25-30, 32) it is indicated that the prices given for each item are real and not fictitiously increased in honor of the bride. In other documents the prices are realistic (e.g., no. 24). In no. 19, the judge dealt with a marriage already in existence.

GROUP 2.

Return to Normalcy after the Conflagration and Pillage of Fustat in 1168:
Eighteen Entries in the Record Book of the Jewish Community, 1182–1186.
All from Bodl. MS Heb. f 56 (Cat. 2821)

	Ms mark and description	Date	Marriage gift	Dowry and other details
1.	f. 46*b* Engagement	Spring, 1182 (Sivan)	20 + 50 (= 70)	(Of the 20 dinars, 12 were given in cash and for the balance two rings.)
2.	f. 47*a-b* Trousseau list	(1182)	—	Jewelry 42 Clothing 83 Bedding 55 Copper 30 210
3.	f. 53*a* M. with a freedwoman	Spring, 1184 (Adar)	10 + 30 = 40	130 ("Total" at end of document refers to the dowry alone.)
4.	f. 57*a* and *b* Betrothal	Sept. 13, 1184	5 + 20 (= 25)	(Father will maintain couple for five years.)
5.	f. 51 *a* and *b* Engagement	May 23, 1185 (Sivan)	5 + 15 = 20	(Wedding three years later. Ring given "as deposit.")
6.	f. 53*b*	1185	10 + 25 = 35	(Dowry detailed with realistic prices: 60 +) 35 = 95 Total.
7.	f. 53*b*-54*a*	May, 1185 (Sivan)	10 + 25 = 35	(Dowry, detailed with realistic prices: 55 +) 35 = 90 total.
8.	f. 55*a*, item I	Spring, 1186 (Nisan)	5 + 20 (= 25)	44 ("Total" refers to dowry).

9.	f. 55*a*, item II-*b*	Spring, 1186 (Nisan)	B:30	Dowry 40, maid 15, total of husband's obligations 85.
10.	f. 54, item I	Spring, 1186	B:10	75 ("Total" refers to the dowry alone, as an addition of the details proves).
11.	f. 54*b*, item II	Spring, 1186 (Sivan)	B:10	Books 5, cash for buying a maid 15, jewelry 7, clothing 16 3/4, bedding 7, copper 7, varia 7 1/4 (= 65), total (with m. gift) 75. Scribe wrote 65.
12.	f. 55*b*, item II	Summer, 1186 (Av)	B:15	Dowry 33, total 48.
13.	f. 48*a*, item II-48*b* in Qalyūb	After July 25, 1186	10 + 40 = 50	264. GT 314.
14.	f. 55*b*, item III-56*a*	Fall, 1186 (Tishri)	5 + 20 (= 25)	Dowry (many details) 15 (total 40).
15.	f. 56*a*, item II	Fall, 1186 (Marheshvan)	5 + 20 (= 25)	Dowry 41 plus half a house at the water-carrier's depot, Fustat.
16.	f. 56*a*, item III	Fall, 1186 (Marheshvan)	2 + 12 (= 14)	23 (seventeen items).
17.	f. 56*b*, item I	Winter, 1186 (Kislev)	10 + 20 (= 30)	150 (my addition: 153). Grand total 180, plus 7/24 house in Cairo.
18.	f. 56*b*, item II	Winter, 1186 (Teveth)	20 + 20 (= 40)	(Clothing 55, jewelry 23, copper 6, bedding 15 1/2, actual total 99 1/2) 100. Total 140.

GROUP 3.

Tenth-Century Items from Damascus
Includes the oldest complete marriage contract preserved in the Geniza

Ms mark and description	Date	Marriage gift	Dowry and other details
1. TS 16.181^{+}, item I Betrothal	Spring, 933	25 local minimum + 10 (= 35)	Groom registers in the bride's name 1 of 4 shares in a house.
2. *Ibid.*, item II Betrothal	Spring, 933	50 + 20 = 70	Groom paid 15 at betrothal, 35 at wedding.
3. *Ibid.*, *v*, item III Betrothal	Spring, 933	10 + 20 = 30	Groom paid 7 at betrothal, 3 at wedding. The bride had inherited an apartment from her father.
4. TS AS 146, f. 66, item I Betrothal, frag.	Spring, 933	25 + 25 nominal 20 + 30 actual	3 at betrothal, 17 at wedding.
5. *Ibid.*, item II Betrothal, frag.	Spring, 933	25 minimum	Delayed m. gift promised.
6. TS 16.181^{+}, item IV M.c.	March 28, 933	25 minimum + 15 (= 40)	Groom delivered ornaments worth 5. Dowry 262 plus an apartment consisting of two rooms.
7. TS NS 320, f. 108^{+} M.c., small frag.	933	GT 90	Valuable. Part in three-story house.
8. Bodl. d 65 (Cat. 2877), f. 30^{+}	March 24, 956	25 + 200 (= 225)	GT 620 (jewelry 150, clothing 100, copper 50, other items not complete. Dowry 395).
9. TS 12.118^{+} M.c., frag.	10th century	25 local minimum	Valuable. Items of jewelry and clothing preserved.

GROUP 4.

Late Tenth- and Early Eleventh-Century Documents from Eight Major Cities
Where no name of a city is indicated, the item is from Fustat.

	Ms mark and description	Date	Marriage gift	Dowry and other details
1.	TS 16.189^{+} M.c., frag.	Ca. 960	B:20	GT 200 + (tens and singles not preserved).
2.	TS 24.35*v*$^{+}$ M.c., much damaged frag.	979/980	A:20	Dowry included a house and another property, a sum of 30 is mentioned.
3.	TS 16.142^{+}	June, 982	—	Dowry 150. See B, 4, n. 65.
4.	TS 16.105 M.c. (see *Med. Soc.*, I 145)	March, 986	5 (paid in 150 dirhems) +15 (= 20)	Bride is a widowed freedwoman. Dowry 45; GT 60 d., plus 162 1/2 dirhems (this includes 12 1/2 dirhems basic m. gift due at second m).
5.	Bodl. a 2 (2805), f. 2^{+} M.c., Barqa, Libya	Aug. 990	50 + 100 = 150 plus 50 dirhems double basic m. gift "according to the custom of Tripoli"	The bride was "the prospective sole heiress" and therefore received no dowry. The first installment was to be used by her "to buy what she liked and needed for the wedding."
6.	TS 16.70 M.c., frag.	Jan./Feb., 995	Total 150	Gold ornaments valued at 300 and a maid at 80. Most of the trousseau list lost.
7.	ENA NS 17, f. 24 Karaite betrothal	May/June, 999	40 + 60 = 100	No details about dowry.

GROUP 4. (Continued)

	Ms mark and description	Date	Marriage gift	Dowry and other details
8.	ENA 4020, f. 37 M.c., frag., exquisite script, center piece torn from all four sides	Late 10th century	—	GT 600 + (tens and singles not preserved) plus house.
9.	TS 8.97 M.c., frag.	Early 11th century	—	GT 281, second m. of bride.
10.	TS 24.7 Karaite m.c., Cairo, frag.	1003/1004	A: 100 + 50 = 150 (plus 50 dirhems, Karaite basic m. gift)	The headings of the sections Gold, Silver, Copper, Clothing (Bedding) are indicated, but the sums are lost.
11.	TS 12.452 M.c., frag.	Same period	—	Copper 20, GT (inclusive A + B) 113.
12.	Bodl. d 65 (2877), f. 26+ ENA NS 3, f. 24+, Bodl. b 3, f. 28 (2806, n. 26)+, TS 12.128+ M.c., Tinnis, Egypt, all frag.	Ca. 1005/1006	5 + 15 = 20 plus a golden ring and two golden bracelets totaling 10	774 (actual total, it seems, 773 1/3). Widow will receive domicile, food, and clothing from her husband's estate, unless she prefers to receive her m. gift.
13.	TS 18 J 1, f. 3+ Betrothal	June, 1007	100 + 150 = 250	The first installment of 100 was paid at the betrothal; rings given to the father served as the basic m. gift.
14.	TA 6 J a, f. 2 Testimony on Karaite m.c., frag.	1012/1013	—	GT 47 1/2; twelve witnesses.

15.	TS 12.155 Renewal of m.c., frag.	Feb./March, 1013	15 + 20 = 35	Dowry 100 + (tens and singles lost). Husband: cantor and scribe.
16.	TS 13 J 1 f. 2+ Ramle	1015	B:10	
17.	JNUL Heb. 4°577/4, no. 98+ M.c., Tyre, Lebanon, frag.	Nov., 1023	5 + 20	After the husband's death the widow will live in his house and be maintained by his estate, unless the heirs prefer to pay her the m. gift. 40 + (singles not preserved) 1/3.
18.	Bodl. a 3 (2873), f. 39 M.c., frag.	Some years before 1027	20 + 30 = 50	GT 290 (dowry 240).
19.	TS 12.12 Trousseau list	1020s (husband signed TS 16.45 in 1032 when his father was dead; here his father is alive)	40 + 60	Total value of trousseau: 865.
20.	Westminster College Frag. Cairens., 125 Frag.	1023/1024	A:15	High-priced pieces of trousseau (e.g., 15, 40).
21.	PER H 18+ M.c., Aleppo, Syria, frag.	Feb., 1026	Total 50	Same condition as in no. 17.
22.	TS 8 J 6, f. 18*a-c* Three depositions on a lawsuit	Nov. 1026	A:15	Agreement on m. between groom and mother of bride. A given to her brother "as pledge."

GROUP 4. (Continued)

	Ms mark and description	Date	Marriage gift	Dowry and other details
22*a*.	TS 8 J 4, f. 2*b*	Dec., 1026	—	See B, 2, n. 83, above.
23.	Bodl. d 66 (2878), f. 121*v* Betrothal	Dec., 1027	10 + 10 (= 20)	See B, 2, n. 69, above.
24.	TS 12.167 M.c.	1027/1028	Total 15	GT 42 (dowry 27).
25.	ULC Add. 3430 Karaite m.c., Jerusalem	Feb., 1028	5 + 35 = 40 (plus 50 dirhems Karaite basic m. gift)	Dowry 61 1/2 (total 101 1/2).
26.	Bodl. a 2 (2805), f. 4+ M.c.	Oct., 1029	5 + 10 = 15	Jewelry and clothing (all specified) 20, bedding 10, furniture 10, copper 10, total 50. GT 65.
27.	TS 24.2 M.c., frag.	1020s	5 + 10 = 15	Second m. of bride. GT 810 (dowry 795).
28.	TS NS 324, f. 107 M.c., frag.	1018-1028	Total 25	Second m.
29.	ENA 2738, f. 33 Settlement	Shortly before 1028	20 + 30	676. See C, 1, n. 234.

30.	TS 13 J 6 f. 14+ Tyre, frag.	Ca. 1030	—	Father gives daughter a house in Acre, Palestine, on condition that he and his immediate family are entitled to live there, if needed. For the first year the couple will stay in Tyre with the bride's parents.
31.	TS 13 J 17, f. 14 Draft of a deposition on a release, frag.	1030/1031	—	A wife releases her husband from his responsibility for her dowry (which included a house) after he had granted her complete disposition of it. Details totaling about 540 visible.
32.	TS J 3, f. 47, formerly TS 13 J 32 + Karaite betrothal (note in Arabic characters)	July, 1033	200 + 300 = 500 (plus 50 dirhems Karaite basic m.g.)	See B, 4, n. 96.
33.	Bodl. a 3 (2873), f. 45 M.c., frag.	1033/1034	3 + 15 = 18	Dowry (twenty items) 32. GT 50.
34.	Westminster College Arabica I, fs. 76 and 40*b*, and frag. Cairens., f. 105	1033/1034	A:4 (4 1/6)	Second m. of bride.
35.	TS 24.12 M.c., frag.	1033/1034	Total 150	Only the minor part of the trousseau, totaling ca. 600, is visible.

GROUP 4. (Continued)

	Ms mark and description	Date	Marriage gift	Dowry and other details
36.	TS 20.6+ M.c., frag.	Sept., 1037	A:25	Half an old house, plus outfit, whose sections are valued thus: Jewelry 30 Clothing 70 Copper 40 Bedding 80 Lingerie 20 (Total) 240 GT[?]80, most probably 380 M.g. 25 [+ 45 = 70] [House 70] + 240 = 310 380
37.	TS 12.180	1037/1038	5 + [1]5	Of dowry, items valued at 30 visible. The complete document could not have contained much more. Second marriage.
38.	TS 24.80 M.c.	Oct., 1039	10 + 20 = 30	GT 140 (dowry 110, remarkably low prices).
39.	ULC Or 1080 J 7 Settlement in Fustat about a broken marriage and a property in Qayrawān	Several years before Feb., 1040	B:100	200. A divorcée from Qayrawān, a mother of several children, receives from her husband a property in Qayrawān worth 295, as against 100 + 200 = 300. He still owes her 5.
40.	TS 16.80 Karaite m.c., large frag.	From this period	—	Total dowry, immovables included, 1,170 (or 1,171–1,179, singles lost).

GROUP 5.

A PERIOD OF RICH DOCUMENTATION: DATED ITEMS FROM THE EGYPTIAN CAPITAL (AND ALEPPO), 1105–1135

Ms mark and description	Date	Marriage gift	Dowry and other details
1. TS NS Box 323, f. 4 M.c., frag.	Nov., 1105	1 + 2 = 3	Widow. GT 3 (i.e., no dowry). Both fathers dead.
2. TS 28.23 + 16.217 + 8.225 M.c., frag.	Oct., 1106	10 + 30 = 40	Total 100 (dowry 60).
3. TS 10 J 27, f. 3*a* Betrothal, Cairo	May/June, 1107	10 + 30 (= 40)	One half of A, 5, delivered at betrothal. Wedding two years later.
4. TS 16.107 M.c., Aleppo, frag.	1107/1108	A:100	High-priced items of dowry, extant prices total 230, about 1/3 of the original [ca. 700].
5. TS 8 J 4, f. 22*v* Betrothal, Cairo	Oct., 1108	5 + 20 = 25	One ring of gold and three of silver at betrothal.
6. TS 12.488 M.c., frag.	Spring, 1109-1119	10 (+ 15) = 25	Dowry contains clothing, bedding, and copper.
7. TS 8.116⁺	After 1109	B:100	Barren wife, saved in 1109 with her husband during the capture of Tripoli, Lebanon, by the Crusaders, permits him under certain conditions, to take another wife.
8. TS 8 J 4, f. 23*c* Betrothal, Cairo	Oct., 1110	5 + 20 = 25	Perhaps cousins (both Levi).

GROUP 5. (Continued)

	Ms mark and description	Date	Marriage gift	Dowry and other details
9.	TS 24.5 M.c., frag.	Spring, 1111	3 + 10 = 13	A freedman marries a virgin. Her dowry: 14 cash for buying half a house, plus clothing, bedding, and copper, worth, as far as visible, about 20.
10.	Antonin 634 M.c.	Approx. same	3 + 10 = 13	Dowry 7, GT 20; a widow.
11.	TS 24.3 M.c.	Jan., 1115	5 + 10 = 15	GT 43 1/3 (dowry 28 1/3).
12.	Bodl. b 12 (2875), f. 19 + TS 12.164 + 8.210 M.c., frag.	Oct., 1116	1 + 15 (= 16)	A divorcée on whose earnings the husband will have no right, but who will provide her clothing by herself.
13.	TS 24.75 Rider on m.c.	Nov., 1116	—	The husband if traveling, even with his wife, is not permitted to take any item of the dowry with him, even with her consent.
14.	Bodl. a 3 (2873), f. 42+ M.c., Karaite, frag.	Fall, 1117	20 + 50 = 70	Total 719 (dowry 649, intended 650). Son of a physician marries a Karaite widow and promises to bring up her daughter.
15.	Westminster College Frag. Cairens., 42 Engagement	Nov., 1119	—	Mother of bride receives three golden rings and one of amber.

16.	TS NS Box 226, fs. 10-11, Two betrothals, frag.	Dec., 1119	—	No payment of first installment in first betrothal. The bride was declared trustworthy with regard to her trousseau in that one but not in the second one.
17.	TS 12.163 M.c., frag.	1120 or earlier	Total 35	See group 8, no. 8, below.
18.	TS NS J 185, nos. 8 and 12 Court record	Fall, 1120	—	A father, who had given his daughter 1/8 house, two maidservants, and all furniture in her apartment, takes ornaments worth 25 from the trousseau "readied for her by her [late] mother" to use their price on a business trip. He promises to pay back "with his best money."
19.	TS 8 J 5, f. 3*c* Engagement, frag.	April, 1124	—	Father received ring.
20.	TS Arabic Box 51, f. 103 Court record	June, 1124	—	After a girl had received half of a newly built house from her father, the dates for the assessment of her trousseau and for her marriage are set.
21.	TS 16.52, M.c., frag.	Dec., 1124	5 + 10 = 15	GT, 20, dowry, described as clothing, 5. Divorcée whose father was dead. Groom son of a cantor.

GROUP 5. (Continued)

	Ms mark and description	Date	Marriage gift	Dowry and other details
22.	TS 20.62 + 24.15 M.c., frag.	1124/1125	7 + 30	GT 185. In April 1126, the wife receives from her mother ornaments worth 6 3/4, to be included in the trousseau. For remarriage see group 8, no. 11, below.
23.	TS 8 J 5, f. 3*a-b* Engagement, frag.	May/June, 1125	10 + 30	The bride is the daughter of a freedman. Wedding after a year.
24.	TS 8 J 32 f. 1+, Bodl. b 13, f. 48+ (Cat. 2834, no. 29) M.c., frag.	1125/1126	3 + . . .	Second marriage of bride. Her trousseau occupies a line and a half. Prices visible amount to 5.
25.	TS 8.138 Court record (betrothal), frag.	Jan./Feb., 1126	—	After the girl "had received the entire outfit [probably: of her mother] and the entire house," she was betrothed.
26.	TS 12.613 + 16.44 Court record (deathbed declaration), frag.	April, 1126	—	After a dying woman had given part of her house to her manumitted maid, a man swore to marry and never to divorce her.
27.	TS 12.453 Frag.	1126/1127	(5 +) 20 = 25	List of trousseau almost completely lost.
28.	TS 8.208 Note of clerk	May/June, 1127	12 1/2 dirhems + 25 dirhems (37 1/2 dirhems = 1 dinar)	Widow with son marries a foreigner.

28*a*.	Bodl. a 2 (2805), f. 6	May/June, 1127	—	Dowry 174, as far as extant.
29.	TS Misc. Box 25, f. 140 Court record	Aug., 1127	Less than 9, probably 5	Remarriage of divorcee. See group 8, no. 9, below.
30.	Bodl. a 3 (2873), f. 40 M.c.	May, 1128	5 + 25	GT 76 (dowry 46).
31.	Bodl. b 11 (2874), f. 3 Settlement, frag.	Oct., 1130	—	Wife receives her dowry back from her husband "to sell and to buy with it."
32.	TS 8 J 17, f. 9*a-c* Betrothal	Nov., 1131	20 + 30 = 50	See B, 2, n. 80.
33.	*Ibid*., f. 9*d* Betrothal	Jan., 1132	1 (+ 10)	Father received ring. Wedding to be "before Passover" (three months later), but she was divorced before.
33*a*.	TS 24.15*v*, item II M.c.	March, 1132	7 + 30	Dowry 148, GT 185.
34.	TS 8 J 5, f 2*a-c* Engagement	April, 1132	2 + 2 = 4 + 12 (= 16)	A silver ring, "as deposit." Both parties were divorcés.
35.	*Ibid*., f. 2*c-d* Engagement	April, 1132	3 or 4 + 20	Both bride and groom had no father.
36.	JNUL 4° 577 3, no. 83, item I+ Engagement	Aug., 1132	5 + 30 (= 35)	The first installment was delivered at the engagement.
37.	JNUL 4° 577 3, no. 83, item II+ Engagement	Aug., 1132	4 + 20	The first installment was delivered at the engagement. Fines.

GROUP 5. (Continued)

	Ms mark and description	Date	Marriage gift	Dowry and other details
38.	TS 12.653 M.c., small frag.	1132/1133	2 + . . .	Second marriage of bride. Few items of trousseau preserved.
39.	Bodl. a 3 (2873), f. 40*v* Settlement	Jan., 1133	—	Wife receives her dowry back from her husband, who remains responsible only for the m. gift. Cf. no. 31, above.
40.	ENA 2806, f. 11 + 2727, f. 18*v* Engagement	March, 1133	20 + 40 [= 60]	See B, 5, n. 76.
41.	TS 16.147 *recto* and *verso* M.c. and settlement, frag.	June, 1135	B:15	The dowry includes (part of) a house. Husband returns dowry and remains responsible for m. gift only.
42.	Bodl. d 80. f. 42 Note of clerk, frag.	Fall, 1135	—	Husband confirms wife's free disposal (of what, is not preserved).
43.	TS 16.233 Court record	Ca. 1135	B:100	Settlement: husband has to bear the cost of medical treatment of his wife (50) in addition to (and not as part of) the m. gift.
44.	Bodl. b 12 (2875), f. 18 M.c., small frag.	Ca. 1135	B:7	See group 8, no. 24, below.

GROUP 6.

MARRIAGE DOCUMENTS WRITTEN BY JUDGE NATHAN B. SAMUEL, CA. 1140–1147

Ms mark and description	Date	Marriage gift	Dowry and other details
1. TS 13 J 3, f. 1+ Court record	Nov., 1141	—	A childless woman agrees that her husband take a second wife on condition that his silver and carpets serve as surety for her delayed marriage gift (B).
2. *Ibid.*, f. 2+ Deposition of witness	1141/1142	B:30	In a declaration made a day before his death a husband mentions as an afterthought that his wife has to be given 30 as B.
3. Gottheil-Worrel, XLV, pp. 220-222 Trousseau list	(1142)	—	Jewelry 107, clothing 453, carpets and hangings (as far as preserved) 155 [total dowry ca. 750].
4. TS NS J 27 *d* Note of judge	1143	10 + 20 (= 30)	1/8 house.
5. ULC Or 1080 J 286 M.c., frag	1144/1145	1 + 1 = 2	No dowry (carefully written, but only left side is preserved).
6. ULC Or 1080 J 65 End of court record, frag.	Fall, 1145	—	Divorcée releases her former husband, after having received her B completely.

GROUP 6. *(Continued)*

	Ms mark and description	Date	Marriage gift	Dowry and other details
7.	ULC Or 1080 J 49 Court record	Sept., 1146	—	Complete list of items of trousseau (without prices) returned to Sitt al-Ḥasab on order of the Nagid: jewelry ca. 30 items, clothing ca. 50, bedding 20, copper etc. - 17 items. Total value at least 300 dinars.
8.	Bodl. d 66 (2878) f. 47-48+* Engagement contract, see B, 2, above	Nov., 1146	40 + 100 (= 140)	About 125 items having a total value of 640, "1 dinar being worth 1 dinar." Her (late) father and grandfather had been India traders, her maternal grandfather was a physician.
9.	TS 12.544* Court record with depositions, made first by husband, then by wife	Nov./Dec., 1147	—	Widow brings in 1/6 house (received as B:40, plus other dues from a former marriage) and stands surety to her husband in case he will be sued by her two sons and/or a fourth party in the house, a Muslim, with the claim that he occupies more than one-sixth.
10.	TS K 6, f. 118*b* Note of judge	Ca. 1140	—	Wife gives 1/4 house to son and another 1/4 to daughter and states that her husband has the right to live in those parts (as long as he keeps them in repair) but not to inherit them.

11.	TS 20.33 Left lower corner of m.c., frag.	Ca. 1140	—	350 (+, singles not extant; nine lines of trousseau preserved).
12.	TS J 1, f. 29+* List of bridegroom's responsibilities (originally attached to his m.c.)	Ca. 1140	500	Jewelry 471, clothing 373, carpets and hangings 198, copper etc. 208, two maidservants and two chambermaids 100, total outfit 1,350, books 250, m. gift 500. GT 2,100.
13.	TS 12.673	Ca. 1140	2 + 10 = 12	No dowry.
14.	TS 16.246*v*	Ca. 1140	Total 5	Remarriage; see group 8, no. 14.
15.	TS 12.771	Ca. 1140	B:25	Remarriage; see group 8, no. 15.
16.	TS 8.168 Settlement with widow, frag.	Ca. 1140	40 + 60 = 100	D [3] 90. A and copper and other items had been received by her before. The total due the widow was reduced to one third and received by her. Her brother released the heirs in her name from any further claims.
17.	TS AS 147, f. 9	Ca. 1140	15 + 30	D 102 + a house

GROUP 7.

MARRIAGE DOCUMENTS FROM THE RĪF (PROVINCIAL TOWNS OR VILLAGES IN EGYPT), 945–1492

	Ms mark and place	Date	Marriage gift	Dowry and other details
1.	TS 12.154[+] Qūjandīma	July, 945	2 + 4 = 6	16 1/3 (eleven items).
2.	ENA 2556, f. 1 al-Ramle	Fall, 997	—	A mother gives her daughter 1/2 of a house for her dowry.
3.	TS 16.132 al-Banā near Fāqūs	Fall, 998	—	After having given 1/4 of 1/3 of a house inherited from her father to her daughter, a woman sells another fourth to her son-in-law for 3 dinars. Eighteen signatures.
4.	Dropsie 335 Ṣahrajt	March, 1041	—	A brother gives to his sister (a second draft: two sisters) a house worth 10 for her (their) dowry.
5.	Bodl. d 66 (Cat. 2878), f. 22 Abyār	Dec., 1069	—	(No numbers because used as form.)
6.	TS 16.53[+] Ṣā (Saïs)	March, 1081	2 + 10 = 12	5 1/3. The bride is a divorcée and both she and her husband have no father.
7.	PER H 24[+] Damsīs	April, 1083	10 + 20 = 30	19 (thirteen items). The fathers of both the bride and the groom were dead.
8.	TS 12.494(+) Minyat Ziftā, not completed	Aug., 1110	1 + 5 = 6	The groom agrees to be like a father to the son of his bride, a divorcée, and to teach him his craft.

9.	TS 13 J 2, f. 17 Sambuṭya = Sunbāṭ	Spring, 1116	—	A wife releases her husband from all claims that she or her three sons might have against him. He still owes her the delayed m. gift and her dowry. She has the right to live in a house assigned to her for five years.
10.	TS 12.547 Minyat Ziftā, frag.	Ca. 1120	Total 40	GT 90 (dowry 50).
11.	Bodl. b 12 (2875), f. 1 Sambuṭya = Sunbāṭ	Feb., 1133	1 + 3 = 4	5 (husband takes repudiated wife back).
12.	TS NS J 228 Malīj	March, 1134	6 + 20	Dowry 70, GT 90. The first installment is not included in the grand total.
13.	Bodl. c 28 (Cat. 2876), f. 69 Minya Ziftā	Jan., 1160	—	A wife conveys to her husband full proprietorship in half a house given to her by her father and renounces her rights in a house of her husband serving as a collateral for her m. gift.
14.	TS 8 J 5, f. 21 al-Maḥalla, betrothal	May, 1160	30 + 60 (= 90)	One ring of gold and two of silver given at betrothal.
15.	Bodl. f 56 (2821), f. 48*a-b* Qalyūb	Fall, 1186	10 + 40 = 50	264. GT 314.
16.	TS 13 J 5, f. 5* Bilbays	Aug., 1204	B:60	Widow receives her dowry back, valued 186. (In Bilbays, in clothing section 4 = 1, in jewelry and copper, 2 = 1). She had not yet received her B.

GROUP 7. (Continued)

	Ms mark and place	Date	Marriage gift	Dowry and other details
17.	ULC Add. 3339 b Bilbays	Dec., 1218	B:60	Wife had agreed to a reduction of B to 30 (probably because two minor daughters had to be provided for).
18.	TS 8 J 6, f. 12 Qūṣ	1215/1216	—	A physician gives to his two minor daughters the dowry of his late wife, worth 200, which he had inherited from her.
19.	TS 8.239 Qūṣ, small frag.	—	Total 15	(Beautifully written.)
20.	TS 12.39+ Minyat Ghamr, engagement	Sept., 1315	10 + 30 = 40	The bride, a widow, will look after the husband's son for ten years.
21.	TS Misc. Box 28, f. 71+ Malīj, engagement	May, 1492	5 + 5 = 10 ashrafis	The ashrafi dinar is defined as worth 300 copper dirhems. The bride was a widow.
22.	TS 16.85 M.c. of a couple from Qalyūb issued in the capital, frag.	13th century	B:17	"The bride produced her outfit in court" (eight pieces worth 7).

GROUP 8.

REMARRYING ONE'S DIVORCÉE

Ms mark and description	Date	Marriage gift	Dowry and other details
1. TS 8.89 M.c., frag.	1048-1057	—	Poor people, as the frag. of the trousseau list shows.
2. TS 16.123+ Ramle, Palestine, m.c.	Dec., 1052	2 + 5 = 7	17 1/3.
3. TS 12.98 M.c., frag.	1058-1067	1 (+ 5) = 6	Ca. 30 (ca. 1/3 preserved, 8 items of total value of 10).
4. ULC Or 1080 J 187 M.c., frag.	1066/1067	—	Addition to first m. gift promised.
5. ULC Or 1080 J 260 Frag.	1068-1079	1 + 3 = 4	—
6. Bodl. b 12 (2875), f. 26+ M.c.	Sept., 1094	5 + 15 = 20	Dowry of four items. Value 2. The divorcée was a virgin.
7. Bodl. e 98, f. 60 Court record, frag.	Jan., 1100 (date of first marriage)	(See next column)	Debt of 62 1/2, house in Cairo, and an amber-and-gold band, worth 35, mentioned.
8. TS 12.163*v* Agreement written on back of m.c., frag.	Sept., 1120	Total 35	Much lost. Eight items of total value of ca. 65 preserved. Addition to first m. gift promised.
9. TS Misc. Box 25, f. 140 Court record	Aug., 1127	Less than 9, probably 5	The bill of divorce had been written, but not yet delivered. Wife consents now to (continue to) live with husband's parents and not to demand "separation" from them.

GROUP 8. (Continued)

Ms mark and description	Date	Marriage gift	Dowry and other details
10. TS 8.228 Court record	Ca. 1130	—	A betrothal is renewed after the future husband promises by oath not to take away wife's earnings nor to interfere with her work.
11. TS 24.15*v*, item II Court record	March, 1132	[7 + 30]	(Dowry 148). GT 185. For the marriage in 1124/1125 see Group 5, no. 22.
12. Bodl. b 12 (2875), f. 1 Sambuṭya = Sunbāṭ, m.c.	Oct., 1133	1 + 3 = 4	5.
13. TS 13 J 3, f. 13 Court record	Feb., 1137	—	Husband grants wife a loan of 5 and she gives a golden bracelet as collateral. The marriage is renewed according to the original conditions.
14. TS 16.246*v* Court record	Ca. 1140	Total 5 plus 1 owed the divorcée	No dowry mentioned.
15. TS 12.771 Court record	Ca. 1140	B:25	Wife's earnings belong to her; husband will not provide her with clothing, "whether she has work or not." B in the first m.c. had been higher.
16. TS 8.223 Court record	Ca. 1145	—	Karaite wife, remarried to a Rabbanite husband, is threatened with loss of her delayed m. gift, if she again breaks her promise to observe Rabbanite ritual.

17.	ULC Or 1080 J 206 M.c., frag.	April, 1147	—	—
18.	ULC Or 1081 J 40 M.c.	Sept., 1229	A:2 1/2	Not mentioned. She had been divorced on Jan. 22, 1229 (Mosseri A, f. 56).
19.	TS 20.10+ M.c., frag.	Dec., 1310	5 + 40 = 45	Many items, but much lost; prices visible: Ca. 55 (real value of each estimated = 1/2).
20.	TS 12.815+ M.c., frag.	15th century	—	The groom is described as "the esteemed notable."
			Special cases	
21.	ENA NS 17, f. 31*b*, col. II, item II + 31*a*, margin	1084	5 + 20 (= 25)	Married and divorced before consummation in Tyre, remarried in al-Maḥalla. GT 74. See B, 4, n. 89.
22.	ENA NS 17, f. 28*a*	1089	See C, 1, n. 206	Husband about to marry another wife. Wishes to remarry divorcée if she consents to live with the other one. Meanwhile he maintains her for four years.
23.	TS 13 J 20, f. 17, 1. 13	Ca. 1065	—	3 dirhems paid for the issue of a m.c. at remarriage. See *Med. Soc.*, II, 230.
24.	Bodl. b 12 (2875), f. 18 M.c., small frag.	Ca. 1135	B:7	
25.	ENA 2727, f. 18d *v*	Ca. 1140	(B:35)	Wife agrees to her husband's remarriage of his second wife after he had issued her a promissory note for 35 before a Muslim notary. The Jewish court orders the deposition of the amount with a third person.

Part II. General Data about Marriage Gift and Dowry and the Status of Bride and Groom

See pp. 99–100, above.

ABBREVIATIONS

A	marriage gift at the conclusion of the marriage contract
B	payment at the termination of the marriage
d	divorcée
D	dowry
dr	divorcée remarried to original husband
fb	father of bride noted as dead
fg	father of groom noted as dead. (The absence of a mark does not prove that the father was alive. In lists of trousseaux and other marriage documents copied in the record books the clerks often did not care to enter this detail.)
GT	grand total of marriage gift and dowry
sm	second marriage (widowed or divorced)
T	total of A and B
w	widow

All numbers designate dinars; 1 dinar = approximately 40 dirhems.

When not otherwise indicated, the document was issued at Fustat, or the relevant detail is lost.

Bodleian manuscripts, usually written, e.g., Bodl. MS Heb. d 66 (Cat. 2878), f. 47, appear thus: d 66 (2878), f. 47.

1 + 1 = 2 means that the MS notes A, B, and T.

1 + 1 indicates that the MS mentions solely A and B.

As a rule, the marriage contracts contain A + B = T, whereas the records or drafts about a marriage note solely A and B.

Marriage gift	Dowry	Status	Place, date	MS mark
		A, B, AND T MENTIONED		
1. 12 1/2 + 25 = 37 1/2 dirhems	No D	—	1127	TS 8.208
2. 1 + 1 = 2	—	—	1144/1145	ULC Or 1080 J 286
3. 1 + 1 (or more)	—	sm	Cairo, 1088-1189	d 65 (2877), f. 16
4. 40 + 50 dirhems	D 150 dirhems	(freedwoman)	Aleppo, 1201	TS AS 145, f.1
5. 1 + 2 = 3	—	sm	1058	b 12 (2875), f. 14
6. 1 + 2 = 3	No D	sm	Cairo, 1071	ULC Or 1080 Box 5, f. 17
7. 1 + 2 = 3	—	fb, w, fg	1105	TS NS Box 323, f. 4
8. (1 +) 2 = 3	No D	—	—	TS 12.442
9. 1 + 3 = 4	—	dr	1068-1079	ULC Or 1080 J 260
10. 1 + 3 = 4	No D	d	1102	ULC Or 1080 J 289
11. 1 + 3 = 4	D 5	dr	1133	b 12 (2875), f. 1
12. 1 + 5 = 6	No D	d	Minyat Ziftā, 1110	TS 12.494
13. 1 + 5 = 6	No D	d	Alexandria, 1160	TS 12.490
14. 1 + 5 = 6	D frag.	dr	—	TS 12.98
15. 1 (+ 7) = 8	—	—	1156	Firkovitch II, 1700, f. 16*a*
16. 1 (+ 14) = 15	—	w	1241	TS 20.64
17. 2 + 4 = 6	D 16 1/3	—	Qūjandīma, 945	TS 12.154^{+}
18. 2 + 5 = 7	D 17 1/3	dr	Ramle, 1052	TS 16.123^{+}
19. 2 + 5 = 7	D 30	w	Ca. 1090	TS 20.116*v*, item II

Marriage gift	Dowry	Status	Place, date	MS mark
20. 2 + 6 = 8	D 5 1/3 + 1/2 house worth 25	—	Ca. 1064	a 3 (2873), f. 32*v*$^{+}$
21. 2 + 10 = 12	D 16 3/4	fg	Tyre, 1079	PER H 1^{+}
22. 2 + 10 = 12	D 5 1/3	fb, d, fg	1081	TS 16.53^{+}
23. 2 + 10 = 12	No D	—	Ca. 1145	TS 12.673
24. 2 + 10 = 12	GT 93	proselyte bride	—	TS K 25, f. 166
25. 2 + 12 (= 14)	D 23	—	Fall, 1186	f 56 (2821), f. 56*a* item III
26. 2 + 13 = 15	D 35, GT 50	sm	11th century	ENA NS 3, f. 8 (vellum)
27. 2 + 15 = 17	D 26, GT 43	sm	1050	ENA NS 18, f. 21
28. 2 + 15 = 17	—	fb	1156	Firkovitch II, 1700, f. 10*a*
29. 3 + 5 = 8	No D	sm	Cairo, 1083	TS 12.541
30. 3 + 5 corrected to 1 (+ 7) = 8	—	—	1156	Firkovitch II, 1700, f. 16*a*
31. (3 +) 6 = 9	D 15	sm	Cairo, ca. 1080	d 65 (2877), f. 15
32. 3 + 10 = 13	Jewelry 30	sm	Ca. 1080	ENA NS 18, f. 29
33. 3 + 10 = 13	D 1/2 house = 14+	—	1111	TS 24.5
34. 3 + 10 = 13	—	d	Ca. 1111	Antonin 634
35. 3 + 10 = 13	D 37	—	11th century	TS 16.74
36. 4 + 10 (= 14) "in bad money"	D 32 items	—	—	TS NS J 461

37. 4 + 12 = 16	—	d	1132	TS 8 J 5, f. 2*a-c*
38. (3 or) 4 + 20 = 24	—	fg, fb	1132	*Ibid.*, f. 2*c-d*
39. 4 + 20 = 24	—	—	1132	JNUL 83, no. 4, item II+
40. 5 + 5	D 70, GT 80	d	Ca. 1020	TS 16.2
41. 5 + 5 (Ashrafi)	—	fg, w	Malīj, 1492	TS Misc. Box 28, f. 71+
42. 5 + 10	D 24, GT 39	—	Ca. 1000	ENA NS 17, f.12
43. 5 + 10	D 795, GT 810	sm	Ca. 1020	TS 24.2
44. 5 + 10	D 50, GT 65	—	1029	a 2 (2805), f. 4
45. 5 + 10	D 20 (cash), GT 35	sm	1063	Dropsie 339 + TS 20.12
46. 5 + 10	—	d	1065	Antonin 460
47. 5 + 10	No D	—	1066	TS 12.685
48. 5 + 10	D 28 1/3, GT 43 1/3	fb, fg	Jan., 1115	TS 24.3
49. 5 + 10	D 5, GT 20	d, fb	1124	TS 16.52
50. 5 + 10	No D	—	1100-1138	TS AS 147, f. 1
51. 5 + 10	—	—	1164	BM Or 5561 B, f. 3
52. 5 + 10	—	fb	12th century	TS 12.762
53. 5 + 10	—	fg	1331	b 3 (2806), f. 9*v*
54. 5 + 10	D incomplete	sm	—	TS 16.75
55. 5 + 10	—	—	—	TS Misc. Box 8, f. 97

Marriage gift	Dowry	Status	Place, date	MS mark
56. 5 + 12	D 11 +	—	1083/4	TS 16.71^{+}
57. 5 + 15	D 45	w	986	TS 16.105
58. 5 + 15	D 774	—	Ca. 1005/1006	d 65 (2877), f. 26^{+} ENA NS 3, f. 24^{+} b 3 (2806), f. 28^{+} TS 12.128^{+}
59. 5 + 15	D 30+	sm	1037/1038	TS 12.180
60. 5 + 15	D 36 1/2+	d	Tyre, 1054-1059	Antonin 635
61. 5 + 15	D incomplete	sm, fg	1067	a 3 (2878), f. 38
62. 5 + 15	D 2	fb, fg, d	Sept. 27, 1094	b 12 (2875), f. 26^{+}
63. 5 + 15	(D 40), GT 60	—	11th century	TS AS 147, f. 25
64. 5 + 15	D mostly copper preserved	—	Ca. 1160	TS 10 J 7, f. 6*c*
65. 5 + 15	—	—	May 23, 1185	f 56 (2821), f. 51
66. 5 + 17 = 22	D 20, GT 42	—	1159	TS 13 J 3, f. 10, item IV
67. 5 + 20	D 40 1/3+	—	Tyre, 1023	JNUL Heb. 4° 577/4, f. 98
68. 5 + 20	D 75, GT 100	—	1045	ULC Or 1080 J 140
69. 5 + 20	D 27, GT 52	—	1050	TS 12.165
70. 5 + 20	D 49, GT 74	dr	1084	ENA NS 17, f. 31*v* item III
71. 5 + 20	—	fg	Cairo, 1108	TS 8 J 4, f. 22*v*
72. 5 + 20	—	fg	Cairo, 1110	TS 8 J 4, f. 23*c*

73. 5 + 20	D frag.	—	1126/1127	TS 12.453
74. 5 + 20	No D remains	fb	1158	TS 12.457
75. 5 + 20	D 25, GT 50	—	1160	TS 8 J 9, f. 17*a*
76. 5 + 20	D 60	—	Ca. 1160	TS K 15, f. 65, item I
77. 5 + 20	Father maintains for 5 years	fb	1184	f 56 (2821), f. 57 *a* and *b*
78. 5 + 20	D 44	—	1186	f 56 (2821), f. 55*a*, item 1
79. 5 + 20	D 15	—	Fall, 1186	f 56 (2821), f. 55*b*, Item III, 56*a*
80. 5 + 20	D 41 + 1/2 house	—	Fall, 1186	f 56 (2821), f. 56*a*, item II
81. 5 + 20	No D	w	1292-1297	TS Misc. Box 28, f. 264
82. 5 + 25	D 46, GT 76	fb, fg	May, 1128	a 3 (2873), f. 40
83. 5 + 25 (100 + 500 nuqra, see B, 4, n. 5)	—	w, d	Late 13th century	TS 20.109
84. 5 + 25	D 55 + 1/2 house	fb	—	TS 12.558
85. 5 + 25	GT 85	—	—	TS 20.1
86. 5 + 25	—	fb, fg	—	TS 10 J 21, f. 5
87. 5 + 25	—	both sm	1324	ENA 2727, f. 14, item II
88. 5 + 30	—	—	Ca. 1050	Mosseri A 52.1

Marriage gift	Dowry	Status	Place, date	MS mark
89. 5 + 30	D little remains	fb, fg	Town on seashore, 11th century	TS 16.169+
90. 5 + 30	D 90, GT 125	—	Ca. 1100	TS K 15, f. 79
91. 5 + 30	—	—	1132	JNUL 83, no. 4+
92. 5 + 30	D many items	fg	1225	TS NS J 231
93. 5 + 30	—	d	Cairo, 1379	TS 13 J 4, f. 15 (1)+
94. 5 + 30	D poor, two lines	—	—	TS 12.144
95. 5 + 35	D 61 1/2, GT 101 1/2	—	Jerusalem, 1028	ULC Add. 3430+
96. 5 + 40	D incomplete, ca. 55, actual value 22 1/2	dr	1310	TS 20.10+
97. 6 + 20	D (64), GT 90	—	Malīj, 1134	TS NS J 228
98. 7 + 30	—	w	Cairo, late 12th century	TS 12.440
99. 7 + 30	D 148	fb (dr)	1124/1125	TS 20.62 + 24.15
100. 10 + 5	D 30 + 30 (house)	sm	1088 or earlier	16.155 + Dropsie 333
101. 10 + 10	—	—	1027	d 66 (2878), f. 121*v*+
102. 10 + 15	D frag.	fg	1109-1119	TS 12.488

103. (7 + 3 =) 10 + 20	Inherited apartment	—	933	TS 16.181, item III[+]
104. 10 + 20	—	—	Ca. 1030	TS 16.78
105. 10 + 20	D 110, GT 140	—	1039	TS 24.80
106. 10 + 20	D incomplete, at least 100	—	1069	d 65 (2877), f. 1
107. 10 + 20	D 19	fb, fg	Damsīs, 1083	PER H 24[+]
108. 10 + 20 = 30 (originally 25)	—	fb, fg, sm	1089/90	TS NS Box 313, f. 4[+]
109. 10 + 20	D 79, GT 109	—	Ca. 1090	TS 20.116*v* I
110. 10 + 20	D 343, GT 373	fb, fg	Ca. 1100	b 12 (2875), f. 11
111. 10 + 20	D 115	—	Ca. 1100	Westminster College, Frag. Cairens., 47
112. 10 + 20	1/8 house	—	1143	TS NS J 27 d
113. 10 + 20	—	fb, fg	1161	TS 8 J 5, f. 22[*]
114. 10 + 20	D 150, GT 180 + 7/24 house	—	Winter, 1186	f 56 (2821), f. 56*b* I
115. 10 + 20	D 59, GT 89	—	1301	Mosseri V 8[+]
116. 10 + 20	D incomplete	—	—	TS 12.526
117. 10 + 20	D little preserved	fg	—	TS 12.443
118. 10 + 20	D 203, GT 233	—	—	TS NS J 410
119. 10 + 20	D frag.	—	—	ULC Or 1080 J 100
120. 10 + 25	D two lines	—	1013	TS 12.155

	Marriage gift	Dowry	Status	Place, date	MS mark
121.	10 + 25	D 316 (overvalued)	fb	Ca. 1080	ENA 2727, f. 8 A
122.	10 + 25	—	fb	Alexandria, ca. 1140	TS 20.5
123.	10 + 25	D 60, GT 95	—	1185	f 56 (2821), f. 53*b*
124.	10 + 25	D 55, GT 90	—	1185	*Ibid.*, f. 53*b*-54*a*
125.	10 + 30	D 85, GT 125	fb	1106	TS 28.23 + TS 16.217 + TS 8.225
126.	10 + 30	5 at betrothal	fg	Cairo, 1107	TS 10 J 27, f. 3, item I
127.	10 + 30	—	freedman's daughter	1125	TS 8 J 5, f. 3*a-b*
128.	10 (+ 30) = 40	D not preserved	fb, fg	June, 1164	BM Or 5561 B, f. 2
129.	10 + 30	D 210, GT 250	—	Ca. 1170	ENA 3626, f. 6
130.	10 + 30	D 130	—	1184	f 56 (2821), f. 53*a*
131.	10 + 30	D 100, GT 140	—	—	TS K 15, f. 65, item II
132.	10 + 30	—	fg	Cairo	TS 12.159
133.	10 + 30	—	—	—	TS 16.106
134.	10 + 40	D 30 + part of house	—	Ca. 1090	TS 10 J 7, f. 13
135.	10 + 40, groom to bear cost of wedding	—	—	1140	TS NS J 475
136.	10 + 40	D incomplete	fb, fg	1157	TS 8 J 5, f. 18*d*
137.	10 + 40	D 264	—	After July 25, 1186	f 56 (2821), f. 48*a*, item II-48*b*

138.	10 + 40	D incomplete	fb	1241	ULC Add. 3349
139.	10 + 40 "in bad money"	D 65	—	—	ENA 2727, f. 11 A
140.	10 + 40	D incomplete	fb	13th century	TS Misc. Box 27, f. 22*a*+
141.	10 + 40	—	sm, maybe dr	13th century	d 65 (2877), f. 8
142.	10 + 40 (perhaps groom paid only 5)	—	fb	1270	TS Misc. Box 27, f. 26+
143.	10 + 40	(plus 5 at betrothal)	—	1093	TS 13 J 2, f. 3
144.	10 + 50	No D	—	1243	TS 12.121
144*a*.	10 + 60	D promised	fb	Bilbays, 1218	TS 8 J 9, f. 13
145.	15 + 20	D 135	—	1199	TS K 15, f. 100
146.	15 + 30	D 102 + house	—	Ca. 1140	TS AS 147, f. 9
147.	15 + 35 (30 + 70)	GT 280 (560)	fg	13th century	TS Misc. Box 29, f. 29+
148.	15 + 50	D 535, GT 600	—	1059	a 3 (2873), f. 43
149.	15 + 60	—	betrothal	Ca. 1220	TS AS 147, f. 12
150.	20 + 20	D 455, GT 495	—	Ca. 1100	TS Arabic Box 6, f. 2
151.	20 + 30	D 200	—	Early 11th century	ENA 4100, f. 8
152.	20 + 30	D 240, GT 290	—	Before 1027	a 3 (2873), f. 39
153.	20 + 30	D 676	—	Ca. 1028	ENA 2738, f. 33
154.	20 + 30	—	Karaites	1040/1041	Mosseri A 90.1
155.	20 + 30	—	—	1131	TS 8 J 17, f. 9*a-c*

Marriage gift	Dowry	Status	Place, date	MS mark
156. 20 + 40	—	—	1133	ENA 2806, f. 11 + 2727, f. 18*bv*+
157. 20 + 40	D incomplete	—	1156	Firkovitch II, 1700, f. 13*b*
158. 20 + 50	—	—	1025	Mosseri A 7*v*
159. 20 + 50	D 649, GT 719	Karaite w	1117	a 3 (2873), f. 42+
160. 20 + 50	D incomplete	—	1156	Firkovitch II, 1700, f. 27
161. (5 + 15 =) 20 + 50/60	—	fg	Ca. 1140	Mosseri A 10.1
162. 25 + 10 (= 35)	—	See B, 2, nn. 84-90	Spring, 933	TS 16.181, item I+
163. 25 + 15 (= 40)	D 262 + apartment	See B, 2, nn. 84-90	March, 933	TS 16.181, item IV+
164. 25 + 200 (= 225)	D 395	See B, 2, nn. 84-90	March, 956	d 65 (2877), f. 30+
165. 30 + 50	D several hundred	—	10th century	TS 16.173
166. 30 + 50	D about 640, GT 720	fg	1050	TS 20.7
167. 30 + 50	D 340, GT 420	—	Probably Cairo, ca. 1110	TS 10 J 21, f. 4
168. 30 + 60	(No D)	—	al-Maḥalla, 1160	TS 8 J 5, f. 21
169. 30 + 70	D not preserved	—	Ca. 1250	TS 8.102

170.	30 + 80	D incomplete, jewelry 155	—	1159	TS 13 J 3, f. 10, item III
171.	30 + 100	D 450 at least	—	Ca. 1100	ENA 2808, f. 13
172.	40 + 57	D 130	fg	1499	b 12 (2875), f. 3
173.	40 + 60	—	Karaite	Cairo, 999	ENA NS 17, f. 24
174.	40 + 60	D 390	w	Ca. 1145	TS 8.168
175.	40 + 60	D 60	(d)	Ca. 1510	TS Misc. Box 28, f. 266
176.	40 + 60	See B, 5, n. 2	—	—	TS 13 J 8, f. 24
177.	40 + 80	D large frag.	fg	—	ENA 2747, fs. 1 and 2, and ENA 3652, f. 8
178.	40 + 100	D 500	fb	1146	d 66 (2878), f. 47-48+*
179.	40 + 100	—	—	Alexandria, 1201	Maimonides, 138-144
180.	(15 + 35 =) 50 + 20	—	—	Damascus, 933	TS 16.181 II+
181.	50 + 40	D 18 lines	—	—	ENA 2743, f. 2
182.	(20 + 30=) 50 + 70/90 = 120/140	—	fg	Ca. 1100	TS 8 J 9, f. 9
183.	51 + 60	See B, 2, nn. 31, 32	—	Ca. 1200	TS 8.112
184.	50 + 100	heiress	—	Barqa, 990	a 2 (2805), f. 2+
185.	50 + 100	D 80	—	Ca. 1080	d 65 (2877), f. 11
186.	50 + 100	D 520, GT 670	fb	1156	Firkovitch II, 1700, f. 24*a*-25*b*
187.	50 + 100	D 723+	—	1156	Firkovitch II, 1700, f. 25*b*-26*b*

Marriage gift	Dowry	Status	Place, date	MS mark
188. 55 + 100	D not preserved	—	1094	TS 18 J 1, f. 14
189. 80 + 120	—	fb, w	11th century	TS 24.45
190. 100 + 150 = 250	—	—	1007	TS 18 J 1, f. 3+
191. 100 + 150	See B, 1, n. 38	—	1051	Mosseri A 2+
192. 100 + 200	See B, 4, n. 92	—	Ca. 1030	TS 16.50
193. 100 + 200	See B, 1, n. 33	—	Ca. 1050	TS Misc. Box 29, f. 58
194. 100 + 200	D 800, GT 1100 (+)	fg	1082	TS 24.1+
195. 200 + 100 = 300	—	—	(Tyre), 1080	8.129+
196. 200 + 300	See B, 4, n. 96	—	1033	TS 13 J 32+
		ONLY A KNOWN		
197. A 20 dirhems	—	fb	—	TS Arabic Box 30, f. 8
198. A 1	See B, 2, n. 81	—	1132	TS 8 J 17, f. 9*d*
199. A 1 1/2 or 2 1/2	—	dr	1229	ULC Or 1081 J 40
200. A 2	D 1/2 line	sm	Ca. 1100	TS 8.238
201. A 2	D 19 items	fg	1100-1138	TS NS 184, f. 90
202. A 2	D frag.	sm	1132/1133	TS 12.653
203. A 3	—	sm	1125/1126	TS 8 J 32, f. 1+
204. A 3	D 77 1/2, incl. 1/2 house worth 20	Karaite	—	b 12 (2875), f. 31

205. A 4	—	sm	1033/1034	Westminster College, Arabica, I, fs. 76 and 40b, Frag. Cairens., 105
206. A 5	—	Karaite	Ca. 1050	ENA NS 18, f. 37
207. A 5	GT 55	—	1063	b 11 (2874, 33), f. 34
208. A 5	—	—	—	TS 12.640
209. A 5	D (part of) house	—	—	TS 10 J 28, f. 1
210. A 5 (2 cash, 3 jewelry)	D frag.	fb	Tyre, ca. 1100	TS 16.198
211. A 10	D 81 1/2	Karaite	Ca. 1000	TS 20.156
212. A 10	GT 95	—	Ca. 1125	TS 20.151
213. A 10	GT 200	fg, d	Ca. 1125	TS 24.16
214. A 10	D only beginning	—	1030	TS 12.489
215. A 18 (only 10 received)	See D, n. 163	—	1095	TS 8 J 5, f. 16
216. A 10 plus 1/2 house	—	—	—	ENA NS 3, f. 19*a*
217. A 15	—	—	1023/1024	Westminster College, Frag. Cairens., 125
218. A 15	—	fb	Nov., 1026	TS 8 J 6, f. 18*a-c*
219. A 15	See B, 2, n. 83	—	Dec., 1026	TS 8 J 4, f. 2*b*
220. A 15	See B, 2, n. 2	(d)	1138	TS NS J 278
221. A 15	GT 360. 1/4 house	fg	Oct., 1155	TS 20.8 + 12.552

Marriage gift	Dowry	Status	Place, date	MS mark
222. A 15	—	broken engagement	1241	JNUL 4° 577/5, f. 41*v*
223. A 20	D 30 (house and part of other property)	fb	979/980	TS 24.35*v*$^{+}$
224. A 20	D house in Cairo, servant	—	Ca. 1030	TS 16.32
225. A 20	D frag.	—	Ca. 1040	TS 12.131
226. A 20	D substantial	—	Ca. 1130	ENA NS 7, f. 20
227. A 20	D 200^{+}	—	12th century	TS NS J 390
228. A 20	—	—	1239/1240	TS 20.77
229. A 25	D 250+, GT 380+	fb, fg	Sept., 1037	TS 20.6^{+}
230. A 25	D valuable	—	(Damascus?) 10th century	TS 12.118^{+}
231. A 30	D valuable	—	Early 11th century	Westminster College, Frag. Cairens., 98
232. A 30	See B, 4, n. 38	—	—	TS 10 J 21, f. 13
233. A 50	—	fg	13th century	TS 24.8
234. A 50	D 500 + (1 = 1/2)	—	14th century	TS Misc. Box 28, f. 217^{+}
235. A 50 (fine)	See B, 5, n. 7	—	—	TS NS J 378
236. A 100	D ca. 700	—	Aleppo, 1107/1108	TS 16.107

237.	A (100 + 50 =) 150	—	Karaite	Cairo, 1003/1004	TS 24.7
			ONLY B KNOWN		
238.	B 2	See C, 3, n. 6	Deathbed declaration	1241	TS 8 J 6, f. 14
239.	B (70 nuqra =) 5	—	Paid at divorce	1268	Mosseri A 18
240.	B 5	See C, 3, n. 8	Deathbed	1241	TS 13 J 3, f. 17
241.	B 7	—	dr	Ca. 1135	Bodl. b 12 (2875), f. 18
242.	B 8	—	Deathbed	1104	TS 18 J 1, f. 15
243.	B 10	See C, 1, n. 180	—	Ramle, 1015	TS 13 J 1, f. 2+
244.	B 10	See C, 1, n. 104	—	Ca. 1027	ENA 4010, f. 43
245.	B 10	—	fg, fb	Ḥāṣōr, ca. 1060	ENA NS 16, f. 6+
246.	B 10	D 73 (originally 75)	fb	1160	TS 8 J 9, f. 17*c*, item II, and *ibid*., f. 17*d*, item I
247.	B 10	D 13 1/2	—	Feb. 1164	Merx, pp. 39-43
248.	B 10	—	At divorce	Cairo, 1170	TS 13 J 3, f. 14
249.	B 10	D 75	—	Spring, 1186	f 56 (2821), f. 54, item I
250.	B 10	D 75	—	Spring, 1186	f 56 (2821), f. 54*v*, item II
251.	B 10 no A	House but no trousseau	d, w	1180-1191	ULC Or 1080 J 186
252.	B 10	—	Karaite, sm, fg	Fall, 1200, Cairo	TS 16.67
253.	B 15	See B, 5, n. 82	—	Ca. 1040	TS NS J 358

	Marriage gift	Dowry	Status	Place, date	MS mark
254.	B 15	—	Paid after death	Ca. 1060	Mosseri A 89.4
255.	B 15	—	At divorce	1148	Mosseri A 30
256.	B 15	D 33	—	1186	f 56 (2821), f. 55*v*, item II
257.	B 15	—	Deathbed declaration	1188	a 2 (2805), f. 9+
258.	B 15	—	At divorce	1217	TS NS J 412
259.	B 17	D 7	—	(Qalyūb), 13th century	TS 16.85
260.	B 20	D 200+	—	Ca. 960	TS 16.189+
261.	B 20	D little remains	—	Ca. 1030	TS 12.656
262.	B 20	See C, 1, n. 94	—	Ca. 1030	TS 8.110
263.	B 20	D 50+	—	Ca. 1030	TS 8.173
264.	B 20	D (small) and house	—	1100-1138	TS NS J 443
265.	B 20	House	—	1100-1138	BM Or 5566A 1
266.	B 25	See C, 3, n.125	—	—	TS Arabic Box 7, f. 29
267.	B 25	—	bf	Tinnīs 10th century	TS 8.133+, TS 16.210+
268.	B 25	See B, 4, n. 80	—	Ca. 1140	TS 12.771
269.	B 30	—	Deathbed	1142	TS 13 J 3, f. 2+
270.	B 30	D 55	—	1186	f 56 (2821, 16), f. 55*a* item II-*b*
271.	B 30	See B, 3, n. 106	At divorce; husband bankrupt	Alexandria, 1213	TS 24.34

272.	B 30	See C, 4, n. 28	Will of a dyer	1215	Mosseri A 11^{+}
273.	B 30, reduced from 60	See C, 3, nn. 3, 7	—	Bilbays, 1217	ULC Add. 3339 (b)
274.	B 30	D valuable	—	15th century?	TS 20.101
275.	B 30	See B, 4, n. 53	Claim after death of husband	—	TS 13 J 3, f. 10, item V
276.	B 40	D overvalued	—	11th century	TS AS 148, f. 6
277.	B 40	See D, n. 100	Paid after death of husband	1147	TS 12.544*
278.	B 40	See C, 3, n. 45	Paid after death of husband	1151	BM Or 5551*
279.	B 50 (200)	See C, 3, n. 5	Deathbed	1006	TS 18 J 1, f. 4*
280.	B 50	—	—	Ca. 1030	TS NS J 364
281.	B 50	GT 807-897	sm	1040-1050	TS 16.184
282.	B 50	D partly preserved	—	Ca. 1050	b 12 (2875), f. 5
283.	B 50	—	Deathbed + 10 gift	Ca. 1120	TS 8 J 34, f. 10 + ENA 1822 A, f. 17
284.	B 50	See C, 1, n. 207	—	Ca. 1135	TS 16.214^{+}
285.	B 50	See A, 3, n. 15	Deathbed	Ca. 1150	TS 13 J 22, f. 2^{+*}

Marriage gift	Dowry	Status	Place, date	MS mark
286. B 50	D 530	—	Ca. 1170	ULC Or 1080 Box 5, f. 15
287. B 50	(See *Med. Soc.*, I, 613, n. 5)	After death of husband	1203	c 28 (2876), f. 54
288. B 50	Important D	—	Ca. 1240	TS NS Box 324, f. 144
289. B 50	D 40 1/2 + 1/3 new house	—	—	TS 12.119+
290. B 60	—	—	11th century	ENA 3030, f. 7
291. B 60	—	Reaffirmed in will	Alexandria, ca. 1100	Westminster College, Frag. Cairens., 113
292. B 60	—	Litigation after death of husband	Ca. 1100	TS 28.19
293. B 60	D 400+	Settlement (in 1169)	1157	TS 12.585+
294. B 60, not yet received	D 186	(All overestimated?)	Bilbays, 1204	TS 13 J 5, f. 5*
295. B 60, reduced to 30	—	(All overestimated?)	Bilbays, 1217	ULC Add. 3339 (b)
296. B 70, reduced to 20	See C, 3, n. 39	—	1126	TS 18 J 1, f. 20
297. B 75 (representative of merchants)	—	Divorce	1091	ENA 4020, f. 47+*
298. B 75 (rich goldsmith)	—	Deathbed	1114	TS 8 J 5, f. 1*
299. B (or T) 100 (+?)	Jewelry 500(+?)	—	Ca. 1030	TS 20.25*v*

300. B 100	See B, 3, n. 77	–	1109-1138	TS 8.116+
301. B 100	–	–	Ca. 1135	TS 16.233
302. B 100	See C, 4, n. 72	–	Alexandria, 1207	TS 24.81*
303. B 200	See C, 1, n. 195	–	(Ca. 1030)	ULC Or 1080 J 7*
		Only (A + B =) T known		
304. T 12	–	sm	–	b 12 (2875), f. 22
305. T 15	D 27, GT 42	–	1027/8	TS 12.167
306. T 15	–	–	Qūṣ	TS 8.239
307. T 20	D incomplete	–	Ca. 1100	TS 12.95
308. T 25	–	sm	1018-1028	TS NS Box 324, f. 107
309. T 30	–	After death of husband	1159	TS 13 J 3, f. 10*e*
310. T 30	–	–	Ca. 1250	TS 8.127
311. T 31 (A 20+?)	D valuable	–	Ca. 1000	TS 16.58
312. T 35	D jewelry, house	sm	1056	b 12 (2875), f. 28
313. T 35	–	fb, fg	1120	TS 12.163
314. T 40	D 50, GT 90	fb	Minyat Ziftā, ca. 1120	TS 12.547
315. T 45	(No D)	–	13th century	d 65 (2877), f. 20
316. T 62	D incomplete	–	1100-1138	TS 8.147

Marriage gift	Dowry	Status	Place, date	MS mark
317. T 150	D jewelry 300, maid 80, most lost	—	Jan./Feb., 995	TS 16.70
318. T 150	D 600+, most lost	—	1033/1034	TS 24.12
319. T 250	D items arranged so as to form rhymes	—	—	TS K 25, f. 183
320. T 500	D 1,600, GT 2,100	—	—	TS J 1, f. 29+
		Only (T + D =) GT known		
321. GT 47 1/2	—	—	1012/1013	6 J a, f. 2
322. GT 86	—	fg	(Alexandria, ca. 1100)	ENA NS 18, f. 34
323. GT 113 (copper 20)	—	—	1003/1004	TS 12.452
324. GT 140	—	—	Ca. 1160	ENA NS 3, f. 5 (vellum)
325. GT 281	—	sm	Early 11th century	TS 8.97
326. GT 305+	—	—	Ca. 1140	TS 20.33
327. GT 600 (– 699)	—	—	Late 10th century	ENA 4020, f. 37
328. GT 700 (– 799)	—	—	11th century	TS Misc. Box 25, f. 14

		SUPPLEMENT		
329. 1 + 15 (= 16)	—	d, fg	Oct., 1116	b 12 (2875), f. 19 + TS 12.164 + TS 8.210
330. 3 + 15 = 18	D 32, GT 50	—	1033/1034	a 3 (2873), f. 45
331. 5 + 10 = 15 ashrafiyya	D 10	w	Jerusalem, Dec., 1450	b 12 (2875), f. 12
332. 6 + 10 = 16	—	sm	11th century	b 3, f. 11 (2806, 10)
333. 7 + 30	D 148, GT 185	dr	March, 1132	TS 24.15*v*, item II
334. (2 + 8 =) 10 + 20	—	fg, sm	March, 1099	TS NS J 457, p. 1
335. 10 + 30 = 40	—	—	April, 1157	BM Or 5536 II
336. 10 + 30 = 40	—	w	Minyat Ghamr, Sept., 1315	TS 12.39+
337. 10 + 60 = 70	(Promised)	fb	Bilbays, 1218	TS 8 J 9, f. 13
338. 11 + 3 = 14	(No D)	—	11th century	ENA 2779, f. 3+
339. 15 + .5	D rare items	—	11th century	b 3, f. 12 (2806, 11)
340. 20 + 20 (= 40)	D 100	—	Winter, 1186	f 56, f. 56 b II
341. (3 + 17 =) 20 + 30	—	—	Damascus, Spring, 933	TS AS 146, f. 66 I+
342. 20 + 40	"A included in D"	—	Damascus, 1089/1090 or 1189/1190	Antonin 164+
343. 20 + 50 (= 70)	—	fb	Spring, 1182	f 56 (2821), f. 46 v
344. 40 + 60	865	—	1020s	TS 12.12
345. 50 + 20	D = A	sm, fb, fg	1316	TS Misc. Box 28, f. 26+

Marriage gift	Dowry	Status	Place, date	MS mark
		Only A known		
346. A 1	—	b "a stranger"	Ca. 1158	ENA 4011, f. 5, top
347. A 11-19	D valuable	fb, fg	Tyre, 11th century	TS Arabic Box 50, f. 181 b$^+$
348. A 25	—	—	Damascus, 933	TS AS 146, f. 66, item II
		Only B known		
349. B 15	D includes part of house	—	June, 1135	TS 16.147
350. B 20	—	w	Karaite	a 3 (2873), f. 44
351. B 31-39	—	—	1089-1099	TS AS 146, f. 183$^+$
		Only T known		
352. T 5	—	dr	Ca. 1145	TS 16.246*v*
353. T 20	D visible 25	—	11th century	b 13, f. 47 (2834, 28)
354. T 40	D valuable	—	1164/1165	f 56 (2821), fs. 14*v*, 18*v*
355. T 50	—	—	Aleppo, Feb., 1026	PER H 18$^+$
		Only GT known		
356. GT 90	—	—	Damascus, 933	TS NS 320, f. 108$^+$
357. GT 230-239	—	—	12th century	TS NS 258, f. 155

TROUSSEAU LISTS UNACCOMPANIED BY DATA ABOUT MARRIAGE GIFTS FROM PART I

	Dowry	Date	Group and item in Part I	MS mark
358.	30	Ca. 1161	1, no. 20*a*	d 66 (2878), f. 77
359.	56	1171	1, no. 26	PER H 20$^+$
360.	150	982	4, no. 3	TS 16.142$^+$
361.	174	1127	5, no. 28*a*	a 2 (2805), f. 6
362.	210	(1182)	2, no. 2	f 56 (2821), f. 47*a-b*
363.	Approx. 300	1146	6, no. 7	ULC Or 1080 J 49
364.	Approx. 540	1030/1031	4, no. 31	TS 13 J 17, f. 14
365.	Approx. 750	(1142)	6, no. 3	Gottheil-Worrel XLV, pp. 220-222
366.	1,170-1,179	Early 11th century	4, no. 40	TS 16.80

Summary

The demarcation lines between the various socioeconomic groups were drawn not only in accordance with the amount of the marriage gift but also in consideration of other circumstances, such as the status of the spouses and, especially, the value of the dowry or of gifts of houses or parts of them.

Category	Item number	Total
	I. Destitute	
A less than 5	1-39, 197-203, 205, 329-330, 346	50
B less than 10	238-242	5
T 12	304, 352	2
		57
	IIa. Poor	
A + B less than 5 + 20	41/2, 45-57, 59-62, 64-66, 331-332	24
A 5	206-210	5
B 10-17	243-245, 247/8, 251-259, 349	15
T 15-20	305-307, 353	4
D 30	358	1
		49
	IIb. Very modest	
A + B 5 + 20 through 10 + 15	67, 69-89, 91-94, 96-98, 100-102	32
A 10	211/2, 214/5	4
B 20-30	261-275, 350	16
T 25	308	1
GT 47 1/2-90	40, 44, 63, 204, 246, 249, 250, 314/5, 321/2, 356	12
D 56	359	1
Special	107	1
		67
	IIc. Modest	
A + B 10 + 20 through 10 + 60	103-106, 108/9, 111-113, 115-117, 119-128, 130-136, 138-144, 334-337	39
T 30-35	309-313	5
GT 100-140	68, 90, 95, 323-324	5
		49

Category	Item number	Total
	IIIa. Lower middle class	
A + B 15 + 20 through 20 + 60	145-147, 149, 151/2, 154-158, 160-163, 339-343	21
A 15-25	216-230, 347/8	17
B 31-40	276-278, 295/6, 351	6
T 40-62	314-316, 354/5	5
GT ca. 150-380	99, 110, 114, 118, 129, 137, 172, 185, 213, 289, 294, 325, 326, 333, 357	15
D 150-359	360-363	4
		68
	IIIb. Upper middle class	
A + B 30 + 50 through 55 + 100	165-171, 173-184, 186-188, 344	23
A 30-50	231-235	5
B 50-100	279-288, 290-293, 297-302	20
GT ca. 450-800	43, 58, 148, 150, 153, 159, 164, 281, 327/8	10
D ca. 500-750	364/5	2
		60
	IV. Wealthy	
A + B 80 + 120 through 200 + 300	189-196	8
A 100	237/8	2
B 200	303	1
T 150-500	317-320	4
D 1000+	366	1
		16
	Totals	
	I. Destitute	57
	IIa. Poor	49
	IIb. Very Modest	67
	IIc. Modest	49
	Subtotal	165
	IIIa. Lower Middle Class	68
	IIIb. Upper Middle Class	60
	Subtotal	128
	IV. Wealthy	16
	Total	366

Since the poor had more opportunity to leave their family papers with the courts, and hence in the Geniza, than those better off, the actual economic situation of the community might have been somewhat better than indicated by the analysis. But their business letters and contracts (*Med. Soc.*, I. 214-217) indicate that there could not have been much difference between the picture emerging from the Geniza and reality.

The lists and the summary are a first attempt at arranging the vast Geniza material on the economic aspects of marriage in a semblance of statistics. The pronounced stratification of the society emerging from them is remarkable. Naturally, no claim to completeness is made. The multifarious realities of the economics of marriage must be studied in the light of the entire material presented in this volume.

Additional Items

These items are not included in the preceding Summary. The socioeconomic group to which each case belongs is indicated in the last column.

(Note: no. 144*a* (IIc) is not included in the Summary.)

	Marriage gift	Dowry	Status	Date	MS mark	Socioeconomic group
367.	5 + 9	4 items!	sm	Ca. 1100	TS K 15, f. 111, col. II, item *b*	I
368.	5 + 20	(70) GT 95	fb	Ca. 1100	*Ibid*., col. I	IIb
369.	5 + 20 (or 15)	—	—	1081	TS 12.1*v*, see B 3, n. 79	IIa
370.	10 + 12 ?	GT 238	—	1100-1138	TS J 1, f. 48	IIIa
371.	10 + 30 = 40	95 +	(sm, see B 2, n. 2)	Before 1080	TS 20.47v	IIc
372.	20 (+ 30) = 50	GT 400 +	—	11th century	TS 13 J 7, f. 8	IIIa
373.	B 35	160	—	Early 13th century	TS K 25, f. 269, see B 4, n. 63	IIIa
374.	—	GT 95	—	Ca. 1165	ENA 1822 A, f. 10, see App. I, 31	IIc

Additional Items (Continued)

Marriage gift	Dowry	Status	Date	MS mark	Socioeconomic group
375. 15 Malikī (Yemen) worth ca. 5	120 +	w	Ca. 1060	ENA NS 2, f. 25, cont. in ENA NS 1, f. 13	IIc
376. A 10	277	fb	Karaite, Ca. 1020	TS 13 J 37, f. 11	IIIa
377. 30 + 70	GT 500^{+}	see C, 3 n. 114	divorced 1114	ULC Or 1081 J 56	IIIb
378. –	GT 322	–	12th century	TS 12.519	IIIa
379. –	145	see B, 4, n. 37	Ca. 1230	TS 13 J 6, f. 9	IIc

Notes

Notes

CHAPTER VIII: *The Family*

A. "THE HOUSE OF THE FATHER": THE EXTENDED FAMILY

Introduction

[1]Thus in the old Palestinian marriage contracts: *'bhth,* ENA 4010, f. 36 + PER H 1, Tyre, 1079, ed. Friedman, *Marriage,* no. 11.

[2]The usual designation for the extended family is *bayt,* "house," taking the strange form *baytat* when combined with a name, for instance, *baytat al-dayyān,* "the House of the Judge" (TS K 15, f. 63*v*, l. 1) and so throughout the superscriptions of the pedigrees of twenty Karaite families (Mann, *Texts,* II, 257–283). Occasionally, *bayta* is used unconnected with a name. Thus a grandfather is described as *nūr al-bayta,* "the light of the [extended] family" (TS 20.174*v*, l. 15). Equally common is the term *'itra,* popular perhaps at that time because the dynasty ruling Egypt was referred to thus. For instance, *'itrat al-Ghuzūlī* (Maker of Fishnets) (TS K 15, f. 27) or in the genealogy of Maimonides in Mann, II, 319, and others edited there, pp. 282 and 318.

Although only men appear in the genealogies of the memorial lists, the women, too, belonged, of course, to the 'itra. Thus a woman writes of a relative: "She is the only one in the 'itra who has preserved feelings of family attachment (*ḥanīn*)" (TS 13 J 21, f. 18, margin).

Alternately with bayt, the synonym *dār* was used. "You spoke in your letter about your marriage into the house, dār, of the Kohen. I was very happy about this; for there is no family, bayt, in Egypt better than this" (TS 13 J 16, f. 7, ll. 7–8; *Nahray* 47).

Occasionally, the term *'ashīra,* clan, tribe, is introduced, when one wishes to emphasize the extended family over the smaller one. "All close and distant relatives of hers should stop this," *an yazūl kull min ahl-hā wa-min 'ashīrat-hā* (ENA 4011, f. 17).

A man's nuclear family and his wife are referred to as *ahl* (the ancient Semitic word for "tent"), and often it is not evident whether the wife or the family is meant.

The word most commonly used today, *'ā'ila,* has retained in the Geniza its original sense of "dependents," "household." E.g., TS 18 J 3, f. 5: *'abd-hā fī 'ashara min al-'ā'ila,* "your servant's household comprises ten dependents."

[3]Heb. *ba'alē battīm* is probably influenced by Ar. *ahl al-buyūt,* see TS 12.146, l. 24; Mann, *Texts,* I, 190; TS 10 J 13, f. 13, l. 12; TS 13 J 21, f. 5, l. 25^{+}; see also A, 3, n. 68.

1. *Honoring Ancestors and Agnates: Memorial Services and Family-oriented Names*

[1]For a bibliography of memorial lists published see Mann, *Texts,* II, 257 n. 4, and *Med. Soc.,* II, 163 and 554 nn. 28–31. Many more have been found since.

[2]Rabbi David Ibn Abī Zimra (born in Spain in 1479, arrived in Egypt around 1512), cited by Mann, *Texts,* II, 256 n. 1.

[3]Dropsie 461, ed. Julius H. Greenstone, *JQR NS,* 1 (1910–1911), 58–59. The Nagid mentioned: Moses [b. Mevōrākh], 1115–1126 (not 1124, as in *Med. Soc.,* II, 25. See Mann, I, 229, n. 1, and Mann (1970), I, xxviii).

[4]Hebrew Union College, Cincinnati, Geniza MS 4, ed. Mann, *Texts,* I, 472; *shlwm* (see *ibid.,* n. 76) is correct and is to be read *shillūm.*

[5]Such as the detailed memorial of twenty Karaite families, edited by Mann, *Texts,* II, 256–283. It lists also the living members and notes at some of them "deceased," which shows that the list was executed with a view to be used for a prolonged period.

[6]This merchant was a descendant in the fifth generation of Judah b. Joseph ha-Kohen, the leading religious authority of the Jewish community in Egypt in the third quarter of the eleventh century. See about him Goitein, *Letters,* p. 173, n. 2.

[7]ULC Or 1080 J 149. The sequence of generations is the same as in the memorial list edited in Mann, II, 319, and that given by Maimonides himself in the concluding sentence of his commentary of the Mishna, ed. Joseph Qāfeḥ (Jerusalem, 1968), VI, 738. There the editor, a Yemenite rabbi, provides his own pedigree (thirteen generations).

[8]The letter: TS 12.780, bottom, addressed to Nahray b. Nissīm. The inscription: *EJ,* III, 335 (photo and full translation).

[9]ULC Add. 3348, 1. 13.

[10]Collapse of a house: ENA 2592, f. 24, 1. 13. Drowning: *ibid.,* 1. 12. Shipwreck, e.g., TS K 15, f. 4*v*, Arabic Box 6, f. 28, 1. 11. Murder: Mann, *Texts,* II: p. 270, l. 246; p. 276, l. 361; p. 281, l. 484. Dying for God's sake: Dropsie 461[+] (see n. 3, above), p. 57, 1. 17. Six sons: see sec. C, 2, n. 113, below.

[11]Cf. Mann, II, 50 ff., 281 ff.

[12]TS K 15, f. 4*v*: *bayt f'ṭl,* which is to be understood as Fāḍil.

[13]E.g., in a marriage contract from Aswān, A.D. 948, Oriental Institute, Chicago, Nr. 10552, ed. N. Abbott, *ZDMG,* 95 (1941), 59–77, ll. 18, 19, 23, 25, 26, 27 etc.; Grohmann, *APEL,* I, 111, 1. 27.

[14]Mann, II, 319, see my corrections in the 1970 reprint, p. xxxv. Maimonides had at least three sisters; we know the name of one, Miriam, who wrote him the letter TS 10 J 18, f. 1, ed. S. D. Goitein, *Tarbiz,* 32 (1963), 188–191, see C, 2, n. 94, below.

[15]ULC Add. 3343, margin and *verso,* 1. 3. The family of the writer of this letter, Solomon b. Elijah, originated in Palestine; thus the wife of his uncle probably was from one of the ancient Gaonic families there.

[16]TS K 15, f. 7, Mann, II, 270. The lineage contains each of the names Joshua and Dosa four times. For *sār*(?) I am inclined to read *mār*, lord.

[17]Samuel b. Hanania: Bodl. MS Heb. f 61, f. 46 (Cat. 2855, no. 8), ed. Mann, II, 282. Ben bat Shā'ūl: Mosseri A, f. 7 (settlement between Dā'ūd b. Mūsa, "the Son of the daughter of Saul," and his divorcée ʿAzīza b. Ḥusayn b. David, March, 1038, in Arabic). "Name of the fathers": TS AS 147, f. 2, l. 24, a letter from Jerusalem, written around 1085.

[18]TS Arabic Box 6, f. 28. A Levite is second in rank to a Kohen (that is, descendant of the priests who officiated in the Temple of Jerusalem) and has precedence over a simple Jew at the synagogue service. In many Geniza documents Levites sign beneath Kohens and above others.

[19]See Goitein, *Letters,* nos. 38, 39, 41. Further details about the family in *India Book.*

[20]Mann, *Texts,* I, 185–186.

[21]For Ibn Yijū (today, in French spelling: Bénichou) see M. Eisenbeth, *Les Juifs de l'Afrique du Nord, démographie et onomastique* (Algiers, 1936), p. 98; for Ibn Jāmi see *EI,* s.v. Gabes.

[22]S. D. Goitein, "La Tunisie du XIe siècle a la lumière des documents de la Geniza du Caire," *Lévi-Provençal Memorial Volume* (Paris, 1962), p. 568. Details in this genealogy have been corrected in subsequent publications.

[23]Goitein, *Letters,* pp. 186 and 206. Moses b. Ghulayb, TS Arabic Box 18 (2), f. 4 (end of eleventh century), ed. Assaf, *Texts,* pp. 43–47, was a grandson of

Moses b. Ghulayb, AIU VII D 4*c**, dated July 24, 1027. The editor, who was not aware of the repetition of the names in the family, had great difficulty in placing the document chronologically.

[24]Mann, II, 102 and passim.

[25]"They cannot be his sons, as one of them was called Joseph, and Judah's father was still alive" (Mann, *Texts,* I, 116 n. 15).

[26]Dropsie 332, ed. Schechter, *Saadyana,* pp. 23–26, who omits, however, the detailed Arabic address, from which the information provided by me is derived. "Grandfather" translates Heb. *zeqēnkhem,* but it is not excluded that Saadya may have used the word in the sense of Ar. *shaykh,* where it may also mean "father." But the letter is addressed "to the store of 'Alī b. Sulaymān" and the Gaon writes to the three sons because they had been his beloved students. In any case, Sulaymān II was the firstborn.

[27]Judah ha-Levi, *Diwan,* ed. H. Brody (Berlin, 1894), II, 171.

[28]Midrash Bamidbar Rabba, chap. 12, sec. 10, shows that it must have been ancient Jewish usage to call a beloved little daughter "Mom": *lō zāz mēhabbevāh 'ad she-qārā ōtāh immō.*

[29]BT, Bava Mesi'a 85*a*. See also Proverbs 17:6.

[30]TS 12.425*. See C, 2, n. 6, below.

[31]The repetition of names in the kingly houses of Ghassān, who were Christians and attached to the Byzantine Empire, and of Lakhm, who ruled over the Christian town of Ḥīra and were vassals of the Sasanid kings, probably was an imitation of the ruling houses which they served.

[32]Leopold Zunz, *Namen der Juden* (Lepizig, 1837; Hildesheim, 1971), pp. 36–37. Leopold Löw, *Beitraege zur juedischen Altertumskunde,* Vol. II (Szeged, 1875), p. 94. The name Onias (Ḥōnyō), for instance, recurs six times in the genealogy of the high priests of Jerusalem (later in Egypt). Similarly, the lineage of the heads of the medieval Karaite community, who derived their origin from the kingly house of Judah, contains the name David five times, Joshiah four times, Solomon three, as well as the names of seven other members of the house of David (see Mann, II, 215).

[33]Simeon's role in the Bible was insignificant and negative. But since it sounded like Simon, a genuinely Greek name, it was popular among Jews in Hellenic times. It is extremely common in the Talmud, but not in the Geniza. Sam'ān (or Sim'ān), equally rare in the Geniza, is a genuine Arabic name.

[34]Oriental Institute, Chicago, no. 10552, ed. N. Abbott, *ZDMG,* 95 (1941), 60–65.

[35]It must be emphasized, however, that in this, as in other matters, the consistency of the Geniza people was by no means strict. I believe that at least half the people whose grandfathers are known to us did not bear the latters' names. It could be argued, of course, that in all these cases the persons concerned were not first sons. But that assumption is unlikely. Edgar R. Samuel ("New Light on the Selection of Jewish Children's Names," *Transactions of the Jewish Historical Society of England,* 23 [1971], 65) states with regard to "Portuguese" Jews of Amsterdam, London, and elsewhere: "The patterns of choosing names is rigidly prescribed; the first son is named after his paternal grandfather." It is interesting that the custom traced in the Geniza is still observed by the descendants of the Jews expelled from Spain and Portugal about five hundred years ago. But consistency was not a characteristic of the Geniza people. I owe the reference to Dr. S. C. Reif of Cambridge University.

[36]BT Gittin 84*b*–85*a*.

[37]The one case where "Lion" is rendered by Hebrew Arye was that of a man from Palermo, probably an Italian Jew: TS 8 J 5, f. 16, dated 1095.

[38]TS 24.73, dated 1047, ed. S. Assaf, *Yerushalayim* (Jerusalem, 1953), p. 115.

[39]1133: JNUL 5, ed. S. D. Goitein, *Kirjath Sepher,* 41 (1966), 267–271. 1149: TS 13 J 30, f. 2. 1150: Gottheil-Worrell VII, 32 ff. 1151: Bodl. MS Heb. a 3 (Cat. 2873), f. 5, l. 14. 1153: Bodl. MS Heb. b 11 (Cat. 2874), f. 36. 1164: Dropsie 346. 1165: TS 13 J 3, f. 12.

[40]MS (J. M.) Toledano, ed. by him in *Mizraḥ u-Ma'arav,* 1 (1920), 346.

[41]MS Friedenberg* (private proprietor in New York).

[42]1109: TS 10 J 26, f. 2. The full name Judah b. Samuel b. Judah is provided in the validation of the court. Samuel was then still alive. al-Maḥalla: Bodl. MS Heb. d 66 (Cat. 2878), f. 78, dated 1161.

[43]TS 12.815. Fifteenth century.

[44]E.g., Abū Sulaymān and Abū Saʿīd Dāʾūd [David] Ben Shaʿyā, TS 12.229, 12.372*v*, l. 4, 13 J 23, f. 15, l. 16, and his son Joseph, TS 13 J 23, f. 15, l. 31.

[45]For instance, Abu ʾl-ʿAlāʾ Yūsuf (Joseph) b. Dāʾūd Ibn Shaʿyā, see preceding note, and Goitein, *Letters,* pp. 89–95, *Med. Soc.,* I, 243; or Abū Yūsuf Yaʿqūb Ibn Shaʿyā, TS 16.150 (1057).

[46]"The well-known representative of the merchants Ben Shaʿyā," BM Or 5529, see Mann, II, 107 (dated 1055); *Med. Soc.,* I, 191. Or Abu ʾl-Faraj Ben Shaʿyā, TS 13 J 22, f. 20; TS 13 J 26, f. 8, l. 27.

[47]Caliphal rescript to be obtained through Ben Shaʿyā, TS 8 J 22, f. 10 margin, l. 5, *Nahray* 3. Also the two members of the family mentioned next.

[48]TS 20.113, l. 14⁺*, trans. S. D. Goitein, *JJS,* 3 (1952), 172.

[49]TS 16.14: "The young man Joseph b. Jacob "Head of the Assembly" (*rōsh kallā*) b. Joseph Ben Isaiah (= Ibn Shaʿyā)," Damascus 1007. The person mentioned second in n. 45, above, might have been a son of this Joseph.

[50]One prominent member of the family, a banker called Shaʿyā, lived around 1016, when the poet was at the height of his poetical creativity. TS 16.64, l. 27, where cashier's checks drawn on him are to be paid to the Jerusalem yeshiva.

[51]R. A. Nicholson, *Studies in Islamic Poetry* (Cambridge, 1921), p. 284 (Ar. text), p. 196 (trans.).

[52]*Ibid.,* p. 195, n. 3.

[53]TS NS J 9*v*, ll. 7–8*. Brockelmann, *GAL*², I, 885, l. 1. The spelling Shāya there is a mistake.

[54]TS 8 K 22, f. 6, ed. Mann, II, 318, with my correction on p. xxxv.

[55]1156: Firkovitch II, 1700, f. 1. 1160: TS 18 J 1, f. 9.

[56]Goitein, *Letters,* p. 68 n. 14. An Abū Saʿd Ibn Nānū was prominent in Alexandria in 1216: TS 10 J 25, f. 3, l. 9.

[57]TS 8 Ja 1, f. 3*v*, ll. 6–7, *India Book* 183.

[58]Ar. Azraq, Aḥwal, Ashqar, Ibn Sunaynāt, Ḥaṭib, Muzaghlil, Fashshāṭ.

[59]Also in a dated document TS 16.150 (1057).

[60]Solomon I b. Saadya I Ben Ṣaghir: TS 10 J 5, f. 15 (1021); TS 10 J 5, f. 11 (1022); TS 8 J 4, f. 2 (1026; for this and the immediately preceding item see Mann, II, 97); TS 18 J 2, f. 16*, ed. S. Assaf, *Yerushalayim* (Jerusalem, 1953), pp. 113–114 (also 1026). Saadya II b. Solomon I: TS 18 J 1 f. 7, ed. S. Assaf, *Eretz-Israel,* I (1951), 142 (where the shelf mark of the MS is misprinted as 18 J 17), dated 1037 and showing his father still alive. Public appeals: *Med. Soc.,* II, App. C, secs. 7, 8, and 137.

[61]JNUL 11, ed. Avinoam Yellin, *Kirjath Sepher,* 1 (1924), 55–61, where the name is spelled (p. 59) with *S* instead of *Ṣ,* a change commonly found.

[62]Ibn Duqmāq, V, 46.

[63]"Small" is *kuchek* in Persian; but people writing Arabic render *ch* by *j* or even *sh.* Ḥassūn b. Kushik, in the list of beneficiaries, TS NS J 179, l. 3, *Med. Soc.,* II, 441, sec. 11.

[64]ʿAmīd al-Dawla, "Support of the Government," in whose warehouse sales are made (TS 20.80*v*, ll. 20–24, *India Book* 273), who is known to the Nagid and reports to him about the practices of other merchants (TS 13 J 20, f. 2*v*, l. 10), who issues promissory notes (TS K 15, f. 91*), and who provides money to free an imprisoned man (Bodl. MS Heb. e 98, f. 63*v*, item 2).

[65]The accountancy office, *dīwān al-taḥqīq,* 1226–1228, Ibn Muyassar, p. 42.

[66]*Al-shaykh al-thiqa al-qārā Ibn Kushik,* "the trusted elder, the Karaite," sent by the sultan, TS 13 J 18 f. 7, l. 2 (a letter by the judge Elijah b. Zechariah).

[67]TS Arabic Box 41, f. 141, where he receives this appointment.

[68]Strauss, *Mamluks,* I, 281–282.

[69]*Ibid.*, p. 290.

[70]Yūsuf b. Shuʿayb Ibn *al-Naghira* (signature in document, Fez, 1138, TS 8 J 5, f. 13*, *India Book* 115*b*); *Qaṭāʾif* (*Med. Soc.*, II, 231); *Baqara* (see below); *Kammūna* (see nn. 77–81, below).

[71]Magical practices are described in *Med. Soc.*, IV, chap. X, in preparation.

[72]al-Balādhurī, *Ansāb al-Ashrāf*, vol. 5, ed. S. D. Goitein (Jerusalem, 1936), p. 75, l. 2.

[73]Ibn Abī d-Dunyā, *The Noble Qualities of Character*, ed. James A. Bellamy (Wiesbaden, 1973), p. 40, sec. 178.

[74]Abramson, *Bamerkazim*, pp. 67–68, 103–104.

[75]TS 8 Ja 2, f. 1, see Mann, II, 102–103 (who makes no mention of the addition in Arabic characters).

[76]TS 16.42, l. 35, ed. S. D. Goitein, *Tarbiz*, 38 (1968/9), 20; TS 12.367, ed. *ibid.*, 37 (1968), 70.

[77]Bodl. MS Heb. f 56 (Cat. 2821), f. 18, ed. S. D. Goitein, *JQR*, 43 (1952), 68.

[78]Ibn al-Sāʿī, *al-Jāmiʿ al-mukhtaṣar* (Baghdad, 1934), p. 165, see also Fischel, *Jews*, p. 136. "Underground prison" translates *maṭmūra*, see Dozy, *Supplément*, II, 60*b*.

[79]*Letters by Samuel b. Eli*, ed. S. Assaf (Jerusalem, 1930), p. 109, l. 5 (*Fakhr al-kufāt*). The translation "benefactors" would be appropriate for the second *kufāt*, in l. 6, if the reading is correct.

[80]Moshe Perlmann, *Ibn Kammūna's Examination of the Three Faiths* (Los Angeles and Berkeley: University of California Press, 1971), p. 1 n. 1, who mentions also a Muslim family bearing that name (descendants of a convert?).

[81]TS NS J 98, *Med. Soc.*, II, 452, sec. 47. He is referred to as the brother of a woman, Umm ʿAzīza, who is listed as a recipient of charity here and in TS NS J 239, *Med. Soc.*, II, 462, sec. 83.

[82]The founder of the family, it seems, was the cantor al-Kāmukhī (without Ben) living in Jerusalem around 1045: DK XV, l. 12. The "member of the Academy," Ben al-Kāmukhī, probably his son, appears in many communal lists in the capital of Egypt late in the eleventh and early in the twelfth century: Bodl. MS Heb. c 28 (Cat. 2876), f. 6, l. 6, TS K 15, f. 70, l. 9, both ed. Mann II, 246 and 247, TS K 15, fs. 50 and 97, see *Med. Soc.*, II, 443 and 446, as well as in a letter, TS 12.493*; also his daughter: TS NS Box 321, f. 6, l. 2, see *Med. Soc.*, II, 456. Another "member" with this name, presumably his son, lived in Fustat around the middle of the twelfth century: TS NS 246, f. 22, l. 45, ed. N. Allony, *Sefunot*, 8 (1964), 132. At the very beginning of the thirteenth century a Ben al-Kāmukhī is again in a communal list: TS NS Box 320, f. 41*a*, l. 24, see *Med. Soc.*, II, 460.

[83]TS K 15, f. 36*v*, l. 9, see *Med. Soc.*, II, 486.

[84]TS K 15, f. 70, l. 11[+]. 1229: TS 8 J 6, f. 7. 1241: 13 J 3, f. 17.

[85]See, e.g., Goitein, *Letters*, pp. 111 ff.

[86]TS 20.83; 20.122; 8.20*; 12.275; NS J 269; DK 170*b*, BM Or 5542, f. 19 (TS 12.530*).

[87]*Med. Soc.*, II, 14–15, 319–320, and *passim*. For "illustrious houses" in general see *ibid.*, I, 76–78.

[88]Scribes: *ibid.*, II, 240. Cantors: Japheth b. David (*ibid.*, p. 227), whose grandfather had been a cantor, was succeeded by his son Bishr. Eli II ha-Kohen b. Ezekiel II b. Eli I b. Ezekiel I b. Solomon, all cantors and scholars: *ibid.*, p. 575.

[89]*Med. Soc.*, I, 181.

[90]Eight generations of physicians: *Med. Soc.*, II, 245. Families connected with the government: the Ibn Faḍlāns, *ibid.*, pp. 18, 525.

[91]See C, 1, n. 215, below, and Goitein, *Letters*, p. 178, and *passim*.

[92]*Med. Soc.*, II, 446 and 460.

[93]See, e.g., W. K. Lacey, *The Family in Classical Greece* (London, 1968), pp. 16–17, 193, 219, and *passim*.

[94]Urbach, *The Sages*, pp. 439–451; *Rabbinic Anthology*, p. 819, *s.v.* "merit(s) of ancestors."

[95]The recipient's ancestors: e.g., TS 13 J 9, f. 3, l. 21 and margin*, a letter from Jerusalem to Mubārak b. Sa'āda, later, as Nagid, known as Mevōrākh b. Saadya, or TS 13 J 8, f. 4, a letter addressed to Maṣlī'aḥ Gaon. "Man's success depends on his social position," Ar. *al-insān bi-jāhih,* TS 13 J 8, f. 27, l. 27, see B, 1, n. 46, above.

2. *Horizontal Coherence: Brothers and Sisters. Endogamy*

[1]TS 13 J 26, f. 18*v*, 1. 18; *ibid.*, 11. 13–15.

[2]Known in various versions, see, e.g., Goitein, *Jemenica,* p. 5, no. 17. Here the rhyme *ummī* - *'iẓāmī* is in the mind of the writer.

[3]TS 13 J 28, f. 15, *India Book* 291, 11. 7–22.

[4]*Ibid., verso,* ll. 23–27. Another, earlier, letter by the same writer to his brother, and in the same spirit, in Gottheil-Worrell, IX, pp. 45–57, *India Book* 174. Unfortunately, the English translation does not render the text and spirit of the letter correctly. A third letter by the same sender to his brother was discovered by Dr. Gershon Weiss amid a collection of legal responsa, TS Box G 1, f. 61, *India Book* 371.

[5]Labrāṭ I had at least one son of his own: Moses II.

[6]TS 16.179*.

[7]INA, D-55, f. 13, ed. S. D. Goitein, *Tarbiz,* 36 (1966), 56–72; trans. Goitein, *Letters,* pp. 163–168.

[8]Bodl. MS Heb. b 13, f. 49 (Cat. 2834, no. 30), ll. 19–21, a letter in which the judge congratulates his brother Judah on his marriage into a fine family in Egypt.

[9]"Your ransom," e.g., TS 13 J 13, f. 12, *India Book* 98, address; TS NS J 7, *India Book* 206, l. 2. Brother's misdeeds: TS 13 J 20, f. 6, ll. 25-m*.

[10]"Your servant, his son, and that who is with him (his wife) regard themselves as belonging to your family." A cantor writing to a notable, TS 13 J 26, f. 6, l. 16.

[11]Bodl. MS Heb. f 102, f. 52, l. 2 (a lovely note to a brother). TS NS J 24*v*, l. 4 (here, even the hands of the brother's *son* are kissed).

[12]TS 13 J 13, f. 10*v*, *India Book* 125, l. 3. Feet: TS 13 J 19, f. 13, *India Book* 127, top.

[13]E.g., TS 16.264, l. 1, Joseph b. Mūsā b. Barhūn I, writing a long business letter to his brother Barhūn II. "Crown of my head": TS 10 J 29, f. 15.

[14]TS 10 J 9, f. 27, ll. 3–5, *India Book* 126.

[15]TS 13 J 22, f. 29, ll. 24–30. Peraḥyā b. Manasse and his brother Ḥalfōn (see *Med. Soc.,* II, 231) are addressed. TS 12.322, Joseph II, son of judge Peraḥyā II (Yijū), writes to his relative Samuel.

[16]MS Tchufut Kale, Crimea, 39, often quoted; of late discussed in detail by N. Allony, *Textus* (Jerusalem), 6 (1968), 108.

[17]Dropsie 332⁺, see A, 1, n. 26, above.

[18]Abraham and Tanḥūm, sons of Jacob, were addressed by the Gaons Samuel b. Ḥofnī (TS 10 J 9, f. 15 [seemingly not noted thus far]) and Sherīrā (TS 12.829, dated 1007, ed. Mann, *Texts* I, 114–123). About their questions submitted to the latter see Mann, *Texts,* I, 114 n. 11.

[19]The letters of the Berechiah brothers: Bodl. MS Heb. d 65 (Cat. 2877), f. 9, ed. S. Assaf, *J. N. Epstein Jubilee Volume* (Jerusalem, 1950), 179–185 (now available in Arabic transcript and French trans. by N. Stillman, *Hespéris Tamuda,* 13 [1972], 51–59); TS 12.175, this and the following ed. S. D. Goitein, *Tarbiz,* 34 (1965), 169–174; TS 13 J 36, f. 1, ed. *ibid.*, pp. 174–181 (trans. Stillman, *Hespéris Tamuda* pp. 42–51); TS 16.42, ed. S. D. Goitein, *Tarbiz,* 38 (1968), 18–22; TS 16.64, ed. *ibid.*, pp. 22–26.

[20]Abu 'l-Khayr Tāhertī became *ḥāvēr* in, or around 1022, TS NS Box 320, f. 16, ed. S. D. Goitein, *Salo W. Baron Jubilee Volume* (New York, 1974), pp. 506–515. His brother Isma'īl also dealt with the affairs of the yeshivas, Bodl. MS Heb. d 65 (Cat. 2877), f. 9⁺ (see preceding note), 11. 15 and 29.

[21]TS 13 J 9, f. 4*, ed. by Ashtor in Assaf, *Texts,* pp. 108–113; re-ed. with Spanish trans. E. Ashtor, *Sefarad,* 24 (1964), 47–59.

[22]*India Book* 86, ed. S. D. Goitein, *Sinai,* 16 (1953), 234–237; *India Book* 87, ed. *ibid.,* pp. 230–233. Also *India Book* 88, 89, 304 (all referring to Aden). *India Book* 99, 100 (referring to Spain), ed. *Tarbiz,* 24 (1955), 143–146, trans. with transcript into Arabic characters in *Pareja Jubilee Volume* (Madrid, 1974), pp. 133–139, esp. p. 137.

[23]Four sons: TS 13 J 34, f. 5. Five brothers with the title *ḥāvēr*: Mosseri X 107, sons of Japheth b. Yeshūʿā. Poets: Abraham Ibn Ezra praising the sons of Samuel b. Jacob Ibn Jāmiʿ, see Mann, *Texts,* I, 186; Judah al-Ḥarīzī, *Taḥkemōnī,* no. 46.

[24]Wood panel: *Med. Soc.,* II, 148, 551, n. 14. Case of Torah Scroll: ENA NS 11, f. 3, dated 1216/7.

[25]TS 13 J 8, f. 9, l. 18: four sons; 13 J 18, f. 11: the two other sons are mentioned later, in l. 15; 13 J 20, f. 28*v*, ll. 15–17: several brothers, but not mentioned by name or number.

[26]TS 13 J 19, f. 14*v*, l. 14.

[27]TS 13 J 20, f. 22, top, ll. 3–4*.

[28]E.g., TS 16.286* (brother to sister). TS 13 J 20, f. 22* (the reverse).

[29]Greeted before younger brother: TS NS J 29*v* m, ll. 2–3. "My mistress": *sayyidatī al-ukht*: TS 13 J 6, f. 22, Dropsie 411, *Nahray* 254, Moses b. Jacob writing from Jerusalem. For mother and grandmother, *sitt* is preferred to *sayyida.*

[30]Communicated to me by a woman from lower, rural Yemen, and, therefore, not included in my book *Jemenica,* which describes the language and life of the urban Jews in the High Yemen.

[31]Herodotus, 3, 119. I owe this and the following passage to Professor Erich S. Gruen of the University of California, Berkeley. The story does not fit well into the frame of the report on the plot against King Darius and might well have been invented to illustrate the idea expressed in the saying discussed.

[32]Sophocles, *Antigone,* 905–912.

[33]Henry Rosenfeld, *Hamizrah Hehadash,* 9 (1958), 34.

[34]I understand that Dr. Hasan Moh. el-Shamy of the American University, Cairo, worked during 1973–74 at the Folklore Institute of Indiana University on "The Brother-Sister Syndrome in Arabic Folkculture." Actually, this relationship is multifaceted and differs from one culture to another. For its biblical and ancient Mesopotamian type see E. A. Speiser, "The Wife-Sister Motif in the Patriarchal Narratives," *Collected Writings,* ed. J. J. Finkelstein and Moshe Greenberg (Philadelphia, 1967), pp. 62–82; A. Skaist, "The Authority of the Brother at Arrapha and Nuzi," *JAOS,* 89 (1969), 10–17.

[35]DK II, ed. Vilmos Steiner, see Shaked, *Bibliography,* p. 349, *29 (*meaning there: manuscript mark not indicated). I have not seen this Hungarian publication; I used, instead, a photostat of the original manuscript, DK II.

[36]TS 10 J 24, f. 20, l. 28, and *v*, l. 7*.

[37]For *karīma* as term for sister, not daughter, see Gaston Wiet, "Matériaux pour un Corpus Inscriptionum Arabicarum," *Mémoires . . . de l'Institut Français d'Archéologie Orientale,* 52 (Cairo, 1930), 201, and Goitein, *Studies,* p. 286. In Ḥaḍramaut *karīma* still means sister, see R. B. Serjeant, "Kinship Terms in Wādī Ḥaḍramaut," *Otto Spies Jubilee Volume* (Wiesbaden, 1967), p. 627. Dr. Mark Cohen drew my attention to Wiet's article. The term *karīm* for brother has been found by me only once, TS 10 J 15, f. 8, l. 10, an extremely polite letter addressed to Judah, "the great Rāv b. Joseph, the Kohen" (on him see Goitein, *Letters,* p. 173 n. 2).

[38]Aramaic letter: Bodl. MS Aram. e 1 (P) (Cat. 2809), written on papyrus. ENA 2738, f. 32. Mosseri L 49. See *Med. Soc.,* I, 163.

[39]TS 10 J 9, f. 1*. Trans. *Hadassah Magazine,* October 1973, pp. 38–39.

[40]TS 12.262*. Trans. with omissions *ibid.,* p. 38.

[41]TS 13 J 23, f. 18*v*, ll. 13–16.

[42]Mosseri L 206, 2.

[43]ENA 4020, f. 30*. About this obligation of the brother to visit the sister in childbed and bring her a present see Goitein, *Jemenica,* p. 109, no. 770. It is a very widespread custom.

[44]TS 13 J 21, f. 18, ll. 5–8. Approximately a third of the letter was torn away on its left side.

[45]*Commentary of Abraham Maimonides on Genesis and Exodus* (Arabic with Hebrew trans. by E. Wiesenberg), ed. S. D. Sassoon (London, 1959), p. 57.

[46]TS 16.286*. See *Med. Soc.*, I, 98–99.

[47]TS 10 J 7, f. 4. Cf. *Med. Soc.*, II, 373.

[48]TS 10 J 9, f. 32. Standard price: *Med. Soc.*, I, 139.

[49]TS 24.25 (around 1158).

[50]Bodl. MS Heb. f 56 (Cat. 2821), f. 12*v*, a fragment in the hand of Ḥalfōn b. Manasse, issued under Maṣlī'aḥ Gaon (1127–1139).

[51]JNUL 10, ll. 10–15.

[52]ULC Or 1080 J 40. In the hand of Ḥalfōn b. Manasse (1100–1138).

[53]TS NS J 2*, ed. and trans. S. D. Goitein, *Gratz College Anniversary Volume* (Philadelphia, 1971), pp. 92–93, 105–106.

[54]TS 10 J 17, f. 22, ll. 20–23.

[55]DK II. Bashful brother: see n. 35, above. Sisters versus wife: see C, 1, nn. 69–75.

[56]BM Or 5542, f. 6 + TS 20.169*, ll. 1 and 45, dated 1026. See Mann, II, 78 n. 7, where it was not yet recognized that the missing part of the Cambridge manuscript is found in the British Museum. A Muslim designated as sister's son: Abū Muḥammad 'Abdallah, son of the sister of the Faqīh (Muslim religious scholar), ENA 2591, f. 13, l. 16.

[57]Bodl. MS Heb. b 11 (Cat. 2874), f. 8, l. 9, ed. Mann, II, 29. This fragmentary document is at least twenty years older than the one dated 1026 and cited in the preceding note. No "sister's son" should be added here as assumed by Mann. A similar case of the son of the sister of a representative of merchants in Goitein, *Letters,* p. 109 n. 5 (in Ramle, Palestine). Muḥsin b. Sham'ān: MS Reinach IV, ed. M. Schwab, *REJ,* 70 (1920), 59.

[58]Mann, *Texts,* II, 323.

[59]TS NS Box 312, f. 82, ed. Abramson, *Bamerkazim,* p. 33.

[60]See *Med. Soc.*, II, 577 n. 37.

[61] 'Arūs: see *Med. Soc.*, I, 531, s.v. "My father" (Ar. *wālidī*): TS 10 J 16, f. 1. *India Book* 143, l. 1; *abbā mārī, ibid.,* address. TS 12.7 *India Book* 144*a,* l. 11. Debts: Gottheil-Worrell, I, pp. 1–11.

[62]TS 16.293, letter of congratulation on a marriage with a girl whose brother was a fine scholar. BT, Bava Batra 110*a*. Goitein, *Jemenica,* nos. 437 and 922. S. Hayat, "The Family in the Proverbs of Iraqi Jews," *Folklore Studies* (Jerusalem), 3 (1972), 80, no. 21 (Heb.), more than twenty parallels from other Arabic vernaculars.

[63]Ar. *al-tarbiya wal-ahliyya wal-maḥabba,* ENA 1822 A, f. 49*v*, l. 2.

[64]BM Or 5542, f. 5, dated 1064.

[65]TS 13 J 24, f. 23. Late, perhaps fourteenth century.

[66]Legal document: TS 12.8 + 10 J 4, f. 9 (two fragments that belong together), Alexandria, 107(0–9), last digit of year not preserved. Contributors: e.g., Bodl. MS Heb. e 94, f. 21, col. II, ll. 3–4, *Med. Soc.*, II, 476, sec. 15 (around 1100). Passengers: TS 8 J 27, f. 2, *Nahray* 95, l. 8. Information: DK XV, l. 6 (ca. 1040); TS 8 J 19, f. 25, l. 5 (same time, approximately), TS 13 J 14, f. 25, ll. 6–7 (ca. 1140); Westminster College, Frag. Cairens. 43*v*, l. 2 (ca. 1230). Letter of Gaon: TS 10 J 25, f. 8, ll. 8, 16–17, ed. S. Assaf, *Tarbiz,* 11 (1940), 158.

[67]For instance, Ibn Abī 'Uqba's sister's son in TS 12.124, l. 11, ed. S. D. Goitein, *Tarbiz,* 37 (1968), 59, is no doubt identical with Ya'qūb b. Isma'il Ibn ukht Ibn Abī 'Uqba in TS 8 J 18, f. 14, l. 7, ed. *ibid.,* p. 48. In line 12 he is again referred to simply as his uncle's nephew. A sister's son growing up in his uncle's house: see n. 80, no. 11, below.

[68]The sister's daughter is the wife whom a husband would never disgrace, even if she conceived from another man in his absence, BT, Gittin 17*a*, 26*b*, and elsewhere. It is interesting that the gaonic commentator remarks: "It could be of course

also his brother's daughter, or any other wife [whom her husband would be reluctant to expose]" (A. Harkavy, *Responsen der Geonim* [Berlin, 1887], p. 185, no. 366).

Since statistics about the marriage to a niece are difficult to come by, I might provide details from my own family. Among the fifteen children of my great-great-grandmother there were two such cases:

	I	II
Sister born in	1826	1829
Brother born in	1846	1851
Niece born in	1852	1855

A difference of four to six years in the ages of the spouses was normal in those days. A daughter of couple I married a cousin. Couple II produced two sons.

[69]Qayrawān: TS 13 J 18, f. 13, *Nahray* 170, section F, l. 1: Nissīm b. Isḥāq Tāhertī, making accounts for his dead brother Barhun II, notes very considerable sums spent for the alimony of the latter's "sister's daughter." Had this been merely a relative of the two brothers, the entire wording of the passage had to be different. Divorce threatened: TS 10 J 19, f. 7, l. 12. Engagement broken off: JNUL 4⁰ 577/4, f. 41, Fustat, 1241.

[70]TS 18 J 3, f. 4. The family relations in this important letter by a woman are understood by me thus:

Joshia
- Son (married to the writer)
- Moses I
  - The writer of the letter
    - Abu 'l-Khayr (that is, Moses II)
- Joseph
  - Sitt al-Nās, (married to Abu 'l-Khayr)

'Amma, "paternal aunt," designates not only the father's sister, but also his sister-in-law.

[71]Leon Nemoy, "The Epistle of Sahl Ben Maṣlīaḥ," *Proceedings of the American Academy for Jewish Research,* 38–39 (1972), 155.

[72]Paul Bourdieu, *Esquisse d'une théorie de la pratique précédé de trois études d'ethnologie kabyle* (Geneva, 1972), pp. 71–151. See also J. Chelhod, "Le mariage avec la cousine parallele dans le système arabe," *L'Homme,* 5 (1965), 113–173, and Richard T. Antoun, "Anthropology," in *The Study of the Middle East,* ed. L. Binder (New York, 1976), pp. 166–169.

[73]Harvey E. Goldberg, "FBD Marriage and Demography among Tripolitanian Jews in Israel," *Southwestern Journal of Anthropology,* 23 (1967), 176–191. See also the same author's *Cave Dwellers and Citrus Growers* (Cambridge University Press, 1972), pp. 34–45; Meinardus, *Christian Egypt,* p. 283.

[74]Bodl. MS Heb. b 13, f. 49 (Cat. 2834, no. 30), l. 15. Z. W. Falk ("Endogamy in Israel," *Tarbiz,* 62 [1963], 19–34) treats ancient times, not the Middle Ages.

[75]Wherever husband and wife appear as co-owners of a property, they were heirs to, or had received gifts from, their parents who had inherited or been given it from their father, mother, or another relative. See, e.g., n. 81, below.

[76]Tosefta Qiddushin 1:4: "A man should not marry until his sister's daughter grows up, or until he finds a girl from a family with his own standards." See also n. 68, above.

[77]Private MS marked AJ (acquired in Cairo in summer 1972), ll. 17–18. (AJ are the initials of the proprietor, who wishes to remain anonymous.)

[78](1) TS 24.7 (Heb., as all Karaite documents); incomplete. (2) TS 8 J 6, f. 18 *d.* (3) TS 18 J 13, f. 2, transl. C, 1, n. 242, below. (4) TS 13 J 19, f. 2, margin. (5) Firkovitch II, 1700, f. 10 *a,* no. I. (6) *Ibid.,* f. 27, *India Book* 334. (7) Bodl. MS Heb. f 56

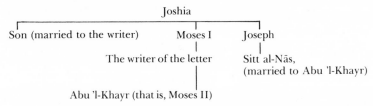

(Cat. 2821, no. 16), f. 51. (8) TS 12.678. (9) TS NS J 183. (10) TS Misc. Box 29, f. 29, ed. Strauss-Ashtor, *Mamluks,* III, 32–37. (11) Bodl. MS Heb. b 12 (Cat. 2875), f. 10, written by Ḥalfōn b. Manasse.

[79](1) TS 12.252; Misgaviyā (a pseudo-biblical name) b. Moses writes to the well-known Jacob *he-ḥāvēr* b. Joseph *Av.* (2) DK 3, see Goitein, *Letters,* p. 243 n. 13 (3–4) TS 10 J 9, f. 13; an extraordinary document of female suffering, see C, 1, n. 82, below. (5) TS 10 J 15, f. 26*. (6) TS 13 J 21, f. 14. (7) ULC Or 1081 J 5. (8) TS 12.789. (9) Mosseri L 268. (10) TS 24.67, see *Med. Soc.,* II, 250, 576 n. 44. (11) Dropsie 398, cf. l. 11. (12) TS 12.69*v*, l. 19, ed. L. A. Motzkin, *Z. Avneri Memorial Volume* (Haifa, 1970), pp. 171–172; also Bodl. MS Heb. c 28 (Cat. 2876), f. 64 and TS 13 J 8, f. 22; L. A. Motzkin's remarks about the family in *JJS,* 21 (1970), 157 n. 59 need some slight revision. (13) TS 16.286*v*, ll. 15 and 28*. (14) TS 18 J 3, f. 4; see n. 70, above. (15) ENA NS 22, f. 27.

[80](1) ENA 4020, f. 24, ed. Mann, II, 115, see *ibid.,* n. 1, and Mann (1970); happy marriage: *ibid.,* l. 4. "I am 'found,' not 'f[ind]' "; Heb. *anī māṣā lō m[ōṣē],* see C, 1, n. 28, below. (2) ULC Or 1080 J 90; the writer calls his future mother-in-law "maternal aunt," which can be a term of endearment; otherwise, this might be a case of a marriage with the daughter of a mother's sister. (3) Bodl. MS Heb. d 66 (Cat. 2878), f. 58. (4) Bodl. MS Heb. c 28 (Cat. 2876), f. 52 margin, end. (5) TS 13 J 3, f. 3*, ed. S. D. Goitein, *Sefunot,* 8 (1964), 122–125. (6) Mosseri A 156. (7) Bodl. MS Heb. f 56 (Cat. 2821), f. 45*a*. (8) See n. 79, no. 12, above. (9) TS Arabic Box 6, f. 28, l. 16, see. C, 1, nn. 208–210, below. (10) TS 10 J 11, f. 13, margin. (11) TS NS Box 184, fs. 58 + 62 + 50, combined with fs. 71 + 70 + 74, and f. 72.

[81]TS NS J 32, see *Med. Soc.,* I, 141.

[82]See n. 79, no. 12, and n. 78, no. 4, above.

[83]Sittūna bint Sulaymān b. Hiba, known as *Sirāj,* was married to Mūsā b. Khalaf (deceased) in 1063 (TS 20.187), and her sister Nājiya to Isaac b. Khalaf (deceased) in 1074 (TS 28.6, sec. C).

[84]Goitein, *Letters,* p. 211 n. 18.

[85]*Ahimaaz Chronicle,* ed. Benjamin Klar (Jerusalem, 1944), pp. 32–34, the poem on pp. 72 ff., bibliography on p. 130.

[86]*The Toledoth Ha-Ari* (Luria's Biography), ed. Meir Benayahu (Jerusalem, 1967), pp. 152–153.

3. *Economic and Legal Aspects of the Extended Family*

[1]BM Or 5566 D, f. 6, *India Book* 152, trans. Goitein, *Letters,* pp. 197–201 (in, or around, 1141). I assumed there that the India traveler might have left a sum for the common household.

[2]TS 13 J 18 f. 27*.

[3]The continuation of the letter shows that the addressee lived in the house of his mother-in-law and had not reported her estate, which contained among other things books, in which the writer was particularly interested and which he asked to be forwarded to him.

[4]This blessing normally refers to a dead person. But, as the continuation shows, here it is used ironically. Four thousand gold pieces had a purchasing power of about half a million dollars—probably a vastly exaggerated figure.

[5]The kerchief (*mandīl*) was a present to the recipient's wife (mentioned first, because she was the writer's sister), the turban to Mufaḍḍal himself. A Muslim was chosen as the go-between to keep the matter secret, so that the father of the girl would not lose face, in case the other side stalled. As the preceding paragraph shows, Jews did commute between Egypt and India in those days.

[6]A son should "serve" his mother and not travel away from her when she is old. She should die in his arms. See C, 2.

[7]TS 10 J 18, f. 10, *India Book* 175, ll. 1–20.

[8]Joseph Ḥubārāh, *Hardships in Yemen and in Jerusalem* (in Heb.) (Jerusalem, 1970), pp. 26–28. Historic documents about family synagogues in the Jewish town

outside San'a in *Boi Teman,* ed. J. Ratzaby (Tel Aviv, 1967), pp. 230–243. About the ancient quarter within the city walls see my Appendix to Carl Rathjens, *Jewish Domestic Architecture in San'a, Yemen* (Jerusalem, 1957). Map of the Jewish town in Joseph Kafih (Qāfeḥ), *Jewish Life in San'a* (Heb.) (Jerusalem, 1961), at the end of the volume. The Ḥubārāhs held that their synagogue was particularly holy and told awesome stories about its magical power; I narrated one in *Davar Literary Supplement,* Nov. 13, 1931. Ḥubārāh (actually ḥubārā) is "bustard" in classical Arabic, a bird proverbial for its foolishness because, allegedly, it forsakes its own nest and guards the nests of others. No one today knows the meaning of the name, a sign of its antiquity.

[9]See *Med. Soc.,* II, 243.

[10]Like the letters translated in Goitein, *Letters,* pp. 34–38, 73–79, or MS Meunier, ed. I, Ben-Zvi, *Zion,* 3 (1938), 180.

[11]See the prominence of foreigners in the lists of beneficiaries, *Med. Soc.,* II, 429, 432, 438, 440–543, and passim.

[12]TS 28.3. See *Med. Soc.,* I, 192 and 447 n. 26.

[13]Mosseri A 82.

[14]Bodl. MS Heb. b 12 (Cat. 2875), ff. 6 and 29+*.

[15]TS 12.499 (969), ed. S. Assaf, *Tarbiz,* 9 (1938), 205–206; TS 13 J 22, f. 2* (ca. 1140), ed. S. D. Goitein, *Sefunot,* 8 (1964), 111–113; Firkovitch II, 1700, f. 22 (1156). Here a brother gives one half of the house and the adjacent ruin to his sister.

[16]TS K 25, f. 251*, ed. and trans. S. D. Goitein, *Robert S. Lopez Jubilee Volume* (New Haven, in press); *ibid.,* f. 284+*, ed. and trans. S. D. Goitein, *Mélanges Le Tourneau* (Aix-en-Provence, 1973), pp. 406–412.

[17]TS 8 J 34, f. 4*.

[18]Half a century: TS 16.5 (1076) and TS 16.356 (1120). Litigation: TS 18 J 2, f. 5. Written by Ḥalfōn b. Manasse (1100–1138).

[19]Gift at marriage: Firkovitch II, 1700, ff. 24–25. Deathbed: TS Misc. Box 24, f. 137, p. 4*v**.

[20]Mosseri A 67, 2 (1040–1140).

[21]TS Arabic Box 53, f. 60, l. 2, "abandoned": *al-dārayn al-kharāb al-wāqifa,* "still standing." The site: *al-'araṣa allatī fīhā al-dārayn* (l. 6). The buyer Ḥassān b. Ibrāhīm b. Azhar is known from documents dated 1076 through 1103. Baghdad: George Makdisi, "Topography of Eleventh Century Baghdad," *Arabica,* 6 (1959), 287.

[22]TS Arabic Box 38, f. 102, a small fragment of a large document in Arabic characters, sufficiently preserved for establishing the main points.

[23]TS 8 J 4, f. 13, and TS 20.92, ed. S. D. Goitein, *Eretz-Israel,* 8 (1967), 288–293, dated 1094 and 1095.

[24]TS Arabic Box 51, f. 103. Ṣedāqā b. Abraham Ibn Warda ("Mr. Rose") gives, with the consent of his wife, one half of a newly erected house to his daughter Sitt al-Khawāt ("Mistress of her sisters") on her marriage to Hillel b. Naḥmān, spring, 1124.

[25]TS 13 J 3, f. 3+*, see A, 2, n. 80, no. 5. above. Dated 1143.

[26]Dropsie 335, March 15, 1041. Two drafts: in the first Nahum b. Faraḥ gives his sisters Munā and Sittūna a house in the Mashshāṭ street, al-Ja'fariyya quarter of Ṣahrajt; in the second part of the second draft only Sittūna is mentioned.

[27]TS 16.132. al-Banā near Fāqūs in Lower Egypt. Dated 998.

[28]ULC Or 1080 J 30. Good hand and style. "Good company": *ḥusn al-'ishra.* Boy writing to father: DK X*, translated in full below, see C, 1, nn. 159–163, below.

[29]TS 12.780*v*, ll. 1–4. Religious merit: *zekhūth* (Heb.).

[30]TS 10 J 4, f. 7* (1181). See *Med. Soc.,* I, 182.

[31]TS 20.174, ll. 38–39, Solomon b. Elijah, writing, it seems, to his uncle. TS NS J 29, l. 22, Abū Zikrī, the physician, Solomon's brother, using similar expressions of such desires.

[32]Subsections B, 4, and C, 1, below.

[33]INA D-55, f. 8* (Jan., 1061).

[34]Bodl. MS Heb. a 3 (Cat. 2873), f. 16* (Summer, 1240). Cf. *Med. Soc.,* I, 367.

[35]TS NS Box 321, f. 50* (together with TS Box 28, f. 263*, *India Book* 212).

[36]Mosseri A 125*.

[37]Goitein, *Letters,* p. 116; also pp. 255–257, where the very young son elicits from his father the promise to send him overseas. See also *Med. Soc.,* II, 191.

[38]Goitein, *Letters,* p. 30.

[39]Not requesting accounts: *Med. Soc.,* I, 204–205. Three brothers and two cousins: TS 10 J 12, f. 4.

[40]TS 16.279+, ll. 7–11.

[41]TS 10 J 7, f. 6, sec. a.

[42]TS 13 J 8, f. 20*.

[43]TS 13 J 18, f. 27,* see n. 2, above.

[44]TS 12.16*v*, ed. Mann, II, 71; see Mann (1970), I, xxx.

[45]TS 20.169* and others (see n. 54, below), (1025/6). MS Friedenberg* (ca. 1155), see A, 1, n. 41, above.

[46]ENA 4020, f. 1, l. 6, *India Book* 265.

[47]Bodl. MS Heb. c 28 (Cat. 2876), f. 52*.

[48]Isaiah 58:7. E.g., TS 16.293*v*, l. 24. The word for "family" used here is *sulāla,* lineage, race, stock.

[49]About Ephraim b. Shemarya see *Med. Soc.,* II, Index, p. 621.

[50]Commercial mail service between Palestine and Egypt *Med. Soc.,* I, 291 ff.

[51]Bodl. MS Heb. b 13, f. 54 (Cat. 2834, no. 35), ll. 10–24.

[52]TS 13 J 37, f. 10, ll. 10–27.

[53]TS 16.287, ed. Strauss-Ashtor, *Mamluks,* III, 101–103. The marginal printed on p. 102 is the direct continuation of l. 26 on p. 101. For *mq'rb* on p. 102 read *'qārib.* For interpretation of the letter see *Tarbiz,* 41 (1971), 68–73.

[54]The document is almost complete, although cut up today into three fragments: TS 20.169*, TS 10 J 8, f. 9*, BM Or 5542, f. 6* (dated 1025/6). See also n. 45, above.

[55]Partnership: TS 28.6, sec. A, ll. 23 and 38 (Summer, 1079). Female relatives: TS 18 J 1, f. 32 (1227/8).

[56]ULC Add. 3337. In *Med. Soc.,* I, 251, I had assumed that this was a family partnership. But a new examination of the document and the parallel cases recommend the interpretation provided here.

[57]This is Judaic law. More about this in C, 3 and 4. In Islam, too, the wife is not regarded as an heir, but she receives a "portion," especially allotted to her in the Koran: if there are no children or son's children, one quarter, and if there are, one eighth. See Joseph Schacht, *An Introduction to Islamic Law* (Oxford, 1964), p. 171.

[58]TS 10 J 6, f. 6, especially *verso,* ll. 5–6, and TS 12.684, which refers to the same affair. Moses b. Jekuthiel was exclusive heir to his cousin Moses b. Isaac and gave a release to Usayd ("Little Lion") b. Abraham, after the latter had paid him all he had owed his dead cousin. Spring, 1041.

[59]Bodl. MS Heb. a 2 (Cat. 2805), f. 3, ed. S. Assaf, *Tarbiz,* 9 (1938), 211.

[60]There was no need to declare this, since, according to Jewish law, an only daughter is by statute the sole heir. The will says so expressly, because in Islam a daughter can never inherit more than one half of her father's estate, cf. *Med. Soc.,* II, 395.

[61]TS 13 J 14, f. 4, *India Book* 259 (shortly after 1100).

[62]See A, 2, nn. 6–8, above.

[63]TS 13 J 14, f. 12, l. 3. "My brother" could perhaps also mean "my former friend."

[64]Dirty trick: TS 13 J 18, f. 29. Physical attack: Bodl. MS Heb. e 101 (no Cat.), f. 15.

[65]Bodl. MS Heb. d 76 (no Cat.), f. 60.

[66]ENA 4020, f. 52 (July 1132). The object of litigation: some household goods and dirhems inherited from the brother's mother. TS 16.148*, an embezzler sues his brother (May, 1086). BM Or 5566 D, f. 11, and Dropsie 340: protracted

lawsuits. Between sisters: ENA 3697, f. 8, a fragment, *daʿāwī zawjat al-rayyis ʿalā ukhtihā zawjat. . . .*

[67]TS 16.191 (ca. 1000): an uncle releases a nephew, after the latter returned a piece of land to him, illegally taken from him by his late sister. TS 18 J 2, f. 5 (incomplete, hand of Hillel b. Eli, 1066–1108): The cantor Ghālib b. Ḥalfōn al-Zayyāt ("maker of olive oil") claims that his sister Bārra was given by their father only the upper floor of the small house adjacent to the brother's own, whereas she had laid her hands on the whole house. TS 8 J 5, f. 4 c (1127): a woman, with the consent of her husband, appoints an attorney against her brother (in what matter, is not stated).

[68]TS 13 J 21, f. 5, l. 16, ed. S. D. Goitein, *Harel* (Tel Aviv, 1962), p. 146. The word is used in an informal way in a letter from Qayrawān, TS 16.269, l. 24, where *mu'ākhāt,* brotherhood, parallels *mawadda,* love, in l. 21.

[69]Firkovitch II, 236, f. 5, ed. Mann, *Texts,* I, 472–474, see S. D. Goitein, "Formal Friendship in the Medieval Near East," *Proceedings of the American Philosophical Society,* 115 (1971), 488.

[70]TS 13 J 27, f. 15, ll. 21–22, 29–30.

B. MARRIAGE

1. *The Nature of the Marriage Bond*

[1]Mishna Yevamot 6, 6. BT Yevamot 65*b*, Maimonides, *Code,* book "Women," chap. "Marriage," 15:2.

[2]S. D. Goitein, "A Report on Messianic Troubles in Baghdad in 1120–21," *JQR,* 43 (1952), 57–76. Cf. D, n. 206.

[3]Dropsie 386, ll. 4–15, ed. Mann, *Texts,* I, 460, written in a Hebrew style which shows that Arabic was not the writer's mother tongue. Divorce of the local wife: TS 13 J 20, f. 28, l. 19. The Talmudic quotation: BT Yevamot 62*b*. A similar story in C, 1, nn. 175–177, below.

[4]TS 13 J 21, f. 36, ll. 17–18*.

[5]Congratulation on birth of girl: TS 12.262, l. 19*.

[6]ULC Or 1080 Box 1, f. 3*v*, ll. 9–10, see Friedman, *Ethics,* p. 84; Bodl. MS Heb. a 3 (Cat. 2873), f. 32*v*, l. 7, ed. Friedman, *Marriage,* no. 12.

[7]Damascus, 933: TS 16.181⁺. Qūjandīma, Egypt, 945: TS 12.154⁺. Jerusalem, 1028 (see next n.). Fustat, 1067: Bodl. MS Heb. a 3 (Cat. 2873), f. 38. Fustat, 1115: TS 24.3. Fustat, 1292: TS 16.76, ed. Strauss-Ashtor, *Mamluks,* III, 62. Ruth's marriage: see A, 2, n. 74, above.

[8]Jerusalem, 1028: ULC Add. 3430, ed. A. M. Luncz, *Yerushalayim,* 6 (1903), 237–239, see Shaked, *Bibliography,* p. 41, without the trousseau list included in it. A complete edition is included in Goitein, *Palestine in Its Arab and Crusader Periods* (in press). Formulary, 1081: BM Or 5532, ed. Mann, *Texts,* II, 174–176. Cairo, 1117: Bodl. MS Heb. a 3 (Cat. 2873), f. 42, ed. *ibid.,* II, 177–180. Cairo, 1200: TS 16.67. Karaite prayerbook: trans. Leon Nemoy, *Karaite Anthology* (New Haven, 1952), pp. 283–284.

[9]As in Malachi 2:14.

[10]Based on Genesis 2:18.

[11]Reference to Genesis 3:16, God's curse pronounced over Eve after she had taken the unfortunate initiative to feed her obedient husband the forbidden fruit.

[12]The verb *ḥūs,* "to pity," "to spare," is common in Hebrew, but the noun *ḥīsā* derived from it and common in the Karaite marriage contracts is not known to me from any other source.

[13]Text: *lehit'ōnēn,* trans. according to *Kitāb Jāmiʿ al-Alfāẓ* by David ben Abraham al-Fāsī, ed. S. L. Skoss (New Haven, 1936), p. 120. Same use in letter to a Gaon of Jerusalem, PER H 135, ed. D. H. Müller and D. Kaufmann, *Mittheilungen aus der Sammlung der Papyrus Erzherzog Rainer,* Vol. V (Vienna, 1892), pp. 127–132, ll. 28 and 33.

[14]Grohmann, *APEL,* I, no. 44, pp. 98–99.

[15]*Ibid.,* no. 45, pp. 102–104. The verse from the Koran is cited in a marriage contract from the year 1030, University Museum, Philadelphia, E.16309, ed. G. Levi Della Vida, *Eretz-Israel* (L. A. Mayer Memorial Volume), 7 (1964), 65–66.

[16]The Christian marriage contracts are civil documents written by Muslim notaries and therefore contain only the legal, not the moral, obligations of the couple.

[17]See Z. W. Falk, *Matrimonial Law,* passim, and Friedman, *Ethics,* p. 85.

[18]Saadya Gaon, *The Book of Beliefs . . . ,* X, 7, ed. Qāfeḥ (Jerusalem, 1970), p. 303.

[19]E.g., TS 16.123, Ramle, 1052, ed. S. Assaf, *Yerushalayim* (Jerusalem, 1953), p. 104. Instead of being torn, this ketubba is crossed out by four vertical strokes, leaving, of course, the superscription, containing the reference to God, intact. Antonin 635, Tyre, probably 1054 (see Friedman, *Marriage,* no. 29), ed. S. Assaf, *Musaf Tarbiz* (Jerusalem, 1930), p. 60. ENA 4010, f. 36+ and PER H 1+, Tyre, 1079. TS NS Box 99, f. 45, Tyre, ed. Friedman, *Marriage,* no. 20. PER H 2, Damsīs, Lower Egypt, 1083, ed. S. Assaf, *A Tribute to Alexander Marx* (New York, 1943), p. 76. An old-Palestinian ketubba from Aleppo, 1029, is superscribed: "In the name of the All-merciful, may his name be praised." PER H 18, ed. S. Assaf in *Ha-Zofeh,* 10 (1926), 28–30, corrections in Friedman, *Marriage,* no. 7.

[20]See preceding note, first item.

[21]Mosseri L 197, l. 15, verso, l. 2: *al-ʿuzūbiyya lil-aḥrār wa-dhawi 'l-ʿiffa fi 'l-qāhira ṣaʿba jiddan.* The word *aḥrār,* translated as "blameless," literally means "free," a usage probably influenced by Greek and Coptic.

[22]Mosseri A 68, based on BT Yevamot 62*b*, where, however, various sages bring together only 3 + 2 + 1 = 6 laudatory aspects of marriage.

[23]PT Bikkurim 3, 3; fol. 65*d*.

[24]Hamburger Staats- und Universitäts-Bibliothek, A.P. 1, ed. Albert Dietrich, "Eine arabische Eheurkunde aus der Aiyūbidenzeit," *Documenta Islamica Inedita* (Berlin, 1952), p. 125, ll. 2–3. A shorter version in Museum of Islamic Art, Cairo, 14982, ed. Suʿād Māhir, *ʿUqūd al-zawāj* p. 5 (dated 1278).

[25]Museum of Islamic Art 4224, l. 5, ed. *ibid.,* p. 14 (dated 1334). Cf. 1 Corinthians 7:5: "Lest Satan tempt you."

[26]BT Ketubbot 7*b*, and found in every Jewish prayerbook. As so often with Jewish-Islamic correlations, one wonders whether there was a historical connection between that ancient Jewish benediction and the very similar formula in the proemiums to the Muslim marriage contracts (emphasizing what is permitted and what prohibited in marriage), or whether both grew independently out of similar or identical religious concepts. Wedding song: E. Fleischer, *Hebrew Liturgical Poetry in the Middle Ages* (Jerusalem, 1975), p. 163, ll. 25–26 (Heb.) (from an ancient piece of liturgy in honor of a wedding, based on Proverbs 5:15–21). Talmud: BT Yevamot 63*a–b*.

[27]E.g., TS 10 J 13, f. 4, l. 20, trans. Goitein, *Letters,* p. 239; TS 10 J 14, f. 9, l. 8; P. Heid. 913, l. 7.

[28]BT Ḥagiga 27*a*. Hospitality, partaking of food with the needy, is given by the commentators as reason for the atoning power of a man's table.

[29]The seven benedictions consist of the official betrothal benediction discussed above, three benedictions extolling procreation as the perpetuation of God's image on earth, and three others praising God as the dispenser of happiness to the young couple and to Zion redeemed.

[30]B. Spuler, *Die Morgenländischen Kirchen* (Leiden, 1961), p. 209. David Herlihy, *The Family in Renaissance Italy,* Forums in History (St. Charles, Miss., 1974), p. 10. For a detailed discussion of the history of the participation of priests in wedding ceremonies in the Church in comparison with the Jewish usages see Falk, *Matrimonial Law,* pp. 66–85.

[31]TS 13 J 20, f. 20*v*, ll. 1–5*. Poor: *ṣaʿlūka*; well off: *mastūra.*

[32]TS 12.337, ll. 21–25, *India Book* 73. Firkovitch II, 1700, 27+.

[33]Sahlawayh's son: Bodl. MS Heb. e 108, f. 70, frag. in Heb., written in small, beautiful cursive. In this document another granddaughter of Manasse, Mu'am-

mala ("The One Hoped for") releases Mulūk, Mulūk's husband, two brothers-in-law, Mulūk's son, Sahlawayh II, and her grandson Ḥayyīm III, from all claims on an inheritance from a daughter of Manasse (including a palace of his in Tyre, Lebanon).

Sahlawayh's daughter: TS 12.621. Frag. of a Karaite ketubba, written in huge, calligraphic letters.

The granddaughter: TS Misc. Box 29, f. 58. Ḥusn, the daughter of Hayyīm II b. Sahlawayh I, marries Azhar (Meir) b. Jābir, otherwise unknown, and receives a nuptial gift of 100 (+ 200 =) 300 dinars. Frag. of Karaite document.

[34]Antonin 904, l. 42, ed. S. Assaf, *Epstein Jubilee Volume* (Jerusalem, 1950), p. 185: *banī Barhūn aṣhārnā* (Tāhertī). Bodl. MS Heb. d 65 (Cat. 2877), f. 9, l. 34, ed. *ibid.*, p. 180: *akhūhum abu 'l-Faḍl ṣihrna.* TS 16.64, l. 26, ed. S. D. Goitein, *Tarbiz,* 38 (1968), 25: *Abū 'Imrān* (i.e., Mūsā) *ṣihrnā wa-ṣāḥibnā Ibn al-Majjānī.*

[35]Nahray b. Nissīm, see Goitein, *Letters,* p. 148; Judah b. Moses Ibn Sighmār, see next note; and Zakariyyā b. Tammām, see n. 37, below.

[36]Bodl. MS Heb. b 13, f. 49 (Cat. 2834, no. 30), ll. 10–15. The writer: Labrāṭ I b. Moses I.

[37]Goitein, *Letters,* p. 106.

[38]Mosseri A 2, ed. J. Mann, *HUCA,* 3 (1926), 281–283 (available now in Mann (1970) pp. 455–457). The name of the bridegroom: "Shela b. Amram al-Qirqīsānī [from Qarqīsiya on the Euphrates], who is at present in Tyre."

[39]TS 13 J 25, f. 20, written in oblong, monumental letters, ed. S. Assaf, *Yerushalayim* (Jerusalem, 1953), pp. 106–107. The name of the girl, Dhukhr ("Treasure"), is rare. I found it only in the lists discussed in *Med. Soc.,* II, 459, sec. 71, and p. 462, sec. 85. The first two signatures were misread. They are: Samuel ha-Kohen b. Wahb; Musāfir b. Simḥā.

[40]See the discussion in *Tarbiz,* 24 (1955), 139–140. Samuel, in his younger days, seems to have been a commuter between Spain and Egypt, see TS 10 J 16, f. 17, l. 20, *Nahray* 37, a letter to Nahray written by his cousin Nathan (where the name is spelled Lukhtūj). Qualifying or, at least, clarifying what has been said in *Tarbiz,* I assume now that Nethanel, the father of Ḥalfōn, was not Nethanel b. Moses "The Sixth," but his cousin.

[41]See Goitein, *Letters,* pp. 62–65 (Maḥrūz to Judah), 181–185 (Maḍmūn to Judah), 203 n. 6.

[42]Bodl. MS Heb. c 28 (Cat. 2876), f. 60, ll. 7–8, *India Book* 136. It is possible, although unlikely, that the congratulation refers to Judah ha-Kohen's second marriage, see C, 4, n. 29, below. Letters from Maḍmūn's cousins in Goitein, *Letters,* pp. 185–197. For overseas marital links between the families of Jewish religious dignitaries see *Med. Soc.,* I, 48. The Talmudic saying in BT Pesaḥim 49*a*.

[43]TS 16.293. See A, 2, n. 62, above.

[44]TS 10 J 30, f. 11, ed. S. D. Goitein, *Tarbiz,* 33 (1964), 195–196. BT Pesaḥim 49*b*.

[45]TS 13 J 35, f. 14. He quotes: "One who marries his daughter to an uneducated common fellow is like one throwing her fettered before a lion," meaning that such persons lack the consideration required in intimate relations. BT Pesahim 49*b*. This saying is found only a few lines below the quotation referred to in n. 44, but is, of course, inappropriate in the letter of a son-in-law. The cantors and beadles, who knew everyone in the community, were the natural matchmakers.

[46]TS 13 J 8, f. 27*. As motto of his letter he quotes Ecclesiastes 11:6, which is explained in BT Yevamot 62*b*, that a man should marry again in his later years, after having been married once in his youth. The letter certainly was composed and written by a professional clerk, while the suitor only added two lines at the end requesting an immediate reply.

[47]TS 13 J 9, f. 4 (dated 1053), ed. E. Ashtor, *Sefarad,* 24 (1964), 49, l. 11, with Spanish translation. *Ibid.,* p. 48, reference to a prior Heb. edition.

[48]Ar. *tawfīq al-'ārifīn.* Was the little schoolmaster aware that he used here a term of Islamic mysticism?

[49]Ar. *mahr,* referring here to the gift made at the betrothal.

[50]TS 13 J 18, f. 22. In several other letters Solomon had complained about bad health. Hence the assurance that he now enjoyed good health.

[51]See A, 2, n. 79, no. 12, above.

[52]*Med. Soc.*, II, 144 and 183.

[53]As described in TS 13 J 28, f. 15+, see A, 2, n. 3, above.

[54]See the story of the orphan girl reported in *Med. Soc.*, I, 49.

[55]TS Arabic Box 53, f. 37, l. 1, *verso*, l. 19, ed. S. D. Goitein, *Sefunot*, 11 (1973), 15 and 19. The letter was written in Arabic language by a scholarly Jew from Egypt who lived in Salonika. "Much favored": *lahā ḥaẓẓ*.

[56]BM Or 12186.

[57]TS 24.27*v*, "the yoke of a household": *ōl ha-bayit* (Heb.). The husband writes. See B, 2, nn. 17–22.

[58]TS 10 J 29, f. 1*v*, ed. Assaf, *Texts*, p. 29. Assaf ascribes the fragment to the ninth century, at the latest. Friedman, *Marriage*, no. 13, discovered another fragment of this document, ENA NS 2, f. 27, whose content puts it into the second quarter of the eleventh century.

[59]TS 13 J 2, f. 8. The estate itself was in Aleppo. But it was not difficult to find in Fustat three competent witnesses to confirm the heir's claim.

[60]PER H 90.

[61]Bodl. MS Heb. b 13, f. 52 (Cat. 2834, no. 33). Their mother is wished to see their "joy."

[62]ULC Or 1080 J 24, ll. 10–15, *India Book* 124. A wife's highest praise was that she lived up to the standards set by her husband's mother, see below, *passim*. It might be, however, that Ḥalfōn excused himself for not marrying by asserting that he could not find a wife in any way comparable to his mother. Chapter IV of my *India Book* is devoted to Ḥalfōn, where TS 13 J 33, f. 1*v*, l. 2, *India Book* 85, *wa-ahlak* is also discussed.

[63]BT Yevamot 63*b*.

[64]Maimonides, *Code*, book "Women," chap. "Marriage," 15:3. Paragraph 2 permits a man engaged in study to postpone marriage. Forty as age of spiritual perfection: Mishna Avot 5:21, see the Commentary on Genesis ascribed to David, the son of Abraham Maimonides, ed. Abraham I. Katsh under the title *Midrash David Hanagid* (Jerusalem, 1964), p. 101. David was born Dec. 19, 1222, see S. D. Goitein, *Tarbiz*, 41 (1972), 74. Woman of forty: BT Bava Bathra 119*b*.

[65]The contemporary visionary of Catania, Sicily, was in her ninth month of pregnancy, Mann, *Texts*, I, 34 ff.

[66]Ar. *rūmī*, which could mean also: Italy and elsewhere in Europe.

[67]Two persons living together sometimes received three instead of four loaves. There were five such cases in this list.

[68]Ar. *al-mukhilla*. Everyone knew what she had done.

[69]Ar. *juhaybidh*, a nickname.

[70]Ar. *lwsyd* for *al-usayd*, also a nickname.

[71]The chamberlain of the Persian king Ahasvẹrus, Book of Esther 7:9. Again a nickname.

[72]A Berber, or at least, a Maghrebi name.

[73]Heb. *ḥālāl*. The status of Kohens in the Geniza society is treated in Vol. IV (in preparation).

[74]Ar. *kurb al-dawā*, "Pain Caused by Medication." One can well understand why a person who became more unbearable the more one tried to please him should be so nicknamed.

[75]TS 24.76*.

[76]See *Med. Soc.*, II, 469, Table I, listing only persons who received 10 loaves and more. These were not paupers, but communal officials.

[77]TS Misc. Box 8, f. 25*, see *Med. Soc.*, II, 443–444.

[78]Ar. *imra'a ibna*.

[79]TS K 15, f. 48, see *Med. Soc.*, II, 444. The many persons referred to as *bayt* were women whose husbands were alive.

[80]I mean aspects of women's lives other than that treated here, e.g., the large number of single women from places and countries other than Fustat.

[81]See C, 3, nn. 143–151; C, 4, nn. 117, 127, 135–137, 142.

2. *Engagement and Betrothal*

[1]Normally expressed in Arabic by *ṭalab* "asking (her father for her hand:), e.g., TS Arabic Box 53, f. 37*v*, l. 19+, TS 12.337, l. 24+, or *khāṭab*, "proposing," TS 8 J 14, f. 25*v*. The latter term is used also for the engagement, Firkovitch II, 1700, f. 10 (May, 1156).

[2]Whether *'rs* originally designated a legal obligation (cf. *arīs*, sharecropper), or had some sexual connotation, is irrelevant. Since biblical times (e.g., Deuteronomy 20:7) it was the term for the conclusion, and not necessarily consummation, of marriage.

The root *qdsh* means "holy," that is, belonging exclusively to God. Similarly, *qaddēsh*, originally meant "taking a wife into one's exclusive possession." But since the idea of holiness had become connected with the root, the untranslatable term must be circumscribed and rendered, according to the circumstances, by expressions such as "formal conclusion of a marriage," or "consecration."

"A virgin divorced after betrothal": ENA 4011, f. 18, a ketubba (1134); TS NS J 278, a betrothal document (1138); TS Misc. Box 28, f. 266, a ketubba (ca. 1510). TS Arabic Box 50, f. 197, ed. M. A. Friedman, *Michael*, 5 (Tel Aviv, 1978), 213–238. Documents on both the betrothal and the marriage of a couple: TS 16.109, betrothal contract (only lower part extant, ca. 27 lines) of Mubāraka, daughter of Faraḥ ha-Kohen, to David b. Ephraim, the parnas, both Karaites; about twelve witnesses. TS 20.47*v*: the ketubba of same couple (middle part, 14 lines extant). This vellum is ca. 20 inches wide. Eleventh century.

[3]Entering: Ar. *dukhūl*, which is most commonly used, e.g., Bodl. MS Heb. d 66 (Cat. 2878), f. 47, l. 10, ed. S. D. Goitein, *AJS review*, 2 (1977), 104–106, dated 1146; in Heb. *kinnūs*, e.g., Bodl. MS Heb. f 56 (Cat. 2821, no. 16), f. 57, l. 8 (1184). For the double meaning of "entering" see n. 85, below. Taking: *nissū'īn*, the general Heb. term. Rare: *zifāf*, the bridal procession, TS 18 J 1, f. 28 (1187), TS NS J 401, no. 2 (Ḥalfōn b. Manasse), l. 1. In Italy, too, this procession symbolized the consumation of marriage, see D. Herlihy, "The Family in Renaissance Italy," *Forums in History* (St. Charles, Miss., 1974), p. 10, bottom.

[4]For instance, TS 12.121, l. 5: *shiddēkh we-qiddēsh* (as late as 1243). TS AS 147, f. 12, l. 2: *shiddēkh we-ērēs*.

[5]TS 12.39 and BM Or 5566 D, f. 22, the latter forming the upper right corner of the document, ed. Strauss-Ashtor, *Mamluks*, III, 74–76. In l. 11, the MS has the word *al[mānā]*, "widow." In l. 14, *ha-Levi*, the family name of the prospective husband, Isaac b. Moses, is omitted. The father of the second signatory, who displays a very careful handwriting, spells his name *ḥlfn*, not *ḥlfwn*. I have dealt with this document in various connections, see Strauss-Ashtor's notes, and *Med. Soc.*, II, 524, n. 58, and 560, n. 25. At that time, I did not yet have BM photostats.

[6]Records for the United States show 12.5–13.0 as age for the first menstrual period observed in white girls in 1940–1945 (Peter Laslett, "Age at Menarche in Europe since the 18th Century," *Journal of Interdisciplinary History*, 11 [1971], 222).

[7]In Heb. *bōgeret . . . birshūt nafshāh*, ENA 2779, f. 3, l. 8, or . . . *'aṣmāh*, JNUL Heb. 4° 577/4, no. 26, both ed. Friedman, *Marriage*, nos. 25 and 2, respectively.

[8]A common blessing for a living person. We see that the father of the bride was alive.

[9]Heb. *parnās*, see *Med. Soc.*, II, 77–82.

[10]All over the Middle East the dyeing of the bride's hands, feet, and face with the reddish-brown color of henna was (and in some places still is) an occasion for a big party, the costs of which were borne here by the bridegroom. For this detail see also n. 31, below. It is found also in a tenth-century Muslim marriage contract from Tunisia, Idris, "Mariage," p. 46.

[11]Ar. *khuyūṭ*. I assume the reference is to the pearl strings and other ornaments borrowed (against a compensation) for the bride during the wedding festivities. Also attested in contemporary Muslim marriage contracts, see *ibid.*, and known to me from Yemenite usage, still alive in the twentieth century, see also n. 31, below.

[12]That is, six months later.

[13]TS 12.121, see n. 4, above. A similar contract with a virgin in ULC Add. 3349 (1241).

[14]As in the story of Cassia, A, 2, n. 82, above, where, however, the father made the final decision.

[15]Mother: Bodl. MS Heb. d 66 (Cat. 2878), fs. 47 and 48, l. 22+* (1146); Firkovitch II, 1700, f. 18 b (1156); BM Or 5536 (1157); TS 8 J 14, f. 25*v*.

[16]Sister of father: Firkovitch II, 1700, f. 10 b (1156). Grandmother: *ibid.*, f. 15 a (1156). The grandmother was assisted by the bride's brother, when the court handed over to her the very considerable sum of 238 dinars for the outfit of the orphan girl.

[17]TS 13 J 16, f. 5*. The name of the girl is given with great precision: Bushr ("Good Tidings"), the daughter of Asad ("Lion"), the son of al-Salār (from Persian *sālār,* chieftain), the market crier (*munādī*) in the bazaar of the wool merchants. For the Qayrawānese practice see C, 1, n. 226, below.

[18]TS 20.122, ll. 11–12, a letter by Ḥayyīm b. ʿAmmār, representative of the merchants in Palermo. See *Med. Soc.*, I, 49 and 403, n. 47.

[19]TS 13 J 14, f. 3. The entire letter deals with this matter. "The dear lady": Ar. *al-sitt al-nfsyh,* a slight slip for *nfysh.* The name of the matchmaker certainly was not *Umm Sawdā',* but *Umm Bayḍā'* "Mother of the White [i.e., beautiful] girl."

[20]TS NS Box 184, fs. 58 + 62 + 50 + 71 + 70 + 74 + 98 + 72 (in this order), stating that the betrothal had taken place in 1118/1119.

[21]JNUL 11, ed. Avinoam Yellin, *Kirjath Sepher,* 1 (1925), 55–61. About the Karaite Ibn Ṣaghīrs (spelled here, as often, with *s*), see A, 1, n. 61, above. A similar contest over a girl in TS 16.231, see n. 83, below.

[22]TS 13 Ja 1. "Nougat" is an approximate translation of *al-jawziyya,* which designated a special sweetmeat made of walnuts in Palestine. In Spain the word was used for a fish sauce made with nuts, see Dozy, *Supplément,* I, 234*a*.

On the reverse side of the letter a clerical note states that Abu 'l-Surūr (= Faraḥ) Ibn al-Qābisī [known from other sources] will pay to the *ḥāvēr* [Solomon], the son of Joseph, the president of the court of the Jerusalem yeshiva, 25 dinars, the balance of a debt, in [twelve] installments of 2 dinars and [one] of 3 dinars as from Nisan 1 = Dhu l-Ḥijja, 1, 477 (= March 29 or 30, 1085). Thus, our letter must have been written sometime before that date.

[23]BT Qiddushin 41*a*. See Friedman, "Ethics," pp. 86–87, where the rabbinical opinions about the marriage of minors are thoroughly discussed.

[24]Maimonides, *Code,* book "Women," sec. "Marriage," para. 19.

[25]ENA 1822 A, f. 23, signed *yeshūʿā,* "salvation," which is a "motto," not a proper name. The writer probably was David b. Daniel b. Azarya. Same script and signature in ENA 4011, f. 17. See S. D. Goitein, "Daniel b. Azarya, Nasi and Gaon," *Shalem,* 2 (Jerusalem, 1976), pp. 72 and 96.

[26]Maimonides, *Responsa,* I, 49. See D, nn. 152–155, below.

[27]Ar. *yastaghīth,* ll. 14 and 21, see *Med. Soc.,* II, 824 and 597 n. 54.

[28]TS 12.242, ll. 13–23.

[29]TS Arabic Box 47, f. 244, dated Adar I 1047, only left side preserved. Since the court decided that she was permitted to stay in the house of her brother (and not her father) it is evident that she was an orphan. Bilbays: TS 8 J 9, f. 13*r* (1221), *v* (1218). Saffron also in TS Arabic Box 30, f. 8*, a list of objects collected for a poor orphan's wedding. See Grohmann, *World of Arabic Papyri,* p. 156. Safflower: Maimonides-Meyerhof, p. 147, no. 300.

[30]See C, 5, below.

[31]Ornamental costume: *jalā',* a term almost identical with the Maghrebī *jalwa,*

see nn. 10 and 11, above. Henna is called here *ṣabāgh,* a common substitute for *ḥinnā'*.

[32]TS 8.112*. The bottom of the document is torn away, but it does not seem that much has been lost.

[33]Deathbed declaration: TS 13 J 3, f. 3+*. See A, 2, n. 80, no. 5, above. Seven years waiting period: ENA NS 1, f. 89*a* (Lam. 146*a*), eleventh century.

[34]TS 13 J 8, f. 31*. The original document is from June 1042, the qadi's statement from October/November of the same year. The Jewish judge is called by the qadi: *Yūsuf b. Sulayman al-ma'rūf bildayyān.* This is the well-known Joseph, judge in Alexandria, succeeded by his even better-known son Yeshū'ā, see *Med. Soc.,* II, 72. The Alexandrian teacher Sariyy b. Ḥayyim mentioned here, l. 9, appears also in TS 13 J 1, f. 7 (dated 1033).

[35]Maimonides, *Responsa,* II, 352–354. "Simon" means So-and-so, and is not a proper name. See the explanation given at the beginning of this section.

[36]S. Hayat, "The Family in the Proverbs of the Iraqi Jews" (see A, 2, n. 62, above), p. 134, nos. 447 and 448.

[37]See *Med. Soc.,* I, 66–67.

[38]In many cases we know this not from the signatures under such a contract, but from the handwriting of the copyist who had made it out.

[39]Abraham Maimuni, *Responsa,* p. 54.

[40]TS 8 J 14, f. 25. Line 3: *ittafaq zīja* should not be taken as meaning that the new marriage had already taken place. The bride's late father was Mufaḍḍal b. al-Dimyāṭī al-Kohen, whose son Bahā is mentioned in TS NS Box 325, f. 8, ll. 2–3. He is probably Mufaḍḍal al-Kohen, partner in a tannery in Minyat Ziftā, March, 1232, see *Med. Soc.,* I, 366, sec. 24. Thus the Nagid concerned was Abraham Maimonides (d. 1237).

[41]TS 8.111. The very wording of the document supports my interpretation: "When the Creator decreed that [these women] should die." The continuation: *wa-qutil allatī kān (!) tazawwaj (!) Sitt al-Ḥusn lahumā jamī'an fi waqt wāḥid* is clumsy.

[42]Bodl. MS Heb. d 66 (Cat. 2878), f. 133*v*, item *b,* ed. E. Ashtor, *Braslavi Jubilee Volume* (Jerusalem, 1970), pp. 484–485. The date 1085 is on a document on the first page, signed by Mevassēr b. Ḥalfōn, who also signed our entry. For *lahū,* l. 9, read *lahā.*

[43]1153: Bodl. MS Heb. b 3 (Cat. 2806), f. 4*v*, ed. D. Z. Baneth *Alexander Marx Jubilee Volume* (New York, 1950), II, 84. 1159: TS 10 J 7, f. 6, p. 2, item *a**. Date not preserved: Bodl. MS Heb. e 94, f. 18.

[44]Ar. *'ulqa dīniyya* or *shar'iyya* and *sulṭāniyya.* ENA 4011, f. 35 (dated 1166). The name *Ibn al-Baṭṭ,* Mr. Duck, was borne also by the physician of a battleship mentioned in *Med. Soc.,* II, 380. TS Misc. Box 25, f. 25 (Spring, 1174), signed by the judge Jacob ha-Kohen b. Joseph. *Med. Soc.,* II, 513, sec. 21, is to be corrected accordingly.

[45]Higher society: TS Misc. Box 25, f. 63. *Abū Naṣr b. Mevōrākh ha-sār ha-addīr sār ha-bīnā* (Heb.) marries *Sitt al-Khāṣṣa b. al-shaykh al-'Afīf Abi 'l-Ma'ālī Mevōrākh b. Yaḥyā ha-sār p'ēr ha-yeshīva.* The girl 'Amā'im: TS 10 J 17, f. 16, cf. *Med. Soc.,* II, 591, n. 9.

[46]The document enumerates here all the situations disqualifying a person as a suitable match according to Mishna Qiddushin 4:1–2. "Bastard" means progeny of an incestuous connection, such as brother and sister.

[47]TS 13 J 3, f. 26*, ENA 190 (2559). For the identity of her benefactor, al-As'ad, see C, 1, n. 120, below. The girl's name: *Akramiyya,* probably after her former master *al-shaykh al-Akram,* "the most honored elder." For a similar pious deed see *Med. Soc.,* I, 135, and TS Misc. Box 24, f. 137, p. 4*v*, (ca. 1160).

[48]Maimonides, *Responsa,* II, 624–625. Abraham Maimuni, *Responsa,* p. 182. The three judges signing the decree, besides Maimonides, Isaac b. Sāsōn, Samuel b. Saadya, Manasse b. Joseph, are frequently mentioned in *Med. Soc.,* e.g., II, 514 (all three together). For Abraham Maimuni see also *Med. Soc.,* II, 74.

[49]Maimonides, *Responsa,* I, 22–24.

[50]*Ibid.,* II, 625–627. See *Med. Soc.,* II, 398 ff. Yet Maimonides' younger contemporary, Solomon b. Elijah, writes to a notable: "I was told that you have made a marriage contract for your daughter at a Muslim court. I cannot believe it." TS NS J 102.

[51]Nabia Abbott, "Arabic Marriage Contracts among Copts," *ZDMG,* 95 (1941), 59–81. The two other contracts in Grohmann, *APEL,* I, nos. 40 and 43, dated 855 and 918, respectively.

[52]The idea that capital amounting to 20 dinars might bring about 1 dinar profit per month also in Bodl. MS Heb. a 3 (Cat. 2873), f. 5, see C, 4, n. 91, below. Here, a minimum profit of 2 dinars was expected which the fiancés would divide. It is likely that the preceding engagement contract was made before a Muslim notary.

[53]Mosseri A 7, 2, partly defective. In Arabic characters.

[54]Mosseri A 27*, dated 1032. The name of the place is here spelled *Ṣahrasht,* see *Med. Soc.,* II, 50–51. "No affairs with women": *verso,* l. 17, *lā ya'riḍ lil-nisā,* cf. *recto,* l. 13, she said bad things about her husband.

[55]See above, nn. 34 and 36.

[56]For details see *Med. Soc.,* II, 327.

[57]A messianic name, see Zechariah 3:8 and *Med. Soc.,* IV, chap. x, in preparation.

[58]Bodl. MS Heb. d 66 (Cat. 2878), fs. 47–48⁺, see n. 3, above.

[59]See B, 1, n. 45. Mufaddāt means one for whom one—namely, the mother—is prepared to give her life. The mother of this girl was dead.

[60]TS Arabic Box 54, f. 78. Outfit: *raḥl.* Bedding and hangings were listed between jewelry and clothing on the one hand and copper and household goods on the other; in l. 14 I read *alkly* (not *ḥly*), which could, however, hardly stand for *killah,* bed awnings.

[61]JNUL 83, no. 4, item I, ed. S. D. Goitein, *Kirjath Sepher,* 41 (1966), 273 and 276. On p. 273 I noted that the bride received the 5 dinars in person. This is not correct. True, her father is not mentioned as the one who received it. But the text says "*he* received." It is taken for granted that the father, and not the bride, makes the financial arrangements. The judge Nathan ha-Kohen b. Solomon, who wrote and signed this note, often makes such elliptic statements.

[62]*Ibid.,* p. 276, item II.

[63]TS 8 J 5 f. 22* (November, 1161). The orphan's fiancé was a schoolmaster. He planned perhaps having her partly take over his classes with his mother continuing to run the household while he earned additional money by copying books.

[64]Bodl. MS Heb. f 56 (Cat. 2821, no. 16), f. 46*v*, (Summer, 1182). The orphan Mu'azzaza ("Highly Esteemed") was represented by her brother.

[65]Example of a detailed trousseau list, simply superscribed *al-taqwīm,* "the estimate" (without any names, which means that it originally formed the continuation of another document): TS 10 J 21, f. 4 (perhaps in the hand of Moses ha-Levi b. David of Cairo, ca. 1110). Engagement contract referring to the bride's outfit: TS 13 J 8, f. 24.

[66]Bodl. MS Heb. f 56 (Cat. 2821, no. 16), f. 51 (Spring, 1185).

[67]See B, 1, nn. 26 and 29.

[68]Heb. *shiddūkhīn,* that is, the word that also means: engagement. The basic meaning of the word is "to appraise, to gratify, to make familiar with." cf. Ar. *sadika,* "to be familiar with."

[69]Bodl. MS Heb. d 66 (Cat. 2878), f. 121*v*, ed. S. Assaf, *Tarbiz,* 9 (1938), 213–214. The document might have been prepared in order to accompany a legal inquiry, cf. TS 10 J 19, f. 15, an instruction to prepare such a document.

[70]*Teshuvot ha-Geonim Sha'are Ṣedeq* (Jerusalem, 1966), p. 40, no. 12 (in the original edition [Salonika, 1792]: f. 18*a*).

[71]TS 18 J 1, f. 3, ed. Norman Golb, *JSS,* 20 (1958), 39–40. The text needs some corrections. The name of the bride was Sittūna. The document is discussed in Friedman, *Marriage,* no. 50.

[72]BT Shabbat 130*a*. Examples of such squabbles in B, 5, below.

[73]ULC Or 1080 J 6, l. 15 ff., where the messenger for the legally valid conveyance of the bill is appointed. See *Med. Soc.,* I, 403 n. 44.

[74]1082: TS AS 146, f. 7. "My betrothed," *mumallakatī.* 1121: TS 16.119, in the hand of Ḥalfōn b. Manasse.

[75]TS 10 J 27, f. 3, item 1. The left margin of the manuscript is damaged. In l. 13 read *walidayh[ā.*

[76]TS 8 J 4, f. 22*v*. Written and signed by the clerk Moses ha-Levi b. David. In Bodl. MS Heb. d 68, f. 106 (Cat. 2836, no. 28) the judge Abraham b. Nathan calls him "the scholar."

[77]TS 8 J 4, f. 23*v* (c). Written by Abraham b. Nathan, the judge.

[78]TS 8 J 9, f. 9. The bridegroom Peraḥya b. Āraḥ (corresponding to Arabic Faraḥ b. Musāfir) signs calligraphically TS 13 J 2, f. 8 (Nov., 1099), where he calls himself *ha-melammed,* teacher, probably as a title of honor, see *Med. Soc.,* II, 190. The . . .]*r* in l. 5 is the end of the word *antila]r,* Greek *entolarios,* representative, attorney, cf. Mann, II, 356 n. 3. I prefer 170 or 190 to 70 or 90, for the space available on l. 10 before *]ʿīn,* requires a text such as *al-mu'akhkhar mi'ah wa-sab]ʿīn* (or *tis]ʿīn*). In TS 16.169, ed. Friedman, *Marriage,* no. 31, the bride receives an "Egyptian robe," *sādīn miṣrī* (Heb.), from her groom. On the wife's trustworthiness, see B, 5, nn. 8–16.

[79]Letter from Jerusalem: TS AS 147, f. 2, l. 22. Betrothal of 1093: TS 13 J 2, f. 3. An explanation of the strange amount of 4 1/6 dinars as obligatory betrothal gift is offered in B, 4, nn. 22 and 23.

[80]TS 8 J 17, f. 9*a-c,* written by Ḥalfōn b. Manasse.

[81]*Ibid.,* f. 9*d,* written and signed by the judge Nathan ha-Kohen b. Solomon (about him see *Med. Soc.,* II, 513). A delayed marriage gift of 10 dinars might have been promised (detail effaced).

[82]Bodl. MS Heb. f 56 (Cat. 2821, no. 16), f. 57. The judges: Samuel ha-Levi b. Saadya and Manasse b. Joseph, see *Med. Soc.,* II, 514. A betrothal contract from the same year (Dec., 1184) is contained in Bodl. MS Heb. f 56 (Cat. 2821, no. 16), f. 58. It stipulates Fustat as the future domicile of the couple. Another case of a grown-up son under the jurisdiction of his father (*walā'*) in TS Arabic Box 50, f. 197⁺.

[83]TS 8 J 4, f. 2*b,* signed by eight men with good handwritings, among them three of the four arbiters. In ENA 1822 A, f. 4, a Nagid is requested to interfere when brothers wished to cancel the betrothal of their sister which had lasted for years, when they learned that the groom had suffered grave financial losses. The groom had frequently sent them presents. Offended family: TS 16.231.

[84]TS 16.181, documents I-III, ed. Assaf, *Texts,* pp. 64–69. Many corrections in Friedman, *Marriage,* no. 53. For the expression "small synagogue" see *Med. Soc.,* II, 520, n. 3. Friedman has recently identified some fragments of the same type and time: *Marriage,* nos. 54 and 55, see App., part I, group 3, nos. 4–5, 7, below.

[85]The editor thought that Heb. *ʿal* stood for *el* and took the phrase throughout as meaning "*to* her." But this is not correct. The bride was not present. The clerk consistently and properly wrote *ʿal* in the sense of "*for* her." Also in TS 16.181⁺, doc. II, l. 6, *beʿēt kenīsatō ʿalēhā,* "at the time of his entering her chamber," and doc. III, l. 6, *beʿēt kenīsātāh ʿalāw,* "at the time of her entering his house," *ʿal* is not a misuse of *el,* but regular medieval Hebrew usage, which was influenced by Arabic *dakhal ʿalā.*

[86]TS 16.181⁺, Doc. I, l. 4; doc. II, l. 5. Exodus 22:16.

[87]TS 16.181⁺, Doc. III, l. 3.

[88]The literary evidence for 25 gold pieces as minimum marriage gift in Babylonia, adduced by the editor of TS 16.181, I–III, is by no means unequivocal.

[89]Details in *Med. Soc.,* II, 423 n. 107.

[90]Ceremonial: *Med. Soc.,* II, 595 nn. 6, 7. I disagree with the surmise of the editor of TS 16.181 that this *shōfeṭ,* or head of the congregation, also wrote the

records. The script of the records is oblong and rather irregular, whereas that of the signature is quadrangular and even.

[91]Mosseri A 37 and 76, which are parts of one document. The bride was a widow, and the day was the eve of the New Year holiday, when everyone is busy with preparations for the festivities.

[92]See *Med. Soc.,* II, 343–344. To the material referred to there, should be added ULC Or 1080 J 140, where a woman named Fā'iza ("Favorite") asks to copy her marriage contract in the communal records so that she might hand over the original to her brother for suing her husband who had deserted her. The original was written in Fustat on October 15, 1045, and Fā'iza's request was made in the same city—how many years after her marriage, we do not know. Anyhow, we see that, in this case, the court possessed no record of the original action.

To the items listed in *Med. Soc.,* II, 597, n. 41, of *one* witness signing a record, while the handwriting of the clerk serves as the second witness, add TS NS J 226*v*, item I, September, 1244, where Solomon ha-Kohen b. Sār Shalōm signs alone.

[93]Falk, *Jewish Matrimonial Law,* p. 68 n. 1, referring to J. Dauvillier and C. de Clercq, *Le mariage en droit canonique oriental* (Paris, 1936), pp. 48 ff.

[94]TS NS J 401, no. 2, l. 8, a fragment in the hand of Ḥalfōn b. Manasse; *ibid.* ll. 5–6: "there was no other stipulation in the contract except for the case that one of the parties canceled [the betrothal] prior to the marriage." Other parts of this interesting document may come to light.

3. *Wedding and the Marriage Contract*

[1]E.g., ENA 4020, f. 47, a detailed description of divorce proceedings, ends thus: "M. Yekuthiel [the husband] was sitting there until the bill of divorce was written and delivered to her; then he received the ketubba and tore it asunder crosswise."

[2]See nn. 76–79, below.

[3]Bodl. MS Heb. d 65 (Cat. 2877), f. 26⁺, Friedman, *Marriage,* no. 1. The name of the place is lost. Its geographic definition in l. 4, . . . *n* . . *miṣrayim,* was ingeniously reconstructed by Friedman as *['al leshō]n [yam] miṣrayim,* being the end of the phrase "situated in the Great Sea, and at 'the tongue' of the River of Egypt," a description referring to Tinnīs (see Golb, *Topography,* p. 143. The document referred to there as quoted in S. Schechter, *Saadyana,* is ENA 4020, f. 57. Schechter omitted the two concluding words: *'al gabbāh.*) Tinnīs in those days was not only a great industrial center, but a commercial emporium as well, where merchants from Iraq, Syria-Palestine, and the Maghreb mixed with the local business men, see *Med. Soc.,* I, 548, s.v. Tinnīs.

[4]TS 16.374, ed. Mann, I, 94–95, translated and often discussed, see Shaked, *Bibliography,* p. 71.

[5]Era of the destruction of the Second Temple: e.g., Bodl. MS Heb. d 65 (Cat. 2877), f. 26⁺, Friedman, *Marriage,* no. 1, PER H 18⁺, *ibid.,* no. 7. It is already mentioned in the Mishna Gittin 8:5, and was used on Jewish tombstones of the sixth century found on the southern shores of the Dead Sea, see E. L. Sukenik and others in *Kedem: Studies in Jewish Archaeology,* Vol. II (Jerusalem, 1945), pp. 83–98. The era begins in A.D., 68, not 70, when the destruction actually took place. The Karaite court of Ramle, Palestine, used a fifth era, "from the exile of King Yehoyakhin" (which occurred in 596 B.C., II Kings 24:15), e.g., in the form of a betrothal act from the year 1009/10 (see Mann, *Texts,* II, 158 and 168 [TS Loan 10]). As is to be expected, the Karaite chronology is far off the mark.

[6]E.g., JNUL 4º 577/4, Friedman, *Marriage,* no. 2; Bodl. MS Heb. a 3 (Cat. 2873), f. 32*v*, *ibid.,* no. 12.

[7]See B, 2, nn. 86–87, above, where in the Damascus documents of 933 the phrase "nuptial gift for virgins" parallels "according to the custom."

[8]Joseph Kafih (Qāfeḥ), *Jewish Life in San'a* (Jerusalem, 1961), pp. 110–156; Judah Levi Nahum, *Miṣefūnōt Yehūdē Tēmān* (Tel Aviv, 1962), pp. 147–169 (both in Hebrew).

[9]M. A. Friedman's letter to me of July 31, 1974. TS Arabic Box 49, f. 166*, a number of cases, it seems, brought before the gaon Daniel b. Azarya, cf. *Med. Soc.*, II, 436, sec. 179.

[10]Abraham Maimuni, *Responsa,* pp. 173–175.

[11]Mann, *Texts,* II, 189–190 (BM Or 2538, f. 88, ll. 94–107). About this custom among the Jews from Yemen and Kurdistan see E. Brauer, *Ethnologie der Jemenitischen Juden* (Heidelberg, 1934), p. 163 n. 1, and *The Jews of Kurdistan* (Jerusalem, 1947), p. 116. About Muslim usages see *EI,* Vol. IV, s.v. *'Urs,* sec. 6. Ezra Fleischer draws my attention to TS H 11, f. 78, TS NS Box 110, f. 20, ULC Or 1080, Box 1, f. 2, Rabbanite (Palestinian) "blessings of virginity," a custom prohibited in the strongest terms by Maimonides, *Responsa,* II, 366.

[12]"Widowed and divorced" e.g., TS 20.109, ULC Or 1080 J 186. For "a virgin divorced after betrothal" see B, 2, n. 2, above.

[13]For (presently) "unmarried," meaning "divorced" compare Antonin 635, l. 5+, where "unmarried, divorced" corresponds to simple "unmarried" in Bodl. MS Heb. c 13 (Cat. 2807, no. 13), f. 16, l. 6, Friedman, *Marriage,* no. 19. "The woman": TS 16.67, l. 13.

[14]"Previously married," *be'ūlā* (Heb.), which should not be translated "deflowered," but "one who had had a *ba'al,* or husband, before"; extremely rare, e.g., TS 16.245 (April 1015). The term is regularly used by Karaites (See Mann, *Texts,* II, 185 n. 74).

[15]Freedwoman: common. Captive: e.g., ULC Add. 3388, Friedman, *Marriage,* no. 27. See *Med. Soc.*, II, 169 n. 56. Widow's late husband: TS 12. 116*v*, item II.

[16]The intricacies of Jewish law in this matter and their reflection in the Geniza documents are discussed in M. A. Friedman, "The Minimum *Mohar* Payment as Reflected in the Geniza Documents: Marriage Gift or Endowment Pledge," *PAAJR* 44 (New York, 1976) 15–47.

[17]E.g., Grohmann, *APEL,* I, 67, 83, 86, 97; Su'ād Māhir, *'Uqūd,* pp. 17, 30; Dietrich, *Eheurkunde* (see B, 1, n. 24, above), p. 126.

[18]TS 20.47, l. 3: *hā-re'ūyā le-qiyyūm ha-miṣvōt* (Heb.), the same in other contracts where this detail is preserved.

[19]E.g., JNUL 4° 577/4+ (1023), where the physical indications of maturity are detailed, TS Misc. Box 29, f. 29+ (late thirteenth century), and TS Misc. Box 28, f. 226 (ca. 1510); in the two latter cases the simple term *bōgeret* (Heb.) is used, spelled *pōgeret* in Mosseri V 8, ed. Mann, *Texts,* I, 430 (1301).

[20]TS 24.7 (1003/4, Karaite), TS Misc. Box 29, f. 29+ (Rabbanite), cf. A, 2, n. 78, nos. 1 and 10.

[21]Five generations, headed by *hā-rāv ha-gādōl* (Heb.), "grand mufti," highest juridical authority, in TS 8 J 11, f. 16, frag. of engagement contract. Italian nobility: Matteo Camera, *Memorie . . . di Amalfi* (reprint; Salerno, 1972) I, 89–90 and *passim.* Arab amirs: Su'ād Māhir, *'Uqūd,* pp. 17 and 29.

[22]Bodl. MS Heb. e 98, f. 59, going back to Judge Maṣlīaḥ, probably identical with Maṣlīaḥ b. Elijah, the chief judge of Palermo; see about him *Med. Soc.*, I, 52, II, 338.

[23]For the presence of such rivalry see A, 1, n. 15, above.

[24]Firkovitch II, 1700, fs. 13*v* and 24.

[25]TS 20.1.

[26]TS 12.494. There is no space for the profession in the slightly damaged l. 5.

[27]Abraham Maimuni, *Responsa,* p. 231 (a note by Professor S. Lieberman).

[28]I retain the spelling (and pronunciation) *ketubba,* which is in common living use among both Near Eastern and European Jews, and do not write *ketuba* or *ketuva,* as some scholars fancy at present. About the spelling in the Geniza documents see Friedman, *Marriage,* excursus no. 1.

[29]Bodl. MS Heb. d 65 (Cat. 2877), f. 30+, l. 10 (Damascus, 956), TS 16.123, l. 9+ (Ramle, 1052), TS 16.67, l. 17 (Cairo, 1200, Karaite), all referring to the late installment of the marriage gift. Loan, *milve* (Heb.) for dowry; TS Misc. Box 28, f. 266, 1 (Cairo, ca. 1510).

[30]E.g., TS 20.7 (Fustat, 1050), ll. 5 and 17.

[31]See B, 5 nn. 5–18.

[32]Yemen: Joseph Kafih (Qāfeḥ), *Jewish Life in San'a* (Heb.) (Jerusalem, 1961), p. 141 n. 8. Maimonides, *Code,* book "Knowledge", sec. "Moral dispositions and ethical conduct" (*Dē'ōt*), 5: 11, partly based on BT Sota 44*a*.

[33]TS 16.181*v*, item II, l. 4+ (Damascus, 933). "Women's quarters": TS 20.77 (1239/40), TS 24.8 (late thirteenth century).

[34]PER H 1, ll. 20–21+ (Tyre, 1079). Fathers—in the plural, see A, Introduction, n. 1: "The All-merciful," *raḥmānā,* is the Talmudic name of God and should not be taken as borrowed from Islam.

[35]TS 12.154, l. 14+ (Qūjandīma, an Egyptian village, 945).

[36]Bodl. MS Heb. a 3 (Cat. 2873), f. 40, l. 14 (Fustat, 1128).

[37]Firkovitch II, 1700, f. 25*v*: *al-shurūṭ al-ma'lūma* (with four general conditions specified), expanded on f. 27+ to *shurūṭ banāt Yisrael al-ma'lūma* (with no specifications). Also f. 24*a*.

[38]See B, 1, n. 7. Occasionally, especially in Karaite ketubbas, this wish is repeated at the end: TS 16.109, l. 13.

[39]Good omen: *be-naḥshā ṭāvā* (Aramaic), TS 16.245 (1015), TS 16.153 (1054), TS 24.2.

[40]Excellent augury: *be-sīmānā me'alyā* (Aramaic), TS 20.6 (1037).

[41]TS 20.7 (1050).

[42]Propitious hour: *be-shā'ā me'ullā we-'ōnā mehullālā* (Heb.) TS 16.330 (1080), TS 16.91 (1104).

[43]See n. 101, below.

[44]Dropsie 331, ed. S. D. Goitein in *Lešonenu,* 30 (1966), 200.

[45]ULC Or 1080 J 260 (1068–1079). TS 12.98 (1048–1058, partly rhymed). TS 16.91 (Dec. 31, 1103) and TS 24.5 (1111) in honor of the Nagid Mevōrākh b. Saadya; TS 24.3 (1115) and TS 16.52 (1124), for his son Moses. TS 16.246 and ULC Or 1080 J 206 (1147) for Samuel b. Hananya. TS 16.76 (1292) ed. Strauss-Ashtor, *Mamluks,* III, 62–63, for David Maimonides.

[46]TS 16.109, l. 13. Messianic: TS 24.7 (1003/4). TS 24.13 (1064).

[47]TS 16.71 (1084), ed. Friedman, *Marriage,* no. 21. A poem with a similar tendency precedes the Karaite ketubba, see Mann, *Texts,* II, 171, 174, 177, 181.

[48]See A, 1, nn. 19 and 20.

[49]Bodl. MS Heb. a 3 (Cat. 2873), f. 45 (1033/4); Mosseri A 37, 2 and A 76 (1043); TS 16.78; TS 16.178 (dates not preserved).

[50]TS 16.112 (Cairo, 1534).

[51]TS 12.689, a small fragment of a magnificent huge ketubba. Elkana's love: TS 16.211, l. 5, ed. Friedman, *Marriage,* no. 17.

[52]E.g., TS 12.689.

[53]TS 12.715, Karaite. See also Mann, *Texts,* II, 180.

[54]TS 20.42 (1062), see Mann, *Texts,* II, 173.

[55]*Near Eastern Numismatics, Iconography, Epigraphy and History: Studies in Honor of Georges C. Miles,* ed. Dickran K. Kouymjian (Beirut, 1974), pp. 297–318. One of the inscriptions discussed by Ettinghausen reads: "In the name of God, the All-merciful, the Beneficient. Praise be . . . ," that is, ending with an incomplete sentence. But every Muslim reading it would understand that "Praise be . . ." is the first word of the first chapter of the Koran, thus inviting him to pray. Similarly, when a ketubba is superscribed "He who finds (etc.)," the reader knows that the verse "He who finds a wife, finds happiness" (Proverbs 18:22) is intended.

[56]Turfa: TS 16.52, written by Ḥalfōn b. Manasse. The two others: TS 24.3 (also by Ḥalfōn, 1115); TS 24.5 (in another hand, 1111). In the ketubba of a widow without any dowry and a marriage gift of 1 + 2 = 3 dinars only, the good wishes are written in one line, but in six groups, each crowned by a fleur-de-lis, but the whole document makes a neat, pleasant impression (TS NS Box 323, f. 4, Ḥalfōn, 1106). The ketubba of another widow, written by the same scribe, is headed by

8 + 7 + 8 groups of wishes, each crowned by that floral design; the text is lost almost in its entirety (TS 20.86).

[57]David Davidovitch, *The Ketuba [thus]: Jewish Marriage Contracts through the Ages* (Tel Aviv, 1968), pp. 10 and 110, presenting Bodl. MS Heb. c 13, fs. 25–26 (Cat. 2807, no. 20), the ketubba of Sitt al-Sāda ("The Mistress over the Masters"), see Franz Landsberger, "Illuminated Marriage Contracts," *HUCA*, 46 (1955), 506. The head decoration consists of two intersecting round arches, filled with intersecting circles of minute script, each having a floral nucleus; the magnificent, large and oblong letters of the text are written alternatively in black contours with gold filling in one line and the reverse in the other.

The second reproduction in *EJ*, X, 926, in the article "Ketubbah," is a tiny fragment, all that is preserved from the marriage contract of Ghāliya ("The Dear One"). The aesthetic effect of the piece is much impaired by the reduction of its size and by the darkness of the photo. The date is not 1125, but 1126/7 (hand of Ḥalfōn b. Nethanel).

[58]See D. Guenzburg and H. V. Stassoff, *L'Ornement hébreu* (Berlin, 1903). For examples reproduced in full color see, e.g., *EJ*, III, opp. p. 524, showing the Bible lection discussed in *Med. Soc.*, II, 152, and IV, opp. p. 812; not in color, although the originals are: *EJ*, IV, 951–954, and XI, 904. An important art history study of the topic: Leila R. K. Avrin, *The Illuminations in the Moshe Ben-Asher Codex of 895 C.E.*, Xerox University Microfilms (Ann Arbor, 1975).

[59]E. L. Sukenik, *Otzar ha-Megillot ha-genuzot* (Jerusalem, 1954), e.g., plates 36–39.

[60]Full illustration *EJ*, XV, 1270; of the Hebrew part only and better visible, *ibid.*, II, 722.

[61]I am obliged to Professor Mark R. Cohen of Princeton University, who, in summer 1974, checked the colors for me in Cambridge, England. I had noted the colors before, but my photostats are black on white.

[62]TS 16.107. These were well-to-do people, see App., part I, group 5, no. 4.

[63]See n. 56, above.

[64]Bodl. MS Heb. a 3 (Cat. 2873), f. 40, see n. 36, above.

[65]The huge, colored ketubba TS 20.62 + 24.15 (see App., part I, group 5, no. 22), the most elaborate we have from Ḥalfōn b. Manasse's hand, is too damaged to lend itself to aesthetic evaluation. Example of a neat, but less pleasing, ketubba written by a colleague of Ḥalfōn: TS 24.16.

[66]TS 12.443, written by Mevōrākh b. Nathan.

[67]Quadrangular: Bodl. MS Heb. a 3 (Cat. 2873), f. 42+ (Karaite, Jerusalem, 1117). Quadruple quadrangular: TS 12.624 (Alexandria, ca. 1090).

[68]*Tabula ansata*: TS 20.33. Hollow letters: TS 12.449.

[69]Border consisting of four bands: TS 8.90.

[70]TS 24.17. The bridegroom's father: Levi ha-Levi [b. Abraham].

[71]TS Misc. Box 28, f. 266 (ca. 1510), an interesting example of late Mamluk style. Fragments: TS 12.438 (late thirteenth century). Other fragments of this ketubba in Westminster College, Frag. Cairens., fs. 106 and 119. Later fragments: *ibid.*, f. 77 (dated 1506); TS 12.596 (dated 1612); ENA 1822 A, f. 84 (lovely rustic illuminations). Gershon Weiss drew my attention to the particularly charming ULC Or 1080, Box 9, f. 21.

[72]TS 13 J 2, f. 14, l. 11 (Dec. 1105).

[73]Addition: TS 24.15*v* (1126). Control over dowry: TS 16.147*v* (1135). Remarrying: TS 16.246*v*. Docket: TS 12.489*v*, Ḥalfōn b. Netanel marrying Karīma b. Joseph (ca. 1030); recto has only Karīma.

[74]TS 8 J 11, f. 15, esp. ll. 3–4.

[75]TS Arabic Box 7, f. 9*.

[76]Replacements of lost ketubbas: e.g., TS 12.155 (1013); Dropsie 333 + TS 16.155 (1088 or shortly before); TS 12.688; TS Box J 3, f. 25(x) (Cairo 1115/6); TS 16.112 (Cairo, 1534); Merx, *Paléographie hébraique*, pp. 39–44 (1164) = Bodl. MS Heb. b 12 (Cat. 2875), f. 26. ENA NS J 3 vellum, f. 3, frag., has the superscription with the good wishes (written 1100–1138).

[77]TS 8.116, ed. M. A. Friedman, *Tarbiz,* 40 (1971), 327–332.

[78]TS Misc. Box 29, f. 6, ed. Strauss-Ashtor, *Mamluks,* III, 14–15.

[79]TS 12.1*v*. The form of such a renewal was the unilateral declaration of the husband that he stands by all the obligations incurred in the original ketubba.

[80]Mosseri L 7; TS 18 J 1, f. 28; ULC Or 1080 J 90.

[81]TS 13 J 3, f. 10, item IV (1159), see App., part I, sec. 1, no. 16.

[82]The so-called Omer period (between Passover and Pentecost) was meticulously observed. There were a few engagements immediately after the Passover week: 25th and 26th of Nisan, TS 8 J 5, f. 2*a-c**, d (1132), remarriage of a divorcée on 29th of Nisan, ULC 1080 J 206 (1147), and practically no Rabbanite wedding in the subsequent month of Iyar. A wedding on the eve of Pentecost, Bodl. MS Heb. a 2 (Cat. 2805), f. 5 (1057), follows the widely diffused custom of celebrating that family event immediately before a holiday, see n. 84, below.

The three weeks of mourning preceding the Ninth of Av, the memorial day of the destruction of the Temple (June–July), were also taboo for weddings. Exceptions: TS 16.357 (20 Tammuz, 1066), TS 16.125 (24 Tammuz, 1492).

[83]A cursory survey revealed this distribution of the frequency of weddings between the weekdays: Sunday, 10; Monday, 14; Tuesday, 19; Wednesday, 23; Thursday, 30; Friday, 12. The Mishna Ketubbot 1:1 recommends Wednesday for virgins and Thursday for second marriages. No such distinction can be observed in the Geniza documents. For Muslim customs see *EI,* IV, 1129–1131, s.v. "*'Urs,*" secs. 4–6.

[84]One or two days before Passover: TS 16.105 (986), TS 16.245 (1015), TS 12.440, PER H 24⁺ (1083), Bodl. MS Heb. b 12 (Cat. 2875), f. 22, TS Arabic Box 38, f. 11. Before the Feast of Tabernacles: Bodl. MS Heb. b 12 (Cat. 2875), f. 26 (1094), TS 12.163 (1119), Bodl. MS Heb. f 56, f. 57 (Cat. 2821, no. 16), a betrothal (1184), TS 16.67, Karaite (1200), Bodl. MS Heb. a 3 (Cat. 2873), f. 46 (1296). Mosseri V 8⁺ (1301, probably a mistake for 1300). On Purim: Bodl. MS Heb. a 3 (Cat. 2873), f. 39 (ca. 1020), TS NS Box 320, f. 15*v* (1048), JNUL 83, no. 4, l. 10⁺ (1132), TS 8 J 5, f. 22, l. 14 (1161). TS 13 J 8, f. 24. Eve of New Year: Mosseri A 37 + 76 (second marriage, 1043). For a ketubba written during a holiday week see S. Assaf, *Gaonica* (Jerusalem, 1933), p. 92. "Mixing joy with joy": BT Mo'ed Qatan 8*b*. See also n. 82, above.

[85]TS 10 J 7, f. 5, ll. 6–12, a note, *ruq'a,* not a letter.

[86]TS 10 J 13, f. 5*v*, ll. 7–8.

[87]Nahray's factotum: TS 10 J 20, f. 18, ll. 10–16, *Nahray* 36. (Abu 'l-Ḥaqq probably is a slip for Abu 'l-Ḥayy). Solomon b. Elijah: TS Arabic Box 7, f. 22: *ḥattā zayyanū 'l-ṣaghīra bi-ālāt al-zīna.* For Solomon's own wedding plans see B, 1, n. 50, above.

[88]"Both women and men": TS NS J 475 (1140). "Luxuries" (Ar. *zukhrufāt al-miṣriyyīn*): TS NS Box 184, f. 65, l. 10. Agreements on the expenditure for the wedding: e.g., B, 2, n. 77, above, C, 1, n. 55, below.

[89]See B, 2, nn. 10, 11, 29, 31, above. The bride's procession: *ibid.,* n. 3. "Tray" and congratulation reception: *Med. Soc.,* II, 492, sec. 54; 495, secs. 63–65.

[90]Bridegroom's procession to synagogue: TS 24.55*v*.

[91]E.g., TS 12.128, TS 16.209, TS 16.107 (Aleppo, 1108). In TS 16.3, ed. Mann, *Texts,* I, 97, l. 26, Sherira Gaon writes to a certain Allūf in Egypt that he was obliged to exert himself for his yeshiva, since the Allūf's brother had been the Gaon's friend and "best man." *Shōshevīn* is usually pronounced today *shushfin.*

[92]Bodl. MS Heb. a 2 (Cat. 2805), f. 2⁺.

[93]See B, 2, n. 51, above, and S. D. Goitein, *Interfaith Relations in Medieval Islam: The Yaakov Herzog Memorial Lecture, Columbia University* (New York, 1973), pp. 15–18.

[94]TS 13 J 34, f. 9, ll. 9–16. About the dignity of a *nāsī* see *Med. Soc.,* II, 19. By chance, a reference to the same wedding is preserved in ULC Add. 3343, see A, 1, n. 15, above.

[95]TS 12.262, top*. "Terrific": *shanīʿ*.

[96]TS 13 J 15, f. 26*.

[97]TS 13 J 29, f. 2, l. 15, ed. S. D. Goitein, *Tarbiz,* 36 (1967), 384: *ta'ahhalt min man kallafnī.*

[98]BM Or 5542, f. 20, ll. 12–14, *Nahray* 210.

[99]TS Misc. Box 25, f. 62m, *Nahray* 118.

[100]See B, 1, nn. 36 and 37. Another good example in Bodl. MS Heb. c 28 (Cat. 2876), f. 60, *India Book* 136.

[101]TS 13 J 25, f. 3*v*, ll. 1–4. The reference is to BT Ḥullin 95 *b*, where success after the acquisition of a house, the birth of a child, and marriage is regarded as an augury for good luck in the future.

[102]Letter of Sahlān (also full of messianic wishes): ENA 4020, f. 33. Letter to Abraham b. Isaac b. Furāt (see *Med. Soc.,* II, 243): TS 18 J 4, f. 11, written by Eli ha-Kohen he-ḥāvēr, son of Ezekiel the cantor, son of Solomon he-ḥāvēr (see *Med. Soc.,* I, 292).

4. *The Economic Foundations of Marriage.*

[1]Tosefta Ketubbot 4:9, *The Tosefta,* ed. S. Lieberman (New York, 1967), p. 68. See also B, 3, n. 32, above.

[2]Tosefta Ketubbot 6:8, ed. *ibid.,* pp. 77–78.

[3]S. Lieberman, *Tosefta Ki-fshuṭah,* Part VI (New York, 1967), p. 282.

[4]See B, 3, n. 30, above.

[5]The case of TS 8.208, where a widow receives as her marriage gift, besides the legal minimum of 12½ dirhems, only an additional 25 dirhems is absolutely exceptional (see App., part I, group 5, no. 28.) This document shows, by the way, that the minimum nuptial gift was actually paid. TS Arabic Box 30, f. 8, where the first installment consists of 20 dirhems, is a collection for a poor girl which was not yet completed. A ketubba of a widow and divorcée from the late thirteenth century, TS 20.109, notes 100 *nuqra* silver dirhems as immediate, and 500, as delayed marriage gift, which, according to *Med. Soc.,* I, 386, sec. 79 (dated 1289), would correspond to 5 and 25 dinars, respectively. Gold had become scarce by that time. It is characteristic for this late period that a betrothal document of a widow written on November 13, 1379, notes 400 dirhems (not nuqra) as delayed installment (no first given), while the record of the betrothal of a divorcée with a young son written by the same clerk on the evening of the same day noted 5 + 30 = 35 dinars as marriage gift (TS 13 J 4, f. 15*a* and *b,* two sheets, ed. Strauss-Ashtor, *Mamluks,* III, 91–93).

[6]Mishna Pe'a 8:8.

[7]The so-called *niṣāb,* see *EI,* IV, 1303, s.v. "Zakāt."

[8]The legal history of the minimum nuptial gift and its reflection in the Geniza documents is lucidly discussed in M. A. Friedman's paper mentioned in B, 3, n. 16, above.

[9]Grohmann, *APEL,* I, 69, 89, 99, 103 f. 112, and elsewhere, and in all the Muslim marriage contracts mentioned *passim,* above. For exceptional payments in silver in Jewish contracts see n. 5, above.

[10]See M. A. Friedman, "The Division in the Geniza Documents of the 'Additional Ketubba' into Early and Late Installments," in the forthcoming *Proceedings of the Seventh World Congress of Jewish Studies held in 1974* (Jerusalem) (Heb.). "Responsibility for her ketubba": TS 16.123 , l. 9, ENA NS 16, f. 6, l. 9, ed. Friedman, *Marriage,* no. 34.

[11]See B, 2, n. 79, above. There the reference is to the gift made at betrothal.

[12]Remarriage to one's own divorcée: App., part I, group 8, nos. 2, 3, 5, 12, 14, 18.

[13]Marriage to divorcée: TS 16.53⁺ (1081), marriage gift (1102), m.g. (= marriage gift) 1 + 3 = 4, no dowry; TS 12.494 (1110), see App., part I, group 7, no. 8;

TS 8 J 5, f. 2*a-c** (1132), see App., part I, group 5, no. 34; TS 12.490 (Alexandria, 1160), m.g. 1 + 5 × 6, no dowry.

[14]Marriage to widow: TS 20.116*v*, item II (ca. 1090), m.g. 2 + 5 = 7, dowry 30; TS NS Box 323, f. 4 (1105), m.g. 1 + 2 = 3. Antonin 634 (ca. 1120), m.g. 3 + 10 = 13; TS 8.208 (1127), see App., part I, group 5, no. 28; TS 12.64 (1241), m.g. 1 (+14) = 15.

[15]Second or third marriage of bride: Bodl. MS Heb. d 65 (Cat. 2877), f. 15 (Cairo, ca. 1080), m.g. (3 +) 6 = 9, dowry 15; TS 8.238 (ca. 1100), m.g. 2 + . . . , dowry occupies half a line; TS 8 J 32, f. 1 (1125/6), see App., part I, group 5, no. 24; TS 12.653 (1132/3), see *ibid.*, no. 38; TS 16.67 (Cairo, 1200), no first installment, only the minimum gift of 25 dirhems obligatory at Karaite second marriage.

[16]Orphans: TS 8 J 5, f. 2*c-d* (1132), see App., part I, group 5, no. 35; Firkovitch II, 1700, f. 10*a*, see App., part I, group 1, no. 4; Firkovitch II, 1700, f. 16*a*, see *ibid.*, n. 7; TS Arabic Box 30, f. 8 (20 dirhems, collected for her).

[17]Status of bride not defined: Bodl. MS Heb. b 12 (Cat. 2875), f. 14 (1058), m.g. 1 + 2 = 3.

[18]TS 12.154⁺ (Qūjandīma, 945), m.g. 2 + 4, dowry 16⅓; special cases: PER H 1⁺ (Tyre, 1079), m.g. 2 + 10 = 12, dowry 16¾; Bodl. MS Heb. b 12 (Cat. 2875), f. 31, right half of Karaite marriage contract, m.g. 3, grand total 77½; TS 24.5 (1111), see App., part I, group 5, no. 9; Bodl. MS Heb. a 3 (Cat. 2873), f. 32*v*⁺ (Ramle, Palestine ca. 1064), m.g. 2 + 6 = 8, dowry 5⅓ (seven items), plus half a house worth 25.

[19]Incomplete data: ULC Or 1080 J 286 (1144/5) m.g. 1 + 1 = 2 (left side only), see App., part I, group 6, no. 5.

[20]ULC Or 1080 Box 5, f. 17 (Cairo, 1071), m.g. 1 + 2 = 3; TS 12.442 (same place and time) (1 +) 2=3, no dowry. Bodl. MS Heb. d 65 (Cat. 2877), f. 15 (see n. 15, above) is written in the same hand and arrangement.

[21]See *Med. Soc.,* I, 390, para (*c*).

[22]Sum of 4 1/6 dinars: TS 13 J 2, f. 3, and TS 8 J 17, f. 9*a-c,* see B, 2, nn. 79 and 80, above. Also TS NS Box 320, f. 15 (to which M. A. Friedman drew my attention).

[23]Minimum obligatory marriage gift of 8⅓ dinars: TS 16.374⁺ (Mastaura, Asia Minor, 1022). For "Jerusalem" see Gulak, *Otzar,* p. 36, top, from a late literary source, which is, however, based on an old model, as proved by the characteristic "Palestinian" stipulations, see Friedman, *Marriage, passim.* The sum of 8⅓ dinars assumes an exchange rate of 1 dinar = 24 zūz (8⅓ × 24 = 200).

[24]See C, 1 and C, 3, below. Cases where the early installment of the marriage gift was larger than the delayed one are extremely exceptional and are traceable to special circumstances, e.g., ENA 2779, f. 3, Friedman, *Marriage,* no. 25 (11 + 3 dinars) where the early installment was used for buying the bride's outfit. TS 12.659, *ibid.,* no. 6 (20 + 8, interpretation doubtful). These are ancient Palestinian ketubbas. I also have doubts about similar cases from the Mamluk period, where an early installment of 50 dinars seems to have been standard for a certain class of people. When, as in TS 24.8, the dowry was large, or in TS Misc. Box 28, f. 217, ed. Strauss-Ashtor, *Mamluks,* III, 72, worth 500 dinars, an early installment of 50 dinars seems reasonable. But when, as in TS Misc. Box 28, f. 26, ed. *ibid.,* p. 77, the daughter of a synagogue beadle, who had no dowry at all, receives 50 dinars as wedding gift at her second marriage, some face-saving or other special circumstances must have been involved, for instance, that the money was given to her in order to buy the outfit, which her father was unable to provide. A similar circumstance seemingly in TS Misc. Box 8, f. 87 (a legal opinion).

[25]Wedding gifts of 6 or 7 dinars were exceptional. I have not found any of 8 or 9 dinars. TS NS J 228 (Malīj, 1134), 6 + 20 (+64 dowry) = 90, grand total. TS 12.440 (Cairo, late twelfth century), 7 + 30, a widow. TS 20.62 + TS 24.15 (1124/5), 7 + 30 = 37, dowry 148, i.e., exactly four times as much.

[26]Note also that those providing wedding gifts of 40 to 50 dinars are far more numerous than those giving 25 to 35.

[27]See C, 1, and C, 2, n. 143, below. Mortgage of a specific piece of property: Bodl. MS Heb. c 28 (Cat. 2876), f. 69 (1160), see App., part I, group 7, no. 13. But here, too, it is not sure that the husband's house (inherited from his brother) was earmarked in the ketubba as a mortgage.

[28]Woman: JNUL 83, f. 3+. Old man: TS 24.14.

[29]See B, 2, n. 23, above.

[30]BT Qiddushin 30*b*.

[31]Another Aramaic term, *'alaltā* ("What comes in," TS 16.181*v*, IV, l. 20+ (Damascus 933) is extremely rare.

[32]*Jihāz,* e.g., TS 13 J 8, f. 24, l. 18. Cf. B, 2, n. 65, above. TS NS J 226, item III (1244).

[33]*Raḥl* designating the dowry in general: TS 12.12*v* (docket), *raḥl Ben Levi,* meaning the total dowry received by the husband; clothing and bedding specifically: TS Arabic Box 54, f. 78, l. 19, where it is opposed to "silver" and, l. 18, to *jihāz,* see preceding note.

[34]*Shuwār*: TS 10 J 27, f. 12. l. 8 (November 1009). In the same document, l. 22, *raḥl* (see preceding note) designates the movable possessions of the *husband,* cf. Idris, "Mariage," p. 46, sec. 9. Shuwār also in TS 13 J 6, f. 9 (ca. 1230), and often between these two dates. Shuwār is still in use in the Egyptian countryside. Beautiful clothing: *shawār.*

[35]TS 20.48, l. 1: *shūra(t) Ma'ānī,* "the trousseau of M." TS 13 J 6, f. 26, l. 6: *man katab qīmat al-shūra,* "the clerk who wrote the assessment of the trousseau." (Both thirteenth century.) See Idris, "Mariage," p. 46, sec. 9, p. 48, sec. 18.

[36]See B, 2, n. 65, above.

[37]TS 13 J 6, f. 9 (see n. 34, above), written and signed by Moses b. Peraḥya, judge in Minyat Ghamr, cf. TS 13 J 4, f. 1 (dated 1226); several documents and letters, written by him, dated and undated, from the years 1220–1234 have been preserved. The order of *recto* and *verso* in this manuscript has to be reversed. Because of the reading in the synagogue of the Targūm, the Aramaic translation of the Bible lection, see *Med. Soc.,* II, 175–177, Aramaic was fairly well known. "Iron sheep": *(nikhsē) ṣōn barzel* (Heb.).

[38]TS 20.48, written and signed by Joseph, son of Moses the judge, during the latter's lifetime. A similar record about the groom's acceptance of the taqwīm in TS 10 J 21, f. 13.

[39]Bodl. MS Heb. d 66 (Cat. 2878), fs. 47–48+, see B, 2, no. 58, above.

[40]ENA 4020, f. 3. The rubric "late marriage gift" was written, but the space provided for it was left blank.

[41]TS Arabic Box 51, f. 103, see App., part I, group 5, no. 20. Ar. *taqdīs* renders Heb. *qiddūshīn,* betrothal (see B, 2, n. 1, above), which more often than not was combined with the wedding.

[42]TS NS J 226*r*. The record is dated Sunday, 8th of Tishri. But that Sunday was the 7th. It is not a mistake: the assessment was made in the evening, and the evening belongs to the following day. Such seemingly wrong dating of evening events is common. For weddings held close to a holiday see B, 3, n. 84.

[43]Bodl. MS Heb. d 66 (Cat. 2878), fs. 47–48+, and TS J 1, f. 29+*, ed. S. D. Goitein in *AJS review,* 2 (1977), 107–110, are models of comprehensively detailed trousseau appraisals. The second example is the most extensive trousseau traced thus far, but does not include houses.

[44]"Dowry receipt": *sheṭār nedunyā,* ULC Or 1080 J 185, written by Immanuel b. Yehiel (ca. 1231–1279, see *Med. Soc.,* II, 515, sec. 32). M. A. Friedman drew my attention to ENA 3755, f. 6, where Ḥalfōn b. Manasse drafts the form of such a document. Cf. TS 8.166, l. 6: a husband agrees that his wife sells her outfit and buys immovables ("because of the insecure times"), TS NS J 112, l. 11 (similar agreement), both written by Ḥalfōn b. Manasse. PER H 20 (dated Oct. 18, 1171), ULC Or 1080 Box 5, f. 15, l. 29, see App., part I, group 1, nos. 26 and 27.

[45]Empty boxes: *EI,* IV, p. 1130, "'Urs," near the end of sec. 4.

[46]BT Baba Meṣi'a, 104*b*. Saadya Gaon: Bodl. MS Heb. d 48 (Cat. 2760), f. 31, ed. S. Assaf in *Rav Saadya Gaon* (Heb.), ed. J. L. Fishman (Jerusalem, 1943), p. 82. TS 12.647, which complements the Bodleian fragment thus: *an yaktubū 'l-jihāz [bi-ḍi'f qīmatih]*.

[47]Ḥalfōn: ENA 3755, f. 6, ll. 21–22, see n. 44, above. Widow: ENA 4011, f. 67. Saladin's time: Bodl. MS Heb. b 12 (Cat. 2875), f. 11, l. 12.

[48]Bilbays: TS 13 J 5, f. 5. Alexandria: Maimonides, *Responsa,* II, 547. See *ibid.*, n. 2, literature on this question. Al-Maḥalla: Bodl. MS Heb. d 74 (no Cat.), f. 35.

[49]ENA 3755, f. 6, ll. 21–22, see n. 47. TS Misc. Box 29, f. 29, l. 20+ (thirteenth century). TS Misc. Box 28, f. 267, l. 11+ (fourteenth century). Responsibility, *qablānūt* (Heb.): Westminster College, Frag. Cairens. 120, ll. 10–12.

[50]See App., part I, *passim,* especially the note at the end of group 1. Thirteenth century: e.g., TS 16.85; TS NS J 306. Parties requesting that prices should be doubled: TS K 15, f. 65, pp. 3–4.

[51]Free disposition: TS 13 J 17, f. 14, see App., part I, group 4, no. 31.

[52]Claims: TS 20.187 + TS 28.6, item III.

[53]Receipts after termination of marriage: TS 13 J 3, f. 10, item V, see App. part I, group 1, no. 17; ULC Or 1080 J 49. Inheritance: TS 10 J 21, f. 6.

[54]Special cases: TS 10 J 7, f. 13; TS K 25, f. 171 (a husband sells the outfit inherited from his wife, probably because he had no daughter).

[55]E.g., TS 28.23, where jewelry comes last obviously because it amounted to only 3 out of a total of 60 dinars, see App., part I, group 5, no. 2; Bodl. MS Heb. f 56 (Cat. 2821), f. 56*b* II, where it is grouped together with copper after clothing, see App., part I, group 2, no. 18; Antonin 460 (Spring 1065): same, but before clothing.

[56]No divisions: TS 12.12 (long list, totaling 865 dinars). The sections separated by special signs: TS 16.86 (very rare).

[57]Chest: *muqaddama,* extremely common, but not yet found by me elsewhere and seemingly used solely for lingerie: trunk: *sundūq,* serving also other purposes. Worth 1 dinar: e.g., TS 20.1, l. 10; TS 10 J 21, f. 5, l. 21. Worth 50 dinars: TS 20.7, ll. 16–17 (1050); TS NS Box 164, f. 13, l. 14 (ca. 1100). Worth 80 dinars: TS 16.107, l. 12 (Aleppo).

[58]The distribution of the various items of clothing varied widely from one social class to the other and from person to person.

[59]Bedding by far the largest item: TS 20.7 (1050).

[60]No jewelry: Bodl. MS Heb. a 3 (Cat. 2873), f. 45 (1033/34); b 12 (Cat. 2875), f. 26 (1094); b 12 (Cat. 2875), f. 15 (1133); ENA 4020, f. 3. TS 16.74.

[61]See App., part II.

[62]TS J 1, f. 29+*, see App., part I, group 6, no. 12. See n. 95, below.

[63]Jewelry 9 dinars, total 203: TS NS J 410. Jewelry 53, total 160: TS K 25, f. 269.

[64]The distinct proof for the absence of a dowry is (*a*) in a marriage contract, when the summary of the husband's obligations follows immediately the details of his marriage gifts, and (*b*) in a court record, when none is mentioned.

[65]TS 16.142, ed. Mann, *Texts,* I, 363–365. The circumstances show that "local custom" could not refer to the fictive evaluation of dowries, see nn. 45–48, above. (The signatory in l. 21 is David Allūf b. Ḥōtām, not Yōtām, and the one in l. 22, *Isaac,* not *Ḥasan,* b. Fashshāṭ. Hebrew *she-tāvō* in l. 10 is influenced by Arabic and should not be corrected according to standard Hebrew grammar). Marriage gift customary among the Muslim of Qayrawān: Idris, "Mariage," p. 47, sec. 14.

[66]Bodl. MS Heb. b 12 (Cat. 2875), f. 3+ (1499), outfit worth 70 dinars, cash 60 dinars. The father was called Moses b. Maimon (as Moses Maimonides, who also emigrated from Spain to Egypt) and the bride Esther, which was common in the West, but not in Egypt, where the women had Arabic names. Similarly TS Misc. Box 28, f. 266 (ca. 1510).

[67]Firkovitch II, 1700, fs. 15*a* and 25*b*–26*b*, see App., part I, group 1, nos. 9 and 10.

[68]See nn. 12–28, above.

[69]See App., part II. David Herlihy's findings are conveniently summarized in the paper cited in B, 1, n. 30, above.

[70]TS 24.2 (1020s), see App., part I, group 4, no. 27.

[71]Bodl. MS Heb. d 65 (Cat. 2877), f. 26+ etc. See App., part I, group 4, no. 12, and B, 3, n. 3, above.

[72]The chores a wife was obliged to do: Maimonides, *Code,* book "Women," sec. "Marriage," chap. 21.

[73]PER H 2, l. 15+. The document speaks in general of "work with flax and wool." Maimonides, following the Talmud, expressly excludes spinning of flax as damaging health, but in those days flax was the main thread produced in Egypt.

[74]See Epstein, *The Jewish Marriage Contract* (New York, 1927), pp. 153–159.

[75]BT Pesaḥim 50*b*.

[76]BT Ketubbot 47*b*.

[77]TS Box J 3, f. 27(z). About the writer of the Aramaic section, Abraham b. Aaron b. Ephraim, see *Med. Soc.,* II, 597 n. 38.

[78]No right on wife's earnings: TS 8.210, l. 3, a tiny fragment. On Bodl. MS Heb. b 12 (Cat. 2875), f. 19, which belongs to the same document, the word *bkswth[*' is visible. A third fragment is preserved in TS 12.164, see App., part I, group 5, no. 12. The identification was made by M. A. Friedman.

[79]TS 8.228. Although the piece is fragmentary, no room for the mention of clothing is left.

[80]TS 12.771, ll. 16–22, see App., part I, group 6, no. 15, sec. 8, n. 15.

[81]BM Or 5536 II, see App., part I, group 1, no. 12.

[82]TS NS J 287, margin. The wife was the daughter of a cantor; her marriage contract is recorded in Bodl. MS Heb. f 56 (Cat. 2821, no. 16), f. 55*a*, item I (1186), see App., part I, group 2, no. 8. The beautifully written petition is probably in her father's hand.

[83]ENA 2560, f. 2. (1260).

[84]Bodl. MS Heb. a 3 (Cat. 2873), f. 46.

[85]TS NS J 363: *māḥal lāh maʿasē yadehā* (Heb.) ENA 2727, f. 5: *ʿamalhā lahā wa-kiswathā ʿalayh* (Ar.; extensive trousseau). Same: TS 20.109 (a divorcée). TS 24.8 (her wedding gift was 50 dinars; long trousseau list). TS 24.9 (also large trousseau).

[86]E.g., TS 12.537, see n. 83, above, and most marriage documents in Strauss-Ashtor, *Mamluks,* III. Fairly well-preserved documents without reference to the wife's work are rare in this period, e.g., TS Misc. Box 29, f. 29, ed. Strauss-Ashtor, *Mamluks,* III, pp. 32–34; TS Misc. Box 28, f. 267, *ibid.,* pp. 70–71.

[87]Widows and divorcées: TS 20.10 (1310), ed. Strauss-Ashtor, *Mamluks,* III, p. 69; TS Misc. Box 28, f. 26 (1316), *ibid.,* p. 78; TS 13 J 4, f. 15 (1379, two cases), *ibid.,* pp. 91–92. Bride with large trousseau: TS Misc. Box 28, f. 217, *ibid.,* pp. 72–74.

[88]Bodl. MS Heb. b 12 (Cat. 2875), f. 3+ (1499); TS Misc. Box 28, f. 266 (ca. 1510); Gottheil-Worrell XL, pp. 178, l. 8, p. 182, l. 7 (both 1511); one of the brides had a Spanish, the other a biblical name.

[89]See n. 76, above. Rent and water: ENA NS 17, f. 31*a*, margin (continued from ENA NS 17, f. 31*b*, col. II, item 2). M. A. Friedman informs me that the question of the wife's earnings formed the topic of his paper at the meeting of the American Oriental Society held in 1971. He intends to revise the paper before publication. For the interesting case where a wife was permitted to retain her earnings, while her mother, who moved in to her son-in-law's house, had to give up to him hers, see C, 4, below.

[90]See sec. D, below.

[91]Lane, *Modern Egyptians,* p. 194 (chap. VI). Heinrich Freiherr von Maltzan, *Reise nach Südarabien* (Braunschweig, 1873), p. 50.

[92]TS 16.50, described in the caption as *sēfer ērūs* (betrothal document, Heb.), a draft, it seems. For Abū Saʿd see *Med. Soc.,* II, 351–352, for his son Ḥasan, Fischel, *Jews,* p. 87 n. 3. The Tustarī brothers mentioned so often in my *Letters of Medieval Jewish Traders* (see the Index) are those of the first generation in Egypt.

[93]TS Misc. Box 29, f. 58. See B, 1, n. 33, above.

[94]The daughter of the treasurer: TS 8.129, Friedman, *Marriage,* no. 43, a tiny fragment. The family name of the girl was al-Qazzāz, "Silk-worker," or "-merchant," the same as that of Manasse Ibn al-Qazzāz, the administrator of Syria for the Fatimid caliph al-ʿAzīz (975–996). But her father was a Kohen, and Manasse was not; thus she could not have been an offspring of that powerful man. The genealogical list TS 8 K 22, f. 1, ed. Mann, II, 320, might refer to her family, but it does so in a confused way. Like other such genealogical lists, the document enumerates the ancestors of both the father and the mother of a person. Mann, II, 318 writes that this list was written at Maimonides' time (ca. 1200). That is correct, but the more orderly version, contained in TS K 15, f. 69, lists eight generations and reaches thus back beyond the year 1080. Since the groom is described as being from Damascus, the ketubba must have been written elsewhere, but not in the Egyptian capital, for the document is dated from the Creation, which was not customary there. Tyre is the most likely place under the circumstances. For the "treasurer" see *Med. Soc.,* I, 249.

[95]TS 24.1, partly ed. S. Schechter, *JQR,* 13 (1900/01), 220–221, see Shaked's *Bibliography,* p. 76. Schechter omitted the trousseau list, the prices of which add up to close to 900 dinars. In the MS the tens and singles after the number 1100 – 300 = 800 are lost. As above, n. 62, the gold and silver ornaments were of a higher value than clothing.

[96]TS 13 J 32 (containing one document; now marked TS J 3, f. 47), ed. S. Assaf, *Joseph Klausner Jubilee Volume* (Jerusalem, 1937), p. 230. For *hdhh* . . . in the printed edition, the MS has *nẓr l-ṣbyh* = *Naẓar al-ṣabiyya,* "The girl Naẓar." Letter addressed to David b. Amram: TS 13 J 13, f. 21, partly ed. Mann, II, 80. The writer, Eli ha-mumḥe b. Abraham, had sent a letter to Ḥesed Abū Naṣr during the latter's lifetime, DK 123, f. 1*a*, ed. A. Scheiber, *Acta Orientalia Hungaria,* 16 (1963), 99–105. About Eli see *ibid.,* p. 101. A Heb. version of Scheiber's article: *Tarbiz,* 32 (1963), 180–183. Letter from Ramle: TS 13 J 26, f. 18, ll. 2–5, ed. S. D. Goitein, *Shalem,* 2 (1976), 65–72. The David b. Amram ha-Kohen, who signed a letter from a provincial town and lived at least two generations later, see *Med. Soc.,* II, 591 n. 38, or the Yemenite Nagid bearing this name, see *ibid.,* p. 26, should not be confused with the Karaite notable.

[97]Taqwīm: TS J 1, f. 29+, see App., part I, group 6, no. 12. Aden: ENA NS 4, f. 13.

[98]Museum of Islamic Art, Cairo, no. 4224, ed. Suʿād Māhir, *ʿUqūd,* pp. 17–18. See B, 1, n. 24, above.

[99]TS 20.7. The details of the dowry, which is preserved almost in its entirety, add up to 596 dinars plus the copper and pots, which are listed, but their prices are lost.

[100]TS 20.6, ed. S. Assaf, *Tarbiz,* 9 (1938), 30–32. The editor, *ibid.,* p. 30 n. 2, erroneously assumed that [?]80 (i.e., the first digit lost) was the total of the marriage gift; it was the grand total, comprising also the dowry. In *Med. Soc.,* I, 48, "daughter" has to be replaced by "granddaughter." For the calculation see App., part I, group 4, no. 36.

[101]Ephraim b. Meshullām: Mosseri A 10.1. Yijū: Firkovitch II, 1700, f. 27+, see App., part I, group 1, no. 11.

[102]Idris, "Mariage," p. 47, sec. 13.

[103]"Perfumer": Bodl. MS Heb. d 66 (Cat. 2878), fs. 47–48+. Two others: see App., part I, group 1, nos. 8 and 10. Jekuthiel: ENA 4020, I, f. 47*v*, TS 8.184, *India Book* 269*c-d*; see about him *Med. Soc.,* II, 477, sec. 16, p. 479, sec. 21, and Goitein, *Letters,* pp. 178 ff.

[104]David B. Shekhanya: TS 12.155, see App., part I, group 4, no. 15, and *Med. Soc.,* II, 227. The widowed cantor Meir b. Yākhīn (in Ar., Abu 'l-Majd b. Thābit) marries the daughter of Ṭāhōr (in Ar., Ṭāhir), the beadle: TS 20.1. For Ṭāhir see *Med. Soc.,* II, 450, sec. 40. He is the beadle who receives 14 loaves of bread at the semiweekly distributions, *ibid.,* pp. 451, 452. The two poorer cantors: see nn. 81 and 82, above.

[105]Second-hand items bought in the bazaar, even of clothing, were by no means ruled out for the bride's outfit.

[106]BT Baba Meṣi'a 74*b*; cf. Ketubbot 54*a*.

[107]For the question of fictive prices in the marriage documents see nn. 45, 46, above.

[108]For mother's trousseau forming daughter's outfit, see C, 2–4, below.

[109]See C, 1, below.

[110]See nn. 65, 98, 102, above. Coptic clergy: Nabia Abbott, "Arabic Marriage Contracts among Copts," *ZDMG,* 95 (1941), 70. The learned editor tried to avoid the then usual translation of *ṣadāq* (which, in practice, is the same as *mahr*) with "bride price"; but dowry, of course, is wrong.

5. *Social Safeguards*

[1]Purim: see B, 3, n. 84, above.

[2]TS 13 J 8, f. 24.

[3]At the annulment of a betrothal a regular bill of repudiation was required in order to enable the bride to marry another man, see B, 2, above, *passim.*

[4]The part of the line torn away no doubt contained the detail concerning the slave girl. The regular conditions are styled in the stereotyped form known from many other documents written by Ḥalfōn b. Manasse. See n. 7, below.

[5]Possibly also the consent of the parents was required.

[6]The conditional bill of divorce stipulated that the wife would be free to marry another man if the husband did not return at the time fixed in the bill. See n. 67, below.

[7]TS NS J 378, written by Ḥalfōn b. Manasse. The upper part and the right and left sides of the document are torn away, but because of the repetitious character of the wording its contents can be restored. It is not evident, however, whether the fine was imposed on the breach of any of these conditions or only the last one, never to separate the wife from her parents.

[8]See C, 3, nn. 39–41, below.

[9]TS 8 J 17, f. 9 *a-c* (Nov. 1131), see App., part I, group 5, no. 32. On "ban in general terms" see *Med. Soc.,* II, 340–341. Similar versions in the hand of Ḥalfōn b. Manasse, e.g., in TS NS Box 226, f. 10 (Dec. 1119) and Bodl. MS Heb. a 3 (2873), f. 40 (May 1128). In TS 8 J 9, f. 9, l. 11, written a short time before Ḥalfōn's activities, the details appear in reverse order: "She is trustworthy in the management of the house and in her statements . . . ," putting the deeds before the words.

[10]TS 8 J 5, f. 2*c-d* (April 1132), see App., part I, group 5, no. 35.

[11]TS NS Box 226, f. 11, l. 4 (Dec. 1119), see App., part I, group 5, no. 16.

[12]ENA 1822A, f. 60. The note is of extreme brevity and therefore somewhat cryptic for us: "My lady, Sitt Ṣalaf visited me and reported to me what you have said to her. Now, my lady, I have children; so if you deem fit that he (or: it) should be left in my engagement agreement, it is fine with me; but if you transfer him (or: it) for me to someone else, you would do me a great favor. I am also *trustworthy etc.* in this matter. So, if you will do this for me, your action will be highly appreciated." The mysterious "he (or: it)" could have been a male slave who had become the property of the widow with children in payment of what was due her after the death of her husband. For reasons of propriety he was admitted to the household of "the Lady," who suggested to include him in the dowry the widow would bring into her new marriage. But she preferred cash, since a male slave was high-priced, but of little practical value to her and her children. The transfer of the proprietorship of a slave was a delicate matter; therefore the widow emphasizes that in her first marriage she had been granted complete trustworthiness and no one could contest her property rights. Whatever the story behind this little note may have been, the emphasis on the privilege of "trustworthiness" is noteworthy. Sitt Ṣalaf, "Lady Inaccessible," appears also in *Med. Soc.,* II, 432, sec. 162 (thirteenth century), but our note seems to belong to the eleventh century.

[13]TS NS J 287. See B, 4, n. 82, above.

[14]See C, 3, below.

[15]Bodl. MS Heb. f 56 (Cat. 2821, no. 16), f. 57, ll. 14 ff. (1184). Bodl. MS Heb. d 66 (Cat. 2878), f. 47⁺ (1146). Two eminent judges, Samuel b. Saadya ha-Levi and Nathan b. Samuel he-ḥāvēr (see *Med. Soc.,* II, 514, sec. 23, and p. 513, sec. 18), were in charge of these marriage agreements.

[16]Idris, "Mariage," II, 79, sec. 130.

[17]Slave girl only: TS 10 J 21, f. 4*d,* ll. 6–7, see B, 2, n. 65, above. TS 20.160 (Nov. 1047), ed. M. A. Friedman, *Dine Israel,* 6 (1975), 107–114. See n. 75, below.

[18]TS Box J 3, f. 27 (z), sec. II, see *Med. Soc.,* II, 344, where I omitted the interesting stipulation about objects made by the wife, as well as the polygyny clause. The writer of this document, Abraham b. Aaron *ha-mumḥe,* is known from documents dated 1094/5–1107 (The date 1094/5: TS K 6, f. 24, had not yet been noted in *Med. Soc.,* II, 597 n. 39). Thus he was an older contemporary of Ḥalfōn b. Manasse, who wrote the upper, but later, sec. I of our document.

[19]Or close to the end of the eleventh century, see preceding note. M. A. Friedman, "Polygamy in the Documents of the Geniza," *Tarbiz,* 40 (1971), 320–359, with a useful English summary on pp. v–vi. *Idem,* "The Monogamy Clause in Jewish Marriage Contracts," *Perspectives in Jewish Learning,* ed. M. A. Friedman (Chicago, 1972), pp. 20–40. *Idem,* "Polygamy: Additional Information from the Geniza," *Tarbiz,* 43 (1974), 166–198. Attention is drawn also to S. Lowy, "The Extent of Jewish Polygamy in Talmudic Times," *JJS,* 9 (1958), 115–138.

[20]ENA NS 18, f. 27, a much mutilated fragment.

[21]TS 13 J 2, f. 25⁺*, Nov./Dec., 1139, not 1140, as in *Med. Soc.,* I, 407 n. 40.

[22]ENA NS 17, f. 10, ed. M. A. Friedman, *Tarbiz,* 43 (1974), 175–182.

[23]ENA 4010, f. 28 (Summer 1023) contains an obscure reference to a man repudiating a wife and having another one, ed. M. A. Friedman, *Tarbiz,* 40 (1971), 358. The petition; TS NS Box 184, f. 154, written by Ḥalfōn b. Manasse. "Strong document," *sheṭār wāthīq* (Heb.).

[24]See n. 18, above.

[25]Bodl. MS Heb. b 13, f. 48 (Cat. 2834, no. 29) + TS 8 J 32, f. 1 (1125/6), see Friedman, "Monogamy Clause" (n. 19, above), p. 22. Moses b. Mevōrākh is mentioned in the superscription. *Med. Soc.,* II, 25, is to be changed accordingly.

[26]See *Med. Soc.,* II, 110. Besides the two examples given there, I know only of TS 8.199, written by Ḥalfōn b. Manasse. But only the end of this document has been preserved, so that all details about the parties concerned remain unknown. See also n. 7, above.

[27]ENA 3755, f. 6*v,* see Friedman, "Monogamy Clause" (n. 19, above), pp. 28–29, 37–38, nn. 35 and 41.

[28]S. D. Goitein, "Portrait of a Yemenite Weavers' Village," *JSS,* 27 (1955), 21 n. 51. A revised version of this study has been prepared for inclusion in a volume containing my studies on Yemenites to be published by the Ben Zvi Institute, Jerusalem.

[29]*Reallexicon der Assyriologie* (Berlin, 1938), II, 284–298. Friedman, "Monogamy Clause" (n. 19, above), p. 38 n. 45, and p. 40 (Addenda) draws attention to some new studies on the subject.

[30]See the discussion of this matter in Grohmann, *APEL,* I, 72–73.

[31]Grohmann, *APEL,* no. 38, ll. 13–14; no. 41, ll. 7–10. In the latter papyrus it is also stipulated that the wife may sell or set free any slave girl of the husband with whom he had intercourse. For Spain see Idris, "Mariage," p. 78, sec. 130.

[32]Bodl. MS Heb. a 2 (Cat. 2805), f. 23, l. 11, ed. S. Assaf, *Tarbiz,* 9 (1938), f. 216. The document deals with the gift to a stepsister of part of a house.

[33]TS 10 J 15, f. 26, ll. 13, 15–16. See A, 2, n. 79, no. 5, above.

[34]ENA 2727, f. 5: *ṣuḥbat abīh wa-ummih.* TS Misc. Box 25, f. 140 (1127): after the wife had already received a bill of repudiation because she found life with her husband's parents intolerable, she married him anew, promising never to demand *furqa,* separation (from his parents).

[35]TS 8 J 5, f. 22* (1161): harmful to wife—an orphan—to live with her mother-

and brother-in-law in one apartment, *maskan*. TS 20.36. TS 13 J 8, f. 24, ll. 10–11, see n. 2, above. TS Misc. Box 8, f. 97: move out or repudiate!

[36]TS 13 J 2, f. 3 (1093): *ṭabaqa*, see B, 2, n. 79, above. TS 13 J 3, f. 3+ (1143). Also TS 10 J 27, f. 3, item 1 (1107), see B, 2, n. 75 above.

[37]Living one year in the house of the bride's parents: TS 13 J 6, f. 14, ed. S. Assaf, *Eretz Israel*, 1 (1951), 140, ll. 9–15; Friedman, *Marriage*, no. 26. Two years: Bodl. MS Heb. b 12 (Cat. 2875), f. 11, l. 15. The MS is fragmentary; the extant remnant does not contain the detail of a move to another city.

[38]Idris, "Mariage," p. 59, sec. 71.

[39]Mosseri A, f. 10.1. The same engagement contract foresees that the wife may not leave the house except with her husband's permission, see n. 62, below. TS J 3, f. 27 (z). TS 10 J 27, f. 3 a, l. 12.

[40]TS 13 J 6, f. 33.

[41]Bodl. MS Heb. a 3 (Cat. 2873), f. 32, ll. 16–17, Friedman, *Marriage*, no. 12. The property was evaluated as being worth 25 dinars and was included in the dowry. In TS 12.119, Friedman, *Marriage*, no. 41, one third of a house is given to a daughter at the marriage on condition that it would become her property only after her mother's death.

[42]See n. 33, above.

[43]Idris, "Mariage," secs. 41, 168, 187 (Tunisia and Spain, early twelfth century).

[44]TS NS J 378, see n. 7 above.

[45]Karaite: Bodl. MS Heb. a 3 (Cat. 2873), f. 42, ll. 35–36+ (1117). Rabbanite: ENA 2727, f. 14, item II (item I is dated 1324).

[46]Firkovitch II, 1700, f. 25*b*–26*b*. See App., part I, group 1, no. 10.

[47]Prohibition of move from Cairo: TS 10 J 27, f. 3, item I, see B, 2, n. 75, above. Right to move: TS 8 J 4, f. 22*v*, *ibid.*, n. 76.

[48]TS 8 J 17, f. 9*a*–*c* (1131), see B, 2, n. 80, above. Another example is TS 8 J 17, f. 6, ll. 12–19, an official letter referring to such a stipulation. Jewish law does not permit a husband to move from a city to a small town or village or vice versa without the consent of his wife. But no references to this or other relevant Talmudic statutes (BT Ketubbot 110*a*–*b*, and parallels) are made in the marriage contracts.

[49]TS 8 J 5, f. 21 (1160).

[50]TS 13 J 8, f. 24, see n. 2, above.

[51]TS NS J 363: Heb. *rōṣā* is to be understood as Arabic *bi-riḍāhā*, "her consent," TS NS J 297, part 2, l. 8, ed. Strauss-Ashtor, *Mamluks*, III, 57, see *Tarbiz*, 41 (1972), 80, for corrections.

[52]Groom: TS 20.109 (1289), see *Med. Soc.*, I, 386, sec. 79; Bodl. MS Heb. b 3, f. 9 (Cat. 2806, no. 8), 1331, ed. D. H. Baneth, *Alexander Marx Jubilee Volume*, Vol. II (New York, 1950), p. 85, where *wsnh'* is to be read *wsknh'*; Gottheil-Worrell XL, p. 178, l. 11 (1511), where the MS has *whdyrh* (not *whdwrh*). Bride: TS 12.39, l. 16+ (1315), see B, 2, n. 5, above, Bride following the groom: TS AS 147, f. 12.

[53]Idris, "Mariage," secs. 26, 73, 44.

[54]Muslim: Grohmann, *APEL*, I, 74, l. 1. "He will not prevent her [a Karaite wife] from visiting her family": Firkovitch II, 1700, f. 17*b*, see n. 73, below. Alexandria: TS 8 J 5, f. 2*a*–*c** (1132). Free not to visit husband's family: TS 6 J 2, f. 2, l. 6.

[55]Friedman, *Ethics*, esp. pp. 87–95.

[56]Ibn Hishām, *Sīra* (Cairo, 1936), IV, 251, l. 16.

[57]Westminster College, Frag. Cairens. 11, a fragment in the same style, script, and arrangement as TS 13 J 23, f. 7, which bears the name of Samuel b. Eli Gaon.

[58]Maimonides, *Code*, book "Women," sec. "Marriage," 13:11.

[59]Al-Ghazālī, *Iḥyā'* (Cairo, 1939), II, 49, ll. 2–4 (book 12, chap. 3, para. 5).

[60]TS 8 J 7, f. 27. See D, below.

[61]I take this to mean that the gift was noted with double its real value, so that the delayed installment amounted only to 25, or, rather, 30 dinars. See B, 4, n. 47, above.

[62]Mosseri A, f. 10.1. Nathan ha-Kohen b. Solomon was old at that time, and numerous documents of his show a certain slackness in execution. Thus, one would

expect the number 50 to be deleted and several details are not defined with sufficient exactitude.

[63]TS 20.87, ll. 16–19 (Summer 1134), *Med. Soc.*, II, 435, sec. 177. Both in this document and in PER H 31 Yeshūʿā al-Ramlī is referred to as "the scholar."

[64]In TS 20.87 (see preceding n.) *al-ramlī,* "from Ramle," is written after the blessing over Yeshūʿā's dead father, which means that the word referred to him, not to his father.

[65]See *Med. Soc.,* II, 514, secs. 24–26. In sec. 24, the date 1155 refers to TS 13 J 34, f. 4, and to Sāsōn. The father of Sāsōn and Ephraim, Meshullām b. Sāsōn *he-ḥaver,* signed a document in Jan. 1133, Bodl. MS Heb. a 3 (Cat. 2873), f. 40*v*.

[66]TS 8 J 5, f. 7. In TS 12.624, l. 4 (right lower corner of a marriage agreement), the phrase "the bride will not leave the house except when he chooses so" seems to have another meaning, for l. 2 says: "If the bride wishes to leave the house and live somewhere else, she cannot rent the place to anyone else except her sister." Another clause provides that any income from their father's inheritance "in the Maghreb" will be divided equally between the two sisters. Thus, the phrase in l. 4, which is worded like l. 2, obviously means that the apartment in the house jointly owned by the two sisters cannot be vacated except with the husband's consent. Friedman, *Ethics,* p. 100 n. 41, rightly puts a question mark after TS 12.634 (misprint for 12.624).

[67]Muslims: Idris, "Mariage," secs. 54 (absence of four months), 163 and 178 (six months). Jews: TS NS J 378, see n. 7, above. Goitein, *Letters,* pp. 316–319.

[68]See Goitein, *Letters,* pp. 249–251, and C, 1, nn. 140–165, below.

[69]TS 20.160 (1047); Bodl. MS Heb. f 56 (Cat. 2821, no. 16), f. 46*v* (1182).

[70]TS 16.286, ll. 19–20*. October 1219.

[71]TS 8 J 5, f. 4*v*, item IV (top of margin). "For the end of Tammuz and Av," summer 1127.

[72]TS 20.62 + 24.15 (1125). At the abortive repudiation (1132) the father, characterized as meshōrēr, singer, was still alive. For Judah al-Ḥarīzī's derision of the synagogue singers in his twenty-fourth *maqāma,* see E. Fleischer, *Yuval* (Jerusalem), 3 (1974), 47.

[73]No oaths: Firkovitch, II, 1700, f. 17*b*, item II (1156). Repudiation and reconciliation after oath: TS 16.246*v*, l. 4.

[74]Ibn Zaffān, merchant: TS NS J 198, col. I, ll. 16 and 25, trans. S. D. Goitein, *JESHO,* 9 (1966), 47 (on p. 46 I counted him erroneously among the Christian customers of Nahray b. Nissīm). Members of the family were contributors to public appeals in the lists described in *Med. Soc.,* II, 474, sec. 8, and 507, sec. 135. The physician Ephraim Ibn Zaffān (Ibn Abī Uṣaybiʿa, II, 105) could have been a grandson of Ephraim b. Ḥalfōn Ibn Zaffān, who had had a partnership in a textile business with a Muslim and a Jew (before 1085), TS 16.11. The groom's name was Ṭōvia b. Eli b. Khalaf, known as Ibn Zaffān (*not* al-zaffān).

[75]TS 20.160⁺. This document contains also the promise not to buy a slave girl, except with the wife's consent or at her request, but not the polygyny clause which was redundant, see n. 17, above.

[76]ENA 2727, f. 18*bv* (main part) + ENA 2806, f. 11 (left upper corner) ed. M. A. Friedman, *Dine Israel,* 6 (1975), 115–122. The main part was torn into two halves, which were afterward pasted together, but incorrectly; the first line of the left half is the continuation of l. 6 of the right half. The name of the month and the hundreds of the year are torn away, but the document was written by Ḥalfōn b. Manasse (1100–1138), and in the year concerned only the new moon day of Nisan fell on a Thursday, wherefore Monday, 5th of [. . . 14] 44 must be March 13, 1133. Name of the bride: Sitt al-Banāt ha-niqrēt Saʿīda, "Mistress over the Girls Named Propitious."

[77]Wife beating: TS NS J 378, see n. 7, above, TS 8 J 5, f. 2*c–d,* see C, 1, nn. 121–137, below. Bedding: TS 13 J 6, f. 33.

[78]See *Med. Soc.,* II, 277, 302.

[79]See Idris, "Mariage," secs. 21 and 31, and the divergent opinions adduced there. See also secs. 92, 110, and 111, where the right faith of the wife is a matter of concern. For the Ibāḍīs see *EI*², III, 648–662, and, specifically for North Africa, pp. 653–657.

[80]Meinardus, *Christian Egypt,* p. 283.

[81]For Samaritans in the Geniza see *Med. Soc.,* II, 7–8, 520 n. 5.

[82]TS NS J 358, the ketubba of Baṭrīqa (Patricia) b. Aaron.

[83]ENA 4020, f. 3. First installment: 10 dinars. Dowry: 200 dinars.

[84]TS NS Box 313, f. 4 (1089/90), ed. Friedman, *Marriage,* no. 9. TS 8 J 5, f. 2*c*–*d* (April 1132). Not crossed out: Mosseri A, f. 10.1, see n. 62, above.

[85]TS Misc. Box 28, f. 26, l. 8, ed. Strauss-Ashtor, *Mamluks,* III, 77.

[86]TS 13 J 8, f. 24, see n. 2, above.

[87]ENA NS 21, f. 6, see n. 34, above.

[88]Rider: TS 24.75 (Nov. 1116). Second version: Antonin 637, ed. Friedman, *Marriage,* no. 30.

[89]No signature: TS 24.80 (1039). One signature: Bodl. MS Heb. a 3 (Cat. 2873), f. 46 (1296).

[90]Private MS marked AJ (acquired in Cairo, summer 1972), ll. 14–23.

[91]TS 16.142, see B, 4, n. 65, above; TS 20.62 + 24.15, see App., part I, group 5, no. 22. Cf. also n. 72, above; ENA NS 2, f. 20, see C, 1, n. 93, below.

[92]See B, 1, n. 5, and B, 3, n. 86, above. It must be noted that the names of girls, when mentioned at all, are usually not accompanied by any good wish. The reference in B, 1, n. 5, is taken from a letter of an aunt writing about her nieces.

[93]BT Ketubbot 17*a*.

C. "THE HOUSE" OR NUCLEAR FAMILY

1. *Husband and Wife*

[1]ENA 2739, f. 16, *India Book* 176, trans. in Goitein, *Letters,* pp. 220–226. I do not include here letters addressed to authorities describing sexual incompetence and similar matters, since they are items of correspondence, not legal documents.

[2]"I am upset because 'the house' (*bayt*) is ill," TS 13 J 18, f. 5, l. 8; "because 'the inhabitants of the house' are in a grave condition," *ahl ad-dār,* TS 12.373, f. 15 (Jewish husband): TS NS Box 321, f. 23, *India Book* 320 (Muslim); "your house (*dār*) and boys are well," ULC Or 1080 J 145; *manzil,* "domicile," TS 28.20*v*, l. 2, *India Book* 280. Heb. *ba'alē ha-bayit*: TS 12.252, l. 30, a letter addressed to a Jewish judge of Aleppo (early eleventh century). The writer in Arabic, too, felt *ahl* to be a plural. In cases where we positively know that only the recipient's wife is greeted we find after *ahl* the plural: PER H 85, margin, l. 6; TS 10 J 18, f. 6, l. 19.

[3]To a son: "Take good care of your mother [the writer's wife], of the one that is with you, *man 'indak,* and your brothers," ULC Or 1080 J 80, l. 16. "The one that is with me": PER H 85, l. 7. A man writing to his brother-in-law refers to his sister as "the dear house," *al-bayt al-'azīza,* TS 18 J 3, f. 15, l. 14.

[4]"One should not inquire about the well-being of any woman," BT Qiddushin 70*b*. Nahray's third wife and widow is known from a contract of the purchase of a slave girl, see *Med. Soc.,* I, 137, n. 39 (Nov. 1108).

In ENA NS 22, f. 27, Nahray b. Nathan, the cousin and brother-in-law of Nahray b. Nissīm, comforts him on the death of a baby girl, conveys greetings "from my sister [i.e., Nahray b. Nissīm's wife] and the girls," and asks his cousin whether he should remain with the family in Alexandria or join him in the capital.

The Gaon Daniel b. Azarya, in writing a personal letter to his brother, sends neither regards to the latter's wife, nor greetings from his own spouse, see Goitein, *Shalem,* 2 (1976), 98.

[5]TS 16.179*v*, ll. 3–6, 8–10*, see A, 2, n. 6, above.

[6]*Mose b. Maimon Epistulae*, ed. D. H. Baneth (Jerusalem, 1946), p. 71.

[7]TS 13 J 21, f. 23, probably thirteenth century. I Samuel 25:6 as superscription: TS 13 J 20, f. 6 (Mevōrākh b. Nathan), at end: TS NS J 97 (Solomon b. Elijah), and often.

[8]E.g., TS 13 J 22, f. 26, l. 21; the writer uses *jōza* (for classical *zawja*), as is common in present-day Arabic speech.

[9]TS 8 J 14, f. 27: "Yehiel b. Isaac, the Frenchman, living in Jerusalem" sends greetings (in Hebrew, of course) to the widow of R. Anatolī (of Marseilles, living in Alexandria), her daughter, and granddaughter, wishing the latter to bear male children.

[10]ULC Or 1080 J 71*. The wife of Judah b. Moses Ibn Sighmār, writing to him in Alexandria from Fustat.

[11]TS 10 J 15, f. 12, l. 8*, written by Israel b. Nathan. See n. 248, below.

[12]TS 16.274*v*, l. 26.

[13]Common, e.g., private MS AJ, l. 10.

[14]TS Arabic Box 54, f. 91, ll. 9, 11, *margin*, l. 3, *verso*, ll. 2, 11.

[15]ENA NS 2, f. 16, l. 15; ULC Or 1080 J 28*v*, l. 7.

[16]TS 20.135, ll. 11–12. "Maidservant": see *Med. Soc.*, I, 131.

[17]PER H 22 * (1137), ed. S. D. Goitein, *Sefunot*, 8 (1964), 115–119.

[18]Genesis 24:1–27. See N. Wieder, *S. Assaf Jubilee Volume* (Jerusalem, 1953), pp. 246–249, and D. Pagis, *J. Schirmann Jubilee Volume* (Jerusalem, 1970), p. 274. I am grateful to Dr. E. Fleischer for drawing my attention to this custom.

[19]BT Pesaḥim 78*a*.

[20]See nn. 2–3, above.

[21]TS 16.277, l. 18*.

[22]Government: TS 13 J 2, f. 25+*, see *Med. Soc.*, I, 68, and B, 5, n. 21, above. Jewish authorities: TS 12.597, l. 25, *Med. Soc.*, II, 49 n. 53. Population: Dropsie 389*v*, ll. 36–44, see *Med. Soc.*, II, 68, n. 150.

[23]Mishna Yoma 1:1, referring to Leviticus 16:17, where the original meaning, no doubt, was "his family," and not "his wife." Separate living quarters: see nn. 69–74, below.

[24]TS 13 J 8, f. 23, l. 13, ed. L. A. Motzkin, *Zvi Avneri Memorial Volume* (Haifa, 1970), pp. 124–127.

[25]TS 13 J 21, f. 36, ll. 11, 13, 16*, cf. B, 1, n. 4: *ṣāḥibat al-bayt*. TS 10 J 12, f. 24, l. 17, *verso* 3.

[26]Dropsie 398, ll. 14–15: *rubbat* [for: *rabbat*] *baytak*. TS 10 J 12, f. 28, l. 16.

[27]Cf. the superscriptions of the marriage contracts, B, 3, nn. 39–43, 51.

[28]"I am 'found' not 'find,' " writes a jubilant young husband who had married his maternal cousin in Damascus and was returning with her to Egypt via Jerusalem, ENA 4020, f. 24, ed. Mann, II, 115, margin, 3. See Mann (1970) p. xxxii. For *m* . . . read *m*[*ōṣē*].

[29]See B, 1, nn. 45, 50–56; B, 2, nn. 18–22.

[30]B, 1, n. 62.

[31]TS 16.277*.

[32]Kindness, tenderness, and consideration: *ḥanna* (for *ḥanān*), *shafaqa, ra'iyya* (for *ri'āya*).

[33]ULC Or 1080 J 23, see n. 244, below. Incantation: TS AS 145, f. 24.

[34]Maimonides, *Responsa*, II, 410. Ar. *lam tazal fī ḥūbbin lahu.*

[35]TS 12.246, l. 6, *Nahray* 132.

[36]DK XIII, l. 18*: *bāzila, naẓīfa, ṣāliḥa, qayyima bi-umūrha.* I do not believe that *ṣāliḥa* means "pious" here; it is, rather, another term for "efficient."

[37]Cf. A, 1, n. 12, above. When the writer of ULC Or 1080 J 23 implores his wife to follow him to the capital he praises her as "a pious woman like you," see n. 244, below.

[38]As in 16.277*, see n. 31, above.

[39]TS 8 J 1, f. 1, ll. 25–26, ed. Schechter, *Saadyana*, p. 66, In l. 25 read *neḥmeshet* for *bḥmsht*, in l. 26, *kā'ēle* for *bowēle*. The daughters are referred to on p. 66,

l. 23, the sons on p. 68, l. 22. The poet's wish that the lady should give birth to another son was fulfilled. We learn this from another poem, BM Or 5554 B, f. 20, ed. J. Mann, *JQR*, 9 (1919), 159.

[40]TS 13 J 8, f. 23, ll. 3–4+, see n. 24, above.

[41]TS 20.47*v*, l. 11; TS NS J 390, l. 9: *ghilāla sharb.* Dozy, *Supplément*, II, 809*b*: *ghilāla khafīfa taṣifu mā warā'ahā min al-thadyayn.*

[42]See B, 1, nn. 6, 7, above, and C, 2, below.

[43]See n. 32, above, "Love, approval, and a generous mind, as God has ordered us," *maḥabba wa-riḍā wa-ahavā [Heb.] wa-jūdat ḍamīr*, Mosseri L, f. 197, 19.

[44]TS 13 J 8, f. 23, ll. 18, 19, 24–25+.

[45]BM Or 10599*v*.

[46]TS NS J 227.

[47]Last minute order: n. 12, above. Sister reminding: TS 12.262, l. 17*, addressed to Isma'īl b. Barhūn Tāhertī.

[48]ULC Or 1080 J 35, ll. 11, 20–22, 30, addressed to Ṣāliḥ and Isma'īl b. Barhūn Tāhertī, now back in Tunisia. Their brother: Abu 'l-Khayr.

[49]TS 13 J 28, f. 19*v*, ll. 19 and 21.

[50]TS 8 J 34, f. 10. The main part of the document is on verso. Because of the many corrections it was continued on recto in the form of a draft, written in another hand.

[51]ENA 2739, f. 16+. See n. 1, above.

[52]Coming home for the Sabbath: Westminster College, Arabica, II, f. 51, see n. 169, below. No Sabbath: TS 10 J 16, f. 14, ll. 20–21.

[53]Islam: *EI²*, II, 593, s.v. "Djum'a." Athens: see S. B. Pomeroy, *Goddesses, Whores, Wives and Slaves: Women in Classical Antiquity* (New York, 1975), p. 87.

[54]See Ephraim Isaac, *A New Text: Critical Introduction to Maṣḥafa Berhān* (Leiden, 1973), p. 90. Dr. Isaac told me that continence on Sunday is still observed in certain circles of the Ethiopian Church.

[55]TS 10 J 4, f. 11.

[56]TS K 25, f. 205. For Judge Nathan b. Samuel see *Med. Soc.*, II, 513, sec. 18.

[57]*Bint al-ẓāmiya*: TS NS J 293, col. II, bottom, *Med. Soc.*, II, 448, sec. 33. See also M. A. Friedman, *Tarbiz*, 43 (1974), 171, with references to TS Misc. Box 25, f. 6. "Son of the Mule": *Med. Soc.*, II, 504, sec. 121.

[58]Prescription: TS Arabic Box 39, f. 338. Amulet: TS K 1, f. 91 c. Magical interfering: ENA 4020, f. 49.

[59]See B, 2, n. 28, above.

[60]Cf. Idris, "Mariage," p. 51, sec. 36 (and notes), p. 99, sec. 241.

[61]ENA NS 18, f. 35, ll. 35–36. Labrāṭ I b. Moses I Ibn Sighmār writing to his brother Judah. See also B, 1, nn. 35–37, above.

[62]Sophocles: see R. Flacelière, *A Literary History of Greece* (Chicago, 1964), p. 191. Letter to sister: ULC Or 1080 J 25*v*, ll. 28–31. Another version in TS 8 J 24, f. 4. For the understanding of the Song of Songs as a piece of female creation see S. D. Goitein, *Bible Studies* (in Heb.) (Tel-Aviv, 1967), pp. 283–317, "The Song of Songs: A New Approach."

[63]TS 13 J 24, f. 10*v*, ll. 5–12. "Her heart is bound to yours": This is not a translation of the biblical phrase, Genesis 44:30, but idiomatic Arabic.

[64]TS 13 J 18, f. 15, l. 12.

[65]Bodl. MS Heb. c 28 (Cat. 2876), f. 64*v*, ll. 7–8: *fī wadā'at allāh wa-wadā'atik.*

[66]TS 10 J 29, f. 15, ll. 15–19: *rā'iḥat al-umm.* Wife of a stepson: TS 13 J 2, f. 16, see C, 3, n. 59.

[67]TS NS 236*, see *Med. Soc.*, II, 567, n. 27.

[68]See nn. 30, 31, above. I learned about that American song from Miss Ellen J. Seidman.

[69]See B, 5, nn. 32–45.

[70]The medieval match (*'ūd kibrīt*, "sulphur chip") was, of course, different from ours.

[71]TS 16.35* (1118).

[72]TS 13 J 2, f. 22 (1135). Slightly damaged at the beginning.

[73]Mosseri A, f. 16. No date preserved.

[74]TS Misc. Box 28, f. 79, nos. 4 and 18, which form parts of one document (1119). The husband: Abu 'l-Khayr, son of Saadya. Father-in-law: Joseph, son of Mevōrākh ha-Kohen (dead).

[75]ENA NS 16, f. 30. The husband, Sulaymān b. Hānī: a pauper in the list ULC Or 1081 J 67, *Med. soc.*, II, 463, sec. 89. Shoe or foot: *qadam.*

[76]A "slave girl" might have been a captive and, therefore, once a free woman. The daughter of a slave girl, that is, born in slavery, was a real slave.

[77]She writes *w'lty* for *wāldtī.* For my mother's sake, Ar. *li-ḥadaqatayn ummī*, lit., "for my mother's eyes." The same phrase in TS K 25, f. 244*v*, l. 21.

[78]Dammūh: a locality near Cairo. MS: *dwmh* for *dmwh.* I do not believe the writer uses here Heb. *dūmā*, "Underworld," "Hell," (Psalm 94:17, 115:17), although it would be a perfect term for the family house out of which she was thrown by her mother-in-law, and although this use occurs in the Geniza, TS 16.287, l. 25+, and in Yemenite speech, see S. D. Goitein, *Lĕšonénu*, 3 (1931), 366, "The Hebrew Elements in the Vernacular of the Jews of Yemen."

[79]The reader should not be irritated by the fact that the writer refers to her mother-in-law first (and later also) by "your sister" and here by *ʿammatī*, "my mother-in-law." It was not exceptional in the style of Geniza letters and even documents, but the rule, see *Med. Soc.*, II, 236–237. In letters one related a person first and mostly to the person addressed, to oneself only when the circumstances, as here, required or recommended it.

[80]This might have been a third sister of the addressee. But it is possible that the writer refers here to her own mother, meaning that she was falsely suspected like herself. After *wa-nafsak* in l. 13 the word *taʿrif* was omitted.

[81]Grave palsy: *shallā' adīda.* The Geniza letters often speak about the adverse physical effects of strong emotions.

[82]TS 10 J 9, f. 13. It is not excluded that the young woman wrote the letter herself.

[83]Letter of proxy: TS 12.288. Successful marriage: DK XIII*, see n. 36, above. Repudiation of the betrothed: ULC Or 1080 J 6, l. 14.

[84]Maimonides: see Goitein, *Letters*, p. 211 n. 26. Miriam, in writing to her brother Moses Maimonides, also sends regards to her sisters, see *ibid.* Nahray: *ibid.*, p. 282 n. 16. Maimonides, as far as we know, was not married at that time, and was accompanied also by his old father.

[85]TS 8 J 5, f. 16: About the name see A, 1, n. 37. Arye had been married to another woman in the Egyptian capital, Karīma, daughter of ʿAmmār, with the same early installment of 10 dinars, and a dowry priced fantastically high: ENA 2727, f. 8 A. See D, nn. 159–162, below.

[86]TS 13 J 16, f. 7, l. 25, *Nahray* 47, ed. J. Starr, *Zion*, 1 (1936), 446. Cf. TS 13 J 16, f. 4, l. 5, *Nahray* 53, ed. *ibid.*, p. 443.

[87]TS 10 J 12, f. 18, a fragment, see Braslavsky, *Our Country*, p. 74.

[88]TS 13 J 28, f. 19, see n. 97, below.

[89]ULC Or 1080 J 276.

[90]ULC Or 1080 J 23. The woman from the Rīf: TS 6 J 3, f. 22.

[91]ENA 4011, f. 34. From al-Maḥalla to Minyat Ziftā.

[92]TS 6 J 3, f. 16. The note is an urgent request to issue the summons since the week before the husband had already deposited his complaint.

[93]ENA NS 2, I, f. 20.

[94]TS 8.110. No date. In the Hebrew script of the early eleventh century.

[95]TS 8.121. Fragment of an old Hebrew document.

[96]TS 10 J 31, f. 14; TS 8 J 20, f. 16, both fragmentary.

[97]TS 13 J 28, f. 19, margin. See n. 88, above. See Goitein, *Jemenica*, p. 164, no. 1276, and the story of the deserted wife who was forsaken by her family, n. 173, below.

[98]See nn. 145–163, below.

[99]TS 18 J 3, f. 2, see n. 242, below.

[100]Mosseri L, f. 197*v*, ll. 7–9.

[101]See B, 4, nn. 66–71, above.

[102]The question of the married woman's economic independence is discussed in D, below.

[103]TS 13 J 22, f. 21, l. 18 (early eleventh century), ed. S. D. Goitein, *Joshua Finkel Jubilee Volume* (New York, 1974), p. 122, court warning the husband; TS 13 J 1, f. 12 (Nov., 1049), settlement; cf. n. 74, above, where the husband refuses to move his furnishings to the wife's new residence.

[104]ENA 4010, f. 43; (fs. 43*v*–44 are from Summer 1029).

[105]TS 24.28 (Spring 1105).

[106]TS 13 J 3, f. 13 (Feb. 1137).

[107]Bodl. MS Heb. a 2 (2805), f. 9, l. 15 (Dec. 1188), ed. S. D. Goitein, *Sefunot*, 8 (1964), 125.

[108]Mosseri A, f. 4.3, a clerk's memo written on a small piece of paper, noting only "to be paid back by the month of Iyyar."

[109]See B, 4, n. 37, above; Baruch Levine, "Muluga," *JAOS*, 88 (1968), 271 ff.; Epstein, *Marriage Contract*, p. 314, Index, s.v. "Mulug." (The pronunciation *melug* is more common.)

[110]TS 13 J 17, f. 14, see B, 4, n. 51, above.

[111]TS 16.144: [. . .], *bayt, makān*. The man's Hebrew name: *mhll* (*Mehullāl* or Mahalāl, cf. Prov. 27:21), "Praised" or "Praise."

[112]Bodl. MS Heb. a 3 (Cat. 2873), f. 40*, see n. 131, below.

[113]The settlement: Bodl. MS Heb. b 11 (Cat. 2874), f. 3, Oct. 1130. The divorce: TS 8.131 (he sent his wife away to her father's house and, two months later, applied for a divorce); Summer 1132. The husband: Ṣedāqā ha-meshōrēr b. Ṣemaḥ. About synagogue singers see B, 5, n. 72, above.

[114]TS 8.166. The husband: Abū Manṣūr Kohen b. Qasāsā. His meritorious and highly praised relative: Abu 'l-Faraj b. Qasāsā, Bodl. MS Heb. f 56 (Cat. 2821, no. 40), f. 130, ll. 5–11, ed. E. Ashtor, *Zion*, 30 (1965), 153.

[115]TS 16.220, written by Mevōrākh b. Nathan, left side only, but containing the main points. In view of "the changing times," *taghāyur al-ḥidthān*, a special document is made out by *Abū ʿAlī al-qazzāz*, the silk worker, son of Khalaf, the silk worker, for his wife Khulla ("Friendship") b. Nathan (deceased), stating that he had received from her 19 dinars, for which he has mortgaged his possessions and his estate after his death just as if they had formed part of her ketubba. She might have inherited the money from her father.

[116]See B, 5, nn. 8–16, above.

[117]Cf. n. 103, above.

[118]TS 13 J 1, f. 12 (Nov. 1049).

[119]TS 10 J 9, f. 32, a draft. Her brother's name Faraḥ ("Joy") was common in a Qābisī family of the eleventh century.

[120]TS 10 J 12, f. 1. The copy of a Bible referred to as given to a newborn in *Med. Soc.*, II, 181, was also a family Bible. (Ibn) Sabra is better known under the name Asʿad (al-dīn) Yaʿqūb b. Isḥāq al-Maḥallī, see Ibn Abī Uṣaybiʿa, II, 218. The identity is established by PER H 181, col. I (see *Med. Soc.*, II, 502, sec. 114; see also *ibid.*, p. 485, sec. 36). The same man in B, 2, n. 47, above.

[121]See n. 124, below.

[122]Sources in Dinur, *Yisrael ba-Gola*, II (2), p. 361, and Finkelstein, *Self-government*, pp. 70–71 and 217. For wife-beating in medieval Europe see G. G. Coulton, *Medieval Panorama*, (New York, 1958), pp. 614–617 (with an illustration: a husband striking his wife with a club. Another scene in Sibylle Harksen, *Die Frau im Mittelalter* (Leipzig, 1974), p. 9: a strong woman battering her spouse with a broom).

[123]*Otzar ha-Geonim*, Ketubbot, para. 428, quoted by Dinur, *Yisrael ba-Gola* I (4), p. 37. For references in the Gaonic literature see S. Assaf, *Kirjath Sepher*, 2 (1926), 183, including a responsum of the Spaniard Joseph Ibn Abitur, who was approached in this matter while in Egypt. Maimonides, *Code*, book "Women," sec. "Marriage," 21:10.

[124]TS 13 J 8, f. 23+. See n. 24, above.

[125]Maṣlīaḥ was the head of the Jewish High Council of Jerusalem, named "the Pride of Jacob," which at that time had its seat in Cairo.

[126]Written in one word *kmsṭ'shr* (*khamsṭa'shar*).

[127]Spelled *by'ml*. The Hebrew introduction certainly was copied from another letter and contains only one mistake.

[128]TS 8 J 22, f. 27.

[129]TS NS J 118, fragment 10, in the hand of Ḥalfōn b. Manasse, see *Med. Soc.*, II, 231. The woman is called Maḥfūẓa ("Guarded," namely by God) of the Ḥātimiyya family, which frequently appears in the lists of poor people receiving bread from the community, e.g., TS Misc. Box 8, f. 100; ENA Uncatalogued 89*v*; TS K 15, f. 2, see *Med. Soc.* II, 450, sec. 41; 451, sec. 44*b*; *ibid.*, sec. 43.

[130]Gottheil-Worrell, XLV, p. 218. See n. 237, below.

[131]Bodl. MS Heb. a 3 (Cat. 2873), f. 40. See B, 3, nn. 36 and 64, above.

[132]TS 8 J 5, f. 2*c-d* (1132). Poor people: see B, 4, n. 16; B, 5, n. 10. TS 13 J 2, f. 22 (1135), see n. 72, above. A similar case, about a century older, is found in TS 6 J 2, f. 2, where the husband promises to rent for her a separate apartment, not to beat her, and to provide her with adequate means, while she agrees not to leave the house except with his permission. The document is badly preserved. It seems to say that she may go to the bazaar for buying flax, unless he brought it home so that she could work it "and all could be clothed"—again an indication of extreme poverty. A promise not to curse or to beat his wife is given by a husband in the frag. Mosseri A, 4. 16, ll. 4–5, see n. 73, above.

[133]Bodl. MS Heb. c 28 (Cat. 2876), f. 7. The document is much effaced, but can be restored almost in its entirety. The printed Catalogue describes it as "a deed of sale." This mistake is attributable to the phrase "the symbolic purchase was made from him," the usual expression describing a formal undertaking, see *Med. Soc.*, II, 329–330, and here, *passim*. The stipulation that the late installment was to be paid from "the most available properties" of the husband was an additional imposition on him.

[134]TS 8 J 6, f, 16, ed. Strauss-Ashtor, *Mamluks*, III, 6–7. For *y'w* in l. 2, read *ya'ūd*, followed by a lacuna of about four letters. The elder *Muḥriz b. Ṭāhōr* signed the document TS 8 J 5, f. 25, of May 1, 1261, referred to in *Med. Soc.*, II, 568, n. 44, and is mentioned (without his father's name) as an almoner in 1241: TS K 15, f. 25.

[135]TS 12.129, written on vellum in the beautiful hand of Abraham, son of Aaron "the expert" (dated documents: 1094–1107).

[136]TS NS J 185, fragments 8 and 12 (being parts of one document), where he is referred to thus: the esteemed M. Abraham, son of the late elder Hananel, known as al-Amshāṭī. For the woodwork see, e.g., I. Ben Ze'eb, *Sefunot*, 9 (1965), 267. Photo *ibid.*, opposite p. 172, and *Med. Soc.*, II, 551, n. 14.

[137]Arabic terms: *shtm, l'n*, together in ENA NS 16, f. 30, see n. 75, above. In TS NS J 133 a husband promises not to harm (*yaḍīr*) or to curse his wife, and she vows "to be with him with all her heart" (*be-lēvāv shālēm*, Hebrew).

[138]See B, 5, nn. 68–71.

[139]As in the court record cited in n. 135, above.

[140]TS NS Box 321, f. 100. Fragmentary.

[141]TS 8 J 34, f. 1. The notary: Abraham b. Mevassēr.

[142]See B, 5, nn. 5, 6, 67, above.

[143]Mosseri A, f. 40.2, a fragment in the hand of Ḥalfōn b. Manasse referring to a conditional bill of repudiation made out four years back *'alā al-tiqqūn* (Heb.) *alladhī awjabahu*, "in accordance with the statute made obligatory by. . . ." For *tiqqūn* as "statute" see A. Scheiber, *Sinai*, 46 (1960), 269.

[144]ULC Or 1080 J 22, trans. Goitein, *Letters*, pp. 318–319.

[145]TS 8 J 4, f. 18*c*, ed. S. D. Goitein, *JQR*, 66 (1976), 74–79. Written in the beautiful hand of a scribe from the Holy Land, see n. 193, below. The first signatory is Nathan ha-Kohen b. Solomon, also a Palestinian, who, about a quarter of a century later, became judge in Fustat, see *Med. Soc.*, II, 513, sec. 17. The head and the left edge of the document are cut away. The words [per week] were written on the lost

margin and are complemented by me on the basis of the considerations explained in the text above. See also next note. For "local emission" see *Med. Soc.*, I, 380–381, sec. 48. The marriage contract (TS 16.198, only the beginning is preserved) is written in Tyre and by the same scribe. The name of the wife is Sitt al-Bayt b. Jacob (d.), the same as in the document from 1102 (where, however, her father's name is not mentioned), and she is an orphan in both documents.

[146]TS 8 J 5, f. 4*v*, item IV, summer 1127. See B, 5, n. 71, above. TS 8 J 26, f. 17, l. 9, *Nahray* 236: The representative of an Alexandrian merchant sojourning in Cairo paid to the family 3/4 of a dinar—1/2 for maintenance, 1/4 for clothing. In TS 8 J 25, f. 13, ll. 20–21, *Nahray* 234, he paid 1/2 dinar per month, and in ll. 11–12 three waybas wheat per month. Wheat was measured, not weighed, see *Med. Soc.*, I, 361. In the first letter cited the relative remarks also: "Your family is all the time with us and my family visits them; they are fine."

[147]TS 8 J 10, f. 17, written and signed by Nathan ha-Kohen b. Solomon, this time in Fustat, see n. 145, above. The remark concerning the poll tax shows that it could be paid in very small installments, as proved by Arabic papyri found in Egypt, see *Med. Soc.*, II, 392. In the phrase "work or spinning" the first term refers to regular earnings, while spinning was, at least in theory, a common occupation of women, in the East, as well as in Europe. The dirhems mentioned here no doubt were regular dirhems, 20 of them equaling approximately half a dinar.

[148]Maimonides, *Responsa*, I, 44–45.

[149]TS 13 J 3, f. 3, ll. 15–18⁺. On her deathbed she stipulates 2 dinars per month and 8 irdabbs of wheat per year for her boy. Males obviously were assumed to have far greater appetites than females.

[150]The agreement: TS 12.585 (*recto* and *verso*), *India Book* 356. The bill of repudiation: TS 8 J 5, f. 23 (1169) *India Book* 357, both in the hand of Mevōrākh b. Nathan. The parties: (Bū Saʿd) Moses, son of Japheth, the parnās, the trustee, head of the parnāsīm, and Sitt al-Fakhr ("Glory"), daughter of Tovia, the esteemed elder; both fathers dead. The girls are referred to in TS 12.585, l. 3 as "her daughters," in l. 7 as "his daughters"; one sees how misleading the predilection for variety of the medieval notaries can be (see *Med. Soc.*, II, 236–237). Reading l. 3 I assumed the children referred to were the husband's stepdaughters. The payments to the family were made from the rents of a house belonging to the husband. In TS 13 J 37, f. 2 (frag.) the wife receives both part or all of her dowry and an alimony, but for what reason is not preserved.

[151]Westminster College, Frag. Cairens. 18 + Glasses 3, forming one document. The twelve months: Tishri-Av 1358 (1046/47), a leap year having two months of Adar, see *Med. Soc.*, I, 356. The circumstances of the case are not stated.

[152]TS NS Box 320, fs. 54 and 57. The wife, as usual, had applied directly to the Nagid, who then ordered the court and the elders to propose an equitable solution; cf. f. 54, l. 3: *imtathalnā marsūmha 'l-sharīf*, "we carried out your high order." See *Med. Soc.*, II, 34.

[153]TS NS J 401, no. 6. "Fine people etc.": *ṭūvē hā-ʿīr* (Heb.) *al-maṣūnāt fī buyūt[hin]*. This and the preceding document were written by Ḥalfōn b. Manasse.

[154]E.g., TS 10 J 10, f. 18 (money for wheat and clothing, but not all that promised); TS 13 J 18, f. 12 (a weaver: "I am sending you a *malḥafa*, cloak, take from its price 6 *nuqra* dirhems and return to me the balance"); TS 13 J 18, f. 26 (sends several items to be sold and their proceeds to be used for the purchase of wheat); TS 8 J 26, f. 5 (a merchant sends consignments of hazel- and walnuts, as well as of textiles).

[155]TS 13 J 17, f. 23 (unemployed, sends nothing, danger on the roads). BM Or 5542, f. 10*v* (no work, sends nothing, but in good spirits). TS 10 J 10, f. 30, l. 22, *Nahray* 140. TS 12.92, ll. 5–6 ("I regret you did not charge me with the care for your family"). TS 8 J 19, f. 33 (a Jew from Byzantium writing to his family in Egypt).

[156]ENA NS 19, f. 131. A long, interesting letter.

[157]Mosseri L 230 (marked VII-162.3 in the Jerusalem collection of photocopies).

[158]TS 13 J 17, f. 23*v*, l. 7, see n. 155, above.

[159]Text: *al-ʿatal wal-suyūf*. Levers (see Dozy, *Supplément*, II, 94*b*) may have been found in the house of a merchant, where heavy loads had to be moved. Swords might have been kept as protection against burglars, but the word designated perhaps another implement, cf. *sayf nasīj* in TS 13 J 28, f. 16, l. 11, and TS 13 J 15, f. 7 (mentioned together with *sukkān*, rudder).

[160]Text: *tmlh*, rendering *tammulih* for *taʾammulih*.

[161]The writer of the letter. The "pearls" probably were coral strings, normally brought home from the western Mediterranean.

[162]The grandfather. Possibly also the paternal uncle referred to before, if he was the elder brother of the addressee.

[163]DK X. ʿAllān: *India Book* 46, 144, 358.

[164]INA D-55, f. 3, addressed to the judge Elijah b. Zechariah.

[165]TS Arabic Box 38, f. 14, ll. 10–12, in Arabic characters. The traveler, writing from Damascus, which apparently was his native town, had left a quantity of honey, a commodity frequently exported from Syria to Egypt, with the addressee, who delivered the entire proceeds to the wife instead of paying her the sum required for her maintenance.

[166]Letter: TS 12.299*v*, margin, ed. Goitein, *Palestine during Its Arab and Crusader Periods* (in press). Excommunication: TS AS 146, f. 4, ll. 10–15 (ca. 1240).

[167]TS 13 J 2, f. 22. See n. 72, above.

[168]TS 18 J 3, f. 2. See n. 242, below.

[169]Westminster College, Arabica II, f. 51, see n. 52, above.

[170]Maimonides, *Responsa*, I, 20.

[171]TS 8 J 5, f. 8. The phrase *ayn ant min Allah* means "worlds separate you from God," whereas his nearness is the highest good (Psalm 73:28). For the signatory see nn. 145 and 146, above.

[172]Stands probably for Ibn al-Ṣiqilliyya ("Son of the Sicilian woman"). This affair seemed to have occupied the court in Fustat before.

[173]TS 13 J 8, f. 19. The ḥāvēr addressed no doubt was Eli b. Amram, the spiritual head of the Jerusalemite congregation of Fustat during the third quarter of the eleventh century, see *Med. Soc.*, II, Index.

[174]TS 13 J 21, f. 2, *Nahray* 28. In his later years Nahray b. Nissim became spiritual leader of the two Rabbanite congregations in Fustat, see Goitein, *Letters*, pp. 173–174.

[175]TS 10 J 26, f. 1 (upper part) + Bodl. MS Heb. d 66 (Cat. 2878), f. 4, ed. S. Assaf, *Tarbiz*, 9 (1938), 201–202.

[176]See *Med. Soc.*, I, 292.

[177]TS 13 J 15, f. 23, ed. Mann, *Texts*, I, 346–352. The text printed needs revision. The circumstances show that the letter was sent from Ramle, not Jerusalem, as Mann, in *ibid.*, p. 346, assumes. Mann also omitted the address written in Arabic characters, which calls Evyatar b. Elijah, the future Gaon, Abu ʾl-Faḍl.

[178]TS 10 J 11, f. 30, partly written in rhymed prose.

[179]Gottheil-Worrell, V, pp. 26–29, see Mann, *Texts*, I, 312–315.

[180]TS 13 J 1, f. 2, ed. S. Assaf, *Gaonica* (Jerusalem, 1933), pp. 206–207.

[181]TS 13 J 1, f. 6, partly ed. S. Assaf, *Sefer ha-Yishuv*, pp. 57–58.

[182]TS J 2, f. 26. The style is that of Solomon b. Judah, but the script differs from those used in his chancellery, including his own.

[183]ULC Or 1080 J 105, especially ll. 26–30; ULC Or 1080 J 107, ll. 15–32.

[184]ENA 3787, f. 10, ed. M. A. Friedman, *Lešonénú* (in press).

[185]TS 20.140*v*, ed. S. D. Goitein, *Tarbiz*, 32 (1963), 269–270, and Abramson, *Bamerkazim*, pp. 168–170. Sister's son: A, 2, nn. 56–67.

[186]Maimonides, *Responsa*, I, 36.

[187]TS Arabic Box 40, f. 96, *India Book* 309. The document does not say that she, too, embraced Islam. On the reverse side, Hebrew religious poetry is written. See C, 3, n. 93, below.

[188]TS 12.681 (1098/9). The terms for absence: *mutasahhib ʿanhā* and *ghāb ʿanhā*

ghaybat harab (Ar.). The pair: Ṣedāqā b. Hillel and Sitt al-Bayt b. Joseph (both fathers dead). The Hebrew terms for grass widow: *almenūt ḥayyūt* (see II Samuel 20:3); *ʿagūnā*, see n. 200, below.

[189]See B, 1, n. 3.

[190]TS 12.347, l. 33 and margin, ed. Mann, *Texts*, I, 385 (The man from Byzantium:) "Would that girl died instead of staying with that adulterous woman." TS 13 J 16, f. 7, l. 26 + (The Tunisian) see n. 86, above.

[191]See *Med. Soc.*, II, 173–175, p. 557, n. 34; Goitein, *Letters*, p. 319.

[192]TS Arabic Box 38, f. 14, l. 14 ("See to it that the boy is not ruined"), in a letter to a relative, see n. 165, above.

[193]University Museum, Philadelphia, E. 16516, trans. S. D. Goitein, *Gratz College Annual of Jewish Studies*, Vol. IV (Philadelphia, 1975), pp. 50–55. See n. 145, above.

[194]TS 13 J 29, f. 7. Abu 'l-Faḍl is probably Ṣāliḥ b. Barhūn Tāhertī, for his brother Moses, a close relative of the writer (Joseph or Nissīm b. Berechiah?) seems to be referred to at the end as having brought to Palestine a Mishna originally belonging to the writer's dead father. For wives refusing to emigrate with their husbands to a foreign country see nn. 85–87, above; women as travelers: D, below.

[195]ULC Or 1080 J 7*, two drafts, one abortive (18 ll.), one final (about 85 ll. with the margins). The parties: Surūra b. Solomon the physician, b. Rabīʿ; Isaac, called Surūr, b. Jacob b. Aaron, known as al-Jāsūs.

[196]Bodl. MS Heb. c 28 (Cat. 2876), f. 41, ed. S. Assaf, *Tarbiz*, 9 (1938), 214–215. A document on the reverse side is dated winter 1043.

[197]TS 13 J 8, f. 2. The debt amounted to 280 silver pieces, worth 23.33 dinars, see *Med. Soc.*, I, 370, sec. 4 (as explained by Philip Grierson). Surūra's appeal quotes the document of 1029 verbatim. A fourth document in this matter, TS NS J 149, seems to be a draft for TS 13 J 8, f. 2.

[198]Bodl. MS Heb. c 28 (Cat. 2876), f. 48. The cantor was Mawhūb b. Shālōm, not to be confused with another cantor and clerk with this name.

[199]Alexandria— Fustat: ENA 4010, f. 19 (1088/89): "The children are left without food and clothing." The woman probably was herself from Fustat since her identity was established by Eli ha-Kohen the welfare official, see *Med. Soc.*, II, 78. Fustat—Cairo: TS 8 J 4, f. 25*v*. Abraham (b. Nathan) Yesōd ha-yeshiva was judge in Cairo. The couple clearly had lived in Cairo, whereas the husband, at the time of the suit, was found in Fustat.

[200]Sittūna's complaint: ULC Or 1080, Box 4, f. 15. Several places in Tunisia are named Raḥba, see Idris, *Zirides*, pp. 419, 451. For *ʿagūnā*, grass widow (see n. 188, above), the MS has *ʿagūmā*, mournful, as in PT Ḥagiga 2:5, f. 77*d*. Transaction: ULC Or 1081 J 30. No fee: TS 13 J 20, f. 17, l. 17, see *Med. Soc.*, II, 230. The family name of the husband, Faraḥ ("Joy") b. Joseph, was *Bānūqa*, the name of the beloved daughter of the caliph al-Ma'mūn (813–833).

[201]TS NS Box 320, f. 20. This judge Samuel is referred to in TS 10 J 16, f. 6, margin, see *Med. Soc.*, II, 111, bottom (instead of "return" read there "arrival").

[202]TS Arabic Box 39, f. 57. It appears from the letter that the writer had applied to the Nagid before. See n. 244, below.

[203]TS 8 J 14, f. 2. About Ḥisday see Mann, *Texts*, II, 137–138.

[204]See B, 5, nn. 17–31 above.

[205]See, for instance, nn. 75 and 88, above.

[206]ENA NS 17, f. 28 a. Text: *ḥifẓ li-ṣuḥbathā wa-raʿfa minnī lahā*. Parties: David b. Mevōrākh, known as Ben Khuzayr, and Sitt al-Bayt b. Joseph, both fathers dead. Their son: Abu 'l-ʿAlā.

[207]For this and the next paragraph see the sources quoted in M. A. Friedman's articles on polygyny, mentioned B, 5, n. 19, above, especially TS 8.116+, TS 13 J 3, f. 1+, TS 16.214+, TS 13 J 2, f. 25+*, Bodl. MS Heb. c 28 (Cat. 2876), f. 14+ (BM Or 5566 A I, fragmentary, seems to be a similar case, where the bride undertakes to look after the children of her future husband's first wife, still married to him), all edited in *Tarbiz*, 40 (1971), 320–359. Unfit for cohabitation: TS 12.242, l. 19, see B,

2, n. 28, above. Separate domicile: TS 8 J 5, f. 3 *a-b*. Special conditions (maid will belong to first wife; house earmarked for her cannot be sold, etc.): TS NS J 490, frag. by Hillel b. Eli.

[208]TS Arabic Box 6, f. 28, ll. 14–16. The woman with the make-up: *muḥammara*, see Dozy, *Supplément* I, 321*a*; *ben* before *khālih* should be *bint*, or, rather, should have been written after the name of the maternal uncle.

[209]See Goitein, *Letters*, pp. 224, 227–228.

[210]Cf. TS 10 J 10, f. 15, *India Book* 68, the story of the India trader Abraham Yijū, trans. Goitein, *Letters*, pp. 201–206.

[211]Documents: TS 12.684 and TS 10 J 6, f. 6 (1041), Mosseri A, fs. 37 + 76 (parts of one document; 1043). Letter: ULC Or 1081 J 17 (frag.), where he calls himself al-Andalusī, the Spaniard. The name Jekuthiel appears in literature sporadically in the fourteenth and fifteenth centuries, see Steinschneider, *Die Arabische Literatur der Juden*, p. 245, para. 187 (1316), Bodl. MS Heb. d 70 (Cat. 2902), dated 1481. For Abū Zikrī the Physician see Goitein, *Letters*, pp. 295–296. For Abū Ya'qūb see n. 214, below.

[212]For the history of the Fayyūm district under Islam see *EI* (first edition) s.v. "al-Faiyūm" (spelled thus).

[213]We find them closely cooperating in ULC Or 1081 J 17, where the parnās's father is called by his Arabic name Ya'īsh (b. Abraham), see *Med. Soc.*, II, 78. Ya'īsh-Yaḥyā died before 1060, see TS 28.7, bottom.

[214]TS 10 J 9, f. 16, *India Book* 269*b*. Persons from Qalhā are frequently mentioned, especially as receivers of alms in Fustat, e.g., TS 16.185, l. 9; TS K 15, f. 50, col. II (1107); TS K 15, f. 102, col. II; TS Misc. Box 8, f. 9, col. III; TS NS J 41, col. II; TS NS J 191, l. 19. Not to be confused with Qalhāt, a port city of Oman in southeast Arabia, ENA 1822A, f. 8, l. 5, *India Book* 238.

[215]See Lane-Poole, *History of Egypt*, pp. 145–146. I have the impression that I have seen other Geniza papers in the beautiful, strong scripts (Heb. and Ar.) of Mūsā b. Jekuthiel, ULC Or 1081 J 17. But it takes time and luck to find them. For Abū Ya'qūb al-Ḥakīm see *Med. Soc.*, I, 447, n. 23; II, 477, secs. 16, 17; 479, sec. 21; 498, sec. 79; 503, sec. 119; 504, sec. 124; 507, sec. 135; and *India Book, passim*; also A, 1, n. 91, above.

[216]TS NS J 380, written with a thick and a fine pen, changing in midst of a sentence (l. 28), but, it seems to me, in the same hand. For Anatoli (he writes *nṭwly* without ') see *Med. Soc.*, I, 53, 67, for Menaḥēm *Med. Soc.*, II, 514, sec. 26. Elijah, *ibid.*, 515, sec. 29, was not yet a judge at the writing of the letter, as indicated by the way in which he is addressed. The writer: Abu 'l-Faraj b. Khalaf (not sure).

[217]See the story in TS NS Box 320, f. 20, n. 201, above.

[218]ULC Or 1080 J 173, l. 16. Oppression: *nakāl*, written *nkyl* with Imāla, as in the opposite way, the name of the girl, *l'l'*, for Laylā, pronounced Lēlā, in l. 5. The Rūm woman: TS 12.575, l. 19. See C, 4, n. 116, below.

[219]For the Islamic custom of levirate see Idris, "Mariage," p. 71, no. 90.

[220]The Karaite reasoning was this: the Bible prohibits intercourse with a brother's wife (Leviticus 18:16). Had the command of the levirate followed that prohibition immediately, it would have formed an exception to it. Since it did not (it appears in Deuteronomy), that prohibition stands, and the word "brother" in Deuteronomy 25, 5–9, must have the meaning of "distant relative," as, in addition, is proved by the story of Ruth and Boaz in the Book of Ruth, chap. 4. This method of argumentation is the Mu'tazilite *ta'khīr al-bayān*, as I learned from Professor Moshe Zucker, who is preparing a study on the influence of Islamic Koran interpretations on the Jewish study of the Bible.

[221]This dissension between Moses Maimonides and his Cairene colleague Isaac b. Sāsōn (see *Med. Soc.*, II, 314, sec. 25) was a *cause celèbre*, see Maimonides, *Responsa*, II, 650–655.

[222]S. D. Goitein, "Zur heutigen Praxis der Leviratsehe bei orientalischen Juden," *Journal of the Palestine Oriental Society*, 13 (1933), 159–166.

[223]Some Geniza cases of levirate: BM Or 5536 I (Jan. 1015): Farjiyyah b. Sahlān is

released from the levirate by her brother-in-law. TS NS J 51 (Aug. 1027) and ENA NS 7 I, f. 24*v* (Nov. 1027): Jacob b. ʿAyyāsh, a minor coming of age, wishes to marry his widowed sister-in-law after years of waiting, while she who is, of course, far older, rejects him. ENA 1822 A, f. 48, and TS 12.234: similar cases, brother-in-law is a little boy. TS 10 J 24, f. 1*c-d* (1090): complicated negotiations between the widow and her brother-in-law who lives in another town. ULC Or 1080 J 47 (same period): alimony for a widow waiting to be married or released. TS 13 J 2, f. 12 (1105): on his deathbed a man asks his brother to write a release for his wife. Bodl. MS Heb. b 12 (Cat. 2875), f. 10, written by Ḥalfōn b. Manasse, and TS 12.678 (1202): widows are released by their paternal cousins, see A, 2, n. 78, nos. 8 and 11. TS J 3, f. 46, and ENA 4011, f. 11: procedures of releases to widows and documents to this effect. TS 6 J 2, f. 1 (1204, not 1404, as in Strauss-Ashtor, *Mamluks*, III, 100, see *Tarbiz*, 41 [1972], 69): a widow appoints an attorney to sue her brother-in-law with the demand either to marry or to free her. ULC Or 1080 J 68: question addressed to the judge Yehiel (see *Med. Soc.*, II, 515, sec. 30) with regard to the outfit of a widow in levirate status.

[224]TS 13 J 4, f. 16, ed. Strauss-Ashtor, *Mamluks*, III, 112–115. On *verso*, l. 3 read *n*ʿ for *l.*, "(may he) r(est in) E(den)"; *al-muntaqil* does not mean "the payment due to her," but "the deceased, the one who has passed away." Whether the payment of 15 1/2 ashrafīs for *kiswa*, clothing, l. 21, and *verso*, l. 1, refers to the visit in Dammūh, or to a period, such as one year, I cannot say. See also M. A. Friedman, *Tarbiz*, 40 (1971), 346, for important remarks on this document.

[225]TS 13 J 8, f. 31*, see B, 2, n. 34, above.

[226]TS Arabic Box 50, f. 197⁺, see B, 2, n. 2, above.

[227]Mosseri A, f. 27*, see B, 2, n. 54, above. "He replaced her with her sister," *khalafa ʿalā ukhtihā, The Ansāb al-Ashrāf of al-Balādhurī*, ed. S. D. F. Goitein (Jerusalem, 1936), V, 379, l. 1.

[228]Case studies of such procedures are provided in *Mediterranean People*, volume I, *passim*.

[229]TS 8 J 41, f. 8, ll. 7–10. Solomon b. Elijah writes to the address of his father, the judge, but the part of the sheet on which the name of the recipient was written is cut away. Most probably, the writer's brother Abū Zikrī is addressed.

[230]TS NS J 120, ll. 1–7. In the second part of the letter a poor Spanish cantor proceeding to Fustat is recommended.

[231]TS 10 J 10, f. 13. The entire letter is dedicated to this matter.

[232]ENA 2958, f. 2. See *Med. Soc.*, II, 224.

[233]ULC Or 1081 J 38. Ar. *ṣālaḥ marʾatoh*. See *Med. Soc.*, II, 424, sec. 116.

[234]The court record: ENA 4010, f. 44, ending on f. 43*v*. The list of the outfit: ENA 2738, f. 33, signed by Yeshūʿā ha-Kohen b. Ghālib. In the record he is referred to as Yeshūʿā ha-Kohen b. Ghulayb ("Little Ghālib"), as he used to be called in daily conversation. Since the court record emphasizes *Rabbanite* Jewish law, one of the parties might have been Karaite. One of the signatories, Ḥasday b. Nathan Parnās (without the article), might also have been a Karaite, since the name Ḥasday was common among the Karaite and other nāsīs but not among Egyptian Rabbanites.

[235]TS 8 J 4, f. 15*a*: the silk weaver Jacob of Rūm, Byzantium, deposits the outfit of his wife with the beadle of the court (1098).

[236]PER H 82, ed. S. Assaf, *Sepher ha-Yovel: Alexander Marx Jubilee Volume* (New York, 1943), pp. 74–76. At that time the manuscript had no mark. My photostat bears the number 2. But the mark today is PER H 82; *Med. Soc.*, II, 597, n. 51, is to be corrected accordingly. The upper part of the sheet is damaged, and the date is only partly preserved. All three dates proposed by Assaf, 978, 998, 1008, are feasible. Joseph b. Saʿdʾēl, who signs here, is party to the contract 12.198, ed. Abramson, *Bamerkazim*, pp. 172–173, and signs Bodl. MS Heb. b 12 (Cat. 2875), f. 7, albeit in a slightly more monumental script. Both these documents were validated by R. Shemarya b. Elhanan (ca. 980–1010, *Med. Soc.*, II, 511, sec. 2). The husband in our document is twice called Abraham, and twice Ibrahīm, cf. *Med. Soc.*, II, 236–237, because of the scribes' predilection for variety. Joseph b. Saʿdʾēl

might have been a relative of the unhappy woman and might have come to the Fayyūm in order "to make peace." The signature read by Assaf as *al-gharrās* is *al-giddēm* (Heb.), cripple, unable to use his hands. The scribe signed for him. He was perhaps a V.I.P. in the locality or specifically connected with the family. Altogether there are seven signatories, a number perhaps purposely chosen, cf. *Med. Soc.*, II, 59.

[237]Gottheil-Worrell, XLV, p. 218–220. The translation is entirely faulty. In the text make these corrections: l. 7, *al-sana*, r. al-*bint*; l. 8, Obadiah is rightly written with one *y*; l. 16. *l'lm'wṭ*, r. *lil-'aniyyīm*; l. 17, *tkd'*, r. *tabarra'*; in l. 24, r. *bal ayy shay amaroh.*

[238]TS 8 J 29, f. 13, "obligation to stay at home," *bayt farḍ*, which might have a specific meaning, such as staying in a particular room or part of the house. At the time of the settlement her father was still alive. The divorce: INA D 55, f. 2. In bills of divorce it was not customary to add a blessing to the name of a dead father. A similar case C, 1, n. 113. Cf. also, B, 4, n. 72.

[239]This, I assume, was added so that the listeners should not ask themselves: where and how does *she* spend her nights.

[240]Ar. *ra's al-kull*, which is an Arabicized rendering of *rōsh kallā*, an honorific title conferred by the Babylonian yeshivas to learned communal leaders. The reference is to Sahlān b. Abraham b. Sahlān, the leader of the Babylonian congregation of Fustat as from 1032, see Mann, I, 97, and passim.

[241]Ar. *tawakkal 'alayhā wa-aṣāb rīḥ al-khayra.*

[242]TS 18 J 3, f. 2. See *Med. Soc.*, II, 170, 324. Another such appeal: TS 13 J 18, f. 18.

[243]TS 13 J 4, f. 7. See *Med. Soc.*, II, 191. Silversmithing was a high art and required two years of training. For mastering the technique of weaving only four months were needed, and a small compensation, 15 dirhems per month, was paid to the apprentice. ENA NS 2, f. 41, trans. S. D. Goitein, *Gratz College Annual of Jewish Studies* (Philadelphia, 1975), pp. 47–50.

[244]ULC Or 1080 J 23. Cf. nn. 90, 202, above. For *ḥanbal* carpet see Dozy, *Supplément*, I, 331*a*.

[245]A pun on Isaiah 38:17.

[246]The phrase has its origin in the custom that one kissed a child on his eyes. Mann, II, 308 n. 1, took *'ynyy* erroneously as a name.

[247]Like the Lord in Isaiah 19:1. Mann read *t[ḥshvy]*. But the manuscript has clearly *tid'agī.*

[248]A humorous reference to the usual wish for a traveler on business to come home with a happy heart and a full purse, e.g., TS 10 J 15, f. 12*, cf. *Tarbiz*, 24 (1955), 42, where the manuscript mark and some other details are wrong.

[249]A well-known phrase, meaning that the prayers of one in great distress are sure of finding their way to God's ear. BT Berakhot 32*b*.

[240]She might, or might not, be identical with the woman to whom the previous letter was addressed.

[251]The lady might have ordered the Pentateuch for donating it to a school or a synagogue, or perhaps for her own use. Cantors usually worked as copyists too.

[252]His father-in-law.

[253]When mentioning a New Moon day or a holiday, Muslims and Jews often add that they should be a blessing for the addressee and his people.

[254]Benhā is a town in the Nile delta about 30 miles north of Cairo. The writer does not state from where he had journeyed to Benhā, as this probably was known to the addressee. Perhaps he had gone there directly from Fustat.

[255]TS 13 J 20, f. 9, ed. Mann, II, 307–308. Corrections of Mann's text made in my Reader's Guide in Mann (1970), p. xxxv, are not repeated here.

[256] The head of the page, containing most of the first line, is torn away. The opening of the letter is restored according to TS 13 J 27, f. 11, ll. 7–8. It is unusual and perhaps reflects the mood of the writer.

[257]Written above the line. Added perhaps in order to make sure that his wife had not paid in advance, as sometimes was done. Several other words are written above the line.

[258]Text: *lā min . . . walā min*, the same strange construction as that found 250 years later in Ibn Khaldūn's *Muqaddima*, cf. Dozy, *Suppléments*, II, 507*a*. Here one sees how this construction originated, as a negative sentence precedes. It is found in some Geniza papers also in an affirmative sentence.

[259]Literally, "a Have Mercy." These Hebrew litanies correspond in form and content to the Kyrie eleison ("O Lord, have mercy"), in use in Christian churches. No doubt, each of these types of religious poetry was chanted to a different tune.

[260]Heb. *rāhāṭ*. See E. Fleischer, *Sinai*, 67 (1970), 181 n. 9, and H. Merhavya, *Tarbiz*, 41, (1971), 95 n. 4.

[261]On the destruction of the Temple of Jerusalem or other calamities that had befallen the community.

[262]The Jewish Sabbath begins on Friday night. The solemn lighting of the candles is the prerogative of the wife, and only in her absence is it done by the husband.

[263]About this phrase from the daily prayer according to the Palestinian ritual see Goitein, *Jews and Arabs*, p. 50.

[264]This combination shows that the judge Nathan b. Samuel, by-named "The Diadem," was married to the writer's maternal aunt. About her see C, 3, n. 146, below.

[265]Obviously the same man who wrote one of the letters referred to before.

[266]He had come to the very bottom of the margin and there was no more room left.

[267]TS 16.278.

2. *Parents and Children*

[1]Lois Wladis Hoffman, "The Value of Children to Parents and the Decrease in Family Size," *Proceedings of the American Philosophical Society*, 119 (1975), 430–438; Lois Wladis Hoffman and Martin L. Hoffman, "The Value of Children to Parents," *Psychological Perspectives on Population*, ed. J. T. Fawcett (New York, 1973), pp. 19–76. For Islamic and Jewish literary sources on children see n. 69. See also L. Weisner, "Kindersegen und Kinderlosigkeit im altrabbinischen Schrifttume," *Monatsschrift für Geschichte und Wissenschaft des Judentums*, 66 (1922), 34–48, 138–148 (on the status of having children or being deprived of them in classical rabbinic literature).

[2]Charity has the effect of preserving the life of one's children, BT Pesahim 8*a*, bottom.

[3]See B, 1, nn. 1 and 27.

[4]Joseph: TS 13 J 18, f. 17, l. 17. Job: ENA NS 2, I, f. 12*v*.

[5]TS 13 J 35, f. 6, and common.

[6]PT Shabbath 1:2, f. 3*a*. See A, 1, nn. 29–30, above.

[7]TS 13 J 18, f. 13, l. 12: *wīgaddelēhū be-tōrā uv-ma'asīm ṭōvīm* (*be*, not *le*).

[8]TS 16.179, l. 9* (Labrāṭ I b. Moses I congratulating his brother Judah on his firstborn, ca. 1060, see n. 17, below); TS 18 J 4, f. 2 (Abraham "the Delight," son of Nathan "the Seventh," is addressed, ca. 1100); TS 13 J 34, f. 8, l. 7 (letter to Moses Maimonides at a time when his only son Abraham, born 1186, is already called *rabbēnū*, "our master"; this in Heb.); TS 18 J 3, f. 15, ll. 8–10 (the judge Elijah b. Zechariah is congratulated on the success in study of his younger son Abu 'l-Barakāt (Solomon), ca. 1210).

[9]See *Med. Soc.*, I, 180–183, II, 89–91. Goitein, *Letters*, p. 35. Prestige: *majd* (Ar.), TS 16.179, l. 9*; *le-shēm we-lithillā* (Heb.), TS 13 J 18, f. 17, l. 15.

[10]TS 16.291 (Moses Maimonides). TS 18 J 3 f. 19, l. 19* (family letter to brother, 1089).

[11]TS 13 J 19, f. 14, l. 14.

[12]E.g., Bodl. MS Heb. d 66 (Cat. 2878), f. 91*v*, l. 18 (*Nahray* 30); TS 10 J 16, f. 18, l. 14 (*Nahray* 35), Nathan b. Nahray referring to his own son Nissīm (*not* to Nahray's son bearing that name), TS 13 J 17, f. 23, l. 1, and *verso*, ll. 3–4.

[13]"Lovely flower": *peraḥ na'īm* (Heb.), TS 13 J 18, f. 13, l. 11, and often. "Blossoming rose": *ha-shōshanna ha-pōraḥat*, TS 8.152, ll. 2–3, addressed as "the elder." Ar. *muhja*: ULC Or 1080 J 28, l. 4.

[14]TS NS J 42, ll. 2–3*, where the *ḥamūd* already bears an honorary title from the yeshiva. The use of ḥamūd as "son" has lived on among Middle East Jews. Isaac Benjamin Yahuda, an elder brother of the famous Professor A. S. Yahuda (whose precious collection of Arabic manuscripts is now in the Library of Princeton University) and author of *Proverbia Arabica* (in Heb.), Jerusalem 1932 and 1934, calls himself on the title page of that book Isaac *ḥr.* Benjamin, which stands for *ḥamūd rabbī* (son of rabbi).

[15]See A, 2, nn. 6–8.

[16]"Seven sons" are the acme of bliss in the Bible (Job 1:2 and elsewhere). The hyperbolic expression "seven and even eight" is derived from Kohelet-Ecclesiastes 11:2. See also S. Abramson, *R. Nissīm Gaon* (Jerusalem, 1965), p. 275 n. 204.

[17]TS 16.179*, see n. 8, above.

[18]ENA NS 18, f. 7, sent by Joseph b. Samuel to "his brother from father(!) and mother" Ṣadaqa b. Ḥakmūn.

[19]TS 12.262, l. 19*, see B, 1, n. 5, above. Ar. *khalāṣ*, e.g.: ENA NS 2, I, f. 16, l. 17; TS 13 J 21, f. 32, margin and verso, l. 1: *bint ṭayyiba*, "a healthy girl" (fourteenth[?] century); Bodl. MS Heb. c 50 (no Cat.) f. 20; here the wish is added "may God increase his numbers and let him see the wedding (*faraḥ*) of his sons (*awlādoh*)." See also n. 25, below. In TS Arabic Box 54, f. 46, an instruction for letter writing, there is a faint attempt at formulating a congratulation on the birth of a girl: *anbithā bil-baraka wal-sa'āda*, "make her grow [like a plant] in bliss and happiness." But even this modest wish has not been found by me in a real letter.

[20]BT Ḥagiga 3*a*, bottom, expounding Deuteronomy 31:12.

[21]TS 8.104*.

[22]Hebrew: PT Yevamot 6:6, f. 7*c*, bottom. Arabic: Sa'īd 'Abbūd, *5000 arabische Sprichwörter aus Palästina* (Berlin, 1933), p. 2, no. 23 ("Your son's son belongs to you, but not your daughter's son"). Goitein, *Jemenica*, p. 43, no. 229, and in many other collections of Arabic maxims.

[23]13 J 23, f. 5, margin*. Text: *wa-kam yaq'ud insān fī buyūt al-nās.*

[24]*Ibid.*, ll. 19–20. Koran 12:92, and cf. Genesis 45:27. The smell of Joseph's shirt and its revivifying effect is an important item in Islamic mysticism and hence in popular tales.

[25]TS 12.250, ll. 20–21. Joseph and Nissīm, sons of Berachia, Qayrawān, writing to their relative Barhūn b. Ṣāliḥ Tāhertī, sojourning in Egypt. Although the plural is used, with "family" and "they" probably the recipient's wife is meant. Atonement: ENA NS 22, f. 27, l. 14, see A 2, n. 79, no. 15, above. Father's sins: BT Shabbat 32*b*.

[26]DK XIX*v*, P.S. Egyptian local.

[27]TS 10 J 13, f. 18, ll. 15–16. At the end of the letter, *verso*, ll. 9–10, "the little one" greets the recipient's "family," that is, wife, and is distressed not to have heard from her, probably after the announcement of the girl's death. "The little one" is spelled *w'yṣghyrh*, that is, *wiṣ-ṣghīra*.

[28]BT Bava Bathra 141*a*, see Tosafot on this saying. Cf. G. Adamek, *Das Kleinkind* (see n. 69, below), pp. 42–43, and L. Wiesner, "Die Wertung der Geschlechter im altrabbinischen Schrifttume," *Jahrbuch für jüdische Volkskunde* (Frankfurt, 1924/5), pp. 80–97.

[29]Here and elsewhere the male form *walad* is used to mean "child," although the reference is to a girl. See n. 33, below.

[30]TS 10 J 15, f. 23*, especially ll. 7–12, and *verso*, ll. 3–4.

[31]See the passage from TS 16.179*, n. 8 above.

[32]These two reasons given in BT Bava Bathra 141*a*.

[33]Ar. *waladī*, as n. 29, above.

[34]Bodl. MS Heb. c 28 (Cat. 2876), f. 58, ll. 13–14, 16–20, 24–26*.

[35]See C, 1, n. 255.

[36]See B, 1, n. 3.

[37]TS 12.347, l. 33, ed. Mann, *Texts*, I, 385. Reprinted in Z. Ankori, *Essays on Jewish Life* (New York, 1959), p. 31.

[38]See C, 1, nn. 2–4, above.

[39]Thus, in the passage from the letter of the little cantor just translated, see n. 34, above, yearnings are expressed first for the wife, but a report is requested first in respect of the child.

[40]*Commentary of Abraham b. Moses Maimonides on Genesis and Exodus*, ed. E. J. Wiesenberg (Letchworth, 1959), pp. 98–99 (Heb.).

[41]DK XIII, ll. 19–20*. The husband is described in *ṣabī ṣaghīr*, "a young boy." See H. Ritter, "Ein arabisches Handbuch der Handelswissenschaft," *Der Islam*, 7 (1916), 87, and Basim F. Musallam, "Birth Control and Middle Eastern History," *Princeton Conference on the Economic History of the Near East* (in preparation).

[42]Maimonides, *Responsa*, I, 40.

[43]Ar. *ẓihra*, explained on the reverse side as *ẓihrat al-ḥaml*, derived from *ẓahara*, "to become apparent."

[44]The year is omitted, but must have been 1094, for only in that year did the 16th of both the Muslim and Jewish months mentioned fall on a Thursday.

[45]"A miscarrying woman is quick in conceiving," *al-musguṭah mulguṭah* (g = q), Goitein, *Jemenica*, p. 82, no. 550.

[46]ULC Or 1080 J 190. For ʿArūs see the index and Goitein, *Letters*, pp. 232–239, in particular, p. 239.

[47]ENA 2727, f. 4.

[48]TS 13 J 21, f. 18, ll. 5, 13, 26.

[49]TS 8 J 24, f. 4, and ULC Or 1080 J 25. A third letter, written about the same time, tells about the children and complains about neglect: Westminster College, Arabica II, f. 129.

[50]TS 8 J 22, f. 6, l. 15. Plague: *dever* (Heb.). The writer's wife had a son before.

[51]ENA NS 18, f. 35, margin, see n. 18, above. "Busy" in the sense of "with child": *mashghūla*. Cf. TS 18 J 3, f. 19, l. 21 *balaghnī annak zawwajt ibnātak al-wāḥida dakhalat wal-ukhra fī ashghālhā*, "I learned that you married your daughters, the one had just had her wedding, and the other is already expecting."

[52]Dropsie 386, ll. 35–39, ed. Mann, *Texts*, I, 462. "Lady of the house": *gevīrā* (Heb.).

[53]For instance, TS 13 J 13, f. 13, frag. B, see n. 134, below; ENA NS 17, f. 31*b*, col. I, see n. 175 below.

[54]PER H 89, ed. S. D. Goitein, *Sefunot*, 8 (1964), 119–122 (dated 1137), ENA 4101, f. 16*b* (ca. 1090).

[55]See *Med. Soc.*, I, 127–128. For another task of the midwife see C, 1, n. 75, above. Umm Baqā, the midwife mentioned there, appears in TS NS Box 320, f. 33 (see *Med. Soc.*, II, 463, sec. 88), as a receiver of emoluments or alms from the community, probably for attending poor mothers. The family consulting Umm Baqā were paupers.

[56]An army doctor, absent at the delivery of his wife, asks her grownup son three times to buy her everything she wishes to offer to the visiting women, TS 13 J 18, f. 20, ll. 9, 10, 17.

[57]TS 13 J 36, f. 4*v*, l. 12. Ar. *maḥfil ʿaẓīm*. The special liturgies recited: *reshūt, qaddīsh, yōṣēr, ahavā lil-mīlā*, with a *sillūq*, or concluding poem, by the Spanish Hebrew poet Isaac Ibn Ghiyāth (Ghayyāth), 1038–1089.

[58]See *Med. Soc.*, II, 89. TS 6 J 6, f. 17, the cantor Abu 'l-Majd asks whether the father wishes to have the celebrations on the preceding Sabbath or on the day of the circumcision. ENA NS 2, I, f. 9, the judge Nathan b. Abraham Āv apologizes for

being unable to attend a ceremony in Fustat, because he had been scheduled for a similar one in Cairo before, and asks that his letter of apology be read out during the celebrations.

[59]Many such poetical creations have been preserved, e.g., TS 20.66. Begging letters on occasion of a circumcision, e.g., ENA 4020, f. 13; ENA NS 2, f. 21 (Karaite). A lamb and a hundred loaves of bread for the poor: n. 47, above.

[60]TS 10 J 6, f. 5. See Meinardus, *Christian Egypt*, pp. 318–341.

[61]About eras see *Med. Soc.*, I, 355–357. TS Arabic Box 54, f. 74; INA D-55, f. 9. The writer was not familiar with the Arabic script, and, what is more surprising, the Muslim months. In the year 1149, the Jewish month of Iyyar corresponded to the Muslim month of Dhu'l-Ḥijja, the last month of the Muslim year 543, as is rightly corrected in Arabic characters written beneath the Hebrew entry. In Hebrew the preceding month Dhu'l-Qa'da is listed—and even twice. Professor Bernard Goldstein of the University of Pittsburgh is dealing with this and other horoscopes extant in the Geniza.

[62]TS 12.512, to be edited by B. R. Goldstein, see preceding note.

[63]See A, 1, nn. 19–35, above; D, nn. 9–30, below.

[64]Abu 'l-Barakāt: TS 16.179*v*, l. 23, see n. 8, above. Abu 'l-Fakhr, ENA 2727A, f. 4, see n. 47, above.

[65]TS 16.57, ed. with trans. G. Weiss, *Gratz College Anniversary Volume* (Philadelphia, 1971), pp. 275–283.

[66]ULC Or 1080 J 190, see n. 46, above.

[67]DK X*. Trans. C, 1, n. 163, above.

[68]Bodl. MS Heb. c 50 (no Cat.), f. 23, a letter to the judge Elijah b. Zechariah.

[69]Cf. the Bonn Ph.D. thesis *Das Kleinkind in Glaube und Sitte der Araber im Mittelalter* (The small child in the beliefs and customs of the Arabs in the Middle Ages) by Gerhard Adamek (Bonn 1968), based, of course, on literary sources (important bibliography), cf. n. 28, above. For Jewish literary sources see "Children," *EJ*, V, 426–427.

[70]Goitein, *Education*, pp. 28–74, and "Side Lights on Jewish Education from the Cairo Geniza," *Gratz College Anniversary Volume* (Philadelphia, 1971), pp. 83–110.

[71]TS 10 J 11, f. 13, ll. 6–10. It was a short time after Elijah b. Solomon had taken office (1063). The letter is in the hand of Abūn b. Ṣadaqa, its recipient was Nahray b. Nissīm, see S. D. Goitein, "Daniel b. Azaria, Nāsī and Gaon, New Sources," *Shalem*, 2 (1976) 98. The father was alive, but, it seems, not present in the town at the time of the death of his wife.

[72]TS 12.494, Summer 1110, cf. *Med. Soc.*, II, 47, and 191.

[73]About the importance of being well dressed in school see Goitein, *Education*, pp. 59, 65.

[74]TS 13 J 24, f. 1, ll. 8–13. Ar. *hū ṭayyib munsharih al-khāṭir ma'hum* etc.; "plays": *yatafarraj*.

[75]TS 13 J 20, f. 3, ll. 11–13, ed. Mann, II, 302.

[76]The father's name Yeshū'ā he-ḥāvēr b. rabbi Nathan, *gūr aryē*, ("the Lion's cub," meaning from the royal family of David). The boy died on Friday, March 11, 1026. The long poem is contained in several widely dispersed Geniza texts, critically assembled by E. Fleischer, "Remarks on Medieval Hebrew Poetry," *Studies in Literature: Presented to Simon Halkin* (Jerusalem, 1973), pp. 183–189 (Heb.). Questions: *Med. Soc.*, II, 209–210.

[77]ENA 2935, fs. 16–17. The passage ed. in *Gratz College Anniversary Volume* (see n. 70, above), p. 87. For *b't, ibid.*, l. 2 of n. 10, read *k't*.

[78]TS 13 J 25, f. 19, ll. 18–19 (*Nahray* 181). Joseph b. Mūsā Tāhertī writing to Nahray b. Nissīm.

[79]TS 10 J 16, f. 14, ll. 14–16.

[80]TS 8 J 27, f. 5*v*, ll. 2–4. Gottheil-Worrell XXXIV, ll. 4–6, p. 156. For *'lyk* the MS has *'llh*, Allah: *'dywny* is not Heb. *adōnī*, but Ar. *addiyūnī* "bring me"; for *'ndn'* the MS has *'ndh*. This Nathan b. Nahray was the son of Nahray b. Nathan, Nahray b. Nissīm's first cousin, mentioned in C, 1, n. 4, above.

[81]See *Med. Soc.*, II, 173, bottom.

[82]*Ibid.*, p. 183.

[83]The passage from TS 10 J 7, f. 5 (trans. above. B, 3, n. 85) is a good example.

[84]TS 12.493*, see *Gratz College Anniversary Volume* (Philadelphia, 1971), pp. 88–89.

[85]The legal opinion is by Joseph Ibn Abitur, early eleventh century, see *Med. Soc.*, I, 567, n. 30. For the text quoted see S. Assaf, *History of Jewish Education*, Vol. III (Jerusalem, 1936), p. 22 n. 2 (Heb.).

[86]TS 16.171, ll. 17–19+, see Mann, *Texts*, II, 198.

[87]Maimonides, *Responsa*, II, 317.

[88]Maimonides, *Code*, book "Property," sec. "Sales," chap. 29, para. 12–17.

[89]Bilbays: ULC Add. 3339 (a), esp. ll. 19 and 28. Maimonides, *Commentary on the Mishna*, ed. J. Kafih, 7 (Jerusalem, 1969), 738.

[90]ENA NS 2, f. 41, see C, 1, n. 243 above. The remark in *Med. Soc.*, I, 99, that no apprenticeship agreement has been found thus far in the Geniza is to be qualified accordingly.

[91]Consider only the role of the fathers in the conclusion of their son's marriages, see sec. B, above.

[92]Summer 1232: ULC Add. 3417*v*, item II. Ar. *bāligh wa-yaẓhar minoh al-'ān annoh ḥariq mujtahid fī taḥṣīl shay ya'ūd bih 'alā nafsoh.* The term *ḥariq* (spelled *ḥryq*), not found by me elsewhere, is derived from the fifth form of the verb; cf. TS 16.272, l. 12 and *verso*, l. 21: *taḥarruqoh fī iqḍā' (!) ḥawa'ij al-nās*, "his readiness to look after other people's affairs," cf. Dozy, *Supplément*, I, 273*b*, bottom. Renowned for his probity: TS AS 147, f. 4, l. 12. Adolescents: TS 12.9, l. 10 (letter of the Nagid Mevōrākh to the community of al-Maḥalla) *taḥnīk awlādhim wa-nawāshīhim.*

[93]In the numerous cases when, in memorial lists, a person is described as "short-lived," I assume the reference is not to a mere child but to a young man who died before marrying, or before having children.

[94]TS 10 J 18, f. 1+. See my remarks in *Tarbiz*, 32 (1963), 189.

[95]See *Med. Soc.*, II, 140. There, the average size of a household, not that of a nuclear family, is estimated.

[96]TS 20.169* (1025/6), see A, 3, n. 54, above.

[97]TS 16.262, *India Book* 307 (ca. 1100).

[98]TS 8.104*. See C, 3, n. 20, below.

[99]ULC Or 1080 J 6, a claim made in Fustat by one of the heirs; TS 16.241, ll. 15 ff.; ENA 3793, f. 1; TS NS J 383.

[100]Single daughter: TS 13 J 14, f. 4+, *India Book* 259; Bodl. MS Heb. d 66 (Cat. 2878), f. 121 (1028), ed. S. Assaf, *Tarbiz*, 9 (1938), 213. See C, 4, nn. 16–21. Single son: ENA NS 17, f. 21 (1040; wife alive).

[101]TS 10 J 17, f. 14, *India Book* 37. Maimonides, *Responsa*, I, 182.

[102]TS 18 J 3, f. 5, cf. *Med. Soc.*, II, 88, n. 110. The writer had no sons, for he says "I and my five daughters pray for you." Other dependents, such as a sister, mother, or aunt, lived in his household, which comprised a total of ten persons, see A, *Introduction*, n. 2, end.

[103]TS NS Box 31, f. 8*. See *Med. Soc.*, II, 501, sec. 95.

[104]TS 13 J 17, f. 9 (Heb.). The writer asks also for expenses for the voyage back to his children's country.

[105]*India Book*, chapters III and IV.

[106]Cf., e.g., TS 10 J 13, f. 12; TS 13 J 22, f. 29. The sisters are referred to in the plural, not in the dual, which had become almost obsolete by the time of the Geniza. If there had been more than two sisters, I feel, they would have been mentioned in a different way.

[107]ENA NS 18, f. 35, l. 41: "Your paternal cousins are well; to your sister a boy was born." The sister, as usual, was married to a paternal cousin. See also n. 51, above.

[108]TS 13 J 21, f. 35, where this wish is expressed both in the address and in ll. 7–9 of the text, which conclude the proem; TS 16.241, l. 5, a letter of theoretical and practical questions. On *verso* the answers addressed to a man named R. Nathan.

[109]TS 13 J 9, f. 4 + *, see A, 2, n. 21, above.

[110]TS 18 J 3, f. 19*. The daughters Miriam and Berākhā, mentioned in ll. 32 bottom and in the margin, were from the first marriage, while "my sister" was from the second. The letter was written by the sender's elder son.

[111]TS 8 J 22, f. 23*. I do not quite understand why the writer states: "I have *one* wife." Perhaps "one" simply stands for "a."

[112]As in the fragment TS 12.13, l. 9, a report to a brother who had returned from being abroad: "Berākhā is well, she has four boys (*ghilmān*, rare) and one daughter, whom she has married off."

[113]E.g., government servants: Mann, *Texts*, II, 270, l. 245 (six); Maimonides' five brothers-in-law. Judges: The judge Saadya, the father of Samuel b. Saadya, see *Med. Soc.*, II, 514, sec. 23 (six), TS Box K 15, f. 92. Physicians: Saadya, the father of the Nagids Judah and Mevōrākh, see Mann, II, 250, or Aaron Ibn al-ʿAmmānī, physician and judge in Alexandria, see *Med. Soc.*, II, 245 (five). Bearers of titles: TS 13 J 18, f. 9, l. 17; TS 13 J 34, f. 5, l. 23; ENA 4020, f. 51 (four). See also A, 2, n. 23, above.

[114]Six cases of two sons and six others of one son on two pages of the memorial lists, Mann, *Texts*, II, 274–275.

[115]Cecil Roth, "The Ordinary Jew of the Middle Ages," *Abraham A. Neuman Jubilee Volume* (Leiden, 1962), p. 428 n. 3, contrasts the restricted size of the natural family of the Middle Ages with the large families of the English bourgeoisie of the nineteenth century. (Some details in Roth's study need revision. He adduces Moses Maimonides and his brother David as an example of a singularly small family; but they had at least three sisters.) The studies of Peter Laslett, *The World We Have Lost* (New York, 1971), and *Household and Family in Past Time* (CUP, Cambridge, 1972), show that, in the centuries preceding the industrial revolution, households, that is, nuclear families plus members of the extended family and even servants or apprentices, were smaller than generally believed, comprising an average of about five persons (see S. S. Boocock, "The Social Context of Childhood," *Proceedings of the American Philosophical Society*, 119 [1975], p. 425).

The father of my great-grandmother, Hänle(in) Kohn (1803–1880), had eight sons and seven daughters from his wife Zierle, all but one of whom survived him (the exception died of a contagious disease at the age of twenty-six). Hänle was a pious and wealthy man, who spent his whole life in the small Bavarian town in which he and all his known ancestors had been born—a typical example of a nineteenth-century bourgeois family. I owe the details to an unpublished book on the family by Dr. Jean Kohn of Paris. My own father was one of seven brothers, with one sister, the jewel of the family.

[116]Hands, e.g., DK X*, trans. in C, 1, n. 163, above (son-father); TS 10 J 17, f. 3, l. 1 (son-parents). Feet, e.g., ULC Or 1081 J 5*v*, l. 12* (daughter-mother). TS 16.265 (son-mother). TS 13 J 24, f. 22, l. 3 (daughter-father).

[117]TS 10 J 7, f. 3, margin: "I kiss your eyes and the eyes of my mother." The writer refers to himself in the address as "Your servant, your son." DK XXVIII*v*, l. 6, ed. Samuel Kandel, *Genizai kéziratok* (Budapest, 1909) p. iv: "Your boy kisses your eyes." For "father kissing his son's eyes" see C, 1, n. 246, above. Other young relative: TS 10 J 17, f. 8, l. 15.

[118]Heb. *adonēnū*, "our lord" (without "father"), TS NS Box 298, f. 27, ed. A. Scheiber, *Kirjath Sepher*, 40 (1965), 571. Aramaic: *imma martha* "the (not: my) mother, the lady," ENA 4020, f. 18, l. 42, ed. J. Mann, *Tarbiz* 6 (1935), 83. Hence the name Martha. Weaver: TS 13 J 18, f. 26, *ya sīdī*, probably pronounced thus, for otherwise the spelling would be *syydy*, as in *sayyidī wāldī*, "my lord, my father," TS 13 J 24, f. 22, l. 1 (daughter).

[119]John Rylands Library, Manchester, Gaster Collection, L 213* (1090), ed. S. D. Goitein, *Bulletin of the John Rylands Library*, 54 (1971), 94–102.

[120]TS 16.277*, see C, 1, n. 31, above.

[121]Holiday: TS AS 145, f. 22. Parents: DK XIII*.

[122]TS 13 J 9, f. 4+* (1053), see n. 109, above.

[123]TS 24.49, l. 23 Evyatar "The Fourth," referring to his father, the Gaon Elijah b. Solomon. TS 10 J 18, f. 10, ll. 18–19+, referring to mother, see A, 3, n. 7, above.

[124]TS 10 J 14, f. 6, ll. 27 and 32. ULC Add. 3417 (Cat. 839), l. 15.

[125]Sassoon Collection 713*v*, ll. 31–35, *India Book*, 263 (1148), ed. H. Z. Hirschberg, *I. F. Baer Jubilee Volume* (Jerusalem, 1961), pp. 134–153.

[126]TS 10 J 11, f. 22, ll. 8–9.

[127]AIU VII A 17, ed. B. Chapira, *Mélanges H. Derenbourg* (Paris, 1909), p. 125.

[128]TS 12.780*v*, ll. 1–2, cf. A, 3, n. 29, above.

[129]ENA NS 2, f. 11, ll. 14–16, and *verso*, l. 12.

[130]TS 10 J 13, f. 10, ll. 8–9, 22, *verso*, l. 4. See *Med. Soc.*, II, 379, n. 27.

[131]TS 10 J 9, f. 1*, See A, 2, n. 39, above.

[132]TS 10 J 13, f. 24, ll. 10–11, *li-khaṣā'ilha 'l-malīḥa ma' ummhā wa-ma' a[l]-nās.*

[133]"You honor God in accordance with your means, but your parents, even if you must go begging," PT Peah I, f. 15*d*, with reference to Proverbs 3:9.

[134]The case of the old cantor and court clerk Japheth (Ḥusayn) b. David, who was forced to apply for an additional job because he expended all his possessions on the treatment of his daughter who died in childbed, is particularly impressive, TS 13 J 13, f. 13 B, see S. D. Goitein, *Shalem* (Jerusalem), 2 (1976), 75.

[135]Tosefta Kiddushin 1:11, ed. Saul Lieberman, *The Tosefta*, (New York, 1973), p. 279, l. 49 (with parallels).

[136]PSR 1451 in Arabic characters; on the reverse side the son is called Yeshū'ā b. Elazar b. Judah b. Japheth ha-Levi in Hebrew, which corresponds to Faraj Allah b. Manṣūr b. Abi 'l-Futūḥ b. Abi 'l-Ḥasan in the Arabic document.

[137]TS 12.50, frag. in the hand of Ḥalfōn b. Manasse, The "Mosque of the Lemon," *masjid al-laymūna*, given as one of the borders of the house, is not noted in Casanova, *Reconstitution* (in *Med. Soc.*, I, xx, erroneously *Reconstruction*).

[138]ULC Or 1080 J 117*v*. Abū Sahl b. Ibrāhīm making the gift to his son Abu 'l-Ḥasan. In the original document, dated December 1088, Khulayf b. 'Ubayd b. 'Alī b. Khulayf sells the house to Hārūn b. Khulayf b. Hārūn, the perfumer, a Jew.

[139]TS Arabic Box 38, f. 102.

[140]TS 12.177, TS NS J 338 and 382, ed. S. D. Goitein, *Eretz-Israel*, 8 (1967), 293–297.

[141]TS 16.65 (Oct.–Nov. 1117). The house bordered on a Muslim pious foundation, *ḥubs yūnus*, administered by "the office of the Friday- and other mosques," *diwān al-jawāmi' wal-masājid.*

[142]See B, 4, n. 27, above.

[143]ENA 4011, f. 56. The house was situated between the two synagogues of Fustat. Probably poor people, since father and son are not even honored with the title M. or R., corresponding to our Mr.

[144]TS 8.206. The property was near al-Qamra, a Jewish neighborhood in Alexandria and in a lane leading to "the great pilgrims road," *al-maḥajja al-'uẓmā*. In the excellent hand of the court clerk Mawhūb, the cantor, son of Aaron, the cantor (cf., e.g., TS 28.6 C, written and signed by him).

[145]She ordered that a *ḥujra*, or chamber, be erected above her tomb, which was quite exceptional.

[146]TS K 6, f. 118v*.

[147]TS 13 J 6, f. 14+, see B, 5, n. 37, above.

[148]TS 16.241. The much damaged document contains six questions, with the answers on the reverse side. One of the other questions: whether a man, vowing a gift "to the poor in general" has fulfilled his pledge by distributing gifts to a number of individual poor. The jurisconsult addressed had one son, a description fitting both Maimonides and his son and successor Abraham, but the answers are in neither the script nor the style of either.

[149]Goitein, *Jemenica*, p. 72 n. 458: *di'it loh ummoh.*

[150]ENA 1822 A, f. 71.

[151]TS 10 J 15, f. 15, ll. 17–18. Isma'īl b. Faraḥ addressing his son Faraḥ, cf.

Goitein, *Letters*, p. 153. The Bible quotation is inexact *(kī ta'arīkh yāmīm*, reminiscent of Deuteronomy 4:40, said in another context).

[152]DK XIII, ll. 23–24*. "By these lines," that is, just as this letter is real, so are my words. "Intensive prayer," Ar. *du'ā jayyid*. The concluding words are Islamic religious phraseology.

[153]Son to mother: "I request from you only this favor and charity: be so kind and pray for me day and night, as you are accustomed to do," TS 16.277, ll. 24–*verso*, l. l. When a man writes to his brother "convey to the lady, our mother, my greetings, prayers, and thanks," TS 13 J 33, f. 10, ll. 26–28, the word translated as *du'ā'ī*, "prayer," means "gratitude," not intercessional prayer. In countless business letters thanks are expressed in this way.

[154]Bodl. MS Heb. g 2 (Cat. 2700), f. 2, ed. Margalioth, *Hilkhot*, p. 134, an eleventh-century hand, it seems, see plates 24–25. The Talmudic phrase "May I become a ransom for his [the father's] rest," *harēnī kappārat mishkāvō* (BT Kiddushin 31*b*) is not used in the Geniza. The corresponding Arabic phrase, *ju'ilt fidāh*, "may I become his ransom," is not said for the dead and not specifically for parents. In ENA 2742, f. 6, a *muqaddam*, or head of a Jewish local community, demands that his name be included in the *kaddish*, as had been done for his predecessors, see M. A. Friedman, *Gratz College Annual of Jewish Studies*, 1 (1972), 57 n. 4.

[155]The Talmudic "a son brings merit to his father" (BT Sanhedrin 104*a*) means: if a son is better than his father, he somehow atones for his father's sins. That saying does not refer to intercessional prayer. To a father: TS 12.133, see Goitein, *Letters*, p. 74 n. 12 *(khayr)*; TS 10 J 16, f. 19, ll. 11–12, see *Letters*, p. 256 n. 2 *(afḍal)*. To a son: TS 13 J 20, f. 6, ll. 9–11*, a Hebrew letter by Mevōrākh b. Nathan ("may He make your fine name even higher than that of your ancestors"), noting 1 Kings 1:47.

[156]See S. 'Abbūd, *5000 arabische Sprichwörter aus Palästina* (Berlin, 1933), p. 9 n. 181; Goitein, *Jemenica*, p. 19, no. 94. J. Theodor and Ch. Albeck, *Bereschit Rabba*, Vol. II (Berlin, 1927), pp. 870–871, with parallels, based on Genesis 31:46, where the sons of the Patriarch Jacob are referred to as his brothers. An even stronger, also all-Arabic, version: "When your son's beard grows, shave off your own beard," S. Hayat, "The Family in the Proverbs of Iraqi Jews," *Folklore Studies*, Vol. 3 (Jerusalem, 1972), p. 101, no. 198 (with ten parallels, Hebrew).

[157]Thus, the son writing to his father in Goitein, *Letters*, pp. 51–56, had reached a higher degree of independence than the son addressed by his father in *ibid.*, pp. 197–201. The letters of Isma'īl b. Faraḥ to his son (see n. 151, above) are hardly different in tone from those sent to a regular business friend or partner. See also *Med. Soc.*, I, 315, n. 14.

[158]TS 13 J 22, f. 22, ll. 15–16. Ar. *wa-tukhallī 'annak al-ishtighāl bil-jīza* (=*zīja*) *wal-umūrāt al-hadhayāniyya*. First I took *bljyzh* as *bil-ijāza* (with Imāla) in the sense of *tazkiya*, see *Med. Soc.*, II, 250. But the reading suggested here seems to be preferable. Later in the letter the father says: *ant muḥārif*, "you are a poor man."

[159]Bodl. MS Heb. d 66 (Cat. 2878), f. 57*, trans. in *Gratz College Annual*, 4 (1975), 58–61. The two sons were Abū Zikrī and Raḍī (who died as a young man), both physicians. Abu 'l-Barakāt Solomon b. Elijah is referred to in the letter as a schoolboy.

[160]TS NS J 14, l. 14*, ed. S. D. Goitein, *Shalem*, 1 (1974), 44–46. See Mann, *Texts*, II, 63, and Goitein, *Tarbiz*, 45 (1976), 75.

[161]Dropsie 400, ll. 16–18.

[162]TS 8.9*.

[163]TS 13 J 18, f. 29*v*, l. 15.

[164]Bodl. MS Heb. d 66 (Cat. 2878), f. 21, *India Book* 177.

[165]DK 2, Zayn ("Beauty") b. Abu 'l-Faḍl is addressed.

[166]TS NS J 58*v*, ll. 6–9, in the hand of Abū Naṣr b. Abraham.

[167]TS 24.78*v*, ll. 11 and 40–41*, ed., transcribed into Arabic characters, and trans. by S. D. Goitein, *Hamilton A. R. Gibb Jubilee Volume*, ed. G. Makdisi (Leiden, 1965), pp. 270–284.

[168]TS 8 J 4, f. 17*b-d*, Shemarya b. Ḥalfōn and his son Eli.

[169]Summer 1045: ENA 4010, f. 26. Alms fund: *heqdēsh* (Heb.). 1065: TS 13 J 1, f. 17. It is not stated whether the mother was a widow or a divorcée.

[170]JNUL 12, ll. 5–8, 26, letter of ʿAllūsh b. Yeshūʿā, Qayrawān, to Ismaʿīl b. Abraham, Fustat. The shipowner: Muhammad *al-jwj'ly* or *jwgh'ly*, hardly Djidjelli. The story of the lost bale happened in connection with the ship of Ibn Abī Ronda, often mentioned in the Geniza.

[171]TS 13 J 16, f. 3*, lacking beginning and address. The letter is in the hand of the judge Shēla b. Mevasser (dated documents: 1075–1101), referring, in l. 10, to his colleague Abraham (b. Jacob) Derʿī.

[172]TS 16.90, a fragment. Khazariyya's father bore an Arab name: Munajjā, "the Saved One," usually corresponding to Heb. Joseph.

[173]See C, 3, nn. 40, 42, below.

[174]ENA 2808, f. 15a*, ed. S. D. Goitein, *JQR*, 66 (1975), 86–88.

[175]ENA NS 17, f. 31*b*, col. I, trans. S. D. Goitein, *Gratz College Annual*, 4 (1975), 65–67.

[176]"How can one do a good work every minute? By bringing up an orphan boy and an orphan girl in one's house and marrying them to one another." BT Ketubbot 50*a*.

[177]TS AS 146, f. 5. David ha-Nasī (not to be confounded with his namesake David ha-Nāsī b. Daniel, who lived in the second part of the eleventh century) orders three communal officials to pay a quarter dinar to the foster sons of al-Afḍal out of the revenue from the houses donated "for Jerusalem" (where, at that time, no Jews lived). Another order of payment by this David ha-Nāsī, dated 1165, is preserved in TS Arabic Box 52, f. 248, see *Med. Soc.*, II, 458, sec. 69. For the upbringing of slave girls see B, 2, n. 47, above.

[178]Mentioning one's real father, TS 24.49, ll. 13 and 23 (Evyatar b. Elijah, the future Gaon, addressing Eli b. Yaḥya-Ḥiyyā, the parnās); *ḥamūdō*, TS 18 J 4, f. 4, in address and signature (addressed to the same by Nathan ha-Kohen b. Mevōrākh of Ascalon). "Son, brother, and friend" in address of TS 10 J 14, f. 29.

3. *Widowhood, Divorce, and Remarriage*

[1]Men married a second time and produced children in such marriages as frequently, at least, as women, see nn. 143, 156, below.

[2]The passage referred to in *Med. Soc.*, I, 135, n. 23, shows that, before trying to buy a maidservant, one preferred to look for a free woman as help. See also *ibid.*, p. 130, on domestic help in general.

[3]ULC Add. 3339 (b), ll. 27–30 (1217/8). See C, 1, n. 105, above.

[4]About this contingency, and "the widow's oath," in particular, see nn. 31–33, below.

[5]TS 18 J 1, f. 4(Oct. 1006)*, a magnificent document.

[6]TS 8 J 6, f. 14 a (1241), ENA NS 17, f. 21(1040). Debt owed husband: Bodl. MS Heb. a 2 (Cat. 2805), f. 9 (Dec. 1188)+*. See n. 41, below.

[7]ULC Add. 3339 (b), *in tarammalat*, "if she consented to live as a widow" (30 + 10 dinars); TS 8 J 34, f. 10 = ENA 1822 A, f. 17 (50 + 1 dinars); Westminster College, Frag. Cairens. 113 + 115, ll. 20 and 32* (60 + 10 dinars).

[8]TS 13 J 3, f. 17 (July/Aug. 1241). "My wife, their mother, my three sons," ll. 15–19. For the family name Kāmukhī see *Med. Soc.*, I, 424, n. 100.

[9]Westminster College, Frag. Cairens. 113 + 115*, ll. 20–22. Together with her son from a previous marriage the widow was given 100 dinars, see n. 7, above. Another case in TS 8 J 8, f. 12 (1085).

[10]TS NS J 347, ll. 11–13, a fragment. Additional details may have been lost. For male slaves see *Med. Soc.*, I, 147.

[11]TS 12.88 (Dec. 1129/Jan. 1130), a fragment written by Nathan ha-Kohen b. Solomon. "Retrieving," "seeking full payment," *tastawfī minhā ḥaqqhā*.

[12]Firkovitch II, 1700, f. 19*b* (June 1156). Abū ʿImrān al-Ṣāʾigh b. Joseph; *bi-ḥuqūq ketubbahā*. Written by Mevōrākh b. Nathan.

[13]TS 18 J 1, f. 27 (May 1185). Landed property: *amlāk*. Sār Shālōm is styled here "President of the yeshiva of the Land of Delight" (*ereṣ ha-ṣevī*, Israel).

[14]ENA 4011, f. 67 (Spring 1145). A poor man leaves "all that is in the house" to his wife: TS NS J 356, written by Solomon b. Elijah on 17 Nisan 1229, that is, during the Passover week, when normally no documents were made out.

[15]Westminster College, Frag. Cairens. 115*v*.

[16]*Ibid.*, ll. 5–7, where *wld* is to be understood as *wuld*, children. ʿArūs is repeatedly wished to become a father of sons, see Goitein, *Letters*, p. 239, and DK VII, a letter to him by Raḥamīm b. Nissīm; on the other hand, greetings are extended to "the little ones," *ṣighār*, meaning his small children, DK 14*v*, l. 7, in a letter from al-Mahdiyya by Abu ʾl-Surūr b. David.

[17]In the appeals described in *Med. Soc.*, II, 471–509, e.g., secs. 15, 16, 18, 19, 21, 135, also TS AS 145, f. 9, l. 17. Letter to ʿArūs from his brother-in-law Abu ʾl-Ḥasan Ibn Ṭībān: TS 13 J 22, f. 28; another referred to is TS 13 J 22, f. 20, ll. 8–9. Greetings to his brothers-in-law in a letter to ʿArūs: TS 12.350.

[18]ULC Or 1080 J 262. Salāma, daughter of Furayj b. Suhayl Ibn Abu ʾl-Gharīb, widow of Nathan-Hiba ha-Levi b. Ḥakam b. Joseph Ibn (al-) Shumaym, appoints her maternal uncle Bishr b. Abraham to carry her husband's "bones" to Jerusalem. Addressed to Japheth-Abū ʿAlī Ḥasan al-Baghdādī b. Ṭovia-Ṭayyib, her attorney. Several of these names were not common in Egypt.

[19]For the legal consequences of the appointment of a wife as heir see Yaron, *Gifts in Contemplation of Death*, pp. 158–160.

[20]TS 8.104*. Abu ʾl-Munajjā Solomon b. Saadya, father of the girls Mudallila ("Coquette," "Bold"), Naṣr ("Victory"), and Nab(a)ʾ ("Excellence," "Supremacy") and the sons Abū Saʿd ("Lucky") and Maḥāsin ("Virtuous") makes his wife "Lady . . ." *mutaṣarrifa wa-waṣiyya ʿalā jamī ʿmawjūdih*.

[21]Westminster College, Frag. Cairens. 113, l. 12.

[22]For ʿArūs see nn. 15–17, above.

[23]Management: *al-naẓar fī mā yaʿūd bih al-ṣalāḥ li-mār* (Heb. "Mister") Japheth *waladih hādhā*. According to Talmudic law the wife, if appointed as heir, receives the same share as a son. Japheth obviously was the firstborn and only son from a previous marriage and, as such, was assigned by his father two shares, with a third going to Amat al-Qādir. See n. 19, above.

[24]TS 16.23 and TS 10 J 5, f. 2, *India Book* 141*a* and *b*, fragments of one contract, fortunately complementing each other, both written by Hillel b. Eli. The document speaks only of Yemen; the India traders usually undertook to travel as far as Aden. If they did not succeed there, they went farther afield.

[25]TS 12.531*v*.

[26]TS 12.631. "With" *maʿ*, not *ʿind*, which would have meant that the wife owed that sum.

[27]TS 12.553 and TS NS Box 323, f. 19, two fragments of a document written by Ḥalfon b. Manasse, which still leave it very incomplete. "Entrusted with all his affairs": *asnad ilayhā jamī ʿumūroh*.

[28]Mishna Gittin 5:1. About later developments see M. A. Friedman, *Tarbiz*, 43 (1973/4), 181 n. 68.

[29]TS NS J 461, ENA 2727, f. 11 A. The term: *zibbūrīt* (Heb.). The bride was a poor widow or divorcée, who received only 4 dinars as immediate marriage gift.

[30]TS 8 J 21, f. 14 (1085), Bodl. MS Heb. a 2 (Cat. 2805), f. 9+* (1188). ENA NS 17, f. 16 (1353).

[31]TS NS J 392 (Feb. 1128): In court, the widow of Solomon b. Ḥayyīm the Seventh receives from Jacob the perfumer, son of the parnās David, her dowry, a large one, including her personal wardrobe. Whether the dowry had been deposited with Solomon because he was an official trustee of the court, or because the husband, who had had business relations with him (TS 10 J 4, f. 10 [1126]), had willed thus, is not evident. Earnings of wife: TS 13 J 3, f. 10 (e) (1159). The delayed marriage gift of this woman amounted to 30 dinars.

[32]TS 18 J 4, f. 21, a legal opinion by Eli he-ḥāvēr b. Amram, who had, however, the reputation of being a poor scholar, see TS 13 J 26, f. 18*v*, ll. 22 ff., written by the brother of the Gaon Daniel b. Azarya, and ENA NS 2, I, f. 31, ll. 31–40, by Daniel himself, both ed. S. D. Goitein, *Shalem*, 2 (1976), 65–72, and 63–64. As we learn from Mosseri A 89.4, the delayed marriage gift of this widow was 15 dinars. Had she been adjudicated the minimum of half a dirhem per day for nursing (like a divorcée), she would have had an additional income of about 5 dinars for the year or so the baby needed her.

[33]Document conveying the status of trustworthiness: *sheṭār ne'emānūt* (Heb.). TS 10 J 21, f. 16. In TS NS J 496 a widow from another locality presents such a document.

[34]ENA 2728, f. 5*v*. Property of wife: *melūg*, see C, 1, n. 109, above. Had the house been registered as dowry, the legal situation would have been different, since the dowry is a debt owed by the husband. For judge Menaḥēm see *Med. Soc.*, II, 514, sec. 26.

[35]TS NS J 357. The wife: Sutayt ("Little Lady") b. Nadīv ("Noble," Heb.). Upper part only.

[36]TS 12.140 (1145), see *Med. Soc.*, I, 135, n. 28, 138, n. 49. The titles: *ha-rāv ha-gadōl rēsh bē rabbānān*. Written and signed by Nathan b. Samuel.

[37]ENA NS 18, f. 25*, written by Ḥalfōn b. Manasse. The testator: Abu 'l-Ṭāhir Mevōrākh b. Shēlā al-mūrid. The wife's name overleaf in the docket: Sitt al-Dār b. Joseph.

[38]TS 8 J 21, f. 4, and TS 8 J 8, f. 12, in that sequence (June 1085).

[39]TS 18 J 1, f. 20 (April 1126). On Abraham b. Nathan the Seventh see *Med. Soc.*, I, 84; *ibid.*, II, 434, sec. 171, 586, n. 15, p. 587, n. 22; often mentioned.

[40]ULC Or 1080 J 6, case I*. The remark that the father had married off his daughters before means perhaps that they had no claim on the estate.

[41]See nn. 5–8, above.

[42]TS 8.260*v*, much effaced.

[43]ENA 4011, f. 5 (March 1158). For the "ban in general terms" see *Med. Soc.*, II, 340.

[44]ENA 2808, f. 12, ll. 6–11: "The brother of the dead husband [the heir] has not paid the widow a thing." TS 12.125: the head of the community in Sammānūd asks the district judge to come since he was unable to reach a settlement between the heirs and the widow of a deceased member.

[45]Bodl. MS Heb. b 11 (Cat. 2874), f. 12 (Tyre 1037), ed. S. Assaf, *Yerushalayim* (Jerusalem, 1953), pp. 107–108: two daughters release their mother and ask a brother abroad to do the same, so that the widow may claim her husband's goods left in Egypt. TS 13 J 3, f. 11 (1165): a brother and heir releases his sister-in-law. TS 10 J 26, f. 4*: a son releases his mother who was about to marry again, see n. 152, below.

TS 16.49, ed. Assaf, *Yerushalayim* (1953), pp. 110–112 (March 28, 987, not April 26, as in *Med. Soc.*, I, 7): a widow releases her brother-in-law, his two sisters, and the husband of one of the two. TS 16.90: a mother releases her three sons after long litigation, see C, 2, n. 172, above. ENA 4011, f. 55 (1144/5; left half only): accounting with children and complete release. BM Or 5551 (Glass. 1151)*: a mother releases her daughter and the "perfumer," with whom her delayed marriage gift was deposited, and also her father, who obviously had still owed something from the dowry. ENA NS 18, f. 23: a mother releases both son and stepson; written by Hillel b. Eli at his best, but not completed; had she second thoughts? TS 18 J 1, f. 18: The widow of the Cairene judge Abraham b. Nathan (*Med. Soc.*, II, 512, sec. 14) confirms having received from her son-in-law all due her from the estate of her late husband. The judge's daughter, as the only heir, had paid her mother whatever was owed her from her marriage contract or her husband's will (March 1116). TS 13 J 5, f. 5*: a widow declares having received the value of her dowry, but not yet her late marriage gift (Bilbays, Aug. 1204). TS 8.168: another acknowledgment by a widow, interesting, but fragmentary.

[46]ENA 2591, f. 7.

[47]TS 18 J 1, f. 1, frag. The first signature is effaced. One of the signatories, Zur'a ha-Levi b. Abraham, signed also, and with the same faltering hand, TS 16.370, written in Damascus in 995. "The orphans of Ibn Sābā."

[48]TS Arabic Box 41, f. 79* in the name of the survivors, *mukhallaf*, of Mubārak b. Mundhir Ibn Sābā. See *Med. Soc.*, II, 602, n. 40.

[49]The judges groomed their sons to become their successors, see *Med. Soc.*, II, 319–320.

[50]But according to Muslim law debts must be paid before the estate can be divided among the heirs.

[51]TS 28.19*. Jalīla b. Abraham b. Khalfa al-Rashīdī (of Rosetta), widow of Burayk b. Sāsōn.

[52]TS 8 J 17, f. 17. See n. 120, below.

[53]Mosseri A 77, *India Book* 354. "Yemen" stands also for the more distant regions of the India trade.

[54]ENA 2727, f. 15*c*, *India Book* 355. Only partly preserved.

[55]The daughter's family belongs to "other people's houses," see C, 2, n. 23, above. Anthropologist Judith Goldstein, after a year and a half stay in Yazd, Iran (Aug. 1975), tells me that the same expression (in Persian, of course: *khōn* [for *khān*]-*e-mardom*) is used there for the same concept.

[56]Bodl. MS Heb. b 13, f. 46 (Cat. 2834, no. 27), ll. 28–31.

[57]TS NS J 413, an incomplete and much damaged draft in the hand of Solomon b. Elijah, written while visiting the donator Abu 'l-Manṣūr b. al-Rayyis Abu 'l-Faraj in his house. No details about Sitt al-Sāda ("Mistress of the Lords"), his wife.

[58]TS 18 J 1, 23*v* (Feb. 1132).

[59]TS 13 J 2, f. 16 (Sept. 1112). Separate widow's lodgings: *bayt tarammul*. See also C, 1, n. 66, above.

[60]TS 10 J 16, f. 4. The widow of the ḥazzān Ben Naḥmān.

[61]The complainant in n. 60 also calls herself "wife of," not "widow of." See the discussion of the list TS 24.76* in B, 1, n. 75, above ("the wife of the dead elder").

[62]See *Med. Soc.*, II, 432–433, sec. 162.

[63]TS 13 J 16, f. 11, ll. 5–6, TS 13 J 22, f. 21, ll. 7–8, both ed. S. D. Goitein, *Joshua Finkel Jubilee Volume* (New York, 1974), pp. 121–122. TS NS J 459, Ḥasana comes to court: "I wish to ransom myself from my husband by renouncing all my rights." But "we exerted ourselves to settle the affair." See also *Med. Soc.*, II, 84, n. 82.

[64]TS 10 J 2, fs. 1–40. A similar, but small collection: BM Or 5524, fs. 1–8.

[65]TS NS Box 308, f. 25, ed. Margalioth, *Hilkhot*, p. 121. This is a copy to be used as an example.

[66]B. Spuler, *Die morgenländischen Kirchen* (Leiden 1961), p. 292. Meinardus, *Christian Egypt*, p. 284.

[67]TS 10 J 11, f. 13*v*, ll. 16–18. This is a direct continuation of TS 10 J 5, f. 10, *Nahray* 152, a letter by Abūn b. Ṣadaqa to Nahray. "Separation" meaning divorce: *firqa*.

[68]ENA 4100, f. 23*. "She does not like him": *lays lah gharba* [for *raghba*] *fīh*. "Getting rid of" meaning divorce: *khalāṣ*.

[69]TS 10 J 15, f. 9*.

[70]See B, 1, nn. 33–42, above.

[71]TS 13 J 36, f. 1, ll. 10–12+, a letter from Qayrawān, see A, 2, n. 19, above.

[72]TS 10 K 7, no. 1, p. 2, l. 29 - p. 3, l. 8, the Evyatar scroll, ed. Schechter, *Saadyana*, pp. 89–90. The text needs complete revision. *Ibid*, p. 90, l. 8, *ṣbhh b. kfya* is probably Ṣedāqā b. Nufay'. I have not examined the MS.

[73]ENA 4020, f. 47*v**; TS 8.184, *India Book* 269*c* and *d*. Samuel and his brother Faraj contributed to the collection described in *Med. Soc.*, II, 504, sec. 124 (arranged at Munā's wedding?). For Jekūthiel, alias al-Ḥakīm, see *ibid.*, II, App. C, secs. 17, 79, 119, 134, and C, 1, n. 211, above.

[74]TS 8.139. The husband, Manasse b. Samuel, is not known to me from another source. For Japheth b. Abraham see *Med. Soc.*, I, 362, sec. 2; II, App. C, secs. 16, 19–21, 135. Dated documents of Japheth: 1076–1108.

[75]See C, 1, nn. 140–165, 166–203.

[76]TS 13 J 16, f. 24 (ca. 1035). Ed. partly (but faultily) in *Sefer ha-Yishuv*, p. 114, see Braslavsky, *Our Country*, pp. 305–306.

[77]Mosseri A 75 (Aleppo, 1189), the bill of repudiation. TS NS J 455, the court record (frag.).

[78]TS NS J 226*v*, item II. The date (1244) is on the same page, but in another section.

[79]Cf. the Near Eastern maxim warning of such marriages in *Med. Soc.*, I, 48, n. 43.

[80]For 872/3 see n. 65, above. Taṭay: TS 8.154.

[81]TS 13 J 21, f. 5, ll. 19–27⁺.

[82]TS NS J 282. Copy or draft omitting the personal names.

[83]TS AS 152, f. l. Of the date only ..35 is preserved, but the script is of the thirteenth century (1535 Sel. = 1223/4).

[84]TS 10 J 2, f. 39. Remarriage after second divorce: TS NS J 297, part 2⁺, see B, 5, n. 51, above.

[85]Ar.: *ṣuḥba ka'annahā zinā li'annaha ṣuḥba bighayr ṭība.* As a legal term *zinā* denotes any illicit intercourse.

[86]ENA 2808, f. 36*.

[87]E.g., TS 13 J 8, f. 23⁺*, C, 1, nn. 24, 40, 44, 124, above.

[88]This is as literal a translation as possible to me: *armāt* (for classical *ramat*) *al-shawq 'alayya wa-ta'allafat lī.*

[89]Dropsie 398*. The holiday was Passover. See also A. L. Motzkin, "A Thirteenth-Century Jewish Physician in Jerusalem (A Geniza Portrait)," *Muslim World*, 60 (1970), 344–349. Some statements in that paper need revision. The letter cited here is not included there, but see *ibid.*, p. 349.

[90]See Friedman, *Marriage*, and his preliminary publication "Termination of the Marriage upon the Wife's Request: A Palestinian Ketubba Stipulation," *PAAJR*, 37 (1969), 29–55.

[91]See *EI*, "Ṭalāq" (Joseph Schacht).

[92]TS 8 J 11, f. 19. Nadīv b. Isaac, "the son of the brother of Umm Nadīv" (this aunt of his must have been a V.I.P.), asks his teacher, whom he styles: *ha-melammēd Yeshū'ā ha-rāv ha-gādōl*, a curious combination.

[93]TS Arabic Box 40, f. 96⁺, see C, 1, n. 187.

[94]TS Arabic Box 40, f. 56, *India Book* 314, a letter in Arabic characters written by Bū Alī b. Bū 'Amr in 'Aydhāb, while on his way to Aden. (He cites a letter by Khalaf.)

[95]E.g., TS 10 J 2, f. 7*v* (1119); TS 10 J 2, f. 17 (1129); TS 10 J 2, f. 15 (1172).

[96]Hall: *qā'a*; cabinet: *khizāna.*

[97]TS 18 J 2, f. 13 (June 1117). See n. 122, below.

[98]Bodl. MS Heb. b 11 (Cat. 2874), f. 14. The bill is called here by the Arabic term *barā'a,* see n. 113, below.

[99]As in ENA 4020, f. 47*v**, see n. 107, below.

[100]See n. 69, above; JTS Misc. 17, l. 6 (see *Med. Soc.*, I, 502); Mosseri L 197, l. 20; Maimonides, *Responsa*, I, 51. In all these cases the verb for repudiation (by the husband), *ṭallaq*, is applied to the wife. In Mosseri A, f. 27, l. 2* (see C, 1, n. 227, above) the corresponding Heb. term is used: *gērashtō*. See n. 102, below.

[101]Mishna Yevamot 14:1, end.

[102]Mosseri A, f. 27*, see n. 100, above.

[103]See n. 63, above.

[104]TS Arabic Box 54, f. 69 (May 1203).

[105]PT Ketubbot 5:1, p. 29*c*, see M. A. Friedman's article cited in n. 90, p. 31.

[106]TS 24.34* (Jan./Feb. 1213). The document contains other interesting details. As said in its introduction, it is a copy, which means that further litigation was in the offing.

[107]ENA 4020, f. 47+* (Nov. 10, 1091), see n. 73, above.

[108]"Maimonides as Chief Justice," *JQR*, 49 (1959), 198 n. 25. The title of this review article is a misnomer. For Maimonides did not serve as a judge, but as a jurisconsult, see *Med. Soc.*, II, 326.

[109]M. A. Friedman, "The Ransom-Divorce: Divorce Proceedings Initiated by the Wife in Medieval Jewish Practice," *Israel Oriental Studies*, 6 (1976), 288–307. ULC Or 1080 J 141 (Summer 1114), edited in that paper, pp. 303–306, reveals the ransom-divorce as a standard procedure.

[110]E.g., Mosseri A, f. 18 (Jan. 1268). The divorcée agrees to a reduction of her dues from 70 to 30 dirhems of good silver, while the husband agrees to pay the alimony (presumably for a baby of his, the document is not complete), which she had formerly waived. In l. 10 *mnṭqy* is *muṭalliqī*. TS 13 J 3, f. 14 (Cairo, Feb. 1170): Of a delayed marriage gift of 10 dinars, 1 is paid in cash, the balance in payments of ⅓ dinar per month. The reverse side shows only four such payments. TS NS J 412 (Aug. 18, 1217): The cash payment is reduced from 15 to 10 dinars, while the balance is to be paid in weekly installments of 3 dirhems, beginning on Dec. 30; in addition, the children receive 5¼ dirhems per week as of New Year (Sept. 4). In TS 16.134, a letter by Elhanan b. Shemarya to the community in Malīj, where a divorcée receives ⅛ dirhem per day instead of ⅔, as demanded by her, possibly a payment for the nursing of a baby is intended. Ed. Abramson, *Bamerkazim*, p. 116, corrections S. D. Goitein, *Joshua Finkel Jubilee Volume* (New York, 1974), pp. 124–125.

[111]TS 10 J 27, f. 3, item II (Cairo, 1109); TS 16.218 (old).

[112]Illness: TS AS 147, f. 17. Bad character: TS 8 J 14, f. 2.

[113]*Barā'a* and *geṭ* together, e.g., TS 10 J 6, f. 16, l. 14 (spelled *'l-'br'h*). TS 12.288, ll. 14–15, cf. C, 1, n. 83, above. Model of a full-fledged *barā'a*: TS 13 J 3, f. 22 (Aug. 1213), wife and husband from al-Maḥalla appear before the court in Fustat. Barā'a comprising, or designating, *geṭ*: TS 13 J 18, f. 27, ll. 23, 24, margin, l. 12*, cf. A, 3, n. 2, above. Bodl. MS Heb. b 11 (Cat. 2874), f. 14, see n. 98, above.

[114]TS 10 J 27, f. 12 (Nov. 1009), cf. B, 4, n. 34, above. ULC Or 1080 J 141+ (see no. 109, above), ll. 8–9: "They released one another, and we wrote for each of them a release given by the other." ULC Or 1081 J 56 contains their marriage agreement.

[115]Different, of course, from his contemporary and compatriot, the communal leader Barhūn (Abraham) b. Sahlān, the bearer of the highest honorific titles who died in 1032.

[116]TS 8 J 4, f. 3*bv*.

[117]TS 13 J 5, f. 1*c*.

[118]TS 8 K 20, f. 1*v*. Despite the identity of names (Fā'iza d. of Solomon, son of Nethanel) I cannot believe that she is identical with the girl betrothed in 1047, see B, 5, n. 75, above.

[119]Mosseri A, f. 30 (Nov. 1148).

[120]TS 8 J 22, f. 22* (the letter of the wife); TS 18 J 3, f. 12* (written by Abu 'l-Barakāt Solomon, son of the judge Elijah); ULC Or 1080 J 285, all ed. M. A. Friedman, *Tarbiz*, 43 (1974), 182—196.

[121]One day, same scribe, both bills unsigned: TS 10 J 2, fs. 8 and 11 (Cairo, 1088). One month exactly, same scribe, in both cases signatures cut away and no witness of delivery on either bill: TS 10 J 2, fs. 37–38 (1226). Two months exactly, the first bill in mediocre script on irregularly cut paper, lacking witnesses: TS 10 J 2, f. 35, the second, perfectly executed and signed: JNUL Heb. 4° 577/4, no. 27. The girl's father is called in the first bill by his Arabic name Manṣūr, in the second Elazar (6 Nisan–6 Sivan, 1213). Three months exactly, same scribe, both bills signed, but only the second delivered: BM Or 5524, fs. 6 and 7 (Marheshvan 9, 1163–Shevat 9, 1164). Nine months, same scribe, both bills signed: TS NS J 247 (Tammūz 7, 1065), TS 10 J 2, f. 6 (Nisan 4, 1066). Unsigned, e.g.: Mosseri A, f. 80 (1084), Mosseri A, f. 21 (1270).

[122]TS 18 J 2, f. 13 (June 1117, written by Ḥalfōn b. Manasse). Her name: Sitt al-Ḥusn ("Beauty"), daughter of the late Saadya, known as Daughter of the Hunchbacked Woman (Bint al-Hadbā, see n. 146, below.)

[123]A. Harkavy, *Responsen der Geonim* (Berlin, 1887), p. 216, no. 220.

[124]See C, 1, n. 236, above.

[125]TS Arabic Box 7, f. 29. She claimed also that her paternal aunt (and mother-in-law) was on her side, *ibid., verso,* l. 6.

[126]ENA 2808, f. 15*a*[+]*, ed. S. D. Goitein, *JQR*, 66 (1975), 85–88, see C, 2, n. 174, above.

[127]ENA 154 (2558).

[128]Father guaranteeing for his divorcée daughter: TS 8 J 5, f. 2, l. 4 (1131); Mosseri A, f. 124.

[129]Divorcée ordered to appear in person: TS 13 J 6, f. 11, ll. 7–9[+].

[130]Bodl. MS Heb. d 98 (no Cat.), f. 58.

[131]TS 10 J 12, f. 14, l. 5.

[132]ENA 4011, f. 17. See n. 86, above.

[133]Divorce: Mosseri A, f. 56 (Jan. 22, 1229). Remarriage: ULC Or 1081 J 40 (Sept. 18, 1229). In the *geṭ* the name of the husband is lost, but the entry on the marriage calls the bride Maʿānī bint Karīm al-Aqraʿ expressly "his divorcée." (The scribe, Solomon b. Elijah, in his usual negligence, writes *bmṭlqh'* for *bmṭlqth.*)

[134]"Retaking": *murājaʿa,* see Idris, "Mariage," p. 56, sec. 52. Cf. App., part II, group 8, items 4, 8, 9. The marriage gift at a Muslim remarriage in 1069 was 1 + 3 dinars, see Grohmann, *World of Arabic Papyri,* p. 196.

[135]TS 12.613, l. 25 (+ 16.44), written by Ḥalfōn b. Manasse.

[136]ENA NS 7, f. 43, l. 3. For the women of the court sending their hair to a powerful general see Lane-Poole, *History of Egypt,* p. 173.

[137]See B, 1, nn. 1–3, 58–80, above, on this question.

[138]If not otherwise indicated, "second marriage" in this subsection denotes any marriage after the first. In most cases the documents either do not indicate whether a woman was married more than twice, or the relevant detail is not preserved.

[139]See B, 3, nn. 7–19.

[140]Letter of condolence: TS K 25, f. 191. Widow: TS 18 J 1, f. 17, ed. S. Assaf, *Zion,* 5 (1940), 276–277. See *Med. Soc.,* I, 137, n. 39. Nahray's cousin: ENA NS 22, f. 27.

[141]See Mann, II, 255–256, and *Med. Soc.,* II, 532, n. 44, and 576, n. 14.

[142]TS 10 J 12, f. 14, see n. 131, above.

[143]For the few references to widowers making arrangements for their orphaned children see C, 4, nn. 157, 158, below. For traveling merchants cooking for themselves, see the third letter translated at the end of subsection C, l. "A cup of water:" TS NS J 453, l. 8.

[144]The seeming discrepancy between this table and App., part II, is to be explained by the fact that many fragments that contain data about the marriage gift or dowry lack those about the status of the bride, and vice versa. A large part of our information is derived from documents on engagements, betrothals, settlements, or wills, which usually say nothing about the status of the bride.

[145]BM Or 12 186, see B, 1, n. 56, above. Woman from Jerusalem: see n. 67, above.

[146]Sitt al-Ḥusn ("Beauty"), daughter of Saadya (Ar. Saʿāda), known as the Daughter of the Hunchbacked Woman, who was divorced in June 1117, see n. 122, above, was involved in a transaction in July, 1129, where she is not referred to as married, TS 18 J 1, f. 23, and made her deathbed declaration as the wife of Nathan b. Samuel, TS 13 J 22, f. 2[+]* (no date). She could have been the mother of Nathan's sons, since Mevōrākh, his eldest, appears in documents from 1150, see *Med. Soc.,* II, 514, n. 22. But it is more likely that she was Nathan's second wife.

[147]See D, nn. 156–189, below.

[148]Cf. C, 1, n. 34, above.

[149]TS 13 J 20, f. 27: *mā kānat rāmat al-zawāj li-aḥad jumla, wa-lākin lā ḥīla.*

[150]DK XIII*. Cf. the Talmudic saying, that children die because of their mothers' (unkept) vows, BT Ketubbot 72*a*, cited by M. A. Friedman, "Annulling the Bride's Vows: A Palestinian Ketubba Clause," *JQR*, 61 (1971), 223 n. 8.

[151]Westminster College, Arabica, II, f. 129 (the warning of the judge). ULC Or 1080 J 25: *mā 'aqlhā illā fi 'l-zīja wa-sayyabat awlādhā.* A third letter from the same pen, TS 8 J 24, f. 4, does not refer to that woman.

[152]TS 10 J 26, f. 4* (Tishri 1171, under the authority of Maimonides). For the widow's oath see C, 3, n. 31, above.

[153]ULC Or 1080 J 67, beginning of a question addressed to the judge Yehiel b. Eliakim: a woman wished to marry a man with whom she was suspected, while he was prepared to confirm by oath that the allegation was untrue. The same prohibition only in certain Islamic sects, see Schacht, *Islamic Law*, p. 21.

[154]See *Med. Soc.*, I, 134–135, and B, 5, nn. 16–17, above.

[155]Maimonides, *Responsa*, II, 386–388. "Killer," *qaṭlānīt* (Heb.)

[156]More children in second marriage, e.g., TS 18 J 1, f. 4* (one boy—two girls and one boy); TS NS Box 320, f. 46 (one boy—2 girls); Firkovitch, II, 1700, f. 3 (same). ENA NS 18, f. 25 (boy and girl—several children); Mosseri A 89.4 (none—one daughter). More in first marriage: Bodl. MS Heb. b 13, f. 46 (Cat. 2834, no. 27) (several children—one son); Bodl. MS Heb. b 13, f. 34 (Cat. 2834, no. 19) (two sons—one son); Yehuda ha-Nagid had several full brothers, his stepbrother Mevōrākh seemingly not.

[157]See C, 1, nn. 120 and 267, above.

[158]TS 16.335. The physician Elazar ha-Levi b. Tiqva ("Hope") in Ashmūm Tannāḥ (1228).

[159]Bodl. MS Heb. c 28 (Cat. 2876), f. 14⁺, see C, 4, n. 175, below.

4. *Heirs and Orphans*

[1]See C, 3, above.

[2]TS NS J 469* (April 1257); TS NS Box 297, f. 1* (Sept. 1278), see *Med. Soc.*, II, 321; TS Arabic Box 39, f. 189 (Feb. 1284), see H. Rabie, *The Financial System of Egypt A.H. 564–741/A.D. 1169–1341* (London, 1972), p. 130. *Dīwān al-jawālī wal-mawārīth al-ḥashriyya;* see also *EI*², II, 329*a*, *(k)*.

[3]See *Med. Soc.*, II, 395–403, and C, 3, nn. 48–51, above. Cf. A. A. A. Fyzee, "The Fatimid Law of Inheritance," *Studia Islamica*, 9 (1958), 61–70. Fatimid (Ismā'īlī Shī'ite) law differed from general Islamic law, for instance, by giving a single daughter the entire estate of her father, but since the vast majority of the Muslim population of Egypt belonged to the main stock of Islam, it is doubtful how far Fatimid law was applied in that country.

[4]TS 10 J 21, f. 10, frag. in the hand of Samuel b. Saadya ha-Levi (1165–1203), see *Med. Soc.*, II, 514. The name of the official: Abu 'l-Ḥusayn 'Amīd al-Dawla ("Support of the Government"), Yiḥye, son of the late Abraham Segullat ha-yeshiva. It seems that before his death Abu 'l-Ḥusayn had instructed Abu 'l-Ma'ālī Samuel, "The Master of the Discerning," b. Judah (see A, 1, n. 39) how to get the ruler's rescript for the release of the estate.

[5]Tāj al-Dīn al-Subkī, *Tabaqāt al-Shāfi'iyya* (Cairo, 1323/4 [1905/6]), IV, 47, quoted in Strauss, *Mamluks*, II, 223. For later developments see *ibid.*, pp. 224–234.

Whether TS 10 J 21, f. 14, where an official styled *ustādh* was about to sequester the possessions, *qabḍ 'alā mawjūd*, of Rafā'īl b. Abī Rūna (probably a Christian who had deposited some of his belongings with a Jew while another Jew denunciated him), was a case of inheritance or of confiscation is not evident from the fragment. Anyhow, as proved by the name of one of the witnesses, Berākhōt ha-Kohen b. Aaron *ha-mumḥe*, who wrote and signed TS 8 J 4, f. 20, in 1107, the document preceded Saladin's reign by two generations.

[6]Cf. S. Assaf, "Ordinances and Usages with regard to a Husband's Inheritance from his Wife," *Maddā'ē ha-Yahadūt*, Vol. I, (Jerusalem, 1926), pp. 79–94. In

Islamic law a wife receives one quarter of her husband's estate, if there are no children, and one eighth if there are (see Schacht, *Islamic Law*, p. 171).

[7]Such as PER H 89⁺, see C, 2, n. 54, above.

[8]Bodl. MS Heb. f 56, fs. 45*v*, 46 (Cat. 2821, no. 16). Abu 'l-Faraj, who was in charge of the division, is, of course, not the man bearing this name on f. 45 recto, who made the deathbed declaration described in *Med. Soc.*, I, 253, n. 138. Samuel (b. Saadya) and Manasse (b. Joseph), signing only with their first names, are the two judges. The wife's father was a *jashshāsh*, see *Med. Soc.*, I, 115 and 424.

[9]TS 8 J 6, f. 12, written under the authority of the Nagid Abraham Maimonides, whose titles occupy seven of the twenty lines preserved.

[10]ENA 4011, f. 72*d* (Feb. 1100). Samuel b. Nathan he-ḥāvēr (who may have been the father of the judge Nathan b. Samuel he-ḥāvēr) sues Sittān, the daughter of the banker Abū Naṣr, for the estate of his wife, for one half of that of a sister-in-law who had never married, and for one half of the house occupied by Sittān, who denied all these claims. The house had been given to her as a *ṣadaqa*, "charity," by her late husband in a Muslim court.

[11]Bodl. MS Heb. d 66 (Cat. 2878), f. 83. The boy who was known only by his Arabic *kunya*, or by-name, Abū Naṣr ("Victorious"), that is, he had no Hebrew name, is described as a *ḥālāl* (Heb.): his mother had been a divorcée, whom his father, a Kohen, was not supposed to marry. The father is not called "Kohen," since he lost the privileges connected with the title because of his illicit marriage.

[12]*Med. Soc.*, II, 399; A, 2, nn. 25–27; C, 2, n. 148, above. For the elder sister see *Med. Soc.*, I, 176, and A, 2, n. 29, above.

[13]TS NS Box 154, f. 165. Dr. E. Hurvitz of Yeshiva University, New York, drew my attention to this fragment. "Simple, not firstborn": TS AS 153, f. 1 (large sums mentioned).

[14]ENA 2805, f. 15 (right half) + Bodl. MS Heb. b 13, f. 38 (Cat. 2834, no. 19), Oct. 11, 1094. Butcher: *laḥḥām*, trans. in *Med. Soc.*, I, 424, n. 101, as "meat-seller"; cf. ENA 4020, f. 28*v* (1028): *al-harrās al-laḥḥām*, a restauranteur who sells meat.

[15]Especially, *Med. Soc.*, II, 395–397.

[16]Barqa: B, 3, n. 92. India trader: C, 2, n. 100.

[17]Acre: Bodl. MS Heb. d 66 (Cat. 2878), f. 121⁺. Damascus: ENA NS 17, l. 22. Khibā ("Treasure"), daughter of Abraham, releases Solomon b. Musāfir. Written and signed by Elijah ha-Kohen b. Solomon, the future Gaon, who then was only *ḥāvēr*. Aleppo: TS 18 J 2, f. 12*.

[18]Mosseri A, f. 89.4, a frag. in Heb. The name of the *peqīd ha-sōḥarīm* was Abū Sa'īd b. Naḥmān, see TS 10 J 20, f. 3, l. 17, *Nahray* 198. The younger sister: TS 18 J 4, f. 21, l. 13, a legal opinion by Eli b. Amram.

[19]ENA 4010, f. 31, which precedes TS 20.162, dealing with the same matter (ca. 1085). Musāfir with large sums also in TS 16.141 (see n. 51, below) and TS 16.162 (1049), the latter probably acknowledgment of (part of) the estate of his father.

[20]TS AS 145, f. 7.

[21]TS NS Box 226, f. 12: *al-tarika al-mawrūtha lahā*, "the estate left to her." Had this been a legacy, the text would have used the word *waṣiyya*.

[22]TS 10 J 5, f. 9 (July-Aug., 1102). Shēlā b. Elazar, grandson of Elazar ha-Shōfēt, confirms having held the cash and having received the objects from the orphans' stepbrother Japheth b. Nethan'el *ha-mumḥe*. Shēlā, a *sharābī*, or seller of potions (Bodl. MS Heb. a 2 [Cat. 2805], f. 7, l. 4, dated 1103), was a trustee of the court.

[23]Bodl. MS Heb. d 74 (no Cat.), f. 39. This is a complaint by a son-in-law of the deceased addressed to a Gaon. The manuscript breaks off where the complaint begins. Presumably, the father had promised something to his married daughter (from a previous wife). One sixth: TS 12.156. See ll. 6–9: *al-mukhtaṣṣ bi-a[khīhā]*.

[24]Mother: TS K 6, f. 118, see C, 2, nn. 145–146. Grandmother TS 8 J 7, f. 7. Qayrawān (1050): Bodl. MS Heb. a 2 (Cat. 2805), f. 23⁺.

[25]ENA NS 17, f. 18 (ca. 1030).

[26]TS 13 J 8, f. 20, ll. 17–20*, see A, 3, n. 42, above.

[27]TS 8.143+, ed. Strauss-Ashtor, *Mamluks*, III, 4–5, see *Tarbiz*, 42 (1973), 501.

[28]Daughter one third: Mosseri A 11+. S. Assaf, the learned editor, took *bny* as *banay*, "my (two) sons," instead of *benī*, "my son," and understood the document as an additional proof for the equal treatment of sons and daughters, drawing the attention to his Hebrew paper, "The Inheritance of Daughters," *Jacob Freimann Jubilee Volume* (Berlin, 1937), pp. 8–13. If that meaning had been intended, however, the writer would have said: "I give to my daughter and *two* sons each one third." In the subsequent sentence, "when *banay* [which could mean either "sons" or "children"] will be grown up," the word means "children." Daughter one half: Bodl. MS Heb. b 12 (Cat. 2875), f. 30, complete, 43 ll., mostly legal verbiage, no signatures.

[29]Firkovitch II, 1700, f. 3, dated 11 Iyyar (1156); f. 28 (a loose sheet, my numbering), middle decade of the month of Iyyar; f. 5, last day of Iyyar; f. 18, 24 Sivan (the subsequent month).

[30]Dropsie 335. For additional details see A, 3, n. 26, above. For the law referred to see Maimonides' *Code*, book 'Women,' section "Marriage," chap. 20:1–5. An actual decision in these matters by Maimonides, see *Responsa*, I, 94. The court record cites the ancient law, BT Ketubbot 68*a*.

[31]TS 18 J 1, f. 4*, see C, 3, n. 5, above.

[32]TS 12.530*; TS 8 J 5, f. 1*; ULC Or 1080 J 142 + TS Misc. Box 25, f. 53, forming parts of one document.

[33]TS NS J 184, written by Ḥalfōn b. Manasse.

[34]Library: TS K 3, f. 32. Storeroom: ENA 4020, f. 60, superscribed, "List of what was found in the storeroom of the judge Isaac b. Moses, on Friday, 26th of Tishri 1462 according to the Era of the Documents." This corresponds to Oct. 18, 1150, which was not a Friday. For Isaac b. Moses see *Med. Soc.*, II, 537, n. 24; 569, n. 23; 572, n. 15.

[35]TS 10 J 20, f. 6, frag. For Ḥiyyā see *Med. Soc.*, II, 513, sec. 19. Of the items in the house only the line mentioning "wine, carpets, copper, china, pots, and fuel" is preserved.

[36]See also TS 24.81*, n. 72, below.

[37]This aversion is still shared by the Arab oil magnates of our time. "If I knew how much money I had, I wouldn't be rich," says Mahdi al-Tajir (which means "merchant"), one of the world's wealthiest men (*National Geographic*, 148 [October 1975], p. 514).

[38]Alexandria: TS 12.591, ll. 6–8, addressed to a person of high rank requesting him to approach the Nagid Mevōrākh b. Saadya. For "ban in general terms" see *Med. Soc.*, II, 340, for "Monday and Thursday" *ibid.*, p. 342. Al-Maḥalla: TS 10 J 17, f. 25, ll. 11–18.

[39]TS 10 J 29, f. 5, ll. 7–12, see *Med. Soc.*, II, 341, n. 40.

[40]BM Or 5542, f. 11. For ten men as quorum required for public prayer see *Med. Soc.*, II, 58. In Islam it is forty.

[41]Attention is drawn to *Med. Soc.*, I, 391, last paragraph.

[42]This rate for *waraq* corresponds to 1:13⅓ for *nuqra* and was constantly applied by the courts in those days.

[43]TS 8 J 4, f. 21*.

[44]Not to be confused with his namesake and contemporary Jacob Rōsh Kallā b. Joseph Āv, for the latter was still alive in 1028. See S. D. Goitein, "On the History of the Palestinian Gaonate," *Shalem* (Jerusalem), I (1974) 27.

[45]TS 16.14*. From various sources: *neṭālām mi-kammā pānīm* (Heb.), ll. 5, 25–26. *Shahryār* is Persian, meaning sovereign, mayor, person in authority. New house sold: TS Arabic Box 53, f. 53; TS 6 J 2, f. 26 (frag. of another document on the same matter). Smithson: See *Smithsonian*, 6, 10 (1976), 33.

[46]This refers to documents from the Fatimid and Ayyubid periods (969-1250).

[47]TS NS J 385, a complete letter to Nahray b. Nissīm re the orphans and widow of Ben Sāsōn. TS 12.591, fragment of a larger letter. The bribe in l. 9, to my mind, refers not to the qadi but to a notary. About al-Makīn see Ibn Muyassar,

p. 77, ll. 3–6; ULC Or 1080 J 258, ll. 19–28, where the request is made that the poll tax be fixed (again), as regulated by al-Makīn, cf. *Med. Soc.*, I, 147, n. 113. The Alexandrian judge al-Makīn in TS 13 J 3, f. 4* (1143), see *Med. Soc.*, I, 62–63, n. 21, was probably his son. Sons strove to obtain the same titles as their fathers had.

[48]TS Misc. Box 28, f. 44, *India Book* 335 (Ḥalfōn b. Manasse). Sole heir: TS 8 J 5, f. 25 (1261, a maternal uncle). PER H 90 (1150, two daughters of a paternal uncle, see B, 1, n. 60, above). For other sole heiresses see nn. 16—20, above.

[49]TS Misc. Box 8, f. 72. TS Arabic Box 54, f. 49*v*.

[50]TS 12.714.

[51]TS 16.141 (seems to be written in Damascus around 1060). Cf. n. 19. I was puzzled by the fact that here as there the sum of 350 dinars is involved, but they are two different affairs connected with Musāfir b. Samuel.

[52]TS 8 J 6, f. 18*d*. The reverse where a husband and wife are released in TS 18 J 1, f. 2.

[53]TS 20.23, a large document.

[54]TS 8 J 6, f. 4 (1217/8).

[55]See n. 14, above.

[56]Monday: ENA NS 21, f. 18 (The date *qlḥ* is abbreviated from *'tqlḥ*, meaning 1538= A.D. 1227). Thursday: TS 8 J 6, f. 6. The scribe, Solomon b. Elijah, tried to squeeze the second record on a small blank space in the first, but did not succeed. Both records are written with Solomon's usual incompetence and carelessness.

[57]For the general character of these types of documents see *Med. Soc.*, I, 11.

[58]TS 24.18 + 12.634. *Nahray* 26 and 24. Janūnī-Guenoun, originally the name of a Berber tribe, has remained a North African Jewish family name up till now, see M. Eisenbeth, *Les Juifs de l'Afrique du Nord* (Algiers, 1936), p. 131. The form Janūn (without *ī*) is more common in the Geniza.

[59]TS Misc. Box 25, f. 138, *Nahray* 22.

[60]TS 13 J 3, f. 25. For the symbolic act see *Med. Soc.*, II, 329.

[61]ENA 4020, f. 2. The dead brother was Mevōrākh b. Yeshūʿā, Pe'ēr ha-Qehillōt ("Pride of the Congregations"), b. Saʿdʾēl, Rōsh ha-Qehillōt ("Head of the Congregations"). He is not the India trader Abu 'l-Barakāt Mevōrākh al-Ḥalabī, whose dealings loom large in this document, for the latter's father was called Solomon, cf. Bodl. MS Heb. a 3 (Cat. 2873), f. 20 (1098), *India Book* 162, another partnership of Yaḥyā with this Abu 'l-Barakāt.

While myrobalan, *ihlīlaj*, is extremely common, see *Med. Soc.*, II, 267, I have not yet noted *qinna*, galbanum (see Maimonides-Meyerhof, no. 339,) elsewhere in the Geniza.

[62]TS 13 J 2, f. 8, summarized B, 1, n. 59, above.

[63]ENA 2739, f. 13, taken together with TS 10 J 29, f. 1*v*+, and ENA NS 2, f. 27, see B, 1, n. 58, above. Mufrij b. Mawhūb was the elder brother of Mevōrākh and Japheth.

[64]TS 18 J 1, f. 7+, see A 1, n. 60, above (not noted as edited in Shaked, *Bibliography*, p. 140). For "Mr. Small" see A, 1, nn. 59–61.

[65]TS AS 147, f. 23. In the hand of Mevōrākh b. Nathan, therefore probably later than 1150. The name of the girl was Sumr, which is an abbreviation of Sitt al-Sumr, "Queen of the Dark Brown," cf. *Med. Soc.*, I, 433, n. 42. This color was loved, wherefore the name was also frequently borne by free women. The uncle may have been the grandfather of his namesake mentioned C, 3, n. 58, above.

[66]Mosseri A, f. 1, ed., with a facsimile and an important linguistic commentary, by Shaul Shaked, *Tarbiz*, 41 (1971), 49–58. In the first line p, [...]'z(?), the word following *pā* must be a place, presumably [Ahw]āz. Shaked is preparing a volume of Persian Geniza texts, mostly literary and mostly Karaite.

[67]TS 16.150*. For Ḥayyim II b. Sahlawayh II see B, 1, n. 33, on Ibn Shaʿyā, A, 1, nn. 44–51, and on "Mr. Small," n. 64, above.

[68]See *Med. Soc.*, II, 299–303.

[69]TS 18 J 1, f. 22 (March 17, 1141). For the Fatimid law see the article of Fyzee cited in n. 3, above, p. 67.

[70]The first line is to be read: *[thab]at mā in[ṣ]alaḥ fī nawā'ib*, as Dr. Gershon Weiss, with whom I discussed this much damaged text, rightly suggested.

[71]TS Box K 15, f. 95* (May 1150).

[72]TS 24.81*. For *kātib*, government official (pl. *kuttāb*), see *Med. Soc.*, II, 230.

[73]See, e.g., nn. 8–13, 20–23, 25, 28–31, 40, 43, 47, 63, 72, above.

[74]TS 16.256, l. 10, a letter addressed to the Nagid Mevōrākh.

[75]BT Gittin 37*a*: "Rabbān Gamliel and his court are the father of the orphans." As the medieval commentator Rashi explains, "Gamliel" stands for public authority in general.

[76]A responsum by the nāsī Daniel b. Azarya, TS Arabic Box 49, f. 166, p. 4, l. 13*, cites the wording of the original.

[77]TS 18 J 2, f. 16⁺*, (Iyyar = April/May 1026). AIU VII, D, 4*c** (July 24, 1027). Another case where a grandfather (a maternal one) approaches the courts with the request to appoint a guardian for his grandson in TS 8.13, a magnificently written Hebrew appeal, but too fragmentary for admitting full understanding.

[78]See n. 67, above.

[79]TS Arabic Box 49, f. 166, p. 4. Twenty long lines, but the beginning and end are missing. See n. 76 above. Looting: *nahb*.

[80]TS 18 J 2, f. 16, l. 18⁺*, *mistākhē* (spelled *mst'ky*) *'alōhī*, from *sky*, to see (Aramaic).

[81]ENA NS 18, f. 4*a*. The document was written in or after April 1019 (dated 133?, Era of Documents), but long before January 1026, when the orphan was declared as having come of age, see n. 84 below.

[82]TS 16.27*, TS 10 J 30, f. 7, both in Arabic and both mentioning as senders also the supervisor, designated here by the Arabic term *mushrif*. "Live up to your reputation": *fa-kun 'ind al-ẓann fīk*, TS 10 J 30, f. 7, l. 17. The guardians: Joseph b. Benjamin, the banker (*ṣayrafī*, Ar., *shulḥānī*, Heb.), Japheth ha-Levi b. Toviya ha-Bavlī (Ḥasan b. Ṭayyib al-Baghdādī al-Nīlī). The latter is praised in ULC Or 1080 J 262 (see C, 3, n. 18 above) for having taken care of the affairs of a compatriot in foreign parts both during his last illness and after his death. The supervisor: Mevōrākh ha-Kohen b. Joseph (Abu 'l-Ḥusayn al-Mubārak b. Yūsuf b. Yazdād).

[83]TS 20.60. In line 13, the supervisor is referred to with the Heb. term *mashqīf*, see nn. 80, 82, above. The partner: Shemaryah b. Solomon Ibn Mahāra (Son of the Oyster, a nickname), see Goitein, *Letters*, p. 104.

[84]ENA NS 7, f. 25*. Flogging: *ulzimnā* (Ar.) *be-ōnes al-malqōt* (Heb.).

[85]TS 13 J 5, f. 1*. The session was held in the synagogue of the Palestinians, but is signed solely by Samuel b. Ṭalyūn, head of the Iraqian congregation, assisted by seven associates. Ephraim b. Shemarya, head of the Palestinians, expected to preside, was not present.

About Samuel (Isma'īl) b. Barhūn Tahertī see Goitein, *Letters*, pp. 80, 275, 316. ENA 2747, f. 19*v* contains the laudatory rhymed opening of a letter to Samuel, The Delight of the Yeshiva, in the hand of Japheth b. David.

When I used this document in *Med. Soc.*, II, 322 (and elswhere), I did not know the circumstances involved, because the new series of the ENA collection was not yet available. After having found ENA NS 7, f. 25, see n. 84, above, I was able to identify the four other documents connected with the case.

[86]TS 10 J 7, f. 17. The father of the orphan was called She'ērīt b. Japheth ha-Kohen, *verso*, l. 22, not to be confused with his namesake who lived at the time of Abraham Maimonides, Bodl. MS Heb. b 3 (Cat. 2806), f. 6.

[87]TS 16.256. The orphans and their mother speak in the letter, see l. 24.

[88]See A, 1, nn. 39–42.

[89]TS 13 J 3, f. 10, item II (March 1159).

[90]ENA 4010, f. 42, and 4011, f. 22, two complementary fragments, not providing a complete document. Among the real estate there were a *furn*, bakery, and three other items in Minyat Ziftā. In ENA 4011*v*, f. 22, margin and postscript, the orphan Abu 'l-Ghayth confirms sums received, one of 8 dinars in Dec. 1166/Jan. 1167.

[91]Bodl. MS Heb. a 3 (2873), f. 5*.

[92]Maimonides, *Code*, book "Civil Laws," sec. "Loans," chap. 4:14, based on BT Bava Meṣi'a 70*a*.

[93]See n. 90, above.

[94]TS NS J 465. For Nathan b. Samuel see *Med. Soc.*, II, 513, sec. 18.

[95]TS NS J 163* (1191 or 1201).

[96]ULC Add. 3339*a*.

[97]Wife: C, 3, nn. 11 and 20. Son: C, 4, n. 31, above. Brother: Bodl. MS Heb. b 13, f. 46 (Cat. 2834, no. 27), ll. 33-37*, where it is expressly stated that no court may interfere with any action of the executor.

[98]See nn. 80–85, above.

[99]Repairs: Bodl. MS Heb. a 2 (Cat. 2805), f. 7 (1103). Complete, but no signatures. Alexandria: TS 12.591, see n. 47, above. Malıj: Bodl. MS Heb. a 3 (Cat. 2873), f. 5*, see n. 91, above. Government: Bodl. MS Heb. a 3 (Cat. 2873), f. 6* (1169).

[100]ULC Or 1080 J 8* (April/May 1173).

[101]TS AS 145, f. 25* (for the period May 30–July 25, 1161).

[102]TS NS J 90 (June 1099). The document states that the rights of three elder brothers, who had come of age before, had been preserved.

[103]See, e.g., nn. 21, 45, 63, above.

[104]Cf. nn. 32–33, above.

[105]See n. 77, above.

[106]TS 20.100, ed. Mann. *Texts*, I, 122, ll. 31–35, also 151–152. The letter was written in Aug. 1006; Hay died at the age of ninety-nine in 1038.

[107]TS 10 J 4, f. 3, ed. Jacob Mann, *JQR*, 9 (1918/19), 152. For *yāfe* in l. 2 the MS has *pūkh*, the Heb. equivalent of Ar. *kuḥl*, antimony (the well-known eye-powder). Had Joseph and Nahum come of age by the time their father died, there was no point in mentioning that their mother and sisters had died too, since they were the heirs, who could have acted immediately after their father's death. For the Baradānī brothers in the West see TS 10 J 11, f. 13*v*, TS 13 J 17, f. 18, Bodl. MS Heb. c 28 (Cat. 2876), fs. 20 and 61, *Nahray* 152 B, 164, 166, 190; also TS 12.2.

[108]TS 13 J 2, f. 2. The record remained unsigned for a curious technical reason: in line 10, the scribe wrote "God" instead of "the father." He tried to correct the mistake, but without success. It is forbidden to strike out the word God. Sequestered: *mūqaf*. *Verso* contains interesting details about the settlement between the investor's attorney and the teen-age orphan. One of the debtors was "the Lady, the daughter of the head [of the yeshiva]." A letter of this enterprising woman is preserved in ENA 4100, f. 21 A, ed. S. D. Goitein, *Tarbiz*, 45 (1976), 70–74.

[109]Cf. *Med. Soc.*, II, 338–339.

[110]Cf. *ibid.*, p. 59, n. 110. See next note.

[111]PER H 94 (the present MS mark), ed. Assaf, *Texts*, pp. 31–37. The signatures are arranged in two columns of seven. The letter states that one of the three nephews is "with you," meaning probably that he defended the case of the sister's progeny. In l. 5, the MS has *maggī'a* (Heb.), "he is traveling," not *shāv*, "he returns," as printed.

[112]TS 16.256, ll. 19–20. See n. 87, above.

[113]TS 8.101, truncated on all sides, but the hand of the judge, Abraham b. Nathan (see *Med. Soc.*, II, 512–513, sec. 14), is unmistakable. The saying: BT Bava Meṣi'a 70*a*.

[114]See *Med. Soc.*, I, 200–201.

[115]TS Misc. Box 28, f. 184*v*, col. I, l. 25*. See *Med. Soc.*, II, 457, sec. 66.

[116]TS 12.575, ll. 9 and 17: *qiṭ'at laḥm munqaṭi'īn mutayattimīn*. The word *munqaṭi'* is used in the Geniza in the meaning of lonely, deserted. For the story of the Byzantine woman see also C, 1, n. 218, above. Desertion: see C, I, nn. 166–203, above.

[117]See *Med. Soc.*, II, 117, 133–134, 181, 187.

[118]TS AS 145, f. 17, a frag. in Heb. See also n. 141, below.

[119]See *Med. Soc.*, II, 184.

[120]TS NS J 249, top.

[121]As in ULC Or 1080 J 8, l. 6, above, n. 100, and in TS 13 J 9, f. 8*, n. 131, below.

[122]Uncle: Bodl. MS Heb. a 3 (Cat. 2873), f. 6*. Little girls: Bodl. MS Heb. d 66 (Cat. 2878), f. 32.

[123]TS 10 J 11, f. 13⁺, see C, 2, n. 71.

[124]TS 13 J 22, f. 7, ll. 7–13, 20–21. The physician's widow writes. The tone of the letter proves that she was a relative of the judge.

[125]TS K 15, f. 102*v*, bottom, see *Med. Soc.*, II, 446 sec. 31; TS K 15, f. 97, col. II, see *ibid.*, sec. 29; John Rylands Library, Manchester, Gaster Collection, A 923, see *ibid.*, sec. 30.

[126]TS 6 J 6, f. 21. The last word in l. 4 is ya'w̱[ūhū]. The same cantor in TS NS Box 31, f. 7, where he is ordered to arrange a collection for a traveler and warned "do not cause me to blame you," and in TS Arabic Box 54, f. 52, col. III, sec. 3, lection Noah, *Med. Soc.*, II, 464, sec. 93, dated Sept. 14, 1387, where he is in charge of one of the weekly collections.

[127]ENA 1822 A, f. 50, a classic example. But even the widow of the physician of Bilbays̱, see n. 124, who was on quite familiar terms with the judge, made a similar complaint. TS 10 J 5, f. 4: "She has a house under the administration of the court, but no answer to her letters has been given." TS 8 J 17, f. 6, ll. 5–8, a letter to the judge Elijah b. Zechariah does not belong here exactly: the physician Abū Zikrī, his son, had taken "an Arabic book," certainly a medical treatise, belonging to orphans, but had not paid for it. Now the local official asks the judge either to have his son pay, or to return the book. See also *Med. Soc.*, II, 170 and 501, secs. 94 and 96.

[128]His family name *al-jn'wy* or *ghn'wy*, hardly meaning "Genoese," for this is spelled *jnwy* (without '), but see next note.

[129]Written twice *al-dnw'r*, which I take as an awkward spelling for *dīnwar* (Persian *dīnver*).

[130]Ar. *maliyy*, see Dozy, *Supplément*, II, 609*b*. In TS 10 J 10, f. 23, *India* 251, l. 8, this is even said of God: *innhū qādir 'ala dhālik wa-maliyy bih.*

[131]TS 13 J 9, f. 8*, addressed to Abraham Maimonides, perhaps the second (early fourteenth century). Complete, but the sender's name and place are not indicated.

[132]TS NS J 249 margin. See n. 120, above.

[133]TS 12.289, l. 14⁺*.

[134]TS 10 J 15, f. 27.

[135]The very fact that she is anonymously described as "a widow in debt and mother of four" was an endeavor "to keep her face covered," or, as we would say, "to save face."

[136]TS 13 J 18, f. 10*. Real estate: see n. 99, above. Dishonest: see *Med. Soc.*, II, 319. Also C, 3, nn. 47–52.

[137]TS 8 J 16, f. l.

[138]See Goitein, *Jemenica*, nos. 817, 943, 1375.

[139]Bibliography about him in *EJ*, 10, pp. 1200–1201.

[140]See, in particular, *Med. Soc.*, II, 127 and 469.

[141]TS 13 J 6, f. 27* (1160), ed. S. D. Goitein, *Gratz College Anniversary Volume* (Philadelphia, 1971), pp. 94–95, 107. Cf. *Med. Soc.*, II, 124, n. 15. See also n. 118, above.

[142]BM Or 5542, f. 33, ll. 14–21. The collection brought 9 7/8 dinars, a considerable sum for a small place.

[143]Maimonides, *Code*, book "Seeds (Agriculture)," sec. "Gifts to the poor," ch. 10:17, trans., e.g., in Baron, *History of the Jews*, IV, 196, and Isadore Twersky, *A Maimonides Reader* (New York, 1972), p. 138.

[144]See B, 2, n. 18, above.

[145]TS 8 J 19, f. 29, ll. 6–12. The letter is addressed to Tripoli, Libya and, most probably was sent from Egypt.

[146]TS 12.242, ll. 13–21, see B, 2, n. 28, above.

[147]TS 13 J 22, f. 25, left side preserved, a letter to Ephraim he-ḥaver (b. Shemarya, for which erroneously Ephraim was repeated).

[148]TS 18 J 1, f. 28 (1187), cf. B, 3, n. 80.

[149]TS NS J 68*. For the ban see *Med. Soc.*, II, 340.

[150]TS 12.289*, see n. 133, above.

[151]See C, 2, n. 119, above.

[152]DK III. The orphan was a relative of the groom.

[153]See A, 3, nn. 51–52.

[154]TS 16.115+* (1006), sec. D: a woman on her deathbed gives one-sixth, worth about 30 dinars, of her house to a girl for marriage. Outfit of orphan bride: TS Arabic Box 30, f. 8*.

[155]See B, 2, n. 81.

[156]See C, 3, nn. 1–2. For the role of a domestic in the upbringing of a motherless orphan cf. *Med. Soc.*, I, 135, n. 25.

[157]ENA 4010, f. 14, written and signed by the cantor Japheth b. David. The second witness who was present during the ceremony in the house of the widower was represented by someone else. In twelve out of the sixteen lines of the document a large part is cut away on the left side.

[158]TS 16.134*v*, a draft written on the reverse side of a letter sent at least twenty years earlier, by the spiritual leader of the Jews of Egypt of that time, Elhanan b. Shemarya, to the community in Malīj, see C, 3, n. 110, above. The other half of the house in which the widower lived, probably belonged to him. His name was Jacob, and the grandfather of the two widows was called by the same name. It is likely that Jacob's mother was an elder sister of the two widows, and the house had been legated to Jacob and his infant cousin in equal parts.

[159]Father remarrying: C, 1, n. 66; C, 3, n. 59, above. Mother: C, 3, n. 151, above.

[160]Bodl. MS Heb. a 3 (Cat. 2873), f. 42+*, l. 34, see B, 1, n. 8.

[161]TS 20.39. End of a marriage contract between Eli b. David and Ḥusn b. Sa'dān ha-Kohen.

[162]TS 12.445. Frag., signed by the cantor Isaac b. Ghālib (ca. 1125).

[163]The father might have died meanwhile. More likely, the term "orphan" is used in the sense of a child whose father does not support him.

[164]TS 12.494, trans. Goitein, *Education*, p. 29. Whether TS 13 J 4, f. 15(1), ed. Strauss-Ashtor, *Mamluks*, III, 92–93, belongs here, is doubtful, for there, l. 15, "her father" is to be read rather than "her child." According to the Library's handlist, the mark of the MS is TS 13 J 4, f. 15(1), not (2) as in Strauss-Ashtor.

[165]TS 16.153, trans. Goitein, *Education*, p. 30.

[166]TS NS J 226*v*, item I, trans. *ibid.*, p. 29, to be corrected according to the details given here.

[167]TS 13 J 2, f. 1, ll. 9–13, 16–19*, trans. *ibid.*, p. 30. The mother was the widow of a cantor. A wife supporting her orphans: C, 1, n. 243, above. TS 16.127 (summer 1101) is too fragmentary to be instructive. It is not evident whether l. 14: *wa-yurabbīh* "and he will bring him up," refers to the husband, or the wife's father.

[168]TS NS J 86, frag., containing important details about the bride's outfit.

[169]Bodl. MS Heb. e 98 (no Cat.), f. 63*v*, item I. Item II on the same page is dated Oct. 1138. Hand of Nathan b. Samuel he-ḥāvēr. The former husband's name: Abū Manṣūr b. Qasāsā. The statement is docketed "the wife [meaning, widow] of Ibn Qasāsā." Thus her second marriage probably took place not long after the death of her former husband. Real estate acquired: TS 8.166, cf. B, 4, n. 44, above.

[170]ULC Or 1080 J 172*. The writer of the letter must have been the father of the deceased woman, for he asks the addressee to take deeds on the proprietorship of an orchard, *ḥākūra*, from her husband and her brother, while he, the writer, wishes to register that property in the names of the two orphans. A somewhat similar case in a question addressed to Maimonides, *Responsa*, I, 108–109.

[171]TS 13 J 2, f. 17, Sambuṭya-Sunbāt, 1116. See D, n. 97, below.

[172]As the unhappy physician in TS 10 J 12, f. 1, see C, 1, n. 120, and *passim*, above.

[173]TS 12.39, ll. 19–20⁺. See B, 2, n. 5, above. Trans. Goitein, *Education*, p. 30. Her marriage gift: 10 + 30 = 40 dinars.

[174]Bodl. MS Heb. a 2 (Cat. 2805), f. 10, trans. *ibid.*

[175]TS 20.1, see B, 4, n. 104, above (ca. 1200). ENA 2560, f. 1 (Spring 1260). Bodl. MS Heb. c 28 (Cat. 2876), f. 14, ed. M. A. Friedman, *Tarbiz*, 40, 1971, 341. See Goitein, *Education*, pp. 30–31. Betrothal contract: TS NS J 457 (March 1099).

[176]Westminster College, Frag. Cairens. 113*, see C, 3, n. 9 (for the husband's stepson). The document mentions the gifts made to the merchant's son from his first marriage.

[177]TS 12.763. Ar. *yuzawwaj*, which could hardly be *yazzawwaj* = *yatazawwaj*.

[178]ENA 2727, f. 14, item II (1324), see B, 5, n. 45, above. Her marriage gift: 5 + 25 = 30 dinars.

[179]Beneficiary: TS K 15, f. 93, col. II, l. 1, see *Med. Soc.*, II, 440, sec. 6. Contributor: TS Misc. Box 8, f. 29*v*, col. II, see *Med. Soc.*, II, 477, sec. 17. Letter: TS 13 J 18, f. 6, ll. 18–19. R. B. Serjeant, "Kinship Terms in Wādī Ḥaḍramaut," *Otto Spies Jubilee Volume* (Wiesbaden, 1967), p. 627, notes: stepson, *ibn al-zawja*; step-daughter, *rabība*.

[180]TS 13 J 19, f. 12*v*, l. 8, a letter from Damīra, Lower Egypt. The spelling *ṣ* for *s* is common (almost "required by usage") in this name. Maimonides, *Responsa*, I, 129.

[181]ULC Or 1080, Box 6, f. 25*v* (ca. 1039), ed. S. D. Goitein, *Eretz-Israel* (Z. Shazar Jubilee Volume), 10 (1971), 113.

[182]See C, 2, nn. 174–177.

[183]TS 16.291, a letter to Maimonides by Ibn al-Hamadānī, see S. D. Goitein, "The Life of Maimonides in the Light of New Finds from the Cairo Geniza" (in Heb.), *Perāqīm*, 4 (New York, 1966), 36–37.

[184]See n. 124, above.

[185]Poll tax: TS 8 J 41, f. 13*v*, see *Med. Soc.*, II, 460–461, sec. 75. Alexandria: TS 13 J 21, f. 30, l. 15*, ed. J. Braslavi, *Eretz-Israel*, 3 (1954) 207–209.

D. THE WORLD OF WOMEN

[1]See Lionel Tiger, *Men in Groups* (New York, 1969). The author emphasizes (Introduction, p. xix), that his book is not based on field research, but represents an attempt to develop a new theoretical position. For this a vast array of scientific literature is adduced, as is evidenced also by the comprehensive bibliography. I thank Professor Carmel Schrire of Rutgers University for drawing attention to this book, which lies outside my own fields of research and competence.

[2]Al-Balādhurī, *Ansāb al-Ashrāf*, ed. S. D. Goitein, Vol. V (Jerusalem, 1936), pp. 173–174. (On Bishr, the brother of the caliph 'Abd al-Malik b. Marwān.)

[3]Qāsim Amīn, *Taḥrīr al-mar'a* (Cairo, 1899). Since the appearance of Qāsim Amīn's *Woman's Liberation*, articles and books on the position of women in the Middle East and the progress made in their modernization have been proliferating. A good survey, especially of the crop of the last twenty years, is to be found in Roxann A. van Dusen, "The Study of Women in the Middle East: Some Thoughts", *Middle East Studies Association Bulletin* 10 (May 1, 1976), 1–19. The paper is accompanied by a bibliography containing over 150 items. The same *Bulletin*, pp. 20–23, contains a report and brief commentary by Elizabeth Fernea and Suad Joseph on the roundtable on women's roles in the Middle East held at the 1975 meeting of the Association. See also *Abstracts of Papers Delivered at the Tenth Annual Meeting of the Middle East Studies Association at Los Angeles, November 10–13, 1976*, pp. 36–39.

[4]BT Yevamot 39*b*. The phrase is used even when the woman is known: TS 24.81, ll. 18 and 35*, see C, 4, n. 72, above. TS NS Box 184, fs. 58 etc., see B, 2, n. 20, above. In a few cases it is stated expressly who made a judge or notary cognizant

of the woman with whom he was dealing, as when in Damascus, 1031, a woman is introduced by the local cantor (the cantors were the confidants of women, see *Med. Soc.,* II, 223–224) together with another "trustworthy" man, who was, however, not among the nine witnesses signing the document besides the judge (ENA NS 17, f. 22, see C, 4, n. 17, above). As a rule, at least in Fustat, the introduction was informal, not requiring "two trustworthy witnesses," and could be made by one person, even a close relative, who otherwise was legally disqualified to testify, as when one record states: "This widow was introduced to us by her son so-and-so" (TS 12.618, l. 22, frag.). When the energetic orphan 'Amā'im, who at her marriage had acted on her own, a few years later made an agreement with her husband, she was "made known" to the judge by a single man (whose relationship to her is not indicated). The same judge, incidentally, presided on both occasions (Bodl. MS Heb. a 3 [Cat. 2873], f. 40*v*, ll. 12–14, see C, 1, n. 131, above). Umm Abu 'l-Faraj, a woman from Jerusalem, established the identity of another woman, probably a stranger in the Egyptian capital, who appeared in court with her husband. The woman from Jerusalem herself clearly needed no introduction (TS 8 J 5, f. 4*a*, l. 7, July 12, 1127).

[5]Missing, e.g.: TS 13 J 1, f. 2+ (Ramle, 1015), see C, 1, n. 180. TS 24.73 (Malīj, 1047), ed. S. Assaf (Yerushalayim, 1953), pp. 115–117. Rayyisa b. Manṣūr appoints her brother Asad to "take" from Ḥesed b. Yāshār, that is, Abū Naṣr b. Sahl al-Tustarī, her share (Pseudo-Heb. *ha-qshṭ* is Ar. *qisṭ*) in the inheritance of her paternal uncle Joseph b. Asad. ENA 4020, f. 52*v** (Fustat, 1132), a woman sells half a house to another woman. Bodl. MS Heb. b 3 (Cat. 2806), fs. 7* and 8* (Fustat, April 20, 1232; the lawsuit originated in Bilbays).

[6]S. D. Goitein, "Individualism and Conformity in Classical Islam," in *Individualism and Conformity in Classical Islam,* ed. A. Banani and S. Vryonis, Jr. (Wiesbaden, 1977), pp. 1–17.

[7]The name *Amat al-Qādir,* "Maidservant of the Almighty" is found in some Karaite ketubbas, TS 18 J 5, f. 10; Harkavy 60.9 (private MS), ed. Mann, *Texts,* II, 182; Firkovitch, II, 1071, ed. *ibid.,* p. 184. Also in one Rabbanite noble family, see C, 3, n. 24, above, and University Museum, Philadelphia, E.16510, see S. D. Goitein, *JQR,* 49 (1958), 36–39. Two other such names, *Amat al-'Azīz,* "Maidservant of the Omnipotent." TS 16.50, see B, 4, n. 92; and *Amat al-Wāḥid,* "Maidservant of the Unique," ENA NS 17, f. 24 (betrothed to Ḥalfōn ha-Levi b. Daniel b. Bundār, Cairo, 999) have been found only once, and both in Karaite documents.

[8]For a list of names of Yemenite women see E. Brauer, *Die Ethnologie der Jemenitischen Juden* (Heidelberg, 1934), p. 198.

[9]Laylā: C, 1, n. 218, above. 'Abla: *Med. Soc.,* II, 120. 'Ātika: Bodl. MS Heb. d 65 (Cat. 2877), f. 30, l. 3+ (Damascus, 956). Bānūqa: C, 1, n. 200, above. The classical Arabic names of women are discussed by E. Gratzl, *Die altarabischen Frauennamen* (Leipzig, 1906). A more complete inventory is to be found in Ibn al-Kalbī, *Ǧamhara.*

[10]For Arabic folktales see n. 217, below.

[11]Cf. 12.262, l. 18*: "To your brother a daughter was born. I called her by the name of my [= our] mother" (a woman in Tunisia, writing to a brother traveling abroad). "A daughter is generally named by her mother," Lane, *Modern Egyptians,* p. 54. In biblical times, female neighbors suggested a name even for a son, cf. Ruth 4:17. Sa'īd A. Ashūr, "Les femmes du Caire a l'époque des sultans Mamlūks," *Colloque international sur l'histoire du Caire* (Cairo, [1972]), p. 41, regards the names composed with *Sitt* as given by husbands to their wives and their daughters as an expression of "veneration." The Geniza shows that such names were already commonplace in Fatimid times and were borne by girls before marriage. Compounds formed with *Sitt* as *titles* are rare,, e.g., *Amat al-qādir Sitt al-Gharb,* "The Maidservant of the Almighty, the Mistress of the West," University Museum, Philadelphia, E.16510, see n. 7, above; in the document TS 16.23+, she is called Sitt al-Gharb without her first name. TS 12.461: *Sitt al-Aqrān Mufaddāt* "Mistress of her Peers, Beloved," (lit., one for whom one gives his own life). TS 16.188: *Zayn*

Sitt al-Dār, "Beauty, the Mistress of the House." TS 10 J 28, f. 11*v*: *Turfa Sitt al-Kamāl,* "Cherished gift, Lady Perfection." See also B, 5, n. 76, above, and here, n. 24, below. *Sitt* and its derivatives, as well as *Sayyida,* which means the same, appear also as names without being followed by an attribute, e.g., al-Sitt b. Ḥalfōn, ULC Or 1080 J 206, 11. 8, 10. A woman in Damietta called her daughters Sayyida and Sutayt, "Little Lady," Bodl. MS Heb. a 2 (Cat. 2805), f. 3+ (ca. 990). Sutayt was common, e.g., TS 16.70 (995), Gottheil-Worrell VIII, p. 40, l. 5 (1231).

[12]See n. 6, above. The name 'Amā'im is found elsewhere, e.g., TS NS J 47, dated 1156, and TS 10 J 17, f. 16. Sometimes, a name appears with and without *Sitt* in the same document. Thus in the deed of gift, discussed in C, 4, n. 8, above, *Ḥasab,* "Distinction," is referred to in Bodl. MS Heb. f 56, f. 45*v*, l. 12 with, and in the subsequent section, f. 46, l. 16, without Sitt. Even stranger: TS 16.172*v*, l. 17, *Naba',* "Excellence," l. 18, *Sitt Naba'.*

[13]The mother of Ibn Ḥajar al-'Asqalānī, an eminent Muslim author (1372–1449), was called *Tujjār*; her brother was a Kārimī, that is, member of a group of rich merchants, engaged in the India trade [see *EI²*, III, 776–778 (Franz Rosenthal)]. The frequently found name *Rayyisa,* "chief" (fem.), should be understood as "head physician." A doctor was normally addressed as *rayyis,* meaning chief of a department in a hospital. Since there is no name parallel to "Merchants," "Clerks," "Kings" for girls from doctors' families, I assume that Rayyisa fulfilled this role.

[14]I noted at random fifteen examples of the name *Sitt al-Dār,* which is also found in a Muslim marriage contract, University Museum, Philadelphia, E.16309+ (ca. 1030). *Sitt A'dāhā*: TS 8.224, TS 16.238. *Sitthum* (repeatedly voweled thus): Bodl. MS Heb. a 2 (Cat. 2805), f. 6; *Sitthim*: TS Misc. Box 25 f. 129*v* col. II, l. 13 (see *Med. Soc.*, II, 432, sec. 162). No vowels: BM Or 5536 II.

[15]*Qā'ida*: TS 12.576. Signed by Japheth b. David (ca. 1030). The commanders of the Berber contingents then stationed in Egypt and Palestine were called *qā'id.* I have not found in the Geniza the name Sulṭāna, common in later centuries, probably because in Fatimid times *sulṭān* had the meaning of "government" rather than "ruler." But *Malika,* "Queen," is rather frequent: ENA 4010, f. 28 (1023); TS 12.658 (Karaite), TS 16.32, ENA NS 18, f. 26 (all ca. 1030), TS 16.153 (1053/4), TS 13 J 1, f. 18 (1078), Karaite. The name *'lm* is to be read *'alam,* "Flag," not *'ilm,* "Knowledge." (In *Med. Soc.*, I, 434, n. 64, as name of slave girls, I was still in doubt.) It is used as an honorary title for a man, as *al-shaykh al-'alam ibn al-'ūdī,* TS Misc. Box 8, f. 99, col. II, B, l. 11 (in a list of contributors, *Med. Soc.*, II, 492, sec. 55), also Westminster College, Arabica I, f. 53. As female name it appears in three forms: simply *'lm,* as in TS Arabic Box 54, f. 69, see C, 3, n. 104, above; *Sitt 'lm,* TS NS J 325, l. 1; and with article, e.g., ULC Or 1080 J 28, l. 15; ULC Or 1081 J 5*v*, l. 12; ULC Add. 3343, l. 17; Bodl. MS Heb. f 56, f. 54*v* (Cat. 2821, no. 16). The names of slave girls frequently designate them as the best of their kind. In Persian *'alam* means inter alia "lord, prince."

[16]The apocryphal Third Book of Ezra, chap. 4.

[17]For Muslim parallels see nn. 13 and 14, above, and the names of women on epitaphs from eleventh-century Qayrawān, Idris, *Zirides,* p. 588, especially *Sitt al-Ahl* and *Sitt al-Sayyid,* "Mistress over the Master." The biographical dictionaries from the Mamluk period are replete with female names formed with *Sitt,* see n. 11, above.

[18]"Woman is hit with the stick of bashfulness," Goitein, *Jemenica,* p. 64, no. 396.

[19]Mūnisa: TS 24.76, l. 12*, in list of beneficiaries, see *Med. Soc.*, II, 438, sec. 1. *Muwānis*: Bodl. MS Heb. b 12 (Cat. 2875), f. 11, l. 4 (a bride). Saying: *shāf aḥbābō nisī aṣḥābō,* S. Hayat, "Proverbs of Iraqi Jews" (see A, 2, n. 62, above), p. 123, no. 371.

[20]*Zakiyya* (b. Isaac b. Ephraim, Westminster College, Glass, f. 39, ll. 1, 8, *verso,* l. 15 [1038]), means "bright, intelligent" in the Geniza, not "pure."

[21]TS AS 145, f. 7 (Alexandria, 1088), see C, 4, n. 20, above.

[22]Grohmann, *APEL,* I, 97, n. 44. See A, 2, n. 37, above.

[23]*Khibā',* "hidden treasure," the name of the bride in the Muslim marriage contract Hamburger Staats- und Universitäts-Bibliothek, A. P. 1, see B, 1, n. 24, above, for which the editor could not find another example, occurs repeatedly in the

Geniza, e.g., ENA NS 17, f. 22 (Damascus 1031), TS 16.79 (Fustat 1050), Dropsie 338 (1053), TS 20.1 and 24.17, the latter two probably referring to the same person (end of twelfth century).

[24]E.g., *Sitt al-Yumn ha-qerū'ā Nājiya,* "Lady Good Augury, called Nājiya," ENA 2728, f. 2. The corresponding male name *Nājī,* "Saved," is less frequent because another derivative, *Munajjā,* was used in this sense for men.

[25]Especially *Ḍiyā,* "Light," "Brightness," serving as a common name for Jewish girls in the second half of the eleventh century and found in a Muslim marriage contract of 1069, Grohmann, *APEL,* I, 102, no. 45. But dark brown, (Sitt al-)*Sumr, Samrā',* also was regarded as a color of beauty, TS 8 J 11, f. 15 (c. 1130); TS NS J 27, IV, no. 5 (1143); TS 12.544 (1148); TS 13 J 22, f. 2 (1150)+*; Westminster College, Frag. Cairens. 46 (1180); TS Arabic Box 38, f. 116 (Bilbays, 1519). This may be compared with the tan-madness of our women (and men).

[26]Turayk: see A, 3, n. 54, above. Khuzayr b. Ḥasan (a bride): TS 24.35 (979/80). ENA NS 17, f. 28*a* (Dec. 1089): David b. Mevōrākh, known as the son of (the woman) Khuzayr.

[27]TS 12.262*. Early eleventh century. In this context attention is drawn to TS 13 J 1, f. 21: "Sitt al-Ahl daughter of Abraham, known as the daughter of *Bint al-Wuḥsha,* 'the Daughter of Wuḥsha' ". Since her grandmother had been a remarkable person, she was commonly known by that relationship. See n. 165, below.

[28]Ahimaaz Chronicle, ed. B. Klar (Jerusalem, 1945), pp. 32–38. See A, 2, n. 85.

[29]In the rather short letter TS 12.262*, see n. 27, above, the comparatively rare name *Mawlāt* (meaning "Mistress," like *Sitt*) occurs twice in the same family.

[30]1029: TS 10 J 2, f. 4. 1334: see B, 4, n. 98. All the female names mentioned in this subsection, and many more, of course, are entered in my card index of persons together with the marks of the manuscripts in which they occur. Thus, *Sitt al-kull,* "The Mistress over everyone," has fifteen entries. Once a name occurs three times or more one can be sure that additional examples of it will be found. The purpose of this subsection is to provide a fairly exhaustive list of *types* of female names.

[31]The passages Jeremiah 44:15, 19, 20, 24, and Nehemiah 5:1, where women speak up in public assemblies, or, as in Nehemiah 8:2–3, are referred to as listeners along with men, are particularly noteworthy.

[32]See *EJ,* VII, 1270–1272, s.v. "Hannah and her Seven Sons." As explained in Gerson D. Cohen's article there, the name Hannah for this woman is a later invention.

[33]The latest comprehensive and highly praised study on women in Greek civilization is Sarah B. Pomeroy, *Goddesses, Whores, Wives, and Slaves; Women in Classical Antiquity* (New York, 1975), which also contains an extensive bibliography on the subject. I am still very much enchanted by the relevant chapter in *The Lady,* by Emily James Putnam, ed., with a Foreword, by Jeannette Mirsky (Chicago, 1970), pp. 3–38. Emily J. Smith-Putnam was a fine Greek scholar. Hers is an inside story.

[34]Mishna Sota 3:4, PT, Sota 19*a,* BT, Yoma 66*b.*

[35]E.g., E. L. Sukenik, "The Mosaic Inscriptions in the Synagogue at Apamea on the Orontes," *HUCA,* 23, part II (1950–1951), 541–554, shows nine women donating alone and three together with their husbands parts of the mosaic (dated A.D. 391). The women donators by far outnumbered the men. Rabbi Aqiba: BT Ketubbot 63*a.* See the dedication of *Med. Soc.,* I.

[36]Y. Sussman, "A Halakhic Inscription from the Beth-Shean Valley," *Tarbiz,* 43 (1974), 88–158, English summary *ibid.,* v–vii.

[37]E. Ashtor, "Migrations de l'Iraq vers les pays méditerranéens dans le haut Moyen Age," *Annales,* 27 (1972), 185–214.

[38]Al-Maqrīzī, *Khiṭaṭ* (Bulāq, A.H. 1270), I, 39. See Mez, *Renaissance,* chap. xx, p. 342. *Muqaddasi,* p. 200, l. 5, and p. 166, l. 3.

[39]See B, 4, nn. 72–91, above.

[40]See C, 1, nn. 1–9 above.

[41]"There was one relief recipient to every four contributors to the charities of the Jewish community in Fustat," see *Med. Soc.*, II, 142, and the number of unmarried women among those recipients was formidable, see B, 1, nn. 66–80, above.

[42]*Med. Soc.*, II, 91–142, 411–510.

[43]TS AS 146, f. 18. Mother of the Little Calf: *Umm al-ʿujayl.*

[44]*Med. Soc.*, II, 427, secs. 135 and 136.

[45]ENA (shelf mark momentarily unavailable). The woman: Umm Ḥasan.

[46]See p. 276, above.

[47]Women without or with children enjoying ample charity from persons with whom they apparently were not related: TS 20.169*, see A, 3, n. 54, and MS Friedenberg, see A, 3, n. 45.

[48]TS 28.3 (July 20, 1004, in Heb.), a huge document, see A, 3, n. 12, above. Interestingly, here the wife's name was consistently inserted above the line ahead of the name of the husband. Another case: TS 12.773, l. 20: "my wife and I."

[49]See C, 3, nn. 11, 13, 14, above.

[50]See B, 5, nn. 36, 41, 42, above.

[51]See B, 3, n. 32, and B, 4, nn. 1–3, above.

[52]ENA NS 2, f. 45, a large fragment of a ketubba in the hand of Ḥalfōn b. Manasse (1100–1138). It was the bride's second or third marriage, as is evident from l. 10.

[53]Bodl. MS Heb. d 66 (Cat. 2878), f. 47*v*, ll. 13–19. Cf. B, 2, nn. 57 and 58, above.

[54]TS 8 J 35, f. 11, *India Book* 269*d*. Small frag.

[55]Donation: TS NS Box 184, f. 57 (frag. in the hand of Ḥalfōn b. Manasse). The Christian women: TS Arabic Box 53, f. 61.

[56]TS 10 J 11, f. 13, l. 4, see C, 2, n. 71, above.

[57]TS 20.126. Left side only preserved. Her name: Sittūna ("Little Lady") b. Japheth.

[58]TS 16.146 and 12.176, *India Book* 286. Sitt al-Sāda.

[59]TS 16.172, a large fragment. The reverse side was written in 1231.

[60]Rent paid to a woman: TS Arabic Box 40, f. 29. Issued by a Muslim notary.

[61]TS Arabic Box 38, f. 116.

[62]TS 8 J 6, fs. 2 and 3, *India Book* 284. The other house: AIU, VII, D, 7, *India Book* 283.

[63]ENA 4020, f. 52* (Dec. 1132).

[64]TS 13 J 25, f. 19 (early thirteenth century). The father was alive and agreed to the sale. Bodl. MS Heb. d 66 (Cat. 2878), f. 92 (Oct. 18, 1229).

[65]See n. 12, end, above.

[66]TS 16.172*v*, a large document, much damaged and effaced, written by Solomon b. Elijah and not completed. For the date see l. 13. Rustic building. *qaṣr*, l. 26, seemingly spelled *qasr*.

[67]See *Med. Soc.*, II, 75 ff. He might have been identical with Ephraim b. Joseph ha-Levi who sold half a house in Cairo around 1100, TS 13 J 30, f. 4*v*, l. 11.

[68]TS 8 J 4, f. 23*d*, written and signed by Abraham b. Nathan, then judge in Cairo, see *Med. Soc.*, II, 512–513, sec. 14. For beekeeping see *Med. Soc.*, I, 125. The husband's consent is implied in the phrase *qabadat-hū min māl ketubbat-hā ʿalā* Mr. Sāsōn b. Japheth, "which she took from the outfit of her ketubba, which is an obligation on Mr. Sāsōn."

[69]TS NS Box 306, f. 1, l. 15. This is a governmental inventory of the pious foundations of the Jewish community, see *Med. Soc.*, II, 419, sec. 39. The house was called Ibn Luffāḥa "Son of the Mandrake," a plant regarded as a powerful love charm, see S. D. Goitein, "Nicknames as Family Names," *JAOS*, 90 (1970), 524.

[70]Bodl. MS Heb. e 94 (no Cat.), f. 19. Jayyida's husband Peraḥyā bore the family name ʿAṣṣār ("Grape-presser"), but probably was a merchant like other persons of that name. He is described as *talmīd* (Heb.), that is, religious scholar. His grandson was a physician with the honorary title "Pride of the Physicians," *Tife'ret ha-Rōfʾīm* (Heb.), see ENA 3150, f. 8, ll. 3–6, a memorial list of the ʿAṣṣār family.

[71]Bodl. MS Heb. e 94, f. 25.

[72]See n. 62, above.

[73]TS 10 J 5, f. 2, see C, 3, nn. 23–24, above.

[74]See nn. 156–189, below.

[75]Firkovitch, II, 1700, fs. 8–9. In *Med. Soc.*, I, 464, n. 153, I noted, instead, f. 20. The reason for the discrepancy: while in Leningrad in summer 1965 I made a detailed handlist of the record book and left a copy of it to the then assistant librarian Dr. Lebedev, who intended to publish the manuscript concerned. Since several court records are often written on one page, I divided the manuscript according to records, not folios, and cited it thus in *Med. Soc.*, I. But since that publication is still outstanding, while it is doubtful how the future editor will proceed, it is preferable to cite the manuscript according to folios. In *Med. Soc.*, I, 255, l. 2, "half-yearly" is to be replaced by "monthly."

[76]See *Med. Soc.*, I, 256, n. 166.

[77]See n. 71, above.

[78]Eli was perhaps Bahiyya's stepbrother. He signs the document together with six others; since two witnesses are sufficient for making a document legally valid, the fact that he might have been a close relative of one of the parties did not impair the validity of the testimony.

[79]TS 20.32. A huge Hebrew document, the beginning of which is missing.

[80]See A, 2, nn. 46–55, and *passim.*

[81]TS NS Box 320, f. 29. Nafīsa ("Precious"), the daughter of Kathīr (Ar. = Ephraim), known as the son of the native of Sepphoris (Ṣaffūriyya, Palestine), the widow of Jacob ha-Kohen, known as the son of "the woman replacing another," *al-mu'awwaḍa,* sells the slave girl Tawfīq ("Success") to the merchant Abu'l-Barakāt Ibn Sha'yā. A note in the hand of Ḥalfōn b. Manasse (1100–1138). Husband sells to wife: PER H 23 (Spring 1126), an extensive document.

[82]Mamlūk: TS AS 147, f. 8.

[83]Wives as executors: C, 2, nn. 20, 21, 25–27, and *passim.* Mother-in-law: C, 1, n. 17. Grandmother: C, 4, n. 95. Sister-in-law: C, 4, n. 25. See S. Assaf, "The Appointment of Women as Executrixes," *Ha-Mishpāṭ ha-'Ivrī* (Hebrew Law), 2 (1927), 75–80 (not based on Geniza texts).

[84]TS 13 J 3, f. 27*v*, dated 1218.

[85]TS 13 J 13, f. 1. Addressed to Ephraim b. Shemarya.

[86]TS 10 J 5, f. 19. Japheth b. Eli of Tinnīs releases his wife Turfa b. Ṭoviah *fī jamī' mā taṣarrafat fīhī fī baytī wa-jamī' mā tawallathū min qibalī.*

[87]TS 28.19, ll. 50–51*, see C, 3, nn. 50, 51, B, 2, n. 54, above, and D, n. 112, below. Maimonides writes about a woman embracing Islam and trying to collect her ketubba through a qadi, Mosseri A 178 (in the course of publication).

[88]A number of Muslim court records containing descriptions of Jewish men are preserved in the Geniza.

[89]ENA 4020, f. 52*, see n. 63, above. A similar case in TS NS J 73 (eleventh century), described in *Med. Soc.*, II, 611, n. 25.

[90]See nn. 70, 71, above. According to Bodl. MS Heb. e 94, f. 19, ll. 7–8, the husband wrote the contract of sale of Jayyida's house stipulating only that the buyer was not permitted to sell it to someone else; but Jayyida's obligation to pay "the rent," i.e., interest, certainly was included.

[91]TS 13 J 25, f. 19, see n. 64, above.

[92]TS 16.172*v*, see n. 66, above.

[93]E.g., B, 2, n. 13, above, from 1243 and 1241, respectively.

[94]For the role of the *Muhandiz* in the supervision of houses see S. D. Goitein, "Geniza Documents on the Transfer and Inspection of Houses," *Mélanges Le Tourneau* (Aix-en-Provence, 1973), p. 405.

[95]He was called Mu'allā b. Raḥmūn, and both he and the "son of the surveyor," Bu 'l-Ḥasan al-Hōd (Heb. "Glory", an honorific title), were involved in the communal service described in ENA 4011, f. 62*v*, see *Med. Soc.*, II, 428, sec. 138.

[96]TS 10 J 6, f. 3. The beginning with the date is torn away. The document is signed by Mevōrākh b. Nathan when his father was still alive. Nathan b. Samuel

he-ḥavēr died between Oct. 8, 1163, when his son mentions him as living (BM Or 5524, f. 6), and Jan. 5, 1164, when Mevōrākh eulogizes him as dead (BM Or 5524, f. 7, both bills of divorce). Thus Nathan remained alive for ten years after the last dated document he signed, as identified thus far, see *Med. Soc.*, II, 513, n. 18. Releases in extended family: A, 3, nn. 55–56 B, 2, n. 83, above.

[97]TS 13 J 2, f. 17, see C, 4, n. 171, above. Although written in a small town, this is a carefully executed document, properly validated by a court of three.

[98]ULC Or 1080 J 175. This is not the final document, but a note taking down the proceedings of the session. Here the wife is informally called Hilāla ("New Moon") b. Hiba ("Gift"), but in TS 13 J 2, f. 17, her father is called by his Hebrew name, Nathan, which means the same, and receives the blessing due a dead person. The husband Sāsōn b. Japheth (d.) is called both times by his Hebrew names. The note is in the hand of the judge Manasse (*he-ḥāvēr*, see Bodl. MS Heb. e 44 [Cat. 2668, no. 25], fs. 98–99*v*), son of Sa'adyāhū *ha-me'ulle ba-ḥavūrā*, "the most excellent member of the Academy." In TS 13 J 6, f. 21*, Manasse informs Abraham b. Nathan Āv the Cairene judge, that our Sāsōn had made peace with his uncle Sa'adya b. Ephraim, the father of his (first) wife, and other notables of the community: There must have been a big and prolonged row, for the letter is signed by seven (including the father-in-law, which is extremely unusual). Judge Abraham is asked to convey the good tidings to Sāsōn's father, Japheth, "the munificent elder of the community," who happened to live in Cairo.

[99]TS 16.119, see B, 2, n. 74, above.

[100]TS 12.544*. The wife's name was Sumr, see n. 25, above.

[101]Bodl. MS Heb. b 12 (2875), f. 2, 1128/9, written by Ḥalfōn b. Manasse. About the introduction of females see nn. 4–8, especially, n. 6, above. In our age, too, one would know adult women of one's wider circle of acquaintances, but not by name. Forms of introduction sometimes state that concerning a woman appearing in court, both the name and the individual (*shakhṣ*) were known, TS 13 J 2, f. 17, l. 2.

[102]TS 13 J 8, f. 1*, Sept. 1052. The payments were to be made to a third person in Cairo, specified in the document.

[103]I do not use the word "attorney," because, as a rule, the persons appointed were not professionals. Occasionally, cantors, who were also court clerks, served as attorneys.

[104]1004: TS 28.3, see A, 3, n. 12, and D, n. 48, above.

[105]TS 13 J 1, f. 5, ed. Braslavsky, *Our Country*, p. 102 (facsimile opposite p. 96), and see *ibid.*, p. 101. The editor did not recognize that l. 18 contains the name of the woman.

[106]AIU VII, D 4 c* (July 24, 1027), see C, 4, n. 77, above.

[107]TS Misc. Box 27, f. 31 (1244), see Friedman, *Ethics*, p. 95 n. 53.

[108]See B, 2, n. 13, above.

[109]TS NS J 383*v* (June 1239). Wife: 'Alam b. Mahfūẓ; husband: Abu 'l-Munā b. Sābiq. The same arrangement on *recto* (July 1238, see C, 2, n. 99, above), written by the same clerk and also signed by one witness only, Uzziel b. Ṭāhōr ha-*nāzīr* (the Nazirean, Heb.).

[110]ULC Or 1080 J 262, see C, 3, n. 18, above.

[111]TS 16.238, a fragment, lacking beginning and end, wherefore the signatures are lost. But the script is undoubtedly that of the judge Meir b. Hillel b. Ṣādōq Āv, who, while writing to Moses Maimonides, treats him as if he was his peer, see *Med. Soc.*, II, 421, sec. 97. Details about him in *Tarbiz*, 34 (1965), 232–236. Whether the widow, *Sitt A'dāhā*, "Mistress over her Enemies," daughter of Hillel ha-Kohen, is identical with her namesake, "the wife of the Rayyis," or head physician, in the highly interesting document TS 8.224, cannot yet be decided. The strange name is found elsewhere.

[112]TS 10 J 20, f. 21*. Written by Mevōrākh b. Nathan and signed in full by Sār Shālōm, which is uncommon and probably underlines the Gaon's displeasure.

[113]TS 8 J 5, f. 2*a*–*c**, see B, 5, n. 54, above.

[114]Naturally, we learn about this aspect of social life mostly from invitations and from letters expressing disappointment that the invited had not come. Occasionally, the hardships of travel are described.

[115]Mother visiting: see C, 1, nn. 63–64; sister: C, 1, n. 62, and *passim.*

[116]TS 20.117*v*, ed. Assaf, *Texts,* pp. 160–162. Left side torn away. In l. 15 the words *illā wa-ma'hā zawjha aw,* "except when accompanied by her husband or" have to be complemented.

[117]ULC Or 1080 J 2, see *Med. Soc.*, II, 502, sec. 113: Ibn *al-ḥājja.*

[118]TS 10 J 32, f. 10, l. 7, *Nahray* 78, Joseph b. Eli b. (al-) Fāsī writing to Nahray b. Nissīm.

[119]TS 13 J 28, f. 16*; "desolate": *sā'ib*; "business season": *mawsim.* "If possible, please return before the Little Fast," i.e., according to Saul Lieberman, the Ninth of Āv, see TS 20.96, p. 37, ed. *Eretz-Israel,* 7 (1964), 86 n. 35.

[120]TS 13 J 27, f. 21, esp. ll. 21–22.

[121]TS NS J 226*v*, item I*, see C, 4, n. 166, above.

[122]Bodl. MS Heb. f 102 (no Cat.), f. 52, ll. 2–3.

[123]ENA NS 2, f. 11, see C, 2, n. 129, above. Umm Farjūn, the widow, seemingly did not live with relatives.

[124]Bodl. MS Heb. d 76 (no Cat.), f. 65.

[125]Ṣahrajt: see B, 2, n. 54. Malīj: see C, 1, n. 231.

[126]Idris, "Mariage," p. 60, sec. 81.

[127]See C, 1, n. 194, above.

[128]C.-A Julien and C. Courtois, *Histoire de l'Afrique du Nord* (Paris, 1951), I, 257.

[129]Balādhurī, *Futūḥ al-buldān* (Cairo, 1932), p. 157, bottom.

[130]TS 8 J 21, f. 7, ll. 8–11, *India Book* 252*c*. For Abu 'l-Faḍl see Goitein, *Letters,* p. 199 n. 10.

[131]See C, 1, n. 145, above.

[132]TS 16.13*v*, l. 3, a large letter by Ḥayyīm's brother, Zakkār b. 'Ammār (see *Med. Soc.*, II, 25), cf. *ibid., verso,* l. 11.

[133]Girl: TS 13 J 20, f. 25, l. 3, ed. Mann, II, 88. Woman: ENA 2804, detached leaf, ed. Mann, II, 88–89, l. 16. Physician and wife: *ibid.*, l. 25.

[134]Overseas marriages: B, 1, nn. 35–42, above. Male travelers accompanied: *Med. Soc.*, II, 347–348. Spirit of adventure: *Med. Soc.*, I, 274–275, Goitein, *Letters,* pp. 255–257.

[135]*Ma'ālim al-Qurba,* p. 89 (Eng. summary), p. 222 (text).

[136]This story of Synesius (who later became a Christian and even a bishop) is told at length in Goitein, *Jews and Arabs,* p. 108.

[137]Unpleasant experiences: Goitein, *Letters,* p. 339.

[138]Shipwreck: *Med. Soc.*, I, 322, n. 67.

[139]TS AS 147, f. 22. A letter of recommendation by the *muqaddam* of Bilbays to Isaac b. Sāsōn, the Cairene member of Maimonides' court, referring to a similar letter received by him from Ascalon.

[140]See C, 1, n. 123.

[141]Cf. *Med. Soc.*, II, 135.

[142]See *Med. Soc.*, I, 114–115.

[143]Fullers appear in the lists of the beneficiaries of communal welfare, e.g., in those analyzed in *Med. Soc.*, II, 438, sec. 1, p. 441, sec. 8, certainly when they had become old and unable to work. A fuller, as usual with craftsmen, would also sell clothing, TS K 15, f. 114 v, col. III, l. 5, *Nahray* 42, and a son of a fuller could become a physician, TS 13 J 20, f. 18, ll. 18 and 24, ed. Mann, II, 300–301. Ar. *qaṣṣār* is borrowed from Aramaic. When the word occurs in a Hebrew text and is spelled without an alif, it must be regarded as Aramaic, see *Med. Soc.*, II, 540, n. 93.

[144]The term "embroiderer" is rare. Male embroiderer, *raqqām*: *Med. Soc.*, II, 467, sec. 107. Female: *ibid.*, I, 430, n. 13.

[145]See, for instance, Goitein, *Letters,* pp. 75–76.

[146]See C, 1, nn. 238 and 145, above. Also B, 5, nn. 55–56, above, and D, n. 149, below.

[147]Cf. A, 2, n. 53, above.

[148]In years past, I often saw such female supplications in the synagogues of Oriental communities.

[149]See "Life in the synagogue," *Med. Soc.*, II, 155–170, and *ibid.*, pp. 144–145, and 183, n. 1.

[150]See "Ḥammām," *EI*², III, 139–146, and H. Grotzfeld, *Das Bad im arabisch-islamischen Mittelalter* (Wiesbaden, 1970).

[151]The story of Zayn al-Mawāṣif ("The woman with beautiful traits") and Masrūr ("Happy") is told in *The Arabian Nights*, nos. 845–863. A short and stringent analysis of this strange and immoral story is found in Mia I. Gerhardt, *The Art of Story-Telling* (Leiden, 1963), pp. 139–140.

[152]Maimonides, *Responsa*, I, no. 34, pp. 49–53, no. 45, pp. 71–73. In the manuscript of the *Responsa* the numbers are 52 and 63.

[153]As mentioned above, B, 2, n. 26.

[154]The letter in favor of the wife states laconically: *ma'hā ḥifẓ min al-miqrā*, "she knows parts of the Bible (*miqrā*, Heb.)," Maimonides, *Responsa*, I, 50, l. 11. The letter in favor of the husband, *ibid.*, p. 72, ll. 5–7, says that originally her husband taught her "a part of the Torah," while she studied others during his absence.

[155]See Mishna Qiddushin 4:13 "A bachelor should not be a school master (because of the mothers bringing their boys), nor should a woman be a school mistress (because of their fathers)." The words in parentheses are from Maimonides, *Code*, book "Knowledge," section "Study of the Torah," 2:4. About women as teachers see nn. 152–155, below.

[156]Broker: *dallāla*. See S. D. Goitein, "A Jewish Business Woman of the Eleventh Century," *The Seventy-Fifth Anniversary Volume of the Jewish Quarterly Review* (Philadelphia, 1967), pp. 225–247. Since then much new material has come to light, qualifying several statements made in that article. Wuḥsha, without *al*, as name, in Bodl. MS Heb. b 12 (Cat. 2875), f. 28, dated 1056, Wuḥsha b. Yeshū'ā, a bride, thus far, the only occurrence.

[157]A fragment in TS NS J 401.

[158]1093: TS 13 J 1, f. 23. 1104: TS 8 J 5, f. 5*b–c*, *India Book* 268, see n. 169, below.

[159]For the practice of overvaluating the dowry see B, 4, nn. 45–50, above. For 150 dinars as "standard" see B, 4, n. 65, above.

[160]See B, 4, n. 25, above.

[161]ENA 2727, f. 8A, an assessment of the trousseau, written by Hillel b. Eli at his very best, probably in the 1080s.

[162]TS AS 145, f. 3, also in the hand of Hillel b. Eli. This Mr. Goldsmith, Abu 'l-Faḍl Ibn al-Dhahabī Joseph b. Joshiah is described in TS 10 J 5, f. 16, a lawsuit about a Bible codex acquired by him, as living in Alexandria.

[163]TS 8 J 5, f. 16, see C, 1, n. 85, above.

[164]ENA 4020, f. 52*v*, see D, nn. 5, 63, above. The document itself was written by Ḥalfōn b. Manasse, but the superscription is in the unmistakable hand of judge Nathan ha-Kohen b. Solomon, see C, 1, n. 145. In this document Arye is called by his Arabic name Sibā' (both mean "Lion," but the Hebrew form was not used in Egypt), and is described as being from Damascus. In the story of his second marriage, see preceding note, we found him traveling with his wife to Palermo, Sicily. He might have been a native of that city, but sojourned some time in Damacus, as the government official whose fortunes are described in TS 13 J 2, f. 25+*, see B, 5, n. 21, above.

[165]TS 13 J 1, f. 21, Sitt al-Ahl b. Ibrahīm, wife of Abu 'l-Ma'rūf Ṣadaqa ("Bounty, Gift"), "known as *ibnat Bint al-Wuḥsha*," leases the ground floor and mezzanine of her house for a duration of eight years against a total rent of 40 dinars, to be spent by the tenant on repairs.

[166]See n. 198, below (daughter). TS 18 J 1, f. 25 (son).

[167]ULC Add. 3420 d, translated in full in the article mentioned in n. 156, above, p. 227.

[168]See nn. 53, 62, above.

[169]TS 8 J 5, f. 5*b–c*, *India Book* 268. Share: *naṣīb.*

[170]For Hillel b. Eli see *Med. Soc.,* II, 222, 231.

[171]Only she is called by name (Ṣabāḥ, "Morning," or Ṣubāḥ, "Beauty"). It makes the impression that al-Wuḥsha was reminded of her by someone present. Such things happened at dispositions in face of death.

[172]For the general upkeep of the cemetery, not for her tomb, which is listed later in the will.

[173]Joseph might have been her late brother, mentioned in the document of 1104, see n. 169, above. The fact that there he is called Abū Naṣr ("Victor") is not decisive, for this *kunya,* or honorific designation, goes together with practically any Hebrew name, including Joseph, as in TS 10 J 25, f. 8+ ("Abū Naṣr Joseph b. Ḥasan, Bundār's sister's son"), see A, 2, n. 66, above. But the details about Joseph's wife and her two brothers are listed after the section on public charity and before that on the orphan. Thus the donation is a charity rather than a legacy to a close relative.

[174]The one encountered in ULC Add. 3420 d, see n. 167, above.

[175]TS Arabic Box 4, f. 5+*, ed. and trans. in the article mentioned in n. 156, above, pp. 229–235, 239–241. The notable Abū Manṣūr b. Ayyūb (Job) contributed to the same public appeal to which al-Wuḥsha pledged, see n. 189, below.

[176]Sitt Ikhtiyār. Does this name express submission to God's choice (that it was a girl and not a boy) or a proud assertion ("it is my preference")? Probably the former. Found by me only once more, and without Sitt: the widow and bride in TS 20.116*v*, item II, see B, 4, n. 14, above.

[177]PER H 31, written by Ḥalfōn b. Manasse, Hillel b. Eli's son-in-law and signed by him and three others. The four signatures are validated by three judges. This Sitt al-Ḥusn probably is not identical with the one mentioned in C, 4, 169, above.

[178]A (Muslim) eulogy on a saintly dead person. At the time of the deposition in court Hillel b. Eli was dead.

[179]Ar. *waqaʿt maʿ,* literally, "I fell with." Possible meaning: "I have got into a quagmire with." Said of a male and with *ʿalā* it simply means: "I slept with."

[180]Ar. *wa-kitābna ʿindī [ʿind] al-muslimīn,* "I have our marriage certificate, issued by Muslims."

[181]Maker and seller of sugar, a common family name, see A, 1, n. 86, above. His first name is given in the second deposition.

[182]This is David b. Daniel b. Azarya, who was head of the Jews in the Fatimid empire until April/May 1094. But he might also have presided over the synagogue of the Iraqians after his downfall.

[183]"Gift of God," the Arabic equivalent of Hebrew Nethanel.

[184]For this family name see A, 1, n. 82, above.

[185]Writer or singer of a type of liturgical poetry, called *rahaṭ,* see *Med. Soc.,* II, 224, n. 34. About rahaṭ see now E. Fleischer, *Hebrew Liturgical Poetry in the Middle Ages* (Jerusalem, 1975), pp. 299 ff. and *passim* (in Hebrew).

[186]TS 10 J 7, f. 10*v*+*, ed. and trans. in the article mentioned above, n. 156, pp. 236–237, 241–242. Facsimile of the much damaged record *ibid.,* p. 226.

[187]TS AS 145, f. 13, a small fragment, a middle piece of the left side of an interesting document, in which al-Wuḥsha's son is mentioned twice.

[188]TS 13 J 3, f. 7 (1148), Abu 'l-Ḥasan *al-ṣayrafī,* "al-Wuḥsha's relative," sells his servant "Wild Rose," Nisrīn, to the Nagid designate, a son of the Nagid Samuel b. Hananiah, see *Med. Soc.,* I, 139, JNUL 4, f. 4 (1133), see S. D. Goitein, *Kirjath Sepher,* 41 (1966), 265–266, a release by Abu 'l-Ḥasan, "al-Wuḥsha's sister's son."

[189]TS Misc. Box 8, f. 102, col. II, ll. 10–11, see *Med. Soc.,* II, 478, sec. 19. Al-Wuḥsha contributed ¼ dinar.

[190]See B, 1, n. 2, above. Ancient Israel had professional female diviners, Ezekiel 13:17–23.

[191]Always referred to as *al-nazīra* (Heb. with the Ar. article), which seems to indicate that at a certain time only one woman was habitually described as such. TS 13 J 8, f. 11*v*, col. II, *Med. Soc.*, II, 429, sec. 146*a*. ENA 3124, f. 13*v*, l. 13, *ibid.*, p. 432, sec. 160. TS 24.76, l. 15, *ibid.*, p. 438, sec. l.

[192]Devout: *Ibn al-dayyina*, in the list TS Misc. Box 28, f. 184*, col. I, l. 23, described in *Med. Soc.*, II, 457–458. Pietist: *al-'ābida*, JTS Geniza Misc. 6+*, n. 198, below.

[193]Mishna Avot 2:5.

[194]One swears by the father, whether dead or alive.

[195]This cannot have been meant too seriously. Only well-to-do families could keep two maidservants, one with a child.

[196]Literally: the lady, *al-sitt.*

[197]Most probably her sister's husband, a physician.

[198]JTS Geniza Misc. 6+*, ed. and trans. S. D. Goitein, *Gratz College Anniversary Volume* (Philadelphia, 1971), pp. 85–87, 100–101. The large beautiful script is of a very individual style and difficult to date. The name of the elder daughter, Sitt al-Sirr ("Secret," a mystical term) has been seen by me elsewhere only once, in the marriage contract of a girl with that name at a time when her father was dead, JTS Geniza Misc. 18. That fragment is in the hand of Halfōn b. Manasse, 1100–1138.

[199]BT Shabbat 62*a*, quoted in connection with some technical detail of the Sabbath laws. "Locked chests," a saying found in practically all Arabic vernaculars and used in a variety of applications, see S. Hayat, "The Family in the Proverbs of Iraqi Jews," *Folklore Studies* 3 (Jerusalem, 1972), 124, no. 377 (with many parallels).

[200]Maimonides, *Code*, book "Knowledge," sec. "Study" 1:1, and its source. Islamic law, to the contrary, makes study obligatory for women as well. The actual state of women under traditional Islam, however, proves the might of the misogynous Greek influence in those parts.

[201]See *Med. Soc.*, II, 182–185, "The Education of Girls," for the sources of some of the items mentioned in these paragraphs.

[202]Al-Balādhurī, *Futūḥ* (Cairo, 1932), p. 458. Of two other wives of Muhammad it is reported, *ibid.* that they knew how to write.

[203]TS J 1, f. 29+*, l. 24, see B, 4, n. 43, above.

[204]ENA NS 2, f. 17. For synagogue = school see *Med. Soc.*, II, 185, bottom, n. 3. This usage remained alive in the vernacular of the Yemenite Jews. Cf. TS 13 J 6, f. 27, l. 5+*, a cantor known as "the son of the [female] teacher," see C, 4, n. 141, above.

[205]Cf. the beautiful chapter "The Lady Abbess" in Emily J. Putnam's *The Lady* (Chicago, 1975), pp. 69–105, and Sibylle Harksen, *Die Frau im Mittelalter* (Leipzig, 1974). Although essentially an elaborate picturebook, the text of this volume is very sensible, and the bibliography, pp. 64–65, contains items not generally known. There is no need to point to the *Histoire mondiale de la femme*, Vol. II (Paris, 1965), where Nada Tomiche contributed the section on Islam.

[206]A recent publication, Ahmad 'Abd ar-Raziq, *La femme aux temps des Mamlouks en Égypte* (Cairo, 1973), deals with a period later than the "classical" Geniza. A very comprehensive treatment of a cognate subject, *Islam et sexualité* by Abdelwahab Bouhdiba (Service de reproduction des thèses, Université de Lille III, 1973, 601 pp.), with an extensive bibliography on women in Islam (pp. 576–597) shows how much is still to be done in this field. Appendix II in Annemarie Schimmel, *Mystical Dimensions of Islam* (Chapel Hill, 1975) is devoted to the role of women in Islamic mysticism. The Geniza sources on Jewish female visionaries are treated in volume IV in connection with Messianism. See also B, 1, nn. 2 and 65, above.

[207]Lane-Poole, *History of Egypt*, pp. 119, 120, 134–135, 137.

[208]See S. M. Stern, "The Epistle of the Fatimid Caliph al-Āmir (al-Hidāya al-Āmiriyya): Its Date and Its Purpose," *Journal of the Royal Asiatic Society*, n.v. (April, 1950), 25–26.

[209]Idris, *Zirides*, pp. 141–142, and *passim.*

[210]Ibn ʿIdhārī, *Al-Bayān al-Mughrib*, ed. G. S. Colin and E. Lévi-Provençal (Leiden, 1948), pp. 271–273.

[211]Bodl. MS Heb. e 74, f. 58 (Cat. 2862, no. 20), l. 3, ed. Mann, II, 256, l. 9. See Mann (1970), Reader's Guide, p. xxxiii–xxxiv. By "The King" is meant most probably al-Malik al-Afḍal (see *Med. Soc.*, II, 349–350).

[212]Firkovitch II, 1700, f. 3, l. 15 (Summer 1156). See C, 4, n. 29, above.

[213]ULC Or 1080 J 223, dated Feb. 9, 1228. One of the Sultan's servants is described as *mē-ḥasīdē ummōt ha-ʿōlām*, or well-disposed toward Jews.

[214]TS NS Box 321, f. 54, dated Aug. 11, 1091. The two judges: Abraham, son of Isaac, the Scholar, and Abraham, the descendant of the Gaon Shemaʿya (*Med. Soc.*, II, 512, secs. 10 and 12).

[215]In his letter to me of Feb. 21, 1975, Professor J. Schirmann, the acknowledged authority in this field, confirms that no Hebrew woman poet can be identified with certainty in the period under discussion. For Qasamūna b. Ismāʿīl, who wrote Arabic verses, Schirmann draws attention to al-Maqqarī, *Nafḥ al-Ṭīb*, II (Cairo, 1886/7), 356.

[216]BM Or 5554 B, f. 20, ll. 12–14⁺, see C, 1, n. 39, above. Dr. Ezra Fleischer, author of many papers and books on Hebrew liturgical poetry, explained "songs" in the sense noted.

[217]Dr. Victor Lebedev of the Saltykov-Shchedrin State Public Library in Leningrad has written a comprehensive Ph.D. dissertation on the folktales from the Geniza preserved in the Firkovitch collection of that library. I understand that Dr. Lebedev is preparing a publication on this topic in a Western language. In my note "The Oldest Documentary Evidence for The Title *Alf Laila wa-Laila* [1001 Nights, commonly known as The Arabian Nights]", *JAOS*, 78 (1959), 301–302, I drew attention to the folktales in the Geniza treasures of the University Library, Cambridge. It seems, however, that thus far no research has been made on this material.

[218]As a rule, women did not participate in public appeals. Their donations were made privately.

[219]I owe this quotation (and interpretation) to James Holly Hanford, *John Milton: Poet and Humanist* (Cleveland, 1966), p. 72.

[220]See n. 33, above.

[221]TS 10 J 12, f. 1, see C, 1, n. 120.

General Index

(Owing to the frequency of their occurrence, the following have not been indexed: Fustat, Islam, Jew[ish], Judaism, Muslim. The section on female names (pp. 314–319), the appendix, and the notes are not indexed. Where necessary, f. is added to designate a woman's name.)